1000
CHOCOLATE
BAKING &
DESSERT RECIPES

1000
CHOCOLATE
BAKING &
DESSERT RECIPES

p

This is a Parragon Publishing Book
First published in 2003

Parragon Publishing
Queen Street House
4 Queen Street
Bath BA1 1HE, UK

ISBN: 1-40540-187-7

Printed in Indonesia

Produced by The Bridgewater Book Company Ltd, Lewes, East Sussex

Thanks to the following contributors Sarah Banbery, Linda Doeser,
Stephanie Horner, Tom Kitch, Lesley Mackley, Gina Steer, Susanna Tee

New photography Ian Parsons
Home economists Richard Green, Brian Wilson

NOTE

Cup measurements in this book are for American cups.
This book also uses imperial and metric measurements. Follow the same units
of measurement throughout; do not mix imperial and metric.
All spoon measurements are level: teaspoons are assumed to be 5 ml and
tablespoons are assumed to be 15 ml.
Unless otherwise stated, milk is assumed to be whole milk,
eggs and individual vegetables such as potatoes are medium,
and pepper is freshly ground black pepper.

The nutritional information provided for each recipe is per serving or per person.
Optional ingredients, variations, or serving suggestions have
not been included in the calculations. The times given for each recipe are an approximate
guide only because the preparation times may differ according to the techniques used by
different people and the cooking times may vary as a result of the type of oven used.

Recipes using raw or very lightly cooked eggs should be
avoided by infants, the elderly, pregnant women, convalescents,
and anyone suffering from an illness.

contents

INTRODUCTION

Enjoy the delicious delights of the 1,000 chocolate, baking, and dessert recipes in this collection. Find old favorites and numerous new and utterly tempting sweet dishes to try out. Whenever you are preparing a family meal, a filling and tasty treat for children's lunchboxes, a slice or cookie for coffee or teatime with friends, or a rich dessert or petit four to round off a dinner party or festive meal— you will find yourself reaching again and again for this book.

Children need little encouragement to eat cookies or muffins, and will enjoy helping to make and decorate many of the small cakes and slices in this book. Each recipe contains the following information: preparation and cooking times, number of portions, and level of difficulty (one chef's hat for an easy recipe, rising to five chef's hats for a difficult one). There are plenty of cook's tips and variations for you to follow.

Since all the recipes in this book are sweet, you may wish to use sweet butter. Sweet butter is specified for any recipe where the salted version would impair the taste, as in many of the cold desserts and gâteaux, petits fours, and confectionery. In less rich recipes—the tea loaves, crêpes, cakes, or cookies, for example—either salted or sweet butter may be used.

Chocolate features in the majority of recipes in this collection. For many of us, chocolate is sheer indulgence. Delicious as a taste in its own right, chocolate is particularly versatile in the kitchen as it pairs so well with all manner of other ingredients: spices, cream, fruit, nuts, liqueurs—and, as a sauce or filling, it

transforms the simple into the sumptuous. Few can resist a slice of rich chocolate cake or a cookie, a chocolate-covered petit four, or a comforting bedtime drink. There are decadent smoothies and chocolate cocktails to try, too.

Types and styles of chocolate

Today there is an impressive range of styles and qualities of chocolate, readily available in our stores, from the basic cooking chocolate to the finest, cocoa-rich varieties. The most suitable variety for each recipe is not necessarily the most expensive: the texture of the different chocolates varies with the amount of cocoa they contain. Mousses, for example, can become much too heavy if the chocolate contains too much cocoa solid, because it acts in the same way as adding too much flour. The recipes only specify good-quality chocolate where its superior flavor enhances the result. In these cases, chocolate containing over 50 percent cocoa is considered to be good quality, with 70 percent-plus indicating the finest chocolate of all, which is probably better for eating rather than cooking.

chocolate-flavored cake covering

This product has an inferior flavor because it contains vegetable fat instead of cocoa butter, but it is useful for making decorations because of the high fat content. As a compromise, add a few squares to a good-quality chocolate.

white chocolate

For color contrast, especially for cake decoration, white chocolate is unbeatable. However, white chocolate has a lower content of cocoa butter, so choose a luxury cooking variety and take care not to overheat it when melting. There is also a vanilla-flavored variety.

semisweet or bittersweet chocolate

These styles of chocolate contain a minimum of 34 percent cocoa solids and are generally around 50 percent. They are ideal for most everyday cooking purposes. For special recipes, choose a luxury chocolate with a cocoa solid content of 70–75% for a richer, more intense flavor but do be aware that the higher the cocoa content, the denser the texture of your dessert or gâteau.

milk chocolate

As the name implies, this chocolate has a milder, creamier flavor, which makes it more popular with children than the semisweet variety. It is also useful for decorations. It must contain a minimum of 10 percent cocoa mass and 12 percent milk solids. Care must be taken when melting milk chocolate, because its milk content makes it more sensitive to heat than the semisweet variety.

chocolate chips

Available in semisweet, milk, or white chocolate, these chips are useful for baking and decoration. They are especially good in cookies, as well as sweets and a whole range of delicious confections. Chocolate buttons (usually milk) are also good for decorating cakes and small cakes and slices intended for children.

unsweetened cocoa

This powder tastes bitter, and gives a good, strong chocolate flavor in cooking. It is mostly used in cakes. Do not use sweetened cocoa unless a recipe specifically calls for it.

Storage

Most chocolate, including unsweetened cocoa, can be stored for up to a year if it is kept in a cool, dry place away from direct heat or sunlight.

Preparing chocolate

Many recipes require chocolate to be melted before it is added with the other ingredients. One of the easiest ways to melt chocolate is on the stove:

1 Break the chocolate into small, equal-size pieces and put into a heatproof bowl.

2 Place the bowl over a pan of gently simmering water, making sure the base of the bowl does not come into contact with the water. Do not allow any hot water to get into the chocolate, or it will harden rather than melt.

3 Once the chocolate starts to melt, stir gently until smooth, then remove from the heat.

This stove method is the one suggested in most of the recipes. Never melt chocolate over direct heat (unless melting with other ingredients, such as cream or butter, and in this case keep the heat very low). You can also melt chocolate in a low oven (160°F/325°C). Break up the chocolate into pieces and place in an ovenproof bowl in the center of the oven for about 10–15 minutes.

microwave method

To melt chocolate in a microwave oven:

1 Break chocolate into small pieces and place in a microwave-proof bowl.

2 Put the bowl in the microwave oven and melt. As a guide, melt 4½ oz/ 125 g dark chocolate on High for 2 minutes, and white or milk chocolate on Medium for 2–3 minutes.

3 Stir the chocolate, leave to stand for a few minutes, then stir again. If necessary, return it to the microwave for a further 30 seconds (different brands melt at different rates).

Note: As microwave oven temperatures and settings vary, you should consult the manufacturer's instructions first.

basic recipes

rich chocolate pie dough

makes: 1 x 8-inch/20-cm tart case
preparation time: 10 minutes,
plus 30 minutes chilling

4 tbsp unsweetened cocoa

scant 1½ cups all-purpose flour, plus extra
  for dusting

3½ oz/100 g butter, softened

4 tbsp superfine sugar

2 egg yolks

few drops of vanilla extract

1–2 tbsp cold water

1 Sift the unsweetened cocoa and flour
into a large bowl. Add the butter and
rub it in with your fingertips until the
mixture resembles fine breadcrumbs. Stir
in the superfine sugar. Add the egg yolks,
vanilla extract, and enough water to mix
to the consistency of a dough.

2 Cover the dough in plastic wrap and
leave to chill in the refrigerator for
about 30 minutes. Roll out the dough on
a lightly floured work counter. It will line
an 8-inch/20-cm tart pan or cake pan.

shortcrust pie dough

makes: 1 x 6-inch/15-cm tart case
preparation time: 10 minutes,
plus 30 minutes chilling

generous ¾ cup all-purpose flour

2 tbsp butter

2 tbsp shortening or white cooking fat

2 tbsp cold water

1 Sift the flour into a mixing bowl. Cut
the butter and fat into small cubes
and add them to the flour. Using your
fingertips, gently rub the fats and flour
together until the fat breaks down into
tiny pieces and the mixture resembles fine
bread crumbs.

2 Use a round-bladed knife to stir in
enough water to make the
consistency of a dough. Gather into a ball
and knead briefly. If it feels sticky, sprinkle
over a little flour. Cover the dough in
plastic wrap and leave to chill in the
refrigerator for about 30 minutes. Roll out
the pie dough on a lightly floured work
counter. It will line an 8-inch/20-cm tart
pan or cake pan.

sweet shortcrust pie dough

makes: 1 x 8-inch/20-cm tart case
preparation time: 10 minutes,
plus 30 minutes chilling

1½ cups all-purpose flour

4 oz/115 g butter

2 tbsp shortening or white cooking fat

2 oz/55 g golden superfine sugar

6 tbsp cold milk

Make in the same way as the shortcrust pie
dough, above, stirring in the sugar after
you have rubbed the butter and fat into
the flour and using milk instead of water.

pâte sucrée

makes: 1 x 8-inch/20-cm tart case
preparation time: 10 minutes,
plus 30 minutes chilling

1½ cups all-purpose flour

4 oz/115 g butter, chilled and cubed

2 oz/55 g golden superfine sugar

1 egg yolk

1 tsp vanilla extract

a little water

Make in the same way as the shortcrust
pie dough, left, stirring in the sugar after
you have rubbed the butter into the flour.
Stir in the egg yolk and vanilla extract,
with a little water if necessary, to make a
smooth dough.

rich shortcrust pie dough

makes: 1 x 8-inch/20-cm tart case
preparation time: 10 minutes,
plus 30 minutes chilling

generous 1 cup all-purpose flour, plus extra
  for dusting

3½ oz/100 g butter, diced

1 tbsp golden superfine sugar

1 egg yolk, beaten with 1 tbsp water

1 Sift the flour into a large bowl. Add
the butter and rub it in with your
fingertips until the mixture resembles fine
bread crumbs, then stir in the sugar. Stir
in the beaten egg yolk.

2 Knead lightly to form a firm dough.
Cover with plastic wrap and leave to
chill in the refrigerator for 30 minutes.

3 Roll out the dough on a lightly
floured work counter and use to line
an 8-inch/20-cm tart pan.

Chocolate Decorations

Decorations add a special touch to a cake or dessert. They can be interleaved with parchment paper and stored in airtight containers. Decorations made with semi-sweet chocolate will keep for 4 weeks, and with milk or white chocolate for 2 weeks.

chocolate curls

1 Choose a thick bar of chocolate, and keep it at room temperature.

2 Using a sharp vegetable peeler, scrape lightly along the chocolate to form fine curls, or more firmly to form thicker ones.

chocolate caraque

It takes a little practice to achieve the professional look of caraque as a decoration for cakes and desserts, although the technique is in itself not difficult.

1 Break a bar of chocolate into pieces and put in a heatproof bowl set over a pan of gently simmering water, stirring until it melts. Spread the melted chocolate over a clean acrylic chopping board or, preferably, a marble slab and let it set.

2 When the chocolate has set, hold the board firmly, position a large, smooth-bladed knife on the chocolate and pull the blade towards you at an angle of 45°, scraping along the chocolate to form the caraque. You should end up with irregularly shaped long scrolls (see below).

3 Using the knife blade, lift the caraque off the board.

chocolate leaves

You need first to select some freshly picked leaves with well-defined veins that are clean, dry, and pliable. Rose leaves and bay leaves are particularly suitable.

1 Holding a leaf by its stem, paint a smooth layer of melted chocolate on to the underside with a small paint brush or pie dough brush.

2 Repeat with the remaining leaves, then place them, chocolate side up, on a cookie sheet lined with waxed paper.

3 Refrigerate for at least an hour until set. When set, peel each leaf away from its chocolate coating.

chocolate sauce

Many dessert recipes include their own version of a chocolate sauce. Here is a basic chocolate sauce, which you can prepare very quickly. A tablespoon of cognac may be added, if preferred.

serves: 4
preparation time: 10 minutes

3 oz/85 g bittersweet chocolate

generous ½ cup light cream

1 Break the chocolate into small pieces and place in a heavy-based saucepan with the cream. Heat very gently over a low heat, stirring constantly, until a smooth sauce is formed.

2 Transfer to a heatproof pitcher and serve warm.

chocolate frosting

4 oz/115 g best-quality semisweet chocolate

4 oz/115 g sweet butter

2 tbsp cold water or dark rum

Melt the chocolate with the water or rum in a heatproof bowl set over a pan of gently simmering water and stir until the chocolate is melted. Whisk in the butter a tablespoon at a time. Allow to cool, whisking occasionally, before use.

homemade crème fraîche

2 tablespoons buttermilk

1¼ cups heavy cream

Put the buttermilk in a preserving jar or a jar with a screw top. Add the cream, then close securely and shake to blend. Let set at warm room temperature for 6–8 hours, then refrigerate for at least 8 hours and up to 4 days. It will develop a slightly tangy flavor. Beat lightly before using.

Small Cakes, Slices & Cookies

Who can resist the smell or taste of fresh-baked cookies, muffins, and biscuits? You will be spoilt for choice in this chapter, which includes such tempting treats as Lemon Chocolate Pinwheels, Chocolate Pretzels, Spiced Almond Cookies, White Chocolate Cookies, Chocolate & Nut Crescents, and Double Chocolate Muffins. You can satisfy hungry children with healthy treats such as Coconut Flapjacks or Chocolate & Apple Oaties, or offer indulgent morsels like Vanilla Hearts or Lavender Cookies during a mid-morning break shared with family or friends.

Chocolate Chip Oat Cookies

Cookies expand during cooking, so it is best to bake them in several batches. Store these chocolate chip cookies in an airtight container for up to a week.

 10 mins 10–12 mins

INGREDIENTS

4 oz/115 g butter or margarine, plus extra for greasing

scant ⅔ cup raw sugar

1 egg

1 tbsp corn syrup

1 tbsp water

1 tsp vanilla extract

½ tsp almond extract

generous 1 cup all-purpose flour, unsifted

½ tsp baking soda

pinch of salt

2 tbsp boiling water

1 cup rolled oats

½ cup semisweet chocolate chips

½ cup white chocolate chips

1 Preheat the oven to 350°F/180°C. Grease 2 large cookie sheets.

2 Put the butter (or margarine), sugar, eggs, corn syrup, water, and vanilla and almond extract in a large bowl or free-standing mixer and beat.

3 In a separate bowl, mix together the flour, baking soda, salt, boiling water, and oats, and then add to the egg mixture. Beat together thoroughly.

4 Stir in the semisweet and white chocolate chips, trying to incorporate them evenly, then put rounded teaspoonfuls of the cookie dough on to the greased cookie sheets, allowing room for the cookies to expand. Transfer the sheets to the preheated oven and bake for 10–12 minutes.

5 Remove the cookies from the oven, then transfer to a wire rack and let them cool completely.

White Chocolate Cookies

These chunky cookies reveal a secret as you bite into them and discover the white chocolate chips scattered through them.

INGREDIENTS

4 oz/115 g butter, softened, plus extra for greasing

⅔ cup brown sugar

1 egg, beaten

1¾ cups self-rising flour

pinch of salt

4½ oz/125 g white chocolate, chopped

⅓ cup chopped Brazil nuts

1 Preheat the oven to 375°F/190°C. Grease several cookie sheets lightly with a little butter.

2 In a large mixing bowl, cream together the butter and sugar until light and fluffy.

3 Gradually add the beaten egg to the creamed mixture, beating well after each addition.

4 Sift the flour and salt into the creamed mixture and blend well.

5 Stir in the white chocolate chunks and the chopped Brazil nuts.

6 Place heaping teaspoonfuls of the dough on the prepared cookie sheets. Put no more than 6 on each sheet because the cookies will spread during cooking.

7 Bake in the oven for 10–12 minutes, or until just golden brown.

8 Transfer the cookies to wire racks and leave until completely cold.

VARIATION
Use semisweet or milk chocolate instead of white chocolate, if you prefer.

Walnut & Chocolate Cookies

These delicious cookies will not be in the cookie jar for long! They are too good, served with a cup of coffee, to resist.

15 mins   10–15 mins

MAKES 24

INGREDIENTS

4 oz/115 g butter, softened, plus extra for greasing

¼ cup golden granulated sugar

scant ½ cup light muscovado sugar

1 egg, beaten

½ tsp vanilla extract

1 cup all-purpose flour

2 tbsp unsweetened cocoa

½ tsp baking soda

¾ cup milk chocolate chips

½ cup walnuts, chopped coarsely

1 Preheat the oven to 350°F/180°C. Grease 2 large cookies sheets. Put the butter, granulated sugar, and muscovado sugar in a bowl and beat until light and fluffy. Gradually beat in the egg and vanilla extract.

2 Sift the flour, cocoa, and baking soda into the cookie dough and stir in carefully. Stir in the chocolate chips and walnuts. Drop spoonfuls of the cookie dough, well apart, on greased cookie sheets.

3 Bake in the oven for 10-15 minutes, until the cookie dough has spread and the cookies are starting to feel firm. Leave on the cookie sheets for 2 minutes, then transfer to wire racks to cool completely.

COOK'S TIP
The minimum cooking time will give cookies that are soft and chewy in the middle. The longer cooking time will produce crisper cookies.

Double Chocolate Chip Cookies

Boasting both white and semisweet chocolate chips, these cookies are the ultimate treat for chocolate lovers.

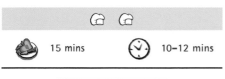

15 mins   10–12 mins

MAKES ABOUT 24

INGREDIENTS

7 oz/200 g butter, softened, plus extra for greasing

1 cup golden superfine sugar

½ tsp vanilla extract

1 large egg

generous 1½ cups all-purpose flour

pinch of salt

1 tsp baking soda

⅔ cup white chocolate chips

⅔ cup semisweet chocolate chips

1 Preheat the oven to 350°F/180°C. Grease 2 cookie sheets with butter. Place the butter, sugar, and vanilla extract in a large bowl and beat together. Gradually beat in the egg until the cookie dough is light and fluffy.

2 Sift the flour, salt, and baking soda over the cookie dough and fold in. Fold in the chocolate chips.

3 Drop heaping teaspoonfuls of the cookie dough on to the prepared cookie sheets, allowing room for the cookies to spread during cooking. Bake in the oven for 10–12 minutes, or until crisp outside but still soft inside. Let cool on the cookie sheets for 2 minutes, then transfer to wire racks to cool completely.

COOK'S TIP
If you prefer crisp cookies, rather than soft, cook them for a little longer, about 13–15 minutes, then proceed as in the recipe.

Viennese Chocolate Fingers

These cookies have a fabulously light, melting texture. You can leave them plain, but for real indulgence dip them in chocolate to decorate.

35 mins

15–20 mins

INGREDIENTS

4 oz/115 g sweet butter, plus extra for greasing

6 tbsp confectioners' sugar

1½ cups self-rising flour, sifted

3 tbsp cornstarch

7 oz/200 g semisweet chocolate, broken into pieces

1 Preheat the oven to 375°F/190°C. Lightly grease 2 cookie sheets. Beat the butter and sugar in a mixing bowl until light and fluffy. Gradually beat in the flour and cornstarch.

2 Put 2¾ oz/75 g of the semisweet chocolate in a heatproof bowl set over a pan of gently simmering water and stir until melted. Beat the melted chocolate into the dough.

3 Place in a pastry bag fitted with a large star tip and pipe fingers about 2 inches/5 cm long on the cookie sheets, allowing room for the cookies to spread during cooking.

4 Bake in the preheated oven for 12–15 minutes. Let cool slightly on the cookie sheets, then transfer to a wire rack and let cool completely.

5 Melt the remaining chocolate as in step 2. Dip one end of each cookie in the chocolate, allowing the excess to drip back into the bowl.

6 Place the cookies on a sheet of parchment paper and let the chocolate set before serving.

COOK'S TIP
If the cookie dough is too thick to pipe, beat in a little milk to thin it out.

Chocolate Chip Cookies

No chocolate cook's repertoire would be complete without a chocolate chip cookie recipe. This recipe can be used to make several variations.

 35 mins   10–12 mins

MAKES 18

INGREDIENTS

4 oz/115 g soft margarine, plus extra for greasing

1½ cups all-purpose flour

1 tsp baking powder

scant ⅔ cup brown sugar

¼ cup superfine sugar

½ tsp vanilla extract

1 egg

⅔ cup semisweet chocolate chips

1 Preheat the oven to 375°F/190°C. Lightly grease 2 cookie sheets. Place all of the ingredients in a large mixing bowl and beat until they are thoroughly combined.

2 Place tablespoonfuls of the cookie dough on to the prepared cookie sheets, allowing room for the cookies to spread during cooking.

3 Bake in the preheated oven for 10–12 minutes, or until the cookies are golden brown.

4 Using a spatula, transfer the cookies to a wire rack to cool completely.

VARIATIONS
For Choc & Nut Cookies, add ½ cup chopped hazelnuts to the basic mixture. For Double Choc Cookies, beat in 1½ oz/40 g melted semisweet chocolate. For White Chocolate Chip Cookies, use white chocolate chips instead of the semisweet chocolate chips.

Chocolate & Coconut Cookies

These delicious, melt-in-the-mouth cookies are finished off with a simple frosting and a generous sprinkling of coconut.

40 mins   15–20 mins

MAKES 24

I N G R E D I E N T S

½ cup soft margarine, plus extra for greasing

1 tsp vanilla extract

½ cup confectioners' sugar, sifted

1 cup all-purpose flour

2 tbsp unsweetened cocoa

1 cup shredded coconut

2 tbsp butter

3½ oz/100 g white marshmallows

grated white chocolate, to decorate

1 Preheat the oven to 350°F/180°C. Lightly grease a cookie sheet. Beat together the margarine, vanilla, and confectioners' sugar in a bowl until fluffy. Sift together the flour and cocoa and beat it into the dough with ⅔ cup coconut.

2 Roll rounded teaspoons of the cookie dough into balls and place on the prepared cookie sheet, allowing room for the cookies to spread during cooking.

3 Flatten the balls slightly with a spatula and bake in the preheated oven for 12–15 minutes, until just firm.

4 Let cool on the cookie sheet for a few minutes before transferring to a wire rack to cool completely.

5 Place the butter and marshmallows in a small pan and heat gently, stirring until melted. Spread a little of the frosting mixture over each cookie and dip in the remaining coconut. Let set. Decorate with grated white chocolate before serving.

Chocolate Vanilla Pinwheels

These two-tone spiral biscuits look impressive, but they are easy to make. Presented in a pretty box, they make an ideal gift.

20 mins plus
1 hr chilling

10–15 mins

MAKES ABOUT 36

INGREDIENTS

8 oz/225 g butter, softened, plus extra
    for greasing

½ cup golden caster sugar

3 cups all-purpose flour, plus extra
    for dusting

1 tbsp unsweetened cocoa

1 tsp vanilla extract

1 Put the butter and sugar in a bowl and beat until light and fluffy. Transfer half the cookie dough to another bowl and add 1¼ cups of the flour and the cocoa. Stir the vanilla extract into the other half of the cookie dough and sift in the remaining flour. Stir both mixtures to make firm pliable doughs.

2 On a floured work counter roll out each dough piece to a rectangle measuring 8 x 11 inches/20 x 28 cm. Place the chocolate dough on a piece of waxed paper and carefully place the vanilla dough on top. Roll up firmly from a long side, using the paper to guide the rolling. Wrap the roll in the paper and chill in the refrigerator for 1 hour, or until firm.

3 Preheat the oven to 350°F/180°C. Grease 2 or 3 cookie sheets. Unwrap the dough and cut into thin slices. Place the cookies on the prepared cookie sheets and bake in the oven for 10-15 minutes, until golden. Cool on the cookie sheets for 2 minutes then transfer to wire racks to cool completely.

COOK'S TIP
Roll up the cookie dough firmly or the cookies will crack.

Chocolate & Apricot Cookies

White chocolate and apricots make a very flavorful combination.
Serve these cookies as an afternoon treat or after dinner with coffee.

 15 mins plus 1 hr to chill   10 mins

MAKES 24

INGREDIENTS

2½ cups white chocolate, chopped into small pieces

1 cup all-purpose flour, sifted, plus extra for dusting

½ tsp baking powder

½ tsp baking soda

pinch of salt

4 tbsp butter, plus extra for greasing

5 tbsp granulated sugar

1 tsp vanilla extract

1 egg

½ cup no-soak dried apricots, chopped, plus 3-4 extra, cut into thin slices, to decorate

1 Put ½ cup of the white chocolate pieces into a heatproof bowl set over a pan of gently simmering water; stir until melted. Remove from the heat. Sift the flour, baking powder, baking soda, and salt into a separate bowl. In another bowl, cream the butter, sugar, and vanilla. Beat in the egg. Add the apricots, melted chocolate, and 1 cup of the remaining chocolate pieces.

2 Add the flour mixture and beat well. Using your hands, form the dough into a ball. Cover the bowl with plastic wrap and chill in the refrigerator for at least 1 hour. Preheat the oven to 350°F/180°C. Grease 1-2 large cookie sheets.

3 Roll out the dough into an oblong ¹⁄₁₆ inch/2 mm thick. Using cookie cutters, make 24 circles. Put on the cookie sheets, place in the preheated oven and bake for 10 minutes. Transfer to a wire rack to cool. Melt the remaining chocolate (see step 1) and dip the cookies in it. Put each one on waxed paper, decorate with apricot slices and let set. Store in an airtight container in the refrigerator.

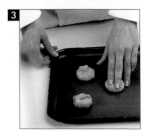

Lemon Chocolate Pinwheels

These stunning cookies will have your guests guessing what are the mystery ingredients that give the pinwheels their exotic flavor!

🍰 15 mins plus 1 hr chilling   🕐 10–12 mins

MAKES 40

INGREDIENTS

6 oz/175 g butter, softened, plus extra for greasing

3 cups all-purpose flour, plus extra for dusting

1⅓ cups superfine sugar

1 egg, beaten

1 oz/25 g semisweet chocolate, broken into pieces

grated rind of 1 lemon

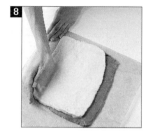
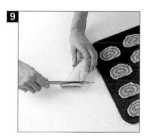

1 Grease and flour several cookie sheets.

2 In a large mixing bowl, cream together the butter and sugar until light and fluffy.

3 Gradually add the beaten egg to the creamed mixture, beating well after each addition.

4 Sift the flour into the creamed mixture and mix thoroughly until a soft dough forms.

5 Transfer half of the dough to another bowl. Put the chocolate in a heatproof bowl set over a pan of gently simmering water until melted. Cool slightly. Beat in the chocolate.

6 Stir the grated lemon rind into the other half of the plain dough.

7 On a lightly floured work counter, roll out the dough to form 2 rectangles.

8 Lay the lemon dough on top of the chocolate dough. Roll up tightly, using a sheet of parchment paper to guide you. Chill the dough for 1 hour.

9 Preheat the oven to 375°F/190°C. Cut the roll into 40 slices, place them on the cookie sheets, and bake in the oven for 10–12 minutes, or until lightly golden. Transfer the pinwheels to a wire rack and let cool completely before serving.

COOK'S TIP
To make rolling out easier, place each piece of dough between 2 sheets of parchment paper.

Molten Chocolate Cookies

The ultimate cookies—chocolate hazelnut spread, from a jar, packed inside a chocolate cookie to produce an irresistible soft chocolate center.

20 mins plus
30 mins chilling   15 mins

MAKES 12–14

INGREDIENTS

4 oz/115 g butter, plus extra for greasing

1½ cups self-rising flour

2 tbsp unsweetened cocoa

½ cup superfine sugar

1 egg, beaten

all-purpose flour, for dusting

7 oz/200 g chocolate hazelnut spread

milk, for brushing

confectioners' sugar, for dusting

1 Preheat the oven to 375°F/190°C. Grease 2 large cookie sheets. Sift the flour and unsweetened cocoa together.

2 Whisk the butter and superfine sugar together until soft and fluffy. Gradually beat in the egg, then the sifted flour. Place the dough on a lightly floured work counter and knead for a short time until smooth. Chill in the refrigerator for 30 minutes.

3 Place the dough between 2 sheets of floured parchment paper, thinly roll out half of it, and cut into circles using a 2¼-inch/5.5-cm cookie cutter.

4 Place the circles on the prepared cookie sheets and place heaping teaspoons of the chocolate hazelnut spread on each. Brush the edges with a little milk.

5 Roll out the remaining dough and cut into circles using a 2³⁄₄-inch/7-cm cookie cutter. Place on top of the chocolate hazelnut spread and seal the edges well.

6 Bake the cookies in the oven for about 15 minutes, until firm. Transfer to a wire rack and let cool. When cold, dust with sifted confectioners' sugar.

Chocolate Butter Cookies

Topping these simple chocolate cookies with a spoonful of chocolate and half a walnut turns them into something quite sophisticated.

20 mins   15 mins

MAKES 24

INGREDIENTS

4 oz/115 g butter, plus extra for greasing

1½ cups all-purpose flour

generous ⅓ cup unsweetened cocoa

½ cup superfine sugar

1 egg, beaten

6 oz/175 g semisweet chocolate, broken into pieces

24 walnut halves

1 Preheat the oven to 350°F/180°C. Grease 2–3 large cookie sheets. Sift the flour and cocoa together into a large bowl.

2 Add the butter to the flour mixture and rub in until the mixture resembles fine bread crumbs. Stir in the sugar then add enough of the beaten egg to form a soft dough.

3 On a lightly floured work counter, roll out the dough to ⅛-inch/3-mm thickness, then cut into circles, using a 2½-inch/6-cm cookie cutter. Place the circles on the prepared cookie sheets, allowing room for the cookies to spread during cooking.

4 Bake the cookies in the oven for about 15 minutes, until firm. Transfer to a wire rack and let cool.

5 When the cookies have cooled, melt the chocolate in a heatproof bowl set over a pan of gently simmering water. Spoon a little of the melted chocolate on to the center of each cookie, then top with a walnut half. Let set before serving.

Chocolate Orange Cookies

These delicious chocolate cookies have a tangy orange frosting. Children love them cut into animal shapes.

🍰 40 mins   🕐 15–20 mins

MAKES 30

INGREDIENTS

3¼ oz/90 g butter, softened

⅓ cup superfine sugar

1 egg

1 tbsp milk

2 cups all-purpose flour, plus extra
 for dusting

2 tbsp unsweetened cocoa

FROSTING

1½ cups confectioners' sugar, sifted

3 tbsp orange juice

a little semisweet chocolate,
 broken into pieces

1 Preheat the oven to 350°F/180°C. Line 2 cookie sheets with sheets of parchment paper.

2 Beat together the butter and sugar until the cookie dough is light and fluffy. Beat in the egg and milk until well combined. Sift the flour and unsweetened cocoa into the bowl and gradually mix together to form a soft dough. Use your fingers to incorporate the last of the flour and bring the dough together.

3 Roll out the dough on a lightly floured work counter until ¼-inch/5-mm thick. Cut out circles using a 2-inch/5-cm fluted round cookie cutter.

4 Place the circles on the prepared cookie sheets and bake in the oven for 10–12 minutes, or until golden.

5 Let the cookies cool on the cookie sheet for a few minutes before transferring them to a wire rack to cool completely and become crisp.

6 To make the frosting, put the confectioners' sugar in a bowl and stir in enough orange juice to form a thin frosting that will coat the back of the spoon. Put a spoonful of frosting in the center of each cookie and let set. Place the semisweet chocolate in a heatproof bowl set over a pan of gently simmering water and stir until melted. Drizzle thin lines of melted chocolate over the cookies and let set before serving.

Chocolate & Apple Oaties

Applesauce and apple juice add a pleasing sweetness to these cookies. They can be stored in an airtight container for several days.

45 mins   15 mins

MAKES 24

I N G R E D I E N T S

4 oz/115 g butter or margarine, plus extra for greasing

⅔ cup applesauce

2 tbsp apple juice

½ cup raw sugar

1 tsp baking soda

1 tsp almond extract

¼ cup boiling water

1⅓ cups rolled oats

2 cups all-purpose flour, unsifted

pinch of salt

⅓ cup semisweet chocolate chips

1 Preheat the oven to 400°F/200°C. Grease a large cookie sheet.

2 Blend the butter (or margarine) and sugar in a food processor until a fluffy consistency is reached. Blend in the apple sauce and apple juice.

3 In a separate bowl, mix together the baking soda, almond extract, and water, then add to the food processor and mix with the apple mixture. In another bowl, mix together the oats, flour, and salt, then gradually stir into the apple mixture and beat well. Stir in the chocolate chips.

4 Put 24 rounded tablespoonfuls of the cookie dough on to the cookie sheet, allowing room for the cookies to spread during cooking. Transfer to the preheated oven and bake for 15 minutes, or until golden brown.

5 Remove the cookies from the oven, then transfer to a wire rack and let them cool completely before serving.

Hazelnut Bites

Toasted hazelnuts and chocolate partner each other very successfully.
Use milk or white chocolate if preferred.

45 mins   10–15 mins

MAKES 24

INGREDIENTS

4 oz/115 g butter, plus extra for greasing

¾ cup raw sugar

1 egg

1 tbsp almond extract

1 cup all-purpose flour

¾ tsp baking powder

pinch of salt

2 cups rolled oats

½ cup semisweet chocolate chips

⅔ cup hazelnuts, toasted and chopped

1¾ cups semisweet chocolate pieces

1 Preheat the oven to 350°F/180°C. Grease a large cookie sheet. Cream the butter and sugar together in a bowl. Add the egg and almond extract and beat well. In a separate bowl, sift together the flour, baking powder, and salt. Beat in the egg mixture. Stir in the oats, chocolate chips, and half of the hazelnuts.

2 Divide the mixture into 24 teaspoonfuls of dough and place on a cookie sheet or sheets. Flatten with a rolling pin. Transfer to the preheated oven and bake for 10 minutes, or until the cookies are golden brown.

3 Remove the cookies from the oven, then transfer to a wire rack and let cool completely. Put the chocolate pieces into a heatproof bowl set over a pan of gently simmering water and stir until melted. Cover the tops of the cookies with melted chocolate, then top with a sprinkling of the remaining hazelnuts. Let cool on waxed paper before serving. Store the cookies in an airtight container in the refrigerator.

Mocha Walnut Cookies

These cookies have a lovely chewy texture. Serve with a cup of coffee for a delicious mid-morning snack.

    20 mins   10–15 mins

MAKES ABOUT 16

INGREDIENTS

4 oz/115 g butter, softened, plus extra for greasing

4 oz/115 g light muscovado sugar

scant ½ cup golden granulated sugar

1 tsp vanilla extract

1 tbsp instant coffee granules dissolved in 1 tbsp hot water

1 egg

1½ cups all-purpose flour

½ tsp baking powder

¼ tsp baking soda

scant ½ cup milk chocolate chips

½ cup walnuts, chopped coarsely

1 Preheat the oven to 350°F/180°C. Grease 2 cookie sheets. Put the butter, light muscovado sugar, and granulated sugar in a bowl and beat until light and fluffy. Put the vanilla extract, coffee, and egg in a separate bowl and whisk together.

2 Gradually add to the butter and sugar, beating until fluffy. Sift the flour, baking powder, and baking soda into the mixture and fold in carefully. Fold in the chocolate chips and chopped walnuts.

3 Spoon heaping teaspoonfuls of the cookie dough on to the prepared cookie sheets, allowing room for the cookies to spread. Bake for 10-15 minutes, until crisp on the outside but still soft inside. Let cool on the cookie sheets for 2 minutes, then transfer to wire racks to cool completely.

COOK'S TIP
Muscovado sugar has a tendency to be lumpy, so it is a good idea to sift it before use.

Chocolate & Nut Crescents

These crisp little cookies are a variation on a cookie that is served in Greece for festivals and on special occasions.

20 mins

20–25 mins

MAKES 40

INGREDIENTS

8 oz/225 g butter, softened, plus extra for greasing

scant ½ cup golden superfine sugar

1 egg yolk

1 tsp dark rum

½ cup shelled walnuts, ground

generous 1½ cups all-purpose flour, plus extra for shaping

scant ½ cup cornstarch

1 tbsp unsweetened cocoa

sifted confectioners' sugar, for dusting

1 Preheat the oven to 350°F/180°C. Grease several cookie sheets. Place the butter and sugar in a bowl and beat together until pale and fluffy. Beat in the egg yolk and rum. Stir in the walnuts. Sift the flour, cornstarch, and unsweetened cocoa over the mixture and stir, adding a little more flour, if necessary, to make a firm dough.

2 With lightly floured hands, break off walnut-size pieces of dough and roll into 3-inch/7.5-cm lengths, thick in the center and tapering into pointed ends. Shape into crescents and place on the prepared cookie sheets.

3 Bake in the oven for 20–25 minutes, or until firm. Let cool on the cookie sheets for 2 minutes, then transfer to wire racks to cool completely. Lightly dust the cookies with confectioners' sugar, before serving.

COOK'S TIP
Do not use ready-ground walnuts as they are too fine. Prepare your own in a food processor if possible, taking care not to over-grind them.

Nutty Chocolate Drizzles

Drizzling a little melted chocolate over these cookies makes a very quick yet attractive decoration.

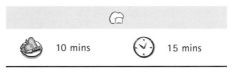

10 mins   15 mins

MAKES 24

INGREDIENTS

7 oz/200 g butter or margarine, plus extra for greasing

1½ cups raw sugar

1 egg

1 cup all-purpose flour, sifted

1 tsp baking powder

1 tsp baking soda

1½ cups rolled oats

¼ cup bran

¼ cup wheat germ

¾ cup mixed nuts, toasted and chopped coarsely

scant 1¼ cups semisweet chocolate chips

⅔ cup raisins and golden raisins

1 cup coarsely chopped semisweet chocolate

1 Preheat the oven to 350°F/180°C. Grease a large cookie sheet. In a large bowl, cream together the butter, sugar, and egg. Add the flour, baking powder, baking soda, oats, bran, and wheat germ and mix together until well combined. Finally stir in the nuts, chocolate chips, and dry fruits.

2 Put 24 rounded tablespoonfuls of the cookie dough on to the greased cookie sheet. Transfer to the preheated oven and bake for 12 minutes, or until the cookies are golden brown.

3 Remove the cookies from the oven, then transfer to a wire rack and let them cool. While they are cooling, put the chocolate pieces in a heatproof bowl set over a pan of gently simmering water until melted. Stir the chocolate, then let cool slightly. Use a spoon to drizzle the chocolate in waves over the cookies, or spoon it into a pastry bag and pipe zig zag lines over the cookies. Store in an airtight container in the refrigerator before serving.

Chocolate Nut Crunchies

If you are a fan of Brazil nuts, these are the cookies for you. Use milk chocolate chips instead of the semisweet chocolate chips if preferred.

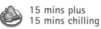

15 mins plus
15 mins chilling   15 mins

MAKES 30

I N G R E D I E N T S

3 tbsp butter or margarine, plus extra
   for greasing

¼ cup shortening

scant ¾ cup raw sugar

1 egg

1 tsp vanilla extract

1 tbsp milk

⅔ cup all-purpose flour, unsifted

1⅓ cups rolled oats

1 tsp baking soda

pinch of salt

1 cup semisweet chocolate chips

½ cup chopped Brazil nuts

1 Preheat the oven to 350°F/180°C. Grease a large cookie sheet.

2 Put the butter (or margarine), shortening, sugar, egg, vanilla extract, and milk in a free-standing mixer and beat for at least 3 minutes, or until a fluffy consistency is reached.

3 In a separate bowl, combine the flour, oats, baking soda, and salt. Stir into the egg mixture, then add the chocolate chips and Brazil nuts, and mix thoroughly. Cover the bowl with plastic wrap. Chill in the refrigerator for 30 minutes.

4 Put 30 rounded tablespoonfuls of the dough on to the greased cookie sheet, allowing room for the cookies to spread during cooking. Transfer to the oven and bake for 15 minutes, or until the cookies are golden brown.

5 Remove the cookies from the oven, then transfer to a wire rack and let cool before serving.

Coffee Whole-Wheat Bakes

These delicious, dark cookies, flavored with coffee and toasted chopped hazelnuts, are perfect served with coffee.

🥧 20 mins 🕐 16–18 mins

MAKES 24

INGREDIENTS

6 oz/175 g butter or margarine, plus extra for greasing

1 cup brown sugar

1 egg

½ cup all-purpose flour

1 tsp baking soda

pinch of salt

½ cup whole-wheat flour

1 tbsp bran

1⅓ cups semisweet chocolate chips

generous 2 cups rolled oats

1 tbsp strong coffee

⅔ cup hazelnuts, toasted and chopped coarsely

1 Preheat the oven to 375°F/190°C. Grease a large cookie sheet. Cream the butter and sugar together in a bowl. Add the egg and beat well, using a hand whisk if preferred.

2 In a separate bowl, sift together the all-purpose flour, baking soda, and salt, then add in the whole-wheat flour and bran. Mix in the egg mixture, then stir in the chocolate chips, oats, coffee, and hazelnuts. Mix well, with an electric whisk if preferred.

3 Put 24 rounded tablespoonfuls of the cookie dough on to the cookie sheet, allowing room for the cookies to spread during cooking. Alternatively, with lightly floured hands, break off pieces of the dough mixture and roll into balls

(about 1 oz/25 g each), place on the cookie sheet and flatten them with the back of a teaspoon. Transfer to the preheated oven and bake for 16–18 minutes, or until the cookies are golden brown.

4 Transfer the cookies to a wire rack and let cool before serving.

Chocolate Wheatmeals

These cookies will keep well in an airtight container for at least 1 week. Dip them in white, light, or semisweet chocolate.

🍰 1 hr   🕐 15–20 mins

MAKES 20

INGREDIENTS

⅓ cup butter, plus extra for greasing

⅔ cup raw sugar

1 egg

¼ cup wheat germ

1 cup whole-wheat self-rising flour

½ cup self-rising flour, sifted

4½ oz/125 g chocolate, broken into pieces

1 Preheat the oven to 350°F/180°C. Lightly grease a cookie sheet. Beat the butter and sugar until fluffy. Add the egg and beat well. Stir in the wheat germ and flours. Bring the dough together with your hands.

2 Roll rounded teaspoonfuls of the dough into balls and place on the prepared cookie sheet, allowing room for the cookies to spread during cooking.

3 Flatten the cookies slightly with the tines of a fork. Bake in the preheated oven for 15–20 minutes, until golden. Let cool on the cookie sheet for a few minutes before transferring to a wire rack to cool completely

COOK'S TIP
These cookies can be frozen very successfully. Freeze them at the end of Step 3 for up to 3 months. Thaw and then dip them in melted chocolate.

4 Put the chocolate in a heatproof bowl set over a pan of gently simmering water until melted. Dip each cookie in the chocolate to cover the flat side and come a little way around the edges. Let the excess chocolate drip back into the bowl.

5 Place the cookies on a sheet of parchment paper in a cool place and let the chocolate set before serving.

Chocolate Temptations

Piping white chocolate lines over these cookies gives them a touch of elegance and sophistication.

15–20 mins   20 mins

MAKES 24

INGREDIENTS

3¼ oz/90 g sweet butter, plus extra for greasing

12½ oz/365 g semisweet chocolate

1 tsp strong coffee

2 eggs

scant ¾ cup brown sugar

generous 1⅓ cups all-purpose flour

¼ tsp baking powder

pinch of salt

2 tsp almond extract

scant ⅔ cup chopped Brazil nuts

scant ⅔ cup chopped hazelnuts

1½ oz/40 g white chocolate

1 Preheat the oven to 350°F/180°C. Grease a large cookie sheet. Put 8 oz/225 g of the semisweet chocolate with the butter and coffee into a heatproof bowl set over a pan of gently simmering water and heat until the chocolate is almost melted.

2 Meanwhile, beat the eggs in a bowl until fluffy. Whisk in the sugar gradually until thick. Remove the chocolate from the heat and stir until smooth. Add to the egg mixture and stir until combined.

3 Sift the flour, baking powder, and salt into a bowl and stir into the chocolate mixture. Chop 3 oz/85 g of semisweet chocolate into pieces and stir into the dough. Stir in the almond extract and nuts.

4 Put 24 tablespoonfuls of the dough on to the cookie sheet, transfer to the preheated oven and bake for 16 minutes. Transfer the cookies to a wire rack to cool.

To decorate, melt the remaining chocolate (semisweet and white) in turn as in step 1, then spoon into a pastry bag and pipe lines on to the cookies.

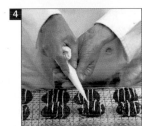

Chocolate Pretzels

If you thought of pretzels as exclusively salted, then think again.
Store these pretzels in an airtight container for up to 1 week.

1 hr 15 mins
plus 15 mins
chilling

10–15 mins

MAKES 30

INGREDIENTS

2¾ oz/75 g sweet butter, plus extra
for greasing

½ cup superfine sugar

1 egg

2 cups all-purpose flour

¼ cup unsweetened cocoa

TO FINISH

1 tbsp butter

3½ oz/100 g semisweet chocolate

confectioners' sugar, for dusting

1 Preheat the oven to 375°F/190°C.
Lightly grease a cookie sheet. Beat
together the butter and sugar in a mixing
bowl until light and fluffy. Beat in the egg.

2 Sift together the flour and cocoa and
gradually beat in to form a soft
dough. Use your fingers to incorporate the
last of the flour and bring the dough
together. Chill for 15 minutes.

3 Break pieces from the dough and roll
into thin sausage shapes about
4 inches/10 cm long and ¼ inch/5 mm
thick. Twist into pretzel shapes by making
a circle, then twist the ends through each
other to form a letter "B."

4 Place on the prepared cookie sheet,
allowing room for the pretzels to
spread during cooking.

5 Bake in the preheated oven for
8–12 minutes. Let the pretzels cool
slightly on the cookie sheet, then transfer
them to a wire rack to cool completely.

6 Put the butter and chocolate in
a heatproof bowl set over a pan of
gently simmering water until the
chocolate has melted. Stir to combine.

7 Dip half of each pretzel into the
chocolate and allow the excess

chocolate to drip back into the bowl. Place
the pretzels on a sheet of parchment paper
and let set.

8 When set, dust the non-chocolate-
coated side of each pretzel with
confectioners' sugar before serving.

Chocolate Roundels

Irresistibly flavored with amaretto, semisweet chocolate chips, hazelnuts, and raisins, these cookies are simple to make.

20 mins   10 mins

MAKES 24

INGREDIENTS

8 oz/225 g butter or margarine, plus extra for greasing

1¼ cups raw sugar

1 tbsp milk

1 egg

1 tsp almond extract

1 tbsp amaretto

1⅔ cups all-purpose flour, sifted, plus extra for rolling

1 tsp baking soda

pinch of salt

1 cup semisweet chocolate chips

½ cup hazelnuts, chopped finely

½ cup raisins

confectioners' sugar, to decorate

1 Preheat the oven to 350°F/180°C. Grease a large cookie sheet. Mix the butter, sugar, and milk together in a bowl. Add the egg, almond extract, and amaretto and beat well.

2 In a separate bowl, sift together the flour, baking soda, and salt. Then mix in the egg mixture, along with the chocolate chips, nuts, and raisins. Mix together thoroughly.

3 Sprinkle flour on a work counter or cutting board. Using your hands, roll the dough into balls, then put them on to the greased cookie sheet, allowing room for them to spread during cooking. Flatten them into roundels with a rolling pin and trim the edges with the cutter if needed.

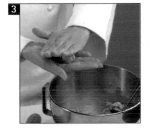

4 Transfer the cookies to the preheated oven and bake for 10 minutes, or until golden brown. Transfer to a wire rack and let cool. Sprinkle over confectioners' sugar before serving.

Chocolate Almond Snowballs

These tasty little cookies are an ideal choice at Christmas. The "snow" on them is simply a generous sprinkling of confectioners' sugar.

20 mins   15–20 mins

MAKES 25

INGREDIENTS

3 oz/85 g butter, plus extra for greasing

1½ cups all-purpose flour

pinch of baking powder

¼ cup superfine sugar

1 egg yolk

few drops almond extract

¼ cup milk chocolate chips

¼ cup confectioners' sugar

1 Preheat the oven to 325°F/160°C. Grease 1–2 large cookie sheets. Sift the flour and baking powder together.

2 Whisk the butter and superfine sugar together until soft and fluffy. Beat in the egg yolk and almond extract, then the sifted flour. Stir in the chocolate chips. Shape the mixture into 1-inch/2.5-cm balls and place on the prepared cookie sheets, allowing room for the cookies to spread during cooking.

3 Bake the cookies in the oven for 15–20 minutes, until firm. Transfer to a wire rack and let cool slightly.

4 Put the confectioners' sugar in a large polythene bag, add a few warm cookies and shake gently until coated. Return to the wire rack and repeat with the remaining cookies. Let cool on the wire rack until cold.

Chocolate Snow Flurries

As their name suggests, these little domes of soft, fudge-like cookies are coated with coconut to give them the appearance of sprinkled snow.

10 mins plus
3 hrs chilling   15 mins

MAKES 32

INGREDIENTS

1¼ cups all-purpose flour

⅓ cup unsweetened cocoa

1 tsp baking powder

5 tbsp sunflower oil

1 cup superfine sugar

2 eggs

1 tsp vanilla extract

⅔ cup dry unsweetened coconut

1 Sift the flour, cocoa, and baking powder together. In a large bowl, whisk the oil, sugar, eggs, and vanilla extract together until well blended, then fold in the flour mixture. Cover the bowl and let chill in the refrigerator for at least 3 hours.

2 Preheat the oven to 350°F/180°C. Line 2–3 large cookie sheets with parchment paper. Shape heaping teaspoonfuls of the mixture into balls using your hands, then roll in the coconut. Place on the prepared cookie sheets, allowing room for the cookies to spread during cooking.

3 Bake the cookies in the preheated oven for 15 minutes, until firm. Transfer to a wire rack and let cool.

Chocolate Macaroons

Classic macaroons are always a favorite for coffee-time: they are made even better by the addition of rich semisweet chocolate.

1 hr   25 mins

MAKES 18

INGREDIENTS

butter, for greasing

2¾ oz/75 g semisweet chocolate, broken into pieces

2 egg whites

pinch of salt

1 cup superfine sugar

1¼ cups ground almonds

shredded coconut, for sprinkling (optional)

1 Preheat the oven to 300°F/150°C. Grease 2 cookie sheets and line with parchment paper or rice paper

2 Melt the semisweet chocolate in a small heatproof bowl set over a pan of simmering water. Let cool slightly

3 Whisk the egg whites with the salt until soft peaks form.

VARIATION
For a traditional finish, top each macaroon with half a candied cherry before baking.

4 Gradually whisk the superfine sugar into the egg whites, then fold in the almonds and cooled melted chocolate.

5 Place heaping teaspoons of the mixture spaced well apart on the prepared cookie sheets and spread into circles about 2½ inches/6 cm across. Sprinkle with shredded coconut (if using).

6 Bake in the preheated oven for about 25 minutes, or until they are firm.

7 Let cool before carefully lifting from the cookie sheets. Transfer the macaroons to a wire rack and let cool completely before serving.

Cookies & Cream Sandwiches

Delicious chocolate shortbread cookies, with a delicate hint of spice, are sandwiched together with chocolate cream. Assemble just before serving.

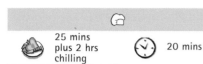

25 mins plus 2 hrs chilling   20 mins

SERVES 4

INGREDIENTS

4½ oz/125 g butter, softened

scant ¾ cup golden confectioners' sugar

scant 1 cup all-purpose flour

⅜ cup unsweetened cocoa

½ tsp ground cinnamon

FILLING

4½ oz/125 g semisweet chocolate, broken into pieces

¼ cup heavy cream

1 Preheat the oven to 325°F/160°C. Line a baking sheet with nonstick parchment paper. Place the butter and sugar in a large bowl and beat together until light and fluffy. Sift the flour, unsweetened cocoa, and ground cinnamon into the bowl and mix to form a dough.

2 Place the dough between 2 sheets of nonstick parchment paper and roll out to ¹/₈ inch/3 mm thick. Cut out 2¹/₂-inch/6-cm circles and place on the prepared baking sheet. Bake in the oven for 15 minutes, or until firm to the touch. Let cool for 2 minutes, then transfer to wire racks to cool completely.

3 Meanwhile, make the filling. Place the chocolate and cream in a pan and heat gently until the chocolate has melted. Stir until smooth. Let cool, then let chill in the refrigerator for 2 hours, or until firm. Sandwich the cookies together in pairs with a spoonful of chocolate cream and serve.

COOK'S TIP
Do not sandwich the cookies together too long before serving, otherwise they will go soft. Store unsandwiched cookies in an airtight container for up to 3 days.

Dutch Macaroons

These unusual cookie treats are delicious served with coffee. They also make an ideal dessert cookie to serve with ice cream.

40 mins   20–25 mins

MAKES 20

INGREDIENTS

rice paper

2 egg whites

1 cup superfine sugar

1⅔ cups ground almonds

8 oz/225 g semisweet chocolate

1 Preheat the oven to 350°F/180°C. Cover 2 cookie sheets with rice paper. Whisk the egg whites in a large mixing bowl until stiff, then fold in the sugar and ground almonds.

2 Place the mixture in a large pastry bag fitted with a ½-inch/1-cm plain tip and pipe fingers, about 3 inches/7.5 cm long, allowing room for the cookies to spread during cooking.

3 Bake in the preheated oven for 15–20 minutes, until golden. Transfer to a wire rack and let cool. Remove the excess rice paper from around the edges.

4 Melt the chocolate and dip the bottom of each cookie into the chocolate. Place the macaroons on a sheet of parchment paper and let set.

5 Drizzle any remaining chocolate over the top of the cookies (you may need to reheat the chocolate in order to do this). Let it set before serving.

COOK'S TIP
Rice paper is edible so you can just break off the excess from around the edge of the cookies. Remove it completely before dipping in the chocolate, if you prefer.

Chocolate Peanut Cookies

Made with peanut butter, chopped peanuts, and chocolate chips, these cookies are always a hit with children.

10 mins plus
1 hr to chill

20 mins

MAKES 24

INGREDIENTS

7 oz/200 g butter or margarine, plus extra for greasing

generous 1⅓ cups brown sugar

1½ cups crunchy peanut butter

1 egg

2 tsp almond extract

2 cups all-purpose flour

1 tsp baking soda

½ cup semisweet chocolate chips

⅔ cup peanuts

1 Preheat the oven to 350°F/180°C. Grease a large cookie sheet. Chop the peanuts and set aside. Cream the butter (or margarine) and sugar together in a bowl until fluffy. Add the peanut butter, egg, and almond extract and mix thoroughly.

2 In a separate bowl, fold in the flour and baking soda; add gradually to the peanut butter mixture. Stir in the chocolate chips and peanuts and mix thoroughly. Cover the bowl with plastic wrap and let chill in the refrigerator for 1 hour, or until the dough is firm.

3 Put 24 rounded balls of the dough on to the greased cookie sheet, then flatten with a spatula. Ensure that they are well spaced because they may expand during cooking. Transfer to the preheated oven and bake for 20 minutes, or until the cookies are golden brown.

4 Remove the cookies from the oven, then transfer to a wire rack and let them cool before serving.

Chocolate Peanut Cookies

These delicious cookies contain two popular ingredients: peanuts and chocolate. The rice flour gives them an original twist.

🍰 40 mins   🕐 10 mins

MAKES 50

I N G R E D I E N T S

1½ cups all-purpose flour

1¼ cups rice flour

2 tbsp unsweetened cocoa

1 tsp baking powder

pinch of salt

5 oz/140 g white vegetable fat

1 cup superfine sugar

1 tsp vanilla extract

1 cup raisins, chopped

¾ cup unsalted peanuts, chopped finely

6 oz/175 g bittersweet chocolate, broken into pieces

1 Preheat the oven to 350°F/180°C. Line several cookie sheets with sheets of parchment paper.

2 Sift the flours, cocoa, baking powder, and salt into a bowl and stir well.

3 Using an electric whisk, beat the fat and sugar in a large bowl for about 2 minutes until light and creamy. Blend in the vanilla extract and the flour mixture to form a soft dough. Stir in the raisins.

4 Put the chopped peanuts on a plate. Pinch off walnut-size pieces of the dough and roll into balls. Drop into the peanuts and roll to coat, pressing them lightly to stick. Place the balls well apart on the prepared cookie sheets.

5 Using the base of a drinking glass dipped in flour, gently flatten each ball to a circle about ¼-inch/5-mm thick.

6 Bake in the preheated oven for about 10 minutes, until golden and lightly set; do not over-bake. Cool on the sheets for about 1 minute, then, using a spatula, transfer to a wire rack to cool.

7 Put the chocolate in a heatproof bowl set over a pan of gently simmering water until melted. Drizzle the tops of the cookies with the melted chocolate when they have cooled. Let set before transferring to an airtight container with waxed paper between the layers.

Chocolate Raisin Cookies

These delicious cookies, flavored with chocolate, raisins, and almonds are especially hard to resist.

15–20 mins   16 mins

MAKES 55

INGREDIENTS

7 oz/200 g butter, plus extra for greasing

2 cups raw sugar

2 eggs

1 tsp almond extract

2 cups all-purpose flour, sifted

pinch of salt

1 tsp baking soda

1 tsp baking powder

3 cups rolled oats

generous 2 cups raisins

4 oz/115 g semisweet chocolate

1½ cups almonds, chopped finely

1 Preheat the oven to 375°F/190°C. Grease several large cookie sheets. Finely chop the chocolate. Cream the butter and sugar together in a bowl until fluffy. Mix in the eggs and almond extract.

2 In a separate bowl, sift together the flour, salt, baking soda, and baking powder. Add the egg mixture, along with the rolled oats, raisins, chopped chocolate, and almonds, and mix together thoroughly.

3 With lightly floured hands, shape the dough into small balls (each about 1 oz/25 g) and place on the prepared cookie sheets, allowing room for the cookies to spread during cooking. Use a spatula or the bottom of a glass to press lightly down on the cookies to flatten them slightly. Transfer the sheet to the oven and bake for 16 minutes, or until the cookies are golden brown.

4 Remove the cookies from the oven, then transfer to a wire rack and let cool before serving.

Easter Cookies

Despite their name, these cookies are good to eat at any time of year! They will be popular with adults and children alike.

40 mins   15 mins

MAKES 20

INGREDIENTS

5½ oz/150 g butter, softened, plus extra for greasing

generous ¾ cup golden superfine sugar

1 egg, beaten

2 tbsp milk

¼ cup chopped candied peel

generous ⅔ cup currants

2½ cups all-purpose flour, plus extra for dusting

1 tsp ground allspice

GLAZE

1 egg white, beaten lightly

2 tbsp golden superfine sugar

1 Preheat the oven to 350°F/180°C. Grease 2 large cookie sheets. Place the butter and sugar in a bowl and beat until light and fluffy. Gradually beat in the egg and milk. Stir in the candied peel and currants, then sift in the flour and allspice. Mix together to make a firm dough. Knead lightly until smooth.

2 On a floured counter, roll out the dough to ¼ inch/ 5 mm thick and use a 2-inch/5-cm round cookie cutter to stamp out the cookies. Re-roll the dough trimmings and stamp out more cookies until the dough is used up. Place the cookies on the prepared cookie sheets and bake in the preheated oven for 10 minutes.

3 Remove from the oven to glaze. Brush with the egg white and sprinkle with the superfine sugar, then return to the oven for an additional 5 minutes, or until lightly browned. Let cool on the cookie sheets for 2 minutes, then transfer to wire racks to cool completely.

VARIATION
If you do not like candied peel, you can substitute another ⅓ cup of extra currants instead.

Chocolate Chip Oaties

Rolled oats give a light texture and a nutty flavor to these cookies. They are superb served with a cup of fresh coffee.

15 mins　　15 mins

MAKES ABOUT 20

INGREDIENTS

4 oz/115 g butter, softened, plus extra for greasing

½ cup firmly packed light brown sugar

1 egg

1 cup rolled oats

1 tbsp milk

1 tsp vanilla extract

scant 1 cup all-purpose flour

1 tbsp unsweetened cocoa

½ tsp baking powder

6 oz/175 g semisweet chocolate, broken into pieces

6 oz/175 g milk chocolate, broken into pieces

1 Preheat the oven to 350°F/180°C. Grease 2 cookie sheets. Place the butter and sugar in a bowl and beat together until light and fluffy.

2 Beat in the egg, then add the oats, milk, and vanilla extract. Beat together until well blended. Sift the flour, unsweetened cocoa, and baking powder into the cookie batter and stir. Stir in the chocolate pieces.

3 Place tablespoonfuls of the cookie batter on the prepared cookie sheets and flatten slightly with a fork. Bake in the preheated oven for 15 minutes, or until slightly risen and firm. Let cool on the cookie sheets for 2 minutes, then transfer to wire racks to cool completely.

Zebra Cookies

These tempting cookies are topped with dark and light chocolate buttons, which makes them a favorite with children. Let cool before serving.

15 mins plus
3 hrs chilling

15 mins

MAKES 18–20

INGREDIENTS

2 oz/55 g semisweet chocolate, broken into pieces

1 cup all-purpose flour

1 tsp baking powder

1 egg

¾ cup superfine sugar

¼ cup sunflower oil, plus extra for oiling

½ tsp vanilla extract

2 tbsp confectioners' sugar

1 small package milk chocolate buttons

1 small package white chocolate buttons

1 Melt the chocolate in a heatproof bowl set over a pan of simmering water. Let cool. Sift the flour and baking powder together.

2 Meanwhile, in a large bowl, whisk the egg, sugar, oil, and vanilla extract together. Whisk in the cooled, melted chocolate until well blended, then gradually stir in the sifted flour. Cover the bowl and let chill for at least 3 hours.

3 Preheat the oven to 375°F/190°C. Oil 1–2 large cookies sheets. Shape tablespoonfuls of the cookie dough into log shapes using your hands, each measuring about 2 inches/5 cm.

4 Roll the logs generously in the confectioners' sugar then place on the prepared cookie sheets, allowing room for the cookies to spread during cooking.

5 Bake the cookies in the oven for about 15 minutes, until firm. As soon as the cookies are done, place 3 chocolate buttons down the center of each, alternating the colors. Transfer to a wire rack and let cool.

Chocolate Ribbon Cookies

Enlist the help of children when you make these cookies, for they will be impressed with the results—both their taste and appearance.

20 mins plus
4 hrs chilling

15 mins

MAKES 50

INGREDIENTS

2 tbsp unsweetened cocoa

2 tbsp water

1 cup butter, plus extra for greasing

½ cup superfine sugar

2⅓ cups all-purpose flour, plus extra
  for dusting

1 tsp vanilla extract

1 Line the bottom of an 8½ x 4½-inch/ 22 x 11-cm loaf pan with parchment paper. Mix the cocoa with the water to form a paste.

2 Whisk the butter, sugar, and flour together until the mixture resembles fine bread crumbs. Divide the mixture in half and add the cocoa paste to one portion. Knead with your hands until the mixture is evenly colored and forms a smooth dough.

3 Add the vanilla extract to the remaining mixture, knead to form a smooth dough and divide it in half.

4 Using your fingertips, evenly press out each piece of dough on a lightly floured work counter to the size of the prepared pan.

5 Layer the flattened pieces of dough in the pan, starting with a chocolate layer. Press well together to remove any trapped air. Cover and let chill in the refrigerator for at least 4 hours.

6 Preheat the oven to 375°F/190°C. Grease 3–4 large cookie sheets. Turn out the dough and cut widthwise into thirds, then slice each third widthwise into ¼-inch/5-mm slices. Place on the prepared cookie sheets, allowing room for the cookies to spread during cooking.

7 Bake the cookies in the oven for 15 minutes, or until firm. Transfer to a wire rack and let cool.

Peanut Butter Cookies

These crunchy cookies will be popular with children of all ages as they contain their favorite food—peanut butter.

MAKES 20

INGREDIENTS

4 oz/115 g butter, softened, plus extra for greasing

½ cup chunky peanut butter

generous 1 cup granulated sugar

1 egg, beaten lightly

generous 1 cup all-purpose flour

½ tsp baking powder

pinch of salt

½ cup chopped unsalted peanuts

1 Preheat the oven to 350°F/180°C. Lightly grease 2 cookie sheets with a little butter.

2 In a large mixing bowl, beat together the butter and peanut butter.

3 Gradually add the granulated sugar and beat well.

4 Add the beaten egg, a little at a time, beating after each addition until it is thoroughly combined.

5 Sift the flour, baking powder, and salt into the peanut butter mixture.

6 Add the peanuts and bring all of the ingredients together to form a soft dough. Wrap and chill for 30 minutes.

7 Form the dough into 20 balls and place them on the prepared cookie sheets about 2-inches/5-cm apart to allow room for the cookies to spread during cooking. Flatten them slightly with your hand.

8 Bake in the oven for 15 minutes, until golden brown. Transfer the cookies to a wire rack and let cool.

COOK'S TIP
For extra crunch and a sparkling appearance, sprinkle the cookies with raw sugar before baking.

40 mins

15 mins

Peanut Butter Oat Cookies

These are easy for children to make because they require no shaping or rolling out and all the ingredients are mixed together in one bowl.

🕐 40 mins   🕐 12 mins

MAKES 26

INGREDIENTS

4 oz/115 g butter, softened

4 oz/115 g crunchy peanut butter

½ cup golden superfine sugar

¾ cup light muscovado sugar

1 egg, beaten

½ tsp vanilla extract

scant 1 cup all-purpose flour

½ tsp baking soda

½ tsp baking powder

pinch of salt

generous 1 cup rolled oats

1 Preheat the oven to 350°F/180°C. Put the butter and peanut butter in a bowl and beat together. Beat in the superfine and muscovado sugars, then gradually beat in the egg and vanilla extract.

2 Sift the flour, baking soda, baking powder, and salt into a bowl and stir in with the oats. Drop teaspoonfuls of the cookie dough, well apart, on to greased cookie sheets. Flatten slightly with a fork.

3 Bake in the oven for 12 minutes, or until lightly browned. Let cool on the cookie sheets for 2 minutes, then transfer to wire racks to cool completely.

VARIATION
Smooth peanut butter
can be used if preferred.

Lavender Hearts

Lavender covers the Provençal landscape during summer, and local bakers incorporate its distinctive flavor into their sweet recipes.

30 mins   10 mins

MAKES 48

INGREDIENTS

2 cups all-purpose flour, plus extra
  for dusting

3½ oz/100 g chilled butter, diced

6 tbsp superfine sugar

1 large egg

1 tbsp dried lavender flowers, chopped
  very finely

TO DECORATE

4 tbsp confectioners' sugar

1 tsp water

2 tbsp fresh lavender flowers

1 Preheat the oven to 350°F/180°C. Line 2 cookie sheets with parchment paper. Put the flour in a bowl, add the diced butter and lightly rub in with your fingertips until the mixture resembles fine bread crumbs.

2 Stir in the sugar. Lightly beat the egg, then add to the flour and butter mixture with the lavender flowers. Stir to form a stiff paste.

3 Turn out the dough on to a lightly floured work counter and roll out until about ¼-inch/5-mm thick.

4 Using a 2-inch/5-cm heart-shaped cookie cutter, press out 48 hearts, occasionally dipping the cutter into extra flour, and re-rolling the trimmings as necessary. Transfer the pastry hearts to the cookie sheets.

5 Prick the surface of each heart with a fork. Place in the preheated oven, and bake for 10 minutes, or until the cookies are lightly browned. Transfer to a wire rack set over a sheet of parchment paper to cool.

6 Sift the confectioners' sugar into a bowl. Add 1 teaspoon of cold water and stir until a smooth frosting forms, adding a little extra water if necessary.

7 Drizzle the frosting from the tip of a metal spoon over the cooled cookies in a random pattern. Immediately sprinkle with the fresh lavender flowers while the frosting is still soft so they stick in place.

8 Let the cookies stand for at least 15 minutes, until the frosting has set. Store the cookies for up to 4 days in an airtight container.

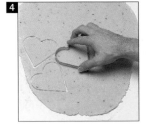

Lavender Cookies

Guests will be surprised and delighted by these original and unusual fragrant cookies.

🐥 15 mins   🕐 12 mins

MAKES 10–12

INGREDIENTS

½ cup butter, softened,
  plus extra for greasing

¼ cup golden superfine sugar,
  plus extra for dusting

1 tsp chopped lavender leaves

finely grated rind of 1 lemon

1¼ cups all-purpose flour

1 Preheat the oven to 300°F/150°C. Grease a large cookie sheet. Place the superfine sugar and lavender leaves in a food processor. Process until the lavender is very finely chopped, then add the butter and lemon rind and process until light and fluffy. Transfer to a large bowl. Sift in the flour and beat until the mixture forms a stiff dough.

2 Place the dough on a sheet of parchment paper and place another sheet on top. Gently press down with a rolling pin and roll out to ⅛–½-inch/ 3–5-mm thick. Remove the top sheet of paper and stamp out circles from the dough using a 2¾-inch/7-cm round cookie cutter. Re-knead and re-roll the dough trimmings and stamp out more cookies.

3 Using a spatula, carefully transfer the cookies to the prepared cookie sheet. Prick the cookies with a fork and bake in the preheated oven for 12 minutes, or until pale brown. Let cool on the cookie sheet for 2 minutes, then transfer to a wire rack and let cool completely.

COOK'S TIP
If you do not have a food processor, you can mix the dough by hand. Knead it into a ball before rolling out in step 2.

Rosemary Cookies

Do not be put off by the idea of herbs being used in these crisp cookies—
try them, and you will be pleasantly surprised.

40 mins plus
30 mins chilling   15 mins

MAKES 25

I N G R E D I E N T S

4 tbsp butter, softened, plus extra
for greasing

4 tbsp superfine sugar

grated rind of 1 lemon

4 tbsp lemon juice

1 egg, separated

2 tsp finely chopped fresh rosemary

scant 1½ cups all-purpose flour, sifted, plus
extra for dusting

superfine sugar, for sprinkling (optional)

1 Preheat the oven to 350°F/180°C.
Lightly grease 2 cookie sheets with a
little butter.

2 In a large mixing bowl, cream
together the butter and sugar until
pale and fluffy.

3 Add the lemon rind and juice, then the
egg yolk, and beat until they are
thoroughly combined. Stir in the chopped
fresh rosemary.

4 Add the sifted flour, mixing well until
a soft dough is formed. Wrap in
plastic wrap and chill in the refrigerator
for 30 minutes.

5 On a lightly floured work counter, roll
out the dough thinly and stamp out
about 25 circles with a 2½-inch/6-cm
cookie cutter. Arrange the dough circles
on the prepared cookie sheets.

6 In a bowl, lightly whisk the egg white.
Gently brush the egg white over the
surface of each cookie, then sprinkle with
a little superfine sugar, if liked.

7 Bake in the preheated oven for about
15 minutes.

8 Transfer the cookies to a wire rack
and let cool before serving.

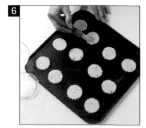

VARIATION
In place of the fresh rosemary,
use 1½ teaspoons of dried rosemary,
if you prefer.

Walnut & Cinnamon Blondies

Blondies are brownies without the chocolate! They taste just as delicious served with a cup of coffee.

🥧 20 mins   🕐 20–25 mins

MAKES 9

INGREDIENTS

4 oz/115 g butter, plus extra for greasing

generous 1 cup brown sugar

1 egg

1 egg yolk

1 cup self-rising flour

1 tsp ground cinnamon

generous ½ cup coarsely chopped walnuts

1 Preheat the oven to 350°F/180°C. Grease and line the bottom of a 7-inch/18-cm square cake pan. Place the butter and sugar in a pan over low heat and stir until the sugar has dissolved. Cook, stirring, for an additional 1 minute. The mixture will bubble slightly, but do not let it boil. Let cool for 10 minutes.

2 Stir the egg and egg yolk into the mixture. Sift in the flour and cinnamon, add the nuts, and stir until just blended. Pour the cake batter into the prepared pan, then bake in the oven for 20–25 minutes, or until springy in the center and a skewer inserted into the center of the cake comes out clean.

3 Let cool in the pan for a few minutes, then run a knife around the edge of the cake to loosen it. Turn the cake out on to a wire rack and peel off the paper. Let cool completely. When cold, cut into squares.

COOK'S TIP
Do not chop the walnuts too finely, as the blondies should have a good texture and a slight crunch to them.

Ranger Cookies

These large cookies are ideal for children when they go off on an adventure trail—even if it is only to the bottom of the yard!

15 mins

15 mins

MAKES 12

INGREDIENTS

4 oz/115 g butter, plus extra for greasing

5½ oz/150 g milk chocolate

generous 1 cup all-purpose flour

½ tsp baking powder

½ cup superfine sugar

½ cup brown sugar

2 eggs, beaten

½ tsp vanilla extract

1 cup rolled oats

½ cup golden raisins

1 Preheat the oven to 375°F/190°C. Grease 3 large cookie sheets. Coarsely chop the chocolate into ¼-inch/8-mm pieces. Sift the flour and baking powder together.

2 Beat the butter, superfine sugar, and brown sugar together until soft and fluffy. Gradually beat in the eggs, then the vanilla extract and sifted flour. Stir in the oats, golden raisins, and chocolate pieces.

3 Place heaped tablespoons of the cookie dough on the prepared cookie sheets, allowing room for the cookies to spread during cooking.

4 Bake the cookies in the preheated oven for about 15 minutes, until lightly browned. Let stand for 5 minutes ,then transfer the cookies to a wire rack and let cool.

Spicy Chocolate Chip Cookies

Chocolate and spices are the perfect marriage so the addition of nutmeg, cinnamon, and cloves turns these popular cookies into something special.

15 mins   15 mins

MAKES 10

I N G R E D I E N T S

4 oz/115 g butter, plus extra for greasing

1 cup self-rising flour

3 tbsp unsweetened cocoa

½ tsp ground cinnamon

¼ tsp ground cloves

¼ tsp grated nutmeg

generous ⅓ cup superfine sugar

½ cup brown sugar

1 egg, beaten

½ cup semisweet chocolate chips

1 Preheat the oven to 350°F/180°C. Grease 2 large cookie sheets. Sift the flour, cocoa, cinnamon, cloves, and nutmeg together.

2 Whisk the butter, superfine sugar, and brown sugar together until soft and fluffy. Gradually beat in the egg, then the flour mixture. Stir in the chocolate chips.

3 Place 10 tablespoonfuls of the cookie dough on the prepared cookies sheets, allowing room for the cookies to spread during baking. Press each one down using the back of a wet spoon.

4 Bake the cookies in the oven for 15–20 minutes, until lightly browned. Leave for 1 minute, then transfer the cookies to a wire rack and let cool.

Chewy Golden Cookies

A little glacé frosting drizzled over these cookies makes for a very effective decoration.

12 mins   12 mins

MAKES 30

INGREDIENTS

6 oz/175 g butter or margarine, plus extra for greasing

scant 1½ cups brown sugar

1 cup corn syrup

3 egg whites

6 cups rolled oats

2 cups all-purpose flour

pinch of salt

1 tsp baking powder

confectioners' sugar, to decorate

1 Preheat the oven to 350°F/180°C and grease a large cookie sheet.

2 In a large mixing bowl, blend the butter (or margarine), sugar, corn syrup, and egg whites together. Gradually add the oats, flour, salt, and baking powder and mix thoroughly.

3 Drop 30 rounded tablespoonfuls of the cookie dough on to the cookie sheet and transfer to the preheated oven.

4 Bake for 12 minutes, or until the cookies are light brown.

5 Remove from the oven and let cool on a wire rack. To make the frosting, combine a little sifted confectioners' sugar with water, drizzle over the cookies and let set. Alternatively, sprinkle over sifted confectioners' sugar and serve.

Caraway Cookies

The caraway seed is best known for its appearance in rye bread.
Here, caraway seeds give these cookies a distinctive flavor.

15 mins   10–15 mins

MAKES 36

INGREDIENTS

3 oz/85 g butter, cut into small pieces, plus
    extra for greasing

2 cups all-purpose flour

pinch of salt

generous 1 cup superfine sugar

1 egg, beaten

2 tbsp caraway seeds

raw sugar, for sprinkling

1 Preheat the oven to 325°F/160°C.
Grease 2 cookie sheets lightly.

2 Sift the flour and salt into a mixing
bowl. Rub in the butter with your
fingertips until the mixture resembles fine
bread crumbs. Stir in the sugar.

3 Reserve 1 tablespoon of the beaten
egg for brushing the cookies. Add the
rest of the egg to the mixture along with
the caraway seeds and bring together to
form a soft dough.

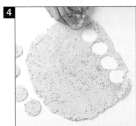

VARIATION
Caraway seeds have a nutty,
delicate anise flavor. If you don't
like this, replace them
with poppy seeds.

4 On a lightly floured work counter, roll
out the cookie dough thinly and then
cut out about 36 circles with a 2½-inch/
6-cm cutter.

5 Transfer the circles to the prepared
cookie sheets, brush with the reserved
egg, and sprinkle with raw sugar.

6 Bake in the oven for 10-15 minutes,
until the cookies are lightly golden
and crisp.

7 Let cool on a wire rack and store in an
airtight container.

Jamaican Rum Cookies

Dark rum and coconut lend a deliciously exotic flavor to these cookies. They are ideal for serving after dinner with coffee.

15 mins   8 mins

MAKES 36

I N G R E D I E N T S

6 oz/175 g butter or margarine, plus extra for greasing

⅓ cup sesame seeds

generous ⅓ cup chopped mixed nuts

1 cup all-purpose flour

¼ tsp baking powder

pinch of salt

1½ cups raw sugar

1 egg

1 tsp dark rum

2 tbsp sweet coconut flakes, to decorate

1 Preheat the oven to 350°F/180°C. Grease a large cookie sheet.

2 Spread the sesame seeds and chopped nuts out on an ungreased cookie sheet and toast them for about 10 minutes, or until slightly browned. Remove from the oven and set aside. Leave the oven on.

3 Sift together the flour, baking powder, and salt in a large mixing bowl. Add the sugar, egg, and rum and beat together well.

4 Put 36 rounded teaspoonfuls of the cookie dough on to the greased cookie sheet, allowing room for them to spread during cooking. Transfer to the preheated oven and bake for about 8 minutes, or until golden brown.

5 Remove from the oven and let cool on a wire rack. Decorate with the coconut flakes and serve.

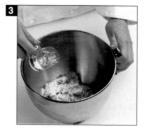

Caribbean Cookies

Flavored with banana, fruit juice, and coconut, these cookies simply melt in the mouth.

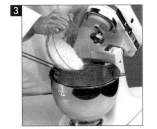

12 mins   10 mins

MAKES 24

INGREDIENTS

butter, for greasing

¼ cup mashed banana

1 tbsp pineapple juice

1 tbsp orange juice

¼ cup peanut oil

1 egg

1 tbsp milk

1 cup all-purpose flour

¼ tsp baking soda

¾ cup dry unsweetened coconut

raw sugar, for sprinkling

1 Preheat the oven to 350°F/180°C. Grease a large cookie sheet.

2 In a large bowl, cream together the banana, fruit juices, oil, egg, and milk. Transfer to a food mixer.

3 With the machine running, sift in the flour and baking soda, beating constantly. Add in the unsweetened coconut and mix well.

4 Drop rounded teaspoonfuls on to the greased cookie sheet, allowing room for the cookies to spread during cooking. Sprinkle with the raw sugar. Transfer to the preheated oven and bake for 10 minutes, or until the cookies are golden brown.

5 Remove the cookies from the oven and transfer to a wire rack to cool before serving.

Chocolate Drop Cookies

These cookies get their name from the method with which they are made—spoonfuls of the mixture are dropped on to the cookie sheets.

10 mins   15–20 mins

MAKES 20

INGREDIENTS

4 oz/115 g butter, plus extra for greasing

⅔ cup all-purpose flour

2 tbsp unsweetened cocoa

¼ cup superfine sugar

½ tsp vanilla extract

1 Preheat the oven to 375°F/190°C. Grease 2–3 large cookie sheets. Sift the flour and cocoa together

2 Whisk the butter, superfine sugar, and vanilla extract together in a large bowl until soft and fluffy. Stir in the flour mixture until well blended.

3 Drop teaspoonfuls of the mixture on to the prepared cookie sheets, allowing room for the cookies to spread during cooking.

4 Bake the cookies in the preheated oven for 15–20 minutes, until firm. Leave for 1 minute, then transfer to a wire rack and let cool.

Mocha Cookies

The word mocha, which describes a combination of chocolate and coffee, comes from the name of a port in Yemen where coffee was first grown.

🍪 25 mins   🕐 15 mins

MAKES 18

INGREDIENTS

4 tbsp butter, plus extra for greasing

1½ cups all-purpose flour

3 tbsp unsweetened cocoa

½ tsp baking powder

⅔ cup semisweet chocolate chips

I tbsp instant coffee granules

⅓ cup superfine sugar

⅓ cup brown sugar

1 egg, beaten

1 Preheat the oven to 350°F/180°C. Grease 3 large cookie sheets. Sift the flour, cocoa, and baking powder together in a large bowl.

2 Put ¼ cup of the chocolate chips and the butter in a pan and heat gently until melted. Add the coffee granules and stir until dissolved, then let cool slightly.

3 When the chocolate mixture has cooled, stir in the superfine sugar, brown sugar, and egg. Stir into the flour mixture, then stir in the remaining chocolate chips.

4 Knead the cookie dough to combine, then drop heaping tablespoons of the cookie dough on to the prepared cookie sheets, allowing room for the cookies to spread during cooking.

5 Bake in the preheated oven for about 15 minutes, until firm. Leave for 5 minutes, then transfer to a wire rack and let cool.

Fruit Morsels

Serve these cookies with coffee or tea, or after dinner to accompany a special-occasion dessert.

 12 mins   10 mins

MAKES 36

INGREDIENTS

4½ oz/125 g butter or margarine, plus extra for greasing

1 cup no-soak dried apricots

½ cup dried dates

1 cup all-purpose flour

scant 1 cup rolled oats

1 cup wheat flakes

½ tsp baking soda

pinch of salt

¾ cup brown sugar, plus extra for dusting

2 eggs

1 tsp almond extract

1 Preheat the oven to 375°F/190°C. Grease a large cookie sheet. Chop the dried apricots and dates.

2 Sift the flour into a large bowl and mix in the oats, wheat flakes, baking soda, and salt.

3 Blend the sugar and butter (or margarine). Beat in the eggs until the mixture is light and fluffy. Add the flour mixture gradually, stirring. Blend in the almond extract and fruit. Mix well.

4 Drop 36 teaspoonfuls of cookie dough on to the cookie sheet, allowing room for the cookies to spread during cooking. Dust with sugar. Bake for 10 minutes, or until the cookies are golden brown.

5 Remove the cookies from the oven, place on a wire rack and let them cool before serving.

Candied Fruit Cookies

A flavorful addition to any cookie jar, these cookies are delicious at any time of the day. Store for up to a week.

12 mins   20 mins

MAKES 20

INGREDIENTS

2 egg whites

1½ cups almonds, ground finely

¾ cup superfine sugar

1 tsp finely grated orange rind

½ tsp ground cinnamon

2 tbsp candied fruit

raw sugar, for sprinkling

1 Preheat the oven to 350°F/180°C. Line 2 large cookie sheets with parchment paper, greasing if necessary.

2 In a large mixing bowl, beat the egg whites until stiff. Using a knife, gently fold in the almonds, sugar, orange rind, cinnamon, and fruit.

3 When the cookie dough is smooth, transfer to a pastry bag with a large tip (at least ½ inch/1 cm in diameter) and pipe filled circles of cookie dough on to the parchment paper, each about 3 inches/ 7.5 cm in diameter. Allow room for the cookies to spread during cooking.

4 Sprinkle with the raw sugar. Transfer to the oven and bake for 20 minutes, or until the cookies are light brown.

5 Remove from the oven and transfer to a wire rack. Decorate with candied fruit and allow to cool completely before serving.

Citrus Crescents

For a sweet treat, try these pretty crescent-shaped cookies, which have a lovely citrus tang to them.

30 mins

12–15 mins

MAKES 25

INGREDIENTS

2¾ oz/75 g butter, softened, plus extra for greasing

⅓ cup superfine sugar, plus extra for sprinkling (optional)

1 egg, separated

scant 1½ cups all-purpose flour, plus extra for dusting

grated rind of 1 orange

grated rind of 1 lemon

grated rind of 1 lime

2–3 tbsp orange juice

1 Preheat the oven to 400°F/200°C. Lightly grease 2 cookie sheets with a little butter.

2 In a mixing bowl, cream together the butter and sugar until light and fluffy, then gradually beat in the egg yolk.

COOK'S TIP

Store the citrus crescents in an airtight container. Alternatively, they can be frozen for up to 1 month.

3 Sift the flour into the creamed mixture and mix until evenly combined. Add the orange, lemon, and lime rind to the mixture, with enough of the orange juice to form a soft dough.

4 Roll out the dough on a lightly floured work counter. Stamp out circles using a 3-inch/7.5-cm cookie cutter. Make crescent shapes by cutting away one-quarter of each circle. Re-roll the trimmings to make 25 crescents.

5 Place the crescents on the prepared cookie sheets, spacing them apart to allowing room for the cookies to spread during cooking. Prick each one with a fork.

6 Lightly whisk the egg white in a small bowl and brush it over the cookies. Dust with extra superfine sugar, if using.

7 Bake in the oven for 12–15 minutes. Transfer the cookies to a wire rack to cool and crispen before serving.

Lemon Disks

Simple but elegant, these cookies combine the sharpness of lemon with the flavor of spices.

🍰 15 mins   🕙 10 mins

MAKES 30

INGREDIENTS

6 oz/175 g butter or margarine, plus extra for greasing

1 cup brown sugar, plus extra for dusting

2 tbsp corn syrup

1 egg

2½ cups all-purpose flour

pinch of salt

1 tsp baking soda

1 tsp ground ginger

1 tsp ground allspice

1 tsp grated lemon rind

cinnamon, for dusting, optional

1   Preheat the oven to 375°F/190°C. Grease a large cookie sheet.

2   Cream the butter (or margarine), sugar, and corn syrup in a large mixing bowl. Beat in the egg.

3   Gradually sift the flour, salt, baking soda, ginger, and allspice into the creamed mixture, stirring constantly. Add the lemon rind and mix thoroughly.

4   Form the dough into 30 or so balls (about 1 rounded tablespoon each). Space the dough balls about 1 inch/2.5 cm apart on the greased cookie sheet and flatten slightly with a spatula. Dust the dough balls with raw sugar. Transfer to the preheated oven and cook for 10 minutes, or until the cookies are light brown.

  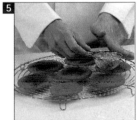

5   Transfer from the oven to a wire rack and let them cool completely. One option is to sprinkle with cinnamon.

Alternatively, leave plain and serve only with the grated lemon rind.

Lemon Drops

Serve these with lemon tea, sweetened with a little honey if liked. They also make a delicious dessert.

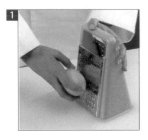
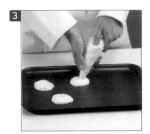

🥚 30 mins   🕐 10 mins

MAKES 24

INGREDIENTS

4 oz/115 g butter or margarine, plus extra for greasing

1 cup superfine sugar

2 tbsp lemon juice

1 tbsp finely grated lemon rind

2 tbsp water

1½ cups all-purpose flour, sifted

1 tsp baking soda

½ tsp cream of tartar

TO DECORATE

confectioners' sugar

candied mixed fruit, chopped finely (optional)

1 Preheat the oven to 350°F/180°C. Grease a large cookie sheet. Beat together the butter, superfine sugar, lemon juice, lemon rind, and water.

2 In a separate bowl, mix together the flour, baking soda, and cream of tartar. Add the butter mixture and blend together well.

3 Spoon the cookie dough into a pastry bag fitted with a star-shaped tip. Pipe 24 fancy drops, about the size of a tablespoon, on to the greased cookie sheet, allowing room for the cookies to spread during cooking. Transfer to the preheated oven and bake for 10 minutes, or until the lemon drops are golden brown.

4 Remove from the oven, then transfer to a wire rack and let cool completely. Dust with confectioners' sugar and sprinkle over the candied fruit, if desired.

Lemon Jumbles

These melt-in-the-mouth cookies are made extra special by dredging them with confectioners' sugar just before serving.

 30 mins · 20 mins

MAKES 50

INGREDIENTS

⅓ cup butter, softened, plus extra for greasing

generous ½ cup superfine sugar

grated rind of 1 lemon

1 egg, beaten lightly

4 tbsp lemon juice

2½ cups all-purpose flour

1 tsp baking powder

1 tbsp milk

confectioners' sugar, for dredging

1 Preheat the oven to 325°F/160°C. Lightly grease several cookie sheets with a little butter.

2 In a mixing bowl, cream together the butter, superfine sugar, and lemon rind, until pale and fluffy.

3 Add the beaten egg and lemon juice, a little at a time, beating well after each addition.

4 Sift the flour and baking powder into the creamed mixture and blend together. Add the milk, mixing to form a firm dough.

5 Turn the dough out on to a lightly floured work counter and divide into about 50 equal-size pieces.

6 Roll each piece into a sausage shape with your hands and twist in the middle to make an "S" shape.

7 Place the cookies on the prepared cookie sheets and bake in the oven for 15–20 minutes. Let cool completely on a wire rack. Dredge generously with confectioners' sugar before serving.

VARIATION
If you prefer, shape the dough into other shapes—letters of the alphabet or geometric shapes—or just make into round cookies.

Sugared Orange Diamonds

Wrapped in cellophane and tied with ribbon, these Cointreau-flavored cookies would make an attractive gift.

  30 mins plus 2 hrs chilling   15 mins

MAKES 24

INGREDIENTS

4 oz/115 g butter or margarine, plus extra for greasing

¾ cup raw sugar

2 tbsp orange juice

1 tbsp Cointreau

2½ cups all-purpose flour, sifted, plus extra for dusting

1½ cups walnuts, chopped coarsely

1 tbsp finely grated orange rind

confectioners' sugar, for dusting

1 Put the butter, sugar, orange juice, and Cointreau in a bowl and beat together until a fluffy consistency is reached.

2 In a separate bowl, mix together the flour, walnuts, and orange rind. Add the butter mixture and mix until thoroughly combined. Cover with plastic wrap and let chill in the refrigerator for 2 hours.

3 When ready to use, preheat the oven to 350°F/180°C. Grease a large cookie sheet.

4 Lightly flour a board or work counter. Roll out the dough into an oblong about ⅛-inch/3-mm thick, then use a sharp knife or cookie cutter to cut out 24 diamond shapes. Put the diamonds on to the greased cookie sheet. Transfer to the oven and bake for 15 minutes, or until the cookies are golden brown.

5 Remove from the oven, transfer to a wire rack and let cool. Dust with confectioners' sugar before serving.

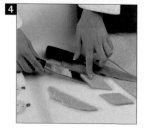

Banana Cookies

Bananas lend a natural sweetness to these cookies. For optimum flavor, use over-ripe bananas in this recipe.

15 mins   20–25 mins

MAKES 20

INGREDIENTS

butter, for greasing

scant 1 cup all-purpose flour

1 tsp baking powder

pinch of salt

1 tsp ground allspice

1½ bananas

¾ cup applesauce

1 tsp cognac

¾ cup corn syrup

generous 1 cup rolled oats

2 tbsp golden raisins

TO DECORATE

1 tbsp chopped candied mixed fruit

1 tbsp chopped dried banana chips

1 Preheat the oven to 350°F/180°C. Grease a large cookie sheet. Sift together the flour, baking powder, salt, and allspice into a large bowl.

2 Coarsely chop the banana and place, with the applesauce, cognac, and corn syrup in a food mixer and blend together until smooth. Stir in the oats and golden raisins. Add the banana mixture to the spiced flour and beat together thoroughly.

3 Put 20 rounded tablespoonfuls of the cookie dough on to the greased cookie sheet, allowing room for the cookies to spread during cooking. Transfer to the oven and bake for 20–25 minutes, or until golden brown.

4 Remove the cookies from the oven and place on a wire rack to cool. Before serving, decorate with the chopped candied mixed fruit and the banana chips.

Banana Pecan Cookies

The mashed banana makes these cookies really moist, while the toasted nuts give them a crunchy texture.

12 mins

15 mins

MAKES 20

INGREDIENTS

5½ oz/150 g butter or margarine, plus extra for greasing

⅔ cup brown sugar

1 egg

1½ cups all-purpose flour

1 tbsp baking powder

¼ tsp baking soda

pinch of salt

2 tsp ground allspice

4 tbsp milk

2 bananas

3 cups rolled oats

⅔ cup pecans, toasted and chopped coarsely

1 Preheat the oven to 375°F/190°C. Grease a large cookie sheet. Mash the banana and set aside. Cream the butter and sugar in a large mixing bowl, then beat in the egg.

2 Gradually sift the flour, baking powder, baking soda, salt, and allspice into the creamed mixture and mix thoroughly. Stir in the milk and the mashed banana. Finally, add the oats and chopped pecans and mix well.

3 Drop 20 rounded tablespoonfuls of the dough on to the greased cookie sheet, allowing room for the cookies to spread during cooking. Transfer to the preheated oven and bake for 15 minutes, or until the cookies are light brown.

4 Transfer from the oven to a wire rack and let them cool before serving.

Ginger Chocolate Chip Squares

These delicious, moist squares are gently spiced with cinnamon, cloves, and nutmeg. Let cool completely, then serve as a dessert or with coffee.

10 mins   30 mins

MAKES 15

INGREDIENTS

4 pieces preserved ginger in syrup

1½ cups all-purpose flour

1½ tsp ground ginger

1 tsp ground cinnamon

¼ tsp ground cloves

¼ tsp grated nutmeg

½ cup brown sugar

4 oz/115 g butter

⅓ cup corn syrup

½ cup semisweet chocolate chips

1 Preheat the oven to 300°F/150°C. Finely chop the preserved ginger. Sift the flour, ground ginger, cinnamon, cloves, and nutmeg into a large bowl. Stir in the chopped preserved ginger and sugar.

2 Put the butter and the syrup in a pan and heat gently until melted. Bring to a boil, then pour the mixture into the flour mixture, stirring all the time. Beat until the mixture is cool enough to handle.

3 Add the chocolate chips to the mixture. Press evenly into a 8 x 12-inch/ 20 x 30-cm jelly roll pan.

4 Bake in the oven for 30 minutes. Cut into squares, then let cool in the pan.

Banana & Chocolate Cookies

Adding mashed banana to the cookie dough of these cookies makes for a really moist texture somewhere between a cake and a cookie.

 10 mins  15 mins

MAKES 30

INGREDIENTS

4 oz/115 g butter, plus extra for greasing

2⅓ cups all-purpose flour

½ tsp baking powder

1 small banana

⅓ cup superfine sugar

⅓ cup brown sugar

1 egg, beaten

½ tsp vanilla extract

½ cup milk chocolate chips

1 Preheat the oven to 375°F/190°C. Grease 2–3 large cookie sheets. Sift the flour and baking powder together. Mash the banana.

2 Whisk together the butter, superfine sugar, and brown sugar until soft and fluffy. Gradually beat in the egg, then beat in the banana and vanilla extract until well mixed. Beat in the flour mixture, then stir in the chocolate chips.

3 Place heaping tablespoons of the mixture on the prepared cookie sheets, allowing room for the cookies to spread during cooking.

4 Bake the cookies in the oven for about 15 minutes, until lightly browned. Transfer to a wire rack and let cool.

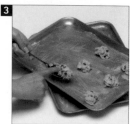

Apricot & Chocolate Cookies

The apricots in these deliciously moist cookies give them a lovely fruity flavor. If there are any left, store in an airtight container.

30 mins

13–15 mins

SERVES 4

INGREDIENTS

3 oz/85 g butter, softened, plus extra for greasing

2 tbsp golden granulated sugar

¼ cup light brown sugar

½ tsp vanilla extract

1 egg

generous 1 cup self-rising flour

4 oz/115 g semisweet chocolate, chopped coarsely

⅔ cup no-soak dried apricots, chopped coarsely

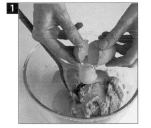

1 Preheat the oven to 350°F/180°C. Grease 2 cookie sheets. Place the butter, granulated sugar, brown sugar, and vanilla extract in a bowl and beat together. Add in the egg and beat until light and fluffy.

2 Sift the flour over the cookie dough and fold in, then fold in the chocolate and apricots.

VARIATION
As an alternative to dried apricots, try other dry fruits such as dried cranberries, cherries, or raisins.

3 Put tablespoonfuls of the cookie dough on to the prepared cookie sheets, allowing room for the cookies to spread during cooking. Bake in the preheated oven for 13–15 minutes, or until crisp outside but still soft inside. Let cool on the cookie sheets for 2 minutes, then transfer the cookies to wire racks to cool completely.

Persian Rice Crescents

These little cookies made with rice flour have a fine texture and a delicate flavor. They are excellent with strong black coffee.

⏲ 30 mins, plus
1 hr resting

🕐 15 mins

MAKES 60

INGREDIENTS

7 oz/200 g butter, sweet for preference, softened, plus extra for greasing

1 cup confectioners' sugar, sifted, plus extra for dusting

2 egg yolks

½–1 tsp ground cardamom or 1 tbsp rose water

1¼ cups rice flour, sifted

1 egg white, beaten lightly

½ cup finely chopped pistachios or almonds

1 Grease several cookie sheets.

2 Using an electric whisk, beat the butter until light and creamy in a large bowl. Gradually add the confectioners' sugar and beat for 2 minutes until light and fluffy. Gradually add the egg yolks, beating well after each addition. Add the cardamom and the rice flour and mix to a soft dough.

3 Turn the dough on to a lightly floured work counter and knead lightly. Turn the mixing bowl over the dough and let rest for about 1 hour.

4 When ready to use, preheat the oven to 350°F/180°C. Roll heaping teaspoonfuls of the dough into balls, then form into crescent shapes. Place 2 inches/5 cm apart on the prepared cookie sheets. Mark a pattern on the tops with a spoon.

5 Brush each crescent with a little beaten egg white and sprinkle with the chopped nuts.

6 Bake in the preheated oven for about 15 minutes until the bases start to color; the tops should remain very pale. Reduce the heat if the tops start to color.

7 Cool on the cookie sheets for about 2 minutes, then transfer the cookies to wire racks to cool completely. Dust with confectioners' sugar before serving.

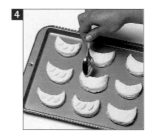

COOK'S TIP

Cooking-oil sprays are ideal for lightly greasing cookie sheets when making cookies.

Melting Hearts

Serve these little heart-shaped cookies with a cup of coffee, or to round off a romantic Valentine's Day dinner.

10 mins plus
8 hrs chilling

 15 mins

MAKES 24

INGREDIENTS

1 cup all-purpose flour, plus extra
   for dusting

1½ tsp ground allspice

½ tsp ground ginger

pinch of salt

½ tsp baking soda

4 oz/115 g butter or margarine, plus extra
   for greasing

½ cup brown sugar

2 small eggs

1 tsp unsweetened cocoa

½ tsp Kahlua

¾ cup hazelnuts, toasted and
   chopped coarsely

12 fresh mint leaves, to decorate

½ cup heavy cream or sour cream, to serve

1 In a large bowl, sift together the flour, spices, salt, and baking soda. In a separate bowl, cream together the butter (or margarine) and sugar. Beat in the eggs, then add the unsweetened cocoa, Kahlua, and flour mixture gradually and continue beating until smooth. Cover with plastic wrap and let chill in the refrigerator for at least 8 hours or overnight if possible.

2 When ready to use, preheat the oven to 350°F/180°C and grease a cookie sheet. Lightly flour a board or work counter. Roll out the dough into an oblong about ⅛ inch/3 mm thick, then cut out

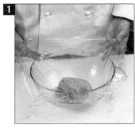

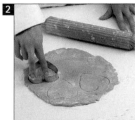

24 heart shapes using a cookie cutter or a sharp knife. Place the hearts on to the greased cookie sheet. Transfer to the preheated oven and bake for 15 minutes, or until the cookies are golden brown.

3 Remove from the oven, then transfer to a wire rack and sprinkle over the hazelnuts. When cool, serve with heavy cream or sour cream topped with fresh mint leaves.

Pistachio & Cardamom Tuiles

These wafer-thin, crisp, nutty cookies are ideal for serving with fresh fruit desserts, or as a delicious alternative to ordinary wafers for ice cream.

30 mins   8–10 mins

MAKES 18

INGREDIENTS

6 cardamoms

4 tbsp butter, melted and cooled, plus extra for greasing

2 egg whites

generous ½ cup golden superfine sugar

scant ½ cup all-purpose flour

scant ¼ cup chopped pistachios

1 Preheat the oven to 350°F/180°C. Crush the cardamoms and remove the husks. Grind the black seeds using a pestle and mortar and set aside. Grease 2–3 cookie sheets and a rolling pin. Place the egg whites and superfine sugar in a bowl. Whisk together with a fork until frothy.

2 Sift the flour into the bowl. Add the pistachios and ground cardamom and mix with a fork. Add the butter and mix together thoroughly. Drop teaspoonfuls of the cookie dough on to the prepared cookie sheets, allowing room for the cookies to spread during cooking. Using a spatula, spread each one out slightly.

3 Bake in the preheated oven, 1 sheet at a time, for 8–10 minutes, or until the edges are firm. Lift the cookies off carefully with a spatula and place over the rolling pin while still warm. Let stand to set for 1–2 minutes, then lift off carefully and transfer to a wire rack to cool. Store in an airtight container.

COOK'S TIP

Do not be tempted to bake more than one tray of cookies at a time, otherwise the second batch will become too firm before you have time to shape them.

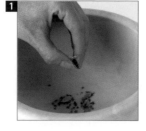

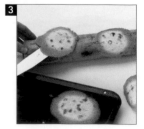

Amaretti

Traditionally, these moreish little Italian macaroons are made with apricot kernels, but almonds are used here.

30 mins  30 mins

MAKES ABOUT 40

INGREDIENTS

¾ cup blanched almonds

¾ cup caster sugar

1 large egg white

confectioners' sugar, for dusting

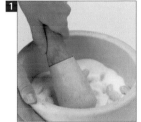  

1 Preheat the oven to 250°F/120°C. Crush the almonds with the superfine sugar using a pestle and mortar, or finely chop the almonds and then combine with the sugar in a bowl.

2 Lightly beat the egg white, then stir it into the almond mixture to form a firm dough. Line 2 cookie sheets with baking paper and place walnut-size portions of the dough, allowing plenty of room for the cookies to spread during cooking. Dust with confectioners' sugar.

3 Bake in the preheated oven for 30 minutes. Transfer to wire racks to cool completely.

Almond Cookies

Almond trees grow in abundance all over the Mediterranean region, so the slightly sweet nut appears frequently in regional dishes.

25 mins   20–25 mins

MAKES 32

INGREDIENTS

generous 1 cup blanched almonds

7 oz/200 g butter, softened

6 tbsp confectioners' sugar, plus extra for sifting

2¼ cups all-purpose flour

2 tsp vanilla extract

½ tsp almond extract

1   Line 2 cookie sheets with parchment paper. Using a sharp knife, finely chop the almonds, or process them in a food processor, taking care not to let them turn into a paste. Set aside. Preheat the oven to 350°F/180°C.

2   Put the butter in a bowl and beat with an electric whisk until smooth. Sift in the confectioners' sugar and continue beating until creamed and smooth.

3   Sift in the flour from above the bowl and beat it in until blended. Add the vanilla and almond extracts and beat the mixture again to form a soft dough. Stir in the chopped almonds.

4   Using a teaspoon, shape the dough into 32 round balls about the size of walnuts. Place on the prepared cookie sheets, allowing room for the cookies to spread during cooking. Bake in the preheated oven for 20–25 minutes, until the cookies are set and just starting to turn brown.

5   Let the cookies stand on the cookie sheets for 2 minutes to firm up. Sift a thick layer of confectioners' sugar over them. Then transfer them to a wire rack and let cool completely.

6   Lightly dust with more confectioners' sugar, just before serving. They can be stored in an airtight container for up to 1 week.

VARIATIONS
Pecans can be used instead of the almonds. If liked, 2 tsp finely grated orange rind can be added to the dough in step 3.

Spiced Almond Cookies

These almond cookies are delicately spiced with ground allspice.
Serve with a cup of tea for a delicious mid-afternoon treat.

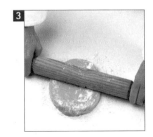

12 mins plus
30 mins chilling   15 mins

MAKES 30

INGREDIENTS

¾ cup butter or margarine, plus extra
    for greasing

½ cup superfine sugar

scant ¼ cup almonds, chopped finely

½ tsp ground allspice

pinch of salt

1 tsp vanilla extract

1⅔ cups all-purpose flour, plus extra
    for dusting

1 egg white, beaten lightly

chopped almonds, to decorate

1 Preheat the oven to 325°F/160°C and grease 2 large cookie sheets. Mix half the sugar with the chopped almonds and allspice and set aside.

2 In a mixing bowl, cream the butter (or margarine) and half the sugar with the salt and vanilla extract. Sift in the flour and mix well. Cover the bowl with plastic wrap and transfer to the refrigerator to chill for 30 minutes.

3 Sprinkle flour on a work counter or cutting board and roll out the dough to ½-inch/1-cm thickness. Cut the dough into circles 2 inches/5 cm in diameter or cut into diamonds. Transfer to the cookie sheets. Brush lightly with egg white and prick with a fork.

4 Sprinkle with the sugar and almond mixture. Transfer to the oven and bake for 15 minutes, or until the cookies are golden. Remove from the oven and sprinkle with chopped almonds before serving.

Spiced Cookies

These spicy cookies are perfect to serve with fruit salad or ice cream for a very easy instant dessert.

35 mins

10–12 mins

SERVES 12

INGREDIENTS

6 oz/175 g butter, sweet for preference, plus extra for greasing

scant 1 cup dark brown sugar

generous 1½ cups all-purpose flour

pinch of salt

½ tsp baking soda

1 tsp ground cinnamon

½ tsp ground coriander

½ tsp ground nutmeg

¼ tsp ground cloves

2 tbsp dark rum

1 Preheat the oven to 350°F/180°C. Grease 2 cookie sheets with a little butter.

2 Cream together the butter and sugar and whisk until light and fluffy.

3 Sift the flour, salt, baking soda, cinnamon, coriander, nutmeg, and cloves into the creamed mixture.

4 Add the dark rum and stir it into the creamed mixture.

5 Using 2 teaspoons, place small mounds of the mixture on the prepared cookie sheets, allowing room for the cookies to spread during cooking.

6 Bake in the preheated oven for 10–12 minutes, until golden brown in color.

7 Transfer the cookies to wire racks to cool and crispen before serving.

COOK'S TIP
Use the back of a fork or spoon to flatten the cookies slightly before baking.

Chocolate Walnut Cookies

These chocolate and walnut cookies are moreish, but topped with a fudge frosting they are divine! Choose a semisweet or milk chocolate topping.

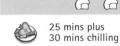

25 mins plus
30 mins chilling   20 mins

MAKES 18–20

I N G R E D I E N T S

C O O K I E S

butter, for greasing

3 oz/85 g semisweet chocolate

1 cup walnut pieces

1 egg, separated

½ cup superfine sugar

¼ cup all-purpose flour

T O P P I N G

3 oz/85 g semisweet or milk chocolate,
   broken into pieces

4 tbsp butter

½ cup brown sugar

2 tbsp milk

1¾ cups confectioners' sugar

1 Grease 2 large cookie sheets. To make the cookies, coarsely grate the chocolate. Finely chop the walnut pieces.

2 Whisk the egg white until stiff, then fold in the superfine sugar. Stir in the grated chocolate, walnuts, flour, and egg yolk. Knead in the bowl for a short time until smooth. Wrap the dough in waxed paper and let chill in the refrigerator for 30 minutes.

3 Preheat the oven to 375°F/190°C. Place the dough between 2 sheets of floured parchment paper and roll out to ¼-inch/8 mm thickness, then cut into circles using a 2-inch/5-cm cookie cutter. Place on the prepared cookie sheets.

4 Bake the cookies in the oven for about 20 minutes, until golden brown. Transfer to a wire rack and let cool.

5 When the cookies are cold, make the topping. Put the chocolate, butter, brown sugar, and milk in a pan and heat gently until the sugar has dissolved. Bring to a boil, then boil rapidly for 3 minutes.

6 Remove the pan from the heat and gradually sift in the confectioners' sugar. Beat with a wooden spoon until smooth, then beat for an additional 2 minutes, until the topping is thick enough to spread.

7 Using a wet spatula, spread the chocolate fudge topping immediately over the top of each cookie. Let set.

Spiced Fruit & Nut Cookies

Bananas, dates, and walnuts make up these delicious cookies, spiced with a little ground allspice. Store in an airtight container for several days.

12 mins   20 mins

MAKES 20

INGREDIENTS

butter, for greasing

1⅓ cups mashed bananas

⅓ cup vegetable oil

1 tsp almond extract

1 egg, beaten

1 tsp ground allspice

pinch of salt

3 cups rolled oats

½ cup raisins

scant ½ cup golden raisins

½ cup dates, chopped finely

⅓ cup walnuts, chopped finely

1 Preheat the oven to 350°F/180°C. Grease a large cookie sheet.

2 Blend the bananas, vegetable oil, almond extract, egg, allspice, and salt together in a large mixing bowl. Add the oats and mix well. Finally, stir in the dried fruit and walnuts until evenly distributed.

3 Drop 20 rounded tablespoonfuls of cookie dough on to the greased cookie sheet, allowing room for the cookies to spread during cooking.

4 Bake in the preheated oven for 20 minutes, or until the cookies are golden brown.

5 Transfer the cookies from the oven to a wire rack and let them cool completely before serving.

Traditional Spiced Cookies

These spicy cookies are delicious served with either coffee or tea. You can replace the golden raisins with chopped mixed nuts if you prefer.

🍰 15 mins plus
1 hr chilling   🕐 12 mins

MAKES 36

INGREDIENTS

1½ cups all-purpose flour

2 tsp ground allspice

1 tsp salt

1 tsp baking soda

6 oz/175 g butter or margarine, plus extra
  for greasing

½ cup granulated sugar

1 cup brown sugar, plus extra for dusting

2 eggs

4 tbsp milk

3½ cups rolled oats

½ cup raisins

scant ½ cup golden raisins

1 Mix the flour, allspice, salt, and baking soda together and sift into a large mixing bowl.

2 One at a time, mix in the butter (or margarine), both sugars, the eggs, and the milk. Beat the mixture until it is smooth.

3 Add the oats and dry fruits and stir thoroughly. Cover the bowl with plastic wrap and chill in the refrigerator for 1 hour.

4 Preheat the oven to 375°F/190°C and grease a large cookie sheet.

5 Put 36 tablespoonfuls of cookie dough on to the greased cookie sheet, allowing room for the cookies to spread during cooking. Dust lightly with brown sugar. Transfer to the preheated oven and bake for 12 minutes, or until the cookies are golden brown.

6 Remove the cookies from the oven and place on a wire rack to cool completely before serving.

Classic Oatmeal Cookies

A no-fuss cookie to enjoy with a morning cup of coffee. These easy-to-make cookies can be stored in airtight containers for several days.

10 mins   15 mins

MAKES 30

INGREDIENTS

6 oz/175 g butter or margarine, plus extra for greasing

scant 1⅓ cups raw sugar

1 egg

4 tbsp water

1 tsp vanilla extract

4⅓ cups rolled oats

1 cup all-purpose flour

1 tsp salt

½ tsp baking soda

1 Preheat the oven to 350°F/180°C and grease a large cookie sheet.

2 Cream the butter (or margarine) and sugar together in a large mixing bowl or free-standing mixer. Beat in the egg, water, and vanilla extract until the mixture is smooth.

3 In a separate bowl, mix the oats, flour, salt, and baking soda. Gradually stir the oat mixture into the butter mixture until thoroughly combined.

4 Put 30 rounded tablespoonfuls of cookie dough on to the greased cookie sheet, making sure they are well spaced. Transfer to the preheated oven and bake for 15 minutes, or until the cookies are golden brown.

5 Remove from the oven and place on a wire rack to cool before serving.

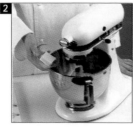  

Oat & Raisin Cookies

These oaty, fruity cookies couldn't be easier to make and are delicious served with a creamy rum and raisin ice cream.

50 mins   15 mins

SERVES 4

INGREDIENTS

4 tbsp butter, plus extra for greasing

⅔ cup superfine sugar

1 egg, beaten

½ cup all-purpose flour

½ tsp salt

½ tsp baking powder

1¾ cups rolled oats

scant 1 cup raisins

2 tbsp sesame seeds

1 Preheat the oven to 350°F/180°C. Lightly grease 2 cookie sheets.

2 In a large mixing bowl, cream together the butter and sugar until light and fluffy.

3 Gradually add the beaten egg, beating well after each addition, until thoroughly combined.

4 Sift the flour, salt, and baking powder into the creamed mixture. Mix gently to combine. Add the rolled oats, raisins, and sesame seeds and mix together until thoroughly combined.

5 Place tablespoonfuls of the cookie dough on the prepared cookie sheets, allowing room for the cookies to spread during cooking, and flatten them slightly with the back of a spoon.

6 Bake the cookies in the preheated oven for 15 minutes.

7 Let the cookies cool slightly on the cookie sheets.

8 Carefully transfer the cookies to a wire rack and let cool completely before serving.

COOK'S TIP
To enjoy these cookies at their best, store them in an airtight container.

Oat & Hazelnut Morsels

Try these delicious cookies with a refreshing cup of mint tea in the afternoon, or give them to hungry children as a healthy snack.

10 mins   12–15 mins

MAKES 30

INGREDIENTS

6 oz/175 g butter or margarine, plus extra for greasing

1¼ cup raw sugar

1 egg, beaten

4 tbsp milk

1 tsp vanilla extract

½ tsp almond extract

¾ cup hazelnuts

1 cup all-purpose flour

1½ tsp ground allspice

¼ tsp baking soda

pinch of salt

3½ cups rolled oats

scant 1 cup golden raisins

1 Preheat the oven to 375°F/190°C. Grease 2 large cookie sheets.

2 Cream the butter (or margarine) and sugar together in a large mixing bowl. Blend in the egg, milk, vanilla extract, and almond extract until thoroughly combined. Chop the hazelnuts finely.

3 In a separate bowl, sift the all-purpose flour, allspice, baking soda, and salt together thoroughly. Add to the creamed mixture slowly, stirring continuously. Mix in the oats, golden raisins, and hazelnuts.

4 Put 30 rounded tablespoonfuls of cookie mixture on to the greased cookie sheets, making sure they are well spaced. Transfer to the preheated oven and bake for 12–15 minutes, or until the cookies are golden brown.

5 Remove the cookies from the oven and place on a wire rack to cool before serving.

Hazelnut & Almond Oaties

These cookies are made with a delectable combination of rolled oats, coarsely chopped nuts, and semisweet chocolate chips.

10 mins   12 mins

MAKES 36

INGREDIENTS

6 oz/175 g butter or margarine, plus extra for greasing

¾ cup raw sugar

1 egg

⅔ cup all-purpose flour

½ tsp salt

1 tsp baking soda

¼ tsp almond extract

1½ cups rolled oats

¼ cup hazelnuts, chopped coarsely

¼ cup almonds, chopped coarsely

1 cup semisweet chocolate chips

1 Preheat the oven to 375°F/190°C and grease a large cookie sheet.

2 Cream the butter (or margarine) and sugar together in a large mixing bowl. Then beat in the egg.

3 In a separate bowl, sift the flour, salt, and baking soda, then stir into the butter mixture.

4 Add the almond extract and oats and beat thoroughly. Finally, mix in the nuts and chocolate chips.

5 Put 36 teaspoonfuls of the cookie mixture on to the greased cookie sheet, making sure they are well spaced. Transfer to the preheated oven and bake for 12 minutes, or until the cookies are golden brown.

6 Remove the cookies from the oven, then place on a wire rack and let them cool before serving.

Fig & Walnut Cookies

Figs and walnuts make a flavorful combination, here complemented by dried dates. Delicious served with coffee.

15 mins   10–15 mins

MAKES 20

INGREDIENTS

1 cup butter or margarine, plus extra for greasing

scant ⅓ cup dried figs

⅓ cup honey

¼ cup raw sugar

2 eggs, beaten

pinch of salt

1 tsp ground allspice

1 tsp baking soda

½ tsp vanilla extract

2 tbsp dried dates, chopped finely

1½ cups all-purpose flour

2 cups rolled oats

⅓ cup walnuts, chopped finely

fig pieces, to decorate (optional)

1 Preheat the oven to 350°F/180°C and grease a large cookie sheet.

2 Finely chop the figs. Mix the butter (or margarine), honey, figs, and sugar together in a large bowl. Beat in the eggs and mix thoroughly.

3 Combine the salt, allspice, baking soda, vanilla extract and dates, stirring constantly. Add them to the creamed mixture gradually. Sift the flour into the mixture, stirring constantly. Finally, mix in the oats and walnuts.

4 Drop 20 rounded tablespoonfuls of cookie dough on to the greased cookie sheet, allowing room for the cookies to spread. Decorate with fig pieces, if desired. Bake in the preheated oven for 10–15 minutes, or until the cookies are golden brown.

5 Transfer the cookies from the oven to a wire rack and let cool before serving.

Oaty Pecan Cookies

These light, crisp cookies are delicious just as they are, but they are also good served with cheese. Let them cool completely before serving.

10 mins   15 mins

MAKES 15

INGREDIENTS

4 oz/115 g butter, softened, plus extra for greasing

⅓ cup light muscovado sugar

1 egg, beaten

⅔ cup all-purpose flour

½ tsp baking powder

½ cup rolled oats

½ cup pecans, chopped

1 Preheat the oven to 350°F/180°C and grease several cookie sheets. Put the butter and sugar in a bowl and beat until light and fluffy. Gradually beat in the egg.

2 Sift the flour and baking powder into the mixture and add the oats and pecans. Stir together until well combined. Drop tablespoonfuls of the mixture on to the cookie sheets, allowing room for the cookies to spread during cooking.

3 Bake in the oven for 15 minutes, or until pale golden. Let cool on the cookie sheets for 2 minutes, then transfer to wire racks to cool completely.

COOK'S TIP
To save a lot of hard work, beat the butter and sugar together with an electric whisk, or use a food processor.

Oat & Walnut Spice Cookies

These delicately spiced cookies are quick and easy to make and are delicious served with either coffee or tea at any time of the day.

🐷 15 mins 🕐 15–20 mins

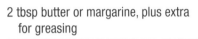

MAKES 20

INGREDIENTS

2 tbsp butter or margarine, plus extra for greasing

1 cup brown sugar

¾ cup walnuts

1 cup all-purpose flour

2 tsp baking soda

pinch of salt

1¼ tsp ground allspice

2 eggs, beaten

2 tsp vanilla extract

2 cups rolled oats

1 cup raisins

1 cup golden raisins

1 Preheat the oven to 350°F/180°C and grease 2 large cookie sheets. Cream the butter (or margarine) and sugar together in a large mixing bowl. Chop the walnuts coarsely.

2 In a separate bowl, sift together the flour, baking soda, salt, and allspice, then stir into the butter mixture. Blend in the eggs, vanilla extract, and oats until they are thoroughly combined. Finally, add the dry fruits and nuts and mix well.

3 Put 10 rounded tablespoonfuls of cookie dough on to each greased cookie sheet, allowing room for the cookies to spread during cooking. Transfer to the oven and bake for 15–20 minutes, or until the cookies are firm.

4 Remove the cookies from the oven and cool before serving.

Cherry & Walnut Cookies

Using slightly bitter maraschino cherries adds an interesting dimension to these cookies. An excellent alternative to after-dinner chocolates.

🥚 12 mins 🕐 10 mins

MAKES 30

INGREDIENTS

6 oz/175 g butter or margarine, plus extra for greasing

1 cup soft brown sugar

2 eggs

2¼ cups all-purpose flour

pinch of salt

2 tsp baking powder

2 tbsp milk

1 tsp almond extract

1 cup chopped walnuts

½ cup raisins

scant ½ cup golden raisins

½ cup maraschino cherries

2 cups wheat flakes, crushed

15 maraschino cherries, to decorate

1 Preheat the oven to 375°F/190°C. Grease a large cookie sheet. Halve the 15 maraschino cherries and set aside.

2 Cream the butter (or margarine) and sugar in a large bowl until a fluffy consistency is reached. Beat in the eggs.

3 Gradually sift the flour, salt, and baking powder into the creamed mixture. Add the milk and almond extract and mix thoroughly. Stir in the walnuts, dry fruits, and maraschino cherries.

4 Form the dough into 30 balls (about 1 rounded tablespoon each) and roll in the crushed wheat flakes. Space the dough balls about 1 inch/2 cm apart on the greased cookie sheet. Place half a maraschino cherry on the top of each dough ball, if desired. Transfer to the preheated oven and cook for 10 minutes, or until the cookies are light brown.

5 Transfer from the oven to a wire rack and let cool.

Prepare-Ahead Cookies

Make the dough for these cookies, then slice and bake it as and when required. The dough keeps in the refrigerator for up to one week.

15 mins plus
3 hrs chilling

10 mins

MAKES 25

INGREDIENTS

1⅓ cups all-purpose flour, plus extra for dusting

¼ cup unsweetened cocoa

1 tsp baking powder

4 oz/115 g butter, plus extra for greasing

scant 1 cup superfine sugar

⅓ cup semisweet chocolate chips

1 egg, beaten

1 Sift the flour, cocoa, and baking powder into a large mixing bowl. Add the butter and rub in until the mixture resembles fine bread crumbs. Stir in the sugar, chocolate chips, and egg and mix together to form a dough.

2 Turn the dough on to a lightly floured work counter and knead for 1 minute then shape into a 2-inch/5-cm long roll. Wrap the dough roll in foil and store in the refrigerator for at least 3 hours, or place in the freezer.

3 When ready to use, preheat the oven to 375°F/190°C. Grease 1–2 cookie sheets. Unwrap the dough roll and cut into ½-inch/1-cm thick slices. Place on the prepared cookie sheets and bake in the oven for about 10 minutes, until firm. Leave for 1 minute, then transfer the cookies to a wire rack and let cool.

VARIATIONS

Replace the chocolate chips with golden raisins, dried apricots, or raisins or add a combination of chopped hazelnuts, almonds, or walnuts, and chocolate chips.

 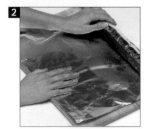 

Milk Chocolate Chunk Cookies

The dough for these large, soft cookies is rich and bursting with chunks of milk chocolate. Serve with tea for a delicious mid-afternoon treat.

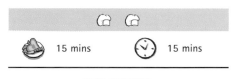

15 mins   15 mins

MAKES 20

INGREDIENTS

¾ cup butter, plus extra for greasing

10½ oz/300 g milk chocolate

2 cups rolled oats

1 cup all-purpose flour

1 tsp baking powder

generous ¾ cup superfine sugar

generous ¾ cup brown sugar

2 eggs, beaten

½ tsp vanilla extract

1 Preheat the oven to 350°F/180°C. Grease 4 large cookie sheets. Coarsely chop the chocolate into ¼-inch/8-mm pieces. Put the oats into a food processor and blend until ground to a powder. Sift the flour and baking powder together.

2 Whisk the butter, superfine sugar, and brown sugar together until soft and fluffy. Gradually beat in the eggs, then beat in the vanilla extract and sifted flour. Stir in the oats and chocolate pieces.

3 Place 20 teaspoonfuls of the cookie dough on the prepared cookie sheets, allowing room for the cookies to spread during cooking. Press each one down using the back of a wet spoon.

4 Bake the cookies in the preheated oven for about 15 minutes, until lightly browned. Leave for 5 minutes, then transfer to a wire rack and let cool.

Mixed Nut Cookies

If you are a lover of nuts, these cookies are a real treat, and will be very hard to resist. Try to let them cool completely before eating.

12 mins   12–14 mins

MAKES 36

INGREDIENTS

4 oz/115 g butter or margarine, plus extra for greasing

scant ¼ cup mixed nuts

½ cup superfine sugar

½ cup brown sugar

pinch of salt

1 tsp almond extract

2 egg whites, beaten lightly

3 tsp water

1 cup all-purpose flour

½ tsp baking powder

½ tsp baking soda

2 cups rolled oats

confectioners' sugar, for dusting (optional)

1 Preheat the oven to 375°F/190°C. Grease 2 large cookie sheets.

2 Finely chop the nuts and set aside. In a large mixing bowl, cream the butter, sugars, salt, and almond extract until the mixture is light and fluffy. Beat in the egg whites and water. Sift the flour, baking powder, and baking soda together and add to the mixture. Blend in the oats and nuts.

3 Drop 36 rounded tablespoonfuls of the cookie dough on to the greased cookie sheets, allowing room for the cookies to spread during cooking. Transfer to the oven and bake for 12–14 minutes.

4 Transfer the cookies to a wire rack, dust with confectioners' sugar, if liked, and let cool completely.

Orange Cream Cheese Cookies

Using cream cheese in these cookies adds lightness and texture to the basic dough. They look particularly attractive decorated with orange rind.

15 mins   10 mins

MAKES 30

INGREDIENTS

1 cup butter or margarine, plus extra
    for greasing

1 cup brown sugar

6 tbsp cream cheese

1 egg, beaten lightly

2⅓ cups all-purpose flour

1 tsp baking soda

1 tbsp orange juice

1 tsp finely grated orange rind

raw sugar, to sprinkle

fine strips of orange rind, to decorate
    (optional)

1 Preheat the oven to 375°F/190°C. Grease a large cookie sheet. In a large mixing bowl, cream together the butter, sugar, and cream cheese until light and fluffy. Mix in the egg and sift in the flour and baking soda. Add the orange juice and rind and mix well.

2 Drop about 30 rounded tablespoonfuls on to the greased cookie sheet, allowing room for the cookies to spread during cooking. Sprinkle with raw sugar.

3 Transfer to the preheated oven and bake for 10 minutes, or until the cookies are light brown at the edges.

4 Remove the cookies from the oven and let cool on a wire rack before serving. Decorate with a few strips of orange rind, if desired.

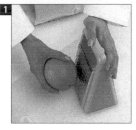

Carrot Cookies

Grated carrot adds a natural sweetness to these delicious cookies, which complements the ground allspice perfectly.

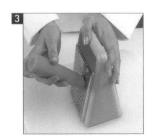

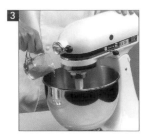

10 mins   12 mins

MAKES 24

INGREDIENTS

4 tbsp butter or margarine, plus extra
    for greasing

1 cup all-purpose flour

½ tsp ground allspice

¼ cup lowfat milk powder

¼ tsp baking soda

1 tsp baking powder

pinch of salt

scant ⅓ cup brown sugar, plus extra
    for dusting

¾ cup corn syrup

1 egg

1½ cups shredded carrots

1 tsp vanilla extract

2⅔ cups rolled oats

1 Preheat the oven to 375°F/190°C and grease a large cookie sheet.

2 In a medium bowl, sift together the flour, allspice, milk powder, baking soda, baking powder, and salt.

3 Blend the butter (or margarine), sugar, and corn syrup together in a large bowl. Beat in the egg thoroughly. Add the dry ingredients gradually, stirring continuously. Shred the carrots and blend in with the vanilla extract and oats.

4 Put 24 tablespoonfuls of cookie dough on to the cookie sheet, allowing room for the cookies to spread during cooking. Dust with brown sugar.

Transfer to the preheated oven and bake for 12 minutes, or until the cookies are golden brown.

5 Remove the cookies from the oven, then place on a wire rack and let them cool completely before serving.

Orange Horns

It is much easier to shape these cookies into horn shapes while they are still warm from the oven. Let them cool before serving.

 10 mins   🕐 7 mins

MAKES 30

INGREDIENTS

4 oz/115 g butter or margarine, plus extra for greasing

1 orange

⅔ cup brown sugar

pinch of salt

1 egg white, beaten lightly

½ tsp baking powder

½ cup oatmeal

1 cup finely chopped Brazil nuts (or hazelnuts)

1 tbsp milk

1 tsp orange juice

1 Preheat the oven to 325°F/160°C and grease a large cookie sheet.

2 Grate the orange and set aside. Blend the butter (or margarine) and sugar together in a bowl until the mixture is fluffy. Add the remaining ingredients and mix thoroughly.

3 Drop 30 rounded teaspoonfuls of the mixture on to the cookie sheet and flatten into small circles using the bottom of a glass. Transfer to the preheated oven and bake for 7 minutes, then remove from the oven.

4 Let cool slightly. Place each cookie in turn on a rolling pin to help start the desired curve, completing the horn shape by hand, while the cookie is still warm.

5 Let the cookies cool on a wire rack before serving.

Party Cookies

These cookies are studded with colorful sugar-coated chocolate beans, and are ideal for children's birthday parties.

10 mins   10–12 mins

MAKES 16

INGREDIENTS

4 oz/115 g butter, softened, plus extra
   for greasing

generous ½ cup brown sugar

1 tbsp corn syrup

½ tsp vanilla extract

1¼ cups self-rising flour

3 oz/85 g sugar-coated chocolate beans

1 Preheat the oven to 350°F/180°C, then grease 2 cookie sheets. Place the butter and sugar in a bowl and beat together with an electric whisk until light and fluffy, then beat in the syrup and vanilla extract.

2 Sift in half the flour and work it into the mixture. Stir in the chocolate beans and the remaining flour and work the dough together with your fingers.

3 Using your fingers, roll the dough into 16 balls and place them on the prepared cookie sheets, allowing room for the cookies to spread during cooking.

COOK'S TIP
To make a slightly less sweet version of these cookies, you could use chocolate chips, cherries, or chopped dried apricots instead of the chocolate beans.

Do not flatten them. Bake in the preheated oven for 10–12 minutes, or until pale golden at the edges.

4 Remove from the oven and let cool on the cookie sheets for 2 minutes, then transfer to wire racks to cool completely.

Christmas Cookies

These festive cookies will quickly become part of your holiday baking repertoire. Store in an airtight container for up to a week.

🍰 30 mins plus 4 hrs chilling   🕐 10 mins

MAKES 24

INGREDIENTS

7 cups all-purpose flour, plus extra for dusting

1 tbsp baking soda

1 tbsp ground ginger

3 tsp ground allspice

pinch of salt

1 cup butter or margarine, plus extra for greasing

1½ cups corn syrup

1 cup raw sugar

½ cup water

1 egg

1 tsp cognac

1 tsp very finely grated orange rind

½ cup confectioners' sugar, plus extra to decorate

1 In a large bowl, sift together the flour, baking soda, ginger, allspice, and salt. In a separate bowl, beat together the butter (or margarine), corn syrup, sugar, water, egg, and cognac until thoroughly combined. Gradually stir in the grated orange rind, then the flour mixture.

2 Halve the dough, then wrap in plastic wrap and refrigerate for at least 4 hours (it will keep for up to 6 days). When ready to use, preheat the oven to 350°F/180°C and grease a cookie sheet.

3 Flour a board or work counter. Roll each half of dough into a ball, then roll it to a thickness of ⅛ inch/3 mm. Using Christmas cookie cutters or a knife, cut festive shapes such as stars and trees. Put the cookies on to the cookie sheet, then transfer to the oven and bake for 10 minutes, or until golden brown. Remove the cookies from the oven and transfer to a wire rack, then set aside.

4 When the cookies have cooled, mix the confectioners' sugar with a little water to make a glacé frosting. Drizzle this frosting over some of the cookies, and decorate the remainder with sifted confectioners' sugar.

Ginger Oat Cookies

These mouthwatering squares are delicately flavored with ground cinnamon, nutmeg, and ginger. They are ideal to serve for dessert.

🕙 10 mins   🕐 20–25 mins

MAKES 24

INGREDIENTS

4 oz/115 g butter or margarine, plus extra for greasing

¾ cup brown sugar

1½ cups all-purpose flour, plus extra for dusting

1 cup rolled oats

1 cup bran

½ tsp ground cinnamon

½ tsp ground nutmeg

1 tsp ground ginger

⅔ cup cold water

1 Preheat the oven to 350°F/180°C and grease a large cookie sheet.

2 In a large mixing bowl, combine the sugar, flour, oats, bran, and spices. Add the butter (or margarine) and mix with your fingers until the mixture resembles bread crumbs. Gradually add the water, continuing to mix with your fingers, until the dough is stiff.

3 Sprinkle flour on to a cutting board or work counter and roll out the dough until it is ½ inch/1 cm thick. Cut into 2-inch/5-cm squares and then place on the cookie sheet.

4 Transfer to the preheated oven and bake for 20–25 minutes, or until the cookies are golden brown. Remove the cookies from the oven and place on a wire rack to cool before serving.

Gingersnaps

Nothing compares with the taste of these freshly baked authentic gingersnaps, which have a lovely hint of orange flavor.

10 mins   15–20 mins

MAKES 30

I N G R E D I E N T S

4 oz/115 g butter, plus extra for greasing

2½ cups self-rising flour

pinch of salt

1 cup superfine sugar

1 tbsp ground ginger

1 tsp baking soda

¼ cup corn syrup

1 egg, beaten lightly

1 tsp grated orange rind

1 Preheat the oven to 325°F/160°C. Lightly grease several cookie sheets.

2 Sift the flour, salt, sugar, ground ginger, and baking soda into a large mixing bowl.

3 Heat the butter and corn syrup together in a pan over very low heat until the butter has melted.

4 Let the butter mixture cool slightly, then pour it on to the dry ingredients. Add the egg and orange rind and mix together thoroughly.

COOK'S TIP

Store these cookies in an airtight container and eat them within 1 week.

5 Using your hands, carefully shape the dough into 30 even-size balls.

6 Place the balls on the prepared cookie sheets, allowing room for the cookies to spread during cooking, then flatten them slightly with your fingers.

7 Bake in the oven for 15–20 minutes. Carefully transfer the cookies to a wire rack to cool and become crisp.

Gingerbread People

This is a favorite with children, who love to make the gingerbread shapes. The recipe makes a pliable dough that is very easy to handle.

30 mins   15–20 mins

MAKES 20

INGREDIENTS

4 oz/115 g butter, plus
   extra for greasing

3½ cups all-purpose flour,
   plus extra for dusting

2 tsp ground ginger

1 tsp ground allspice

2 tsp baking soda

generous ⅓ cup corn syrup

generous ½ cup brown sugar

1 egg, beaten

TO DECORATE

currants

candied cherries

generous ¾ cup confectioners' sugar

3–4 tsp water

1 Preheat the oven to 325°F/160°C, then grease 3 large cookie sheets. Sift the flour, ginger, allspice, and baking soda into a large bowl. Place the butter, syrup, and sugar in a pan over low heat and stir until melted. Pour on to the dry ingredients and add the egg. Mix together to make a dough. The dough will be sticky to start with, but will become firmer as it cools.

2 On a lightly floured work counter, roll out the dough to about ⅛-inch/ 3-mm thick and stamp out gingerbread people shapes. Place on the prepared cookie sheets. Re-knead and re-roll the trimmings and cut out more shapes until the dough is used up. Decorate with currants for eyes and pieces of cherry for mouths. Bake for 15–20 minutes, or until firm and lightly browned.

3 Remove from the oven and let cool on the cookie sheets for a few minutes, then transfer to wire racks to cool completely. Mix the confectioners' sugar with the water to a thick consistency. Place the frosting in a small plastic bag and cut a tiny hole in one corner. Use the frosting to pipe buttons or bows on to the cooled cookies.

COOK'S TIP
At Christmas, cut out star and bell shapes. When the cookies come out of the oven, gently pierce a hole in each one with a skewer. Thread ribbons through and hang on the Christmas tree.

Ginger-Topped Fingers

A delicious sticky ginger topping turns these shortbread fingers into a real treat. To decorate, pipe lines of white frosting on the tops.

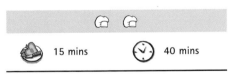

15 mins   40 mins

MAKES 16

INGREDIENTS

¾ cup butter, plus extra for greasing

generous 1½ cups all-purpose flour

1 tsp ground ginger

scant ½ cup golden superfine sugar

GINGER TOPPING

1 tbsp corn syrup

¼ cup butter

2 tbsp confectioners' sugar

1 tsp ground ginger

1 Preheat the oven to 350°F/180°C. Grease an 11 x 7-inch/28 x 18-cm oblong cake pan. Sift the flour and ginger into a bowl and stir in the sugar. Rub in the butter until the mixture starts to stick together.

2 Press the mixture into the prepared pan and smooth the top with a spatula. Bake in the oven for 40 minutes, or until very lightly browned.

3 To make the topping, place the syrup and butter in a small pan over low heat and stir until melted. Stir in the confectioners' sugar and ginger. Remove the shortbread from the oven and pour the topping over it while both are still hot. Let cool slightly in the pan, then cut into 16 fingers. Transfer to wire racks to cool.

COOK'S TIP
The shortbread will be quite soft when it first comes out of the oven, but it will become firm as it cools. Let these fingers cool completely before serving.

Apple Shortcakes

These freshly baked cookies are split and filled with sliced apples and whipped cream. The shortcakes can be eaten either warm or cold.

25 mins   15 mins

MAKES 4

INGREDIENTS

2 tbsp butter, cut into small pieces, plus extra for greasing

1¼ cups all-purpose flour

½ tsp salt

1 tsp baking powder

1 tbsp superfine sugar

¼ cup milk

confectioners' sugar, for dusting

FILLING

3 dessert apples, peeled, cored, and sliced

½ cup superfine sugar

1 tbsp lemon juice

1 tsp ground cinnamon

1¼ cups water

⅔ cup heavy cream, whipped lightly

1 Preheat the oven to 425°F/220°C. Lightly grease a cookie sheet with a little butter.

2 Sift the flour, salt, and baking powder into a mixing bowl. Stir in the sugar, then rub in the butter with your fingertips until the mixture resembles fine bread crumbs.

3 Pour in the milk and mix to a soft dough. On a lightly floured counter, knead the dough lightly, then roll out to ½ inch/1 cm thick. Stamp out 4 circles, using a 5-cm/2-inch cutter. Transfer the circles to the cookie sheet.

4 Bake in the preheated oven for about 15 minutes, until risen and lightly browned. Let cool.

5 To make the filling, place the apple slices with the sugar, lemon juice, and cinnamon in a pan. Add the water, bring to a boil, and simmer, uncovered, for 5-10 minutes, until the apples are tender. Let cool a little, then remove the apples.

6 Split the shortcakes in half. Place each bottom half on an individual serving plate and spoon on a quarter of the apple slices, then the cream. Place the other half of the shortcake on top. Serve dusted with confectioners' sugar.

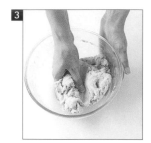

Christmas Shortbread

Make this wonderful shortbread and then give it the Christmas touch by cutting it into different shapes with seasonal cookie cutters.

30 mins plus
10–15 mins
chilling

10–15 mins

MAKES 24

INGREDIENTS

½ cup superfine sugar

8 oz/225 g butter, plus extra for greasing

3 cups all-purpose flour, sifted, plus extra
  for dusting

pinch of salt

TO DECORATE

½ cup confectioners' sugar

silver balls

candied cherries

angelica

1 Beat the sugar and butter together in a large bowl until combined (thorough creaming is not necessary).

2 Sift in the flour and salt and work together to form a stiff dough. Turn out on to a lightly floured work counter. Knead lightly for a few moments until smooth, but avoid over-handling. Chill in the refrigerator for 10–15 minutes. Preheat the oven to 350°F/180°C. Grease several cookie sheets.

3 Roll out the dough on a lightly floured work counter and cut into shapes with small Christmas cutters, such as trees, bells, stars, and angels. Place on greased cookie sheets.

4 Bake in the oven for 10–15 minutes, until pale golden brown. Let cool on the cookie sheets for 10 minutes, then transfer to wire racks to cool completely.

5 Mix the confectioners' sugar with a little water to make a glacé frosting, and use to frost the cookies. Before the frosting sets, decorate with silver balls, tiny pieces of candied cherries, and angelica. Store in an airtight container or wrap the cookies individually in cellophane, tie with colored ribbon, or string, then hang them on the Christmas tree as edible decorations.

Scottish Shortbread

Many traditional recipes for shortbread contain a small amount of rice flour, which gives each wedge a delicate, crisp texture.

25 mins | 1 hr

MAKES 16

INGREDIENTS

6 oz/175 g butter, sweet for preference, at room temperature, plus extra for greasing

2 cups all-purpose flour, plus extra for dusting

⅓ cup rice flour

¼ tsp salt

¼ cup superfine sugar

¼ cup confectioners' sugar, sifted

¼ tsp vanilla extract (optional)

superfine sugar, for sprinkling

1 Preheat the oven to 250°F/120°C. Grease 2 x 8-inch/20-cm cake or tart pans with removable bottoms. Sift the all-purpose flour, rice flour, and salt into a bowl; set aside.

2 Using an electric whisk, beat the butter for about 1 minute in a large bowl until creamy. Add the sugars and continue beating for 1–2 minutes until very light and fluffy. If using, beat in the vanilla extract.

3 Using a wooden spoon, stir the flour mixture into the creamed butter and sugar until well blended. Turn on to a lightly floured work counter. Divide the dough into 2 pieces, knead each lightly, and press into a circle.

4 Press a dough circle into each pan, smoothing the surface. Lightly sprinkle the surfaces of each dough round with a little superfine sugar. Then prick the surface lightly with a fork.

5 Using a sharp knife, mark each dough round into 8 wedges. Prick with a fork and bake in the preheated oven for 50–60 minutes, until the shortbread is pale golden and crisp. Cool in the pans on a wire rack for about 5 minutes.

6 Carefully remove the side of each pan and slide the bottoms on to a heatproof surface. Using the knife marks as a guide, cut each shortbread into 8 wedges while still warm. Cool completely on the wire rack, then store in airtight containers.

Shortbread Fantails

These cookies are perfect for afternoon tea, or they can be served with vanilla or chocolate ice cream for a really delicious dessert.

 40 mins   30–35 mins

SERVES 8

INGREDIENTS

4 oz/115 g butter, softened, plus extra for greasing

scant ¼ cup granulated sugar

2 tbsp confectioners' sugar

generous 1½ cups all-purpose flour, plus extra for dusting

pinch of salt

2 tsp orange flower water

superfine sugar, for sprinkling

1 Preheat the oven to 325°F/160°C. Lightly grease a shallow 8-inch/20-cm round cake pan.

2 In a large mixing bowl, cream together the butter, the granulated sugar, and the confectioners' sugar, until light and fluffy.

3 Sift the flour and salt into the creamed mixture. Add the orange flower water and bring everything together to form a soft dough.

4 On a lightly floured counter, roll out the dough to an 8-inch/20-cm circle and place in the prepared pan. Use a fork to press neatly around the edge. Score 8 triangles with a knife then prick the surface.

5 Transfer the shortbread to the oven and bake for 30–35 minutes, or until the shortbread is crisp and the top is pale golden.

6 Sprinkle with superfine sugar, then cut along the marked lines to make the fantails.

7 Let the shortbread cool before removing the pieces from the pan. Store in an airtight container.

COOK'S TIP

For a crunchy addition, sprinkle 2 tablespoons chopped mixed nuts over the top of the fantails before baking.

Chocolate Shortbread

This delicious buttery chocolate shortbread is the perfect addition to the cookie jar of any chocoholic. Let it cool completely before eating.

40 mins   40 mins

MAKES 12

INGREDIENTS

6 oz/175 g butter, softened, plus extra for greasing

1½ cups all-purpose flour

1 tbsp unsweetened cocoa

4 tbsp superfine sugar

1¾ oz/50 g semisweet chocolate, chopped finely

1 Preheat the oven to 325°F/160°C. Lightly grease a cookie sheet. Place all the ingredients in a large mixing bowl and beat together until they form a dough. Knead the dough lightly.

2 Place the dough on the cookie sheet and roll out to form an 8-inch/20-cm circle.

3 Pinch the edges of the dough with your fingertips to form a decorative edge. Prick the dough all over with a fork and mark into 12 wedges, using a knife.

4 Bake in the oven for 40 minutes, until firm and golden. Let cool slightly before cutting into wedges. Transfer to a wire rack to cool completely.

VARIATION
To make small shortbread cookies, roll out the dough on a lightly floured counter to ¾ inch/ 8 mm thick. Cut out 3-inch/7.5-cm circles with a cookie cutter. Transfer to a greased cookie sheet and bake as above. If liked, coat half the cookie in melted chocolate.

Chocolate Chip Shortbread

Buttery shortbread sprinkled with chocolate chips—nothing could be simpler or more delicious! Store in an airtight jar for several days.

🍰 10 mins   🕐 35–40 mins

MAKES 10

INGREDIENTS

4 oz/115 g butter, diced, plus extra
  for greasing

generous ¾ cup all-purpose flour

⅜ cup cornstarch

generous ¼ cup golden superfine sugar

¼ cup semisweet chocolate chips

1 Preheat the oven to 325°F/160°C. Grease a 9-inch/23-cm loose-bottom fluted tart pan. Sift the flour and cornstarch into a large bowl. Stir in the sugar, then add the butter and rub it in until the mixture starts to bind together.

2 Turn into the prepared tart pan and press evenly over the bottom. Prick the surface with a fork. Sprinkle with the chocolate chips and press lightly into the surface.

3 Bake in the oven for 35–40 minutes, or until cooked but not browned. Mark into 8 portions with a sharp knife. Let cool in the pan for 10 minutes, then transfer to a wire rack to cool completely.

VARIATION
To give the shortbread a crunchier texture, use semolina as a substitute for the cornstarch. Use milk or white chocolate chips in place of semisweet.

Millionaire's Shortbread

These rich squares of shortbread are topped with caramel and finished with chocolate to make a very special treat for both adults and children!

55 mins   30 mins

MAKES 4

INGREDIENTS

4 oz/115 g butter, cut into small pieces, plus extra for greasing

1½ cups all-purpose flour

⅓ cup brown sugar, sifted

TOPPING

4 tbsp butter

⅓ cup brown sugar

1¾ cups condensed milk

5½ oz/150 g milk chocolate

1 Preheat the oven to 375°F/190°C. Lightly grease a 9-inch/23-cm square cake pan.

2 Sift the flour into a mixing bowl and rub in the butter with your fingers until the mixture resembles fine bread crumbs. Add the sugar and mix to form a firm dough.

3 Press the dough into the bottom of the prepared pan and prick the bottom with a fork.

4 Bake in the preheated oven for 20 minutes, until lightly golden. Let cool in the pan.

5 To make the topping, place the butter, sugar, and condensed milk in a nonstick pan and cook over gentle heat, stirring constantly, until the mixture comes to a boil.

6 Reduce the heat and cook for 4–5 minutes, until the caramel is pale golden and thick and is coming away from the sides of the pan. Pour the topping over the shortbread layer and let cool.

7 When the caramel topping is firm, melt the milk chocolate in a heatproof bowl set over a pan of gently simmering water. Spread the melted chocolate over the topping. Let set in a cool place, then cut the shortbread into squares or fingers to serve.

COOK'S TIP
Ensure the caramel layer is completely cool and set before coating it with the melted chocolate, otherwise they will mix together.

Vanilla Hearts

This is a classic shortbread cookie which melts in the mouth. Here the cookies are made in pretty heart shapes.

🍳 30 mins   🕐 15–20 mins

MAKES 16

I N G R E D I E N T S

6 oz/175 g butter, cut into small pieces, plus extra for greasing

2 cups all-purpose flour, plus extra for dusting

½ cup superfine sugar, plus extra for dusting

1 tsp vanilla extract

1 Preheat the oven to 350°F/180°C. Lightly grease a cookie sheet.

2 Sift the flour into a large mixing bowl and rub in the butter with your fingertips until the mixture resembles fine bread crumbs.

3 Stir in the superfine sugar and vanilla extract and bring the mixture together with your hands to make a smooth, firm dough.

4 On a lightly floured work counter, roll out the dough to a thickness of 1 inch/2.5 cm. Stamp out 12 hearts with a heart-shaped cookie cutter measuring about 2 inches/5 cm across and 1 inch/2.5 cm deep.

5 Arrange the hearts on the prepared cookie sheet. Bake in the preheated oven for 15-20 minutes, until the hearts are a light golden color.

6 Transfer the vanilla hearts to a wire rack and let cool.

7 Dust the cookies with a little superfine sugar just before serving.

COOK'S TIP
Place a fresh vanilla bean in your superfine sugar and keep it in a storage jar for several weeks to give the sugar a delicious vanilla flavor.

Chocolate Peanut Butter Slices

Children in particular will love these slices made with crunchy peanut butter and condensed milk. Store in airtight containers.

20 mins   35 mins

MAKES 25

INGREDIENTS

10½ oz/300 g milk chocolate

2½ cups all-purpose flour

1 tsp baking powder

1 cup butter

1¾ cups brown sugar

2 cups rolled oats

½ cup chopped mixed nuts

1 egg, beaten

14 oz/400 g condensed milk

⅓ cup crunchy peanut butter

1 Preheat the oven to 350°F/180°C. Finely chop the chocolate. Sift the flour and baking powder into a large bowl.

2 Add the butter to the flour and rub in until the mixture resembles bread crumbs. Stir in the sugar, oats, and chopped nuts.

3 Put a quarter of the mixture into a bowl and stir in the chopped chocolate. Set aside.

4 Stir the egg into the remaining mixture, then press into the bottom of a 12 x 8-inch/30 x 20-cm roasting pan.

5 Bake the base in the preheated oven for 15 minutes. Meanwhile, mix the condensed milk and peanut butter together. Pour the mixture over the base and spread evenly, then sprinkle the reserved chocolate mixture on top and press down lightly.

6 Return to the oven and bake the slices for an additional 20 minutes, until golden brown. Let cool in the pan, then cut into slices.

Chocolate Chip & Walnut Slices

Although these slices can be made in a matter of moments, the result is truly delicious and they will disappear in moments too!

🍮 10 mins   🕐 25–30 mins

MAKES 18

INGREDIENTS

8 oz/225 g butter, plus extra for greasing

1 cup walnut pieces

1 cup semisweet chocolate chips

1 cup superfine sugar

few drops vanilla extract

2 cups all-purpose flour

1 Preheat the oven to 350°F/180°C. Grease an 8 x 12-inch/20 x 30-cm jelly roll pan. Coarsely chop the walnut pieces to about the same size as the chocolate chips.

2 Whisk the butter and sugar together until pale and fluffy. Add the vanilla extract, then stir in the flour. Stir in the walnuts and chocolate chips. Press the mixture into the prepared pan.

3 Bake the mixture in the oven for 20–25 minutes, until golden brown. Let cool in the pan, then cut into slices.

Mincemeat Crumble Bars

These crumble bars make a change from traditional mince pies, but they are bound to be popular at any time of the year!

40 mins plus
20 mins chilling

32–35 mins

MAKES 12

INGREDIENTS

1⅓ cups mincemeat

confectioners' sugar, for dusting

BOTTOM LAYER

scant ⅔ cup butter, plus extra for greasing

scant ½ cup golden superfine sugar

1 cup all-purpose flour

scant ⅔ cup cornstarch

TOPPING

generous ¾ cup self-rising flour

6 tbsp butter, cut into pieces

scant ½ cup golden superfine sugar

¼ cup slivered almonds

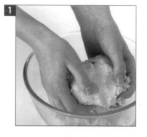

1 Grease a shallow 11 x 8-inch/28 x 20-cm cake pan. To make the bottom layer, place the butter and sugar in a bowl and cream together until light and fluffy. Sift in the flour and cornstarch and, with your hands, bring the mixture together to form a ball. Push the dough into the cake pan, flattening it out and pressing it into the corners, then chill in the refrigerator for 20 minutes. Meanwhile, preheat the oven to 400°F/200°C. Bake the bottom layer in the oven for 12–15 minutes, or until puffed and golden.

2 To make the crumble topping, place the flour, butter, and sugar in a bowl and rub together into coarse crumbs. Stir in the almonds.

3 Spread the mincemeat over the bottom layer and scatter the crumbs on top. Bake in the oven for an additional 20 minutes, or until golden. Let cool slightly, then cut into 12 pieces and let cool completely. Dust with sifted confectioners' sugar, then serve.

COOK'S TIP
Make sure that you bake the bottom layer thoroughly. If it is undercooked, it will not be crisp enough.

Almond Slices

A mouthwatering dessert that is sure to impress your guests, especially if it is served with a spoonful of whipped cream.

10 mins   45 mins

SERVES 8

INGREDIENTS

3 eggs

⅔ cup ground almonds

1½ cups milk powder

1 cup granulated sugar

½ tsp saffron strands

4 oz/115 g butter, sweet for preference

1 tbsp slivered almonds, to decorate

1 Preheat the oven to 325°F/160°C. Heat the eggs together in a mixing bowl and set aside.

2 Place the ground almonds, milk powder, sugar, and saffron in a large mixing bowl and stir to mix well.

3 Melt the butter in a small pan over low heat. Pour the melted butter over the dry ingredients and mix well until thoroughly combined.

4 Add the reserved beaten eggs to the mixture and stir to blend well.

5 Spread the cake mixture evenly in a shallow 8-inch/20-cm ovenproof dish and bake in the preheated oven for 45 minutes, or until a skewer inserted into the center comes out clean.

6 Cut the almond cake into slices. Decorate the almond slices with slivered almonds, and transfer to serving plates. Serve hot or cold.

COOK'S TIP
These almond slices are best eaten hot, but they may also be served cold. They can be made a day or even a week in advance and reheated. They also freeze beautifully.

Apricot Slices

These vegan slices are ideal for children's lunch boxes. They are full of flavor and made with healthy ingredients.

20 mins plus
30 mins chilling

1 hr

MAKES 12

INGREDIENTS

PASTRY

3½ oz/100 g margarine, cut into small pieces, plus extra for greasing

2 cups whole-wheat flour

½ cup finely ground mixed nuts

4 tbsp water

soy milk, to glaze

FILLING

1 cup dried apricots

grated rind of 1 orange

1½ cups apple juice

1 tsp ground cinnamon

generous ⅓ cup raisins

1 Preheat the oven to 400°F/200°C. Lightly grease a 9-inch/23-cm square cake pan. To make the dough, place the flour and nuts in a mixing bowl and rub in the margarine with your fingers until the mixture resembles bread crumbs. Stir in the water and bring together to form a dough. Wrap and let chill for 30 minutes.

2 To make the filling, place the apricots, orange rind, and apple juice in a pan and bring to a boil. Simmer for 30 minutes until the apricots are mushy. Cool slightly, then process in a food processor or blender to a purée. Alternatively, press the mixture through a fine strainer. Stir in the cinnamon and raisins.

3 Divide the dough in half, roll out 1 half, and use to line the bottom of the pan. Spread the apricot purée over the top and brush the edges of the dough with water. Roll out the rest of the dough to fit over the top of the apricot purée. Press down and seal the edges.

4 Prick the top of the dough with a fork and brush with soy milk. Bake in the oven for 20–25 minutes, until the pastry is golden. Let cool slightly before cutting into 12 bars. Serve the slices either warm or cold.

COOK'S TIP
These slices will keep in an airtight container for 3-4 days.

Mexican Pastelitos

These little cookies are traditionally served at Mexican weddings, their confectioners' sugar coating reflecting the white of the bridal gown.

 20 mins 30–40 mins

MAKES 40–50

INGREDIENTS

8 oz/225 g butter, softened, plus extra for greasing

¼ cup golden superfine sugar

generous 1½ cups all-purpose flour

generous ¾ cup cornstarch

1 tsp ground cinnamon

½ cup confectioners' sugar, sifted, to decorate

1 Preheat the oven to 325°F/160°C. Grease 2 cookie sheets. Place the butter and superfine sugar in a bowl and beat until light and fluffy. Sift the flour, cornstarch, and cinnamon into a separate bowl, then gradually work them into the creamed mixture with a wooden spoon. When well mixed, knead until smooth.

2 Take 1 teaspoonful of the cookie dough at a time and roll into a ball. Place the little balls on the prepared cookie sheets. Bake in the preheated oven for 30–40 minutes, or until pale golden.

3 Place the confectioners' sugar in a shallow dish and toss the pastelitos in it while they are still warm. Let cool on wire racks.

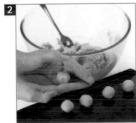

Gingerbread Squares

Gingerbread is delicious either on its own or served with a spoonful or two of vanilla ice cream as a quick and easy dessert.

40 mins | 10 mins

MAKES 24

I N G R E D I E N T S

6 oz/175 g butter, plus extra for greasing

¼ cup brown sugar

5 tbsp molasses

1 egg white

1 tsp almond extract

scant 1½ cups all-purpose flour

¼ tsp baking soda

¼ tsp baking powder

pinch of salt

½ tsp ground allspice

½ tsp ground ginger

scant ½ cup dessert apples, cooked

1 Preheat the oven to 350°F/180°C. Grease a large cake pan and line it with parchment paper. Chop the apple and set aside. Put the butter, sugar, molasses, egg white, and almond extract in a food processor and beat until smooth.

2 In a separate bowl, sift together the flour, baking soda, baking powder, salt, allspice, and ginger. Add to the creamed mixture and beat together well. Stir the prepared apples into the mixture, then pour the mixture into the lined cake pan.

3 Transfer to the preheated oven and bake for 10 minutes, or until golden brown. Remove from the oven and cut into 24 pieces. Transfer the gingerbread to a wire rack and let cool completely before serving.

Gingerbread

This spicy gingerbread is made even more moist and flavorful by the addition of chopped fresh apples. Serve as a mid-afternoon snack.

40 mins   30–35 mins

MAKES 12 BARS

INGREDIENTS

6 oz/175 g butter, plus extra for greasing

scant 1 cup brown sugar

2 tbsp molasses

generous 1½ cups all-purpose flour

1 tsp baking powder

2 tsp baking soda

2 tsp ground ginger

⅔ cup milk

1 egg, beaten lightly

2 dessert apples, peeled, chopped, and coated with 1 tbsp lemon juice

1 Preheat the oven to 325°F/160°C. Grease a 9-inch/23-cm square cake pan and line with parchment paper.

2 Melt the butter, sugar, and molasses in a pan over low heat. Remove the pan from the heat and let cool.

3 Sift the flour, baking powder, baking soda, and ginger together into a large mixing bowl.

4 Stir in the milk, beaten egg, and the cooled buttery liquid, followed by the chopped apples coated with the lemon juice.

5 Mix together gently, then pour the mixture into the prepared pan.

6 Bake in the preheated oven for 30–35 minutes, until the cake has risen and a skewer inserted into the center comes out clean.

7 Let the cake cool in the pan before turning out and cutting into 12 bars.

VARIATION

If you enjoy the flavor of ginger, try adding 1 tablespoon finely chopped preserved ginger to the mixture in step 3.

Cinnamon Squares

These moist, cakelike squares have a lovely spicy flavor. Sunflower seeds give them a nutty texture. Let cool before cutting into squares.

🕐 1 hr   🕐 45 mins

MAKES 12

INGREDIENTS

8 oz/225 g butter, softened, plus extra for greasing

1¼ cups superfine sugar

3 eggs, beaten lightly

1¾ cups self-rising flour

½ tsp baking soda

1 tbsp ground cinnamon

⅔ cup sour cream

½ cup sunflower seeds

1 Preheat the oven to 350°F/180°C. Grease a 9-inch/23-cm square cake pan with a little butter and line the bottom with parchment paper.

2 In a large mixing bowl, cream together the butter and superfine sugar until the mixture is light and fluffy.

3 Gradually add the beaten eggs to the mixture, beating thoroughly after each addition.

4 Sift the flour, baking soda, and cinnamon together into the creamed mixture and fold in, using a metal spoon in a figure-of-eight movement.

5 Spoon in the sour cream and sunflower seeds and mix gently until well combined.

6 Spoon the mixture into the prepared cake pan and smooth the surface with the back of a spoon or a knife.

7 Bake in the preheated oven for about 45 minutes, until the mixture is firm to the touch when pressed with a finger.

8 Loosen the edges with a round-bladed knife, then turn out on to a wire rack to cool completely. Slice into 12 squares before serving.

COOK'S TIP

These moist squares will freeze well and will keep for up to 1 month.

Hazelnut Squares

These can be made quickly and easily for an afternoon tea treat.
The hazelnuts can be replaced by any other nut if preferred.

40 mins   25 mins

MAKES 16

INGREDIENTS

2¾ oz/75 g butter, cut into small pieces, plus extra for greasing

generous 1 cup all-purpose flour

pinch of salt

1 tsp baking powder

¾ cup brown sugar

1 egg, beaten lightly

4 tbsp milk

1 cup halved hazelnuts

raw sugar, for sprinkling (optional)

1 Preheat the oven to 350°F/180°C. Grease a 9-inch/23-cm square cake pan and line with parchment paper.

2 Sift the flour, salt, and baking powder into a large bowl.

3 Rub in the butter with your fingertips until the mixture resembles fine bread crumbs. Stir in the brown sugar.

4 Add the beaten egg, milk, and nuts to the mixture and stir well until thoroughly combined.

5 Spoon the mixture into the prepared cake pan, spreading it out evenly, and smooth the surface. Sprinkle with raw sugar (if using).

6 Bake in the preheated oven for about 25 minutes, or until the mixture is firm to the touch when pressed gently with a finger.

7 Let cool for 10 minutes in the pan, then loosen the edges with a round-bladed knife and turn out on to a wire rack. Cut into squares and let cool completely before serving.

VARIATION
For a coffee-time cookie, replace the milk with the same amount of cold, strong black coffee—the stronger the better.

Mocha Brownies

A hint of coffee gives these brownies a sophisticated flavor and will quickly become a firm family favorite.

40 mins   25–30 mins

MAKES 16

INGREDIENTS

4 tbsp butter, plus extra for greasing

4 oz/115 g semisweet chocolate, broken into pieces

½ cup pecans

generous 1 cup dark muscovado sugar

2 eggs

1 tbsp instant coffee granules dissolved in 1 tbsp hot water

⅔ cup all-purpose flour

½ tsp baking powder

1 Preheat the oven to 350°F/180°C. Grease and base-line an 8-inch/20-cm square cake pan. Put the chocolate and butter in a pan and heat very gently until melted. Stir and let cool.

2 Coarsely chop the pecans and set aside. Put the sugar and eggs in a bowl and cream together until light and fluffy. Fold in the chocolate and cooled coffee and mix thoroughly. Sift in the flour and baking powder and lightly fold into the mixture. Carefully fold in the chopped nuts. Pour the mixture into the prepared pan and bake in the oven for 25–30 minutes, until firm and a skewer inserted into the center comes out clean.

3 Let cool in the pan for a few minutes, then run a knife around the edge of the cake to loosen it. Turn the cake out and peel off the paper. Place the cake on a wire rack to cool completely. When cold, cut into squares.

COOK'S TIP
The brownies will sink slightly and crack as they cool.

Pecan Brownies

Pecans and chocolate complement each other very successfully in this version of brownies. Dust with confectioners' sugar if liked.

40 mins   30 mins

MAKES 20

INGREDIENTS

8 oz/225 g butter, sweet for preference, plus extra for greasing

2½ oz/70 g semisweet chocolate

scant 1 cup all-purpose flour

¾ tsp baking soda

¼ tsp baking powder

⅓ cup pecans

½ cup raw sugar

⅛ tsp almond extract

1 egg

1 tsp milk

1 Preheat the oven to 350°F/180°C. Grease a large cookie sheet and line it with parchment paper.

2 Put the chocolate in a heatproof bowl set over a pan of gently simmering water and heat until it is melted. Meanwhile, sift together the flour, baking soda, and baking powder in a large bowl.

3 Finely chop the pecans and set aside. In a separate bowl, cream together the butter and sugar, then mix in the almond extract and the egg. Remove the chocolate from the heat and stir into the butter mixture. Add the flour mixture, milk, and chopped nuts to the bowl and stir until well combined.

4 Spoon the cookie dough on to the greased cookie sheet and smooth it. Transfer to the preheated oven and cook for 30 minutes, or until firm to the touch (it should still be a little soft in the center). Remove from the oven and let cool completely. Cut into 20 squares and serve.

Cappuccino Squares

These cakes are made by the all-in-one method and baked in one pan, so they are very easy to put together. Store in airtight containers.

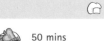

50 mins   40–45 mins

MAKES 15

INGREDIENTS

8 oz/225 g butter, softened, plus extra
    for greasing

generous 1½ cups self-rising flour

1 tsp baking powder

1 tsp unsweetened cocoa, plus extra
    for dusting

generous 1 cup golden superfine sugar

4 eggs, beaten

3 tbsp instant coffee powder dissolved in
    2 tbsp hot water

FROSTING

4 oz/115 g white chocolate, broken
    into pieces

4 tbsp butter, softened

3 tbsp milk

1¾ cups confectioners' sugar

unsweetened cocoa, to decorate

1 Preheat the oven to 350°F/180°C. Grease and line the bottom of a shallow oblong 11 x 7-inch/28 x 18-cm pan. Sift the flour, baking powder, and unsweetened cocoa into a bowl and add the butter, superfine sugar, eggs, and coffee. Beat well, by hand or with an electric whisk, until smooth, then spoon into the pan and smooth the top.

2 Bake in the oven for 35–40 minutes, or until risen and firm. Let cool in the pan for 10 minutes, then turn out on to a wire rack and peel off the lining paper. Let cool completely. To make the frosting, place the chocolate, butter, and milk in a bowl set over a pan of simmering water and stir until the chocolate has melted.

3 Remove the bowl from the pan and sift in the confectioners' sugar. Beat until smooth, then spread over the cake. Dust the top of the cake with sifted cocoa, then cut into squares.

COOK'S TIP
When melting the frosting ingredients, make sure that the bottom of the bowl does not touch the simmering water, otherwise the chocolate will seize and become unusable.

Almond Biscotti

These hard Italian cookies are traditionally served at the end of a meal for dipping into a sweet white wine. Try them with coffee or ice cream.

30 mins   25 mins

SERVES 4

INGREDIENTS

1¾ cups all-purpose flour,
  plus extra for dusting

1 tsp baking powder

pinch of salt

¾ cup golden superfine sugar

2 eggs, beaten

finely grated rind of 1 unwaxed orange

⅔ cup whole blanched almonds,
  toasted lightly

1 Preheat the oven to 350°F/180°C. Lightly dust a cookie sheet with flour. Sift the flour, baking powder, and salt into a bowl. Add the sugar, eggs, and orange rind and mix to a dough, then knead in the toasted almonds.

2 Roll out the dough into a ball, cut in half, and roll out each portion into a log about 1½ inches/4 cm in diameter. Place on the floured cookie sheet and bake in the oven for 10 minutes. Remove from the oven and let cool for 5 minutes.

3 Using a serrated knife, cut the logs into ½-inch/1-cm thick diagonal slices. Arrange the slices on the cookie sheet and return to the oven for an additional 15 minutes, or until slightly golden. Transfer to a wire rack to cool and become crisp.

Chocolate Biscotti

Italian-style dry cookies are a traditional accompaniment to black coffee after dinner, but you may find yourself nibbling them the morning after.

30 mins   40 mins

MAKES 16

INGREDIENTS

butter, for greasing

1 egg

½ cup superfine sugar

1 tsp vanilla extract

generous 1 cup all-purpose flour

½ tsp baking powder

1 tsp ground cinnamon

1¾ oz/50 g bittersweet chocolate, chopped coarsely

½ cup toasted slivered almonds

½ cup pine nuts

1 Preheat the oven to 350°F/180°C. Lightly grease a large cookie sheet with a little butter.

2 Whisk the egg, sugar, and vanilla extract in a mixing bowl with an electric mixer until thick and pale—the mixture should leave a trail when the whisk is lifted.

3 Sift the flour, baking powder, and cinnamon into a separate bowl, then sift the ingredients into the egg mixture and fold in gently. Stir in the chocolate, almonds, and pine nuts.

4 Turn on to a lightly floured work counter and shape into a flat log, measuring 9 inches/23 cm long and ¾ inch/2 cm wide. Transfer to the prepared cookie sheet.

5 Bake the biscotti in the preheated oven for 20–25 minutes, or until golden. Remove from the oven and let cool for 5 minutes, or until firm.

6 Transfer the log to a cutting board. Using a serrated bread knife, cut the log on the diagonal into slices about ½ inch/1 cm thick and arrange them on the cookie sheet. Return to the oven for 10-15 minutes, turning the biscotti on to the other side halfway through the cooking time to bake evenly.

7 Let cool for about 5 minutes, then transfer the biscotti to a wire rack to cool completely.

Chocolate Pistachio Cookies

These crisp Italian biscotti are made with fine cornmeal as well as flour, to give them an interesting texture. They are perfect served with coffee.

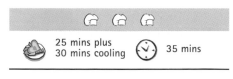

25 mins plus
30 mins cooling   35 mins

MAKES 24

INGREDIENTS

2 tbsp butter, sweet for preference,
plus extra for greasing

6 oz/175 g semisweet chocolate, broken
into pieces

2½ cups self-rising flour, plus extra
for dusting

1½ tsp baking powder

scant ½ cup superfine sugar

½ cup cornmeal

finely grated rind of 1 lemon

2 tsp amaretto

1 egg, beaten lightly

¾ cup coarsely chopped pistachios

2 tbsp confectioners' sugar, for dusting

1 Preheat the oven to 325°F/160°C. Grease a cookie sheet with butter. Put the chocolate and 2 tablespoons of butter in a heatproof bowl set over a pan of gently simmering water. Stir over low heat until melted and smooth. Remove from the heat and cool slightly.

2 Sift the flour and baking powder into a bowl and mix in the superfine sugar, cornmeal, lemon rind, amaretto, egg, and pistachios. Stir in the chocolate mixture and mix to a soft dough.

3 Lightly dust your hands with flour, divide the dough in half, and shape each piece into an 11-inch/28-cm long cylinder. Transfer the cylinders to the prepared cookie sheet and flatten, with the palm of your hand, to about 2 cm/ ¾ inch thick. Bake the cookies in the preheated oven for about 20 minutes, until firm to the touch.

4 Remove the cookie sheet from the oven and let the cooked pieces cool. When cool, put the cooked pieces on a cutting board and slice them diagonally into thin cookies. Return them to the cookie sheet and bake for an additional 10 minutes, until crisp. Remove from the oven, and transfer to a wire rack to cool. Dust lightly with confectioners' sugar.

Chocolate Marshmallow Fingers

These rich slices are packed with crunchy pieces of graham crackers, mini marshmallows, and lots of white chocolate chips.

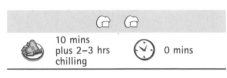

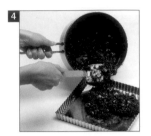

10 mins
plus 2–3 hrs
chilling

0 mins

MAKES 18

INGREDIENTS

12 oz/350 g graham crackers

4½ oz/125 g semisweet chocolate, broken into pieces

8 oz/225 g butter

⅛ cup superfine sugar

2 tbsp unsweetened cocoa

2 tbsp honey

⅔ cup mini marshmallows

½ cup white chocolate chips

1 Put the graham crackers in a polythene bag and, using a rolling pin, crush into small pieces.

2 Put the chocolate, butter, sugar, cocoa, and honey in a pan and heat gently until melted. Remove from the heat and let cool slightly.

3 Stir the crushed crackers into the chocolate mixture until well mixed. Add the marshmallows and mix well then finally stir in the chocolate chips.

4 Turn the mixture into an 8-inch/ 20-cm square cake pan and lightly smooth the top. Put in the refrigerator and let chill for 2–3 hours, until set. Cut into fingers before serving.

Macadamia Nut Caramel Bars

These delicious caramel cookie bars are bursting with macadamia nuts and topped with a layer of chocolate. Store in airtight containers.

10 mins   20 mins

MAKES 16

INGREDIENTS

BASE

1 cup macadamia nuts

2 cups all-purpose flour

1 cup brown sugar

4 oz/115 g butter

TOPPING

4 oz/115 g butter

½ cup brown sugar

1 cup milk chocolate chips

1 Preheat the oven to 350°F/180°C. Coarsely chop the macadamia nuts. To make the base, whisk together the flour, sugar, and butter until the mixture resembles fine bread crumbs.

2 Press the mixture into the bottom of a 12 x 8-inch/30 x 20-cm jelly roll pan. Sprinkle over the chopped nuts.

3 To make the topping, put the butter and sugar in a pan and, stirring constantly, slowly bring the mixture to a boil. Boil for 1 minute, stirring constantly, then carefully pour the mixture over the macadamia nuts.

4 Bake in the preheated oven for about 20 minutes, until the caramel topping is bubbling. Remove from the oven and immediately sprinkle the chocolate chips evenly on top. Leave for 2–3 minutes, until the chocolate chips start to melt then, using the blade of a knife, swirl the chocolate over the top. Let cool in the pan, then cut into bars.

VARIATIONS
Walnuts or pecans could be used if preferred.

Chocolate & Apricot Squares

These squares are made with white chocolate, which makes them extremely rich, so keep them quite small, or slice them thinly to serve.

50 mins | 30–35 mins

MAKES 12

INGREDIENTS

4½ oz/125 g butter, plus extra for greasing

6 oz/175 g white chocolate, chopped

4 eggs

½ cup superfine sugar

1¾ cups all-purpose flour, sifted

1 tsp baking powder

pinch of salt

3½ oz/100 g no-soak dried apricots, chopped

1 Preheat the oven to 350°F/180°C. Lightly grease a 20-cm/8-inch square cake pan and base line with a sheet of parchment paper.

2 Melt the butter and chocolate in a heatproof bowl set over a pan of gently simmering water. Stir frequently with a wooden spoon until the mixture is smooth and glossy. Let the mixture cool slightly.

3 Beat the eggs and superfine sugar into the butter and chocolate mixture until well combined.

4 Fold in the flour, baking powder, salt, and chopped dried apricots and mix thoroughly.

5 Pour the mixture into the pan and bake in the preheated oven for about 25–30 minutes.

6 The center of the cake may not be completely firm, but it will set as it cools. Leave in the pan to cool.

7 When the cake is completely cold turn it out carefully and slice into bars or small squares.

Chocolate Coconut Squares

These cookies consist of a chewy coconut layer resting on a crisp chocolate cookie base. Let cool, then cut into squares to serve.

🍰 1 hr   🕐 35 mins

MAKES 9

INGREDIENTS

⅓ cup butter or margarine, plus extra for greasing

8 oz/225 g semisweet chocolate graham crackers

¾ cup canned evaporated milk

1 egg, beaten

1 tsp vanilla extract

2 tbsp superfine sugar

⅓ cup self-rising flour, sifted

1⅓ cups shredded coconut

1¾ oz/50 g semisweet chocolate (optional)

1 Preheat the oven to 375°F/190°C. Grease a shallow 8-inch/20-cm square cake pan and line the bottom.

2 Crush the crackers in a polythene bag with a rolling pin or process them in a food processor.

3 Melt the butter (or margarine) in a pan and stir in the crushed crackers until well combined.

4 Press the mixture into the bottom of the cake pan.

5 Beat together the evaporated milk, egg, vanilla, and sugar until smooth. Stir in the flour and shredded coconut. Pour over the cracker layer and use a spatula to smooth the top.

6 Bake in the oven for 30 minutes, or until the coconut topping has become firm and just golden.

7 Let cool in the cake pan for about 5 minutes, then cut into squares. Let cool completely in the pan.

8 Carefully remove the squares from the pan and place them on a cutting board. Melt the semisweet chocolate (if using) and drizzle it over the squares to decorate them. Let the chocolate set before serving.

VARIATION
Store the squares in an airtight container for up to 4 days. They can be frozen, undecorated, for up to 2 months. Thaw at room temperature.

Chocolate Caramel Squares

It is hard to resist these wonderfully rich cookies, which consist of a crunchy oat layer, a creamy caramel filling, and a chocolate topping.

🍳 40 mins   🕐 35 mins

MAKES 16

INGREDIENTS

generous ⅓ cup soft margarine

⅓ cup brown sugar

1 cup all-purpose flour

½ cup rolled oats

CARAMEL FILLING

2 tbsp butter

2 tbsp brown sugar

generous ¾ cup condensed milk

TOPPING

3½ oz/100 g semisweet chocolate

1 oz/25 g white chocolate (optional)

1 Preheat the oven to 350°F/180°C. Beat together the margarine and brown sugar in a bowl until light and fluffy. Beat in the flour and the rolled oats. Use your fingertips to bring the mixture together, if necessary.

2 Press the mixture into the base of a shallow 8-inch/20-cm square cake pan.

3 Bake the cookies in the preheated oven for 25 minutes, or until just golden and firm. Cool in the pan.

4 Place the ingredients for the caramel filling in a saucepan and heat gently, stirring until the sugar has dissolved. Bring slowly to a boil over very low heat, then boil very gently for 3–4 minutes, stirring constantly, until thickened.

5 Pour the caramel filling over the oat layer in the pan and let set.

6 Melt the semisweet chocolate and spread it over the caramel. If using the white chocolate, place in a heatproof bowl set over a saucepan of gently simmering water until melted. Pipe lines of white chocolate over the semisweet chocolate. Using a toothpick, feather the white chocolate into the semisweet chocolate. Let set, then cut into squares to serve.

COOK'S TIP

If liked, you can line the pan with parchment paper so that the oat layer can be lifted out before cutting into pieces.

Sticky Chocolate Brownies

Everyone loves chocolate brownies and these are particularly moist and delicious. Serve as a mid-afternoon treat or as an instant dessert.

🍰 1 hr 20 mins ⏰ 35 mins

MAKES 9

I N G R E D I E N T S

generous ⅓ cup butter, sweet for preference, plus extra for greasing

¾ cup superfine sugar

½ cup dark brown sugar

4½ oz/125 g semisweet chocolate

1 tbsp corn syrup

2 eggs

1 tsp chocolate or vanilla extract

¾ cup all-purpose flour

2 tbsp unsweetened cocoa

½ tsp baking powder

1 Preheat the oven to 350°F/180°C. Lightly grease an 8-inch/20-cm shallow square cake pan and line the bottom with parchment paper.

2 Place the butter, sugars, chocolate, and corn syrup in a heavy-based saucepan and heat gently, stirring until the mixture is well blended and smooth. Remove from the heat and let cool.

3 Beat together the eggs and chocolate or vanilla extract. Whisk in the cooled chocolate mixture.

4 Sift together the flour, unsweetened cocoa, and baking powder and fold carefully into the egg and chocolate mixture using a metal spoon or spatula.

5 Spoon the cake batter into the prepared pan and bake in the preheated oven for 25 minutes, until the top is crisp and the edge of the cake is starting to shrink away from the pan. The inside of the cake batter will still be quite stodgy and soft to the touch.

6 Let the cake cool completely in the pan, then cut it into squares to serve.

Double Chocolate Brownies

Semisweet chocolate, unsweetened cocoa, and white chocolate chips make these delicious brownies a chocolate-lover's dream.

🕐 25 mins   🕐 55–60 mins

MAKES 9 LARGE OR 16 SMALL

I N G R E D I E N T S

4 oz/115 g butter, plus extra for greasing

4 oz/115 g semisweet chocolate,
  broken into pieces

1⅓ cups golden superfine sugar

pinch of salt

1 tsp vanilla extract

2 large eggs

1 cup all-purpose flour

2 tbsp unsweetened cocoa

½ cup white chocolate chips

F U D G E   S A U C E

4 tbsp butter

generous 1 cup golden superfine sugar

⅔ cup milk

generous 1 cup heavy cream

⅔ cup corn syrup

7 oz/200 g semisweet chocolate,
  broken into pieces

1 Preheat the oven to 350°F/180°C. Grease and line the bottom of a 7-inch/18-cm square cake pan. Place the butter and chocolate in a small heatproof bowl set over a saucepan of gently simmering water until melted. Stir until smooth. Let cool slightly. Stir in the sugar, salt, and vanilla extract. Add the eggs, one at a time, stirring well, until blended.

2 Sift the flour and unsweetened cocoa into the cake batter and beat until smooth. Stir in the chocolate chips, then pour the batter into the pan. Bake in the preheated oven for 35–40 minutes, or until the top is evenly colored and a toothpick inserted into the center comes out almost clean. Let cool slightly while preparing the sauce.

3 To make the sauce, place the butter, sugar, milk, cream, and syrup in a small saucepan and heat gently until the sugar has dissolved. Bring to a boil and stir for 10 minutes, or until the mixture is caramel-colored. Remove from the heat and add the chocolate. Stir until smooth. Cut the brownies into squares and serve immediately with the sauce.

Chocolate Brownies

You really can have a lowfat chocolate treat. These moist bars contain a dry fruits paste, which enables you to bake without adding any fat.

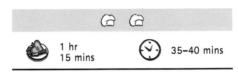

1 hr 15 mins   35–40 mins

MAKES 12

INGREDIENTS

butter, for greasing

⅓ cup unsweetened pitted dates, chopped

⅓ cup no-soak dried prunes, chopped

6 tbsp unsweetened apple juice

4 medium eggs, beaten

2 cups dark brown sugar

1 tsp vanilla extract

4 tbsp lowfat drinking chocolate powder, plus extra for dusting

2 tbsp unsweetened cocoa

1½ cups all-purpose flour

scant ½ cup semisweet chocolate chips

FROSTING

¾ cup confectioners' sugar

1–2 tsp water

1 tsp vanilla extract

1 Preheat the oven to 350°F/180°C. Grease and line a 7 x 11-inch/18 x 28-cm cake pan with parchment paper. Place the dates and prunes in a small pan and add the apple juice. Bring to a boil, cover, and simmer for 10 minutes until soft. Beat to form a smooth paste, then set aside to cool.

2 Place the cooled fruit in a large mixing bowl and stir in the eggs, sugar, and vanilla extract. Sift in 4 tablespoons of drinking chocolate powder, the unsweetened cocoa, and the flour, and fold in with the chocolate chips until thoroughly incorporated.

3 Spoon the batter into the prepared pan and smooth over the top. Bake for 25–30 minutes, until firm to the touch or until a skewer inserted into the center comes out clean. Cut into 12 bars and let cool in the tin for 10 minutes. Transfer to a wire rack to cool completely.

4 To make the frosting, sift the sugar into a bowl and mix with sufficient water and the vanilla extract to form a soft, but not too runny, frosting.

5 Drizzle the frosting over the chocolate brownies and let set. Dust with the extra chocolate powder before serving.

COOK'S TIP
Make double the amount, cut one of the cakes into bars, and open-freeze, then store in polythene bags. Take out pieces of cake as and when you need them—they'll take no time at all to thaw.

Chocolate Chip Brownies

Choose a good-quality semisweet chocolate for these chocolate chip brownies to give them a rich flavor that is not too sweet.

45 mins | 35–40 mins

MAKES 12

I N G R E D I E N T S

8 oz/225 g butter, softened, plus extra for greasing

5½ oz/150 g semisweet chocolate, broken into pieces

2 cups self-rising flour

½ cup superfine sugar

4 eggs, beaten

½ cup chopped pistachios

3½ oz/100 g white chocolate, chopped coarsely

confectioners' sugar, for dusting

1 Preheat the oven to 350°F/180°C. Lightly grease a 9-inch/23-cm baking pan and line with waxed paper.

2 Melt the semisweet chocolate and butter in a heatproof bowl set over a pan of gently simmering water. Let cool slightly.

3 Sift the flour into a separate mixing bowl and stir in the superfine sugar.

4 Stir the eggs into the melted chocolate mixture, then pour this mixture into the flour and sugar mixture, beating well. Stir in the pistachios and white chocolate, then pour the cake batter into the pan, spreading it evenly into the corners.

5 Bake in the preheated oven for 30–35 minutes, until firm to the touch. Let cool in the pan for 20 minutes, then turn out on to a wire rack.

6 Let cool completely, then cut into 12 pieces and dust with confectioners' sugar.

COOK'S TIP
The brownie won't be completely firm in the center when it is removed from the oven, but it will set when it has cooled.

Sour Cream Brownies

Sour cream in the topping gives these brownies a more sophisticated flavor. They make a fabulous dessert.

🍫 1 hr   🕐 30 mins

MAKES 9 LARGE OR 16 SMALL

INGREDIENTS

2 oz/55 g butter, plus extra for greasing

4 oz/115 g semisweet chocolate,
  broken into pieces

¾ cup dark brown sugar

2 eggs

2 tbsp strong coffee, cooled

generous ½ cup all-purpose flour

½ tsp baking powder

pinch of salt

¼ cup shelled walnuts, chopped

FROSTING

4 oz/115 g semisweet chocolate,
  broken into pieces

⅔ cup sour cream

1 Preheat the oven to 350°F/180°C. Grease an 8-inch/20-cm square cake pan with butter and line with parchment paper. Place the chocolate and butter in a small heatproof bowl and set over a saucepan of gently simmering water until melted. Stir until smooth. Remove from the heat and let cool.

2 Beat the sugar and eggs together until pale and thick. Fold in the chocolate mixture and coffee. Mix well. Sift the flour, baking powder, and salt into the cake batter and fold in. Fold in the walnuts. Pour the cake batter into the pan and bake in the oven for 20–25 minutes, or until set. Let cool in the pan.

3 To make the frosting, melt the chocolate in a heatproof bowl set over a saucepan of gently simmering water until melted. Stir in the sour cream and beat until evenly blended. Spoon the topping over the brownies and make a swirling pattern with a spatula. Let set in a cool place. Cut into squares, then remove from the pan and serve.

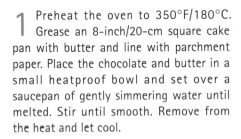

VARIATION
These brownies can be made without the frosting and served warm with vanilla ice cream or whipped cream.

Chocolate Fudge Brownies

Here, a traditional brownie mixture has a cream cheese ribbon through the center and is topped with a delicious chocolate fudge frosting.

1 hr 20 mins   45–50 mins

MAKES 16

INGREDIENTS

generous ⅓ cup butter, plus extra for greasing

scant 1 cup lowfat soft cheese

½ tsp vanilla extract

2 eggs

generous 1 cup superfine sugar

3 tbsp unsweetened cocoa

¾ cup self-rising flour, sifted

⅓ cup chopped pecans

FUDGE FROSTING

4 tbsp butter

1 tbsp milk

⅔ cup confectioners' sugar

2 tbsp unsweetened cocoa

pecans, to decorate (optional)

1 Preheat the oven to 350°F/180°C. Lightly grease an 8-inch/20-cm square shallow cake pan and line the bottom.

2 Beat together the cheese, vanilla extract, and 5 teaspoons of superfine sugar until smooth, then set aside.

3 Beat the eggs and remaining superfine sugar together until light and fluffy. Place the butter and unsweetened cocoa in a small pan and heat gently, stirring until the butter melts and the mixture combines, then stir it into the egg mixture. Fold in the flour and nuts.

4 Pour half of the cake batter into the pan and smooth the top. Carefully spread the soft cheese over it, then cover it with the remaining cake batter. Bake in the preheated oven for 40–45 minutes. Let cool in the pan.

5 To make the frosting, melt the butter in the milk. Stir in the confectioners' sugar and unsweetened cocoa. Spread the frosting over the brownies and decorate with pecans (if using). Let the frosting set, then cut into squares to serve.

VARIATION
Omit the cheese layer if preferred. Use walnuts in place of the pecans.

White Chocolate Brownies

Made with white chocolate and walnut pieces, these moist brownies make a pleasant change from the more usual semisweet chocolate ones.

15 mins   30 mins

MAKES 9

INGREDIENTS

4 oz/115 g butter, plus extra for greasing

8 oz/225 g white chocolate

⅔ cup walnut pieces

2 eggs

1 cup brown sugar

1 cup self-rising flour

1 Preheat the oven to 350°F/180°C. Lightly grease a 7-inch/18-cm square cake pan.

2 Coarsely chop 6 oz/175 g of the chocolate and all the walnuts. Put the remaining chocolate and the butter in a heatproof bowl, set over a pan of gently simmering water. When melted, stir together, then set aside to cool slightly.

3 Whisk the eggs and sugar together, then beat in the cooled chocolate mixture until well mixed. Fold in the flour, chopped chocolate, and the walnuts. Turn the mixture into the prepared pan and smooth the surface.

4 Transfer the pan to the preheated oven and bake the brownies for about 30 minutes, until just set. The mixture should still be a little soft in the center. Let cool in the pan, then cut into 9 squares before serving.

VARIATIONS
You can vary the nuts by using almonds, pecans, or hazelnuts instead of the walnuts.

Checkerboard Cookies

Children will love eating these two-tone chocolate cookies. If you do not mind a little mess, let them help to form the cookies.

1 hr plus
30 mins chilling   10 mins

SERVES 18

INGREDIENTS

¾ cup butter, softened, plus extra
for greasing

6 tbsp confectioners' sugar

1 teaspoon vanilla extract or grated rind
of ½ orange

2¼ cups all-purpose flour

1 oz/25 g semisweet chocolate, melted

1 egg white, beaten

1 Preheat the oven to 350°F/180°C. Lightly grease a cookie sheet. Beat the butter and confectioners' sugar in a mixing bowl until light and fluffy. Beat in the vanilla extract or grated orange rind.

2 Gradually beat in the flour to form a soft dough. Use your fingers to incorporate the last of the flour and bring the dough together.

3 Divide the dough in half and beat the melted chocolate into one half. Keeping each half of the dough separate, cover, and let chill for about 30 minutes.

4 Roll out each piece of dough to a rectangle measuring 3 x 8 inches/ 7.5 x 20 cm, and 1½ inches/4 cm thick. Brush one piece of dough with a little egg white and place the other on top.

5 Cut the block of dough in half lengthwise and turn over one half. Brush the side of one strip with egg white and butt the other up to it, so that it resembles a checkerboard.

6 Cut the block into thin slices and place each slice flat on the cookie sheet, allowing enough room for them to spread a little during cooking.

7 Bake in the preheated oven for about 10 minutes, until just firm. Let cool on the cookie sheets for a few minutes, before carefully transferring to a wire rack with a spatula. Let cool completely.

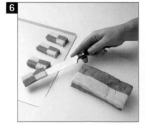

Chocolate Crispy Bites

A favorite with children, this version of crispy bites has been given a new twist, which is sure to be extremely popular.

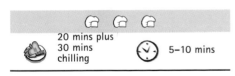

20 mins plus
30 mins chilling

5–10 mins

MAKES 16

INGREDIENTS

WHITE LAYER

4 tbsp butter, plus extra for greasing

1 tbsp corn syrup

5½ oz/150 g white chocolate

1¾ oz/50 g toasted rice cereal

DARK LAYER

4 tbsp butter

2 tbsp corn syrup

4½ oz/125 g semisweet chocolate, broken into small pieces

2¾ oz/75 g toasted rice cereal

1 Grease an 8-inch/20-cm square cake pan and line with parchment paper.

2 To make the white chocolate layer, melt the butter, corn syrup, and chocolate in a bowl set over a pan of gently simmering water.

3 Remove from the heat and stir in the rice cereal until it is well combined.

4 Press into the prepared pan and smooth the surface.

5 To make the semisweet chocolate layer, melt the butter, corn syrup, and semisweet chocolate in a bowl set over a pan of gently simmering water.

6 Remove from the heat and stir in the rice cereal. Pour the semisweet chocolate over the hardened white chocolate layer, let cool, then let chill until hardened.

7 Turn out of the cake pan and cut into small squares, using a sharp knife.

COOK'S TIP
These bites can be made up to 4 days ahead. Keep them covered in the refrigerator until ready to use.

No-Bake Chocolate Squares

Combining chocolate, cereal, nuts and cherries, these little treats not only taste delicious but look fantastic.

30 mins plus
2 hrs chilling

5 mins

MAKES 16

INGREDIENTS

9½ oz/275 g semisweet chocolate,
  broken into pieces

6 oz/175 g butter

4 tbsp corn syrup

2 tbsp dark rum, optional

6 oz/175 g plain cookies

1 oz/25 g toasted rice cereal

½ cup chopped walnuts or pecans

½ cup candied cherries,
  chopped coarsely

1 oz/25 g white chocolate, to decorate

1 Place the semisweet chocolate in a large mixing bowl with the butter, syrup, and dark rum (if using) and set over a pan of gently simmering water until melted, stirring until blended.

2 Break the cookies into small pieces and stir into the chocolate mixture along with the toasted rice cereal, nuts, and cherries.

3 Line a 7-inch/18-cm square cake pan with parchment paper. Pour the mixture into the pan and smooth the top, pressing down well with the back of a spoon. Let chill for 2 hours.

4 To decorate, melt the white chocolate and drizzle it over the top of the cake randomly. Let it set. To serve, carefully turn out of the pan and remove the parchment paper. Cut the cake into 16 squares.

VARIATION
Cognac or an orange-flavored liqueur can be used instead of the rum if you prefer. Cherry cognac also works well.

Chocolate Slices

Packed with cherries, graham crackers, chocolate, and almonds, these slices make a popular after-school snack for children.

15 mins plus
2 hrs chilling

0 mins

MAKES 16

INGREDIENTS

8 oz/225 g graham crackers

8 candied cherries

8 oz/225 g semisweet chocolate, broken into pieces

1 cup butter

2 tbsp corn syrup

4 tbsp golden raisins

1 cup slivered almonds

1 Put the graham crackers into a polythene bag and, using a rolling pin, crush into small pieces. Slice the cherries into quarters.

2 Put the chocolate, butter, and corn syrup in a pan and heat gently until melted. Remove from the heat and let cool slightly. Stir in the crushed graham crackers, cherries, sultanas, and almonds until well mixed.

3 Turn the mixture into an 8 x 12-inch/20 x 30-cm jelly roll pan and lightly spread over the base. Put in the refrigerator and let chill for 2–3 hours, until set. Cut into slices before serving.

Chocolate Madeleines

These tasty little French cakes are baked in ribbed oval molds, which give them their delicate shell-like appearance.

15 mins   10 mins

MAKES 12

INGREDIENTS

4 tbsp butter, plus extra for greasing

7 tbsp all-purpose flour, plus extra for dusting

2 tbsp unsweetened cocoa

1 egg

½ tsp vanilla extract

½ cup confectioners' sugar

confectioners' sugar, for dusting

1 Grease and flour a 12-mold madeleine sheet, then let chill. Preheat the oven to 375°F/190°C.

2 Melt the butter, then let cool. Sift the flour and cocoa together. In a large bowl, whisk the egg and vanilla extract for 2 minutes. Sift in the icing sugar, then whisk for an additional 3 minutes, until thick and smooth. Gradually fold in the flour mixture, then fold in the butter, being careful not to knock out any air. Spoon a little of the mixture equally into the prepared molds.

COOK'S TIP
Don't be tempted to dust the madeleines with confectioners' sugar before they have cooled or it will soak into them.

3 Bake the madeleines in the oven for about 10 minutes, until just firm to the touch. Carefully ease them out of the molds, transfer to a wire rack, molded-side uppermost, and let cool. When cold, dust with sifted confectioners' sugar.

Chocolate Chip Flapjacks

Turn flapjacks into something special with the addition of chocolate chips. Use white rather than semisweet chocolate chips if preferred.

40 mins   40 mins

MAKES 12

INGREDIENTS

4 oz/115 g butter, plus extra for greasing

⅓ cup superfine sugar

1 tbsp corn syrup

4 cups rolled oats

½ cup semisweet chocolate chips

⅓ cup golden raisins

1 Preheat the oven to 350°F/180°C. Lightly grease a shallow 8-inch/20-cm square cake pan.

2 Place the butter, superfine sugar, and corn syrup in a pan and cook over low heat, stirring constantly until the butter and sugar melt and the mixture is well combined.

3 Remove the pan from the heat and stir in the rolled oats until they are well coated. Add the chocolate chips and the golden raisins and mix well to combine everything.

4 Turn into the prepared pan and press down well.

5 Bake in the preheated oven for 30 minutes. Cool slightly, then mark into fingers. When almost cold cut into bars or squares and transfer to a wire rack to cool completely.

COOK'S TIP
The flapjacks will keep in an airtight container for up to 1 week, but they are so delicious they are unlikely to last that long!

Hazelnut Chocolate Crunch

These chewy, nutty oat crunch bars are very filling, so they are great for a snack at any time of the day or for packing into a lunch box.

30 mins   25–30 mins

MAKES 12

INGREDIENTS

4 oz/115 g butter, plus extra for greasing

2⅓ cups rolled oats

⅜ cup hazelnuts, lightly toasted and chopped

scant ½ cup all-purpose flour

⅜ cup light brown sugar

2 tbsp corn syrup

⅓ cup semisweet chocolate chips

1 Preheat the oven to 350°F/180°C. Grease a 9-inch/23-cm shallow square pan with butter. Place the oats, hazelnuts, and flour in a large bowl and mix.

2 Place the butter, sugar, and syrup in a large pan and heat gently until the sugar has dissolved. Pour in the dry ingredients and mix well. Stir in the chocolate chips.

3 Turn the mixture into the prepared pan and bake in the preheated oven for 20–25 minutes, or until golden brown and firm to the touch. Mark into 12 rectangles using a knife and let cool in the pan. Cut the oat crunch bars with a sharp knife before removing from the pan.

COOK'S TIP
Instead of using a pan, heat the butter, sugar, and syrup in a microwave oven on Medium for 2½ minutes.

Nutty Oat Squares

These delicious oat squares are really quick and easy to make, and have a delightful texture that is irresistible.

30 mins

30–35 mins

MAKES 16 PIECES

INGREDIENTS

4 oz/115 g butter, plus extra for greasing

scant 2¾ cups rolled oats

¾ cup chopped hazelnuts

6 tbsp all-purpose flour

2 tbsp corn syrup

scant ½ cup brown sugar

1 Preheat the oven to 350°F/180°C. Lightly grease a 9-inch/23-cm square ovenproof dish or cake pan. Place the rolled oats, chopped hazelnuts, and flour in a large mixing bowl and stir together.

2 Place the butter, syrup, and sugar in a pan over low heat and stir until melted. Pour on to the dry ingredients and mix well. Turn into the prepared ovenproof dish and smooth the surface with the back of a spoon.

3 Bake in the oven for 20–25 minutes, or until golden and firm to the touch. Mark into 16 pieces and let cool in the pan. When completely cold, cut through with a sharp knife and remove from the dish.

Coconut Flapjacks

Ever-popular, freshly baked, chewy flapjacks are just the thing to serve with a fresh cup of coffee, or as an after-school snack.

45 mins

35 mins

MAKES 16

INGREDIENTS

7 oz/200 g butter, plus extra for greasing

1 cup raw brown sugar

2 tbsp corn syrup

3½ cups rolled oats

1 cup shredded coconut

⅓ cup chopped candied cherries

1 Preheat the oven to 350°F/180°C. Lightly grease a 12 x 9-inch/30 x 23-cm cookie sheet and set aside.

2 Heat the butter, raw brown sugar, and corn syrup in a large pan over low heat until just melted.

3 Stir in the oats, shredded coconut, and candied cherries and mix well until evenly combined.

4 Spread the mixture evenly on to the prepared cookie sheet and gently press down with the back of a spatula to form a smooth surface.

5 Bake the flapjack in the preheated oven for about 30 minutes, until golden.

6 Remove from the oven and let cool on the cookie sheet for 10 minutes.

7 Cut the mixture into squares using a sharp knife.

8 Carefully transfer the flapjack squares to a wire rack and let cool completely.

COOK'S TIP
The flapjacks are best stored in an airtight container and eaten within 1 week. They can also be frozen for up to 1 month.

Fruity Flapjacks

Great favorites with children and popular with moms, too, these tasty cereal bars are healthy, inexpensive, and very easy to make.

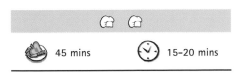

🍲 45 mins   🕐 15-20 mins

MAKES 14

I N G R E D I E N T S

sunflower or corn oil, for brushing

1¼ cups rolled oats

¾ cup raw sugar

½ cup raisins

4 oz/115 g lowfat sunflower margarine, melted

1 Preheat the oven to 375°F/190°C. Lightly brush an 11 x 7-inch/28 x 18-cm shallow rectangular cake pan with oil. Combine the oats, sugar, and raisins with the margarine, stirring well.

2 Spoon the oat mixture into the pan and press down firmly with the back of a spoon. Bake in the preheated oven for 15–20 minutes, or until golden.

3 Using a sharp knife, score lines to mark out 14 bars, then let the flapjack cool in the pan for 10 minutes. Carefully transfer the bars to a wire rack to cool completely.

VARIATION
Substitute the same quantity of dried cranberries for the raisins.

Fruity Muffins

The perfect choice for people on a lowfat diet, these little muffins contain no butter, just a little corn oil. Serve while still warm.

20 mins   25–30 mins

MAKES 10

INGREDIENTS

2 cups self-rising whole-wheat flour

2 tsp baking powder

2 tbsp molasses sugar

3½ oz/100 g no-soak dried apricots, chopped finely

1 medium banana, mashed with 1 tbsp orange juice

1 tsp finely grated orange rind

1¼ cups skim milk

1 egg, beaten

3 tbsp corn oil

2 tbsp rolled oats

fruit spread, honey, or maple syrup, to serve

1 Preheat the oven to 400°F/200°C. Place 10 muffin paper cases in a muffin pan. Sift the flour and baking powder into a mixing bowl, adding any husks that remain in the sifter. Stir in the sugar and chopped apricots.

2 Make a well in the center and add the banana, orange rind, milk, beaten egg, and oil. Mix together well to form a thick batter and divide among the muffin cases.

3 Sprinkle with a few rolled oats and bake in the oven for 25–30 minutes, until well risen and firm to the touch, or until a toothpick inserted into the center comes out clean.

4 Transfer the muffins to a wire rack to cool slightly. Serve the muffins while still warm with a little fruit spread, honey, or maple syrup.

VARIATION
If you like dried figs, they make a deliciously crunchy alternative to the apricots; they also go very well with the flavor of orange. Other no-soak dry fruits, chopped finely, can be used as well.

Cranberry Muffins

These flavorful muffins make a nice change from sweet cakes for serving with coffee. Let cool completely before serving.

1 hr   20 mins

MAKES 18

INGREDIENTS

butter, for greasing

generous 1½ cups all-purpose flour

2 tsp baking powder

½ tsp salt

¼ cup superfine sugar

4 tbsp butter, melted

2 eggs, beaten lightly

generous ¾ cup milk

1 cup fresh cranberries

scant ½ cup freshly grated
    Parmesan cheese

1 Preheat the oven to 400°F/200°C. Lightly grease 2 muffin pans with a little butter.

2 Sift the flour, baking powder, and salt into a mixing bowl. Stir in the superfine sugar.

3 In a separate bowl, combine the butter, beaten eggs, and milk, then pour into the bowl of dry ingredients. Mix lightly together until all of the ingredients are evenly combined then stir in the fresh cranberries.

4 Divide the batter among the prepared pans. Sprinkle the grated Parmesan cheese over the top.

5 Bake in the preheated oven for about 20 minutes, or until the muffins are well risen and a golden brown color.

6 Let the muffins cool slightly in the pans. Transfer the muffins to a wire rack and let cool completely.

VARIATION
For a sweeter alternative, replace the Parmesan cheese with raw sugar in step 4 if you prefer.

Apple & Cinnamon Muffins

These spicy muffins are quick and easy to make with a few stock ingredients and two small apples. The crunchy sugar topping is a treat.

🕒 15 mins

⏱ 20–25 mins

MAKES 6

INGREDIENTS

⅔ cup whole-wheat all-purpose flour

½ cup white all-purpose flour

1½ tsp baking powder

pinch of salt

1 tsp ground cinnamon

scant ¼ cup golden superfine sugar

2 small dessert apples, peeled, cored, and finely chopped

½ cup milk

1 egg, beaten

4 tbsp butter, melted

TOPPING

12 brown sugar lumps, crushed coarsely

½ tsp ground cinnamon

1 Preheat the oven to 400°F/200°C. Place 6 muffin paper cases in a muffin pan.

2 Sift the 2 flours, baking powder, salt, and cinnamon into a large bowl and stir in the sugar and chopped apples. Place the milk, egg, and butter in a separate bowl and mix. Add the wet ingredients to the dry ingredients and gently stir until just combined.

3 Divide the batter among the paper cases. To make the topping, mix together the crushed sugar lumps and cinnamon and sprinkle over the muffins. Bake in the oven for 20–25 minutes, or until risen and golden. Serve the muffins warm or cold.

VARIATION
If you like, you can split this batter into 12 portions to make small muffins.

Banana Pecan Muffins

This is a good way of using up ripe bananas. Do not over-mix the mixture or the muffins will be tough. Use hazelnuts instead of pecans if preferred.

🍞 🍞 🍞

🥘 15 mins   🕐 20–25 mins

MAKES 8

INGREDIENTS

1¼ cups all-purpose flour

generous ¼ cup golden superfine sugar

1½ tsp baking powder

pinch of salt

1 cup pecans, chopped coarsely

2 large ripe bananas, mashed

¼ cup milk

2 tbsp butter, melted

1 egg, beaten

½ tsp vanilla extract

1 Preheat the oven to 375°F/190°C. Place 8 muffin paper cases in a muffin tray. Sift the flour, baking powder, and salt into a bowl, add the sugar and pecans and stir to combine.

2 Put the mashed bananas, milk, butter, egg, and vanilla extract in another bowl and mix together. Add the wet ingredients to the dry ingredients and gently stir until just combined.

3 Divide the batter among the paper cases and bake in the preheated oven for 20-25 minutes, until risen and golden. Transfer to a wire rack to cool.

Rice Muffins with Amaretto

Italian rice gives these delicate muffins an interesting texture. The amaretti cookies complement the flavors and add a crunchy topping.

20 mins   15 mins

MAKES 12

INGREDIENTS

butter, for greasing

1 cup all-purpose flour

1 tbsp baking powder

½ tsp baking soda

½ tsp salt

1 egg

¼ cup honey

½ cup milk

2 tbsp sunflower oil

½ tsp almond extract

1 cup cooked risotto rice

2–3 amaretti cookies, crushed coarsely

AMARETTO BUTTER

4 oz/115 g butter, sweet for preference, at room temperature

1 tbsp honey

1–2 tbsp amaretto

1–2 tbsp mascarpone cheese

1 Preheat the oven to 400°F/200°C. Grease a 12-cup muffin pan or 2 x 6-cup pans. Sift the flour, baking powder, baking soda, and salt into a large bowl, and stir. Make a well in the center.

2 In another bowl, beat the egg, honey, milk, oil, and almond extract with an electric whisk for about 2 minutes, or until light and foamy. Gradually beat in the rice. Pour into the well and, using a fork, stir lightly until just combined. Do not beat too long or the batter can become lumpy.

3 Spoon the batter into the prepared muffin pans. Sprinkle each with some of the amaretti crumbs, and bake in the oven for 15 minutes, or until risen and golden. The tops should spring back lightly when pressed.

4 Cool in the pans on a wire rack for about 1 minute. Carefully remove the muffins, and let cool slightly.

5 To make the amaretto butter, put the butter and honey in a small bowl and beat until creamy. Add the amaretto and mascarpone and beat together. Spoon into a small serving bowl and serve with the warm muffins.

COOK'S TIP

Line the muffin pan with muffin paper cases to avoid sticking.

Fudge Nut Muffins

Chewy pieces of fudge give these muffins a lovely texture and contrast with the crunchiness of the nuts. Store in airtight containers.

🐾 30 mins   🕐 20-25 mins

MAKES 12

INGREDIENTS

scant 2 cups all-purpose flour

4 tsp baking powder

⅜ cup golden superfine sugar

6 tbsp crunchy peanut butter

1 egg, beaten

4 tbsp butter, melted

¾ cup milk

5½ oz/150 g vanilla fudge, cut into small pieces

3 tbsp coarsely chopped unsalted peanuts

1 Preheat the oven to 400°F/200°C. Line a 12-hole muffin pan with double muffin paper cases. Sift the flour and baking powder into a bowl. Stir in the sugar. Add the peanut butter and stir until the mixture resembles bread crumbs.

2 Place the egg, butter, and milk in a separate bowl and beat together until blended, then stir into the dry ingredients until just blended. Lightly stir in the fudge pieces. Spoon the muffin batter into the muffin cases.

3 Sprinkle the chopped peanuts on top and bake in the preheated oven for 20-25 minutes, or until well risen and firm to the touch. Let cool for 2 minutes, then remove the muffins to a wire rack to cool completely before serving.

Chocolate Chip Muffins

Muffins are always popular and are so simple to make. Mini muffins are fabulous bite-size treats for young children—and perfect for parties.

45 mins   25 mins

MAKES 12

INGREDIENTS

3 tbsp soft margarine

1 cup superfine sugar

2 large eggs

⅔ cup whole milk unsweetened yogurt

5 tbsp milk

2 cups all-purpose flour

1 tsp baking soda

1 cup semisweet chocolate chips

VARIATION
The mixture can also be used to make 6 large or 24 mini muffins. Bake mini muffins for 10 minutes, or until springy to the touch.

1 Preheat the oven to 400°F/200°C. Line a muffin pan with 12 paper cases.

2 Place the margarine and sugar in a mixing bowl and beat with a wooden spoon until light and fluffy. Beat in the eggs, yogurt, and milk until combined.

3 Sift the flour and baking soda together and add to the mixture. Stir until just blended.

4 Stir in the chocolate chips, then spoon the batter into the paper cases and bake in the preheated oven for 25 minutes, or until a fine skewer inserted into the center comes out clean. Let the muffins cool in the pan for 5 minutes, then turn out on to a wire rack to cool completely.

Double Chocolate Muffins

Chocolate-flavored muffins with a white chocolate frosting are sure to please children and adults alike.

45 mins   25 mins

MAKES 12

INGREDIENTS

scant 1½ cups all-purpose flour

¼ cup unsweetened cocoa,
   plus extra for dusting

1 tbsp baking powder

1 tsp ground cinnamon

generous ½ cup golden superfine sugar

6½ oz/185 g white chocolate,
   broken into pieces

2 eggs

generous ⅓ cup corn oil

1 cup milk

1 Preheat the oven to 400°F/200°C. Line a 12-hole muffin pan with muffin paper cases. Sift the flour, unsweetened cocoa, baking powder, and cinnamon into a large mixing bowl. Stir in the sugar and 4¹/₂ oz/125 g of the white chocolate.

2 Place the eggs and oil in a separate bowl and whisk until frothy, then gradually whisk in the milk. Stir into the dry ingredients until just blended. Spoon the batter into the paper cases, filling each three-quarters full. Bake in the preheated oven for 20 minutes, or until well risen and springy to the touch. Let cool for 2 minutes, then remove the muffins and transfer to a wire rack to cool them completely.

3 Melt the remaining white chocolate in a heatproof bowl set over a pan of gently simmering water until melted and spread over the top of the muffins. Let set then dust the tops with a little unsweetened cocoa and serve.

COOK'S TIP
When stirring the muffin batter together, do not overstir or the muffins will be tough. The muffin batter should be quite lumpy.

Triple Chocolate Muffins

Packed with melting semisweet and white chocolate, these creamy muffins are a chocoholic's delight. Serve with coffee for a real treat.

15 mins   20 mins

MAKES 11

INGREDIENTS

1¾ cups all-purpose flour

¼ cup unsweetened cocoa

2 tsp baking powder

½ tsp baking soda

generous ½ cup semisweet chocolate chips

generous ½ cup white chocolate chips

2 eggs, beaten

1¼ cups sour cream

scant ½ cup brown sugar

6 tbsp butter, melted

1 Preheat the oven to 400°F/200°C. Line 11 cups of 1 or 2 muffin pans with muffin paper cases. Sift the flour, cocoa, baking powder, and baking soda into a large bowl, add the semisweet and white chocolate chips, and stir.

2 Place the eggs, sour cream, sugar, and butter in a separate mixing bowl and mix well. Add the wet ingredients to the dry ingredients and stir gently until just combined.

3 Using 2 spoons, divide the batter among the paper cases and bake in the preheated oven for 20 minutes, or until well risen and firm to the touch. Serve warm or cold.

COOK'S TIP

As with all muffins, these chocolate delights taste best if they are eaten fresh, on the day they are made.

Marshmallow Muffins

Children adore these muffins filled with mini marshmallows and chocolate chips and will no doubt enjoy making them too.

15 mins　　20–25 mins

SERVES 4

INGREDIENTS

5 tbsp butter

2¼ cups all-purpose flour

6 tbsp unsweetened cocoa

3 tsp baking powder

½ cup superfine sugar

⅔ cup milk chocolate chips

⅔ cup white mini marshmallows

1 egg, beaten

1¼ cups milk

1 Preheat the oven to 375°F/190°C. Place 12 muffin paper cases in a muffin pan. Melt the butter.

2 Sift the flour, cocoa, and baking powder together into a large bowl. Stir in the sugar, chocolate chips, and marshmallows until well mixed.

3 Whisk the egg, milk, and melted butter together then gently stir into the flour to form a stiff batter. Gently stir in the chocolate chips and marshmallows. Spoon the batter into the muffin cases.

4 Bake the muffins in the preheated oven for 20–25 minutes, until well risen and golden brown. Let cool in the pan for 5 minutes then transfer to a wire rack and let cool completely.

COOK'S TIP
Don't over-beat the batter (there should still be a few lumps of flour) or the muffins will be crusty.

Chocolate Orange Muffins

These muffins are a favorite with children of all ages. They are best served warm and are particularly good served for breakfast.

10 mins

20–25 mins

MAKES 8–10

INGREDIENTS

sunflower oil, for oiling

1 cup self-rising flour

⅔ cup whole-wheat self-rising flour

¼ cup ground almonds

scant ½ cup brown sugar

2 oz/55 g semisweet chocolate chips

rind and juice of 1 orange

¾ cup cream cheese

2 eggs

1 Preheat the oven to 375°F/190°C. Thoroughly oil the muffin pans.

2 Sift the flours in a mixing bowl and add the ground almonds and sugar.

3 Mix together the orange rind and juice, the cream cheese, and the eggs. Make a well in the center of the flour mixture and stir in the liquid then add the chocolate chips. Beat well to combine all the ingredients.

4 Spoon the mixture into the muffin pans, filling them no more than three-quarters full.

VARIATION
Use ¼ cup dry unsweetened coconut instead of the ground almonds.

5 Bake in the center of the preheated oven for 20–25 minutes, or until well risen and golden brown.

6 Let cool slightly on a wire rack but eat them as fresh from the oven as possible.

Potato & Raisin Muffins

Using potatoes in sweet dishes may seem an odd idea, but, in fact, they add a lightness and lift to all kinds of baked goods.

10 mins   30 mins

MAKES 12

INGREDIENTS

butter, for greasing

⅔ cup self-rising flour, plus extra for dusting

6 oz/175 g mealy potatoes, diced

2 tbsp brown sugar

1 tsp baking powder

scant 1 cup raisins

4 eggs, separated

1 Preheat the oven to 400°F/200°C. Lightly grease and flour 12 muffin pans. Cook the diced potatoes in a pan of boiling water for 10 minutes, or until tender. Drain well and mash until smooth.

2 Transfer the mashed potatoes to a mixing bowl and add the flour, sugar, baking powder, raisins, and egg yolks. Stir well to mix thoroughly.

3 In a clean, greasefree bowl, whisk the egg whites until they are standing in peaks. Using a metal spoon, gently fold them into the potato mixture until fully incorporated.

4 Divide the mixture among the prepared pans.

5 Cook the muffins in the preheated oven for 10 minutes. Reduce the oven temperature to 325°F/160°C and cook the muffins for 7–10 minutes, or until risen.

6 Remove the muffins from the pans and serve warm, buttered, if liked.

COOK'S TIP
Instead of spreading the muffins with plain butter, serve them with cinnamon butter made by blending 5 tablespoons of butter with a large pinch of ground cinnamon.

New Orleans Rice Cakes

This classic New Orleans breakfast dish is a cross between a doughnut and a fritter. Serve the cakes hot, sprinkled with confectioners' sugar.

40 mins   40 mins

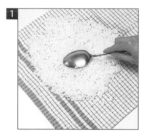

MAKES ABOUT 12 CAKES

INGREDIENTS

½ cup long-grain white rice

1 egg

2–3 tbsp sugar

1½ tsp baking powder

½ tsp ground cinnamon

¼ tsp salt

2 tsp vanilla extract

9 tbsp all-purpose flour

vegetable oil, for frying

confectioners' sugar, for dusting

1 Bring a pan of water to a boil. Sprinkle in the rice and return to a boil, stirring once or twice. Reduce the heat and simmer for 15–20 minutes until the rice is tender. Drain, rinse, and drain again. Spread the rice on to a dry dish towel to dry completely.

2 Using an electric whisk, beat the egg for about 2 minutes until light and frothy. Add the sugar, baking powder, cinnamon, and salt and continue beating until well blended; beat in the vanilla. Add the flour and stir until well blended, then gently fold in the rice. Cover the bowl with plastic wrap and let rest at room temperature for about 20 minutes.

3 Meanwhile, heat 4 inches of oil in a deep-fat fryer to 375°F/190°C, or until a cube of bread browns in about 25–30 seconds.

4 Drop rounded tablespoons of the batter into the oil, about 3 or 4 at a time. Cook for 4–5 minutes, turning gently, until puffed and golden and cooked through.

5 Using a slotted spoon, transfer to double-thickness paper towels to drain, then transfer to a low oven to keep warm while frying the rest. Continue with the remaining batter until it is used up. Dust the rice cakes with confectioners' sugar to serve.

Rock Drops

These fruit rock drops are more substantial than a crisp cookie. Serve them fresh from the oven to enjoy them at their best.

🕐 20 mins   🕐 15–20 mins

SERVES 4

I N G R E D I E N T S

4 tbsp butter, cut into small pieces, plus extra for greasing

scant 1½ cups all-purpose flour

2 tsp baking powder

⅓ cup raw sugar

½ cup golden raisins

2 tbsp candied cherries, chopped finely

1 egg, beaten lightly

2 tbsp milk

1 Preheat the oven to 400°F/200°C. Lightly grease a cookie sheet with a little butter and set aside.

2 Sift the flour and baking powder together into a mixing bowl. Rub in the butter with your fingertips until the mixture resembles bread crumbs.

3 Stir in the raw sugar, golden raisins, and candied cherries.

4 Add the egg and the milk to the mixture. Mix to form a soft dough.

5 Spoon 8 mounds of the cookie dough on to the prepared cookie sheet, allowing room for the cookies to spread during cooking.

6 Bake in the preheated oven for about 15–20 minutes, until firm to the touch when pressed with a finger.

7 Remove the rock drops from the cookie sheet. Either serve piping hot from the oven or transfer to a wire rack and let cool before serving.

COOK'S TIP
For convenience, prepare the dry ingredients in advance and just before cooking, stir in the liquid.

Cherry & Raisin Rockies

Rock cakes are always popular and they are very quick and easy to make. To be at their best they should be eaten the day they are made.

40 mins   10–15 mins

MAKES 10–12

INGREDIENTS

6 tbsp butter, plus extra for greasing

1¾ cups self-rising flour

1 tsp ground allspice

scant ½ cup golden superfine sugar

¼ cup candied cherries, quartered

⅓ cup golden raisins

1 egg

2 tbsp milk

raw brown sugar, for sprinkling

1 Preheat the oven to 400°F/200°C. Lightly grease a cookie sheet. Sift the flour and allspice into a bowl. Add the butter and rub in until the mixture resembles bread crumbs. Stir in the sugar, cherries, and golden raisins.

2 Break the egg into a bowl and whisk in the milk. Pour most of the egg mixture into the dry ingredients and mix with a fork to make a stiff, coarse dough, adding the rest of the egg and milk, if necessary.

3 Using 2 forks, pile the dough into 10 rocky heaps on the prepared cookie sheet. Sprinkle with raw brown sugar. Bake in the oven for 10–15 minutes, or until golden and firm to the touch. Let cool on the cookie sheet for 2 minutes, then transfer to a wire rack to cool completely.

VARIATION
Mixed dry fruits could be used as an alternative to the cherries and golden raisins in these rock cakes.

Coconut & Cherry Cakes

Coconut and candied cherries make these little cakes really moist, and give them a sweet flavor that will make them a hit with children.

40 mins   20–25 mins

MAKES 8

INGREDIENTS

4 oz/115 g butter, softened

generous ½ cup golden superfine sugar

2 tbsp milk

2 eggs, beaten

⅔ cup self-rising flour

½ tsp baking powder

1 cup dry unsweetened coconut

generous ½ cup candied cherries, quartered

1 Preheat the oven to 350°F/180°C. Line 1 or 2 muffin pans with 8 muffin paper cases. Place the butter and sugar in a bowl and cream together until light and fluffy, then stir in the milk.

2 Gradually beat in the eggs. Sift in the flour and baking powder and fold in with the coconut. Gently fold in most of the cherries. Spoon the batter into the paper cases and scatter the remaining cherries on top.

3 Bake in the preheated oven for 20–25 minutes, or until well risen, golden, and firm to the touch. Transfer to a wire rack to cool.

Mini Orange Rice Cakes

These mini rice cakes, fragrant with orange or sometimes lemon rind, are found in many of the bakeries and coffee shops in Florence.

1 hr 30 mins   40 mins

MAKES ABOUT 16

INGREDIENTS

3 cups milk

pinch of salt

1 vanilla bean, split, seeds removed, and reserved

scant 1 cup risotto rice

½ cup sugar

2 tbsp butter

grated rind of 2 oranges

2 eggs, separated

2 tbsp orange-flavored liqueur or rum

1 tbsp freshly squeezed orange juice

1 orange, cut into small wedges, to decorate

confectioners' sugar, for dusting

1 Bring the milk to a boil in a large pan over medium-high heat. Add the salt and vanilla bean and seeds, and sprinkle in the rice. Return to a boil, stirring once or twice. Reduce the heat and simmer, stirring frequently, for about 10 minutes.

2 Add the sugar and butter and simmer for about 10 minutes, stirring frequently, until the mixture is thick and creamy. Pour into a bowl and stir in the orange rind. Remove the vanilla bean. Let cool to room temperature, stirring occasionally. Meanwhile, preheat the oven to 375°F/190°C.

3 Beat the egg yolks with the liqueur and orange juice, then beat into the cooled rice mixture.

4 Beat the egg whites until almost stiff, but not too dry. Stir in a spoonful into the rice mixture to lighten it, then gently fold in the remaining whites.

5 Line a muffin pan with 16 muffin paper cases. Spoon the batter into the paper cases, filling them to the brim. Bake in the preheated oven for 20 minutes, until golden and cooked through. Place on a wire rack to cool for 2 minutes, then remove the liners. Let cool completely.

6 Decorate with tiny wedges of orange and dust with confectioners' sugar just before serving.

Lemon Butterfly Cakes

Butterfly cakes may remind you of children's birthday parties, but these attractive, creamy, miniature delights are for adults too!

40 mins   15–20 mins

MAKES 12

INGREDIENTS

generous ¾ cup self-rising flour

½ tsp baking powder

4 oz/115 g butter, softened

generous ½ cup golden superfine sugar

2 eggs, beaten

finely grated rind of ½ lemon

2–4 tbsp milk

confectioners' sugar, for dusting

FILLING

¼ cup butter

generous 1 cup confectioners' sugar

1 tbsp lemon juice

1 Preheat the oven to 375°F/190°C. Place 12 paper cases in a muffin pan.

2 Sift the flour and baking powder into a bowl. Add the butter, sugar, eggs, lemon rind, and enough milk to give a medium-soft consistency. Beat thoroughly until smooth. Divide the batter among the paper cases and bake in the preheated oven for 15–20 minutes, or until well risen and golden. Transfer to wire racks to cool.

3 To make the filling, place the butter in a bowl, then sift in the confectioners' sugar and add the lemon juice. Beat well until smooth and creamy. When the cakes are quite cold, use a sharp-pointed vegetable knife to cut a circle from the top of each cake, then cut each circle in half.

4 Spoon a little of the buttercream into the center of each cake and press the 2 semi-circular pieces into it to resemble wings. Dust the cakes with sifted confectioners' sugar before serving.

Chocolate Butterfly Cakes

Filled with a tangy lemon buttercream, these appealing little cakes will become an all-time favorite with both adults and children.

30 mins   15 mins

MAKES 12

INGREDIENTS

4 oz/115 g soft margarine

½ cup superfine sugar

1¼ cups self-rising flour

2 large eggs

2 tbsp unsweetened cocoa

1 oz/25 g semisweet chocolate, melted

confectioners' sugar, for dusting

LEMON BUTTERCREAM

6 tbsp butter, sweet for preference, softened

1⅓ cups confectioners' sugar, sifted

grated rind of ½ lemon

1 tbsp lemon juice

1 Preheat the oven to 350°F/180°C. Line a shallow muffin pan with 12 muffin paper cases. Place all of the ingredients for the cakes, except for the melted chocolate, in a large bowl, and beat with an electric whisk until the mixture is just smooth. Beat in the melted chocolate.

2 Spoon equal amounts of the batter into each paper case, filling them three-quarters full. Bake in the preheated oven for 15 minutes, or until springy to the touch. Transfer to a wire rack and let cool.

3 Meanwhile, make the lemon buttercream. Place the butter in a mixing bowl and beat until fluffy, then gradually beat in the confectioners' sugar. Beat in the lemon rind and gradually add the lemon juice, beating well.

4 When cold, cut the top off each cake, using a serrated knife. Cut each cake top in half.

5 Spread or pipe the buttercream frosting over the cut surface of each cake and push the 2 cut pieces of cake top into the frosting to form wings. Dust with confectioners' sugar.

VARIATION
For a chocolate buttercream, beat the butter and confectioners' sugar together, then beat in 1 oz/25 g melted semisweet chocolate.

Chocolate Parfait Sandwiches

This is a novel way of serving a creamy white chocolate parfait in a crisp pastry "sandwich." It is the perfect finale to any dinner-party meal.

30 mins
plus 5–6 hrs
freezing

15 mins

SERVES 4

INGREDIENTS

3 large egg whites

¾ cup superfine sugar

1¾ cups whipping cream, whipped

5 oz/140 g white chocolate, grated

12 oz/350 g ready-rolled puff pastry

1 To make the parfait, beat the egg whites and the sugar together in a heatproof bowl, then set the bowl over a pan of gently simmering water. Using an electric whisk, beat the whites over the heat until you have a light and fluffy meringue. This will take up to 10 minutes. Remove from the heat, add the chocolate, and keep whisking to cool. Fold in the whipping cream.

2 Spoon the parfait into a shallow rectangular freezerproof container and freeze for 5–6 hours.

3 Meanwhile, preheat the oven to 350°F/180°C and line a cookie sheet with parchment paper. Cut the pie dough into regular-size rectangles to accommodate a slice of the parfait. Place the pie dough rectangles on the sheet and top with another cookie sheet, which will keep the pie dough flat but crisp. Bake in the oven for 15 minutes, transfer to a wire rack and let cool.

4 About 20 minutes before you are ready to serve, remove the parfait from the freezer. When it has softened, cut the parfait into slices and put each slice between 2 pieces of pie dough to make a "sandwich."

COOK'S TIP
For a more elegant version, drizzle a little melted semisweet chocolate over the sandwiches or sprinkle with a little sifted confectioners' sugar.

Chocolate Rum Babas

A little fiddly to make, but well worth the effort. Indulge in these tasty cakes with coffee, or serve them as a dessert with summer fruits.

40 mins plus 1 hr rising

15 mins

SERVES 4

INGREDIENTS

2 tsp melted butter, for greasing

¾ cup white bread flour

2 tbsp unsweetened cocoa

⅛ oz/5 g active dry yeast

pinch of salt

1 tbsp superfine sugar

1½ oz/40 g semisweet chocolate, grated

2 eggs

3 tbsp tepid milk

4 tbsp butter, melted

SYRUP

4 tbsp honey

2 tbsp water

4 tbsp rum

TO SERVE

whipped cream

unsweetened cocoa, for dusting

fresh fruit (optional)

1 Preheat the oven to 400°F/200°C. Lightly grease 4 individual ring pans. Sift the flour and unsweetened cocoa into a large, warmed mixing bowl. Stir in the yeast, salt, sugar, and chocolate. In a separate bowl, beat the eggs, add the milk and butter, and beat until mixed.

2 Make a well in the center of the dry ingredients and pour in the egg mixture, beating to mix to a batter. Beat the batter for 10 minutes, ideally in a food processor with a dough hook. Divide the batter among the pans—it should come halfway up the sides of the pans.

3 Place the pans on a cookie sheet and cover with a damp dish towel. Set aside in a warm place until the mixture rises almost to the tops of the pans. Bake in the preheated oven for 15 minutes.

4 To make the syrup, gently heat all of the ingredients in a small pan. Turn out the babas and put on a wire rack placed above a tray to catch the syrup.

Drizzle the syrup over the babas and leave for at least 2 hours to let the syrup soak in. From time to time, spoon the syrup that has collected in the tray back over the babas.

5 Fill the center of the babas with whipped cream and sprinkle a little unsweetened cocoa over the top. Serve the babas with fresh fruit, if desired.

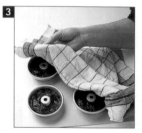

Malted Chocolate Wedges

These tasty malted cookie wedges are perfect with a bedtime drink, although you can enjoy them at any time of the day.

🍰 45 mins 🕐 5 mins

MAKES 16

INGREDIENTS

6 tbsp butter, plus extra for greasing

2 tbsp corn syrup

2 tbsp malted chocolate drink

8 oz/225 g malted milk cookies

2¾ oz/75 g light or semisweet chocolate, broken into pieces

2 tbsp confectioners' sugar

2 tbsp milk

1 Grease and base-line a shallow 7-inch/18-cm round cake pan or tart pan.

2 Place the butter, corn syrup, and malted chocolate drink in a small pan and heat gently, stirring all the time until the butter has melted and the mixture is well combined.

3 Crush the cookies in a polythene bag with a rolling pin, or process them in a food processor. Stir the cookie crumbs into the chocolate mixture and mix well.

4 Press the mixture into the prepared pan and then chill in the refrigerator until firm.

5 Place the chocolate pieces in a small heatproof bowl with the sugar and the milk. Place the bowl over a pan of gently simmering water and stir until the chocolate melts and the mixture is combined.

6 Spread the chocolate frosting over the cookie base and let the frosting set in the pan. Using a sharp knife, cut into wedges to serve.

VARIATION
Add chopped pecans to the cookie crumb mixture in step 3, if liked.

Chocolate Cup Cakes

A variation on an old favorite, these delicious little cakes will appeal to both kids and grown-ups. Let the cakes chill before serving.

20 mins plus
1 hr chilling

20 mins

MAKES 18

INGREDIENTS

6 tbsp butter, softened

½ cup superfine sugar

2 eggs, lightly beaten

2 tbsp milk

⅓ cup semisweet chocolate chips

1¼ cups self-rising flour

¼ cup unsweetened cocoa

FROSTING

8 oz/225 g white chocolate

5½ oz/150 g lowfat cream cheese

1 Preheat the oven to 400°F/200°C. Line a shallow muffin pan with 18 muffin paper cases.

2 Beat together the butter and sugar until pale and fluffy. Gradually add the eggs, beating well after each addition. Add a little of the flour if the mixture starts to curdle. Add the milk, then fold in the chocolate chips.

3 Sift together the flour and cocoa and fold into the batter with a metal spoon or spatula. Divide the batter equally among the muffin paper cases and smooth the tops.

4 Bake in the preheated oven for 20 minutes, or until well risen and springy to the touch. Cool on a wire rack.

5 To make the frosting, melt the chocolate in a heatproof bowl set over a pan of gently simmering water. Cool slightly. Beat the cream cheese until softened, then beat in the chocolate. Spread a little of the frosting over each cake and let chill for 1 hour before serving.

VARIATION

Add white chocolate chips or chopped pecans to the mixture instead of the semisweet chocolate chips if you prefer. You can also add the finely grated rind of 1 orange for a chocolate and orange flavor.

Cup Cakes

These pretty little cakes are light and moist, with a tempting fudgy chocolate topping. Perfect for serving at any time of the day.

🍰 50 mins   🕐 35 mins

MAKES ABOUT 20

INGREDIENTS

generous ¾ cup water

6 tbsp butter

⅜ cup golden superfine sugar

1 tbsp corn syrup

3 tbsp milk

1 tsp vanilla extract

1 tsp baking soda

2 tbsp unsweetened cocoa

generous 1½ cups all-purpose flour

FROSTING

1¾ oz/50 g semisweet chocolate, broken into pieces

4 tbsp water

1¾ oz/50 g butter

1¾ oz/50 g white chocolate, broken into pieces

3 cups confectioners' sugar

TO DECORATE

candied rose petals

candied violets

1 Preheat the oven to 350°F/180°C. Line 2 muffin pans with 20 muffin paper cases.

2 Place the water, butter, sugar, and syrup in a pan. Heat gently, stirring, until the sugar has dissolved, then bring to a boil. Reduce the heat and cook gently for 5 minutes. Remove from the heat and let cool. Place the milk and vanilla extract in a bowl. Add the baking soda and stir to dissolve. Sift the unsweetened cocoa and flour into a separate bowl and add the syrup mixture. Stir in the milk and beat until smooth.

3 Carefully spoon the batter into the paper cases to come within two-thirds of the tops. Bake in the oven for 20 minutes, or until well risen and firm to the touch. Let cool on a wire rack. To make the frosting, place the semisweet chocolate in a small heatproof bowl with half the water and half the butter and set the bowl over a pan of gently simmering water until melted. Stir until smooth and let stand over the water. Repeat with the white chocolate and remaining water and butter.

4 Stir half the confectioners' sugar into each bowl and beat until smooth and fudgy. Divide the frostings among the cakes, filling to the top of the paper cases. Let cool, then place a rose petal on each of the semisweet chocolate frosted cakes and a violet on each white chocolate frosted cake. Let set before serving.

VARIATION
Instead of the candied flower petals, the cakes could be decorated with chocolate curls or chopped hazelnuts.

White Chocolate Florentines

These attractive jeweled cookies are coated with white chocolate to give them a delicious flavor. They make particularly attractive gifts.

40 mins   15 mins

MAKES 24

INGREDIENTS

7 oz/200 g butter

1 cup superfine sugar

generous 1 cup walnuts, chopped

generous 1 cup almonds, chopped

⅓ cup golden raisins, chopped

scant ¼ cup candied cherries, chopped

¼ cup candied peel, chopped finely

2 tbsp light cream

8 oz/225 g white chocolate

1 Preheat the oven to 350°F/180°C. Line 3–4 cookie sheets with nonstick parchment paper.

2 Melt the butter over low heat and then add the sugar, stirring until it has dissolved. Boil the mixture for exactly 1 minute. Remove from the heat.

3 Add the walnuts, almonds, golden raisins, candied cherries, candied peel, and cream to the pan, stirring well to mix.

4 Drop heaping teaspoonfuls of the cookie dough on to the cookie sheets, allowing plenty of room for them to spread during cooking. Bake in the preheated oven for 10 minutes, or until golden brown.

5 Remove the cookies from the oven and neaten the edges with a knife while they are still warm. Let cool slightly, and then transfer them to a wire rack to cool completely.

6 Melt the chocolate in a heatproof bowl placed over a pan of gently simmering water. Spread the underside of the cookies with chocolate and use a fork to make wavy lines across the surface. Let cool completely.

7 Store the florentines in an airtight container, kept in a cool place.

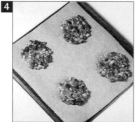

COOK'S TIP

A combination of white and semisweet chocolate florentines looks very attractive, especially if you are making them as gifts. Pack them in pretty boxes, lined with tissue paper and tied with some ribbon.

Florentine Twists

These famous and delicious florentine cookies are twisted into curls or cones before the ends are dipped in a little chocolate.

🍰 40 mins   🕐 20 mins

MAKES 20

INGREDIENTS

6 tbsp butter, plus extra for greasing

½ cup superfine sugar

½ cup blanched or slivered almonds, chopped coarsely

3 tbsp raisins, chopped

¼ cup chopped candied peel

scant ¼ cup candied cherries, chopped

3 tbsp dried apricots, chopped finely

finely grated rind of ½ lemon or ½ small orange

4 oz/115 g semisweet or white chocolate

1 Preheat the oven to 350°F/180°C. Line 2–3 cookie sheets with nonstick parchment paper; then grease 4–6 cream horn molds, or a fairly thin rolling pin, or wooden spoon handles.

2 Melt the butter and sugar together gently in a large heavy-based pan and then bring to a boil for 1 minute. Remove the pan from the heat and stir in all the remaining ingredients, except for the chocolate. Let cool.

3 Put heaping teaspoonfuls of the cookie dough on to the cookie sheets, allowing plenty of room for the cookies to spread during cooking, perhaps only 3–4 cookies per sheet, and flatten slightly.

4 Bake in the preheated oven for 10–12 minutes, or until golden. Let cool until they start to firm up. As they cool, press the edges back to form a neat shape. Remove each one with a spatula and wrap quickly around a cream horn mold, or lay over the rolling pin or spoon handles. If they become too firm to bend, return to the oven for a few minutes to soften.

5 Leave until cold and crisp and then slip carefully off the horn molds or remove from the rolling pin or spoons.

6 Melt the chocolate in a heatproof bowl set over a pan of gently simmering water and stir until smooth. Either dip the end of each florentine twist into the chocolate or, using a pastry brush, paint chocolate to come about halfway up the twist. As the chocolate sets, it can be marked into wavy lines with a fork. Let set before serving.

Pineapple Florentines

These florentines combine candied pineapple, angelica, and almond in a delicate, crisp cookie with a delicious chocolate coating.

45 mins   10-12 mins

MAKES ABOUT 14

INGREDIENTS

4 tbsp butter

scant ¼ cup raw sugar

1 tbsp corn syrup

⅜ cup all-purpose flour, sifted

2 tbsp angelica, chopped coarsely

⅛ cup candied cherries, chopped coarsely

½ cup slivered almonds, chopped coarsely

¼ cup candied pineapple, chopped coarsely

1 tsp lemon juice

4 oz/115 g semisweet chocolate, broken into pieces

1 Preheat the oven to 350°F/180°C. Line several cookie sheets with parchment paper. Place the butter, sugar, and syrup in a pan and heat gently until melted, then stir in the flour, angelica, cherries, almonds, pineapple, and lemon juice.

2 Place walnut-size mounds of the cookie dough well apart on the baking sheets and flatten with a fork. Bake in the oven for 8–10 minutes, or until golden. Use a spatula to neaten the ragged edges. Let cool for 1 minute, then transfer to a wire rack to cool completely.

3 Melt the chocolate in a heatproof bowl set over a pan of simmering water. Spread melted chocolate over the bottom of each florentine, placing the cookies, chocolate-side up, on a wire rack. Use a fork to mark the chocolate into wavy lines. Let stand until set.

COOK'S TIP
Try serving these with vanilla ice cream for an instant dessert.

Florentines

These luxury cookies will be popular at any time of the year, but they make a particularly wonderful treat at Christmas.

50 mins   15 mins

MAKES 10

INGREDIENTS

4 tbsp butter

¼ cup superfine sugar

scant ¼ cup all-purpose flour, sifted

⅓ cup almonds, chopped

⅓ cup chopped candied peel

¼ cup raisins, chopped

2 tbsp chopped candied cherries

finely grated rind of ½ lemon

4½ oz/125 g semisweet chocolate, broken into pieces

1 Preheat the oven to 350°F/180°C. Line 2 large cookie sheets with parchment paper.

2 Heat the butter and sugar in a small pan until the butter has just melted and the sugar dissolved. Remove from the heat.

3 Stir in the flour and mix well. Stir in the chopped almonds, candied peel, raisins, cherries, and lemon rind. Place teaspoonfuls of the cookie dough well apart on the cookie sheets.

4 Bake in the preheated oven for about 10 minutes, or until the florentines are lightly golden.

5 As soon as the florentines are removed from the oven, press the edges into neat shapes while still on the cookie sheets, using a cookie cutter. Let cool on the cookie sheets until firm, then transfer to a wire rack to cool completely.

6 Melt the chocolate in a heatproof bowl set over a pan of gently simmering water. Spread the melted chocolate over the smooth side of each florentine. As the chocolate starts to set, mark wavy lines in it with a fork. Let the florentines set, chocolate side up.

VARIATION
Replace the semisweet chocolate with white chocolate or cover half of the florentines in semisweet chocolate and half in white.

Ladies' Kisses

These melt-in-the-mouth cookies sandwiched together with chocolate are divine at coffee-time or served as petits fours after dinner.

1 hr plus 2 hrs chilling   **30–35 mins**

SERVES 20

I N G R E D I E N T S

scant ⅔ cup butter, sweet for preference

generous ½ cup superfine sugar

1 egg yolk

1 cup ground almonds

1¼ cups all-purpose flour

2 oz/55 g semisweet chocolate,
    broken into pieces

2 tbsp confectioners' sugar, for dusting

2 tbsp unsweetened cocoa, for dusting

1 Line 3 cookie sheets with parchment paper, or use 3 nonstick sheets. Cream the butter and sugar together until pale and fluffy. Beat in the egg yolk, then beat in the almonds and flour. Continue beating until thoroughly mixed. Shape the dough into a ball, wrap in plastic wrap and chill in the refrigerator for 1½–2 hours.

2 Preheat the oven to 325°F/160°C. Unwrap the dough, break off walnut-size pieces and roll them into balls between the palms of your hands. Place the dough balls on the prepared cookie sheets, allowing space for the cookies to spread during cooking. You may need to cook them in batches. Bake in the preheated oven for 20–25 minutes, until golden. Carefully transfer the cookies, still on the parchment paper (if using) to wire racks to cool.

3 Melt the chocolate in a heatproof bowl set over a pan of gently simmering water. Remove the cookies from the parchment paper (if using). Spread the melted chocolate on the flat sides and sandwich them together in pairs. Return to the wire racks to cool. Lightly dust with a mixture of confectioners' sugar and unsweetened cocoa.

Chocolate Crinkles

These chocolate cookies are popular at Christmas. Children enjoy shaping the mixture into balls so invite them to help you at this busy time of year.

30 mins plus 3 hrs chilling   15 mins

MAKES 24

INGREDIENTS

1 cup all-purpose flour

1 tsp baking powder

¼ cup walnut pieces

1 oz/25 g semisweet chocolate, broken into pieces

4 tbsp butter, plus extra for greasing

⅓ cup superfine sugar

1 tsp vanilla extract

1 egg, beaten

2 tbsp milk

¼ cup confectioners' sugar

1 Sift the flour and baking powder together. Finely chop the walnuts. Melt the chocolate in a heatproof bowl set over a pan of gently simmering water, then set aside to cool slightly.

2 Meanwhile, whisk the butter, superfine sugar and vanilla extract together until soft and fluffy. Gradually whisk in the egg, then whisk in the melted chocolate.

3 Whisk in the flour mixture alternatively with the milk. Stir in the chopped walnuts. Chill the mixture in the refrigerator for at least 3 hours.

4 Preheat the oven to 350°F/180°C. Grease 2–3 large cookie sheets. Put the confectioners' sugar into a large polythene bag.

5 Shape the mixture into 1-inch/2.5-cm balls, then roll each one in the confectioners' sugar. Place on the prepared cookie sheets, allowing room for the cookies to spread during cooking.

6 Bake the cookies in the oven for about 15 minutes, until firm. Transfer to a wire rack and let cool.

VARIATION
Pecans could be used instead of the walnuts.

Raspberry Chocolate Eclairs

These small eclairs are perfect for serving at a summer tea party. They look particularly appealing arranged on a pretty serving plate.

30 mins   40 mins

MAKES 20-24

INGREDIENTS

4 tbsp butter

⅔ cup water

½ cup all-purpose flour, sifted

2 eggs, beaten

FILLING AND TOPPING

¾ cup heavy cream

1 tbsp confectioners' sugar

¾ cup fresh raspberries

3 oz/85 g semisweet chocolate, broken into pieces

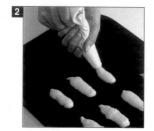

1 Preheat the oven to 425°F/220°C. To make the dough, place the butter and water in a heavy-based pan and bring to a boil over low heat. Add the flour, all at once, and beat thoroughly until the mixture leaves the side of the pan. Let cool slightly, then vigorously beat in the eggs, a little at a time.

2 Spoon the mixture into a pastry bag fitted with a ½-inch/1-cm tip and pipe 20–24 x 3-inch/7.5-cm lengths on to dampened cookie sheets. Bake in the preheated oven for 10 minutes, then reduce the oven temperature to 375°F/190°C and bake for an additional 20 minutes, or until crisp and golden brown. Split the side of each eclair to let the steam escape, and transfer to a wire rack to cool completely.

3 To make the filling, place the cream and confectioners' sugar in a bowl and whip until thick. Spoon into the eclairs. Place a few raspberries in each eclair.

4 Melt the chocolate in a heatproof bowl set over a pan of gently simmering water. Spread a little on each eclair. Let set, then serve.

COOK'S TIP

The raw piped choux mixture can be made a few days ahead and frozen, then baked directly from the freezer for 5 minutes longer than usual.

Chocolate Eclairs

Pastry cream (crème pâtissière) is the traditional filling for eclairs, but if time is short you can fill them with whipped cream.

🥧 1 hr   🕐 35–40 mins

MAKES 10

INGREDIENTS

DOUGH

5 tbsp butter, cut into small pieces, plus extra for greasing

⅔ cup water

¾ cup all-purpose flour, sifted

2 eggs

PASTRY CREAM

2 eggs, beaten lightly

¼ cup superfine sugar

2 tbsp cornstarch

1¼ cups milk

¼ tsp vanilla extract

FROSTING

2 tbsp butter

1 tbsp milk

1 tbsp unsweetened cocoa

½ cup confectioners' sugar

white chocolate, broken into pieces

1 Preheat the oven to 400°F/200°C. Lightly grease a cookie sheet. Place the water in a pan, add the butter, and heat gently until the butter melts. Bring to a rolling boil, then remove the pan from the heat and add the flour all at once, beating well until the mixture leaves the sides of the pan and forms a ball. Let cool slightly, then gradually beat in the eggs to form a smooth, glossy mixture. Spoon into a large pastry bag fitted with a ½-inch/1-cm plain tip.

2 Sprinkle the cookie sheet with a little water. Pipe eclairs 3 inches/7.5 cm long, spaced well apart. Bake in the preheated oven for 30–35 minutes, or until crisp and golden. Make a small slit in the side of each eclair to let the steam escape. Let cool on a wire rack.

3 Meanwhile, make the pastry cream. Whisk the eggs and sugar until thick and creamy, then fold in the cornstarch. Heat the milk until almost boiling and pour on to the eggs, whisking. Transfer to the pan and cook over low heat, stirring until thick. Remove the pan from the heat and stir in the vanilla extract. Cover with parchment paper and let cool.

4 To make the frosting, melt the butter with the milk in a pan, remove from the heat and stir in the unsweetened cocoa and sugar. Split the eclairs lengthwise and pipe in the pastry cream. Spread the frosting over the top of the eclair. Melt a little white chocolate in a heatproof bowl set over a pan of gently simmering water, then spoon over the chocolate frosting, swirl in, and let set.

Chestnut Cream Squares

These little cakes look wonderful, and are well worth the preparation time. The magical combination of flavors is out of this world.

45 mins plus
11–11 hrs 30 mins
freezing/standing

55–60 mins

MAKES 30

INGREDIENTS

BOTTOM LAYER

3 oz/85 g semisweet chocolate, broken into pieces

6 tbsp butter, sweet for preference

4 tbsp confectioners' sugar

4 eggs, separated

½ cup superfine sugar

⅔ cup all-purpose flour

5 tbsp sour cherry jelly

3 tbsp kirsch

DARK LAYER

3½ oz/100 g semisweet chocolate

generous ⅓ cup milk

4 tsp superfine sugar

¼ tsp vanilla extract

1 egg yolk

1 tbsp cornstarch

generous 2 tbsp confectioners' sugar

1¼ cups heavy cream

WHITE LAYER

2 cups heavy cream

1 tbsp confectioners' sugar

CHESTNUT LAYER

1½ cups chestnut purée

4 tsp dark rum

2 tsp superfine sugar

30 cherries, to decorate

1 Preheat the oven to 350°F/180°C. Line a 12 x 10 x 2-inch/30 x 25 x 5-cm cake pan with parchment paper. Melt the chocolate in a heatproof bowl set over a pan of gently simmering water, then cool slightly. Mix the butter, confectioners' sugar, and chocolate together. Beat in the egg yolks, 1 at a time.

2 Whisk the egg whites in a separate bowl until soft peaks form, whisk in the superfine sugar until stiff, then fold into the chocolate mixture. Sift the flour, then fold into the mixture. Spoon into the pan and smooth the surface. Bake for 30 minutes.

3 Remove from the oven, let cool, then cut around the edges with a knife. Invert on to a flat surface. Wash and dry the cake pan and line with parchment paper. Return the bottom layer to the pan. Bring the jelly to a boil in a small pan, strain, and cool. Sprinkle the kirsch over the bottom layer, then spread with the cherry jelly.

4 Melt the chocolate in a heatproof bowl set over a pan of gently simmering water. Remove from the heat. Put the milk, superfine sugar, and vanilla extract into a pan and bring to a boil. Remove from the heat. Mix the egg yolk, cornstarch, and 2 tablespoons of the hot milk in a bowl, add to the milk in the pan, and return to medium heat. Cook, stirring, for 3–5 minutes until thickened. Stir in the confectioners' sugar and melted chocolate. Remove from the heat. Beat the cream until thick, then stir it into the chocolate mixture. Spread over the layer in the pan, cover and freeze for 1½–2 hours.

5 When the dark layer is half-frozen, make the white layer. Whisk the cream with the sugar until thick, then spread over the dark layer. Cover and freeze for 8 hours.

6 Remove the cake from the pan, with the white layer uppermost. Beat together the chestnut purée, rum, and sugar. Pipe or press through a garlic press and spread over the white layer. Cut the cake into 30 squares and top each one with a cherry. Let chill for 30 minutes before serving.

Chocolate Strawberry Slices

Here, strawberry jelly and semisweet chocolate chips are sandwiched between an oat crumble mixture to make delicious cookie slices.

15 mins   30–35 mins

MAKES 16

INGREDIENTS

1½ cups all-purpose flour

1 tsp baking powder

½ cup superfine sugar

½ cup brown sugar

8 oz/225 g butter

1½ cups rolled oats

¾ cup strawberry jelly

½ cup semisweet chocolate chips

¼ cup chopped almonds

1 Preheat the oven to 375°F/190°C. Line a 12 x 8-inch/30 x 12-cm deep-sided jelly roll pan with parchment paper. Sift the flour and baking powder into a large bowl.

2 Add the superfine sugar and brown sugar to the flour and mix well. Add the butter and rub in until the mixture resembles bread crumbs. Stir in the oats.

3 Press three-quarters of the mixture into the bottom of a 9-inch/23-cm square cake pan. Bake in the preheated oven for 10 minutes.

4 Spread the jelly over the cooked base, then sprinkle over the chocolate chips. Mix the remaining flour mixture and almonds together. Sprinkle the mixture over the chocolate chips and press down gently.

5 Return to the oven and bake for an additional 20–25 minutes, until golden brown. Let cool in the pan, then cut into slices.

VARIATION
Seedless raspberry jelly would work equally well in this recipe.

Mocha Rolls

Semisweet and white chocolate are combined with coffee and Kahlúa in these attractive sponge-cake rolls.

35 mins plus
1–2 hrs 30 mins
chilling/setting

50–55 mins

MAKES 16

I N G R E D I E N T S

⅔ cup cold, strong, black coffee

1 tbsp gelatin

1 tsp Kahlúa or other coffee-flavored liqueur

1 cup ricotta cheese

10 oz/280 g white chocolate, broken into pieces

1 oz/25 g semisweet chocolate

S P O N G E   C A K E

3 eggs, plus 1 egg white

scant ½ cup superfine sugar

generous ¾ cup all-purpose flour

2 tbsp butter, melted

1 Preheat the oven to 350°F/180°C. For the sponge cake, base-line a 12 x 8 x 1½-inch/30 x 20 x 4-cm cake pan with parchment paper. Put the eggs, egg white, and sugar in a heatproof bowl set over a pan of gently simmering water. Whisk until pale and thickened.

2 Remove the mixture from the heat, then whisk until cool. Sift the flour over the mixture and fold in. Fold in the melted butter, a little at a time. Pour the cake batter into the prepared pan and bake for 25–30 minutes, until the cake is firm to the touch and has shrunk slightly from the sides of the pan. Remove from the oven and transfer to a wire rack, still standing on the parchment paper, to cool.

3 Meanwhile, put 2 tablespoons of the coffee into a small heatproof bowl and sprinkle the gelatin on the surface. Let

it soften for 2 minutes, then set the bowl over a pan of gently simmering water and stir until the gelatin has dissolved. Remove from the heat. Put the remaining coffee, liqueur, and ricotta in a food processor and process until smooth. Add the gelatin mixture in a single stream and process briefly. Scrape the mixture into a bowl, cover with plastic wrap, and chill in the refrigerator for 1–1½ hours, until set.

4 Peel the parchment paper from the cooled cake. Using a knife, cut horizontally through the cake. Trim off any dried edges. Cut each piece of cake in half lengthwise. Place each piece between 2 sheets of parchment paper and roll with a rolling pin to make it more flexible.

5 Spread the cut side of each cake piece with an even ¼-inch/5-mm thick layer of the coffee filling, leaving a

¼-inch/5-mm margin all round. Cut each strip across into 4 pieces, to give a total of 16. Roll up each piece from the short end, like a jelly roll.

6 Melt the white chocolate in a heatproof bowl set over a pan of barely simmering water. Remove from the heat. Place 1 roll, seam-side down, on a metal spatula and hold it over the bowl of melted chocolate. Spoon the chocolate over the roll to coat. Transfer the roll to a sheet of parchment paper and repeat with the remaining rolls.

7 Put the semisweet chocolate in a heatproof bowl set over a pan of gently simmering water. Remove from the heat. Spoon it into a waxed paper pastry bag fitted with a small, plain tip and pipe zigzags along the rolls. Let set completely before serving.

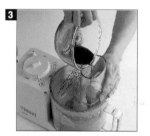

Meringues

These are just as meringues should be—as light as air and at the same time crisp and melt-in-the-mouth. Store in an airtight container.

🥧 8 hrs 15 mins   🕐 1 hr 30 mins

MAKES 13

INGREDIENTS

4 egg whites

generous ½ cup granulated sugar

generous ½ cup superfine sugar

1¼ cups heavy cream, whipped lightly

salt

1 Preheat the oven to 250°F/120°C. Line 3 cookie sheets with sheets of parchment paper.

2 In a large clean bowl, whisk the egg whites with a pinch of salt until stiff, using an electric hand-held whisk or a balloon whisk. You should be able to turn the bowl upside down without any movement from the egg whites.

3 Whisk in the granulated sugar, a little at a time; the meringue should start to look glossy at this stage.

4 Sprinkle in the superfine sugar, a little at a time, and continue whisking until all the sugar has been incorporated and the meringue is thick, white, and stands in tall peaks.

5 Transfer the meringue mixture to a pastry bag fitted with a ¾-inch/2-cm star tip. Pipe about 26 small whirls on to the prepared cookie sheets.

6 Bake in a preheated oven for 1½ hours, or until the meringues are pale golden in color and can be easily lifted off the paper. Let cool in the turned-off oven overnight.

7 Just before serving, sandwich the meringues together in pairs with the whipped cream and arrange them on a serving plate.

VARIATION
For a finer texture, replace the granulated sugar with superfine sugar.

Chocolate Meringues

These melt-in-the-mouth meringues are an ideal choice for an extra-special occasion—pile them high in a pyramid for pure, bite-size magic.

🍮 1 hr 25 mins   🕐 1 hr

MAKES 8

I N G R E D I E N T S

4 egg whites

1 cup superfine sugar

1 tsp cornstarch

1½ oz/40 g semisweet chocolate, grated

TO FINISH

3½ oz/100 g semisweet chocolate

⅔ cup heavy cream

1 tbsp confectioners' sugar

1 tbsp cognac (optional)

1 Preheat the oven to 275°F/140°C. Line 2 cookie sheets with parchment paper. Whisk the egg whites until soft peaks form, then gradually whisk in half of the sugar. Continue whisking until the mixture is very stiff and glossy.

2 Carefully fold in the remaining sugar, cornstarch, and grated chocolate with a metal spoon or spatula.

3 Spoon the mixture into a pastry bag fitted with a large star or plain tip. Pipe 16 large rosettes or mounds on the lined cookie sheets.

4 Bake in the oven for about 1 hour, changing the position of the cookie sheets after 30 minutes. Without opening the oven door, turn off the oven and let the meringues cool in the oven. Once cold, carefully peel off the parchment paper.

5 Melt the semisweet chocolate in a heatproof bowl set over a pan of gently simmering water and carefully spread it over the bottom of the meringues. Stand them upside down on a wire rack until the chocolate has set. Whip the cream, confectioners' sugar and cognac (if using), until the cream holds its shape. Spoon into a pastry bag and use to sandwich the chocolate-coated meringues together in pairs.

VARIATION
To make mini meringues, use a star-shape tip and pipe about 24 small rosettes. Bake for about 40 minutes until crisp.

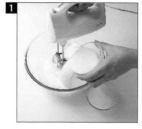

Mexican Meringues

The Mexican name for these delicate meringues is *suspiros*, meaning "sighs"—supposedly the contented sighs of the nuns who created them.

🕐 1 hr 15 mins   ⏰ 2 hrs

MAKES 25

INGREDIENTS

4–5 egg whites, at room temperature

pinch of salt

¼ tsp cream of tartar

¼–½ tsp vanilla extract

¾–1 cup superfine sugar

⅛–¼ tsp ground cinnamon

4 oz/115 g semisweet or bittersweet chocolate, grated

TO SERVE

ground cinnamon, for dusting

4 oz/115 g strawberries

chocolate-flavored cream (see Cook's Tip)

1 Preheat the oven to 300°F/150°C. Whisk the egg whites until they are foamy, then add the salt, and cream of tartar, and beat until very stiff. Whisk in the vanilla, then slowly whisk in the sugar, a small amount at a time, until the meringue is shiny and stiff. This should take about 3 minutes by hand, and under 1 minute with an electric whisk.

2 Whisk in the cinnamon and grated chocolate. Spoon mounds of about 2 tablespoons, on to an ungreased, nonstick cookie sheet. Space the mounds out well.

3 Place in the preheated oven and cook for 2 hours, until set.

4 Carefully remove from the cookie sheet. If the meringues are too moist and soft, return them to the oven to firm up and dry out. Let cool completely.

5 Serve the meringues dusted with cinnamon and accompanied by strawberries and the chocolate-flavored cream (see Cook's Tip).

COOK'S TIP
To make the flavored cream, simply stir half-melted chocolate pieces into stiffly whipped cream, then chill until solid.

Chocolate Ginger Meringues

These meringues are flecked with semisweet chocolate and sandwiched together with a delicious ginger cream. Assemble just before serving.

🍮 1 hr   🕐 1 hr 40 mins

MAKES 8 PAIRS

INGREDIENTS

8 oz/225 g semisweet chocolate

4 egg whites

generous 1 cup golden superfine sugar

FILLING

1¼ cups heavy cream

1 tbsp syrup from the preserved ginger jar

3 pieces preserved ginger, chopped finely

1 Preheat the oven to 250°F/120°C. Line 2 cookie sheets with nonstick parchment paper. Grate half the semisweet chocolate. Put the egg whites in a clean, greasefree bowl and whisk until stiff. Whisk in half the remaining sugar with the grated chocolate.

2 Pipe or spoon 16 tablespoons of the meringue mixture on to the prepared baking sheets. Bake in the oven for 1½ hours, or until dry. Transfer to wire racks to cool. Put the remaining chocolate in a heatproof bowl set over a pan of gently simmering water until melted. Spread a little melted chocolate over the base of each meringue. Let set.

3 To make the filling, put the cream in a bowl and whisk until thick. Stir in the ginger syrup, then add the chopped ginger and stir gently to incorporate. Sandwich the meringues together in pairs with the ginger cream before serving.

COOK'S TIP
Take care not to over-whisk the meringue mixture after adding the grated chocolate.

Chocolate Peppermint Slices

A fresh mint-flavored frosting, sandwiched between a shortbread cookie base and a chocolate coating, make these slices deliciously different.

50 mins

10–15 mins

MAKES 16

INGREDIENTS

4 tbsp butter, plus extra for greasing

¼ cup superfine sugar

¾ cup all-purpose flour

2 cups confectioners' sugar

½ tsp peppermint extract

6 oz/175 g semisweet chocolate, broken into pieces

1–2 tbsp warm water

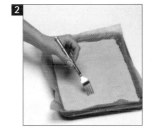

1 Preheat the oven to 350°F/180°C. Grease and line an 8 x 12-inch/20 x 30-cm jelly roll pan with parchment paper. Whisk the butter and sugar together until pale and fluffy. Stir in the flour until the mixture binds together.

2 Knead the mixture to form a smooth dough, then press into the prepared pan. Prick the surface all over with a fork. Bake the base in the preheated oven for 10–15 minutes, until lightly browned and just firm to the touch. Let cool in the pan.

3 Sift the confectioners' sugar into a bowl. Gradually add the water, then add the peppermint extract. Spread the frosting over the base, then let set.

4 Melt the chocolate in a heatproof bowl set over a pan of gently simmering water, then spread over the peppermint frosting. Let set, then cut into slices.

Christmas Tree Clusters

Popcorn is the perfect nibble to have around at Christmas. Wrapped in cellophane, these clusters make ideal decorations for the Christmas tree.

10 mins   20 mins

MAKES 16

INGREDIENTS

1 tbsp vegetable oil

1 oz/25 g unpopped corn

2 tbsp butter

4 tbsp brown sugar

4 tbsp corn syrup

¼ cup candied cherries, chopped

⅓ cup golden raisins or raisins

½ cup ground almonds

2 tbsp slivered almonds

½ tsp ground allspice

1 To pop the corn, heat the oil in a large pan or in a popcorn pan. The oil is hot enough when a kernel spins around in the pan. Add the unpopped corn, cover tightly, and pop the corn over medium-high heat, shaking the pan frequently.

2 Remove the pan from the heat and wait until the popping sound subsides.

3 Put the butter, sugar, and syrup into a pan and heat, stirring frequently, to dissolve the sugar. Do not let boil. Remove from the heat once the sugar is dissolved.

4 Add the popped corn, candied cherries, golden raisins or raisins, ground and slivered almonds, and allspice to the syrup mixture, stirring well. Let cool for a few minutes.

5 Shape the mixture into small balls. Let cool completely, then wrap in cellophane and tie with colored ribbon or string and hang from the Christmas tree.

VARIATION
Omit the cherries, golden raisins, ground almonds and allspice and replace with ½ cup coarsely chopped pecans and ½ tsp ground cinnamon to make Pecan Clusters.

Lebkuchen

These spice cookies are traditionally eaten in Germany on the feast day of St Nicholas but they are good to eat at any time of the year!

🍰 25 mins   🕐 15–20 mins

MAKES ABOUT 60

INGREDIENTS

3 eggs

1 cup golden superfine sugar

½ cup all-purpose flour

2 tsp unsweetened cocoa

1 tsp ground cinnamon

½ tsp ground cardamom

¼ tsp ground cloves

¼ tsp ground nutmeg

generous 1 cup ground almonds

scant ⅓ cup candied peel, chopped finely

TO DECORATE

4 oz/115 g semisweet chocolate

4 oz/115 g white chocolate

sugar crystals

1 Preheat the oven to 350°F/180°C. Line several cookie sheets with nonstick parchment paper. Put the eggs and sugar in a heatproof bowl set over a pan of gently simmering water. Whisk until thick and foamy. Remove the bowl from the pan and continue to whisk for 2 minutes.

2 Sift the flour, cocoa, cinnamon, cardamom, cloves, and nutmeg into the bowl and stir in with the ground almonds and chopped peel. Drop heaping teaspoonfuls of the cookie dough on to the prepared cookie sheets, spreading them gently into smooth mounds.

3 Bake in the oven for 15–20 minutes, until light brown and slightly soft to the touch. Cool on the cookie sheets for 10 minutes, then transfer to wire racks to cool completely. Put the semisweet and white chocolate in 2 separate heatproof bowls set over 2 saucepans of gently simmering water until melted. Dip half the cookies in melted semisweet chocolate and half in white. Sprinkle with sugar crystals and let set.

Cakes
& Gâteaux

There are those dull days or quiet weekends that make us

want to retreat to the warmth and comfort of the kitchen

and what better way to spend an afternoon than to

indulge in some baking? Few things culinary can lift jaded

spirits in quite the same way as a

tempting slice of homemade cake.

Here are everyday cakes and gâteaux

for special occasions, from spicy rich

fruit cakes to sumptuous creamy cheesecakes. Favorites

include Mississippi Mud Cake, Double Chocolate Roulade,

and Tropical Fruit Vacherin. Unleash

your creative genius and get baking.

Chocolate Ganache Cake

Ganache—a divine mixture of chocolate and cream—is used to fill and decorate this rich chocolate cake, making it a chocolate lover's dream.

1 hr plus
2 hrs chilling

40 mins

SERVES 10

I N G R E D I E N T S

6 oz/175 g butter plus extra for greasing

¾ cup superfine sugar

4 eggs, beaten lightly

1¾ cups self-rising flour

1 tbsp unsweetened cocoa

1¾ oz/50 g semisweet chocolate, melted

G A N A C H E

2 cups heavy cream

13 oz/375 g semisweet chocolate,
  broken into pieces

T O   F I N I S H

7 oz/200 g chocolate-flavored
  cake covering

1 Preheat the oven to 350°F/180°C. Lightly grease and base-line an 8-inch/20-cm springform cake pan. Beat the butter and sugar until light and fluffy. Gradually add the eggs, beating well after each addition. Sift the flour and unsweetened cocoa together. Fold into the cake batter. Fold in the melted chocolate.

2 Pour into the prepared pan and smooth the top. Bake in the preheated oven for 40 minutes, or until springy to the touch. Let the cake cool for 5 minutes in the pan, then turn out on to a wire rack and let cool completely. Cut the cold cake into 2 layers.

3 To make the ganache, place the cream in a pan and bring to a boil, stirring. Add the chocolate and stir until melted. Pour into a bowl, cool then chill for 2 hours or until set and firm. Whisk the mixture until light and fluffy and set aside.

4 Reserve one-third of the ganache. Use the rest to sandwich the cake together and spread over the cake.

5 Melt the cake covering and spread it over a large sheet of parchment paper. Let cool until just set. Cut into strips a little wider than the height of the cake. Place the strips around the edge of the cake, overlapping them slightly.

6 Pipe the reserved ganache in tear drops or shells to cover the top of the cake. Let chill for 1 hour.

Swedish Chocolate Cake

This is the ideal snack to eat with a mid-morning cup of coffee.
Serve with whipped cream for a special treat.

🔥 50 mins   🕐 1 hr

MAKES 9-INCH/23-CM CAKE

INGREDIENTS

3¼ oz/90 g butter, unsalted for preference,
   plus extra for greasing

⅓ cup dry white bread crumbs

3 oz/85 g semisweet chocolate,
   broken into pieces

scant 1 cup superfine sugar

2 eggs, separated

1 tsp vanilla extract

1½ cups all-purpose flour

1 tsp baking powder

½ cup light cream

1 Preheat the oven to 300°F/150°C. Grease a deep 9-inch/23-cm round cake pan with butter. Sprinkle the bread crumbs into the pan and press them on to the bottom and sides.

2 Put the chocolate in a heatproof bowl set over a pan of gently simmering water. Stir over low heat until melted, then remove from the heat.

3 Cream the butter with the sugar until pale and fluffy. Beat in the egg yolks, one at a time, and add the vanilla.

4 Sift one-third of the flour with the baking powder, then beat into the egg mixture. Mix together the cream and melted chocolate, then beat one-third of this mixture into the egg mixture. Continue adding the flour and the chocolate mixture alternately, beating well after each addition.

5 Whisk the egg whites in a separate bowl until stiff peaks form. Fold the egg whites into the chocolate mixture.

6 Pour into the prepared pan and bake in the preheated oven for about 50 minutes, until a skewer inserted into the center of the cake comes out clean. Turn the cake out on to a wire rack to cool before serving.

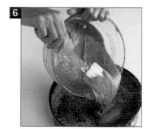

Chocolate Battenberg Cake

Although this cake requires care and patience to prepare, the result is well worth the effort.

🍰 25 mins   🕐 25–30 mins

SERVES 8–10

INGREDIENTS

1 tsp sunflower oil, for oiling

6 oz/175 g butter or margarine, softened

¾ cup superfine sugar, plus extra for rolling and sprinkling

3 eggs, beaten

1 cup self-rising flour

1 tsp vanilla extract

2 oz/55 g semisweet chocolate

6 tbsp apricot jelly

1 tbsp lemon juice

1 lb/450 g ready-made white marzipan

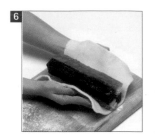

1 Preheat the oven to 375°F/190°C. Lightly oil and line a 10 x 8-inch/26 x 20-cm oblong baking pan with nonstick parchment paper. Make a partition down the center of the pan with the paper.

2 Cream the butter with the sugar until light and fluffy. Gradually beat in the eggs, adding a little flour after each addition. When all the eggs have been added stir in the remaining flour. Spoon half the cake batter into a separate bowl.

3 Add the vanilla extract to one bowl with 1–2 tablespoons of cooled boiled water and mix to form a smooth dropping consistency. Set aside. Melt the chocolate in a heatproof bowl set over a pan of gently simmering water. Stir until smooth then add to the second bowl together with 1–2 tablespoons of cooled boiled water and mix to achieve the same consistency as the vanilla batter.

4 Spoon both batters into the prepared cake pan, placing the vanilla mixture down one side of the pan and the chocolate mixture down the other side. Smooth and level the top then bake in the preheated oven for 25–30 minutes or until a skewer inserted into the center comes out clean. Remove and leave until cold before removing from the pan and discarding the lining paper.

5 Heat the jelly and lemon juice then rub through a strainer. Cut both cakes in half lengthwise and trim to an even shape. Brush the sides with apricot glaze and place the cakes together to form a checkerboard effect. Press together firmly.

6 Roll the marzipan out on a lightly sugared work counter or cutting board to form a 12 x 9-inch/30 x 23-cm oblong. Brush the base of the cake with the apricot glaze and place in the center of the marzipan. Brush all the sides of the cake then bring the marzipan up and around the cake, pressing firmly into the sides and top. Use your forefinger and thumb to make a decorative edge down both sides of the cake. Mark a pattern down the center and sprinkle with a little extra superfine sugar.

Apricot & Cherry Cake

This chocolate cake has a really moist texture and is filled with plump apricots and cherries.

15 mins   50–60 mins

SERVES 8–10

INGREDIENTS

1 tsp sunflower oil, for oiling

6 oz/175 g butter, softened

¾ cup superfine sugar

4 oz/115 g semisweet chocolate

½ tsp almond extract

3 eggs, beaten

1 cup self-rising flour

generous ¼ cup ground almonds

1 cup no-soak apricots, chopped

¾ cup candied cherries, chopped

4–6 white sugar lumps

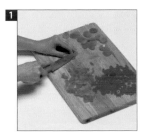

1 Preheat the oven to 350°F/180°C . Lightly oil and line the base of an 8-inch/20-cm cake pan with nonstick parchment paper. Ensure the apricots and cherries are chopped to an even size. Cream the butter with the sugar until light and fluffy. Melt the chocolate in a heatproof bowl set over a pan of gently simmering water then add to the creamed mixture with the almond extract. Stir well.

2 Gradually beat in the eggs, a little at a time and beating well after each addition and adding a little flour after each addition. When all the eggs have been added, stir in the remaining flour with the ground almonds and the apricots. Mix to form a soft dropping consistency, adding 1–2 tablespoons of cooled boiled water, then stir in the candied cherries.

3 Turn into the prepared cake pan and smooth the top. Lightly crush the sugar lumps and scatter over the top of the cake. Bake in the preheated oven for 50–60 minutes or until a skewer inserted into the center comes out clean. Remove from the oven and let cool in the pan before turning out on to a wire rack and discarding the lining paper. Store in an airtight container.

COOK'S TIP
Ground almonds not only help to keep this cake moist, but also improve its keeping qualities.

Date & Chocolate Cake

Moist and moreish, this fruity chocolate cake will prove to be a popular after-school snack.

25 mins plus
20 mins cooling

40 mins

MAKES 7-INCH/18-CM CAKE

INGREDIENTS

4 oz/115 g sweet butter, plus extra
  for greasing

⅔ cup self-rising flour, plus 1 tbsp
  extra for dusting

4 oz/115 g semisweet chocolate,
  broken into pieces

1 tbsp grenadine

1 tbsp corn syrup

4 tbsp superfine sugar

2 large eggs

2 tbsp ground rice

1 tbsp confectioners' sugar, to decorate

FILLING

⅔ cup chopped dried dates

1 tbsp lemon juice

1 tbsp orange juice

1 tbsp raw sugar

¼ cup chopped blanched almonds

2 tbsp apricot jelly

1 Preheat the oven to 350°F/180°C. Grease and flour 2 x 7-inch/18-cm layer cake pans. Put the chocolate, grenadine, and syrup in a heatproof bowl set over a pan of gently simmering water. Stir over low heat until the chocolate has melted and the mixture is smooth. Remove from the heat and let cool.

2 Cream the butter and superfine sugar together until pale and fluffy. Gradually beat in the eggs then the cooled chocolate mixture.

3 Sift the flour into another bowl and stir in the ground rice. Fold the flour mixture into the creamed mixture.

4 Divide the batter among the prepared pans and smooth the surface. Bake in the preheated oven for 20–25 minutes, until golden and firm to the touch. Turn out on to a wire rack to cool.

5 To make the filling, put all the ingredients into a pan and stir over low heat for 4–5 minutes, until fully incorporated. Remove from the heat, let cool, then use it to sandwich the cakes together. Dust the top of the cake with confectioners' sugar to decorate.

Chocolate Tray Bake

This is a good family cake that keeps well. Baked in a shallow rectangular cake pan, the squares are ideal for serving with morning coffee.

50 mins · 30–40 mins

SERVES 15

INGREDIENTS

butter, for greasing

3 cups self-rising flour, sifted

3 tbsp unsweetened cocoa, sifted

1 cup superfine sugar

7 oz/200 g soft margarine

4 eggs, beaten

4 tbsp milk

⅓ cup milk chocolate chips

⅓ cup semisweet chocolate chips

⅓ cup white chocolate chips

confectioners' sugar, for dusting

1 Preheat the oven to 350°F/180°C. Grease a 13 x 9 x 2-inch/33 x 23 x 5-cm cake pan with a little butter.

2 Place all of the ingredients except for the chocolate chips and confectioners' sugar in a large mixing bowl and beat together until smooth.

3 Beat in the milk, semisweet, and white chocolate chips.

4 Spoon the cake batter into the prepared cake pan and smooth the top. Bake in the preheated oven for 30–40 minutes, until risen and springy to the touch. Let cool in the pan.

5 Once cool, dust with confectioners' sugar. Cut into squares to serve.

VARIATION
For an attractive finish, cut thin strips of paper and lay in a criss-cross pattern on top of the cake. Dust with confectioners' sugar, then remove the paper strips.

Chocolate Truffle Cake

Soft chocolate sponge topped with a rich chocolate truffle mixture makes a cake that chocoholics will die for.

🍰 45 mins plus
4 hrs chilling　　🕐 25–30 mins

SERVES 12

INGREDIENTS

2¾ oz/75 g butter plus extra for greasing

⅓ cup superfine sugar

2 eggs, beaten lightly

⅔ cup self-rising flour

½ tsp baking powder

¼ cup unsweetened cocoa

½ cup ground almonds

TRUFFLE TOPPING

12 oz/350 g semisweet chocolate

4 oz/115 g butter

1¼ cups heavy cream

1¼ cups plain cake crumbs

3 tbsp dark rum

TO DECORATE

1¾ oz/50 g semisweet chocolate,
    broken into pieces

cape gooseberries

1 Preheat the oven to 350°F/180°C. Lightly grease and base-line an 8-inch/20-cm round springform pan. Beat the butter and sugar together until light and fluffy. Gradually add the eggs, beating well after each addition.

2 Sift the flour, baking powder, and unsweetened cocoa together and fold into the cake batter along with the ground almonds. Pour into the prepared pan and bake in the preheated oven for 20–25 minutes, or until springy to the touch. Let the cake cool slightly in the pan, then transfer to a wire rack to cool

completely. Wash and dry the pan and return the cooled cake to the pan.

3 To make the topping, heat the chocolate, butter, and cream in a heavy-based pan over low heat and stir until smooth. Cool, then chill for 30 minutes. Beat well with a wooden spoon and chill for an additional 30 minutes. Beat the mixture again, then add the cake crumbs and rum, beating

until well combined. Spoon over the sponge cake and let chill for 3 hours.

4 Meanwhile, put the chocolate in a heatproof bowl set over a pan of gently simmering water until melted. Dip the cape gooseberries in the melted chocolate until partially covered. Let set on parchment paper. Transfer the cake to a serving plate; decorate with the cape gooseberries.

Chocolate Truffle Torte

Chocolate and cream on a thin sponge base make this a wickedly rich cake—a good choice for a party.

40 mins plus
30 mins chilling ⏱ 10–15 mins

SERVES 10

I N G R E D I E N T S

S P O N G E

butter, for greasing

¼ cup golden superfine sugar

2 eggs

¼ cup all-purpose flour

¼ cup unsweetened cocoa

¼ cup cold strong black coffee

2 tbsp cognac

T R U F F L E   F I L L I N G

2½ cups whipping cream

15 oz/425 g semisweet chocolate,
broken into pieces

T O   D E C O R A T E

unsweetened cocoa

confectioners' sugar

1 Preheat the oven to 425°F/220°C. Grease and line a 9-inch/23-cm springform cake pan. Put the sugar and eggs in a heatproof bowl set over a pan of gently simmering water. Whisk together until pale and mousselike. Sift in the flour and unsweetened cocoa and fold gently into the batter. Pour into the prepared pan and bake in the oven for 7–10 minutes, or until risen and firm to the touch.

2 Transfer to a wire rack to cool. Wash and dry the pan and replace the cooled cake in the pan. Mix together the coffee and cognac and brush over the cake. To make the truffle filling, put the cream in a bowl and whisk until just holding very soft peaks. Put the chocolate in a heatproof bowl set over a pan of gently simmering water until melted. Carefully fold the cooled melted chocolate into the cream. Pour the chocolate mixture over the sponge. Chill until set.

3 To decorate the torte, sift unsweetened cocoa over the top and remove carefully from the pan. Using strips of card or waxed paper, sift bands of confectioners' sugar over the torte to create a striped pattern. Cut into slices with a hot knife, to serve.

COOK'S TIP
It is important that the cream is only whipped lightly because it thickens when the chocolate is added.

White Truffle Cake

A light white sponge, topped with a rich creamy-white chocolate truffle mixture, makes an out-of-this-world treat.

40 mins plus
2 hrs chilling

30 mins

SERVES 12

INGREDIENTS

butter for greasing

1¾ oz/50 g white chocolate

2 eggs

¼ cup superfine sugar

½ cup all-purpose flour

TRUFFLE TOPPING

1¼ cups heavy cream

12 oz/350 g white chocolate, broken into pieces

generous 1 cup mascarpone

TO DECORATE

12 oz/350 g semisweet, milk, or white chocolate curls (see page 9)

unsweetened cocoa, for dusting

1 Preheat the oven to 350°F/180°. Grease and base-line a round 8-inch/20-cm springform cake pan. Put the white chocolate in a heatproof bowl set over a pan of gently simmering water until melted.

2 Whisk the eggs and superfine sugar in a mixing bowl for 10 minutes, or until very light and foamy, and a trail is left when the whisk is dragged across the surface. Sift the flour and fold into the eggs with a metal spoon. Add the melted white chocolate. Pour the cake batter into the pan and bake in the preheated oven for 25 minutes, or until springy to the touch. Let cool slightly, then transfer to a wire rack until completely cold. Return the cold cake to the pan.

3 To make the topping, place the cream in a pan and bring to a boil, stirring constantly. Let cool slightly, then add the white chocolate and stir until melted and combined. Remove from the heat and set aside until almost cool, stirring, then mix in the mascarpone. Pour on top of the cake and let chill for 2 hours.

4 Decorate with chocolate curls (see page 9) and sprinkle with unsweetened cocoa.

Chocolate Fudge Cake

This rich chocolate cake with soft fudge frosting makes a perfect birthday cake for a chocolate lover.

25 mins plus
1 hr chilling

35–45 mins

SERVES 8

INGREDIENTS

6 oz/175 g butter, sweet for preference, softened, plus extra for greasing

scant 1 cup golden superfine sugar

3 eggs, beaten

3 tbsp corn syrup

3 tbsp ground almonds

1½ cups self-rising flour

pinch of salt

⅓ cup unsweetened cocoa

FROSTING

8 oz/225 g semisweet chocolate, broken into pieces

½ cup dark muscovado sugar

8 oz/225 g butter, sweet for preference, diced

5 tbsp evaporated milk

½ tsp vanilla extract

1 To make the frosting, put the chocolate, sugar, butter, evaporated milk, and vanilla extract in a heavy-based pan. Heat gently, stirring constantly, until melted. Pour into a bowl and let cool. Cover with plastic wrap and let chill for 1 hour, or until spreadable. Preheat the oven to 350°F/180°C. Grease and base-line 2 x 8-inch/20-cm cake pans.

2 To make the cake, put the butter and sugar in a bowl and beat until light and fluffy. Gradually beat in the eggs. Stir in the syrup and ground almonds. Sift the flour, salt, and unsweetened cocoa into a bowl, then fold it into the cake batter. Add a little water if necessary to make a dropping consistency. Spoon the cake batter into the prepared pans and bake in the preheated oven for 30-35 minutes, until springy to the touch and a skewer inserted into the center comes out clean.

3 Leave in the pans for 5 minutes, then transfer to wire racks to cool. When the cakes are completely cold, sandwich them together with half of the frosting. Spread the remaining frosting over the top and sides of the cake, swirling it to give a frosted appearance.

COOK'S TIP
If the cake batter starts to curdle while you are adding the eggs, beat in a little of the flour.

Chocolate & Orange Cake

A classic favorite combination of flavors makes this cake ideal for a treat. Omit the frosting if preferred, and sprinkle with confectioners' sugar.

🍰 1 hr   🕐 25 mins

SERVES 8

I N G R E D I E N T S

6 oz/175 g butter, plus extra for greasing

¾ cup superfine sugar

3 eggs, beaten

1½ cups self-rising flour, sifted

2 tbsp unsweetened cocoa, sifted

2 tbsp milk

3 tbsp orange juice

grated rind of ½ orange

F R O S T I N G

1½ cups confectioners' sugar

2 tbsp orange juice

a little semisweet chocolate, to decorate

1 Preheat the oven to 375°F/190°C. Lightly grease an 8-inch/20-cm deep round cake pan.

2 Beat the sugar and butter together in a bowl until light and fluffy. Gradually add the eggs, beating well after each addition. Carefully fold in the flour.

3 Divide the cake batter in half. Add the unsweetened cocoa and milk to half, stirring until well combined. Add the orange juice and rind to the other half.

4 Place tablespoonfuls of each cake batter into the prepared pan and swirl together with a skewer, to create a marbled effect. Bake in the preheated oven for 25 minutes, or until the cake is springy to the touch. Let cool in the pan for a few minutes before transferring to a wire rack to cool completely.

5 To make the frosting, sift the confectioners' sugar into a mixing bowl and mix in enough of the orange juice to form a smooth frosting. Spread the frosting over the top of the cake. Melt the chocolate in a heatproof bowl set over a pan of gently simmering water. Pipe thin lines of chocolate over the frosting, then feather the pattern by dragging a clean toothpick across the lines. You need to drag the toothpick alternately from left to right then right to left to create the feathered effect.

VARIATION

Add 2 tablespoons rum or cognac to the chocolate batter instead of the milk. The cake also works well when flavored with grated lemon rind and juice instead of the orange.

Chocolate & Pear Sponge

Fresh pear slices are placed on top of a moist chocolate sponge, making an ingenious combination of flavors for a dessert or snack.

1 hr 15 mins | 1 hr

SERVES 6

INGREDIENTS

6 oz/175 g butter, softened, plus extra for greasing

generous ¾ cup brown sugar

3 eggs, beaten

1⅓ cups self-rising flour

2 tbsp unsweetened cocoa

2 tbsp milk

2 small pears, peeled, cored, and sliced

1 Preheat the oven to 350°F/180°C. Grease an 8-inch/20-cm loose-bottomed cake pan and line the bottom with parchment paper.

2 In a large mixing bowl, cream together the butter and brown sugar until the mixture is pale and fluffy.

3 Gradually add the beaten eggs to the creamed mixture, beating well after each addition to make sure the cake batter is blended smoothly and does not curdle.

4 Sift the flour and unsweetened cocoa into the creamed batter and fold in gently with the milk until combined.

5 Spoon the cake batter into the prepared pan. Smooth the surface with the back of the spoon.

6 Lay the pear slices on top of the cake mixture, arranging them in a radiating pattern.

7 Bake in the preheated oven for about 1 hour, until the cake is just firm to the touch.

8 Let the cake cool in the pan, then transfer to a wire rack to cool completely before serving.

COOK'S TIP
Serve the cake with melted chocolate drizzled over the top for a delicious dessert.

Chocolate Fudge Gâteau

This gâteau is absolutely delicious and combines all of the most wickedly delectable ingredients.

20 mins   35–40 mins

SERVES 10

I N G R E D I E N T S

1 tsp sunflower oil, for oiling

8 oz/225 g butter, softened

1 cup light muscovado sugar

4 eggs, beaten

1½ cups self-rising flour

3 oz/85 g semisweet chocolate

generous ½ cup ground almonds

4 oz/115 g soft vanilla fudge,
   chopped small

F R O S T I N G

6 oz/175 g butter, softened

2½ cups confectioners' sugar, sifted

3–4 tbsp light cream

¼ cup light muscovado sugar

1 tbsp unsweetened cocoa, sifted

T O   D E C O R A T E

2 oz/55 g semisweet chocolate, grated

cocoa-dusted truffles

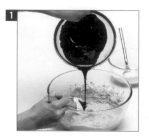

1 Preheat the oven to 350°F/180°C. Lightly oil and line the base of 2 x 8-inch/20-cm shallow cake pans with nonstick baking paper. Melt the chocolate in a heatproof bowl set over a pan of gently simmering water. Cream the butter and sugar together until light and fluffy then gradually add the eggs, beating well between each addition and adding a little flour after each addition. When all the eggs have been added, stir in the melted chocolate and then the remaining flour and mix lightly together.

2 Stir in the ground almonds together with 1–2 tablespoons of cooled boiled water. Mix to form a soft dropping consistency. Stir in the fudge pieces then divide between the 2 lined cake pans and smooth the tops. Bake in the preheated oven for 35–40 minutes or until the tops spring back when touched lightly with a finger. Remove and let cool before turning out on to wire racks and discarding the lining paper. Leave until cold.

3 Beat the butter for the frosting until soft and creamy then gradually beat in the confectioners' sugar, adding a little cream as the mixture becomes stiff. Add the muscovado sugar together with the unsweetened cocoa and stir lightly. Stir in sufficient of the remaining cream to give a soft spreadable frosting.

4 Place the grated chocolate on a sheet of nonstick parchment paper. Split the cakes in half horizontally and sandwich together with a third of the prepared frosting. Spread another third around the sides then roll the cake in the grated chocolate. Place on a serving plate. Spread the top with the remaining frosting, piping rosettes around the outside edge for an attractive finish. Decorate with the truffles before serving.

Praline & Fruit Gâteau

With its chocolate ganache and sponge base, this cake would be ideal to serve at a formal dinner party or a family gathering.

20 mins plus
2 hrs and
8 hrs chilling

🕐 5 mins

SERVES 8

INGREDIENTS

1 tsp sunflower oil, for oiling

2½ cups heavy cream

8 oz/225 g semisweet chocolate

6–8 tbsp Cointreau or Grand Marnier

½ cup granulated sugar

4 tbsp water

⅔ cup whole blanched almonds

1¾ cups fresh fruits such as strawberries (sliced if large), blueberries, and raspberries

12 trifle sponge cakes

1 Lightly oil and line the base of a 2-lb/900-g loaf pan with nonstick parchment paper. To make the ganache, pour 1 cup of the heavy cream into a heavy-based pan. Break the chocolate into small pieces and add to the pan together with 2 tablespoons of the liqueur. Heat gently, stirring until the chocolate has melted and the mixture is smooth. Pour into a bowl, cool then chill for 2 hours, or until set and firm. Whisk the mixture until light and fluffy, and set aside.

2 Place the sugar with the water into a clean heavy-based pan and heat gently until the sugar has dissolved, stirring occasionally. Bring to a boil and boil steadily for 10 minutes or until a light golden caramel forms. Remove from the heat and add the almonds. Pour on to a lightly oiled cookie sheet and leave until cold and set. Place in 1 or 2 thick polythene bags and pound lightly with a rolling pin or mallet until crushed. Set aside. Clean the fruits and set aside.

3 Cut the trifle sponges into thin fingers and place a layer in the base of the loaf pan. Sprinkle with a little of the remaining liqueur. Set aside some pieces of praline for decoration then scatter over half of the remaining crushed praline and then spoon over half of the chocolate ganache. Set aside a few soft fruits for decoration then top with half the prepared fruits. Repeat the layers again, finishing with a layer of sponge.

Cover the top layer with some plastic wrap and weigh down with either clean weights or cans. Leave overnight in the refrigerator.

4 When ready to serve, remove the weights and plastic wrap then invert and turn out. Whip the remaining cream until softly peaking then use to cover the top and sides of the gâteau. Using a fork, make swirls over the cream and decorate with the remaining praline and fruits.

Mincemeat Cake

Use a mincemeat that is suitable for vegetarians so everyone can enjoy this fruity cake.

15 mins

1 hr 45 mins–2 hrs

SERVES 10–12

INGREDIENTS

1 tsp sunflower oil, for oiling

8 oz/225 g butter or margarine, softened

1 cup light muscovado sugar

1 tbsp grated orange rind

4 eggs, beaten

scant 1¾ cups all-purpose flour

3 oz/85 g semisweet chocolate

scant 1 cup ground almonds

1 cup chopped dates

scant ¾ cup candied cherries, chopped

scant ¾ cup glacé fruit, such as mandarins, pineapple, and pears, chopped

14 oz/400 g mincemeat

1 cup whole pieces of glacé fruits, to decorate

1 Preheat the oven to 325°F/160°C. Lightly oil and line the base and sides of a 9-inch/23-cm cake pan with nonstick parchment paper. Cream the butter with the sugar and orange rind until light and fluffy. Gradually beat in the eggs, a little at a time, adding a little flour after each addition. Melt the chocolate in a heatproof bowl set over a pan of gently simmering water.

2 When all the eggs have been added, stir in the remaining flour together with the ground almonds and mix lightly then add the chopped dates, candied cherries, and glacé fruits. Mix lightly.

3 Stir the melted chocolate until smooth then add to the mixture and stir lightly. Finally, add in the mincemeat and mix well then spoon into the prepared cake pan. Smooth the top.

4 Bake in the preheated oven for 25 minutes or until the top is slightly firm. Remove and arrange the whole pieces of glacé fruit on top. Return to the oven and continue to bake for 1 hour 45 minutes–2 hours or until cooked. (Cover the top with foil if the cake browns too quickly.) Remove and let the cake become cold before removing from the pan and discarding the lining paper. Store in an airtight container.

COOK'S TIP

When using melted chocolate in cakes, make sure that the chocolate is thoroughly melted and is cool before adding to the cake mixture.

Caribbean Chocolate Cake

Chocolate and spice are combined in this light cake with a preserved ginger topping.

🕐 1 hr 10 mins   🕐 45–50 mins

MAKES 12 SQUARES

INGREDIENTS

4 oz/115 g butter, plus extra for greasing

1⅔ cups self-rising flour

¼ cup unsweetened cocoa

1 tbsp ground ginger

1 tsp ground cinnamon

½ tsp baking soda

¾ cup light muscovado sugar

2 eggs

1½ tbsp corn syrup

1½ tbsp milk

TOPPING

6 pieces preserved ginger

¾ cup confectioners' sugar

1 tbsp dark rum

a little syrup from the ginger jar

1 Preheat the oven to 325°F/160°C. Grease and base-line a shallow 7-inch/18-cm square cake pan. Sift the flour, unsweetened cocoa, ginger, cinnamon, and baking soda into a bowl. Rub in the butter, then stir in the sugar. Make a well in the center.

2 Put the eggs in a bowl with the syrup and milk. Whisk together, then pour into the dry ingredients and beat until smooth and glossy. Spoon the cake batter into the prepared pan and bake in the preheated oven for 45–50 minutes, until well risen and firm to the touch. Leave in the pan for 30 minutes, then transfer to a wire rack to cool completely.

3 For the topping, cut each piece of preserved ginger into quarters and arrange on top of the cake. Sift the confectioners' sugar into a bowl and stir in the rum and enough of the ginger syrup to make a smooth frosting. Drizzle the frosting over the cake and let set. Cut the cake into squares to serve.

COOK'S TIP
This cake benefits from being kept in an airtight container for a day before eating.

Chocolate & Walnut Cake

This walnut-studded chocolate cake has a creamy butter frosting. It is perfect for entertaining because it can be made the day before.

1 hr   45 mins

SERVES 8

INGREDIENTS

2 tsp melted butter, for greasing

4 eggs

⅔ cup superfine sugar

2¾ oz/75 g semisweet chocolate, broken into pieces

scant 1 cup all-purpose flour

1 tbsp unsweetened cocoa

2 tbsp butter, melted

1 cup walnuts, chopped finely

FROSTING

2¾ oz/75 g semisweet chocolate

4 oz/115 g butter

1½ cups confectioners' sugar

2 tbsp milk

walnut halves, to decorate

1 Preheat the oven to 325°F/160°C. Grease and line a deep, round, 7-inch/18-cm cake pan. Place the eggs and superfine sugar in a bowl and whisk with an electric whisk for 10 minutes, or until foamy, and a trail is left when the whisk is dragged across the surface. Put the chocolate in a heatproof bowl set over a pan of gently simmering water until melted.

2 Sift the flour and unsweetened cocoa together and fold into the eggs and sugar with a spoon or a spatula. Fold in the melted butter, melted chocolate, and chopped walnuts. Pour into the pan and bake in the preheated oven for 30–35 minutes, or until springy to the touch.

3 Let cool in the pan for 5 minutes, then transfer to a wire rack and let cool completely.

4 To make the frosting, melt the chocolate and let it cool slightly. Beat together the butter, confectioners' sugar, and milk until the mixture is pale and fluffy. Whisk in the melted chocolate.

5 Cut the cake into 2 layers of equal thickness. Place the bottom half on a serving plate, spread with some of the frosting, and put the other half on top. Smooth the remaining frosting over the top of the cake with a spatula, swirling it slightly as you do so for a decorative effect. Decorate the cake with walnut halves, and serve.

German Chocolate Cake

This is a classic German cake, made with chocolate and hazelnuts, which is lovely served with a cup of coffee or tea.

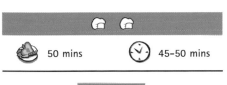

50 mins   45–50 mins

SERVES 8

INGREDIENTS

6 oz/175 g butter, sweet for preference, softened, plus extra for greasing

all-purpose flour, for dusting

generous 1 cup dark muscovado sugar

1 cup self-rising flour

1 tbsp unsweetened cocoa

1 tsp ground allspice

3 eggs, beaten

scant 1 cup ground hazelnuts

2 tbsp black coffee

sifted confectioners' sugar, to decorate

1 Preheat the oven to 350°F/180°C. Grease and flour a 7½-inch/19-cm kugelhopf pan. Put the butter and sugar in a bowl and beat until light and fluffy. Sift the flour, unsweetened cocoa, and allspice into a bowl.

2 Beat the eggs into the creamed mixture, one at a time, adding 1 tablespoon of the flour mixture with the second and third eggs. Fold in the remaining flour, unsweetened cocoa ground hazelnuts, and coffee.

3 Turn into the prepared pan and bake in the preheated oven for 45-50 minutes, until the cake springs back when the top is lightly pressed. Leave in the pan for 10 minutes, then turn out on to a wire rack to cool. Dust generously with confectioners' sugar before serving.

COOK'S NOTE
A kugelhopf pan is a special fluted ring pan. If you do not have one, use a 9-inch/23-cm ring mold instead.

Chocolate Almond Cake

Chocolate and almonds complement each other perfectly in this delicious cake. Be warned though, one slice will never be enough!

2 hrs plus
30 mins chilling

40 mins

SERVES 8

INGREDIENTS

6 oz/175 g butter, plus extra for greasing

6 oz/175 g semisweet chocolate

½ cup superfine sugar

4 eggs, separated

¼ tsp cream of tartar

⅓ cup self-rising flour

1¼ cups ground almonds

1 tsp almond extract

TOPPING

4½ oz/125 g milk chocolate

2 tbsp butter

4 tbsp heavy cream

TO DECORATE

2 tbsp toasted slivered almonds

1 oz/25 g semisweet chocolate, melted

1 Preheat the oven to 375°F/190°C. Lightly grease and base-line a 9-inch/ 23-cm round springform pan. Break the chocolate into small pieces and place in a small pan with the butter. Heat gently, stirring until melted and well combined.

2 Place half of the superfine sugar in a bowl with the egg yolks and whisk until pale and creamy. Add the melted chocolate and butter mixture, beating until well combined.

3 Sift the cream of tartar and flour together and fold into the chocolate cake batter with the ground almonds and almond extract.

4 Whisk the egg whites in a bowl until soft peaks form. Add the remaining superfine sugar and whisk for about 2 minutes by hand, or 45–60 seconds if using an electric whisk, until thick and glossy. Fold the egg whites into the chocolate cake batter and spoon into the pan. Bake in preheated oven for 40 minutes, until just springy to the touch. Let cool.

5 To make the topping, heat the ingredients in a heatproof bowl set over a pan of gently simmering water. Remove from the heat and beat for 2 minutes. Let chill for 30 minutes. Transfer the cake to a serving plate and spread with the topping. Melt the semisweet chocolate in a heatproof bowl set over a pan of gently simmering water. Scatter the cake with the slivered almonds and drizzle with the melted chocolate. Let the topping set for 2 hours before serving.

Family Chocolate Cake

A simple to make cake, ideal for a family treat. Keep the decoration simple—you could use a store-bought frosting or filling, if liked.

🍴 1 hr 🕐 30 mins

SERVES 8

INGREDIENTS

4 oz/115 g soft margarine, plus extra for greasing

½ cup superfine sugar

2 eggs

1 tbsp corn syrup

1 cup self-rising flour, sifted

2 tbsp unsweetened cocoa, sifted

FILLING AND TOPPING

4 tbsp confectioners' sugar, sifted

2 tbsp butter

3½ oz/100 g white or milk cooking chocolate

a little milk or white chocolate, for melting

1 Preheat the oven to 375°F/190°C. Lightly grease 2 x 7-inch/18-cm layer cake pans.

2 Place all of the ingredients for the cake in a large mixing bowl and beat with an electric whisk until smooth.

3 Divide the batter among the prepared pans and smooth the tops. Bake in the preheated oven for 20 minutes, or until springy to the touch. Let cool for a few minutes in the pans, then transfer to a wire rack to cool completely.

4 To make the filling, beat the confectioners' sugar and butter together until light and fluffy. Melt the cooking chocolate in a heatproof bowl set over a pan of gently simmering water. Beat half into the frosting mixture and use to sandwich the cakes together.

5 Spread the remaining melted cooking chocolate over the top of the cake. In a separate heatproof bowl, melt a little milk or white chocolate (see step 4). Pipe circles of contrasting melted milk or white chocolate and feather into the cooking chocolate by dragging lines through the circles using a clean toothpick. Let set before serving.

COOK'S TIP
Ensure that you eat this cake on the day of baking, because it does not keep well.

Chocolate Slab Cake

This chocolate slab cake gets its moist texture from the sour cream, which is stirred into the beaten mixture.

55 mins   50 mins

SERVES 4

INGREDIENTS

7 oz/200 g butter, plus extra for greasing

3½ oz/100 g bittersweet chocolate, broken into pieces

⅓ cup water

2½ cups all-purpose flour

2 tsp baking powder

1⅓ cups brown sugar

⅓ cup sour cream

2 eggs, beaten

FROSTING

7 oz/200 g bittersweet chocolate

6 tbsp water

3 tbsp light cream

1 tbsp butter, chilled

1 Preheat the oven to 375°F/190°C. Grease a 13 x 8-inch/33 x 20-cm square cake pan and line the bottom with parchment paper. Melt the butter and chocolate with the water in a pan over low heat, stirring frequently.

2 Sift the flour and baking powder into a mixing bowl and stir in the sugar.

3 Pour the hot chocolate liquid into the bowl and then beat well until all of the ingredients are evenly mixed. Stir in the sour cream, followed by the eggs.

4 Pour the cake batter into the cake pan and bake in the preheated oven for 40–45 minutes, until springy to the touch.

5 Let the cake cool slightly in the pan before turning it out on to a wire rack. Let cool completely.

6 To make the frosting, melt the chocolate with the water in a pan over very low heat, stir in the cream and remove from the heat. Stir in the chilled butter, then pour the frosting over the cooled cake, using a spatula to spread it evenly over the top of the cake.

COOK'S TIP
Put the cake on the wire rack to frost it, and place a large cookie sheet underneath to catch any drips.

Chilled Rum Chocolate Cake

Apart from melting the chocolate, this delicious refrigerator cake requires no cooking at all!

10 mins
plus 8 hrs
soaking/chilling

2 mins

SERVES 10–12

INGREDIENTS

2 tbsp dark rum

⅓ cup raisins

3 oz/85 g butter, sweet for preference

3 tbsp corn syrup

6 oz/175 g semisweet chocolate

8 oz/225 g graham crackers, crushed

⅓ cup candied cherries, halved

½ cup macadamia nuts, chopped coarsely

grated rind of 1 orange

TOPPING

2 oz/55 g semisweet chocolate, broken into pieces

2 tbsp butter, sweet for preference

a little white chocolate, to decorate

1 Put the rum and raisins in a bowl and let soak for several hours, or preferably overnight. Line a 1-lb/450-g loaf pan with plastic wrap. Put the butter, corn syrup, and chocolate in a pan and heat gently until the chocolate has melted. Remove from the heat and stir in the raisins, crushed graham crackers, cherries, nuts, and grated orange rind.

2 Transfer the cake batter to the prepared pan. Let chill until firm. Turn the cake out on to a serving plate and remove the plastic wrap.

3 To make the topping, put the semisweet chocolate and butter in a heatproof bowl set over a pan of gently simmering water and heat until melted. Stir until smooth, then spread over the top and sides of the cake. In a separate bowl, melt the white chocolate and drizzle over the top of the cake. Let chill until the topping has set. Serve cut into thin slices.

COOK'S TIP
If you omit the chocolate topping, this cake is perfect for cutting into small pieces to serve with coffee after dinner.

No-Bake Refrigerator Cake

Ideal for children to make, with help to melt the chocolate, this cake needs no baking and is quickly prepared—but requires chilling overnight.

20 mins plus 12 hrs chilling

5–8 mins

MAKES 8½ x 4¼-INCH/22 x 11-CM CAKE

INGREDIENTS

7 oz/200 g butter, sweet for preference, diced

8 oz/225 g semisweet chocolate, broken into pieces

⅓ cup chopped candied cherries

½ cup chopped walnuts

12 rectangular semisweet chocolate cookies

1 Line a 1-lb/450-g loaf pan with waxed paper or parchment paper.

2 Put the butter and chocolate in a heatproof bowl set over a pan of gently simmering water. Stir constantly over low heat until they have melted and the mixture is smooth. Remove from the heat and cool slightly.

3 In a separate bowl, mix together the cherries and walnuts. Spoon one-third of the chocolate mixture into the prepared pan, cover with a layer of cookies, and top with half the cherries and walnuts. Make further layers, ending with the chocolate mixture. Cover with plastic wrap and let chill in the refrigerator for at least 12 hours. When chilled, turn the cake out on to a serving dish.

Chocolate Cake with Syrup

An intensely flavored chocolate cake that is particularly good served slightly warm, with sour cream, as a dessert.

🍰 15 mins 🕐 50 mins

SERVES 12

I N G R E D I E N T S

4 oz/115 g unsalted butter,
   plus extra for greasing

8 oz/225 g semisweet chocolate,
   broken into pieces

1 tbsp strong black coffee

4 large eggs

2 egg yolks

generous ½ cup golden superfine sugar

generous ⅓ cup all-purpose flour

2 tsp ground cinnamon

scant ½ cup ground almonds

chocolate-covered coffee beans,
   to decorate

S Y R U P

1¼ cups strong black coffee

generous ½ cup golden superfine sugar

1 cinnamon stick

1 Preheat the oven to 375°F/190°C. Grease and base-line the bottom of a deep 8-inch/20-cm round cake pan. Place the chocolate, butter, and coffee in a heatproof bowl and set over a pan of gently simmering water until melted. Stir to blend, then remove from the heat and let cool slightly.

2 Place the whole eggs, egg yolks, and sugar in a separate bowl and whisk together until thick and pale. Sift the flour and cinnamon over the egg mixture. Add the almonds and the chocolate mixture and fold in carefully. Spoon the cake batter into the prepared pan. Bake in the preheated oven for 35 minutes, or until the tip of a knife inserted into the center comes out clean. Let cool slightly before turning out on to a serving plate.

3 Meanwhile, make the syrup. Place the coffee, sugar, and cinnamon stick in a heavy-based pan and heat gently, stirring, until the sugar has dissolved. Increase the heat and boil for 5 minutes, or until reduced and thickened slightly. Keep warm. Pierce the surface of the cake with a toothpick, then drizzle over half the coffee syrup. Decorate with chocolate-covered coffee beans and serve, cut into wedges, with the remaining coffee syrup.

Chocolate & Mango Layer

Canned peaches can be used instead of mangoes for this deliciously moist cake if you prefer.

1 hr 15 mins   1 hr 10 mins

SERVES 12

INGREDIENTS

butter, for greasing

½ cup unsweetened cocoa

⅔ cup boiling water

6 large eggs

1½ cups superfine sugar

2½ cups self-rising flour

1 lb 12 oz/800 g canned mangoes

1 tsp cornstarch

generous 1¾ cups heavy cream

2¾ oz/75 g grated semisweet chocolate

1 Preheat the oven to 325°F/170°C. Grease a deep 9-inch/23-cm round cake pan and base-line the bottom with parchment paper.

2 Place the unsweetened cocoa in a small bowl and gradually add the boiling water; blend to form a smooth paste.

3 Place the eggs and superfine sugar in a mixing bowl and whisk until the mixture is very thick and creamy. Fold in the cocoa mixture. Sift the flour and fold into the batter.

4 Pour the batter into the pan and smooth the top. Bake in the preheated oven for about 1 hour, or until springy to the touch.

5 Let the cake cool in the pan for a few minutes, then turn out and cool completely on a wire rack. Peel off the lining paper and cut the cake into 3 layers.

6 Drain the mangoes, reserving the juice, and put a quarter of them in a food processor and blend until smooth. Mix the cornstarch with about 3 tablespoons of the mango juice to form a smooth paste. Add to the blended mangoes. Transfer to a small pan and heat gently, stirring until the paste thickens. Let cool.

7 Chop the remaining mango. Whip the cream and reserve about one quarter. Fold the mango into the remaining cream and use to sandwich the layers of cake together. Place on a serving plate. Spread some of the remaining cream around the side of the cake. Press the grated chocolate lightly into the cream. Spread the mango paste over the center and pipe cream rosettes to form a decorative edge.

Devil's Food Cake

This classic melt-in-the-mouth chocolate cake, is given a tangy citrus-flavored frosting in this recipe.

🍰 1 hr   🕐 30 mins

SERVES 6

INGREDIENTS

butter for greasing

3½ oz/100 g semisweet chocolate, broken into pieces

2¼ cups self-rising flour

1 tsp baking soda

1 cup butter

2⅔ cups brown sugar

1 tsp vanilla extract

3 eggs

½ cup buttermilk

scant 1 cup boiling water

FROSTING

1¼ cups superfine sugar

2 egg whites

1 tbsp lemon juice

3 tbsp orange juice

candied orange rind, to decorate

1 Preheat the oven to 375°F/190°C. Grease and base-line 2 x 8-inch/20-cm layer cake pans. Put the chocolate in a heatproof bowl set over a pan of gently simmering water until melted. Sift the flour and baking soda together.

2 Beat the butter and sugar in a bowl until pale and fluffy. Beat in the vanilla extract and the eggs one at a time, beating well after each addition. Add a little flour if the mixture starts to curdle.

3 Fold the melted chocolate into the mixture until well blended. Gradually fold in the remaining flour, then stir in the buttermilk and boiling water.

4 Divide the batter among the pans and smooth the tops. Bake in the preheated oven for 30 minutes, until springy to the touch. Let the cakes cool in the pans for 5 minutes, then transfer to a wire rack to cool completely.

5 Place the frosting ingredients in a large heatproof bowl set over a pan of gently simmering water. Whisk until thickened and forming soft peaks. Remove from the heat and whisk until the mixture is cool.

6 Sandwich the 2 cakes together with a little of the frosting. Spread the remainder over the sides and top of the cake, swirling it as you do so. Decorate with the candied orange rind.

Chocolate & Pineapple Cake

Decorated with thick yogurt and canned pineapple, this is a lowfat cake, but it is by no means lacking in flavor.

40 mins   20–25 mins

SERVES 9

I N G R E D I E N T S

6 oz/175 g lowfat spread, plus extra for greasing

scant ¾ cup superfine sugar

generous ¾ cup self-rising flour, sifted

3 tbsp unsweetened cocoa, sifted

1½ tsp baking powder

2 eggs

8 oz/225 g canned pineapple pieces in natural juice

½ cup lowfat thick plain yogurt

about 1 tbsp confectioners' sugar

grated chocolate, to decorate

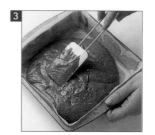

1 Preheat the oven to 375°F/190°C. Lightly grease an 8-inch/20-cm square cake pan with lowfat spread.

2 Place the lowfat spread, superfine sugar, flour, unsweetened cocoa, baking powder, and eggs in a large mixing bowl. Beat with a wooden spoon or electric whisk until smooth.

3 Pour the cake batter into the prepared pan and smooth the surface. Bake in the preheated oven for 20–25 minutes, or until springy to the touch. Let cool slightly in the pan before transferring to a wire rack to cool completely.

4 Drain the pineapple, chop the pineapple pieces, and drain again. Reserve some pineapple pieces for the decoration, then stir the remainder into the yogurt, and sweeten to taste with confectioners' sugar.

5 Spread the pineapple and yogurt mixture over the cake and decorate with the reserved pineapple pieces. Sprinkle with the grated chocolate.

Raspberry Dessert Cake

The raspberries in this cake give it a fresh tangy flavour. Serve with fresh raspberries and whipped cream.

35 mins

40–50 mins

SERVES 8–10

INGREDIENTS

8 oz/225 g butter, plus extra for greasing

9 oz/250 g semisweet chocolate

1 tbsp strong black coffee

5 medium eggs

scant ¼ cup golden superfine sugar

⅔ cup all-purpose flour, sifted

1 tsp ground cinnamon

⅔ cup fresh raspberries

confectioners' sugar, for dusting

TO SERVE

fresh raspberries

whipped cream

1 Preheat the oven to 325°F/160°C. Grease and base-line a 9-inch/23-cm cake pan. Put the chocolate, butter, and coffee in a heatproof bowl set over a pan of gently simmering water and heat until melted. Stir and let cool slightly.

2 Put the eggs and sugar in a bowl and beat until thick and pale. Gently fold in the chocolate. Sift the flour and cinnamon into a bowl, then fold into the chocolate mixture. Pour into the prepared pan and sprinkle the raspberries evenly over the top.

3 Bake in the preheated oven for 35-45 minutes, until the cake is well risen and springy to the touch. Let cool in the pan for 15 minutes before turning out on to a large plate. Dust with confectioners' sugar before serving with raspberries and cream.

VARIATION
Frozen raspberries may be used if fresh are not available. Thaw thoroughly and drain off any excess juice before using.

Chocolate Tropical Fruit Cake

This cake is ideal for a summer lunch party, an informal tea, or an elegant dinner party. You can, of course, vary the fruits.

25 mins plus 2 hrs chilling

20–25 mins

SERVES 10

I N G R E D I E N T S

1 tsp sunflower oil, for oiling

generous ½ cup all-purpose flour

2 tbsp unsweetened cocoa

3 large eggs

½ cup superfine sugar

3 level tbsp sweet butter, melted

1 small mango, peeled, pitted, and chopped

1 papaya, seeded, pitted, and chopped

1 kiwi, peeled and sliced

fresh coconut shavings, to decorate

F R O S T I N G

8 oz/225 g semisweet chocolate

1 cup heavy cream

1 tbsp framboise or cognac

½ cup toasted chopped hazelnuts

1 Preheat the oven to 375°F/190°C. Sift the flour and unsweetened cocoa together twice and set aside. Lightly oil and line the base of a 9-inch/23-cm cake pan with nonstick parchment paper.

2 Place the eggs and sugar in a heatproof bowl set over a pan of gently simmering water. Whisk until very thick and creamy and doubled in volume. Remove the bowl from the pan and continue to whisk until the mixture has cooled.

3 Gently stir in the sifted flour and then the butter in a figure-of-eight action, taking care not to over-mix. Pour the mixture into the prepared pan and bake in

the center of the preheated oven for 20–25 minutes or until the top springs back when touched lightly with a finger. Remove from the oven and let cool for 10 minutes. Turn out on to a wire rack and discard the lining paper. Leave until cold before decorating.

4 Meanwhile make the frosting. Break the chocolate into small pieces and place in a heavy-based pan together with the cream and framboise. Heat gently, stirring frequently until smooth. Pour into a bowl, large enough to accommodate a whisk. Let cool then chill until completely cold. When ready to use whisk the frosting until light and fluffy.

5 Split the cooled cake in half and sandwich together with one-third of the frosting, pressing the halves lightly together.

6 Spread half of the remaining frosting over the sides of the cake and press on the nuts. Spread the remaining frosting over the top, swirling to give a decorative effect. Decorate with the chopped fruits and serve. Store in the refrigerator and use within 2–3 days.

Chocolate & Prune Gâteau

Using prunes in place of any butter may sound a little strange but in fact it works extremely well, giving a very moist, rich cake.

20 mins plus 2 hrs marinating — 30–35 mins

SERVES 10–12

INGREDIENTS

1 tsp sunflower oil, for oiling

scant 1½ cups ready-to-eat dried prunes

4 tbsp cognac

¾ cup superfine sugar

3 eggs, beaten

3oz/85 g semisweet chocolate

generous 1 cup ground almonds

scant ½ cup all-purpose flour, sifted

1 tsp baking powder, sifted

TOPPING

4 oz/115 g semisweet chocolate

1 tbsp butter

1 tbsp corn syrup

generous ½ cup heavy cream

dragees, to decorate

1 Preheat the oven to 375°F/190°C. Lightly oil and line the base of a 23-cm/9-inch cake pan. Snip the prunes into small pieces and place in a bowl. Pour over the cognac and leave for up to 2 hours or until the cognac has been absorbed. Place in a food processor or blender and process to form a purée.

2 Place the prune purée in the bowl of a free-standing mixer or in a bowl set over a pan of gently simmering water. Add the sugar and whisk until well incorporated. Add the eggs and continue to whisk until the mixture is very thick and creamy. (Remove from the heat, if applicable, and continue to whisk until cool.)

3 Melt the chocolate in a heatproof bowl set over a pan of gently simmering water. Stir until smooth and gently mix into the mixture. Add the ground almonds, flour, and baking powder then, stirring very lightly, mix until thoroughly incorporated, adding 2–3 tablespoons of cooled boiled water to give a soft dropping consistency. Turn into the prepared cake pan, tap lightly on the work counter to remove any air bubbles, and level the surface. Bake in the preheated oven for 30–35 minutes or until the top springs back when touched lightly with a clean finger. Remove from the oven

and let cool before removing from the tin and discarding the lining paper.

4 Break the chocolate into small pieces and place in a heavy-based pan and add the butter, syrup, and cream. Heat gently, stirring frequently until the mixture is smooth. Remove from the heat, leave to cool until thickened, stirring occasionally.

5 Spoon the cooled chocolate frosting over the top and sides of the cake, swirling to give a decorative effect. Let set before decorating with the dragees.

Chocolate Passion Cake

What could be nicer than passion cake with added chocolate? Rich and moist, this cake is fabulous with afternoon tea.

55 mins   55 mins

SERVES 6

I N G R E D I E N T S

butter, for greasing

5 eggs

⅔ cup superfine sugar

1¼ cups all-purpose flour

⅓ cup unsweetened cocoa

2 carrots, peeled, grated finely, and squeezed until dry

⅓ cup chopped walnuts

2 tbsp sunflower oil

12 oz/350 g medium-fat cream cheese

1½ cups confectioners' sugar

6 oz/175 g milk or semisweet chocolate, melted

1 Preheat the oven to 375°F/190°C. Lightly grease and base-line an 8-inch/20-cm deep round cake pan.

2 Place the eggs and sugar in a large mixing bowl set over a pan of gently simmering water and whisk until very thick. Lift the whisk up and let the mixture drizzle back—it will leave a trail for a few seconds when thick enough.

3 Remove the bowl from the heat. Sift the flour and unsweetened cocoa into the bowl and carefully fold in. Fold in the grated carrots, walnuts, and oil until they are just combined.

4 Pour into the prepared pan and bake in the preheated oven for 45 minutes. Let the cake cool slightly, then turn out on to a wire rack to cool completely.

5 Beat together the cream cheese and confectioners' sugar until combined. Beat in the melted chocolate. Split the cake in half and sandwich together again with half of the chocolate mixture. Cover the top of the cake with the remainder of the chocolate mixture, swirling it with a knife. Let chill, or serve at once.

COOK'S TIP

The undecorated cake can be frozen for up to 2 months. Thaw at room temperature for 3 hours or overnight in the refrigerator.

Marble Cake

This cake looks impressive but is easy to make. Just drag a skewer through two contrasting cake batters to create a marbled effect.

🍮 45 mins   🕐 60–70 mins

MAKES 10 SLICES

INGREDIENTS

8 oz/225 g butter, softened, plus extra
  for greasing

2 oz/55 g semisweet chocolate

1 tbsp strong black coffee

2 cups self-rising flour

1 tsp baking powder

generous 1 cup golden superfine sugar

4 eggs, beaten

½ cup ground almonds

2 tbsp milk

1 tsp vanilla extract

FROSTING

4½ oz/125 g semisweet chocolate

2 tbsp butter

2 tbsp water

1 Preheat the oven to 350°F/180°C. Grease a 3-pint/1.7-liter ring mold. Put the chocolate and coffee in a heatproof bowl set over a pan of gently simmering water. Heat until melted. Let cool. Sift the flour and baking powder into a bowl. Add the butter, sugar, eggs, ground almonds, and milk. Beat well until smooth.

2 Transfer one half of the batter to another bowl and stir in the vanilla extract. Stir the cooled soft chocolate into the other half of the batter. Place spoonfuls of the 2 batters alternately into the ring mold, then drag a skewer through to create a marbled effect. Smooth the top. Bake in the preheated oven for 50-60 minutes, until risen and a skewer inserted into the center comes out clean. Leave in the mold for 5 minutes, then turn out on to a wire rack to cool.

3 To make the frosting, put the chocolate, butter, and water in a heatproof bowl set over a pan of simmering water. Heat until melted. Stir and pour over the cake, working quickly to coat the top and sides. Let set before serving.

COOK'S TIP

If you prefer a plain cake, omit the frosting and simply dust the top of the cake with sifted confectioners' sugar.

Orange Marble Cake

Separate chocolate and orange cake batters are combined in a ring mold to achieve the marbled effect in this light sponge.

40 mins   30–35 mins

SERVES 8

INGREDIENTS

6 oz/175 g butter, softened, plus extra
   for greasing

¾ cup superfine sugar

3 eggs, beaten

1 cup self-rising flour, sifted

¼ cup unsweetened cocoa, sifted

5–6 tbsp orange juice

grated rind of 1 orange

1 Preheat the oven to 350°F/180°C. Lightly grease a 10-inch/25-cm ring mold.

2 In a mixing bowl, cream together the butter and sugar with an electric whisk for about 5 minutes.

3 Add the beaten eggs a little at a time, whisking well after each addition.

4 Using a metal spoon, fold the flour into the creamed mixture carefully, then spoon half of the cake batter into a separate mixing bowl.

5 Fold the unsweetened cocoa and half of the orange juice into the cake batter in one of the bowls and mix gently.

6 Fold the remaining orange juice and orange rind into the cake batter in the other bowl and mix gently.

7 Place alternate spoonfuls of each cake batter around the mold, then drag a skewer through them to create a marbled effect.

8 Bake in the preheated oven for 30–35 minutes, until well risen and a skewer inserted into the center comes out clean.

9 Let the cake cool in the mold before turning out on to a wire rack.

VARIATION
For a richer chocolate flavor, add ¼ cup chocolate chips to the unsweetened cocoa batter.

Moist Chocolate Cake

The sweetness of whipped marshmallow frosting complements the mouthwatering flavor of this moist semisweet chocolate sponge.

30 mins plus 1 hr cooling

55 mins

MAKES 6-INCH/15-CM CAKE

I N G R E D I E N T S

3¼ oz/90 g butter, sweet for preference, plus extra for greasing

generous 1 cup superfine sugar

½ tsp vanilla extract

2 eggs, beaten lightly

3 oz/85 g semisweet chocolate, broken into pieces

⅔ cup buttermilk

1¼ cups self-rising flour

½ tsp baking soda

pinch of salt

2 oz/55 g milk chocolate, grated, to decorate

F R O S T I N G

6 oz/175 g white marshmallows

1 tbsp milk

2 egg whites

2 tbsp superfine sugar

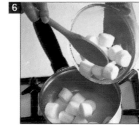

1 Preheat the oven to 325°F/160°C. Grease a 3¾-cup ovenproof bowl with butter. Cream the butter, sugar, and vanilla together until pale and fluffy, then gradually beat in the eggs.

2 Melt the semisweet chocolate in a heatproof bowl over a pan of gently simmering water. When the chocolate has melted, stir in the buttermilk gradually, until well combined. Remove the pan from the heat and let cool slightly.

3 Sift the flour, baking soda, and salt into a separate bowl.

4 Add the chocolate mixture alternately with the flour mixture to the creamed mixture, a little at a time. Spoon the batter into the ovenproof bowl and smooth the surface.

5 Bake in the preheated oven for about 50 minutes, until a skewer inserted into the center of the cake comes out clean. Turn out on to a wire rack to cool.

6 Meanwhile, make the frosting. Put the marshmallows and milk in a small pan and heat very gently until the

marshmallows have melted. Remove the pan from the heat and let cool.

7 Whisk the egg whites until soft peaks form, then add the sugar and continue whisking, until stiff peaks form. Fold the egg white into the cooled marshmallow mixture and set aside for 10 minutes.

8 When the cake is cool, cover the top and sides with the marshmallow frosting. Top with grated milk chocolate.

Rippled Chocolate Gâteau

The frosting on this gâteau has a wonderfully crunchy texture because it includes muscovado sugar, which does not completely dissolve.

30 mins   25–30 mins

SERVES 10

INGREDIENTS

1 tsp sunflower oil, for oiling

6 oz/175 g butter or margarine, softened

1½ cups superfine sugar

1 tsp vanilla extract

3 eggs, beaten

1 cup self-rising flour

¼ cup ground almonds

1 oz/25 g semisweet chocolate

FROSTING

8 oz/225 g semisweet chocolate, broken into pieces

5 tbsp butter

2 tbsp maple or corn syrup

generous ½ cup dark muscovado sugar

TO DECORATE

generous ¼ cup slivered almonds, toasted

chocolate shavings

1 Preheat the oven to 375°F/190°C. Oil and line the bases of 2 x 7-inch/ 18-cm shallow cake pans with parchment paper. Cream the butter, sugar, and vanilla extract until light and fluffy. Add the eggs a little at a time, adding a little flour after each addition. When all the eggs have been added stir in the remaining flour and the ground almonds. Add 1–2 tablespoons of cooled boiled water and mix lightly to form a smooth dropping consistency.

2 Melt the 1 oz/25 g of chocolate in a heatproof bowl set over a pan of gently simmering water. Stir until smooth then pour over the cake batter and gently mix in a figure-of-eight action. Take care not to over-mix or the rippled effect will be lost. Divide between the 2 cake pans and smooth the tops. Tap lightly on the work counter to remove any air bubbles.

3 Bake in the preheated oven for 25–30 minutes or until golden and the top springs back when touched lightly with a finger. Remove from the oven and leave for 10 minutes before transferring to a wire rack and discarding the lining paper. Leave until cold before frosting.

4 To make the frosting, break the chocolate into small pieces and place in a heavy-based pan and add the butter and maple syrup. Heat gently, stirring frequently, until the chocolate has melted and the mixture is smooth. Add the sugar and stir gently until the mixture is well blended. Leave until cool and beginning to thicken. Beat occasionally during this time.

5 Split each cake in half and use one-third of the cooled frosting to sandwich the 4 layers together. Spread an additional third round the sides of the cake and roll in the toasted slivered almonds. Spoon the remaining frosting on top and spread with a swirling action to give a decorative effect. Sprinkle with the chocolate shavings to serve. Store in an airtight container.

Chocolate Chiffon Cake

This delicious cake has a thick layer of crushed praline in the center and on the top which provides a delicious crunch.

30 mins   **25 mins**

SERVES 8–10

INGREDIENTS

1 tsp sunflower oil, for oiling

3 large eggs, separated

¾ cup superfine sugar

4 tbsp sunflower oil

1½ oz/40 g semisweet chocolate

1 tbsp unsweetened cocoa

scant ¾ cup all-purpose flour

1 tsp cream of tartar

PRALINE

½ cup granulated sugar

¼ cup water

½ cup blanched almonds

FROSTING AND DECORATION

4 oz/115 g butter or margarine, softened

2 cup confectioners' sugar, sifted

1 tbsp unsweetened cocoa, sifted

1–2 tbsp strong black coffee

⅓ cup toasted slivered almonds

few whole almonds

1 Preheat the oven to 350°F/180°C. Lightly oil and line the bases of 2 x 7-inch/18-cm shallow cake pans and 1 x cookie sheet.

2 To make the praline, heat the sugar and water together in a heavy-based pan, stirring frequently until the sugar has dissolved. Bring to a boil and boil steadily for 10 minutes or until a golden caramel is formed. Remove from the heat and add the almonds. Pour the praline onto the oiled cookie sheet and leave until cold. Place in a polythene bag and pound with a rolling pin until crushed.

3 Place the egg yolks with the sugar in a mixing bowl set over a bowl of gently simmering water. Whisk until very thick and creamy and a trail is left when the whisk is dragged across the surface. (Alternatively, whisk the egg yolks and sugar in the bowl of a free-standing mixer.) Remove from the heat and whisk until cool.

4 Whisk in the sunflower oil together with 2 tablespoons of cooled boiled water. Melt the chocolate in a heatproof bowl set over a pan of gently simmering water. Gently stir in the melted chocolate. Sift the unsweetened cocoa with the flour and cream of tartar and stir into the egg mixture. Whisk the egg whites until stiff peaks form then fold into the mixture and stir lightly. Spoon into the prepared cake pans and bake in the preheated oven for 25 minutes or until the top springs back when touched lightly with a finger. Remove and let cool before removing from the pans and discarding the lining paper. Leave until cold.

5 To make the frosting, cream the butter until soft then gradually beat in the confectioners' sugar together with the unsweetened cocoa and the strong black coffee to give a soft spreading consistency. Spread over one cake and scatter with most of the crushed praline. Place the second cake on top and press lightly together.

6 Spread half the remaining frosting round the sides of the cake then roll in the slivered almonds and transfer to a serving plate. Spread the remaining frosting over the top and sprinkle with the remaining praline. Arrange a few whole almonds on top and serve.

Orange Mousse Cake

With a semisweet chocolate sponge sandwiched together with a light, creamy orange mousse, this spectacular cake is irresistible.

1 hr 15 mins   40 mins

SERVES 12

INGREDIENTS

6 oz/175 g butter, plus extra for greasing

¾ cup superfine sugar

4 eggs, beaten lightly

1 tbsp unsweetened cocoa

1¾ cups self-rising flour

1¾ oz/50 g semisweet, orange-flavored chocolate, melted

ORANGE MOUSSE

2 eggs, separated

4 tbsp superfine sugar

generous ¾ cup freshly squeezed orange juice

2 tsp powdered gelatin

3 tbsp water

1¼ cups heavy cream

peeled orange slices, to decorate

1 Preheat the oven to 350°F/180°C. Grease and base-line an 8-inch/20-cm springform cake pan. Beat the butter and sugar in a bowl until light and fluffy. Gradually add the eggs, beating well after each addition. Sift the unsweetened cocoa and flour together and fold into the cake batter. Fold in the chocolate.

2 Pour into the prepared pan and smooth the top. Bake in the preheated oven for 40 minutes or until springy to the touch. Let the cake cool for 5 minutes in the pan, then turn out and cool completely on a wire rack.

3 Meanwhile, make the orange mousse. Beat the egg yolks and sugar until light, then whisk in the orange juice. Sprinkle the gelatin over the water in a small bowl and let it go spongy, then place over a pan of hot water and stir until the gelatin has dissolved. Stir into the mousse.

4 Whip the cream until holding its shape, reserve a little for decoration and fold the rest into the mousse. Whisk the egg whites until soft peaks form, then fold in. Let stand in a cool place until starting to set, stirring occasionally.

5 Half the cold cake and place one half in the pan. Pour in the mousse and press the second half on top. Chill until set. Transfer to a dish, pipe cream rosettes on the top, and arrange orange slices in the center.

Chocolate Yogurt Cake

Adding yogurt to the cake mixture gives the finished cake a deliciously moist texture.

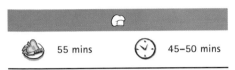

55 mins   45–50 mins

SERVES 8

INGREDIENTS

butter, for greasing

⅔ cup vegetable oil

⅔ cup whole milk unsweetened yogurt

1¼ cups brown sugar

3 eggs, beaten

¾ cup whole-wheat self-rising flour

1 cup self-rising flour, sifted

2 tbsp unsweetened cocoa

1 tsp baking soda

1¾ oz/50 g semisweet chocolate, broken into pieces

FILLING AND TOPPING

⅔ cup whole milk unsweetened plain yogurt

⅔ cup heavy cream

scant 1 cup fresh soft fruit, such as strawberries or raspberries

1 Preheat the oven to 350°F/180°C. Grease a deep 9-inch/23-cm round cake pan and line the bottom with parchment paper.

2 Place the oil, yogurt, sugar, and beaten eggs in a large mixing bowl and beat together until well combined. Sift the flours, unsweetened cocoa, and baking soda together and beat into the bowl until well combined. Put the chocolate in a heatproof bowl set over a pan of gently simmering water until melted. Beat the melted chocolate into the mixture.

3 Pour into the prepared pan and bake in the preheated oven for 45–50 minutes, or until a fine skewer inserted into the center of the cake comes out clean. Let the cake cool in the pan for 5 minutes, then turn out on to a wire rack to cool completely. When cold, split the cake into 3 layers.

4 To make the filling, place the yogurt and cream in a large mixing bowl and whisk well until the mixture stands in soft peaks.

5 Place one layer of cake on to a serving plate and spread with some of the cream. Top with a little of the fruit (slicing larger fruit such as strawberries). Repeat with the next layer. Top with the final layer of cake and spread with the rest of the cream. Arrange more fruit on top and cut the cake into wedges to serve.

Lemon & Yogurt Cake

This cake is served with a rich chocolate sauce but it can be also be served with cream or a fruit coulis.

🍳 15 mins 🕐 50–60 mins

SERVES 10

INGREDIENTS

1 tsp sunflower oil, for oiling

6 oz/175 g butter or margarine, softened

¾ cup superfine sugar

1 tbsp finely grated lemon rind, preferably from an unwaxed lemon

3 eggs, separated

1½ cups self-rising flour

generous ¼ cup ground almonds

½ cup natural yogurt

3 oz/85 g white chocolate, grated

1½–2 tbsp lemon juice

3 tbsp confectioners' sugar, sifted

SAUCE

6 oz/175 g semisweet chocolate

1 tbsp butter

½ cup milk

2 tbsp natural yogurt

1 Preheat the oven to 325°F/160°C. Lightly oil and line the base of a 9-inch/23-cm cake pan with nonstick parchment paper. Cream the butter with the sugar and lemon rind until light and fluffy.

2 Add the egg yolks one at a time, beating well between each addition and adding a little flour after each addition. When all the egg yolks have been added stir in the remaining flour together with the almonds, yogurt, and 1–2 tablespoons cooled boiled water. Mix to form a soft dropping consistency. Add the grated chocolate and stir in carefully.

3 Whisk the egg whites until stiff but not dry then stir into the cake batter. Turn into the prepared pan and bake on the middle shelf of the preheated oven for 50–60 minutes or until it is well risen and the top feels firm when touched with a finger

4 Meanwhile, blend the lemon juice with the confectioners' sugar until smooth. Once the cake is cooked, remove from the oven and pour the lemon frosting over the top. Leave until cold before removing from the pan and discarding the lining paper.

5 To make the sauce, put all the ingredients except the yogurt in a heavy-based pan and heat gently, stirring until smooth. Stir in the yogurt and serve with the cake.

Chocolate Blackcurrant Cake

You can vary the chocolate and fruit in this cake. Try using grated milk or semisweet chocolate and use either summer berries or red currants.

20 mins   30–40 mins

SERVES 10

INGREDIENTS

1 tsp sunflower oil, for oiling

6 oz/175 g butter, softened

¾ cup superfine sugar

3 eggs, separated

1 cup self-rising flour

generous ½ cup buttermilk

½ cup ground almonds

2 oz/55 g white chocolate, grated

TOPPING

scant 1 cup heavy cream

2 tbsp framboise liqueur or Cointreau

10 oz/300 g fresh ripe black currants, or
    other berries of your choice, cleaned

½ cup toasted slivered almonds

chocolate curls, to decorate (see page 9)

1 Preheat the oven to 350°F/180°C 10 minutes before baking. Lightly oil and line the base and sides of a 9-inch/ 23-cm cake pan. Beat the butter and sugar until light and creamy then beat in the egg yolks one at a time, adding a little flour after each yolk. When all the yolks have been added, stir in the remaining flour together with the buttermilk and stir gently until well mixed.

2 Gradually stir in the ground almonds and then the grated chocolate. Whisk the egg whites until soft peaks form then mix into the mixture a spoonful at a time. Turn into the prepared pan and bake in the preheated oven for 30–40 minutes or until the top feels firm and springs back when

touched lightly with a finger. Remove from the oven and leave in the pan until almost cold before turning out and discarding the lining paper. Leave until cold.

3 Whip the cream with the liqueur. Place the slivered almonds on to a large sheet of nonstick parchment paper. Use half the cream to cover the sides of the cake, then roll in the nuts. Spread the remaining cream on top then decorate with the fruit and chocolate curls. Store, lightly covered, in the refrigerator.

Mississippi Mud Cake

Mud cake is a dense chocolate cake perfect for a special occasion. Keep your portions small as it is very rich.

🍰 1 hr 25 mins   🕐 1 hr 30 mins

SERVES 16

INGREDIENTS

9 oz/250 g butter, cut into pieces, plus extra for greasing

5½ oz/15 g semisweet chocolates, broken into pieces

2 cups golden superfine sugar

generous 1 cup hot water

3 tbsp Tia Maria or cognac

2¼ cups all-purpose flour

1 tsp baking powder

¼ cup unsweetened cocoa

2 eggs, beaten

1 Preheat the oven to 325°F/160°C. Grease and base-line an 8-inch/20-cm round cake pan. Put the butter, chocolate, sugar, hot water, and Tia Maria or cognac in a heavy-based pan over a low heat and heat gently until the chocolate melts.

2 Stir until smooth, transfer the mixture to a large bowl, and let cool for 15 minutes. Sift in the flour, baking powder, and unsweetened cocoa and whisk in, then whisk in the eggs. Pour the cake batter into the prepared pan.

3 Bake in the preheated oven for 1½ hours, or until risen and firm to the touch. Leave in the pan for 30 minutes, then turn out and remove the paper. Place on a wire rack to cool completely. Decorate with chocolate curls and serve with raspberries.

COOK'S TIP
Cover the cake loosely with foil if it starts to over-brown.

Layered Meringue Gateau

Surprisingly easy, but somewhat time-consuming to make, this magnificent gâteau makes a wonderfully impressive dinner-party dessert.

🕐 1 hr 40 mins ⏰ 6 hrs, or overnight

SERVES 6

INGREDIENTS

6 egg whites

¾ cup superfine sugar

1½ cups confectioners' sugar

2 tbsp cornstarch

FILLING

1 cup heavy cream

5 oz/140 g semisweet chocolate, broken into pieces

4 tsp dark rum

TO DECORATE

⅔ cup heavy cream

4 tsp superfine sugar

1–2 tsp unsweetened cocoa, for dusting

1 Preheat the oven to 250°F/130°C. Prepare 5 sheets of parchment paper by drawing a 7-inch/18-cm circle on each, then use them to line cookie sheets.

2 Whisk the egg whites until soft peaks form. Mix the sugars and cornstarch together and sift it into the egg whites, a little at a time, whisking constantly until firm peaks form.

3 Spoon the meringue mixture into a pastry bag fitted with a round tip. Starting from the center, pipe 5 spirals, measuring 7 inches/18 cm, on each of the prepared pieces of parchment paper.

4 Bake in a preheated oven, at the lowest possible temperature with the door slightly ajar, for 6 hours, or overnight.

5 After baking, carefully peel the meringue spirals from the parchment paper and place on wire racks to cool.

6 To make the filling, pour the cream into a small pan and place over low heat. Add the chocolate pieces and stir until melted. Remove the pan from the heat and beat the mixture with an electric whisk. Beat in the dark rum, then cover with plastic wrap and let chill overnight or for as long as the meringues are baking.

7 To assemble the gâteau, beat the filling with an electric whisk until thick and smooth. Place 3 of the meringue layers on the work counter and spread the filling over them. Stack the 3 layers, one on top of the other, and place an uncovered meringue layer on top. Crush the fifth meringue into crumbs and set aside.

8 To make the decoration, whisk the cream with the sugar until thick. Carefully spread the mixture over the top of the gateau. Sprinkle the meringue crumbs over the cream and dust the top of the gâteau with cocoa. Serve within 2 hours.

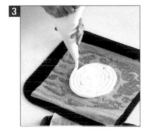

Mocha Walnut Meringue

Walnuts, semisweet chocolate, coffee, and cognac complement each other perfectly in this easy-to-make gâteau.

 50 mins

1 hr 35 mins

SERVES 8

INGREDIENTS

MERINGUE

4 egg whites

generous 1 cup golden superfine sugar

generous 1 cup walnuts, chopped finely

FILLING

6 oz/175 g semisweet chocolate

3 tbsp butter, sweet for preference

2 tbsp strong black coffee

2 tbsp cognac

¾ cup whipping cream

confectioners' sugar, or a little semisweet chocolate, if liked, to decorate

1 Preheat the oven to 275°F/140°C. Line 2 cookie sheets with parchment paper. Put the egg whites in a large bowl and whisk until stiff peaks form, then whisk in half the sugar. Add the chopped walnuts to the remaining sugar and mix together. Fold into the meringue mixture.

2 Spread the meringue in 2 x 8-inch/20-cm circles on the prepared cookie sheets. Bake in the oven for about 1½ hours, until completely dry. Let cool in the oven.

3 To make the filling, break the chocolate into pieces and put in a bowl with the butter, coffee, and cognac. Set over a pan of gently simmering water until melted. Stir and let cool. Put the cream in a bowl and whip lightly, then stir in the chocolate mixture. Sandwich the meringue circles together with the chocolate cream. Dust with confectioners' sugar or drizzle with a little semisweet chocolate, melted in a heatproof bowl over a pan of gently simmering water, just before serving.

VARIATION
Instead of walnuts, chopped toasted hazelnuts or ground almonds may be added to the meringue.

Mocha Layer Cake

Chocolate cake and a creamy coffee-flavored filling are combined in this delicious mocha cake, perfect for any occasion.

50 mins   35–45 mins

SERVES 8

INGREDIENTS

butter, for greasing

1¾ cups self-rising flour

¼ tsp baking powder

4 tbsp unsweetened cocoa

½ cup superfine sugar

2 eggs

2 tbsp corn syrup

⅔ cup sunflower oil

⅔ cup milk

FILLING

1 tsp instant coffee powder

1 tbsp boiling water

1¼ cups heavy cream

2 tbsp confectioners' sugar

TO DECORATE

1¾ oz/50 g chocolate shavings

chocolate caraque (see page 9)

confectioners' sugar, for dusting

1 Preheat the oven to 350°F/180°C. Lightly grease 3 x 7-inch/18-cm layer cake pans.

2 Sift the flour, baking powder, and unsweetened cocoa into a large mixing bowl. Stir in the sugar. Make a well in the center and stir in the eggs, syrup, oil, and milk. Beat with a wooden spoon, gradually mixing in the dry ingredients to make a smooth batter. Divide the cake batter between the prepared pans.

3 Bake in the preheated oven for 35–45 minutes, or until springy to the touch. Let cool in the pans for 5 minutes, then turn out on to a wire rack to cool completely.

4 Dissolve the instant coffee in the boiling water and place in a bowl with the cream and confectioners' sugar. Whip until the cream is just holding its shape. Use half of the cream to sandwich the 3 cakes together. Spread the remaining cream over the top and sides of the cake. Lightly press the chocolate shavings into the cream around the edge of the cake.

5 Transfer to a serving plate. Lay the caraque over the top of the cake. Cut a few thin strips of parchment paper and place on top of the caraque. Dust lightly with confectioners' sugar, then carefully remove the paper. Serve.

Black & White Chocolate Cake

This splendidly dramatic-looking cake should be eaten within 2 or 3 days—if it will last that long!

25 mins   20–25 mins

SERVES 12–14

INGREDIENTS

1 tsp sunflower oil, for oiling

3 large eggs

½ cup superfine sugar

¾ cup all-purpose flour, sifted

2 oz/55 g white chocolate, grated

white and semisweet chocolate curls to
   decorate

FROSTING

6 oz/175 g semisweet chocolate

4 tbsp sweet butter

1 tbsp corn syrup

2 tbsp cognac or Cointreau

4 tbsp raspberry jelly

2 tbsp lemon juice

1 Preheat the oven to 375°F/190°C. Lightly oil and base-line a 9-inch/23-cm shallow cake or tart pan. Place the eggs and sugar in a heatproof bowl set over a pan of gently simmering water. Whisk until very thick and creamy and doubled in volume. Remove the bowl from the pan and continue to whisk until the mixture is cool.

2 Add the grated chocolate and very gently stir into the mixture, then stir in the sifted flour. Spoon into the lined cake or tart pan and tap lightly on the work counter to level. Bake in the preheated oven for 20–25 minutes or until golden and the top springs back when touched lightly with a finger. Remove from the oven and let cool before turning out on to a wire rack and discarding the lining paper. Leave until cold.

3 Break the chocolate into small pieces and place in a heavy based pan. Add the butter, syrup, and cognac, heat gently, stirring frequently until the mixture is smooth and blended. Let cool, stirring occasionally until the mixture has thickened.

4 Heat the jelly and lemon juice together until blended then rub through a strainer and use to coat the top and sides of the cake. Spoon the cooled thickened frosting over the top and sides and decorate with white and semisweet chocolate curls.

COOK'S TIP

With this cake it is very important to ensure that the egg and sugar mixture is very thick and creamy.

Chocolate Brownie Cake

This moist cake, full of dried cranberries and toasted slivered almonds, and with an intense chocolate flavor, is a taste of chocolate heaven.

20 mins | 35–40 mins

SERVES 10

INGREDIENTS

7 oz/200 g butter

4 oz/115 g semisweet chocolate

1¼ cups granulated sugar

½ cup light muscovado sugar

4 eggs

¾ cup all-purpose flour

1 tsp vanilla extract

pinch of salt

½ cup dried cranberries

scant ½ cup slivered almonds, toasted

few almonds, to decorate

FOR THE FROSTING

4 oz/115 g semisweet chocolate

2 tbsp butter

2 cups confectioners' sugar

3–4 tbsp milk

1 Preheat the oven to 350°F/180°C and base-line 2 x 7-inch/18-cm shallow cake pans with nonstick parchment paper. Place the butter in a heavy-based pan, break the chocolate into small pieces and add to the pan. Heat gently, stirring frequently until the mixture has melted. Remove from the heat and stir until smooth. Add the sugars, stir well, then let cool for 10 minutes.

2 Beat the eggs then gradually add to the cooled mixture, beating well after each addition. Stir in the flour, vanilla extract, and salt. Stir in the cranberries and nuts, mix, then divide between the prepared cake pans.

3 Bake in the preheated oven for 25–30 minutes or until the tops feel firm but spring back when touched lightly with a finger. Remove from the oven, let cool before turning out on to a wire rack and leave until cold. Discard the lining paper.

4 To make the frosting, melt the chocolate and butter in a heavy-based pan and stir until smooth. Gradually beat in the confectioners' sugar with sufficient milk to give a smooth spreading consistency. Use to sandwich the two cakes together then spread the top and sides with the remaining frosting, swirling the top to give a decorative effect. Arrange a few almonds on top. Let the frosting set before serving.

Sunken Drunken Cake

This dense rich cake contains no flour and will sink and crack slightly when you take it out of the oven. Let cool completely before decorating.

45 mins   40–45 mins

SERVES 8

INGREDIENTS

4 oz/115 g butter, diced, plus extra
  for greasing

flour, for dusting

5 oz/140 g semisweet chocolate,
  broken into pieces

2 tbsp cognac

⅜ cup golden superfine sugar

6 eggs, separated

1¼ cups ground almonds

1¾ cups whipped cream,
  to decorate

ground cinnamon, for dusting

1 Preheat the oven to 325°F/160°C. Grease a 9-inch/23-cm springform cake pan and line the bottom with nonstick parchment paper. Dust the sides with flour. Place the chocolate and cognac in a heatproof bowl and set over a pan of gently simmering water until the chocolate has melted. Stir until smooth, then let cool slightly.

2 Place the butter in a separate bowl, add the sugar and beat until light and creamy. Add the egg yolks, one at a time, beating well after each addition, then stir in the melted chocolate. Add the ground almonds and beat in. Place the egg whites in a large, spotlessly clean, greasefree bowl and whisk until stiff but not dry. Stir 2 tablespoons of the whisked egg whites into the chocolate batter, then carefully fold in the remainder.

3 Spoon the batter into the prepared pan and bake in the preheated oven for 35–40 minutes, or until well risen and just firm to the touch. Let stand in the pan to cool completely. When cold, remove the cake from the pan and peel away the lining paper, then transfer to a serving plate. Spoon whipped cream over the top to decorate and dust with a little cinnamon. Serve, cut into slices.

COOK'S TIP

This cake is very fragile and benefits from being chilled for at least 10 minutes in the refrigerator before serving. Any uneaten cake should be covered with foil and stored in the refrigerator.

Double Chocolate Gâteau

A chocolate sponge layered with white chocolate cream and covered in semisweet chocolate frosting. Ideal as a celebration cake or a dessert.

1 hr plus
2 hrs chilling

55–65 mins

SERVES 10

INGREDIENTS

8 oz/225 g butter, softened, plus extra for greasing

generous 1 cup golden superfine sugar

4 eggs, beaten

1½ cups self-rising flour

½ cup unsweetened cocoa

a little milk (optional)

FILLING

generous 1 cup whipping cream

8 oz/225 g white chocolate, broken into pieces

FROSTING

12 oz/350 g semisweet chocolate, broken into pieces

4 oz/115 g butter

scant ½ cup heavy cream

TO DECORATE

4 oz/115 g semisweet chocolate curls (see page 9)

2 tsp confectioners' sugar and unsweetened cocoa, mixed

1 To make the filling, put the cream in a pan and heat to almost boiling. Put the white chocolate in a food processor and chop. With the motor running, pour the hot cream through the feed tube and process for 10-15 seconds until smooth. Transfer to a bowl, let cool, then cover with plastic wrap and chill in the refrigerator for 2 hours, or until firm. Whisk until just starting to hold soft peaks.

2 Preheat the oven to 350°F/180°C. Grease and base-line an 8-inch/ 20-cm deep round cake pan. Put the butter and sugar in a bowl and beat until light and fluffy. Gradually beat in the eggs. Sift the flour and cocoa into a bowl, then fold into the mixture, adding milk, if necessary, to make a dropping consistency. Spoon into the prepared pan and bake in the oven for 45-50 minutes, until a skewer inserted into the center comes out clean. Let stand in the pan for 5 minutes, then transfer to a wire rack to cool completely.

3 To make the frosting, put the chocolate in a heatproof bowl set over a pan of gently simmering water until melted. Stir in the butter and cream. Let cool, stirring occasionally until the mixture is a thick spreading consistency. Slice the cake horizontally into 3 layers. Sandwich the layers together with the white chocolate filling. Cover the top and sides of the cake with the frosting and arrange the chocolate curls over the top. Sift the mixed confectioners' sugar and cocoa over the cake.

Chocolate Cognac Torte

A crumbly ginger chocolate shell topped with velvety smooth chocolate cognac cream makes this a blissful treat, ideal if served with coffee.

40 mins plus 2 hrs chilling   5 mins

SERVES 12

INGREDIENTS

BASE
9 oz/250 g gingersnaps

2¾ oz/75 g semisweet chocolate

3 oz/85 g butter

FILLING
8 oz/225 g semisweet chocolate

9 oz/250 g mascarpone cheese

2 eggs, separated

3 tbsp cognac

1¼ cups heavy cream

4 tbsp superfine sugar

TO DECORATE
scant ½ cup heavy cream

chocolate-coated coffee beans

1 Crush the gingersnaps in a bag with a rolling pin or in a food processor. Melt the chocolate and butter together and pour over the gingersnaps. Mix well, then use to line the bottom and sides of a 9-inch/23-cm loose-bottomed fluted flan pan or springform pan. Let chill while preparing the filling.

2 For the filling, melt the semisweet chocolate in a bowl set over boiling water. Remove from the heat and beat in the mascarpone cheese, egg yolks, and cognac.

3 Lightly whip the cream until just holding its shape and fold in the chocolate mixture. Whisk the egg whites in a greasefree bowl until standing in soft peaks.

4 Add the superfine sugar a little at a time and whisk until thick and glossy. Fold into the chocolate mixture, in 2 batches, until just mixed.

5 Spoon the batter into the prepared gingersnap shell and let chill for at least 2 hours. Carefully transfer to a serving plate. To decorate, whip the cream and pipe on to the torte and add the chocolate-coated coffee beans.

VARIATION
If chocolate-coated coffee beans are unavailable, use chocolate-coated raisins to decorate.

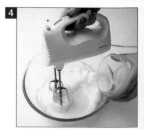

Almond & Apricot Torte

This torte is very moist, so it is best stored, lightly covered, in the refrigerator. It should be eaten within 2 days.

🍰 25 mins   🕐 30 mins

SERVES 10

INGREDIENTS

1 tsp sunflower oil

4 oz/115 g butter, softened

½ cup superfine sugar

1 tbsp finely grated orange rind

1 tbsp finely grated lemon rind

4 eggs, separated

scant ½ cup self-rising flour

generous 1 cup ground almonds

½ cup ricotta cheese

2 tbsp Amaretto

6–8 oz/175–225 g semisweet chocolate, grated

4 tbsp apricot jelly

1 tbsp lemon juice

few fresh apricots, halved and pitted, or no-soak dried apricots, to decorate

TO SERVE

mascarpone cheese

2 tbsp Amaretto

summer berries or extra fresh apricots

1 Preheat the oven to 350°F/180°C. Lightly oil and base-line a 9-inch/23-cm loose bottomed cake or tart pan. Cream the butter, sugar and orange and lemon rind together until light and fluffy. Gradually beat in the egg yolks, adding a little of the flour after each addition. When all the egg yolk has been added, stir in the remaining flour together with the ground almonds.

2 Beat the ricotta cheese with the Amaretto until soft and creamy and stir into the cake batter until well mixed. Add 2 oz/55 g of the grated chocolate to the batter and stir lightly.

3 Whisk the egg whites until soft peaks form and stir into the cake batter. Spoon into the prepared cake or tart pan and smooth the top. Bake in the preheated oven for 30 minutes or until the top is golden and firm to the touch. Remove from the oven, and let cool before removing from the cake pan and discarding the lining paper. Leave until cold.

4 Heat the apricot jelly and lemon juice together then rub through a strainer. Brush the jelly all over the cake, then sprinkle over the remaining grated chocolate, pressing the chocolate lightly into the sides and top. Beat the mascarpone cheese with the Amaretto and place in a serving bowl.

5 Decorate the torte with the fresh or dried apricots and serve with mascarpone cheese and fresh summer berries or more apricots.

Chocolate & Almond Torte

This torte is perfect for serving on a hot, sunny day with a spoonful of whipped cream and a selection of fresh summer berries.

55 mins   50 mins

SERVES 10

INGREDIENTS

¾ cup butter, softened, plus extra
  for greasing

8 oz/225 g bittersweet chocolate,
  broken into pieces

3 tbsp water

¾ cup brown sugar

¼ cup ground almonds

3 tbsp self-rising flour

5 eggs, separated

¾ cup finely chopped blanched almonds

confectioners' sugar, for dusting

heavy cream, to serve (optional)

1 Preheat the oven to 350°F/180°C. Grease a 9-inch/23-cm loose-bottomed cake pan and line the bottom with parchment paper.

2 Put the chocolate and water in a heatproof bowl set over a pan of gently simmering water until melted, stirring until smooth. Add the sugar and stir until dissolved. Remove from the heat.

3 Add the butter in small amounts until it has melted into the chocolate. Lightly stir in the ground almonds and flour. Add the egg yolks one at a time, beating well after each addition.

4 Whisk the egg whites until soft peaks form, then fold into the chocolate batter with a metal spoon. Stir in the chopped almonds. Pour the batter into the cake pan and smooth the surface.

5 Bake in the preheated oven for 40–45 minutes, until well risen and firm (the cake will crack on the surface during cooking).

6 Let cool in the pan for 30–40 minutes. Turn out on to a wire rack to cool completely. Dust with confectioners' sugar and serve with cream, or fresh fruit for a lighter option.

COOK'S TIP

For a nuttier flavor, toast the chopped almonds in a dry skillet over medium heat for 2 minutes until lightly golden.

Frosted Chocolate Torte

If you can't decide whether you prefer bittersweet chocolate or rich, creamy white chocolate, then this gâteau is definitely for you.

1 hr 5 mins   40–45 mins

SERVES 6

INGREDIENTS

butter, for greasing

4 eggs

½ cup superfine sugar

¾ cup all-purpose flour

BITTERSWEET CHOCOLATE CREAM

⅔ cup heavy cream

5½ oz/150 g bittersweet chocolate, broken into small pieces

FROSTING

2¾ oz/75 g white chocolate

1 tbsp butter

1 tbsp milk

4 tbsp confectioners' sugar, sifted

chocolate caraque (see page 9), to decorate

1 Preheat the oven to 350°F/180°C. Grease and base-line an 8-inch/20-cm round springform pan. Beat the eggs and superfine sugar in a large mixing bowl with an electric whisk for about 10 minutes, or until the mixture is very light and foamy and a trail is left when the whisk is dragged across the surface.

2 Sift the flour and fold in with a metal spoon or spatula. Pour into the prepared pan and bake in the preheated oven for 35–40 minutes, or until springy to the touch. Let the cake cool slightly, then transfer to a wire rack to cool completely.

3 While the cake is cooling, make the chocolate cream. Place the cream in a pan and bring to a boil, stirring. Add the

bittersweet chocolate and stir until melted and well combined. Remove from the heat, transfer to a bowl, and let cool. Beat with a wooden spoon until thick.

4 When the cake is cold, cut it in half horizontally. Sandwich the layers with the chocolate cream then place on a wire rack.

5 To make the frosting, melt the chocolate and butter together and stir until blended. Whisk in the milk and confectioners' sugar, and continue whisking until cool. Pour over the cake and spread with a spatula to coat the top and sides. Decorate with chocolate caraque and let the frosting set.

Chocolate Marquise Alice

The smooth filling is delicately flavored with orange, surrounded with crisp chocolate finger cookies, and topped with orange segments and kumquats.

30 mins plus 4 hrs chilling

20 mins

SERVES 8

INGREDIENTS

SPONGE

1 tsp sunflower oil, for oiling

2 eggs

¼ cup superfine sugar

scant ½ cup all-purpose flour, plus 1 tsp for dusting

FILLING AND DECORATION

3 eggs, separated

¼ cup superfine sugar

1 tbsp finely grated orange rind

4 oz/115 g semisweet chocolate

3 tbsp orange juice

2 tsp gelatin

2 cups heavy cream

4 tbsp Cointreau or Grand Marnier

2–3 oranges, peeled and segmented

44 semisweet chocolate finger cookies

kumquats, to decorate

1 Preheat the oven to 400°F/200°C and lightly oil a 7-inch/18-cm tart pan and dust with a teaspoon of flour. Whisk the eggs with the sugar until very thick and creamy then stir in the flour in a figure-of-eight action. Pour into the prepared tart pan and bake in the oven for 12–15 minutes or until well risen and the top feels firm when lightly touched with a finger. Remove and cool slightly before turning out from the tart pan. Set aside.

2 Put the egg yolks with the sugar and orange rind either in the bowl of a free-standing mixer or in a large mixing bowl placed over a pan of gently simmering water. Whisk until thick and creamy. If applicable, remove the bowl from the pan and continue to whisk until the mixture is cool. Melt the chocolate in a heatproof bowl set over a pan of gently simmering water. Stir until smooth then stir into the whisked egg mixture.

3 Heat the orange juice until almost boiling then sprinkle in the gelatin and stir until dissolved. Cool slightly then fold into the mixture, stirring throughout. Whip ⅔ cup of the cream until softly peaking then stir into the egg mixture together with half the Cointreau or Grand Marnier. Whisk the egg whites in a clean bowl until stiff then gently fold into the mixture a little at a time.

4 Place the cake in the base of an 8-inch/20-cm loose-bottomed cake pan or spring form pan. Set aside a few orange segments for decoration then place the rest in the base and sprinkle over the remaining liqueur. Spoon over the prepared chocolate mixture, smooth the top, and leave in the refrigerator for 4 hours or until set.

5 When ready to serve, whip the remaining cream until softly peaking. Remove the gâteau from the cake pan and spread the sides with the cream. Press the chocolate finger cookies into the sides and place on a serving plate. Decorate the top with a little cream, arrange a few orange segments and kumquats on top, and serve.

Chocolate Berry Dacquoise

An excellent choice to serve in the summer when home-grown berries are at their best.

25 mins plus
4 hrs chilling

1–1½ hrs

SERVES 10

I N G R E D I E N T S

4 egg whites

1 cup superfine sugar

generous ½ cup ground hazelnuts

8 oz/225 g semisweet chocolate

1½ cups heavy cream

2 tbsp kirsch

2 cups mixed summer berries, such as baby strawberries, raspberries, and blueberries

1 Preheat the oven to 275°/140°C. Line 3 cookie sheets with nonstick parchment paper and mark 3 x 7-inch/18-cm rounds on each. Whisk the egg whites until very stiff then gradually add the sugar, whisking well after each addition. When all the sugar has been added, stir in the ground hazelnuts. Mix lightly until thoroughly incorporated.

2 Divide the meringue between the 3 cookie sheets and then spread evenly within the circles. Bake in the preheated oven for 1 hour–1 hour 30 minutes or until the meringues feel firm to the touch. Let cool then remove from the cookie sheets. Leave until cold.

3 Break the chocolate into small pieces and place in a heavy-based pan and add 1 cup of the cream and kirsch. Heat gently, stirring until melted and smooth. Remove, pour into a bowl, cool, then chill for at least 2 hours or until set. Once set, whisk until light and fluffy.

4 Spread two-thirds of the chocolate filling over 2 of the meringues and spread to the edges. Arrange most of the fruit over the chocolate filling, reserving the remaining fruit for decoration. Place the meringues one on top of the other, ending with a plain meringue.

5 Whip the remaining cream until stiff then reserve a little for decoration and use the remainder to spread round the sides of the meringues. Spread the remaining chocolate on the top meringue and swirl with the tines of a fork. Decorate the top with the remaining cream and fruits and chill for 2 hours before serving.

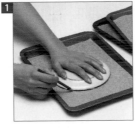

Sachertorte

Do make sure you have a steady hand when writing the name on the top and let the chocolate harden before serving.

3 hrs 30 mins   1–1 hr 15 mins

SERVES 10

INGREDIENTS

5 oz/140 g butter, sweet for preference, plus extra for greasing

6 oz/175 g bittersweet chocolate, broken into pieces

⅔ cup superfine sugar

6 eggs, separated

1¼ cups all-purpose flour

FROSTING & FILLING

6 oz/175 g bittersweet chocolate

5 tbsp strong black coffee

1 cup confectioners' sugar

6 tbsp good-quality apricot jelly

1¾ oz/50 g bittersweet chocolate, melted

1 Preheat the oven to 300°F/150°C. Grease and base-line a 9-inch/23-cm springform cake pan. Put the chocolate in a heatproof bowl set over a pan of gently simmering water until melted. Beat the butter and ⅓ cup of the sugar until pale and fluffy. Add the egg yolks and beat well. Add the chocolate in a thin stream, beating well. Sift the flour; fold it into the mixture. Whisk the egg whites until they stand in soft peaks. Add the remaining sugar and whisk for 2 minutes by hand, or 45–60 seconds if using an electric whisk, until glossy. Fold half into the chocolate mixture, then fold in the remainder.

2 Spoon into the prepared pan and smooth the top. Bake in the preheated oven for 1–1¼ hours, until a skewer inserted into the center comes out clean.

Cool in the pan for 5 minutes, then transfer to a wire rack to cool completely.

3 To make the frosting, melt the chocolate and beat in the coffee until smooth. Sift the confectioners' sugar into a bowl. Whisk in the melted chocolate mixture to give a thick frosting. Halve the cake. Warm the apricot jelly, spread over one half of the cake and sandwich together. Invert the cake on a wire rack.

Spoon the frosting over the cake and spread to coat the top and sides. Let set for 5 minutes, letting any excess drop through the rack. Transfer to a serving plate and let set for at least 2 hours.

4 To decorate, spoon the melted chocolate into a small pastry bag and, with a fine plain tip, pipe the word "Sacher" or "Sachertorte" on the top of the cake. Let it harden before serving.

Bistvitny Torte

This is a Russian chocolate marble cake that is soaked in a delicious flavored syrup and decorated with chocolate and cream.

🍰 1 hr 10 mins   🕐 35 mins

SERVES 10

INGREDIENTS

CHOCOLATE TRIANGLES

1 oz/25 g bittersweet chocolate, broken into pieces

1 oz/25 g white chocolate, broken into pieces

CAKE

butter, for greasing

¾ cup soft margarine

¾ cup superfine sugar

½ tsp vanilla extract

3 eggs, beaten lightly

2 cups self-rising flour

1¾ oz/50 g bittersweet chocolate

SYRUP

½ cup granulated sugar

6 tbsp water

3 tbsp cognac or sherry

⅔ cup heavy cream

1 Preheat the oven to 375°F/190°C. To make the triangles, place a sheet of parchment paper on to a cookie sheet. Put the bittersweet and white chocolate in 2 separate heatproof bowls set over pans of gently simmering water until melted. Place alternate spoonfuls of the melted bittersweet and white chocolate on to the paper. Spread together to form a thick marbled layer, and let the chocolate set. Cut into squares, then into triangles.

2 To make the cake, grease a 9-inch/23-cm ring pan. Beat the margarine and sugar until light and fluffy. Beat in the vanilla extract. Gradually add the eggs, beating well after each addition. Fold in the flour. Divide the batter in half. Melt the bittersweet chocolate and stir into one half.

3 Place spoonfuls of each batter into the prepared pan and swirl together with a skewer to create a marbled effect.

4 Bake in the preheated oven for 30 minutes, or until the cake is springy to the touch. Let cool in the pan for a few minutes, then transfer to a wire rack to cool completely.

5 To make the syrup, place the sugar in a small pan with the water and heat until the sugar has dissolved. Boil for 1–2 minutes. Remove from the heat and stir in the cognac or sherry. Let the syrup cool slightly, then spoon it slowly over the cake, letting it soak into the sponge. Whip the cream and pipe swirls of it on top of the cake. Decorate with the marbled chocolate triangles.

Torta del Cielo

This Italian almond-flavored sponge cake has a dense, moist texture. It makes the perfect accompaniment to a good strong cup of coffee.

 50 mins 40–50 mins

SERVES 4-6

INGREDIENTS

8 oz/225 g butter, sweet for preference, at room temperature, plus extra for greasing

1¼ cups almonds in their skins

1¼ cups sugar

3 eggs, beaten lightly

1 tsp almond extract

1 tsp vanilla extract

½ cup all-purpose flour

pinch of salt

TO SERVE

confectioners' sugar for dusting

toasted slivered almonds

1 Preheat the oven to 350°F/180°C. Lightly grease a round or square 8-inch/20-cm cake pan and line with parchment paper.

2 Place the almonds in a food processor and grind until a crumbly mixture.

3 In a bowl, beat together the butter and sugar until smooth and fluffy. Beat in the almonds, eggs, and almond and vanilla extracts. Blend well.

4 Stir in the flour and salt, and mix together briefly, until the flour is just incorporated.

5 Pour or spoon the cake batter into the greased pan and smooth the surface. Bake in the preheated oven for 40–50 minutes, or until the cake feels spongy when pressed.

6 Remove the pan from the oven, and put on a wire rack to cool completely. To serve, dust the cake with confectioners' sugar and decorate with the toasted slivered almonds.

Dobos Torte

This wonderful cake originates from Hungary and consists of thin layers of light sponge topped with a crunchy caramel layer.

40 mins · 10–16 mins

SERVES 8

INGREDIENTS

3 eggs

½ cup superfine sugar

1 tsp vanilla extract

¾ cup all-purpose flour

FILLING

6 oz/175 g semisweet chocolate, broken into pieces

6 oz/175 g butter

2 tbsp milk

3 cups confectioners' sugar

CARAMEL

½ cup granulated sugar

4 tbsp water

1 Preheat the oven to 400°F/200°C. Draw 4 x 7-inch/18-cm circles on sheets of parchment paper. Place 2 of them upside down on 2 cookie sheets.

2 Beat the eggs and superfine sugar in a large mixing bowl with an electric whisk for 10 minutes, or until the mixture is light and foamy and a trail is left when the whisk is dragged across the surface. Fold in the vanilla extract. Sift the flour and fold in with a metal spoon.

3 Spoon a quarter of the mixture on to one of the cookie sheets and spread out to the size of the circle. Repeat with the other circle. Bake in the preheated oven for 5–8 minutes or until golden brown. Cool on wire racks. Repeat with the remaining mixture.

4 To make the filling, put the chocolate in a heatproof bowl set over a pan of gently simmering water. Cool slightly. Beat the butter, milk, and confectioners' sugar until pale and fluffy. Whisk in the melted chocolate.

5 Place the sugar and water for the caramel in a heavy based pan. Heat gently, stirring, to dissolve the sugar. Boil gently until pale golden in color. Remove from the heat. Pour over one cake layer as a topping. Let harden slightly, then mark into 8 portions with an oiled knife.

6 Remove the cakes from the parchment paper. Trim the edges. Sandwich the layers together with some of the filling, finishing with the caramel-topped cake. Place on a serving plate, spread the sides with the filling mixture, and pipe rosettes on the top of the cake.

Strawberry Chocolate Cake

Strawberries and cream and chocolate cake make the perfect treat for a hot summer's day. Store in the refrigerator for up to 24 hours.

50 mins   30-40 mins

SERVES 8

INGREDIENTS

CHOCOLATE SPONGE

butter, for greasing

3 eggs

generous ½ cup golden superfine sugar

¾ cup all-purpose flour

2 tbsp unsweetened cocoa

TO FINISH

1 cup strawberries

1¼ cups heavy cream

½ tsp vanilla extract

1 tbsp confectioners' sugar

2 tbsp kirsch

chocolate curls (see page 9)

1 Preheat the oven to 375°F/190°C. Grease and line an 8½-inch/22-cm cake pan. Put the eggs and sugar in a bowl and whisk together with an electric whisk, until thick and mousselike and a trail is left when the whisk is dragged across the surface. Sift the flour and unsweetened cocoa together into a bowl, then carefully fold in to the whisked mixture. Turn into the prepared pan and bake in the oven for

30-40 minutes, until the cake springs back when lightly pressed in the center. Let stand in the pan for 5 minutes, then turn out on to a wire rack to cool.

2 Meanwhile, prepare the filling. Set aside 4 strawberries and slice the rest. Put the cream, vanilla extract, and confectioners' sugar in a bowl and whisk until thick. Set aside two-thirds of the cream and fold the sliced strawberries into the remainder. Slice the chocolate sponge across into 2 layers and sprinkle each layer

with 1 tablespoon of kirsch. Place 1 layer on a serving plate and spread over the strawberry cream mixture. Place the other sponge layer on top.

3 Put some of the reserved cream in a pastry bag fitted with a fluted tip and spread the remainder over the top and sides of the cake. Coat the side with chocolate curls. Pipe the cream round the top of the gâteau. Cut the reserved strawberries in half, keeping the stalks intact, and arrange on top of the cream.

COOK'S TIP

If you do not want to make the chocolate curls, decorate the side of the cake with crushed chocolate flake bars.

Chocolate Cherry Gâteau

Chocolate and cherries are a classic combination. It is the perfect cake for all special occasions.

🍰 45 mins   🕐 55 mins

MAKES 9-INCH/23-CM CAKE

I N G R E D I E N T S

3 tbsp butter, sweet for preference, melted, plus extra butter for greasing

5 cups fresh cherries, pitted and halved

generous 1 cup superfine sugar

scant ½ cup cherry cognac

scant 1 cup all-purpose flour

½ cup unsweetened cocoa

½ tsp baking powder

4 eggs

4½ cups heavy cream

TO DECORATE

grated bittersweet chocolate

whole fresh cherries

1 Preheat the oven to 350°F/180°C. Grease and line a 9-inch/23-cm springform cake pan. Put the cherries in a pan and add 3 tablespoons of the sugar and the cherry cognac. Simmer for 5 minutes. Drain, and set aside the syrup. In another bowl, sift together the flour, unsweetened cocoa, and baking powder.

2 Put the eggs in a heatproof bowl and beat in all but 2 tablespoons of the remaining sugar. Place the bowl over a pan of gently simmering water and whisk for 6 minutes until thickened. Remove from the heat, then gradually fold in the flour mixture and the melted butter. Spoon into the cake pan. Bake for 40 minutes. Remove from the oven and let cool.

3 Turn out the cake and cut in half horizontally. Mix the cream with the last of the sugar and whisk until peaking. Spread the syrup over the cut sides of the cake. Arrange the cherries on top of one of the cut sides and fill with cream and cherries on top.

4 Place the other cake half on top of the cherries, cream side-down, then cover the top and sides of the cake with cream. Press grated chocolate over the top and sides. Decorate with whole cherries and serve.

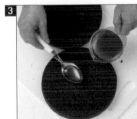

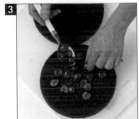

Chocolate Marmalade Cake

This cake will keep for up to 1 week if stored in an airtight container, because the addition of marmalade makes it really moist.

15 mins   1 hr 5 mins

SERVES 12–14

INGREDIENTS

1 tsp sunflower oil, for oiling

8 oz/225 g butter or margarine, softened

1 cup superfine sugar

5 tbsp Temple orange marmalade

4 eggs, beaten

1½ cups self-rising flour

scant ½ cup ground almonds

4 oz/115 g semisweet chocolate, grated

few pieces candied orange peel

1 tsp confectioners' sugar, sifted

1 Preheat the oven to 350°F/180°C. Lightly oil and line the base of an 8-inch/20-cm cake pan with nonstick parchment paper. Cream the butter and sugar together until light and fluffy then stir in the marmalade.

2 Gradually beat in the eggs a little at a time, beating well between each addition and adding a little flour after each addition. When all the eggs have been added, stir in the remaining flour together with the ground almonds and finally stir in the grated chocolate.

3 Spoon into the prepared cake tin and smooth the top. Bake in the preheated oven on the middle shelf for 45 minutes, then remove from the oven and arrange the candied peel on the top of the cake. Return to the oven and continue to bake for an additional 15–20 minutes or until a skewer inserted into the center of the cake comes out clean. Remove and let cool before removing from the pan and discarding the lining paper. Decorate with the peel and sprinkle with the confectioners' sugar to serve.

COOK'S TIP

For a change, chop the chocolate rather than grating it or substitute best-quality white chocolate for the semisweet chocolate. If you cannot find Temple orange marmalade, use another one of your choice.

Giggle Cake

It's a mystery how this cake got its name—perhaps it's because it's easy to make and fun to eat.

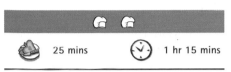

🍮 25 mins   🕐 1 hr 15 mins

SERVES 8

INGREDIENTS

2 cups mixed dry fruits

5½ oz/150 g butter or margarine, plus extra for greasing

¾ cup brown sugar

2 cups self-rising flour

pinch of salt

2 eggs, beaten

8 oz/225 g canned chopped pineapple, drained

¾ cup candied cherries, halved

1 Preheat the oven to 350°F/180°C. Put the mixed dry fruits into a large bowl and cover with boiling water. Set aside to soak for 10–15 minutes, then drain well.

2 Put the butter or margarine and sugar into a large pan and heat gently until melted. Add the drained mixed dry fruits and cook over low heat, stirring frequently, for 4–5 minutes. Remove from the heat and transfer to a mixing bowl. Set aside to cool.

3 Sift together the flour and salt into the dry fruit mixture and stir well. Add the eggs, mixing until the ingredients are thoroughly incorporated.

4 Add the pineapple and cherries to the cake batter and stir to combine. Transfer to a greased and lined 2-lb/ 900-g loaf pan and smooth the surface.

5 Bake in preheated oven for about 1 hour or until a skewer inserted into the center comes out clean. If not, return to the oven for a few more minutes. Transfer the cake to a wire rack to cool completely before serving.

VARIATION

If you wish, add 1 teaspoon ground allspice to the cake mixture, sifting it in with the flour. Bake the cake in a 7-inch/18-cm round cake pan if you don't have a loaf pan of the right size. Remember to grease and line it first.

Chocolate Ring

This light cake has a delicate hint of chocolate and vanilla. In summer, decorate it with edible rose petals but remember to rinse them first.

25 mins   30–35 mins

SERVES 10

INGREDIENTS

1 tsp sunflower oil, for oiling

scant ½ cup all-purpose flour, plus extra for dusting

¾ cup superfine sugar

5 egg whites

½ tsp cream of tartar

salt

1 tsp vanilla extract

2 oz/55 g white chocolate, grated

FROSTING

6 oz/175 g plain semisweet chocolate

2 oz/55 g butter

2 cups confectioners' sugar

2 egg yolks

white and milk chocolate buttons or rose petals, to decorate

1 Preheat the oven to 350°F/180°C 10 minutes before baking. Lightly oil a 2-pint/1.2-liter ring mold, dust with the flour and set aside. Sift the flour with half the superfine sugar at least 4 times. Set aside.

2 Place the egg whites in a large mixing bowl and whisk until soft peaks form. Add the cream of tartar, salt, and vanilla extract and whisk for an additional 1 minute. Gradually whisk in all the remaining sugar, whisking well between each addition. Then carefully stir in the sifted flour and then the grated chocolate.

3 Turn the cake batter into the prepared pan and tap lightly on the work counter to remove any air bubbles. Bake in the preheated oven for 25–30 minutes, or until the top feels firm and springs back when touched lightly with a finger.

4 Remove the pan from the oven and invert on to a wire rack. Let stand until cold, then remove the pan.

5 Break the chocolate for the frosting into small pieces and place in a large heatproof bowl set over a saucepan of gently simmering water and add the butter. Heat, stirring frequently, until melted and smooth. Remove from the heat and stir in 3 tablespoons of the confectioners' sugar. Beat the egg yolks with 2 tablespoons of water, then gradually beat into the frosting. Continue to add the confectioners' sugar, beating well until a smooth, spreadable frosting is formed. Use to cover the entire cake, then decorate with white and milk chocolate buttons or rose petals and let set before serving.

COOK'S TIP
Placing a small circle of baking paper in the bottom of the pan will make the cake easier to remove. Ease the sides of the cake with a round-bladed knife.

Orange Chocolate Ring Cake

The addition of fresh oranges makes this cake very fruity and moist.
The flavor is complemented by the orange and chocolate frostings.

🕐 25 mins   🕐 40 mins

MAKES 8-10 SLICES

INGREDIENTS

6 oz/175 g butter, softened, plus extra
   for greasing

2 small oranges

3 oz/85 g semisweet chocolate

1⅔ cups self-rising flour

1½ tsp baking powder

scant 1 cup golden superfine sugar

3 eggs, beaten

FROSTING

1½ cups confectioners' sugar

2 tbsp orange juice

2 oz/55 g semisweet chocolate, broken
   into pieces

1 Preheat the oven to 325°F/160°C. Grease a 3¾-cup fluted or plain ring mold. Grate the rind from one of the oranges and set aside. Pare the rind from the other orange and set aside. Cut the skin and pith from the oranges, then cut them into segments by cutting down between the membranes with a sharp knife. Chop the segments into small pieces, reserving as much juice as possible. Grate the chocolate coarsely on to a plate.

2 Sift the flour and baking powder into a bowl. Add the butter, sugar, eggs, grated orange rind and any reserved juice. Beat until the batter is smooth. Fold in the chopped oranges and grated chocolate. Spoon the batter into the prepared pan and bake for 40 minutes, or until well risen and golden brown. Leave in the pan for 5 minutes, then turn out on to a wire rack to cool completely.

3 To make the frosting, sift the confectioners' sugar into a bowl and stir in enough orange juice to make a coating consistency. Using a spoon, drizzle the frosting over the cake. Put the chocolate in a heatproof bowl set over a saucepan of gently simmering water until melted. Drizzle the melted chocolate over the cake. Scatter the reserved strips of rind on top. Let set before serving.

COOK'S TIP
You do not need to be skillful at cake decorating to frost a cake as described above. The more untidy it looks the better!

Apricot & Chocolate Ring

A tasty fruit bread in the shape of a ring. You could use golden raisins instead of the dried apricots if preferred.

1 hr   35 mins

SERVES 12

INGREDIENTS

3 oz/85 g butter, cut into pieces, plus extra for greasing

4 cups self-rising flour, sifted

4 tbsp superfine sugar

2 eggs, beaten

⅔ cup milk

all-purpose flour, for dusting

FILLING AND DECORATION

2 tbsp butter, melted

¾ cup no-soak dried apricots, chopped

½ cup semisweet chocolate chips

1–2 tbsp milk, for glazing

1 oz/25 g semisweet chocolate, broken into pieces

1 Preheat the oven to 350°F/180°C. Grease a 10-inch/25-cm cake pan and base-line with parchment paper.

2 Rub the butter into the flour until the mixture resembles fine bread crumbs. Stir in the superfine sugar, eggs, and milk to form a soft dough.

3 Roll out the dough on a lightly floured work counter to form a 14-inch/35-cm square.

4 Brush the melted butter over the surface of the dough. Mix together the apricots and chocolate chips and spread them over the dough to within 1 inch/2.5 cm of the top and bottom.

5 Roll up the dough tightly, like a jelly roll, and cut it into 1-inch/2.5-cm slices. Stand the slices in a ring around the edge of the prepared pan at a slight tilt. Brush with a little milk.

6 Bake in the preheated oven for 30 minutes, or until cooked and golden. Let the bread cool in the pan for about 15 minutes, then transfer to a wire rack to cool.

7 Put the chocolate in a heatproof bowl set over a pan of gently simmering water until melted. Drizzle the melted chocolate over the ring, to decorate.

COOK'S TIP

This cake is best served very fresh, ideally on the day it is made. It is fabulous served slightly warm.

Calypso Fruit Cake

Here's a rich, spicy fruit cake with good keeping qualities which has a moist dense flavor.

20 mins

1 hr 45 mins–2 hrs

SERVES 14–16

INGREDIENTS

1 tsp sunflower oil, for oiling

1¼ cups no-soak dried prunes

5 tbsp water

4 oz/115 g semisweet chocolate

8 oz/225 g butter, softened

1 cup dark muscovado sugar

1 tsp ground cinnamon

1 tsp ground ginger

½ tsp allspice

4 eggs, beaten

1¾ cups all-purpose flour

generous ½ cup ground almonds

1½ cups golden raisins

1 cup raisins

½ cup dried cranberries

1½ cups candied cherries, chopped

½ cup angelica, chopped

1 cup mixed chopped nuts

2 tbsp dark rum or cognac

4–6 crushed brown sugar lumps or 2 tbsp raw sugar

COOK'S TIP

This cake keeps really well. If you want to serve it for a special occasion, prick the bottom lightly and pour over 2 tablespoons of rum before using.

1 Preheat the oven to 325°F/160°C. Oil and line a 9-inch/23-cm cake pan with parchment paper. Place the prunes in a pan with 5 tablespoons water and place over moderate heat. Bring to a boil. Simmer for 5–8 minutes or until the water has been absorbed and the prunes are plump. Let cool, then purée in a food processor or blender. Melt the chocolate in a heatproof bowl set over a pan of gently simmering water. Stir until smooth, then stir into the prune purée. Set aside.

2 Cream the butter with the sugar and spices until light and fluffy, then beat in the prune and chocolate mixture. Add the eggs a little at a time, beating well between each addition and adding a little flour after each addition.

3 When all the eggs have been added, stir in the remaining flour together with the ground almonds. Add all the fruits and nuts and stir lightly, then add the rum and mix to form a soft dropping consistency. Turn into the prepared cake pan and smooth the top. Sprinkle with the crushed sugar lumps or raw sugar.

4 Bake in the preheated oven for 1 hour 45 minutes–2 hours, or until a skewer inserted into the center of the cake comes out clean. Remove from the oven and let cool before removing from the pan and discarding the lining paper. Let stand until cold before cutting. Store in an airtight container or wrap well in waxed paper and cover in foil.

Nutty Chocolate Ring

This cake also makes a delicious dessert with the center filled with soft fruits and served with lightly whipped cream.

15 mins   30–40 mins

SERVES 8–10

INGREDIENTS

1 tsp sunflower oil, for oiling

1 tbsp all-purpose flour, for dusting

4 oz/115 g butter or margarine, softened

½ cup superfine sugar

1 tsp ground cinnamon

2 eggs, separated

scant ¼ cup all-purpose flour

½ tsp baking powder

4 oz/115 g milk chocolate

scant ¾ cup ground almonds

2–3 tbsp cooled boiled water

⅓ cup toasted slivered almonds, plus a few extra to decorate

25 g/1 oz white chocolate

1 Preheat the oven to 350°F/180°C. Lightly oil a 2-pint/1.2-liter ring mold and line the bottom with a circle of parchment paper. Dust lightly with flour. Cream the butter with the sugar and cinnamon until light and fluffy. Add the egg yolks, adding a little flour after each addition. Sift the remaining flour and baking powder together. When all the egg yolks have been added, stir in the flour and baking powder.

2 Melt the chocolate in a heatproof bowl set over a pan of gently simmering water. Stir until smooth, then stir into the mixture and then mix in the ground almonds with the cooled boiled water to give a soft dropping consistency. Add the slivered almonds and stir lightly. Whisk the egg whites until stiff, add to the batter and stir lightly then spoon the batter into the prepared cake pan.

3 Bake in the preheated oven for 25–35 minutes, or until a skewer inserted into the center comes out clean. Remove from the oven and let cool for a few minutes before turning out on to a wire rack. Leave until cold. Melt the white chocolate in a heatproof bowl set over a pan of gently simmering water and drizzle over the cold cake, then sprinkle with a few extra slivered almonds.

COOK'S TIP
The easiest way to toast slivered almonds is to spread them on a cookie sheet and place in the oven at 375°F/190°C for 5–7 minutes.

Tropical Fruit Vacherin

Meringue layers are sandwiched with a rich chocolate cream and topped with tropical fruit. Prepare in advance and make up just before required.

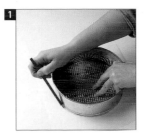

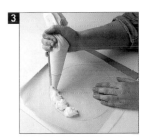

1 hr 30 mins • 1 hr 30 mins

SERVES 10

INGREDIENTS

6 egg whites

1¼ cups superfine sugar

¾ cup shredded coconut

FILLING AND TOPPING

3 oz/85 g semisweet chocolate, broken into pieces

3 egg yolks

3 tbsp water

1 tbsp dark rum (optional)

4 tbsp superfine sugar

2 cups heavy cream

selection of tropical fruits, sliced or cut into bite-size pieces

1 Preheat the oven to 275°F/140°C. Draw 3 × 8-inch/20-cm circles on parchment paper, and place on cookie sheets.

2 Whisk the egg whites until soft peaks form, then gradually whisk in half of the sugar and continue whisking until the mixture is very stiff and glossy. Carefully fold in the remaining sugar and the coconut.

3 Spoon the mixture into a pastry bag fitted with a star tip and cover the circles with piped swirls. Bake in the preheated oven for 1½ hours, changing the position of the cookie sheets halfway through. Without opening the oven door, turn off the oven and let the meringues cool inside the oven, then peel away the parchment paper.

4 While the meringues are cooling, make the filling. Place the chocolate pieces, egg yolks, water, rum (if using), and sugar in a small heatproof bowl and place it over a pan of gently simmering water. Cook over low heat, stirring, until the chocolate has melted and the mixture has thickened. Cover with a disk of parchment paper and set aside until cold.

5 Whip the cream and fold two-thirds of it into the chocolate mixture. Sandwich the meringue layers together with the chocolate mixture. Place the remaining cream in a pastry bag fitted with a star tip and pipe around the edge of the meringue. Arrange the tropical fruits in the center.

Raspberry Vacherin

A vacherin is made of layers of crisp meringue sandwiched together with fruit and cream. It makes a fabulous gâteau for special occasions.

1hr 45 mins   1hr 30 mins

SERVES 10

INGREDIENTS

3 egg whites

¾ cup superfine sugar

1 tsp cornstarch

1 oz/25 g semisweet chocolate, grated

FILLING

6 oz/175 g semisweet chocolate

2 cups heavy cream, whipped

2 cups fresh raspberries

a little melted chocolate, to decorate

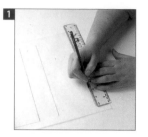

1 Preheat the oven to 275°F/140°C. Draw 3 rectangles, 4 x 10 inches/ 10 x 25 cm, on sheets of parchment paper, and place on 2 cookie sheets.

2 Whisk the egg whites in a mixing bowl until soft peaks form, then gradually whisk in half of the sugar and continue whisking until the mixture is very stiff and glossy.

3 Carefully fold in the rest of the sugar, the cornstarch, and the grated chocolate with a metal spoon or a spatula.

4 Spoon the meringue mixture into a pastry bag fitted with a ½-inch/ 1-cm plain tip and pipe lines across the rectangles.

5 Bake in the preheated oven for 1½ hours, changing the position of the cookie sheets halfway through. Without opening the oven door, turn off the oven and let the meringues cool inside the oven, then peel away the parchment paper.

6 To make the filling, melt the chocolate and spread it over 2 of the meringue layers. Let the filling harden.

7 Place 1 chocolate-coated meringue on a plate and top with about one-third of the cream and raspberries. Gently place the second chocolate-coated meringue on top and spread with half of the remaining cream and raspberries. Place the last meringue on the top and decorate with the remaining cream and raspberries.

8 Put a few pieces of semisweet chocolate in a heatproof bowl set over a pan of gently simmering water until melted. Drizzle a little melted chocolate over the top of the vacherin and serve.

Chocolate Layer Log

This unusual chocolate cake is very popular with children, who love the appearance of the layers when it is sliced.

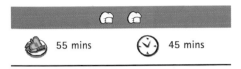

🍰 55 mins   🕐 45 mins

SERVES 8

INGREDIENTS

4 oz/115 g soft margarine, plus extra for greasing

½ cup superfine sugar

2 eggs

¾ cup self-rising flour

¼ cup unsweetened cocoa

2 tbsp milk

WHITE CHOCOLATE BUTTERCREAM

2¾ oz/75 g white chocolate

2 tbsp milk

⅔ cup butter

¾ cup confectioners' sugar

2 tbsp orange-flavored liqueur

chocolate curls (see page 9), to decorate

1 Preheat the oven to 350°F/180°C. Grease and line the sides of 2 x 14-oz/400-g food cans.

2 Beat together the margarine and sugar in a bowl until light and fluffy. Gradually add the eggs, beating well after each addition. Sift the flour and unsweetened cocoa together and fold into the cake batter. Fold in the milk.

3 Divide the cake batter between the 2 prepared cans. Stand the cans on a cookie sheet and bake in the preheated oven for 40 minutes, or until springy to the touch. Let cool for about 5 minutes in the cans, then turn out and cool completely on a wire rack.

4 Meanwhile, make the buttercream. Put the chocolate and milk in a pan and heat gently until the chocolate has melted, stirring until well combined. Let cool slightly. Beat together the butter and confectioners' sugar until light and fluffy. Beat in the orange liqueur. Gradually beat in the chocolate mixture.

5 To assemble, cut both cakes into ½-inch/1-cm thick slices, then sandwich together with some of the buttercream.

6 Place the cake on a serving plate and spread the remaining buttercream over the top and sides. Decorate with the chocolate curls, then serve the cake cut diagonally into slices.

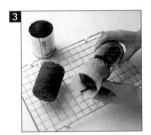

Rich Chocolate Loaf

This chocolate dessert is made without baking, simply by combining its rich ingredients, and then chilling them.

30 mins, plus
1 hr chilling

0 mins

MAKES 15 SLICES

INGREDIENTS

1 tsp melted butter, for greasing

½ cup almonds

5½ oz/150 g semisweet chocolate

6 tbsp butter, sweet for preference

¾ cup canned condensed milk

2 tsp ground cinnamon

2¾ oz/75 g amaretti cookies, crushed

⅓ cup no-soak dried apricots, chopped coarsely

1 Line a 1 lb 7-oz/650-g loaf pan with foil and grease very lightly.

2 Using a sharp knife, coarsely chop the almonds.

3 Place the chocolate, butter, condensed milk, and cinnamon in a heavy-based pan.

4 Heat the mixture over low heat for 3–4 minutes, stirring constantly with a wooden spoon, until the chocolate has melted. Beat thoroughly.

5 Using a wooden spoon, stir the almonds, crushed amaretti cookies, and apricots into the chocolate mixture, until completely incorporated.

6 Pour the mixture into the prepared pan and let it chill in the refrigerator for about 1 hour, or until set.

7 Cut the loaf into slices to serve.

COOK'S TIP

To melt chocolate, break it into manageable pieces. The smaller the pieces, the quicker it will melt.

Chocolate Lamington Cake

This cake is based on an Australian cake named after Lord Lamington, a former Governor of Queensland.

🍰 🍰 🍰

🍲 50 mins   🕐 45 mins

SERVES 8

INGREDIENTS

6 oz/175 g butter or margarine, plus extra for greasing

¾ cup superfine sugar

3 eggs, beaten lightly

1¼ cups self-rising flour

2 tbsp unsweetened cocoa

1¾ oz/50 g semisweet chocolate, broken into pieces

5 tbsp milk

1 tsp butter

¾ cup confectioners' sugar

about 8 tbsp dry unsweetened coconut

⅔ cup heavy cream, whipped

1 Preheat the oven to 350°F/180°C. Lightly grease a 1-lb/450-g loaf pan—preferably a long, thin pan measuring about 3 x 10 inches/7.5 x 25 cm.

2 Cream together the butter or margarine and sugar in a bowl until light and fluffy. Gradually add the eggs, beating well after each addition. Sift the flour and unsweetened cocoa together. Fold into the batter.

3 Pour the batter into the prepared pan and level the top. Bake in the preheated oven for 40 minutes or until springy to the touch. Let cool for 5 minutes in the pan, then turn out on to a wire rack to cool completely.

4 Place the chocolate, milk, and butter in a heatproof bowl set over a pan of gently simmering water. Stir until the

chocolate has melted. Add the confectioners' sugar and beat until smooth. Let the frosting cool until it is thick enough to spread, then spread it all over the cake. Sprinkle with the dry unsweetened coconut and let stand until the frosting has set.

5 Cut a V-shape wedge from the top of the cake. Put the cream in a pastry bag fitted with a plain or star tip. Pipe the cream down the center of the channel and replace the wedge of cake on top of the cream. Pipe cream down either side of the wedge of cake. Serve.

Chocolate & Vanilla Loaf

An old-fashioned favorite, this cake will keep well if stored in an airtight container or well wrapped in a piece of foil in a cool place and left.

50 mins   35 mins

SERVES 10

INGREDIENTS

¾ cup superfine sugar

6 oz/175 g soft margarine, plus extra for greasing

½ tsp vanilla extract

3 eggs

2 cups self-rising flour, sifted

1¾ oz/50 g semisweet chocolate, broken into pieces

confectioners' sugar, for dusting

1 Preheat the oven to 375°F/190°C. Lightly grease a 1-lb/450-g loaf pan.

2 Beat the sugar and soft margarine together in a bowl until the mixture is light and fluffy.

3 Beat in the vanilla extract. Gradually add the eggs, beating well after each addition. Carefully fold the self-rising flour into the batter.

4 Divide the batter in half. Put the semisweet chocolate in a heatproof bowl set over a pan of gently simmering water until melted. Stir the melted chocolate into one half of the batter until well combined.

5 Place the vanilla batter in the pan and smooth the top. Spread the chocolate batter over the vanilla layer.

6 Bake in the preheated oven for 30 minutes, or until springy to the touch.

7 Let the loaf cool in the pan for a few minutes before transferring to a wire rack to cool completely.

8 Serve the loaf dusted with confectioners' sugar.

COOK'S TIP
Freeze the loaf undecorated for up to 2 months. Thaw at room temperature.

Christmas Cake

Christmas would not be the same without a traditional fruitcake. This one is decorated with a delicious lemony white frosting.

🍰 45 mins plus 8 hrs to soak   🕐 3 hrs

MAKES 8-INCH/20-CM CAKE

INGREDIENTS

scant 1 cup raisins

¾ cup pitted dates, chopped

¾ cup golden raisins

generous ½ cup candied cherries, rinsed and drained

generous ½ cup cognac

8 oz/225 g butter, plus extra for greasing

1 cup superfine sugar

4 eggs

grated rind of 1 orange and 1 lemon

1 tbsp molasses

2 cups all-purpose flour

½ tsp salt

½ tsp baking powder

1 tsp allspice

2 tbsp toasted almonds, chopped

2 tbsp toasted hazelnuts, chopped

FROSTING

3 cups confectioners' sugar

1 egg white

juice of 1 lemon

1 tsp vanilla extract

holly leaves, to decorate

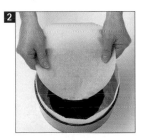

1 Make this cake at least 3 weeks in advance. Put all the fruit in a bowl, pour over the cognac and soak overnight.

2 Preheat the oven to 225°F/110°C. Grease and line an 8-inch/20-cm cake pan with waxed paper. In a bowl, cream together the butter and sugar until fluffy. Gradually beat in the eggs, then stir in the citrus rind and molasses. In a separate bowl, sift together the flour, salt, baking powder, and allspice, then fold it into the egg mixture. Fold in the soaked fruit and cognac, and the chopped nuts. Spoon the batter into the prepared cake pan and bake for at least 3 hours. If it starts to brown too quickly, cover with foil. The cake is cooked when a skewer inserted into the center comes out clean.

Remove from the oven and cool on a wire rack. Store in an airtight container until required.

3 To make the frosting, put the confectioners' sugar, egg white, lemon juice, and vanilla into a bowl and mix until smooth. Spread it over the top and sides of the cake, using a fork to give a textured finish. Decorate with holly leaves.

Easy Christmas Cake

This is an easy way of making a Christmas cake because there is no creaming required. Boiling the fruit mixture first makes a very moist cake.

45 mins

2 hrs 10 mins–
2 hrs 40 mins

MAKES 8-INCH/20-CM CAKE

INGREDIENTS

9 oz/250 g butter, cut into pieces, plus extra
    for greasing

2 cups dark muscovado sugar

2 tbsp molasses

3 lb 5 oz/1.5 kg luxury dry fruits

finely grated rind and juice of
    1 large orange

6 tbsp cognac

5 eggs, beaten

1¾ cups mixed nuts, chopped coarsely

½ cup ground almonds

scant 3 cups all-purpose flour

½ tsp baking powder

1 tbsp allspice

1 Preheat the oven to 300°F/150°C. Put the butter, sugar, molasses, dry fruits, orange rind and juice, and cognac in a large pan. Bring slowly to a boil, then simmer gently for 10 minutes, stirring occasionally. Remove from the heat and let cool.

2 Grease and base-line an 8-inch/ 20-cm deep round cake pan and wrap a double layer of paper round the outside of the pan. Stir the eggs, mixed nuts, and ground almonds into the fruit mixture and

mix well. Sift in the flour, baking powde[r] and allspice. Stir in gently but thoroughl[y.] Spoon into the prepared pan and smoot[h] the top.

3 Bake in the preheated oven for 1 hou[r,] then reduce the heat to 275°F/140°[C] and bake for 2–2½ hours, until a skewe[r] inserted into the center comes out clea[r.] Cool in the pan, then turn out and stor[e] wrapped in waxed paper and foil, unt[il] ready to decorate.

COOK'S TIP
Cover the cake with marzipan and frosting or simply top with nuts and fruit.

Yule Log

A chocolate yule log is a popular alternative to a traditional Christmas cake and is an eye-catching centerpiece on a festive tea table.

45 mins   16–18 mins

SERVES 8

INGREDIENTS

CHOCOLATE SPONGE

butter, for greasing

3 eggs

generous ½ cup superfine sugar

½ cup all-purpose flour

¼ cup unsweetened cocoa

superfine sugar, for sprinkling

SYRUP

generous ¼ cup golden superfine sugar

4 tbsp Cointreau

ORANGE BUTTERCREAM

4 tbsp butter, softened

¾ cup confectioners' sugar, sifted

grated rind of 1 orange

1 tbsp Cointreau

CHOCO BUTTERCREAM

1 tbsp unsweetened cocoa

3 oz/85 g butter

1¼ cups confectioners' sugar, sifted

coarse chocolate caraque (see page 9)

unsweetened cocoa and confectioners' sugar, for dusting

1 Preheat the oven to 400°F/200°C. Grease and line an 8 x 12-inch/20 x 30-cm jelly roll pan. Put the eggs and sugar in a bowl and whisk together with an electric whisk, until thick and mousselike and a trail is left when the whisk is dragged across the surface. Sift the flour and cocoa together into a bowl, then fold into the whisked batter. Turn into the prepared pan and bake in the oven for 8–10 minutes, until the cake springs back when lightly pressed. Wring out a clean dish towel in hot water and place on a work counter. Put a sheet of waxed paper on top and sprinkle with superfine sugar. Turn the sponge on to the paper, peel off the lining paper, and trim the edges of the cake. Roll up the sponge from a long side, with the paper inside. Hold in position for a few seconds, then cool on a wire rack with the join underneath.

2 To make the syrup, put the sugar in a small pan with generous ½ cup water. Heat gently until the sugar dissolves then boil for 2 minutes until syrupy. Stir in the Cointreau and let cool. Unroll the jelly roll and remove the paper. Sprinkle with the syrup. To make the buttercream, put the butter in a bowl and beat until creamy. Gradually beat in the confectioners' sugar, then the orange rind and Cointreau. Beat until smooth. Spread over the sponge and roll up again.

3 To make the chocolate buttercream, put the unsweetened cocoa in a small bowl and stir in 1 tablespoon boiling water. Let cool. Put the butter in a bowl and beat until creamy. Gradually beat in the confectioners' sugar, then beat in the cooled cocoa until smooth. Cut off a quarter of the roll diagonally and attach to the side of the roll with chocolate buttercream. Cover the roll with the remaining buttercream and use a spatula to mark lines to represent bark. Cover the cake with chocolate caraque and sift unsweetened cocoa over. Finish with a dusting of confectioners' sugar.

White Chocolate Yule Log

This log is delicious at Christmas—and can easily be adapted for other occasions! Decorate with marzipan holly berries and leaves if you like.

45 mins

8–10 mins

SERVES 8–10

INGREDIENTS

1 tsp sunflower oil, for oiling

3 eggs

½ cup superfine sugar, plus extra for sprinkling

¾ cup self-rising flour

2 oz/55 g white chocolate, grated

FROSTING

6 oz/175 g butter, softened

3 cups confectioners' sugar

1–2 tbsp milk

1 tsp vanilla extract

4 oz/115 g white chocolate, melted

TO DECORATE

½–1 tsp unsweetened cocoa

marzipan holly berries and leaves

1 Preheat the oven to 425°F/220°C. Lightly oil and line a jelly roll pan with 1 whole sheet of nonstick parchment paper. Place the eggs and sugar in a heatproof bowl set over a pan of gently simmering water. Whisk until very thick and creamy, then remove from the water and continue to whisk until cool. (Alternatively, place the eggs and sugar in the bowl of a free-standing mixer and whisk until thick and creamy.)

2 Sift the flour into the whisked mixture and stir lightly together with 1 tablespoon of cooled boiled water. Melt the chocolate in a heatproof bowl set over a pan of gently simmering water. Stir until smooth, then stir into the batter. Pour into the lined jelly roll pan.

3 Tap the pan lightly on the work counter to smooth the top. Bake in the preheated oven for 8–10 minutes, or until the top springs back when touched lightly with a finger. Remove from the oven and invert on to a sheet of parchment paper sprinkled with superfine sugar. Roll up and leave until cold.

4 Cream the butter with the confectioners' sugar adding sufficient milk to give a smooth spreadable consistency. Stir in the vanilla extract and melted white chocolate.

5 Unroll the cold cake and trim all the edges. Spread one-third of the prepared frosting to within ¼ inch/5 mm of the edges, and roll up as tightly as possible. Cut the jelly roll diagonally in half and arrange in a log shape. Use the remaining frosting to cover the cake completely. Mark the frosting with the tines of a fork to give a bark effect and decorate with a sprinkle of unsweetened cocoa and the marzipan holly berries and leaves.

Panforte di Siena

This famous Tuscan honey and nut cake is a Christmas specialty.
In Italy it is sold in pretty boxes, and served in very thin slices.

45 mins

1 hr 10 mins

SERVES 12

INGREDIENTS

1 cup whole almonds, split

¾ cup hazelnuts

½ cup candied peel, chopped

⅓ cup no-soak dried apricots

⅓ cup candied pineapple

grated rind of 1 large orange

½ cup all-purpose flour

2 tbsp unsweetened cocoa

2 tsp ground cinnamon

½ cup superfine sugar

½ cup honey

confectioners' sugar, for dusting

1 Preheat the oven to 300°F/150°C. Toast the almonds under the broiler until lightly browned, and then place in a bowl.

2 Toast the hazelnuts until the skins split. Place on a dry dish towel and rub off the skins. Coarsely chop the hazelnuts and add them to the almonds, together with the candied peel.

3 Chop the apricots and pineapple fairly finely and add to the nuts, together with the orange rind. Mix well.

4 Sift the flour, unsweetened cocoa, and cinnamon into the nut mixture and mix well.

5 Line a round 8-inch/20-cm cake pan or deep, loose-bottomed flan pan with parchment paper.

6 Put the sugar and honey into a pan and heat until the sugar dissolves. Boil gently for about 5 minutes, or until the mixture thickens and starts to turn a deeper shade of brown. Quickly add to the nut mixture and mix thoroughly. Turn into the prepared pan and smooth the top using the back of a damp spoon.

7 Cook in the preheated oven for 1 hour. Remove the cake from the oven and leave in the pan until completely cool. Take out of the pan and carefully peel off the paper. Before serving, decorate the cake by dredging with sifted confectioners' sugar.

Bûche de Noël

This is the traditional French Christmas cake. It consists of a chocolate cake roll filled with and encased in a delicious rich chocolate frosting.

1 hr   12 mins

SERVES 10

I N G R E D I E N T S

C A K E

butter, for greasing

4 eggs

½ cup superfine sugar

⅔ cup self-rising flour

2 tbsp unsweetened cocoa

F R O S T I N G

5½ oz/150 g semisweet chocolate, broken into pieces

2 egg yolks

⅔ cup milk

4 oz/115 g butter

4 tbsp confectioners' sugar

2 tbsp dark rum (optional)

T O   D E C O R A T E

a little white glacé or royal frosting

confectioners' sugar, for dusting

holly leaves

1 Preheat the oven to 400°F/200°C. Grease and line a 12 x 9-inch/30 x 23-cm jelly roll pan.

2 Beat the eggs and sugar in a bowl with an electric whisk for 10 minutes, or until the mixture is light and foamy and a trail is left when the whisk is lifted off the surface. Fold in the flour and cocoa. Pour into the pan and bake in the preheated oven for 12 minutes, or until springy to the touch. Turn out on to parchment paper sprinkled with superfine sugar. Peel off the lining parchment and trim the edges. Cut a small slit halfway into the cake, ½ inch/ 1 cm from one of the short ends. Roll up tightly, enclosing the parchment paper. Place on a wire rack to cool.

3 To make the frosting, put the chocolate in a heatproof bowl set over a pan of gently simmering water. Beat in the egg yolks, whisk in the milk, and cook, stirring all the time, until the custard thickens enough to coat the back of a wooden spoon. Cover with dampened waxed paper and cool. Beat the butter and sugar until pale. Beat in the custard and rum (if using).

4 Unroll the sponge, spread with one-third of the frosting and roll up. Place on a serving plate. Spread the remaining frosting over the cake and mark with a fork to give the effect of bark. Let set. Pipe glacé frosting to form the rings of the log. Sprinkle with sugar and decorate with holly leaves.

Black Forest Roulade

Do not worry if the roulade cracks when it is rolled up. It has a tendency to do this—and it does not detract from the luscious taste.

25 mins plus overnight standing

25 mins

SERVES 8–10

INGREDIENTS

1 tsp sunflower oil, for oiling

6 oz/175 g semisweet chocolate

2–3 tbsp kirsch or cognac

5 eggs

1 cup superfine sugar

2 tbsp confectioners' sugar, sifted

FILLING AND DECORATION

1½ cups heavy cream

1 tbsp kirsch or cognac

12 oz/350 g fresh black cherries, pitted or 14 oz/400 g canned sour cherries, drained and pitted

chocolate squares, to decorate

1 Preheat the oven to 375°F/190°C. Line a jelly roll pan with 1 whole sheet of nonstick parchment paper. Break the chocolate into small pieces and place in a heatproof bowl set over a pan of gently simmering water. Add the kirsch and heat gently, stirring until the mixture is smooth. Remove from the pan and set aside.

2 Place the eggs and sugar in a large heatproof bowl and set over the pan of gently simmering water. (Alternatively, place in the bowl of a free-standing mixer and use a balloon whisk.) Whisk the eggs and sugar until very thick and creamy and the whisk leaves a trail when dragged across the surface. Remove from the heat and whisk in the cooled chocolate.

3 Spoon into the prepared jelly roll pan, then tap the pan lightly on the work counter to smooth the top. Bake in the preheated oven for 20 minutes, or until the top feels firm to the touch. Remove from the oven and immediately invert on to a whole sheet of parchment paper which is sprinkled with the confectioners' sugar. Lift off the pan and lining paper, then roll up, encasing the parchment paper in the roulade. Leave until cold.

4 Whip the cream until soft peaks form, then stir in the kirsch, reserving 1–2 tablespoons. Unroll the roulade and spread the cream to within ¼ inch/5 mm of the edges. Set aside a few of the cherries for decoration and scatter the remainder over the cream. Carefully roll up the roulade again and place on a serving platter. Decorate the top with small rosettes or small spoonfuls of the reserved cream, the reserved cherries, and squares of chocolate.

Chocolate Roulade

Don't worry if the cake cracks when rolled, this is quite normal. If it doesn't crack, consider yourself a real chocolate wizard in the kitchen!

1 hr   15 mins

SERVES 6

I N G R E D I E N T S

5½ oz/150 g semisweet chocolate, broken into pieces

2 tbsp water

6 eggs

¾ cup superfine sugar

¼ cup all-purpose flour

1 tbsp unsweetened cocoa

FILLING

1¼ cups heavy cream

1 cup sliced strawberries

TO DECORATE

confectioners' sugar, for dusting

chocolate leaves (see page 9)

1 Preheat the oven to 400°F/200°C. Line a 15 x 10-inch/38 x 25-cm jelly roll pan. Put the chocolate and water in a heatproof bowl set over a pan of gently simmering water until melted. Let cool.

2 Place the eggs and sugar in a bowl and whisk for 10 minutes, or until the mixture is pale and foamy and a trail is left when the whisk is lifted off the surface. Whisk in the chocolate. Sift the flour and unsweetened cocoa together and fold into the batter. Pour into the pan and smooth the top.

3 Bake in the preheated oven for 12 minutes. Dust a sheet of parchment paper with confectioners' sugar. Turn out the roulade and remove the lining paper. Roll the roulade with the fresh parchment paper inside. Place on a wire rack, cover with a damp dish towel, and let cool.

4 Whip the cream. Unroll the roulade and scatter over the fruit. Spread three-quarters of the cream over the roulade and re-roll. Dust with confectioners' sugar.

5 Place the roulade on a plate. Pipe the rest of the cream down the center. Make the chocolate leaves and use them to decorate the roulade.

Double Chocolate Roulade

A semisweet chocolate mousse is rolled round white chocolate cream to make a luscious dessert, perfect as a finale to any special-occasion meal.

  30 mins plus standing and chilling   20-25 mins

SERVES 8

INGREDIENTS

ROULADE

4 oz/115 g semisweet chocolate, broken into pieces

4 eggs, separated

generous ½ cup golden superfine sugar

1 tsp instant coffee granules dissolved in 2 tbsp hot water, cooled

FILLING

1 cup whipping cream

5 oz/140 g white chocolate

3 tbsp Tia Maria

TO DECORATE

sifted confectioners' sugar

sifted unsweetened cocoa

1 Preheat the oven to 350°F/180°C. Line a 9 x13-inch/23 x 33-cm jelly roll pan with parchment paper. To make the roulade, put the chocolate in a heatproof bowl set over a pan of gently simmering water until melted. Let cool. Put the egg yolks and sugar in a bowl and whisk together until pale and mousselike. Gently fold in the cooled melted chocolate followed by the cooled coffee. Put the egg whites in another bowl and whisk until stiff but not dry. Stir a little of the egg white into the chocolate batter and carefully fold in the rest. Pour the batter into the prepared pan and bake in the oven for 15-20 minutes, until firm. Cover with a clean damp dish towel and leave in the pan overnight.

2 To make the filling, put the cream in a pan and heat until almost boiling. Put the white chocolate in a food processor and chop coarsely. With the motor running, pour the hot cream through the feed tube. Process for 10-15 seconds, until smooth. Stir in the Tia Maria. Transfer to a bowl and let cool. Cover and chill overnight. When you are ready to assemble the roulade, whisk the chocolate cream until it starts to form soft peaks.

3 Cut a sheet of waxed paper slightly larger than the roulade, place on the work counter and sift confectioners' sugar over it. Turn the roulade out on to the paper and carefully peel away the lining paper. Spread the white chocolate cream over the roulade and roll up, starting at a short side nearest you and pushing away from you with the paper. Transfer seam-side down to a serving dish. Chill for 2 hours.

COOK'S TIP
If you do not have time, it is not essential to chill the roulade for 2 hours before serving. However, the roulade firms up in this time and becomes easier to slice.

Chocolate Coconut Roulade

Here, a coconut-flavored roulade is encased in a rich chocolate coating.
It is served with fresh raspberry coulis, which provides a piquant contrast.

40 mins   15 mins

SERVES 8

INGREDIENTS

butter, for greasing

3 eggs

generous ⅓ cup superfine sugar,
  plus extra for sprinkling

generous ⅓ cup self-rising flour

1 tbsp block creamed coconut, softened
  with 1 tbsp boiling water

⅓ cup dry unsweetened coconut

6 tbsp good-quality raspberry jelly

CHOCOLATE COATING

7 oz/200 g semisweet chocolate

5 tbsp butter

2 tbsp corn syrup

RASPBERRY COULIS

2 cups fresh or frozen raspberries,
  thawed if frozen

2 tbsp water

4 tbsp confectioners' sugar

1 Preheat the oven to 400°F/200°C. Grease and line a 9 x 12-inch/23 x 30-cm jelly roll pan with parchment paper. Whisk the eggs and superfine sugar in a large mixing bowl (with a hand or electric whisk) for about 10 minutes, or until the mixture is very light and foamy and a trail is left when the whisk is dragged across the surface.

2 Sift the flour and fold in with a metal spoon or a spatula. Fold in the creamed coconut and dry unsweetened coconut. Pour the cake batter into the prepared pan and bake in the preheated oven for 10–12 minutes, or until springy to the touch.

3 Sprinkle a sheet of parchment paper with a little superfine sugar and place on top of a damp dish towel. Turn the cake out on to the parchment and carefully peel away the lining paper. Spread the jelly over the sponge and roll up from the short end, using the dish towel to help you. Place seam-side down on a wire rack and let the roulade cool completely.

4 Meanwhile, make the coating. Melt the chocolate and butter, stirring. Stir in the corn syrup; let cool for 5 minutes. Spread it over the cooled roulade and let it set. To make the coulis, purée the fruit in a food processor with the water and sugar; strain to remove the seeds. Cut the roulade into slices and serve with the raspberry coulis.

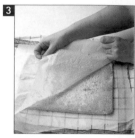

Strawberry Roulade

Serve this moist, light sponge cake rolled up with a creamy almond and strawberry filling for a delicious tea-time treat.

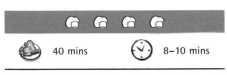

🍰 40 mins   🕐 8–10 mins

SERVES 8

INGREDIENTS

3 large eggs

⅔ cup superfine sugar

scant 1 cup all-purpose flour

1 tbsp hot water

FILLING

¾ cup lowfat mascarpone cheese

1 tsp almond extract

1½ cups small strawberries

TO DECORATE

1 tbsp slivered almonds, toasted

1 tsp confectioners' sugar

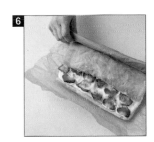

1 Preheat the oven to 425°F/220°C. Line a 14 x 10-inch/35 x 25-cm jelly roll pan with parchment paper.

2 Place the eggs in a heatproof bowl with the superfine sugar. Place the bowl over a pan of gently simmering water and whisk until pale and thick.

3 Remove the bowl from the pan. Sift in the flour and fold into the eggs along with the hot water. Pour the batter into the pan and bake in the preheated oven for 8–10 minutes, until golden and set.

4 Turn out the cake on to a sheet of parchment paper. Peel off the lining paper and roll up the sponge cake tightly along with the parchment paper. Wrap in a dish towel and let cool.

5 Mix together the mascarpone and the almond extract. Reserving a few strawberries for decoration, wash, hull, and slice the rest. Chill the mascarpone mixture and the strawberries in the refrigerator until required.

6 Unroll the cake, spread the mascarpone mixture over the surface, and sprinkle with sliced strawberries. Roll the cake up again and transfer to a serving plate. Sprinkle with almonds and lightly dust with confectioners' sugar. Decorate with the reserved strawberries.

Victoria Sandwich Cake

This cake is extremely versatile, and lends itself to a number of treatments, such as filling with whipped cream and halved strawberries.

40 mins 25–30 mins

SERVES 8

INGREDIENTS

1½ cups self-rising flour

1 tsp baking powder

6 oz/175 g butter, softened, plus extra for greasing

scant 1 cup golden superfine sugar

3 eggs

TO FINISH

3 tbsp raspberry jelly

1 cup heavy cream, whipped

superfine sugar, for dusting

1 Preheat the oven to 350°F/180°C. Grease and base-line 2 x 8-inch/20-cm layer cake pans. Sift the flour and baking powder into a bowl and add the butter, sugar, and eggs. Mix together, then beat well until smooth.

2 Divide the batter evenly among the prepared pans and spread smooth. Bake in the oven for 25-30 minutes, until well risen and golden brown, and the cakes feel springy when to the touch.

3 Leave in the pans for 5 minutes, then turn out and remove the paper. Place on wire racks to cool completely. Sandwich the cakes with the raspberry jelly and whipped cream and sprinkle the superfine sugar on top.

VARIATION
Coffee sandwich cake: Blend 1 tablespoon instant coffee granules with a little hot water and add to the ingredients before mixing. Sandwich with coffee buttercream.

Lemon Syrup Cake

The lovely light and tangy flavor of the sponge cake is balanced by the lemony syrup poured over the top.

1 hr 5 mins   1 hr

SERVES 6–8

INGREDIENTS

butter, for greasing

scant 1½ cups all-purpose flour

2 tsp baking powder

1 cup superfine sugar

4 eggs

⅔ cup sour cream

grated rind of 1 large lemon

4 tbsp lemon juice

⅔ cup sunflower oil

SYRUP

4 tbsp confectioners' sugar

3 tbsp lemon juice

1 Preheat the oven to 350°F/180°C. Lightly grease an 8-inch/20-cm loose-bottomed round cake pan and line the bottom with parchment paper.

2 Sift the flour and baking powder together into a mixing bowl and stir in the sugar.

3 In a separate bowl, whisk the eggs, sour cream, lemon rind, lemon juice, and oil together. Pour the egg mixture into the dry ingredients and mix well until evenly combined.

4 Pour the mixture into the prepared pan and bake in the preheated oven for 45–60 minutes, until risen and golden brown.

5 Meanwhile, to make the syrup, combine the confectioners' sugar and lemon juice in a small pan. Stir over low heat until just starting to bubble and turn syrupy.

6 As soon as the cake comes out of the oven prick the surface with a fine skewer, then brush the syrup over the top. Let the cake cool completely in the pan before turning out and serving.

COOK'S TIP
Pricking the surface of the hot cake with a skewer ensures that the syrup seeps right into the cake and the full flavor is absorbed.

Eggless Sponge

This is a healthy, but still absolutely delicious, variation of the classic sponge layer cake and is suitable for vegans.

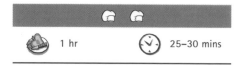

🥣 1 hr   🕐 25–30 mins

SERVES 6

INGREDIENTS

vegan margarine, for greasing

1¾ cups whole-wheat self-rising flour

2 tsp baking powder

¾ cup superfine sugar

6 tbsp sunflower oil

1 cup water

1 tsp vanilla extract

4 tbsp strawberry or raspberry reduced-sugar spread

superfine sugar, for dusting

1 Preheat the oven to 350°F/180°C. Grease 2 x 8-inch/20-cm layer cake pans and line them with parchment paper.

2 Sift the self-rising flour and baking powder into a large mixing bowl, stirring in any bran remaining in the sifter. Stir in the superfine sugar.

3 Pour in the sunflower oil, water, and vanilla extract. Mix well with a wooden spoon for about 1 minute until the mixture is smooth, then divide among the prepared pans.

VARIATIONS
Replace 2 tablespoons of the flour with unsweetened cocoa, or replace 2 teaspoons of flour with instant coffee powder. For a citrus-flavored sponge, add the grated rind of ½ lemon or orange to the flour in step 2.

4 Bake in the preheated oven for about 25–30 minutes until the center of each cake springs back when lightly touched.

5 Let the sponge cakes cool slightly in the pans before turning them out and transferring to a wire rack to cool completely.

6 Remove the parchment paper and place one sponge cake on a serving plate. Cover with the reduced-sugar spread and place the other sponge on top. Dust the eggless sponge cake with a little superfine sugar before serving.

Chocolate & Mandarin Gâteau

The sharp tang of the mandarins, especially if you use fresh fruit, helps cut the richness of this gâteau.

🍰 🍰

🍮 50 mins   ⏱ 25–30 mins

SERVES 4–6

INGREDIENTS

1 tsp sunflower oil, for oiling

3 eggs

½ cup superfine sugar

1 tbsp finely grated orange rind

¾ cup all-purpose flour

4 oz/115 g semisweet chocolate, grated

4 tbsp butter, melted

1¼ cups heavy cream

2 tbsp Cointreau or Grand Marnier

10 oz/300 g canned mandarins or 3 fresh mandarins, peeled and segmented

few maraschino cherries, to decorate

1 Preheat the oven to 350°F/180°C. Lightly oil and line the bottom of a 9-inch/23-cm cake pan. Place the eggs, sugar, and orange rind in a heatproof bowl set over a pan of gently simmering water or in the bowl of a free-standing mixer. Whisk until very thick and creamy and a trail is left when the whisk is dragged across the surface.

2 Remove from the heat, if applicable, and continue to whisk until cool. Carefully stir in 2 oz/55 g of the grated chocolate and then the flour, taking care not to over-mix. Continue to mix gently, then stir in the melted butter. Turn the batter into the prepared cake pan and bake in the preheated oven for 25–30 minutes, or until the top springs back when touched with a finger. Remove and let cool before removing from the pan and discarding the lining paper.

3 Whip the cream and liqueur until thick and spread half round the sides of the cake. Place the remaining grated chocolate on a sheet of waxed paper and roll the sides of the cake in the chocolate. Place on a serving platter. Use the remaining cream to spread over the top and to decorate. Arrange the mandarin segments and cherries attractively over the cream and serve. Store in the refrigerator and eat within 2 days.

COOK'S TIP
If you use canned fruit for decoration, choose fruit in natural syrup. Drain thoroughly and pat dry on absorbent paper towels.

Chocolate Chestnut Gâteau

This spectacular cake tastes as good as it looks and is ideal to serve when entertaining family and friends.

20–25 mins   35 mins

SERVES 8

INGREDIENTS

1 tsp sunflower oil, for oiling

8 oz/225 g butter, softened

1 cup superfine sugar

4 eggs, beaten

1½ cups self-rising flour

2 oz/55 g white chocolate, grated

CHESTNUT FROSTING

4 oz/115 g canned or fresh sweetened chestnut purée

4 tbsp butter, softened

3 cups confectioners' sugar, sifted

1–2 tbsp milk

2 oz/55 g semisweet chocolate

1 tsp vanilla extract

TO DECORATE

⅓ cup chopped hazelnuts, toasted

2 oz/55 g semisweet chocolate

1 tbsp butter

2 tsp corn syrup

few marrons glacés (optional)

1 Preheat the oven to 350°F/180°C. Lightly oil and line the bottom of 2 x 8-inch/20-cm shallow cake pans with nonstick parchment paper. Cream the butter and sugar together until light and fluffy then add the eggs a little at a time, beating well between each addition and adding a little flour after each addition. When all the eggs have been added, stir in the remaining flour together with 1–2 tablespoons of cooled boiled water to give a smooth dropping consistency.

2 Stir in the grated chocolate, mix lightly, and divide among the prepared pans. Smooth the tops and bake in the preheated oven for 25 minutes, or until the top springs back when touched lightly with a finger. Remove from the oven and let cool before turning out and discarding the lining paper. Leave until cold, then split each cake horizontally in half.

3 Cream the chestnut purée and butter together until smooth, then gradually beat in the sifted confectioners' sugar with a little milk to give a spreadable consistency. Melt the chocolate in a heatproof bowl set over a pan of gently simmering water. Stir the vanilla extract and the melted chocolate into the purée.

Set aside 2–3 tablespoons of the frosting, then use half the frosting to sandwich the cakes together. Place the hazelnuts on a sheet of parchment paper. Spread the remaining frosting round the sides of the cake and roll in the nuts. Place on a serving plate. Place the reserved frosting in a pastry bag fitted with a star tip and pipe small rosettes round the top edge of the cake.

4 Place the remaining ingredients in a heavy-based pan and heat gently, stirring until the chocolate and butter have melted. Let cool until starting to thicken, then spoon over the top of the cake. Decorate with marrons glacés (if using) and serve.

Chocolate Madeira Cake

This light cake will certainly become a firm favorite because it has a delicious, velvety chocolate taste without being too rich.

20 mins   50–55 mins

SERVES 8–10

INGREDIENTS

1 tsp sunflower oil, for oiling

scant ½ cup self-rising flour

1 tsp baking powder

4 oz/115 g butter or margarine, softened

½ cup superfine sugar

3 eggs, beaten

¼ cup ground almonds

1 cup drinking chocolate powder

1 tbsp confectioners' sugar, to decorate

FROSTING

2 cups confectioners' sugar

1½ tbsp unsweetened cocoa

2 tbsp butter

3–4 tbsp hot water

1 Preheat the oven to 350°F/180°C. Lightly oil and line the bottom of an 18-cm/7-inch cake pan with nonstick parchment paper. Sift the flour and baking powder together and set aside.

2 Cream the butter with the sugar until light and fluffy, then gradually beat in the eggs, adding a little of the flour after each addition. When all the eggs have been added stir in the remaining flour together with the ground almonds. Sift the drinking chocolate powder into the mixture and stir lightly.

3 Spoon the batter into the prepared cake pan and smooth the top. Bake in the preheated oven for 50–55 minutes, or until a skewer inserted into the center of the cake comes out clean. Remove from the oven and let cool before removing from the pan and discarding the lining paper. Leave until cold.

4 Sift the confectioners' sugar and unsweetened cocoa together into a mixing bowl and make a hollow in the center. Place the butter in the center. Mix with with sufficient hot water to form a smooth spreadable frosting. Coat the top and sides of the cake with frosting, swirling it to give a decorative effect. Dust with confectioners' sugar.

Jewel-Topped Madeira Cake

Brightly colored candied fruits make a stunning topping for this classic Madeira cake.

1 hr

1 hr 30 mins– 1 hr 45 mins

SERVES 8-10

INGREDIENTS

8 oz/225 g butter, softened, plus extra for greasing

generous 1 cup golden superfine sugar

finely grated rind of 1 lemon

4 eggs, beaten

2½ cups self-rising flour, sifted

2–3 tbsp milk

FRUIT TOPPING

2½ tbsp honey

1½ cups candied fruit

1 Preheat the oven to 325°F/160°C. Grease and base-line an 8-inch/20-cm deep round cake pan. Put the butter, sugar, and lemon rind in a bowl and beat together until light and fluffy. Gradually beat in the eggs. Gently fold in the flour, alternately with enough milk to give a soft dropping consistency.

2 Spoon the batter into the prepared pan and bake in the preheated oven for 1½–1¾ hours, until risen and golden and a skewer inserted into the center comes out clean.

3 Leave in the pan for 10 minutes, then turn out, remove the paper, and place on a wire rack to cool. To make the topping, brush the honey over the cake and arrange the fruits on top.

VARIATION
Traditionally a Madeira cake is simply decorated with a slice of candied peel on top. This should be placed on the cake after it has been cooking for 1 hour.

Caraway Madeira

This is a classic Madeira cake made in the traditional way with caraway seeds. If you do not like their flavor, they can be omitted.

🕐 1 hr 15 mins   🕑 1 hr

SERVES 8

INGREDIENTS

7 oz/200 g butter, softened, plus extra
  for greasing

scant 1 cup brown sugar

3 eggs, beaten lightly

2½ cups self-rising flour

1 tbsp caraway seeds

grated rind of 1 lemon

6 tbsp milk

1 or 2 strips citron rind

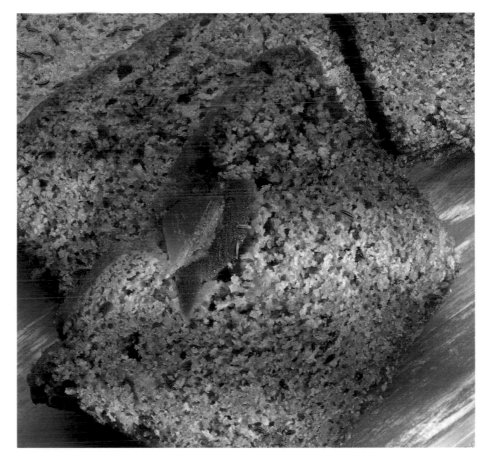

1 Preheat the oven to 325°F/160°C. Grease and line a 2-lb/900-g loaf pan.

2 In a bowl, cream together the butter and brown sugar until pale and fluffy.

3 Gradually add the beaten eggs to the creamed mixture, beating well after each addition.

4 Sift the flour into the bowl and gently fold into the creamed mixture with a figure-of-eight movement.

5 Add the caraway seeds, lemon rind, and milk, and gently fold in until thoroughly blended.

6 Spoon the batter into the prepared pan and smooth the surface.

7 Bake in the preheated oven for 20 minutes.

8 Remove the cake from the oven and gently place the strips of citron rind on top of the cake. Return it to the oven and bake for an additional 40 minutes, or until the cake is well risen, golden brown and a fine skewer inserted into the center comes out clean.

9 Let the cake cool in the pan before turning out and transferring to a wire rack to cool completely.

COOK'S TIP
Citron rind is available in the baking section of large stores. If it is unavailable, you can substitute candied peel.

Caraway Kugelhopf

Kugelhopf is a traditional German specialty which is a cross between a bread and a cake. Caraway seeds add an unusual flavor.

15 mins plus
1 hr 30 mins
rising

30 mins

SERVES 8–10

INGREDIENTS

2 cups white bread flour

generous ¼ cup golden superfine sugar

2 tsp active dry yeast

4 tsp caraway seeds

¼ cup tepid water

4 oz/115 g butter, melted, plus extra
   for greasing

3 eggs, beaten

confectioners' sugar, for dusting

1 Sift the flour into a warmed bowl and stir in the sugar, yeast, and caraway seeds. Make a well in the center. In another bowl, mix together the water, butter, and eggs and pour into the dry ingredients. Beat vigorously until smooth. Cover the bowl with plastic wrap and leave in a warm place until the mixture has doubled in size.

2 Grease an 8-inch/20-cm kugelhopf pan. Stir the batter and turn into the prepared mold. Cover with plastic wrap and leave to prove again until doubled in size. Preheat the oven to 400°F/200°C.

COOK'S TIP

If you do not have a kugelhopf pan, use an ordinary ring mold. Because a kugelhopf pan has a lot of detailed indentations, it is important to grease it thoroughly so that the cake turns out easily.

3 Remove the plastic wrap and bake the kugelhopf in the oven for 20 minutes. Reduce the oven temperature to 375°F/190°C and bake for an additional 10 minutes, until well risen and golden brown. Leave in the pan for 10 minutes, then turn out and place on a wire rack to cool. Sift confectioners' sugar over. Serve with butter while slightly warm.

Fruity Potato Cake

Sweet potatoes mix beautifully with fruit and brown sugar in this unusual cake. Add a few drops of rum or cognac if you like.

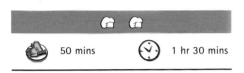

50 mins   1 hr 30 mins

SERVES 6

INGREDIENTS

1 tbsp butter, melted, plus extra
   for greasing

1 lb 8 oz/675 g sweet potatoes,
   peeled and diced

½ cup raw sugar

3 eggs

3 tbsp skim milk

1 tbsp lemon juice

grated rind of 1 lemon

1 tsp caraway seeds

1 cup chopped dry fruits, such as apple,
   pear, or mango

2 tsp baking powder

1 Preheat the oven to 325°F/160°C. Lightly grease a 7-inch/18-cm square cake pan.

2 Bring a large pan of water to a boil. Add the sweet potatoes, bring back to a boil, and cook for 10 minutes or until soft. Drain and mash until smooth.

3 Transfer the mashed sweet potatoes to a mixing bowl while still hot and add the butter and sugar, mixing thoroughly to dissolve.

4 Beat in the eggs, skim milk, lemon juice and rind, caraway seeds, and chopped dry fruits. Add the baking powder and mix well.

5 Pour the batter into the prepared cake pan and smooth the top. Cook in the preheated oven for about 1-1¼ hours, or until a skewer inserted into the center comes out clean.

6 Remove the cake from the pan and transfer to a wire rack to cool. Cut into thick slices to serve or wrap in plastic wrap and store in the freezer.

Carrot & Ginger Cake

This melt-in-your-mouth version of a favorite cake has a fraction of the fat of the traditional cake.

1 hr 15 mins   1 hr 15 mins

SERVES 10

INGREDIENTS

butter, for greasing

2 cups all-purpose flour

1 tsp baking powder

1 tsp baking soda

2 tsp ground ginger

½ tsp salt

¾ cup molasses sugar

1⅔ cups grated carrots

2 pieces chopped preserved ginger

1 tbsp grated gingerroot

generous ⅓ cup raisins

2 eggs, beaten

3 tbsp corn oil

juice of 1 orange

FROSTING

1 cup lowfat cream cheese

4 tbsp confectioners' sugar

1 tsp vanilla extract

TO DECORATE

grated carrot

finely chopped preserved ginger

ground ginger

1 Preheat the oven to 350°F/180°C. Grease and line an 8-inch/20-cm round cake pan with parchment paper.

2 Sift the flour, baking powder, baking soda, ground ginger, and salt into a bowl. Stir in the sugar, carrots, preserved ginger, gingerroot, and raisins. Beat together the eggs, oil, and orange juice, then pour into the bowl. Mix the ingredients together well.

3 Spoon the batter into the pan and bake in the oven for 1–1¼ hours, until firm to the touch or until a skewer inserted into the center of the cake comes out clean. Let cool in the pan.

4 To make the frosting, place the cream cheese in a bowl and beat to soften. Sift in the confectioners' sugar and add the vanilla extract. Mix well.

5 Remove the cake from the pan and spread the frosting over the top. Decorate the cake and serve.

Carrot Cake

This classic favorite is always popular with children and adults alike when it is served for afternoon tea. It is also good served as a dessert.

1 hr 10 mins   20–25 mins

MAKES 12 BARS

INGREDIENTS

butter, for greasing

scant 1 cup self-rising flour

pinch of salt

1 tsp ground cinnamon

⅔ cup brown sugar

2 eggs

scant ½ cup sunflower oil

scant 1 cup finely grated carrot

scant ⅓ cup shredded coconut

2 tbsp chopped walnuts

walnut pieces, to decorate

FROSTING

4 tbsp butter, softened

¼ cup cream cheese

2¼ cups confectioners' sugar, sifted

1 tsp lemon juice

1 Preheat the oven to 350°F/180°C. Lightly grease an 8-inch/20-cm square cake pan with a little butter and line with parchment paper.

2 Sift the flour, salt, and ground cinnamon into a large bowl and stir in the brown sugar. Add the eggs and oil to the dry ingredients and mix well.

3 Stir in the grated carrot, shredded coconut, and chopped walnuts.

4 Pour the batter into the prepared pan and bake in the preheated oven for 20–25 minutes, or until just firm to the touch. Let cool in the pan.

5 Meanwhile, make the cream cheese frosting. In a bowl, beat together the butter, cream cheese, confectioners' sugar, and lemon juice until the mixture is light, fluffy, and creamy.

6 Turn the cake out of the pan and cut into 12 bars or slices. Spread with the frosting and decorate with a few walnut pieces.

VARIATION
For a moister cake, replace the coconut with 1 coarsely mashed banana.

Pear & Ginger Cake

This deliciously buttery pear and ginger cake is ideal with a cup of coffee, or you can serve it with cream for a delicious dessert.

15 mins   40 mins

SERVES 6

INGREDIENTS

7 oz/200 g butter, sweet for preference, softened, plus extra for greasing

generous ¾ cup superfine sugar

1¼ cups self-rising flour, sifted

1 tbsp ground ginger

3 eggs, beaten lightly

1 lb/450 g dessert pears, peeled, cored, and sliced thinly

1 tbsp brown sugar

ice cream or cream, to serve (optional)

1   Preheat the oven to 350°F/180°C. Lightly grease a deep 8-inch/20.5-cm cake pan with butter and base-line with parchment paper.

2   Using a whisk, combine all but 2 tablespoons of the butter with the sugar, flour, ginger, and eggs, and mix to form a smooth consistency.

3   Spoon the cake batter into the prepared pan, smoothing out the surface.

4   Arrange the pear slices over the cake batter. Sprinkle with the brown sugar and dot with the remaining butter.

5   Bake in the preheated oven for 35–40 minutes, or until the cake is golden on top and feels springy to the touch.

6   Serve the pear and ginger cake warm, with ice cream or cream, if you wish.

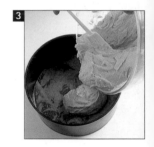

COOK'S TIP

Store ground ginger in an airtight jar, preferably made of colored glass, or store in a clear glass jar in a cool, dark place.

Candied Ginger Cake

Ground ginger, preserved ginger, and ginger syrup make this a really gingery cake!

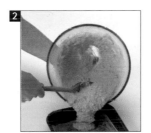

1 hr   45–50 mins

SERVES 12

INGREDIENTS

butter, for greasing

2 cups self-rising flour

1 tbsp ground ginger

1 tsp ground cinnamon

½ tsp baking soda

4 oz/115 g butter

¾ cup light muscovado sugar

grated rind of ½ lemon

2 eggs

1½ tbsp corn syrup

1½ tbsp milk

TOPPING

6 pieces preserved ginger

¾ cup confectioners' sugar

4 tbsp syrup from the ginger jar

lemon juice

1 Preheat the oven to 325°F/160°C. Grease and base-line a 7-inch /18-cm square cake pan. Sift the flour, ginger, cinnamon, and baking soda into a bowl. Rub in the butter, then stir in the sugar and lemon rind. Make a well in the center. Put the eggs, syrup, and milk in a bowl and whisk together. Pour into the dry ingredients and beat until smooth.

2 Spoon the batter into the prepared pan and bake in the preheated oven for 45-50 minutes, until well risen and firm to the touch. Leave in the pan for 30 minutes, then turn out and remove the paper. Leave on a wire rack to cool completely.

3 Cut each piece of preserved ginger into quarters and arrange the pieces on top of the cake. Sift the confectioners' sugar into a bowl and stir in the ginger syrup and enough lemon juice to make a smooth frosting. Put the frosting in a polythene bag and cut a tiny hole in one corner. Drizzle the frosting over the cake. Let set and then cut the cake into squares.

COOK'S TIP
This cake is better if it is kept in an airtight container for 1 day before eating.

Chocolate Banana Cake

The addition of bananas to this cake gives a wonderful moist texture with a subtle hint of banana.

1 hr   50–60 mins

SERVES 10–12

INGREDIENTS

1 tsp sunflower oil, for oiling

2 ripe bananas (about 8 oz/225 g in weight after peeling)

2 tbsp lemon juice

6 oz/175 g butter or margarine, softened

¾ cup light muscovado sugar

2 eggs, beaten

1½ cups self-rising flour

½ cup pecans, chopped coarsely

2 oz/55 g semisweet chocolate

TOPPING

1 oz/25 g white chocolate

few pecans

1 Preheat the oven to 350°F/180°C. Lightly oil and line the base of a 2-lb/900-g loaf pan with nonstick parchment paper. Cut the bananas into pieces, add the lemon juice and mash to form a purée. Set aside.

2 Cream the butter with the sugar until light and fluffy, then gradually beat in the eggs, adding a little of flour after each addition. When all the eggs have been added, stir in the banana purée and then the remaining flour. Add the chopped pecans. Melt the chocolate in a heatproof bowl set over a pan of gently simmering water. Stir until smooth, then stir lightly into the cake batter.

3 Spoon the cake batter into the prepared pan and bake in the preheated oven for 45–55 minutes, or until a skewer inserted into the center comes out clean. Remove from the oven and leave until cool before removing from the pan and discarding the lining paper. Leave until cold.

4 Melt the chocolate in a heatproof bowl set over a pan of gently simmering water. Stir until smooth then drizzle over the cooled cake. Arrange the pecans on top, fixing with melted chocolate, and serve once the chocolate has set. Store in an airtight container and eat within 3 days of making.

COOK'S TIP

Make sure that this cake is eaten quickly. With the addition of bananas it does not last as long as some cakes.

Pear Cake

This is a really moist cake, deliciously flavored with chopped pears and cinnamon and drizzled with lots of honey.

1 hr   1 hr 30 mins

SERVES 8

INGREDIENTS

margarine, for greasing

4 pears, peeled and cored

2 tbsp water

1¾ cups all-purpose flour

2 tsp baking powder

scant ½ cup brown sugar

4 tbsp milk

2 tbsp honey, plus extra for drizzling

2 tsp ground cinnamon

2 egg whites

1 Preheat the oven to 300°F/150°C. Grease and base-line an 8-inch/20-cm cake pan.

2 Put 1 pear in a food processor with the water and process until almost smooth. Transfer to a mixing bowl.

3 Sift in the flour and baking powder. Beat in the sugar, milk, honey, and cinnamon and mix with your fingers.

4 Chop all but 1 of the remaining pears and add to the mixture.

5 Whisk the egg whites until stiff peaks form and gently fold into the mixture until fully blended.

6 Slice the remaining pear and arrange it in a fan pattern on the bottom of the prepared pan.

7 Spoon the cake batter into the pan and cook in the preheated oven for 1¼–1½ hours, or until cooked through and golden.

8 Remove the cake from the oven and let cool in the pan for 10 minutes. Turn the cake out on to a wire rack and drizzle with honey. Set aside to cool completely, then cut into slices to serve.

COOK'S TIP
To test if the cake is cooked through, insert a skewer into the center—if it comes out clean, the cake is cooked. If not, return the cake to the oven and test at frequent intervals.

Fresh Pear & Cinnamon Cake

This cake smells wonderful while it is baking and the combination of pear and cinnamon is divine.

1 hr 15 mins   1 hr 30 mins

SERVES 8

INGREDIENTS

3–4 firm pears, depending on the size

1 vanilla bean

1¼ cups golden superfine sugar

2 large eggs

7 oz/200 g butter, melted and cooled

2¼ cups all-purpose flour

1 tbsp ground cinnamon

½ tsp baking soda

4 tbsp golden confectioners' sugar

1 Preheat the oven to 350°F/180°C. Thoroughly grease an 8-inch/20-cm ring mold. Peel and quarter the pears and remove the cores. Cut the pears into small cubes, place in a pan, and cover with water. Split the vanilla bean to expose the seeds, and add to the pan. Bring to a boil and simmer gently until the pears are tender. Leave in the pan to cool. Drain the pears, reserving their cooking liquid, and pat dry with paper towels.

2 Put the sugar, eggs, and butter in a bowl and whisk together. Sift the flour, cinnamon, and baking soda into another bowl. Fold the flour into the sugar and egg mixture, one-third at a time. Carefully fold in the pears. Transfer the batter to the prepared mold and bake in the oven for 50-55 minutes, until a skewer inserted into the center comes out clean. Leave in the mold to cool for 20 minutes, then turn out on to a wire rack to cool completely.

3 To make the frosting, sift the confectioners' sugar into a bowl and add enough of the reserved pear juice to give a pouring consistency. Drizzle the frosting over the cake and let set before serving.

VARIATION
As an alternative to fresh pears, canned pears could be used.

Coffee Caramel Cake

This intensely flavored coffee cake is complemented perfectly with a delicious caramel frosting, decorated with chocolate-coated coffee beans.

🕒 55 mins   🕐 35 mins

SERVES 8–10

INGREDIENTS

6 oz/175 g butter, softened, plus extra for greasing

scant 1 cup golden superfine sugar

3 eggs, beaten

2 cups self-rising flour, sifted

scant ½ cup strong black coffee

FROSTING

½ cup whole milk

4½ oz/125 g butter

3 tbsp golden superfine sugar

chocolate-coated coffee beans, to decorate

1 Preheat the oven to 350°F/180°C. Grease and base-line 2 x 8-inch/20-cm layer cake pans. Put the butter and sugar in a bowl and beat together until light and fluffy. Gradually beat in the eggs, then fold in the flour and coffee. Divide the batter among the prepared pans and bake in the oven for 30 minutes, until well risen and springy to the touch. Leave in the pans for 5 minutes, then turn out and remove the paper. Place on wire racks to cool completely.

2 To make the frosting, put the milk and butter in a pan and heat gently until the butter has melted. Remove from the heat and set aside. Put the superfine sugar in a heavy-based pan and heat gently until the sugar dissolves and turns a golden caramel. Remove from the heat and stir in the warm milk. Return to the heat and stir until the caramel dissolves.

3 Remove from the heat and gradually stir in the confectioners' sugar, beating until the frosting is a smooth spreading consistency. Sandwich the cakes together with some of the frosting and spread the rest over the top and sides. Decorate with chocolate-coated coffee beans and serve.

Coffee Streusel Cake

This cake has a moist coffee sponge cake on the bottom, covered with a crisp crunchy, spicy topping.

🍰 50 mins 🕐 1 hr

SERVES 8

INGREDIENTS

butter, for greasing

2 cups all-purpose flour

1 tbsp baking powder

⅓ cup superfine sugar

⅔ cup milk

2 eggs

4 oz/115 g butter, melted and cooled

2 tbsp instant coffee powder mixed with 1 tbsp boiling water

⅓ cup chopped almonds

confectioners' sugar, for dusting

TOPPING

½ cup self-rising flour

⅓ cup raw sugar

2 tbsp butter, cut into small pieces

1 tsp ground allspice

1 tbsp water

1 Preheat the oven to 375°F/190°C. Grease and line a 9-inch/23-cm loose-bottomed cake pan.

2 Sift the flour and baking powder into a mixing bowl, then stir in the superfine sugar.

3 Whisk the milk, eggs, melted butter, and coffee mixture together and pour on to the dry ingredients. Add the chopped almonds and mix lightly together. Spoon the batter into the prepared pan.

4 To make the topping, mix the flour and raw sugar together in a bowl.

5 Rub in the butter with your fingertips until the mixture resembles bread crumbs. Sprinkle in the allspice and water and bring the mixture together in loose crumbs. Sprinkle the topping evenly over the cake.

6 Bake in the preheated oven for 50 minutes–1 hour. Cover loosely with foil if the topping starts to brown too quickly.

7 Let cool in the pan, then turn out. Dust with confectioners' sugar just before serving.

Almond Cake

Glazing with a honey syrup after baking gives this cake a lovely moist texture, but it can be eaten without the glaze if preferred.

🍰 2 hrs 5 mins ⏰ 50 mins

SERVES 8

INGREDIENTS

⅓ cup soft margarine, plus extra for greasing

¼ cup brown sugar

2 eggs

1¼ cups self-rising flour

1 tsp baking powder

4 tbsp milk

2 tbsp clear honey

½ cup slivered almonds

SYRUP

⅔ cup honey

2 tbsp lemon juice

1 Preheat the oven to 350°F/180°C. Grease a 7-inch/18-cm round cake pan and line with parchment paper.

2 Place the margarine, brown sugar, eggs, flour, baking powder, milk, and honey in a large mixing bowl and beat well with a wooden spoon for about 1 minute until all of the ingredients are thoroughly mixed together.

3 Spoon into the prepared pan, smooth the surface with the back of a spoon or a knife, and sprinkle with the almonds.

4 Bake in the preheated oven for about 50 minutes, or until the cake is well risen and a fine skewer inserted into the center of the cake comes out clean.

5 Meanwhile, make the syrup. Combine the honey and lemon juice in a small pan and simmer over low heat for about 5 minutes, or until the syrup starts to coat the back of a spoon.

6 As soon as the cake comes out of the oven, pour the syrup over it, letting it seep into the middle of the cake.

7 Let the cake cool for at least 2 hours before slicing.

COOK'S TIP
Experiment with different flavored honeys for the syrup glaze until you find the one that you like best.

Almond & Hazelnut Gâteau

This is a light, nutty cake made with a rich chocolate cream. Simple to create, it is a gâteau you are sure to make again and again.

1 hr plus
1 hr chilling

20–25 mins

SERVES 8

INGREDIENTS

butter, for greasing

4 eggs

½ cup superfine sugar

½ cup ground almonds

½ cup ground hazelnuts

⅓ cup all-purpose flour

½ cup slivered almonds

FILLING

3½ oz/100 g semisweet chocolate

1 tbsp butter

1¼ cups heavy cream

confectioners' sugar, for dusting

1 Preheat the oven to 375°F/190°C. Grease 2 x 7-inch/18-cm layer cake pans and base-line with parchment paper.

2 Whisk the eggs and superfine sugar in a large mixing bowl with an electric whisk for about 10 minutes, or until the mixture is very light and foamy and a trail is left when the whisk is dragged across the surface.

3 Fold in the ground nuts, sift the flour, and fold in with a metal spoon or spatula. Pour into the prepared pans.

4 Scatter the slivered almonds over the top of one of the cakes. Bake both of the cakes in the preheated oven for 15–20 minutes, or until springy to the touch.

5 Let cool slightly in the pans. Carefully remove the cakes from the pans and transfer to a wire rack to cool completely.

6 Meanwhile, make the filling. Melt the chocolate, remove from the heat, and stir in the butter. Let the mixture cool slightly. Whip the cream until just holding its shape, then fold in the melted chocolate until mixed.

7 Place the cake without the extra almonds on a serving plate and spread the filling over it. Let the filling set slightly, then place the almond-topped cake on top and chill for about 1 hour. Dust with confectioners' sugar and serve.

Cherry & Almond Cake

Ground almonds add richness to the cake and help its keeping qualities.
It is good served at any time of day.

50 mins

1 hr 30 mins–
1 hr 45 mins

SERVES 8

INGREDIENTS

6 oz/175 g butter, softened, plus extra for
greasing

1½ cups candied cherries

scant 1 cup golden superfine sugar

3 eggs

scant ½ cup ground almonds

2 cups all-purpose flour

1½ tsp baking powder

scant ½ cup slivered almonds, to decorate

1 Preheat the oven to 325°F/160°C.
Grease and base-line a 7-inch/18-cm
deep cake pan. Cut the cherries in half,
then put them in a strainer and rinse to
remove all the syrup. Pat dry with paper
towels and set aside.

2 Put the butter, superfine sugar, eggs,
and ground almonds in a bowl. Sift in
the flour and baking powder. Beat
thoroughly until smooth, then stir in the
cherries. Spoon the batter into the
prepared pan and smooth the top.

3 Sprinkle the slivered almonds over the
cake. Bake in the preheated oven for
1½–1¾ hours, until well risen and a
skewer inserted into the center of the cake
comes out clean. Leave in the pan for
10 minutes, then turn out, remove the
paper, and place on a wire rack to cool.

COOK'S TIP
Washing and drying the
cherries before use helps
prevent them sinking.

Orange & Almond Cake

This light and tangy citrus cake is better eaten as a dessert than as a cake. It is especially good served at the end of a large meal.

50 mins

35–40 mins

SERVES 8

INGREDIENTS

butter, for greasing

4 eggs, separated

scant ⅔ cup superfine sugar, plus 2 tsp for the cream

finely grated rind and juice of 2 oranges

finely grated rind and juice of 1 lemon

1 cup ground almonds

4 tbsp self-rising flour

scant 1 cup whipping cream

1 tsp ground cinnamon

4 tbsp slivered almonds, toasted

confectioners' sugar, for dusting

1 Preheat the oven to 350°F/180°C. Grease and base-line the bottom of a 7-inch/18-cm round deep cake pan.

2 Blend the egg yolks with the sugar until the mixture is thick and creamy. Whisk half of the orange rind and all of the lemon rind into the egg yolks. Combine the orange and lemon juice with the ground almonds and stir into the egg yolks. Fold in the flour. Whisk the egg whites until stiff and gently fold in.

3 Pour the batter into the pan and smooth the surface. Bake in the preheated oven for 35–40 minutes, or until golden and springy to the touch. Set aside to cool in the pan for 10 minutes and then turn out on to a rack to cool completely.

4 Whip the cream to form soft peaks. Stir in the remaining orange rind, cinnamon, and sugar.

5 Cover the cake with the almonds, dust with confectioners' sugar, and serve with the cream.

VARIATION

To serve with a syrup, boil the juice and finely grated rind of 2 oranges, scant ½ cup superfine sugar, and 2 tablespoons water for 5–6 minutes. Stir in 1 tablespoon orange flavored liqueur just before serving.

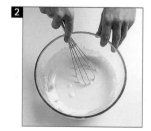

Sicilian Citrus Cake

Serve this delicious fragrant cake after dinner, with a small glass of limoncello or Cointreau if you like.

50 mins	1 hr

SERVES 4

INGREDIENTS

1 tsp olive oil, for oiling

generous 1½ cups all-purpose flour

1 tsp baking powder

1 tsp baking soda

pinch of salt

¾ cup superfine sugar

2 eggs

finely grated rind and juice of 1 orange

2 tbsp limoncello (lemon liqueur) or orange-flavored liqueur, such as Cointreau

TOPPING

1 cup heavy cream, whipped

3 tbsp confectioner's sugar

1 tbsp grated orange rind

strips of candied orange and lemon peel, to decorate

1 Preheat the oven to 350°F/180°C. Oil an 8-inch/20-cm cake pan and line it with parchment paper.

2 Sift the flour, baking powder, baking soda, and salt into a large mixing bowl, then stir in the superfine sugar.

3 In a separate bowl, mix the eggs with the orange rind and juice. Stir in the limoncello or orange liqueur, then pour the mixture into the flour and stir well.

4 Transfer the batter to the prepared cake pan, smooth the surface, and bake in the center of the preheated oven for at least 1 hour, until firm and golden. Remove from the oven and let cool, then turn out the cake on to a serving plate.

5 To make the topping, put the cream into a bowl and add the confectioners' sugar and grated orange rind. Mix well, then spread over the top of the cake. Decorate with strips of candied orange and lemon peel and serve.

Orange Kugelhopf Cake

Baking in a deep, fluted kugelhopf pan ensures that you create a cake with a stunning shape. The moist cake is full of fresh orange flavor.

30 mins   1 hr

SERVES 6–8

INGREDIENTS

7 oz/200 g butter, softened, plus extra for greasing

generous 1 cup superfine sugar

4 eggs, separated

scant 3½ cups all-purpose flour

pinch of salt

3 tsp baking powder

1¼ cups fresh orange juice

1 tbsp orange flower water

1 tsp grated orange rind

SYRUP

¾ cup orange juice

1 cup granulated sugar

1 Preheat the oven to 350°F/180°C. Grease and flour a 10-inch/25-cm kugelhopf pan or deep ring mold.

2 In a bowl, cream together the butter and superfine sugar until light and fluffy. Add the egg yolks, 1 at a time, whisking well after each addition.

3 Sift the flour, a pinch of salt, and the baking powder together into a separate bowl. Fold the dry ingredients and the orange juice alternately into the creamed mixture with a metal spoon, working as lightly as possible. Stir in the orange flower water and orange rind.

4 Whisk the egg whites until they form soft peaks and gently fold them into the batter.

5 Pour into the prepared pan or mold and bake in the preheated oven for 50–55 minutes, or until a metal skewer inserted into the center of the cake comes out clean.

6 Bring the orange juice and sugar to a boil in a small pan over low heat, then simmer gently for 5 minutes until the sugar has dissolved.

7 Remove the cake from the oven and let cool in the pan for 10 minutes.

8 Prick the top of the cake with a fine skewer and brush over half of the syrup. Let the cake cool, still in the pan, for an additional 10 minutes.

9 Invert the cake on to a wire rack placed over a deep plate and brush the syrup over the cake until it is entirely covered. Serve warm or cold.

Clementine Cake

This cake is flavored with clementine rind and juice, creating a rich buttery cake bursting with fresh fruit flavor. Orange would also work well.

50 mins   1 hr

SERVES 8

INGREDIENTS

6 oz/175 g butter, softened, plus extra
    for greasing

2 clementines

¾ cup superfine sugar

3 eggs, beaten lightly

1¼ cups self-rising flour

3 tbsp ground almonds

3 tbsp light cream

GLAZE AND TOPPING

6 tbsp clementine juice

2 tbsp superfine sugar

3 white sugar lumps, crushed

1 Preheat the oven to 350°F/180°C. Grease a 7-inch/18-cm pan and base-line with parchment paper.

2 Pare the rind from the clementines and chop it finely. In a bowl, cream the butter, sugar, and clementine rind together until pale and fluffy.

3 Gradually add the beaten eggs to the batter, beating thoroughly after each addition.

4 Gently fold in the flour, ground almonds, and light cream. Spoon the batter into the prepared pan.

5 Bake in the preheated oven for about 55–60 minutes, or until a fine skewer inserted into the center comes out clean. Let cool slightly.

6 Meanwhile, make the glaze. Put the clementine juice into a small pan with the superfine sugar. Bring to boil over a low heat and simmer for 5 minutes.

7 Turn out the cake on to a wire rack. Drizzle the glaze over the cake until it has been absorbed and sprinkle with the crushed sugar lumps. Let cool completely before serving.

COOK'S TIP
If you prefer, chop the rind from the clementines in a food processor or blender along with the sugar in step 2. Tip the mixture into a bowl with the butter and start to cream the mixture.

Caribbean Coconut Cake

Dry unsweetened coconut and coconut cream make this moist cake rich and delicious, and are complemented by the pineapple jelly.

50 mins   25 mins

SERVES 8

INGREDIENTS

1¼ cups butter, softened, plus
   extra for greasing

scant 1 cup golden superfine sugar

3 eggs

1¼ cups self-rising flour

1½ tsp baking powder

½ tsp freshly grated nutmeg

⅔ cup dry unsweetened coconut

5 tbsp coconut cream

2¾ cups confectioners' sugar

5 tbsp pineapple jelly

dry unsweetened coconut, toasted,
   to decorate

1 Preheat the oven to 350°F/180°C. Grease and line the bottoms of 2 x 8-inch/20-cm sponge cake pans. Place ³/₄ cup of the butter in a bowl with the sugar and eggs and sift in the flour, baking powder, and nutmeg. Beat together until smooth, then stir in the coconut and 2 tablespoons of coconut cream.

2 Divide the batter among the prepared pans and carefully smooth over the tops. Bake in the preheated oven for 25 minutes, or until golden and firm to the touch. Let cool in the pans for 5 minutes, then turn out on to a wire rack, peel off the lining paper, and let cool completely.

3 Sift the confectioners' sugar into a bowl and add the remaining butter and coconut cream. Beat together until smooth. Spread the pineapple jelly on one of the cakes and top with just under half of the buttercream. Place the other cake on top. Spread the remaining buttercream on top of the cake and scatter with the toasted coconut.

COOK'S TIP

Coconut cream comes in small cartons. What remains after making this cake can be used in custards, soups, or curries, or can be poured over fresh fruit in place of cream.

Italian Lemon Rice Cake

This lemony cake should have a crisp crust with a soft moist center. Soaking the currants in dark rum brings out their fruitiness.

1 hr 15 mins   1 hr 15 mins

SERVES 8–10

INGREDIENTS

4 cups milk

pinch of salt

1¾ cups risotto rice

1 vanilla bean, split

¼ cup currants

¼ cup dark rum or water

2 tsp melted butter, for greasing

cornmeal or polenta, for dusting

¾ cup sugar

grated rind of 1 large lemon

4 tbsp butter, cut into pieces

3 eggs

2–3 tbsp lemon juice (optional)

confectioners' sugar

TO SERVE

¾ cup mascarpone cheese

2 tbsp dark rum

2 tbsp whipping cream

1 Bring the milk to a boil. Sprinkle in the salt and rice and bring back to a boil. Add the vanilla bean and seeds. Reduce the heat and simmer, stirring occasionally, for 30 minutes.

2 Meanwhile, bring the currants and rum to a boil, then set aside.

3 Preheat the oven to 325°F/160°C. Brush the bottom and sides of a 10-inch/ 25-cm loose-bottomed cake pan with butter. Dust with about 2–3 tablespoons of cornmeal and shake out any excess.

4 Remove the rice from the heat and remove the vanilla bean. Stir in all but 1 tablespoon of sugar, with the lemon rind and butter, until the sugar has dissolved. Place in ice water to cool. Stir in the soaked currants and remaining rum.

5 Beat the eggs with an electric whisk, for about 2 minutes, until light and foamy. Gradually beat in about half the rice mixture, then stir in the rest. If using, stir in the lemon juice.

6 Pour into the prepared pan and smooth the top. Sprinkle with the reserved sugar and bake in the preheated oven for about 40 minutes until risen, and golden and slightly firm. Cool in the pan on a wire rack.

7 Turn out and dust with confectioners' sugar. Transfer the cake to a serving plate. Whisk the mascarpone with the rum and cream and serve with the cake.

Citrus Honey Cake

This light-textured cake is drizzled with honey and lemon juice while it is still warm from the oven, giving it a rich and zesty flavor.

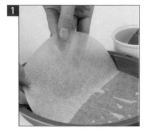

50 mins   35 mins

MAKES 9-INCH/23-CM CAKE

INGREDIENTS

sunflower or corn oil, for brushing

1½ oz/40 g reduced-fat sunflower margarine

4 tbsp honey

finely grated rind and juice of 1 lemon

⅔ cup skim milk

1¼ cups all-purpose flour

1½ tsp baking powder

½ teaspoon allspice

6 tbsp semolina

2 egg whites

2 tsp sesame seeds

1 Preheat the oven to 400°F/200°C. Lightly brush a 9-inch/23-cm round cake pan with oil and line the bottom with parchment paper. Put the margarine and 3 tablespoons of the honey in a heavy-based pan and melt over very low heat. Remove the pan from the heat. Reserve 1 tablespoon of the lemon juice and stir the remainder into the honey mixture with the lemon rind and milk.

VARIATION

For a change, flavor this cake with orange rind and juice instead of the lemon.

2 Sift the flour, baking powder, and allspice into a bowl, then tip the mixture into the pan, together with the semolina, and beat. Whisk the egg whites until soft peaks form, then gently fold them into the batter. Spoon into the prepared pan and smooth the surface. Sprinkle the sesame seeds evenly on top.

3 Bake in the preheated oven for about 30 minutes, or until golden brown and springy to the touch. Combine the remaining honey and lemon juice in a small jug and pour it over the cake. Set aside in the pan to cool before serving.

Honey Spice Cake

This cake benefits from being kept for a day before eating, so it is best made in advance and stored in an airtight container.

15 mins plus cooling

40–50 mins

SERVES 8–10

INGREDIENTS

5½ oz/150 g butter, plus extra for greasing

¾ cup light muscovado sugar

¾ cup honey

1⅔ cups self-rising flour

½ tsp ground ginger

½ tsp ground cinnamon

½ tsp caraway seeds

the seeds from 8 cardamoms, ground

2 eggs, beaten

FROSTING

2½ cups confectioners' sugar

warm water

1 Preheat the oven to 350°F/180°C. Grease a 9-inch/23-cm round cake pan. Put the butter, sugar, honey, and 1 tablespoon water into a pan. Heat gently until the butter has melted and the sugar has dissolved. Remove from the heat and let cool for 10 minutes.

2 Sift the flour into a bowl and mix in the ginger, cinnamon, caraway seeds, and cardamom. Make a well in the center. Pour in the honey mixture and the eggs and beat well until smooth. Pour the batter into the prepared pan and bake in the oven for 40-50 minutes, until well risen and a skewer inserted into the center comes out clean. Leave in the pan for 5 minutes then transfer to a wire rack to cool.

3 To make the frosting, sift the confectioners' sugar into a bowl. Stir in enough warm water to make a smooth flowing frosting. Spoon over the cake, letting it to flow down the sides. Let set before serving.

COOK'S TIP
Choose a strongly flavored honey so that it is not overpowered by the spices.

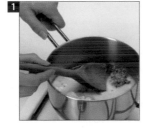

Passion Fruit Angel Cake

Angel cake is wonderfully light and airy. A passion fruit frosting makes it even more delicious.

55 mins   50–55 mins

SERVES 8

INGREDIENTS

⅔ cup all-purpose flour

8 large egg whites

1 tsp cream of tartar

pinch of salt

1½ cups superfine sugar

1 tsp vanilla extract

2 tbsp warm water

FROSTING

4 passion fruit

1½ cups confectioners' sugar

1 Preheat the oven to 350°F/180°C. Sift the flour and 2 tablespoons of sugar on to a sheet of waxed paper. Put the egg whites in a large clean bowl and whisk until frothy, then stir in the cream of tartar and salt. Sprinkle in the vanilla extract and warm water and continue whisking until the egg whites are stiff but not dry. Sift in the remaining sugar, 2 tablespoons at a time, whisking between each addition until the mixture forms soft peaks.

2 Gently fold in the flour and sugar batter, in several batches. Pour the batter into a nonstick angel cake pan with a funnel. It should be about two-thirds full. Bake in the oven for 50-55 minutes, until the top is brown and dry to the touch. Turn the pan upside down and leave until the cake is completely cold. Ease the cake out of the pan with a spatula and place on a serving plate.

3 To make the frosting, halve the passion fruit and scoop out the pulp into a strainer set over a bowl. Press the juice from the pulp with a wooden spoon. Stir in enough confectioners' sugar to make a frosting with the consistency of heavy cream. Pour the frosting over the cake and let set.

COOK'S TIP

If you do not have an angel cake pan, any other pan can be used.

Coconut Cake

This is a great, all-time family favorite. Serve cut into slices with a cup of coffee for an afternoon snack.

50 mins   1 hr

SERVES 6–8

INGREDIENTS

4 oz/115 g butter, cut into small pieces, plus extra for greasing

generous 1½ cups self-rising flour

pinch of salt

½ cup raw sugar

1 cup shredded coconut, plus extra for sprinkling

2 eggs, beaten lightly

4 tbsp milk

1 Preheat the oven to 325°F/160°C. Grease a 2-lb/900-g loaf pan and line the bottom with parchment paper.

2 Sift the flour and salt into a mixing bowl and rub in the butter with your fingertips until the mixture resembles fine bread crumbs.

3 Stir in the sugar, shredded coconut, eggs, and milk and mix to a soft dropping consistency.

4 Spoon the batter into the prepared pan and smooth the surface with a spatula. Bake in the preheated oven, for 30 minutes.

5 Remove the cake from the oven and sprinkle with the extra coconut. Return the cake to the oven and bake for an additional 30 minutes, until well risen and golden and a fine skewer inserted into the center comes out clean.

6 Let the cake cool slightly in the pan before turning out and transferring to a wire rack to cool completely. Serve cut into slices.

COOK'S TIP
The flavor of this cake is enhanced by storing it in a cool dry place for a few days before eating.

Sicilian Cassata

This rich cake with its filling of ricotta cheese, candied peel, almonds, and semisweet chocolate is a specialty of Sicily.

40 mins plus
8 hrs chilling

30–40 mins

SERVES 8

INGREDIENTS

CAKE

6 oz/175 g butter, softened, plus extra
 for greasing

scant 1½ cups self-rising flour

2–3 tbsp unsweetened cocoa

1 tsp baking powder

scant 1 cup golden superfine sugar

3 eggs

FILLING

2 cups ricotta cheese

3½ oz/100 g semisweet chocolate, grated

generous ½ cup golden superfine sugar

3 tbsp Marsala

scant ½ cup chopped candied peel

¼ cup chopped almonds

TO DECORATE

sifted confectioners' sugar

chocolate curls (see page 9)

1 Preheat the oven to 375°F/190°C. Grease and base-line a 7-inch/18-cm loose-ring cake pan. Sift the flour, unsweetened cocoa, and baking powder into a large bowl. Add the butter, sugar, and eggs and beat well until smooth. Pour the batter into the prepared pan and bake in the oven for 30-40 minutes, until well risen and firm to the touch. Leave in the pan for 5 minutes, then turn out on to a wire rack to cool.

2 Wash and dry the cake pan and grease and line it again. To make the filling, rub the ricotta cheese through a strainer into a bowl. Add the chocolate, sugar, and Marsala and beat thoroughly until the mixture is light and fluffy. Stir in the candied peel and chopped almonds.

3 Cut the thin crust off the top of the cake and discard. Cut the cake horizontally into 3 layers. Place the first slice in the prepared pan and cover with half the ricotta mixture. Repeat the layers, finishing with a cake layer. Press down lightly, cover with a weight, and chill overnight. To serve, turn the cake out on to a serving plate. Sift confectioners' sugar over and decorate with chocolate curls.

Nutty Polenta Cake

It is important to use the instant polenta in this recipe, otherwise the texture will be very gritty. Use semisweet or milk chocolate if preferred.

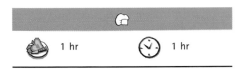

1 hr   1 hr

SERVES 10–12

INGREDIENTS

1 tsp sunflower oil, for oiling

¾ cup mixed nuts, such as hazelnuts, almonds, and pistachios

6 oz/175 g butter, softened

¾ cup light muscovado sugar

1 tbsp grated orange rind

3 eggs, beaten

¾ cup self-rising flour

1½ tsp ground cinnamon

3 oz/85 g milk chocolate, chopped

3 oz/85 g instant polenta

2 tbsp orange juice

1 oz/25 g white chocolate

few whole nuts, to decorate

1 Preheat the oven to 350°F/180°C. Lightly oil and line the bottom of a 2-lb/900-g loaf pan with nonstick parchment paper. Place the nuts in a food processor or blender and process until finely chopped. Set aside.

2 Cream the butter with the sugar and orange rind until light and fluffy. Gradually beat in the eggs, adding a little flour after each addition. When all the eggs have been added stir in the remaining flour together with the ground cinnamon, the chopped chocolate, and the polenta. Stir lightly, adding sufficient orange juice to give a soft dropping consistency.

3 Turn into the prepared loaf pan and smooth the top. Bake in the preheated oven for 50–60 minutes, or until a skewer inserted into the center comes out clean. Remove from the oven and let cool before turning out on a wire rack and discarding the lining paper.

4 Melt the white chocolate in a small heatproof bowl set over a pan of gently simmering water. Stir until smooth, then use to drizzle over the top of the cake. Press the nuts into the melted chocolate and let set before serving.

COOK'S TIP
If you cannot find instant polenta, use ground almonds.

Golden Polenta Cake

Polenta makes an extremely moist cake with a good color. Its texture is quite dense, compared to one made with all wheat flour.

40 mins   1 hr

SERVES 4–6

INGREDIENTS

scant ½ cup butter, plus extra for greasing

scant ½ cup superfine sugar

2 eggs, beaten

6 tbsp self-rising flour

1 tsp baking powder

3½ oz/100 g cornmeal

5½ oz/150 g golden raisins

⅓ cup chopped almonds

grated rind and juice of 1 orange

TO DECORATE

confectioners' sugar

toasted slivered almonds

mascarpone cheese, to serve

1 Preheat the oven to 350°F/180°C. Grease an 8-inch/20-cm cake pan and line it with parchment paper.

2 Cream together the butter and superfine sugar in a bowl, then gradually whisk in the beaten eggs. Fold in the flour, baking powder, and cornmeal. Add the golden raisins, almonds, and the orange rind and juice, and stir together well.

3 Transfer the batter to the prepared cake pan and smooth the surface. Bake in the center of the preheated oven for 1 hour, until firm and golden. Remove from the oven and let cool, then turn out the cake on to a serving plate.

4 Sprinkle over the confectioners' sugar and slivered almonds and serve with generous spoonfuls of mascarpone.

Crispy-Topped Fruit Bake

The crushed sugar lumps give a lovely crunchy texture to this very easy-to-make blackberry and apple dessert.

1 hr   1 hr

SERVES 10

INGREDIENTS

butter or margarine, for greasing

12 oz/350 g cooking apples

3 tbsp lemon juice

2½ cups self-rising whole-wheat flour

½ tsp baking powder

1 tsp ground cinnamon, plus extra
   for dusting

¾ cup prepared blackberries, thawed if
   frozen, plus extra to decorate

¾ cup molasses sugar

1 egg, beaten

scant 1 cup lowfat plain yogurt

2 oz/55 g white or brown sugar lumps,
   crushed lightly

sliced dessert apple, to decorate

1 Preheat the oven to 375°F/190°C. Grease and line a 2-lb/900-g loaf pan with a little butter (or margarine). Core, peel, and finely dice the apples. Place them in a pan with the lemon juice, bring to a boil, cover, and simmer for about 10 minutes until soft and pulpy. Beat well and set aside to cool.

VARIATION
Try replacing the blackberries with blueberries. Use the canned or frozen variety if fresh blueberries are unavailable.

2 Sift the flour, baking powder, and cinnamon into a bowl, adding any husks that remain in the strainer. Stir in ½ cup of the blackberries and the sugar.

3 Make a well in the center of the ingredients and add the egg, yogurt, and cooled apple purée. Mix well to incorporate thoroughly. Spoon the mixture into the loaf pan and smooth the top.

4 Sprinkle with the remaining blackberries, pressing them down into the cake batter, and top with the crushed sugar lumps. Bake in the preheated oven for 40–45 minutes. Remove from the oven and set aside in the pan to cool.

5 Remove the cake from the pan and peel away the lining paper. Serve dusted with cinnamon and decorated with extra blackberries and apple slices.

Blueberry & Lemon Drizzle

The lemon syrup, which is poured over this cake gives it a wonderful fresh tangy flavor. Let cool completely before cutting into squares.

50 mins   1 hr

SERVES 12

INGREDIENTS

8 oz/225 g butter, softened, plus extra for greasing

generous 1 cup golden superfine sugar

4 eggs, beaten

finely grated rind of 1 lemon

2¼ cups self-rising flour, sifted

¼ cup ground almonds

juice of 1 lemon

⅔ cup fresh blueberries

FOR THE TOPPING

juice of 2 lemons

generous ½ cup golden superfine sugar

½ cup confectioners' sugar

1 Preheat the oven to 350°F/180°C. Grease and base-line an 8-inch/20-cm square cake pan. Put the butter and sugar in a bowl and beat together until light and fluffy. Gradually beat in the eggs, adding a little flour toward the end to prevent curdling. Beat in the lemon rind, then fold in the flour and almonds with enough lemon juice to give a dropping consistency.

2 Fold in three-quarters of the blueberries and turn into the prepared pan. Smooth the surface, then scatter the remaining blueberries on top. Bake for about 1 hour, until firm to the touch and a skewer inserted into the center comes out clean.

3 Meanwhile, make the topping. Put the lemon juice and sugar in bowl and mix together. As soon as the cake comes out of the oven prick it all over with a fine skewer and pour the lemon mixture over. Leave in the pan until completely cold, then cut into 12 squares. Decorate with a little drizzled icing if desired.

COOK'S TIP
If you warm a lemon in the microwave for a few seconds on Full Power, it will yield more juice.

Sticky Date Cake

The toffee topping on this sticky cake makes it particularly moreish.
An ideal midweek dessert.

🍱 1 hr

🕐 1hr 10 mins–
1hr 25 mins

SERVES 8

INGREDIENTS

1 cup pitted dates, chopped

1¼ cups boiling water

4 oz/115 g butter, softened, plus extra
  for greasing

scant 1 cup golden superfine sugar

3 eggs, beaten

2 cups self-rising flour, sifted

½ tsp ground cinnamon

1 tsp baking soda

FOR THE TOPPING

¾ cup light muscovado sugar

4 tbsp butter

3 tbsp heavy cream

1 Put the dates in a bowl and cover with the boiling water. Preheat the oven to 350°F/180°C. Grease a 9-inch/23-cm springform cake pan. Put the butter and sugar in a bowl and beat until light and fluffy. Gradually beat in the eggs, then fold in the flour and cinnamon.

2 Add the baking soda to the dates and water, then pour on to the creamed mixture. Mix well. Pour into the prepared pan. Bake in the oven for 1–1¼ hours, until well risen and firm to the touch.

3 To make the topping, put the sugar, butter, and cream in a pan. Heat gently until the sugar has melted. Bring to a boil, simmer for 3 minutes then pour over the cake. Put under the broiler until bubbling. Let cool in the pan then transfer to a wire rack to cool completely.

Apricot Cake

The moist, fruity layer of filling makes this lovely light cake a welcome treat with a cup of mid-morning coffee or as a dessert.

50 mins plus 30 mins chilling

1 hr 15 mins

MAKES 10-INCH/25-CM CAKE

INGREDIENTS

BASE

1⅔ cups all-purpose flour, plus extra for dusting

pinch of salt

generous ¼ cup superfine sugar

grated rind of ½ lemon

4 tbsp water

3¼ oz/90 g butter, sweet for preference, softened

FILLING

1¼ cups short-grain rice

2 cups skim milk

scant ½ cup superfine sugar

grated rind and juice of ½ lemon

1 tbsp apricot jelly

3 eggs, separated

1 lb 12 oz/800 g apricots, peeled, halved, and pitted

confectioners' sugar, for dusting

1 Sift the flour with a pinch of salt into a bowl and add the sugar, lemon rind, water, and butter. Mix well, using an electric whisk or fork, until crumbly. Turn out on to a lightly floured work counter and knead lightly until smooth. Roll out and use to line the bottom and about 1¼ inches/3 cm of the sides of a 10-inch/25-cm springform cake pan. Chill in the refrigerator for 30 minutes, then bake blind (see Cook's Tip) in a preheated oven, 400°F/200°C, for 10 minutes.

2 Meanwhile, make the filling. Put the rice, milk, sugar, and lemon rind in a heavy-based pan and bring to a boil. Reduce the heat and simmer for 30 minutes. Remove the pan from the heat, stir in the lemon rind and juice and apricot jelly and set aside to cool.

3 Stir the egg yolks into the cooled rice mixture. Whisk the egg whites until stiff, then fold gently into the rice mixture. Remove the cooked bottom from the oven, discard the baking beans and lining paper, and reduce the oven temperature to 350°F/180°C. Arrange the apricot halves, flat-side uppermost, over the base. Spoon the rice mixture over the top, spreading it out evenly. Bake for 45 minutes, or until a skewer inserted into the center of the cake comes out clean. Cool on a wire rack and dust with confectioners' sugar before serving.

COOK'S TIP

To bake blind, prick the bottom all over with a fork and then line with parchment paper or waxed paper. Partially fill with baking beans—either store-bought ceramic, or metal beans, or haricot beans kept specially for the purpose.

Banana & Lime Cake

A substantial cake that is ideal served for tea. The mashed bananas help to keep the cake moist, and the lime frosting gives it extra zing and zest.

45 mins   40–45 mins

SERVES 8–10

INGREDIENTS

butter, for greasing

generous 2 cups all-purpose flour

1 tsp salt

1½ tsp baking powder

scant 1 cup brown sugar

1 tsp grated lime rind

1 egg, beaten lightly

1 banana, mashed with 1 tbsp lime juice

⅔ cup lowfat plain yogurt

⅔ cup golden raisins

TOPPING

generous 1 cup confectioners' sugar

1–2 tsp lime juice

½ tsp finely grated lime rind

TO DECORATE

banana chips

finely grated lime rind

1 Preheat the oven to 350°F/180°C. Grease a deep round 7-inch/18-cm cake pan with butter and line with parchment paper.

VARIATION
For a delicious alternative, replace the lime rind and juice with orange, and the golden raisins with chopped apricots.

2 Sift the flour, salt, and baking powder into a mixing bowl and stir in the sugar and lime rind.

3 Make a well in the center of the dry ingredients and add the egg, banana, yogurt, and golden raisins. Mix well until thoroughly incorporated.

4 Spoon the mixture into the pan and smooth the surface. Bake in the preheated oven for 40–45 minutes, until firm to the touch or until a skewer inserted into the center comes out clean. Let cool in the pan for 10 minutes, then turn out on to a wire rack.

5 To make the topping, sift the confectioners' sugar into a small bowl and mix with the lime juice to form a soft, but not too runny frosting. Stir in the grated lime rind. Drizzle the lime frosting over the cake, letting it run down the sides.

6 Decorate with banana chips and lime rind. Let set for 15 minutes and serve.

Rich Fruit Cake

Serve this moist, fruit-laden cake for a special occasion. It would also make an excellent Thanksgiving cake.

🍲 50 mins   🕐 1 hr 45 mins

SERVES 8–10

INGREDIENTS

butter or margarine, for greasing

¾ cup unsweetened pitted dates

½ cup no-soak dried prunes

scant 1 cup unsweetened orange juice

2 tbsp molasses

1 tsp finely grated lemon rind

1 tsp finely grated orange rind

2 cups self-rising whole-wheat flour

1 tsp allspice

scant 1 cup raisins

scant 1 cup golden raisins

½ cup currants

1 cup dried cranberries

3 large eggs, separated

TO DECORATE

1 tbsp apricot jelly, softened

confectioners' sugar, for dusting

generous 1 cup sugarpaste

strips of orange rind

strips of lemon rind

1 Preheat the oven to 325°F/160°C. Grease and line a deep 8-inch/20-cm round cake pan. Chop the dates and prunes and place in a pan. Pour over the orange juice, gently bring to a boil then simmer for 10 minutes. Remove the pan from the heat and beat the fruit mixture until puréed. Add the molasses and lemon and orange rinds. Set aside to cool.

2 Sift the flour and allspice into a bowl and add the dry fruits. When the date and prune mixture is cool, whisk in the egg yolks. In a clean bowl, whisk the egg whites until stiff peaks form. Spoon the fruit mixture into the dry ingredients and mix together.

3 Gently fold in the egg whites. Transfer to the prepared pan and bake in the preheated oven for 1½ hours. Let cool.

4 Remove the cake from the pan and brush the top with jelly. Dust the work counter with confectioners' sugar and roll out the sugarpaste thinly. Lay it over the top of the cake and trim the edges. Decorate with orange and lemon rind and serve.

Vanilla Tea Cake

Slices of juicy fruit soaked in sugar syrup are one of the great delicacies of Provence and southern Italy. Serve as a delicious afternoon treat.

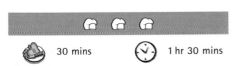

🍰 30 mins   🕐 1 hr 30 mins

SERVES 8

INGREDIENTS

¾ cup butter, softened, plus extra for greasing

1½ cups good-quality candied fruits, such as cherries, and candied orange, lemon, and lime rind

¾ cup ground almonds

finely grated rind of ½ lemon

generous ½ cup all-purpose flour

generous ½ cup self-rising flour

¾ cup plus 2 tbsp vanilla-flavored sugar

½ tsp vanilla extract

3 large eggs, beaten lightly

pinch of salt

candied fruits, to decorate

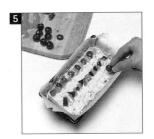

1 Preheat the oven to 350°F/180°C. Grease an 8 x 4 x 2-inch/22 x 12 x 5-cm loaf pan, then line the bottom with a piece of parchment paper.

2 Chop the fruit into even-size small pieces, reserving a few larger slices for the top. Place in a bowl with the ground almonds, lemon rind, and 2 tablespoons of the all-purpose flour, and stir together. Set aside.

3 Beat the butter and vanilla-flavored sugar together until fluffy and creamy. Beat in the vanilla extract and eggs, a little at a time.

4 Sift both flours and the salt into the creamed mixture, then fold in. Fold in the fruit and ground almonds.

5 Spoon into the pan and smooth the surface. Arrange the reserved fruits on the top. Loosely cover the pan with foil, making sure it does not touch the cake batter. Bake in the preheated oven for about 1½ hours, until risen and a skewer inserted into the center comes out clean.

6 Cool in the pan on a wire rack for 5 minutes, then turn out and remove the lining. Cool completely on a wire rack. Wrap in foil and store in an airtight container for up to 4 days. Serve decorated with candied fruits.

COOK'S TIP
Make your own vanilla-flavored sugar by storing a sliced vanilla bean in a closed jar of superfine sugar.

Candied Fruit Cake

This cake is extremely colorful; you can choose any mixture of candied fruits, or stick to just one type if you prefer.

1 hr   1 hr 10 mins

SERVES 8

INGREDIENTS

6 oz/175 g butter, softened, plus extra for greasing

¾ cup superfine sugar

3 eggs, beaten lightly

1¼ cups self-rising flour, sifted

2½ tbsp ground rice

finely grated rind of 1 lemon

4 tbsp lemon juice

⅔ cup candied fruits, chopped

confectioners' sugar, for dusting (optional)

1 Preheat the oven to 350°F/180°C. Lightly grease a 7-inch/18-cm cake pan with a little butter and line with parchment paper.

2 In a bowl, whisk together the butter and superfine sugar until the mixture is light and fluffy.

3 Add the beaten eggs, a little at a time. Using a metal spoon, gently fold in the flour and ground rice.

4 Add the grated lemon rind and lemon juice, followed by the chopped candied fruits. Lightly mix all the ingredients together.

5 Spoon the mixture into the prepared pan and smooth the surface with the back of a spoon or a knife.

6 Bake in the preheated oven for 1 hour–1 hour 10 minutes, until well risen or until a skewer inserted into the center of the cake comes out clean.

7 Let the cake cool in the pan for 5 minutes, then turn out on to a wire rack to cool completely.

8 Dust well with confectioners' sugar (if using) before serving.

COOK'S TIP

Wash and dry the candied fruits before chopping them. This will prevent them sinking to the bottom of the cake during cooking.

Crunchy Fruit Cake

Cornmeal adds texture to this cake, flavored with dry fruits and pine nuts, as well as a golden yellow color.

50 mins

1 hr

SERVES 8

INGREDIENTS

4½ oz/125 g butter, softened, plus extra for greasing

½ cup superfine sugar

2 eggs, beaten

7 tbsp self-rising flour, sifted

1 tsp baking powder

¾ cup cornmeal or polenta

1⅔ cups mixed dry fruits

¼ cup pine nuts

grated rind of 1 lemon

4 tbsp lemon juice

2 tbsp milk

1 Preheat the oven to 350°F/180°C. Grease a 7-inch/18-cm cake pan with a little butter and line the bottom with parchment paper.

2 In a bowl, whisk together the butter and sugar until light and fluffy.

3 Whisk in the beaten eggs, a little at a time, whisking thoroughly after each addition.

4 Gently fold the flour, baking powder, and cornmeal into the mixture until totally incorporated.

5 Stir in the mixed dry fruits, pine nuts, grated lemon rind, lemon juice, and milk.

6 Spoon the batter into the prepared pan and smooth the surface.

7 Bake in the preheated oven for about 1 hour, or until a skewer inserted into the center of the cake comes out clean.

8 Let the cake cool in the pan before turning out.

VARIATION
For a crumblier cake omit the polenta and use 1¼ cups self-rising flour instead.

Sugar-Free Fruit Cake

This cake is full of flavor from the mixed fruits. The fruit gives the cake its sweetness so there is no need for extra sugar.

1 hr 5 mins   1 hr

SERVES 8

INGREDIENTS

4½ oz/125 g butter, cut into small pieces, plus extra for greasing

2½ cups all-purpose flour

2 tsp baking powder

1 tsp ground allspice

⅓ cup no-soak dried apricots, chopped

½ cup chopped pitted dates

⅓ cup candied cherries, chopped

⅔ cup raisins

½ cup milk

2 eggs, beaten lightly

grated rind of 1 orange

5–6 tbsp orange juice

3 tbsp honey

1 Preheat the oven to 350°F/180°C. Grease an 8-inch/20-cm round cake pan with a little butter and line the bottom with parchment paper.

2 Sift the flour, baking powder, and allspice together into a large mixing bowl.

3 Add the butter and rub it in with your fingertips until the mixture resembles fine bread crumbs.

4 Carefully stir in the apricots, dates, candied cherries, and raisins, with the milk, beaten eggs, grated orange rind, and orange juice.

5 Stir in the honey and mix everything together to form a soft dropping consistency. Spoon into the prepared cake pan and smooth the surface.

6 Bake in the preheated oven for 1 hour, until a fine skewer inserted into the center of the cake comes out clean.

7 Leave the cake to cool in the pan before turning out.

VARIATION
For a fruity alternative, replace the honey with 1 mashed ripe banana, if you prefer.

Olive Oil, Fruit & Nut Cake

It is worth using a good-quality olive oil for this cake because this will determine its flavor. The cake will keep well in an airtight container.

🍳 10 mins   🕐 45 mins

SERVES 8

INGREDIENTS

butter, for greasing

2 cups self-rising flour

¼ cup superfine sugar

½ cup milk

¼ cup orange juice

⅔ cup olive oil

¾ cup mixed dry fruits

¼ cup pine nuts

1 Preheat the oven to 350°F/180°C. Grease a 7-inch/18-cm cake pan and line with parchment paper.

2 Sift the flour into a mixing bowl and stir in the superfine sugar.

3 Make a well in the center of the dry ingredients and pour in the milk and orange juice. Stir the mixture with a wooden spoon, gradually beating in the flour and sugar.

4 Pour in the olive oil, stirring well so that all of the ingredients are thoroughly mixed.

5 Stir the mixed dry fruits and pine nuts into the batter and spoon into the prepared pan. Gently smooth the top with a spatula.

6 Bake the cake in the preheated oven for about 45 minutes, until it is golden brown and just firm to the touch.

7 Let the cake cool in the pan for a few minutes before transferring to a wire rack to cool completely.

8 Serve the cake warm or cold and cut into slices.

COOK'S TIP
Pine nuts are best known as the flavoring ingredient in the classic Italian pesto, but here they give a delicate, slightly resinous flavor to this cake.

Spiced Fruit Cake

The addition of cardamom pods gives a wonderful aromatic flavor and smell to this cake. Store in an airtight container for several days.

20 mins   50–60 mins

SERVES 12

INGREDIENTS

1 tsp sunflower oil, for oiling

6 green cardamom pods

6 oz/175 g butter or margarine

¾ cup light muscovado sugar

1 tsp ground cinnamon

½ tsp ground ginger

3 eggs, beaten

1½ cups self-rising flour

½ cup dried cranberries

generous ½ cup no-soak dried apricots, chopped, plus extra, to decorate

½ cup golden raisins

FROSTING

6 oz/175 g semisweet chocolate

2 tbsp butter

2 tbsp corn syrup

2 tbsp milk

1 Preheat the oven to 325°F/160°C. Lightly oil and line the bottom of an 8-inch/20-cm cake pan with nonstick parchment paper. Lightly pound the cardamom pods until cracked open. Scrape out the seeds.

2 Cream the butter with the sugar and spices until light and fluffy. Gradually beat in the eggs adding in a little flour after each addition. When all the eggs have been added, stir in the remaining flour.

3 Add the cardamom seeds, dried cranberries, apricots, and golden raisins and stir lightly, adding 1–2 tablespoons of cooled boiled water to give a soft consistency. Spoon into the prepared cake pan and smooth the top. Bake in the preheated oven for 50–60 minutes, or until a skewer inserted into the center comes out clean. Remove and let cool in the cake pan before removing from the pan and discarding the lining paper. Leave until cold before frosting.

4 Break the chocolate into small pieces and place in a heavy-based pan together with the butter. Heat gently, stirring frequently, until the chocolate and butter have melted and the mixture is smooth. Remove from the heat and stir in the syrup and milk. Beat until the frosting is smooth, then use to coat the top of the cake, swirling to give a decorative effect. Pipe 12 frosting rosettes around the edge of the cake and top with extra apricots.

Caribbean Chocolate Cake

This cake can be stored for a week. Simply let the cake cool completely, then wrap in nonstick parchment paper and foil and leave in a cool place.

2 hrs 30 mins

1 hr 45 mins–2 hrs

SERVES 12–14

I N G R E D I E N T S

8 oz/225 g butter, softened, plus extra for greasing

1 tsp ground ginger

1 tsp ground cinnamon

½ tsp ground cloves

1 cup dark muscovado sugar

4 eggs, beaten

1½ cups all-purpose flour

generous ½ cup ground almonds

4 oz/115 g semisweet chocolate

1 cup no-soak dried apricots

¾ cup no-soak dried papaya

1 cup no-soak dried mango

¾ cup no-soak dried pineapple

1 oz/25 g preserved ginger

¾ cup whole-wheat self-rising flour

2–3 tbsp rum, cognac, or orange juice

T O P P I N G

4 tbsp apricot jelly

1 tbsp lemon juice

1⅓ cups assorted candied fruits

¾ cup mixed nuts

COOK'S TIP

For a different topping, brush the cooked cake with 1–2 tablespoons of apricot glaze, then top with a circle of marzipan and decorate with the candied fruits and nuts if liked.

1 Preheat the oven to 325°F/160°C. Lightly grease and line a 9-inch/23-cm cake pan with nonstick parchment paper. Chop the dry fruits and ginger. Beat the butter with the spices and muscovado sugar until light and creamy. Gradually beat in the eggs, adding a little flour after each addition. When all the eggs have been added, stir in the remaining flour and the ground almonds. Melt the chocolate in a heatproof bowl set over a pan of gently simmering water. Stir the chocolate until smooth, then stir into the cake batter.

2 Add all the fruits and preserved ginger and stir lightly. Sift the whole-wheat flour into the bowl, then add the husks remaining in the sifter to the bowl. Mix lightly, adding sufficient rum, cognac, or orange juice to form a soft dropping consistency. Turn into the pan and smooth the top.

3 Bake in the preheated oven for 1 hr 45 mins–2 hours. Cover the top with foil if it browns too much. Remove from the oven and leave in the pan until almost cold before removing from the pan and discarding the lining paper.

4 Heat the apricot jelly and lemon juice together, then rub through a strainer. Brush over the top of the cake. Arrange the assorted candied fruits and nuts over the top. Brush the fruits and nuts with the remaining apricot glaze and leave for 2 hours to let the jelly set before serving.

Apple Cake with Hard Cider

This can be warmed through and served with cream for a dessert or eaten as a snack with a morning cup of coffee, if preferred.

1 hr 5 mins   40 mins

SERVES 8

INGREDIENTS

3 oz/85 g butter, cut into small pieces, plus extra for greasing

2 cups self-rising flour

1 tsp baking powder

scant ½ cup superfine sugar

4 cups chopped dried apple

⅔ cup raisins

⅔ cup hard cider

1 egg, beaten

1 cup raspberries

1 Preheat the oven to 325°F/190°C. Grease an 8-inch/20-cm cake pan and line with parchment paper.

2 Sift the flour and baking powder into a mixing bowl and rub in the butter with your fingertips until the mixture resembles fine bread crumbs.

3 Stir in the superfine sugar, chopped dried apple, and raisins.

4 Pour in the hard cider and egg and mix together until thoroughly blended. Stir in the raspberries very gently so they do not break up.

5 Pour the cake batter into the prepared cake pan.

6 Bake in the preheated oven for about 40 minutes until risen and lightly golden.

7 Set the cake aside to cool in the pan, then turn out on to a wire rack. Set aside until completely cold before serving.

VARIATION
If you don't want to use hard cider or you are making the cake for children, replace it with clear apple juice.

Spiced Apple Ring

Adding grated fresh apple and crunchy almonds to the cake batter makes this ring beautifully moist yet with a crunch to it.

1 hr 5 mins   30 mins

SERVES 8

INGREDIENTS

6 oz/175 g butter, softened, plus extra
    for greasing

¾ cup superfine sugar

3 eggs, beaten lightly

1¼ cups self-rising flour

1 tsp ground cinnamon

1 tsp ground allspice

2 dessert apples, cored and grated

2 tbsp apple juice or milk

¼ cup slivered almonds

1 Preheat the oven to 350°F/180°C. Lightly grease a 10-inch/25-cm ovenproof ring mold.

2 In a mixing bowl, cream together the butter and sugar until light and fluffy. Gradually add the beaten eggs, beating well after each addition.

3 Sift the flour and spices, then carefully fold them into the creamed mixture with a figure-of-eight movement.

4 Stir in the grated apples and the apple juice or milk and mix to a soft dropping consistency.

5 Sprinkle the slivered almonds around the base of the mold and spoon the cake mixture on top. Smooth the surface with the back of the spoon.

6 Bake in the preheated oven for about 30 minutes, until well risen and a fine skewer inserted into the center comes out clean.

7 Let the cake cool in the pan before turning out and transferring to a wire rack to cool completely. Serve the apple ring cut into slices.

COOK'S TIP
This cake can also be made in a 7-inch/18-cm round cake pan if you do not have an ovenproof ring mold.

Sweet Risotto Cake

Served with your favorite summer berries and a scented mascarpone cream, this baked sweet risotto makes an unusual dessert.

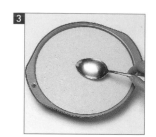

40 mins   25–30 mins

SERVES 6–8

INGREDIENTS

2 tbsp melted butter, for greasing

generous ⅓ cup risotto rice

1½ cups milk

3–4 tbsp sugar

½ tsp freshly grated nutmeg

½ tsp salt, plus a pinch for the
    almond mixture

1⅓ cups all-purpose flour

1½ tsp baking powder

1 tsp baking soda

1–2 tbsp superfine sugar

1 egg

¾ cup milk

½ cup sour cream or yogurt

1 tbsp butter, melted

2 tbsp honey

½ tsp almond extract

2 tbsp toasted slivered almonds

confectioners' sugar, for dusting (optional)

MUSCAT BERRIES

2¼ cups mixed summer berries, such as
    strawberries (halved), raspberries, and
    blueberries

1–2 tbsp sugar

¼ cup Muscat wine

MASCARPONE CREAM

1 cup mascarpone cheese

2 tbsp Muscat wine

1 tbsp honey

½ tsp almond extract

1 cup mascarpone cheese

1 Preheat the oven to 325°F/160°C. Grease a 9–10-inch/23–25-cm loose-bottomed cake pan. Put the rice, milk, sugar, nutmeg, and ½ teaspoon of salt in a heavy-based pan. Bring to a boil, reduce the heat slightly, and cook, stirring constantly, until the rice is tender and the milk is almost absorbed. Let cool.

2 Combine the flour, baking powder, baking soda, pinch of salt, and the superfine sugar. In a bowl, beat the egg, milk, sour cream, butter, honey, and almond extract with an electric whisk until smooth. Gradually beat in the cooled rice. Stir in the flour mixture and the almonds.

3 Spoon the rice and almond mixture gently into the prepared cake pan, smoothing the top evenly. Bake in the preheated oven for about 20 minutes, or until golden. Cool in the pan on a wire rack.

4 While the cake is cooking, put the berries in a bowl and add the sugar and wine. To make the mascarpone cream, stir all the ingredients together and chill.

5 Remove the sides of the pan and slide the cake gently on to a serving plate. Dust the cake with confectioners' sugar and serve warm with the Muscat berries and mascarpone cream piped on top of the cake.

Passion Cake

Decorating this moist, rich carrot cake with sugared flowers lifts it into the celebration class. It is a perfect choice for Easter.

40 mins   1 hr 30 mins

SERVES 10

INGREDIENTS

butter, for greasing

⅔ cup corn oil

¾ cup golden superfine sugar

4 tbsp natural yogurt

3 eggs, plus 1 extra yolk

1 tsp vanilla extract

1 cup walnut pieces, chopped

6 oz/175 g carrots, grated

1 banana, mashed

1½ cups all-purpose flour

½ cup fine oatmeal

1 tsp baking soda

1 tsp baking powder

1 tsp ground cinnamon

½ tsp salt

FROSTING

generous ½ cup cream cheese

4 tbsp plain yogurt

¾ cup confectioners' sugar

1 tsp grated lemon rind

2 tsp lemon juice

TO DECORATE

primroses and violets

1 egg white, beaten lightly

3 tbsp superfine sugar

1 Preheat the oven to 350°F/180°C. Grease and line a 9-inch/23-cm round cake pan. Beat the oil, sugar, yogurt, eggs, egg yolk, and vanilla extract. Beat in the chopped walnuts, grated carrot, and banana.

2 Sift together the remaining ingredients and gradually beat into the mixture.

3 Pour the mixture into the pan and level the surface. Bake in the preheated oven for 1½ hours, or until firm, and a fine skewer inserted into the center comes out clean. Let cool in the pan for 15 minutes, then turn out on to a wire rack.

4 To make the frosting, beat together the cheese and yogurt. Sift in the confectioners' sugar and stir in the lemon rind and juice. Spread over the top and sides of the cake.

5 To prepare the decoration, dip the flowers quickly in the beaten egg white, then sprinkle with superfine sugar to cover the surface completely. Place well apart on parchment paper. Leave in a warm, dry place for several hours, until they are dry and crisp. Arrange the flowers in a pattern on top of the cake.

Simnel Cake

Simnel is a traditional English cake, baked at Easter; this version includes amaretto, which intensifies its almond flavor and keeps it very moist.

1 hr 45 mins   3 hrs–3 hrs 30 mins

SERVES 8–10

INGREDIENTS

8 oz/225 g sweet butter, plus extra for greasing

¾ cup candied cherries

scant ½ cup whole, blanched almonds

2¼ cups golden raisins

2¼ cups currants

2¼ cups raisins

¾ cup candied peel

½ cup ground almonds

rind of 1 lemon

rind of 1 orange

¼ cup amaretto

1½ cups brown sugar

6 eggs

2 lb 4 oz/1 kg ready-made marzipan

1½ tsp baking powder

1 tsp ground cinnamon

2½ cups all-purpose flour

lightly beaten egg white, for brushing

1 Line a 9-inch/23-cm round cake pan with waxed paper and grease it thoroughly.

2 Wash the cherries and pat dry, then halve them. Finely chop the almonds. Mix the dry fruits, nuts, ground almonds, and the lemon and orange rind. Add half the amaretto, and set aside for 1 hour.

3 Preheat the oven to 350°F/180°C.

4 Cream the butter until soft, then add the sugar and beat until pale and fluffy. Whisk the eggs and add little by little, beating well to avoid the batter curdling. Measure off 4 oz/115 g of marzipan and grate it coarsely using a grater. Add this and the soaked fruit to the cake batter. Sift the spice with the flour and fold in gently.

5 Put half of the mixture in the prepared cake pan and smooth over. Roll out half of the remaining marzipan into an 8-inch/20-cm circle and put into the cake pan. Cover with the remaining batter. Smooth over, making a slight dip in the center.

6 Cook in the preheated oven for 1 hour, then reduce the temperature to 325°F/160°C. Cook for an additional 2 hours then test with a skewer inserted into the center. If the skewer does not come out clean, cook for an additional 30–45 minutes.

7 Remove the cake from the oven and prick the surface lightly with a fork or skewer. Pour over the remaining amaretto and let cool completely before removing from the cake pan. Keep the cake covered in waxed paper with a layer of foil until required.

8 Brush the cake surface with a little egg white. Roll out the remaining marzipan to form a 9-inch/23-cm circle and cover the top of the cake. Use the trimmings to make decorations with flowers and leaves on top and twisted strands around the base of the cake.

Chestnut Slab Cake

This quick and simple dessert is a favorite at Christmas in France. It can be made in advance and will keep for up to 1 week in the refrigerator.

20 mins plus 2–3 hrs chilling · 5 mins

SERVES 6–8

INGREDIENTS

10 oz/300 g sweet butter, cubed, plus extra for greasing

1 lb 14 oz/850 g canned unsweetened chestnut purée

4 tbsp confectioners' sugar

7 oz/200 g bittersweet chocolate, grated

3 tsp kirsch

TOPPING

4 oz/115 g bittersweet chocolate

1–2 tbsp warm milk

marrons glacés, to decorate

1 Grease and line a 2-lb/900-g loaf pan. Tip the chestnut purée into a heavy-based pan and heat gently. When it is hot, remove from the heat and add the butter, sugar, grated chocolate, and kirsch. Stir thoroughly. Pour into the prepared loaf pan, smooth the top, and chill in the refrigerator for 2–3 hours.

2 To make the topping, break the chocolate into pieces and place in a heatproof bowl set over a pan of gently simmering water with 1 tablespoon of milk and stir until the chocolate has melted. Add an additional tablespoon of milk if needed to make a smooth, glossy topping.

3 Turn the cake out of the loaf pan on to a serving plate. Cover with the topping, letting it trickle down the sides. Decorate with marrons glacés and cut into slices to serve.

COOK'S TIP

This cake is very rich, so keep your slices thin. It is delicious with tiny cups of black coffee or perhaps a liqueur.

Plum-Topped Chocolate Cake

You can use any type of plums for this recipe, but make sure that they are not too ripe or they will not hold their shape during cooking.

15 mins | 30–40 mins

SERVES 12

INGREDIENTS

1 tsp sunflower oil, for oiling

6 oz/175 g butter or margarine, softened

¾ cup superfine sugar

few drops of almond extract

3 eggs, beaten

scant ½ cup self-rising flour

generous 1 cup ground almonds

3 oz/85 g white chocolate, grated

10 oz/300 g red plums

2 tbsp apricot or raspberry jelly

1 tbsp lemon juice

1 tbsp slivered almonds

1 Preheat the oven to 375°F/190°C. Lightly oil and line the bottom of an 8-inch/20-cm square cake pan with nonstick parchment paper. Cream the butter with the sugar and almond extract until light and fluffy. Gradually beat in the eggs, adding a little flour after each addition. When all the eggs have been added, stir in the remaining flour.

2 Add the ground almonds with 1–2 tablespoons of cooled boiled water and mix to form a smooth dropping consistency. Add the grated chocolate and stir lightly. Spoon into the prepared pan and smooth the top.

3 Rinse the plums, cut in half, pit, and slice thickly. Arrange the plum slices over the cake. Heat the jelly and lemon juice together and brush or spoon over the plums and sprinkle with the slivered almonds.

4 Bake in the preheated oven for 30–40 minutes, or until a skewer inserted into the center of the cake comes out clean. Remove from the oven and let cool before removing from the pan and discarding the lining paper. Cut into squares to serve.

COOK'S TIP
Cover the cake with foil if the top browns too quickly as it cooks.

Raspberry Refrigerator Cake

This is quite the most decadent special-occasion dessert. The rich chocolate filling combines well with the cherries.

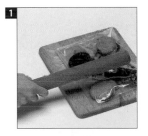

  15–20 mins plus 2–3 hrs chilling 10 mins

SERVES 4

INGREDIENTS

8 oz/225 g half-coated chocolate cookies

6 tbsp butter

2 tbsp corn syrup

10 oz/300 g semisweet chocolate

1¼ cups heavy cream

4 tbsp cognac

1¾ cups fresh raspberries, strawberries, or fruit of your choice

TO DECORATE

¾ cup heavy cream, whipped

fresh cherries or other fruits and 1 tsp confectioners' sugar

1 Place the cookies in a polythene bag and pound lightly until crushed. Alternatively, place in a food processor and process for 1 minute. Heat the butter and syrup together until blended, then stir in the crushed cookies and mix in lightly. Press the cookies into the sides and bottom of an 8-inch/20-cm springform pan. Leave in the refrigerator while preparing the filling.

COOK'S TIP
Use only best-quality chocolate for this recipe.

2 Break the chocolate into small pieces and place in a heavy-based pan. Add the cream and cognac and heat gently until smooth. Remove from the heat and cool, stirring occasionally. Let cool.

3 Pick over the fruit, cutting large ones in half, then arrange over the chocolate cookie base. Stir the chocolate and cream mixture, then pour over the fruit. Leave in the refrigerator until set. Decorate with the whipped cream, cherries, and confectioners' sugar. Store in the refrigerator.

Crêpes, Loaves, Pastries & Cheesecakes

Breakfast, lunch, and teatime are amply catered for in the

delights of this chapter. Here you will find some classic

and some entirely new ideas for baking,

from Scotch Pancakes to Balinese

Banana Crêpes, from traditional

Teacakes and Hot Cross Buns to

Chocolate Nut Soda Bread, along with individual Apricot

Tartes Tatin, Fruity Phyllo Nests, and Maple Pecan Tarts.

Scotch Pancakes

Traditional Scotch pancakes are sometimes known as drop scones. Either way they will always be a very welcome sight on the tea table.

🍂 25 mins   🕐 20 mins

SERVES 4

INGREDIENTS

generous 1½ cups self-rising flour

2 tsp baking powder

pinch of salt

2 tbsp golden superfine sugar

1 egg

scant 1 cup milk

butter, for greasing

ORANGE BUTTER

¾ cup butter

¼ cup confectioners' sugar, strained

finely grated rind of 1 orange and 2 tbsp orange juice

1 To make the orange butter, place all of the ingredients in a bowl and beat together until light and fluffy. Chill in the refrigerator while making the pancakes.

2 To make the pancakes, sift the flour, baking powder, and salt into a bowl. Stir in the sugar and make a well in the center. Place the egg and milk in a separate bowl, whisk together, and pour into the well. Gradually draw the flour into the liquid by stirring with a wooden spoon, then beat thoroughly to make a smooth batter.

3 Grease a griddle or heavy-bottomed skillet and set over medium–high heat. Drop spoonfuls of the batter into the pan and cook for 2–3 minutes, or until bubbles burst on the surface and the underside is golden. Turn over with a spatula and cook for an additional 1 minute, or until golden on the other side. Keep warm in a clean dish towel until all the pancakes are cooked. Serve with the orange butter.

COOK'S TIP
Heat up the griddle or skillet gently and check it is ready by dropping a small amount of pancake batter on to the surface, which should sizzle.

Chocolate Crêpes

Serve these sweet soufflé-filled, golden chocolate crêpes with flambéed summer berries for a superb contrast if you like.

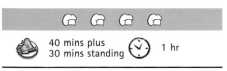

40 mins plus 30 mins standing   **1 hr**

SERVES 6

INGREDIENTS

⅔ cup all-purpose flour

1 tbsp unsweetened cocoa

1 tsp superfine sugar

2 eggs, beaten lightly

¾ cup milk

2 tsp dark rum

3 oz/85 g butter, sweet for preference

confectioners' sugar, for dusting

FILLING

5 tbsp heavy cream

8 oz/225 g semisweet chocolate

3 eggs, separated

2 tbsp superfine sugar

BERRY SAUCE

2 tbsp butter

4 tbsp superfine sugar

⅔ cup orange juice

2 cups mixed berries, such as raspberries, blackberries, and strawberries

3 tbsp white rum

1 To make the crêpes, sift the flour, unsweetened cocoa, and superfine sugar into a bowl. Make a well in the center and add the eggs, beating them in a little at a time. Add the milk and beat until smooth. Stir in the dark rum.

2 Melt all the butter and stir 2 tablespoonfuls into the batter. Cover with plastic wrap and let stand for 30 minutes.

3 To cook the crêpes, brush the bottom of a 7-inch/18-cm crêpe pan or nonstick skillet with melted butter and set over medium heat. Stir the batter and pour 3 tablespoonfuls into the pan, swirling it to cover the bottom. Cook for 2 minutes or until the underside is golden, flip over, cook for 30 seconds, then slide on to a plate. Cook another 11 crêpes in the same way. Stack them interleaved with waxed paper.

4 For the filling, pour the cream into a heavy-based pan, add the chocolate, and melt over low heat, stirring. Remove from the heat. In a heatproof bowl, beat the egg yolks with half of the superfine sugar until creamy, beat in the chocolate cream, and let the mixture cool.

5 In a separate bowl, whisk the egg whites until soft peaks form, add the rest of the superfine sugar, and beat until stiff peaks form. Stir a spoonful of the whites into the chocolate mixture, then fold the mixture into the remaining egg whites with a spoon.

6 Preheat the oven to 400°F/200°C. Brush a cookie sheet with melted butter. Spread 1 crêpe with 1 tablespoon of the filling, then fold it in half and in half again to make a triangle. Place on the cookie sheet. Repeat with the remaining crêpes. Brush the tops with the remaining melted butter and bake for 20 minutes.

7 For the berry sauce, melt the butter in a heavy-based skillet over low heat, stir in the sugar, and cook until golden. Stir in the orange juice and cook until syrupy. Add the berries and warm through, stirring gently. Add the white rum, heat gently for 1 minute, then ignite. Shake the skillet until the flames have died down. Transfer the crêpes to serving plates with the sauce and serve.

Apple Crêpe Stacks

If you cannot wait to get your first chocolate "fix" of the day, serve these crêpes for breakfast. They also make a perfect family dessert.

15 mins   45 mins

SERVES 4

INGREDIENTS

2 cups all-purpose flour

1½ tsp baking powder

4 tbsp superfine sugar

1 egg

1 tbsp butter, melted, plus extra
for greasing

1¼ cups milk

1 dessert apple

¼ cup semisweet chocolate chips

chocolate sauce or maple syrup, to serve

1 Sift the flour and baking powder into a mixing bowl. Stir in the superfine sugar. Make a well in the center and add the egg and melted butter. Gradually whisk in the milk to form a smooth batter.

2 Peel, core, and grate the apple and stir it into the batter with the chocolate chips.

3 Heat a griddle pan or heavy-based skillet over medium heat and grease it lightly. For each crêpe, place about 2 tablespoons of the batter on to the griddle or skillet and spread to make a 3-inch/7.5-cm circle.

4 Cook for a few minutes until you see bubbles appear on the surface of the crêpe. Turn over and cook for an additional 1 minute. Remove from the pan and keep warm. Repeat with the remaining batter to make about 12 crêpes.

5 To serve, stack 2 or 3 crêpes on an individual serving plate and serve them with hot chocolate sauce or maple syrup.

COOK'S TIP
To keep the cooked crêpes warm, pile them on top of each other with waxed paper in between to prevent them sticking to one another.

Crêpes with Apples

The sharpness of the apples contrasts with the sweetness of the butterscotch sauce in this mouthwatering crêpe recipe.

15 mins   45 mins

SERVES 4

INGREDIENTS

generous 1 cup all-purpose flour

pinch of salt

1 tsp finely grated lemon rind

1 egg

1¼ cups milk

1–2 tbsp vegetable oil, plus extra
   for greasing

strips of pared lemon rind, to garnish

FILLING

8 oz/225 g tart cooking apples, peeled,
   cored, and sliced

2 tbsp golden raisins

SAUCE

6 tbsp butter

3 tbsp corn syrup

⅓ cup molasses sugar

1 tbsp dark rum or cognac (optional)

1 tbsp lemon juice

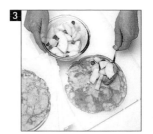

1 Preheat the oven to 325°F/160°C. Sift the flour and salt into a bowl. Add the lemon rind, egg, and milk and whisk to form a smooth batter.

2 Heat a little oil in a heavy-based skillet. Make 8 thin crêpes, using extra oil as required. Stack the cooked crêpes, layering them with waxed paper or parchment paper and keep warm.

3 To make the filling, cook the apples with the golden raisins in a little water over low heat until soft. Divide the mixture evenly among the crêpes and roll up or fold into triangles. Brush an ovenproof dish with a little oil and arrange the crêpes in it. Bake in the preheated oven for about 15 minutes, until warmed through.

4 To make the sauce, melt the butter, syrup, and sugar together in a pan, stirring well. Add the rum or cognac (if using) and the lemon juice. Do not let the mixture boil.

5 Serve the crêpes on warm plates, with a little sauce poured over, and garnished with strips of lemon rind.

Mango & Strawberry Crêpes

Everybody loves crêpes, and when they are filled with exotic fruit they are irresistible. Dust with confectioners' sugar and serve immediately.

20 mins plus
20 mins standing   15 mins

SERVES 4

INGREDIENTS

FILLING

3½ oz/100 g strained plain yogurt

1 cup mascarpone cheese

confectioners' sugar (optional)

1 mango, peeled and diced

scant 1 cup strawberries, hulled and quartered

2 passion fruit

CREPES

scant 1 cup all-purpose flour

2 tbsp unsweetened cocoa

pinch of salt

1 egg, beaten

1¼ cups milk

oil, for frying

confectioners' sugar, for dusting

1 Prepare the filling. Put the yogurt and mascarpone cheese in a bowl and sweeten with confectioners' sugar, if desired. Stir in the mango and strawberries. Cut the passion fruit in half and scoop out the pulp and seeds. Stir into the fruit mixture

2 Make the crêpes. Sift the flour, unsweetened cocoa, and salt into a bowl and make a well in the center. Add the egg and whisk well with a balloon whisk. Gradually beat in the milk, drawing in the flour from the sides to form a smooth batter. Cover and, if possible, let rest for 20 minutes. Heat a small amount of oil in a 7-inch/18-cm crêpe pan or nonstick skillet. Pour in just enough batter to thinly coat the bottom of the pan. Cook over moderately high heat for about 1 minute, then turn and cook the other side for ½–1 minute until cooked through.

3 Transfer the crêpe to a plate and keep hot. Repeat with the remaining batter, stacking the cooked crêpes on top of each other with waxed paper in between each one. Keep warm in the oven while cooking the remainder. Divide the filling among the crêpes, roll up, and dust with confectioners' sugar. Serve at once.

Chocolate & Banana Crêpes

Crêpes are given the chocolate treatment here to make a fabulous dinner-party dessert. Prepare ahead of time for easy entertaining.

🍓 10 mins   🕐 15 mins

SERVES 4

INGREDIENTS

3 large bananas

6 tbsp orange juice

grated rind of 1 orange

2 tbsp orange- or banana-flavored liqueur

HOT CHOCOLATE SAUCE

1 tbsp unsweetened cocoa

2 tsp cornstarch

3 tbsp milk

1½ oz/40 g semisweet chocolate, broken into pieces

1 tbsp butter

½ cup corn syrup

¼ tsp vanilla extract

CREPES

¾ cup all-purpose flour

1 tbsp unsweetened cocoa

1 egg

1 tsp sunflower oil

1¼ cups milk

oil, for frying

1 Peel and slice the bananas and arrange them in a dish with the orange juice and rind and the liqueur. Set aside.

2 Mix the unsweetened cocoa and cornstarch in a bowl, then stir in the milk. Put the chocolate in a pan with the butter and corn syrup. Heat gently, stirring until well blended. Add the cocoa mixture and bring to a boil over gentle heat, stirring. Simmer for 1 minute, then remove from the heat and stir in the vanilla extract.

3 To make the crêpes, sift the flour and unsweetened cocoa into a mixing bowl and make a well in the center. Add the egg and oil. Gradually whisk in the milk to form a smooth batter. Heat a little oil in a heavy-based skillet and pour off any excess. Pour in a little batter and tilt the skillet to coat the bottom. Cook over medium heat until the underside is browned. Flip over and cook the other side. Slide the crêpe out of the skillet and keep warm. Repeat until all the batter has been used.

4 To serve, reheat the chocolate sauce for 1–2 minutes. Fill the crêpes with the bananas and fold in half or into triangles. Pour over a little chocolate sauce and serve.

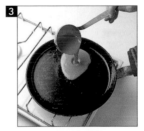

Balinese Banana Crêpes

These little stacks of rich banana crêpes, drizzled with fragrant lime juice, are quite irresistible at any time of the day.

15 mins plus 1 hr chilling

20 mins

SERVES 6

INGREDIENTS

1½ cups all-purpose flour

pinch of salt

4 eggs, beaten

2 large, ripe bananas, peeled and mashed

1¼ cups coconut milk

vegetable oil, for frying

TO DECORATE

sliced banana

6 tbsp lime juice

confectioners' sugar

coconut cream

1 Place the flour, salt, eggs, bananas, and coconut milk in a blender or food processor and process to a smooth batter. Alternatively, if you don't have a food processor, sift the flour and salt into a large mixing bowl and make a well in the center, then add the remaining ingredients, and beat well until smooth.

2 Chill the batter for 1 hour. Remove from the refrigerator and beat briefly again. Heat a small amount of oil in a small skillet until very hot.

3 Drop tablespoonfuls of batter into the pan. Cook until the crêpes are golden underneath.

4 Flip over and cook the other side until golden brown. Cook in batches until you have used up all the batter, making about 36 crêpes. Remove and drain thoroughly on paper towels.

5 Serve the crêpes in a stack, decorated with sliced bananas, sprinkled with lime juice and sugar, and topped with coconut cream.

COOK'S TIP
These little crêpes are best eaten hot and freshly cooked, so keep them hot in a slow oven while the others are cooking.

Pear Crêpes with Chocolate

Chocolate and pears go well together in these crêpes. They are at their best when served immediately.

15 mins plus 30 mins chilling   30 mins

SERVES 4

INGREDIENTS

CREPES

generous 1 cup all-purpose flour

pinch of salt

3 eggs

1 cup milk

2 tbsp lemon oil or vegetable oil

FILLING

9 oz/250 g pears

8 cloves

3 tbsp currants

pinch of allspice

CHOCOLATE SAUCE

4½ oz/125 g semisweet chocolate, broken into small pieces

2½ tbsp butter

6 tbsp water

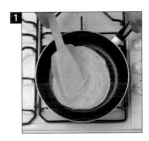

1 To make the crêpes, sift the flour and salt into a bowl. Whisk in the eggs and milk. Cover with plastic wrap and chill for 30 minutes. Preheat the oven to 325°F/160°C. Heat a little oil in a skillet until hot. Add a large spoonful of the batter and cook over high heat until golden, then turn it over and cook briefly on the other side. Cook the other crêpes in the same way, stacking them on a plate.

2 To make the filling, bring a pan of water to a boil. Peel and slice the pears, then add to the pan with the cloves and currants. Reduce the heat and simmer for 5 minutes. Remove from the heat, drain, and discard the cloves. Cool a little. Brush an ovenproof dish with oil. Stir the allspice into the fruit, then divide among the crêpes. Fold into triangles or roll into horns. Arrange in the dish and bake for 15 minutes.

3 To make the sauce, gently melt the chocolate, butter, and water together in a small pan, stirring constantly. Serve the crêpes with the sauce.

Cherry Crêpes

This dish can be made with either fresh pitted cherries or, if your time is very short, you can use canned cherries for extra speed.

10 mins   15 mins

SERVES 4

INGREDIENTS

FILLING

14 oz/400 g canned pitted cherries

½ tsp almond extract

½ tsp allspice

2 tbsp cornstarch

CREPES

¾ cup all-purpose flour

pinch of salt

2 tbsp chopped fresh mint

1 egg

1¼ cups milk

vegetable oil, for frying

confectioners' sugar and toasted slivered almonds, to decorate

1 Put the cherries and 1¼ cups of the can juice in a pan with the almond extract and allspice. Stir in the cornstarch and bring to a boil, stirring until thickened and clear. Set aside.

2 To make the crêpes, sift the flour and salt into a bowl. Add the mint. Make a well in the center and gradually beat in the egg and milk to form a smooth batter.

3 Heat 1 tablespoon of oil in a 7-inch/18-cm skillet, pour off the oil when hot. Add just enough batter to coat the bottom of the skillet and cook for 1–2 minutes, or until the underside is cooked. Flip the crêpe over and cook for 1 minute. Remove from the skillet and keep warm. Heat 1 tablespoon of the oil in the skillet again and repeat to use up all the batter.

4 Spoon a quarter of the cherry filling on to a quarter of each crêpe and fold the crêpe into a cone shape. Dust with confectioners' sugar and sprinkle the toasted slivered almonds over the top. Serve immediately.

Fruit Crêpes

Serve these crêpes with a spoonful of whipped cream to make the perfect finale to a summer barbecue or dinner party.

15–20 mins plus
30 mins chilling

15 mins

SERVES 4

INGREDIENTS

generous 1 cup all-purpose flour

pinch of salt

2 eggs

1¼ cups milk

2–3 tbsp vegetable oil

FILLING

1 banana

1 tbsp lemon juice

2 nectarines, pitted and cut into
   small pieces

1 mango, peeled, pitted and cut into
   small pieces

3 kiwi fruit, peeled and cut into
   small pieces

2 tbsp maple syrup

confectioners' sugar, to decorate

whipped cream, to serve

1 To make the crêpes, sift the flour and salt into a bowl. Whisk in the eggs and milk. Cover with plastic wrap and chill for 30 minutes.

2 To make the filling, peel and slice the banana and put into a large bowl. Pour over the lemon juice and stir gently until coated. Add the nectarines, mango, kiwi fruit and maple syrup and stir together gently until mixed.

3 Heat a little oil in a skillet until hot. Remove the batter from the refrigerator and add a large spoonful to the skillet. Cook over high heat until golden, then turn it over and cook briefly on the other side. Remove from the pan and keep warm. Cook the other crêpes in the same way, stacking them as more are cooked. Keep warm. Divide the fruit filling among the crêpes and fold into triangles or roll into horns. Dust with confectioners' sugar and serve with whipped cream.

Exotic Fruit Crêpes

These crêpes are filled with an exotic array of tropical fruits. Decorate lavishly with tropical flowers or mint sprigs.

10 mins plus
30 mins chilling

35 mins

SERVES 4

INGREDIENTS

BATTER

generous 1 cup all-purpose flour

pinch of salt

1 egg

1 egg yolk

1¼ cups coconut milk

4 tsp vegetable oil, plus extra for frying

FILLING

1 banana

1 papaya

juice of 1 lime

2 passion fruit

1 mango, peeled, pitted, and sliced

4 lychees, pitted and halved

1–2 tbsp honey

flowers or fresh mint sprigs, to decorate

1 Sift the flour and salt into a bowl. Make a well in the center and add the egg, egg yolk, and a little of the coconut milk. Gradually draw the flour into the egg mixture, beating well and gradually adding the remaining coconut milk to form a smooth batter. Stir in the oil. Cover and chill for 30 minutes.

2 Peel and slice the banana and place in a bowl. Peel and slice the papaya, discarding the seeds. Add to the banana with the lime juice and mix well. Cut the passion fruit in half and scoop out the flesh and seeds into the fruit bowl. Stir in the mango, lychees, and honey.

3 Heat a little oil in a 6-inch/15-cm skillet. Pour in just enough of the crêpe batter to cover the bottom of the skillet and tilt so that it spreads thinly and evenly. Cook until the crêpe is just set and the underside is lightly browned, turn, and briefly cook the other side. Remove from the skillet and keep warm. Repeat with the remaining batter to make a total of 8 crêpes.

4 To serve, place a little of the prepared fruit filling along the center of each crêpe and then roll it into a cone shape. Lay on warmed serving plates, decorate with flowers or mint sprigs, and serve.

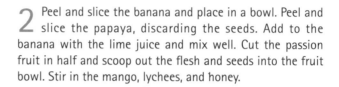

Lemon & Ricotta Crêpes

These thick soft crêpes can be served for breakfast, tea, or even as a delicious dessert. Perfect served with a little cherry or blueberry jelly.

10 mins

20–30 mins

MAKES 15

INGREDIENTS

generous 1 cup ricotta cheese

5 tbsp golden superfine sugar

3 large eggs, separated

finely grated rind of 1 lemon

2 tbsp melted butter

½ cup all-purpose flour

warmed cherry or blueberry jelly, to serve

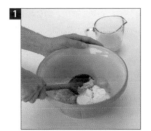

1 Put the ricotta cheese, sugar, and egg yolks in a large bowl and mix together. Stir in the lemon rind and melted butter. Sift in the flour and fold in. Put the egg whites in another bowl and whisk until soft peaks form. Gently fold the egg whites into the ricotta mixture.

2 Heat a large nonstick skillet over medium heat. Add heaping tablespoonfuls of batter, allowing room for them to spread. Cook for 1-2 minutes, until the underside is colored, then turn over and cook on the other side for an additional 2 minutes.

3 Keep warm, wrapped in a clean dish towel until all the crêpes are cooked. Serve with the warmed jelly.

Sicilian Crêpes

These rich crêpes resemble a sweet cannelloni stuffed with sweetened ricotta and are served with a chocolate sauce.

30 mins plus
10 mins resting

30 mins

SERVES 4

INGREDIENTS

1 cup all-purpose flour

1 tsp baking powder

1 cup milk

2 eggs, beaten

4 tbsp sweet butter, melted

finely grated rind 1 lemon

finely grated rind 1 orange

CHOCOLATE SAUCE

5 oz/140 g semisweet chocolate, chopped

½ cup heavy cream

1 tbsp amaretto (optional)

FILLING

9 oz/250 g ricotta cheese

1 tsp vanilla extract

1 cup shelled pistachios, chopped

1 cup blanched almonds, chopped

5 oz/140 g semisweet chocolate, chopped

1 tbsp orange flower water or orange juice

½ cup confectioners' sugar, sifted

⅓ cup golden raisins

⅓ cup candied peel, chopped

1 First, make the filling. Beat the ricotta cheese with the vanilla extract and stir in the other ingredients. Chill the mixture in the refrigerator.

2 To make the sauce, melt the chocolate in a heatproof bowl set over a pan of gently simmering water, cool slightly and stir in the cream and amaretto (if using). Set aside.

3 To make the crêpe batter, sift the flour with the baking powder and whisk in the milk, eggs, and butter, stir in the lemon and orange rinds and whisk. Let rest for 10 minutes.

4 Heat an 8-inch/20-cm nonstick skillet and add a spoonful of batter. Cook for 1–2 minutes, then flip over and cook for an additional minute or so. Repeat until all the batter is used, keeping the prepared crêpes warm in a slow oven until they are all cooked.

5 To assemble, put a spoonful of the ricotta mixture along one side of each crêpe and roll up. Put 3 crêpes on each plate and drizzle with the chocolate sauce to serve immediately.

Walnut Crêpes & Chocolate

These fluffy crêpes are easy to make and could be served with sliced bananas and cream instead of the chocolate cognac sauce.

🐾 🐾

🍲 20 mins   🕐 20 mins

SERVES 4

INGREDIENTS

11½ oz/325 g ricotta cheese

¾ cup milk

4 eggs, separated

1 cup all-purpose flour

1 tsp baking powder

pinch of salt

½ cup chopped walnuts

4 tbsp butter

CHOCOLATE COGNAC SAUCE

⅔ cup heavy cream

5 oz/140 g milk chocolate, chopped

1 tbsp cognac (optional)

1 To make the chocolate cognac sauce, heat the cream until almost boiling, then pour over the chocolate and stir until melted and smooth. Stir in the cognac (if using) and set aside.

2 To make the crêpes, put the ricotta cheese, milk, and egg yolks in a mixing bowl and stir well. Sift in the flour, baking powder, salt, and walnuts and mix well.

3 Whisk the egg whites until stiff, then fold into the ricotta mixture.

4 Heat a nonstick skillet and wipe with a little of the butter, pour a ladleful of batter into the skillet and cook for 2–3 minutes until bubbles appear. Then flip over and cook for an additional 2–3 minutes. Repeat, using a little more butter each time, until you have 8 crêpes.

5 Serve with the chocolate cognac sauce poured over.

Polenta Crêpes with Compôte

Cornmeal gives these crêpes a delicious nutty flavor and the chocolate chips melt into little pools of hot sauce. Serve with sour cream.

  30 mins plus
30 mins standing ⏲ 20 mins

MAKES 12–15

INGREDIENTS

2 oz/55 g all-purpose flour

2 oz/55 g quick-cook polenta

1 tsp baking powder

¼ cup superfine sugar

1 egg, plus 1 egg yolk

1¼ cups milk

1 tsp vanilla extract

1 tbsp melted butter

sunflower oil, for greasing

2 oz/55 g semisweet chocolate chips

BERRY COMPOTE

4½ cups mixed berries, such as
  strawberries, raspberries, black currants,
  red currants

4 oz/115 g confectioners' sugar

½ cup sour cream, to serve

1 First, prepare the crêpe batter. Sift the flours and baking powder together in a large bowl and make a well in the center. Mix the sugar, egg, egg yolk, half the milk, and the vanilla extract together and add to the well in the flour. Whisk the ingredients, gradually drawing in the flour, then beat well to form a smooth thick batter. Add the remaining milk and set aside for at least 30 minutes.

2 Meanwhile, make the berry compôte. Put the fruit into a heavy-based pan with the sugar and heat over very gentle heat until the sugar has melted and the berries have popped, releasing their juice. Remove from the heat and keep warm.

3 Stir the melted butter into the crêpe batter. Heat a very small amount of oil in a heavy-based skillet, then use paper towels to wipe out any excess. When the skillet is smoking hot, reduce the heat to medium, then use a ladle to pour batter into the skillet to make 2 crêpes. Do not tip the pan, as these crêpes are meant to be quite small and thick. Sprinkle a few chocolate chips on the surface. Cook until bubbles appear in the crêpes, then quickly flip each crêpe over, then remove. Repeat the process with the remaining batter and chocolate chips, interleaving the cooked crêpes with waxed paper and keeping them warm in a moderate oven or between 2 plates set over a pan of simmering water.

4 Serve 2 or 3 crêpes per person, arranged overlapping on individual plates, with the warm berries spooned over them, and a generous helping of sour cream.

Chocolate Chip Crêpes

For an impressive dessert, serve these rich crêpes stacked one on top of the other with the toffee sauce poured over.

🥄🥄

🧈 20 mins   🕐 20 mins

SERVES 4

INGREDIENTS

11½ oz/325 g ricotta cheese

¾ cup milk

4 eggs, separated

1 cup all-purpose flour

1 tsp baking powder

pinch of salt

2 oz/55 g milk chocolate, grated

2 tbsp butter

TOFFEE ORANGE SAUCE

4 tbsp sweet butter

3 oz/85 g brown sugar

⅔ cup heavy cream

2–3 tbsp orange juice or Cointreau

1 To make the toffee orange sauce, melt the butter with the brown sugar in a pan over low heat until the sugar has melted, stir in the cream, and bring to a boil. Simmer for 3–4 minutes. Remove from the heat and stir in the orange juice or Cointreau. Set aside.

2 To make the crêpes, put the ricotta cheese, milk, and egg yolks in a mixing bowl and stir well. Sift in the flour, baking powder, and salt, add the chocolate and mix well.

3 Whisk the egg whites until stiff, then fold into the ricotta mixture.

4 Heat a nonstick skillet and wipe with a little of the butter. Spoon in 2 tablespoons of the batter and cook for 2–3 minutes until bubbles appear, then flip the crêpe over and cook for an additional 2–3 minutes. Repeat with a little more butter each time until you have 8 crêpes. Serve with the sauce poured over.

Crêpe Pieces

This is a cheap and cheerful, easy-to-make, and filling dessert that is perfect for midweek family suppers.

10 mins

15 mins

SERVES 4

INGREDIENTS

2 tbsp superfine sugar

1 tsp ground cinnamon

generous 1 cup all-purpose flour

pinch of salt

2 eggs, beaten lightly

½ cup milk

14 oz/400 g canned apricot halves in syrup

sunflower oil, for frying

1 Combine the sugar and cinnamon in a small bowl and set aside. Sift the flour and salt into a bowl. Whisk in the eggs and milk and continue whisking until smooth. Drain the apricots and stir the syrup into the batter. Coarsely chop the apricots and set aside.

2 Heat a large crêpe pan or heavy-based skillet and brush with oil. Pour in all the batter and cook over medium heat for 4–5 minutes, until the underside is golden brown. Turn over using a palette knife or spatula and cook the second side for 4 minutes, until golden. Tear the crêpe into bite-size pieces with 2 spoons or forks.

3 Add the apricots to the skillet and heat through briefly. Divide the crêpe pieces and apricots among individual plates, sprinkle with the sugar mixture, and serve immediately.

VARIATION

These crêpe pieces are also delicious mixed with 14 oz/400 g canned sour cherries in syrup instead of apricots.

Fruity Crêpe Bundles

This unusual crêpe is filled with a sweet cream flavored with ginger, nuts, and apricots and served with a raspberry and orange sauce.

25 mins   35 mins

SERVES 2

INGREDIENTS

BATTER

½ cup all-purpose flour

pinch of salt

¼ tsp ground cinnamon

1 egg

generous ½ cup milk

shortening, for cooking

FILLING

1½ tsp all-purpose flour, sifted

1½ tsp cornstarch

1 tbsp superfine sugar

1 egg

⅔ cup milk

4 tbsp chopped nuts

scant ¼ cup no-soak dried
    apricots, chopped

1 piece preserved or candied ginger,
    chopped finely

SAUCE

3 tbsp raspberry jelly

4½ tsp orange juice

finely grated rind of ¼ orange

1 Preheat the oven to 350°F/180°C. To make the batter, sift the flour, salt, and cinnamon into a bowl and make a well in the center. Add the egg and milk and gradually beat in until smooth.

2 Melt a little shortening in a medium skillet. Pour in half the batter. Cook for 2 minutes until golden, then turn and cook the other side for 1 minute until browned. Set aside and make a second crêpe.

3 For the filling, beat the flour with the cornstarch, sugar, and egg. Gently heat the milk in a pan, then beat 2 tablespoons of it into the flour mixture. Transfer to the pan and cook gently, stirring constantly until thick. Remove from the heat, cover with parchment paper to prevent a skin forming, and set aside to cool.

4 Beat the nuts, apricots, and ginger into the cooled mixture and put a heaping tablespoonful in the center of each crêpe. Gather and squeeze the edges together to make a bundle. Place in an ovenproof dish and bake in the preheated oven for 15–20 minutes, until hot and golden, but not too brown.

5 To make the sauce, melt the jelly gently with the orange juice, then strain. Return to a clean pan with the orange rind and heat through. Serve with the crêpes.

Christmas Rice Crêpes

These delicious crêpes are almost like little rice puddings scented with Christmas mincemeat. They make an elegant festive dessert.

40 mins | 15 mins

MAKES ABOUT 24 CREPES

INGREDIENTS

scant 3 cups milk

salt

½ cup long-grain white rice

1 cinnamon stick

¼ cup sugar

⅓ cup all-purpose flour

1 tsp baking powder

¾ tsp baking soda

2 eggs, beaten

½ cup sour cream

2 tbsp dark rum

1 tsp vanilla extract

½ tsp almond extract

2 tbsp butter, melted

12 oz/350 g mincemeat

melted butter, for frying

confectioners' sugar, for dusting

cherries, for decoration

1 To make the crêpes, bring the milk to a boil in a pan. Add a pinch of salt and sprinkle in the rice. Add the cinnamon stick and simmer gently for about 35 minutes, until the rice is tender and the milk almost absorbed.

2 Remove from the heat, add the sugar, and stir until dissolved. Discard the cinnamon stick and pour into a large bowl. Cool, stirring occasionally, for about 30 minutes.

3 Combine the flour, baking powder, baking soda, and a pinch of salt; set aside. Beat the eggs with the sour cream, rum, vanilla and almond extracts, and the melted butter. Whisk the egg mixture into the rice, then stir in the flour mixture until just blended; do not over-mix. Fold in the mincemeat.

4 Heat a large skillet or griddle pan, and brush with butter. Stir the batter and drop 2–3 tablespoons into the skillet. Cook for about 2 minutes, until the undersides are golden and the tops covered with bubbles that burst open. Gently turn and cook for an additional minute. Keep warm.

5 Top with cherries. Dust the crêpes with confectioners' sugar and serve. A chilled rum and raisin custard goes well with these crêpes (see Cook's Tip).

COOK'S TIP
Soak 1 cup raisins in boiling water. Bring 1½ cups milk, with the seeds out of a vanilla bean and the bean, to a boil. Remove from the heat and let stand for 10 minutes. Beat 5 eggs with sugar to taste; beat in half the milk then return all to the pan. Cook until thick but do not boil. Add drained raisins and 2–3 tbsp dark rum.

Lace Crêpes with Fruit

These super-light crêpes melt in your mouth. They are filled with a gingered fruit salad of melon, grapes, and lychees.

10 mins   5 mins

SERVES 4

INGREDIENTS

3 egg whites

4 tbsp cornstarch

3 tbsp cold water

1 tsp vegetable oil

FRUIT FILLING

12 oz/350 g fresh lychees

¼ Ogen or Charentais melon

¾ cup seedless green grapes

½-inch/1-cm piece gingerroot

2 pieces preserved ginger in syrup

2 tbsp ginger wine or dry sherry

1 To make the fruit filling, peel the lychees and remove the pits. Place the lychees in a bowl. Scoop out the seeds from the melon and remove the skin. Cut the melon flesh into small pieces and place in the bowl.

2 Wash and dry the grapes, remove the stalks, and add to the bowl. Peel the gingerroot and cut into thin shreds or grate finely. Drain the preserved ginger pieces, reserving the syrup, and chop the ginger pieces finely.

3 Stir the gingerroot and preserved ginger into the bowl with the ginger wine or sherry and the preserved ginger syrup. Cover with plastic wrap and set aside.

4 Meanwhile, prepare the crêpes. In a small pitcher, combine the egg whites, cornstarch, and cold water, stirring until very smooth.

5 Brush a small nonstick crêpe pan with oil and heat until hot. Drizzle the surface of the pan with a quarter of the cornstarch mixture to give a lacy effect. Cook for a few seconds until set, then carefully lift out, and transfer to paper towels to drain. Set aside and keep warm.

Repeat with the remaining mixture to make 4 crêpes in total.

6 To serve, place the fruit filling on each of 4 serving plates and top with the crêpes. Serve immediately.

Thai Crêpes & Tropical Fruits

Coconut milk, papayas, and passion fruit give these delicate little crêpes an exotic flavor.

15 mins 20 mins

SERVES 4

INGREDIENTS

2 eggs

½ cup coconut milk

¾ cup milk

1 cup all-purpose flour

½ tsp salt

1 tbsp superfine sugar

1 tbsp butter, melted

oil, for frying

sifted confectioners' sugar, for dusting

FILLING

2 papayas

3 passion fruit

juice of 1 lime

2 tbsp confectioners' sugar

1 In a bowl, whisk the eggs, coconut milk, and milk together. Sift the flour and salt into a large bowl. Stir in the sugar. Make a well in the the flour and gradually beat in the egg mixture to form a smooth batter. Stir in the melted butter.

2 Heat an 8-9-inch/20-23-cm nonstick skillet and brush with oil. Pour in enough batter to coat the bottom of the skillet. Tip the skillet as you pour it in, so the bottom is evenly coated. Cook until browned on the underside and set on top, then turn the crêpe over and cook the other side. Place on a plate, then cover with foil and keep warm while you make the remaining crêpes.

3 Peel the papayas and halve, then scoop out the seeds, reserving a few. Cut into chunks and place in a bowl. Cut the passion fruit in half. Scoop the seeds and pulp into the bowl. Stir in the lime juice and confectioners' sugar. Put a little filling on one-fourth of each crêpe. Fold in half and then into fourths. Dust with sifted confectioners' sugar. Scatter over the reserved papaya seeds and serve.

Coconut Crêpes

These pretty, lacy-thin crêpes, which are often colored a delicate pale-pink or tinted green, are sold by Thai street vendors.

10 mins   20 mins

SERVES 4

INGREDIENTS

⅔ cup rice flour

3 tbsp superfine sugar

pinch of salt

2 eggs

2½ cups coconut milk

4 tbsp shredded coconut

vegetable oil, for frying

2 tbsp jaggery, to decorate

fresh mango or banana, to serve

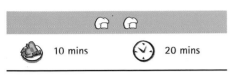

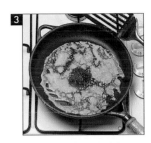

1 Place the rice flour, sugar, and salt in a bowl and add the eggs and coconut milk, whisking until a smooth batter forms. Alternatively, place all the ingredients in a blender and process to a smooth batter. Beat in half the coconut.

2 Heat a small amount of oil in a wide, heavy-based skillet. Pour in a little batter, swirling the skillet to cover the surface thinly and evenly. Cook until pale golden underneath.

3 Turn or toss the crêpe and cook the other side until light golden brown.

4 Turn out the crêpe and keep hot while using the remaining batter to make a total of 8 crêpes.

5 Serve the crêpes folded or loosely rolled, with slices of mango or banana and sprinkled with jaggery and the remaining coconut, toasted.

COOK'S TIP
Rice flour gives the crêpes a light, smooth texture, but if it's not available, use ordinary all-purpose flour instead.

Chocolate Rum & Raisin Crêpes

These sophisticated crêpes are filled with rum-soaked fruits and smothered in a rich chocolate sauce.

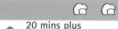

20 mins plus
30 mins macerating
plus 10 mins resting

30 mins

SERVES 4

INGREDIENTS

1 tsp confectioners' sugar

5 tbsp raisins or golden raisins

2 tbsp dark rum

1 cup all-purpose flour

1 tsp baking powder

1 cup milk

2 eggs, beaten

4 tbsp sweet butter, melted

CHOCOLATE SAUCE

⅔ cup heavy cream

5 oz/140 g semisweet chocolate, chopped

1 Put the sugar, raisins or golden raisins, and dark rum in a bowl and mix well. Let soak for at least 30 minutes.

2 To make the sauce, heat the cream until almost boiling then pour over the chocolate. Whisk until the chocolate is melted and smooth. Set aside.

3 To make the crêpes, sift the flour and baking powder together in a large bowl. Whisk the milk, eggs, and butter together and pour into the flour. Whisk until smooth. Let the mixture rest for 10 minutes.

4 Heat an 8-inch/20-cm nonstick skillet and add a spoonful of the batter, swirl to cover the bottom of the pan. Cook the crêpe for 1–2 minutes until brown then flip over and cook for an additional minute or so. Remove the crêpe and keep warm. Repeat until you have used up all the batter.

5 Sprinkle each crêpe with a teaspoonful of raisins, then fold in 4 or roll it up. Put any spare raisins in the chocolate sauce and drizzle over the crêpes to serve.

Crêpes with Honeycomb Butter

These light crêpes are delicious with the rich chocolate butter but are equally good served with maple syrup and blueberries.

20 mins plus 10 mins standing

20 mins

SERVES 4

INGREDIENTS

½ cup buttermilk or plain yogurt

½ cup milk

2 eggs, separated

2 tbsp superfine sugar

2 tbsp sweet butter, melted

1½ cups all-purpose flour

1 tsp baking powder

CHOCOLATE HONEYCOMB BUTTER

2 oz/55 g chocolate-covered honeycomb

4 tbsp sweet butter, softened

1 To make the chocolate honeycomb butter, crush the honeycomb in a polythene bag until it resembles rough bread crumbs and mix thoroughly with the butter. Chill until ready to serve.

2 To make the crêpes, whisk the buttermilk, milk, egg yolks, sugar, and melted butter together in a large bowl. Sift the flour and baking powder together and whisk into the buttermilk mixture until smooth. Let the mixture stand for 10 minutes.

3 Whisk the egg whites until soft peaks form then fold into the batter.

4 Heat a nonstick skillet over a medium heat and add 1 tablespoon of batter. Cook the crêpe for 2–3 minutes until small bubbles appear on the surface then flip over and cook for an additional 2–3 minutes. Repeat until you have 8 crêpes.

5 Serve the crêpes hot with the cold butter melting on to them.

COOK'S TIP

If you cannot find chocolate-covered honeycomb, use chopped chocolate instead.

Pecan and Chocolate Crêpes

American-style crêpes studded with nuts and chocolate are popular at any time of the day.

10 mins   40 mins

SERVES 12

INGREDIENTS

generous 1½ cups self-rising flour

1 tsp baking powder

pinch of salt

1 egg

1¼ cups milk

1 tbsp butter, melted

½ tsp vanilla extract

2 tbsp golden superfine sugar

⅓ cup semisweet chocolate chips

¼ cup shelled pecans, chopped

corn oil, for frying

butter, to serve (optional)

1 Sift the flour, baking powder, and salt into a large bowl and make a well in the center. Place the egg and milk in a small bowl and mix, pour into the well in the dry ingredients and whisk to make a thick, smooth batter.

2 Beat in the melted butter and vanilla extract, then stir in the superfine sugar, chocolate chips, and chopped pecans. Heat a teaspoon of corn oil in a large skillet or flat grill pan. Drop large tablespoonfuls of the batter into the hot pan to make crêpes 3-inches/7.5-cm across. Cook over medium heat for 3 minutes, or until small bubbles appear on the surface of each crêpe.

3 Turn with a spatula and cook for an additional 2–3 minutes, or until golden. Keep the crêpes warm by wrapping in foil or paper towels while cooking the remainder of the batter. Serve with butter.

Sweet Potato Bread

This is a great-tasting loaf, colored light orange by the sweet potato. Added sweetness from the honey is offset by the tangy orange rind.

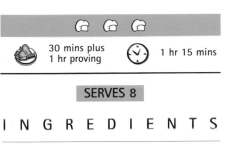

30 mins plus
1 hr proving

1 hr 15 mins

SERVES 8

INGREDIENTS

3¼ oz/90 g butter, plus extra for greasing

8 oz/225 g sweet potatoes, diced

⅔ cup tepid water

2 tbsp honey

2 tbsp vegetable oil

3 tbsp orange juice

scant ½ cup semolina

2 cups white bread flour

2½ tsp active dry yeast

1 tsp ground cinnamon

grated rind of 1 orange

1 Lightly grease a 1 lb 8-oz/675-g loaf pan. Cook the sweet potatoes in a pan of boiling water for about 10 minutes, or until soft. Drain thoroughly and mash until smooth.

2 Meanwhile, mix the water, honey, oil, and orange juice together in a large mixing bowl.

3 Add the mashed sweet potatoes, semolina, three-quarters of the flour, the yeast, ground cinnamon, and grated orange rind and mix thoroughly to form a dough. Set aside for about 10 minutes.

4 Dice the butter and knead it into the dough with the remaining flour. Knead for about 5 minutes until smooth.

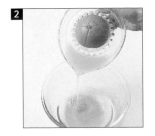

5 Place the dough in the prepared loaf pan. Cover and set aside in a warm place for 1 hour or until doubled in size.

6 Preheat the oven to 375°F/190°C. Cook the loaf for 45–60 minutes, or until the bottom sounds hollow when tapped. Serve warm, cut into slices.

Spicy Carrot-Rice Loaf

Rice flour gives this delicious loaf a tender crumb while the cooked rice adds a chewy texture. Use any kind of cooked rice.

1 hr 30 mins   1–1 hr 15 mins

SERVES 8–10

INGREDIENTS

4 oz/115 g butter, melted and cooled, plus extra for greasing

2 cups all-purpose flour, plus extra for dusting

⅓ cup rice flour

2 tsp baking powder

½ tsp baking soda

½ tsp salt

1 tsp ground cinnamon

½ tsp grated nutmeg

½ tsp ground ginger

⅓ cup cooked risotto or long-grain white rice

½ cup chopped pecans

⅔ cup golden raisins or raisins

3 eggs

1 cup sugar

½ cup brown sugar

2 carrots, grated

confectioners' sugar, for dusting

1 Preheat the oven to 350°F/180°C. Lightly grease a 9 x 5-inch/23 x 12.5-cm loaf pan. Line with nonstick parchment paper and grease with a little butter. Dust lightly with flour.

2 Sift the flour, rice flour, baking powder, baking soda, salt, and spices into a bowl. Add the rice, nuts, and golden raisins or raisins and toss well to coat. Make a well in the center of the dry ingredients and set aside.

3 Using an electric whisk, beat the eggs for about 2 minutes until light and foaming. Add the sugars and continue beating for an additional 2 minutes. Beat in the melted butter, then stir in the grated carrots until blended.

4 Pour the egg and carrot mixture into the well and, using a fork, stir until a soft batter forms. Do not over-mix; the batter should be slightly lumpy.

5 Pour into the prepared pan and smooth the top. Bake in the preheated oven for about 1–1¼ hours until risen and golden. Cover the loaf with foil if it colors too quickly.

6 Cool the loaf in the pan on a wire rack for about 10 minutes. Carefully turn out and let cool completely. Dust with a little confectioners' sugar and cut into thin slices to serve.

Apricot & Walnut Bread

Serve this fruit bread freshly made, sliced and buttered with a cup of tea in the afternoon, or try it for breakfast.

  25 mins plus 1 hr 30 mins proving 🕐 30 mins

SERVES 12

INGREDIENTS

4 tbsp butter, plus extra for greasing

all-purpose flour, for dusting

3 cups white bread flour

½ tsp salt

1 tsp golden superfine sugar

2 tsp active dry yeast

¾ cup no-soak dried apricots, chopped

½ cup walnuts, chopped

⅔ cup tepid milk

¼ cup tepid water

1 egg, beaten

TOPPING

generous ½ cup confectioners' sugar

walnut halves

1 Grease and flour a cookie sheet. Sift the flour and salt into a warm bowl and stir in the sugar and yeast. Rub in the butter and add the apricots and walnuts. Make a well in the center. In another bowl, mix together the milk, water, and egg. Pour into the dry ingredients and mix to a soft dough. Turn on to a floured work counter and knead for 10 minutes until smooth. Put in an oiled bowl, cover with oiled plastic wrap, and leave in a warm place until doubled in size.

2 Turn the dough on to a floured work counter and knead lightly for 1 minute. Divide into 5 equal pieces and roll each piece into a rope 12 inches/ 30 cm long. Plait 3 ropes together, pinching the ends to seal, and place on the prepared cookie sheet. Twist the remaining two ropes together and place on top. Cover lightly with oiled plastic wrap and leave in a warm place until doubled in size.

3 Preheat the oven to 425°F/220°C. Bake the bread in the oven for 10 minutes then reduce the heat to 375°F/190°C and bake for an additional 20 minutes. Transfer to a wire rack to cool. To make the topping, sift the confectioners' sugar into a bowl and stir in enough water to make a thin frosting. Drizzle the frosting over the loaf and decorate the top with walnut halves.

VARIATION
As an alternative to apricots, use candied cherries, dried cranberries, or dates.

Barm Brack

This Irish bread was traditionally baked with a wedding ring in the batter in the belief that whoever received it would be married within the year.

25 mins plus 2 hrs proving

55 mins

MAKES 9-INCH/23-CM LOAF

INGREDIENTS

5⅔ cups white bread flour, plus extra for dusting

1 tsp allspice

1 tsp salt

2 tsp active dry yeast

generous ¼ cup golden superfine sugar

1¼ cups tepid milk

⅔ cup tepid water

4 tbsp butter, softened

2 cups dry fruits

milk, for glazing

1 Sift the flour, allspice, and salt into a warmed bowl. Stir in the yeast and 1 tablespoon of the superfine sugar. Make a well in the center and pour in the milk and water. Mix well to make a sticky dough. Place on a lightly floured work counter and knead the dough until no longer sticky. Put into the clean oiled bowl, cover with plastic wrap, and leave in a warm place for 1 hour until doubled in size.

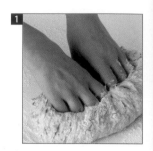

2 Turn the dough out on to a floured work counter and knead lightly for 1 minute. Add the butter and mixed fruits to the dough and work them in until completely incorporated. Return the dough to the bowl, replace the plastic wrap, and let prove for 30 minutes. Grease a 9-inch/23-cm round cake pan. Pat the dough to a neat round and fit in the pan. Cover and leave in a warm place until it has risen to the top of the pan. Preheat the oven to 400°F/200°C.

3 Brush the top of the loaf lightly with milk and bake in the oven for 15 minutes. Cover the loaf with foil, reduce the oven temperature to 350°F/180°C and bake for 45 minutes, until the bread is golden and sounds hollow when tapped underneath. Leave on a wire rack to cool.

COOK'S TIP

Letting the bread prove 3 times gives it its particular open texture, but if time is short, you can omit the second proving.

Chocolate & Nut Soda Bread

This is a delicious sweet version of traditional Irish soda bread which is every bit as good as the original.

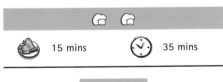

15 mins   35 mins

SERVES 6

INGREDIENTS

4 cups all-purpose flour, plus extra
for dusting

3 tsp superfine sugar

1 tsp salt

1 tsp baking soda

5 oz/140 g milk chocolate, chopped

1¼ cups mixed nuts, chopped

1 egg, beaten

1¼ cups buttermilk

1 Sift the flour into a large bowl and mix in the sugar, salt, baking soda, chocolate, and nuts.

2 Make a well in the center and pour in the beaten egg and buttermilk. Gradually incorporate the flour, a little at a time, until you have a soft dough.

3 Turn on to a floured board and gently knead for a minute or two. Add a little more flour if the dough is too wet.

4 Preheat the oven to 425°F/220°C.

5 Shape the dough into a circle and score the top with a cross. Place the loaf on a lightly floured cookie sheet and bake for 15 minutes, then reduce the oven temperature to 400°F/200°C for an additional 20 minutes.

6 Cool the loaf on a wire rack.

COOK'S TIP
A mixture of walnuts, pecans, and hazelnuts works well but you could also use Brazil nuts, almonds, and macadamia nuts.

Date & Honey Loaf

This bread is full of good things—chopped dates, sesame seeds, and honey. Toast thick slices and spread with cream cheese for a light snack.

40 mins plus
2 hrs proving

30 mins

1 LOAF

INGREDIENTS

butter, for greasing

1¾ cups white bread flour, plus extra for dusting

½ cup brown bread flour

½ tsp salt

¼ oz/7 g active dry yeast

generous ¾ cup tepid water

3 tbsp sunflower oil

3 tbsp honey

½ cup chopped pitted dates

2 tbsp sesame seeds

1 Grease a 2-lb/900-g loaf pan with a little butter.

2 Sift both types of flour into a large mixing bowl, and stir in the salt and dry yeast. Pour in the tepid water, sunflower oil, and honey. Mix together to form a dough.

3 Place the dough on a lightly floured work counter and knead for about 5 minutes until smooth.

4 Place the dough in a greased bowl, cover, and let prove in a warm place for about 1 hour or until doubled in size.

5 Knead in the dates and sesame seeds. Shape the dough and place in the pan.

6 Cover and stand the loaf in a warm place for an additional 30 minutes, or until springy to the touch.

7 Preheat the oven to 425°F/220°C. Bake the loaf for 30 minutes, or until a hollow sound is heard when the bottom of the loaf is tapped.

8 Transfer the loaf to a wire rack and let cool completely. Serve cut into thick slices with butter or cream cheese.

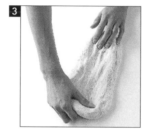

COOK'S TIP

If you cannot find a warm place, sit a bowl with the dough in it over a pan of warm water and cover.

Banana & Cranberry Loaf

The addition of chopped nuts, candied peel, fresh orange juice, and dried cranberries makes this a rich, moist teabread.

45 mins   1 hr

SERVES 8

INGREDIENTS

butter, for greasing

1½ cups self-rising flour

½ tsp baking powder

⅔ cup brown sugar

2 bananas, mashed

⅓ cup candied peel

¼ cup chopped mixed nuts

½ cup dried cranberries

5–6 tbsp orange juice

2 eggs, beaten

⅔ cup sunflower oil

¾ cup confectioners' sugar, sifted

grated rind of 1 orange

1 Preheat the oven to 350°F/180°C. Grease a 2-lb/900-g loaf pan and line the bottom with parchment paper.

2 Sift the flour and baking powder into a mixing bowl. Stir in the brown sugar, bananas, candied peel, nuts, and dried cranberries.

3 Stir the orange juice, eggs, and sunflower oil together until well combined. Add the mixture to the dry ingredients and mix until thoroughly blended. Spoon the mixture into the prepared loaf pan and smooth the top.

4 Bake in the preheated oven for about 1 hour, until firm to the touch or until a skewer inserted into the center of the loaf comes out clean.

5 Turn out the loaf and set aside to cool on a wire rack.

6 Mix the confectioners' sugar with a little water and drizzle the frosting over the loaf. Sprinkle the orange rind over the top. Let the frosting set before slicing.

COOK'S TIP
This teabread will keep for a couple of days. Wrap it carefully and store in a cool, dry place.

Banana & Date Loaf

This fruity bread is excellent for afternoon tea or morning coffee with its moist texture and sweet flavor.

15 mins   1 hr

SERVES 6

INGREDIENTS

2¾ oz/75 g butter, cut into small pieces, plus extra for greasing

generous 1½ cups self-rising flour

⅓ cup superfine sugar

⅔ cup chopped pitted dates

2 bananas, mashed coarsely

2 eggs, beaten lightly

2 tbsp honey

1 Preheat the oven to 325°F/160°C. Grease a 2-lb/900-g loaf pan with a little butter and line the bottom with parchment paper.

2 Sift the flour into a mixing bowl. Rub the butter into the flour with your fingertips until the mixture resembles fine bread crumbs.

3 Add the sugar, chopped dates, bananas, beaten eggs, and honey to the dry ingredients. Mix together to form a soft dropping consistency.

COOK'S TIP

This teabread will keep for several days if stored in an airtight container and kept in a cool, dry place.

4 Spoon the mixture into the prepared loaf pan, spreading it out evenly, and gently smooth the surface with the back of a knife.

5 Bake the loaf in the preheated oven for about 1 hour, or until golden brown on top and a skewer inserted into the center of the loaf comes out clean.

6 Let the loaf cool in the pan before turning out and transferring to a wire rack to cool completely.

7 Serve the loaf warm or cold, cut into thick slices.

Date & Walnut Teabread

This teabread has sticky layers of date purée running through it. It keeps well, stored in an airtight container.

🍰 20 mins

🕐 1 hr 5 mins– 1 hr 35 mins

SERVES 10-12

INGREDIENTS

6 oz/175 g butter, plus extra for greasing

1½ cups pitted dates, chopped into small pieces

grated rind and juice of 1 orange

¼ cup water

generous 1 cup light muscovado sugar

3 eggs, beaten

⅔ cup whole-wheat self-rising flour

⅔ cup self-rising flour

½ cup chopped walnuts

8 walnut halves, to decorate

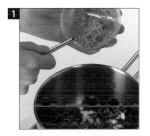

1 Preheat the oven to 325°F/160°C. Grease and line a 2-lb/900-g loaf pan. Put the dates in a pan with the orange rind and juice and the water and cook for 5 minutes until you have a soft purée.

2 Put the butter and sugar in a bowl and beat together until light and fluffy. Gradually beat in the eggs, then sift in the flours and fold in with the walnuts. Spread one-third of the batter over the bottom of the prepared pan and spread half the date purée over.

3 Repeat the layers, ending with the cake batter. Arrange walnut halves down the center of the loaf. Bake in the oven for 1–1½ hours, until well risen and firm to the touch. Leave in the pan for 10 minutes, then turn out and remove the paper and let stand on a wire rack to cool. Serve sliced.

COOK'S TIP
Do not use the dates sold for baking, which are rolled in sugar. They are too sweet.

Glossy Fruit Loaf

This is a rich, sweet fruit loaf, ideal for family celebrations or parties, and tastes superb with a cup of hot tea.

20 mins, plus
8 hrs 20 mins
soaking/cooling

1 hr 30 mins–
1 hr 45 mins

SERVES 10

INGREDIENTS

⅓ cup raisins

½ cup no-soak dried apricots, chopped coarsely

⅓ cup pitted dates, chopped

⅓ cup cold black tea

½ cup butter, plus extra for greasing

generous ½ cup brown sugar

2 eggs, beaten

1¼ cups self-rising flour, sifted

scant ⅓ cup coarsely chopped candied pineapple

scant ½ cup candied cherries, halved

generous ½ cup coarsely chopped Brazil nuts

TOPPING

¼ cup walnut halves

scant ¼ cup Brazil nuts

¼ cup candied cherries, halved

2 tbsp apricot jelly, strained and warmed

1 Place the raisins, apricots, and dates in a bowl, pour over the tea and let soak for 8 hours, or overnight. The following day, preheat the oven to 325°F/160°C. Grease and line a 2-lb/900-g loaf pan. Beat the butter and sugar together until light and fluffy.

2 Gradually beat in the eggs, then fold in the flour alternately with the soaked fruit. Gently stir in the pineapple, cherries, and chopped nuts. Turn the mixture into the prepared pan. To make the topping, arrange the walnuts, Brazil nuts, and cherries on top.

3 Bake in the preheated oven for 1½–1¾ hours, or until a skewer inserted into the center comes out clean. Let cool in the pan for 10 minutes, then turn out and peel off the lining paper. Transfer to a wire rack to cool completely. Warm the apricot jelly and brush over the top of the cake.

COOK'S TIP

Soaking dried fruit in cold black tea makes the fruit plump and juicy, which gives fruitbread extra flavor and moistness.

Welsh Cakes

You do not even have to turn on the oven to make these little scones.
They were traditionally cooked on a flat griddle over a fire.

15 mins   18 mins

MAKES ABOUT 16

INGREDIENTS

2 cups self-rising flour

pinch of salt

4 tbsp shortening

4 tbsp butter

scant ½ cup golden superfine sugar

½ cup currants

1 egg, beaten

1 tbsp milk (optional)

TO FINISH

superfine sugar, for dusting

1 Sift the flour and salt into a bowl. Add the shortening and butter and rub in until the mixture resembles bread crumbs. Stir in the sugar and currants. Add the egg and a little milk, if necessary, to make a soft, but not sticky, dough.

2 On a floured work counter, roll out the dough to ¼-inch/5-mm thickness. Cut into rounds with a 2½-inch/6-cm plain or fluted cutter. Gather the trimmings, re-roll, and cut out more cakes until you have used up the dough.

3 Heat a greased griddle pan or heavy-based skillet. Cook the cakes over low heat, for about 3 minutes on each side, until golden brown. Dust generously with superfine sugar and serve warm or cold.

Sticky Ginger Marmalade Loaf

Ginger marmalade gives a wonderful flavor to this moist sticky teabread, which is very quick to prepare.

10 mins   1 hr

SERVES 10-12

INGREDIENTS

6 oz/175 g butter, softened, plus extra for greasing

½ cup ginger marmalade

generous 1 cup light muscovado sugar

3 eggs, beaten

2 cups self-rising flour

½ tsp baking powder

1 tsp ground ginger

1 cup pecans, chopped coarsely

1 Preheat the oven to 350°F/180°C. Grease and line a 2-lb/900-g loaf pan. Put 1 tablespoon of the ginger marmalade in a small pan and set aside. Put the remaining marmalade in a bowl with the butter, sugar, and eggs.

2 Sift in the flour, baking powder, and ground ginger and beat together until smooth. Stir in three-quarters of the nuts. Spoon the batter into the prepared pan and smooth the top. Sprinkle with the reserved nuts and bake in the oven for 1 hour until well risen and a skewer inserted into the center comes out clean.

3 Leave in the pan for 10 minutes, then turn out and remove the paper. Place on a wire rack to cool. Gently heat the pan of reserved marmalade, then brush over the warm loaf. Serve cut in slices.

COOK'S TIP
If the loaf starts to brown too much before it is cooked, cover lightly with foil.

Banana & Chocolate Chip Loaf

Bananas make this loaf cake beautifully moist, and combining them with chocolate makes this sweet bread a favorite with children.

25 mins plus 30 mins cooling

1 hr 10 mins

SERVES 10

INGREDIENTS

4 oz/115 g butter, softened, plus extra for greasing

1¼ cups all-purpose flour

1 tsp baking soda

pinch of salt

1 tsp ground cinnamon

scant 1 cup golden superfine sugar

2 large ripe bananas, mashed

2 eggs, beaten

5 tbsp boiling water

1 cup semisweet chocolate chips

TO SERVE

whipped cream

ready-made chocolate decorations

1 Preheat the oven to 325°F/160°C. Grease and line the bottom and sides of a 2-lb/900-g loaf pan. Sift the flour, baking soda, salt, and cinnamon into a bowl and set aside. Place the butter and sugar in a bowl and beat together until light and fluffy.

2 Beat in the bananas and then the eggs. The batter may look curdled, but this is perfectly normal. Stir in the flour mixture alternately with the boiling water until just combined, then stir in the chocolate chips.

3 Spoon into the prepared pan and smooth the top. Bake in the preheated oven for 1 hour 10 minutes, or until well risen, golden brown, and firm to the touch. Let cool in the pan for 30 minutes, then turn out and peel off the lining paper. Transfer to a wire rack to cool completely, then serve in slices with a little whipped cream, decorated with chocolate decorations.

Banana & Chocolate Teabread

This is a good loaf to make when you have some over-ripe bananas in the fruit bowl. It will need to be eaten quickly.

10 mins

50–60 mins

SERVES 8

INGREDIENTS

4 oz/115 g butter, softened, plus extra
   for greasing

2 ripe bananas

scant ½ cup golden superfine sugar

2 eggs

1⅔ cups self-rising flour

¼ cup unsweetened cocoa

1 tsp baking powder

2 tbsp milk

½ cup semisweet chocolate chips

1 Preheat the oven to 350°F/180°C. Grease and line a 2-lb/900-g loaf pan. Put the bananas in a large bowl and mash with a fork.

2 Add the butter, sugar, and eggs and sift the flour, unsweetened cocoa, and baking powder. Beat vigorously until smooth, adding sufficient milk to give a thick dropping consistency. Stir in the chocolate chips.

COOK'S TIP
You can mix the ingredients in a food processor, then stir in the chocolate chips by hand.

3 Spoon the batter into the prepared pan and bake in the preheated oven for 50–60 minutes, until well risen and a skewer inserted into the center comes out clean. Leave the teabread in the pan for 5 minutes, then turn out on to a wire rack to cool. Serve sliced, with or without butter.

Mango Twist Bread

This is a sweet bread which has puréed mango mixed into the dough, resulting in a moist loaf with an exotic flavor.

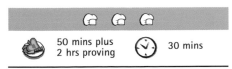

50 mins plus
2 hrs proving

30 mins

1 LOAF

INGREDIENTS

1½ oz/40 g butter, cut into small pieces, plus extra for greasing

3½ cups white bread flour, plus extra for dusting

1 tsp salt

¼ oz/7 g active dry yeast

1 tsp ground ginger

¼ cup brown sugar

1 small mango, peeled, pitted, and blended to a purée

1 cup tepid water

2 tbsp honey

⅔ cup golden raisins

1 egg, beaten lightly

confectioners' sugar, for dusting

1 Grease a cookie sheet with a little butter and set aside.

2 Sift the flour and salt into a large mixing bowl. Stir in the dry yeast, ground ginger, and brown sugar. Rub in the butter with your fingertips until the mixture resembles bread crumbs.

3 Stir in the mango purée, water, and honey and mix to form a dough.

4 Place the dough on a lightly floured work counter and knead for about 5 minutes until smooth. Alternatively, use an electric mixer with a dough hook. Place the dough in a greased bowl, cover, and let prove in a warm place for about 1 hour until it has doubled in size.

5 Knead in the golden raisins and shape the dough into 2 sausage shapes, each 10 inches/25 cm long. Carefully twist the 2 pieces together and pinch the ends to seal. Place the dough on the cookie sheet, cover, and leave in a warm place for an additional 40 minutes.

6 Preheat the oven to 425°F/220°C. Brush the loaf with the egg and bake in the oven for 30 minutes, or until golden brown. Let cool on a wire rack. Dust with confectioners' sugar before serving.

COOK'S TIP
You can tell when the bread is cooked because it will sound hollow when tapped on the bottom.

Citrus Bread

This sweet loaf is flavored with citrus fruits. It is excellent served at breakfast with a glass of freshly squeezed orange juice.

20 mins plus
1 hr 40 mins
proving

30 mins

1 LOAF

INGREDIENTS

4 tbsp butter, cut into small pieces, plus extra for greasing

3½ cups white bread flour, plus extra for dusting

½ tsp salt

¼ cup superfine sugar

¼ oz/7 g active dry yeast

5–6 tbsp orange juice

4 tbsp lemon juice

3–4 tbsp lime juice

⅔ cup tepid water

1 orange

1 lemon

1 lime

2 tbsp honey

1 Lightly grease a cookie sheet with a little butter.

2 Sift the flour and salt into a large mixing bowl. Stir in the sugar and dry yeast.

3 Rub in the butter with your fingertips until the mixture resembles bread crumbs. Add all of the fruit juices and the water and mix to form a dough.

4 Place the dough on a lightly floured work counter and knead for 5 minutes. Alternatively, use an electric mixer with a dough hook. Place the dough in a greased bowl, cover, and let prove in a warm place for 1 hour.

5 Meanwhile, grate the rind of the orange, lemon, and lime. Knead the fruit rinds into the dough.

6 Divide the dough into 2 balls, making one slightly bigger than the other.

7 Place the larger ball on the cookie sheet and set the smaller one on top.

8 Push a floured finger through the center of the dough. Cover and let prove for about 40 minutes, or until springy to the touch.

9 Preheat the oven to 425°F/ 220°C. Bake the loaf for 35 minutes. Remove from the oven and transfer to a wire rack. Glaze with honey and let cool completely.

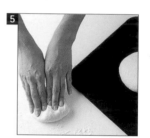

Fruit & Nut Loaf

This fruit bread may be served warm or cold, perhaps spread with a little butter, or topped with apricot jelly.

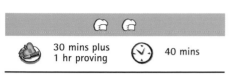
30 mins plus 1 hr proving   40 mins

SERVES 4

INGREDIENTS

2 cups white bread flour, plus extra for dusting

½ tsp salt

1 tbsp margarine, plus extra for greasing

2 tbsp brown sugar

⅔ cup golden raisins

¼ cup no-soak dried apricots, chopped

½ cup chopped hazelnuts

2 tsp active dry yeast

6 tbsp orange juice

6 tbsp lowfat plain yogurt

2 tbsp strained apricot jelly

1 Sift the flour and salt into a bowl. Rub in the margarine and stir in the sugar, raisins, apricots, nuts, and yeast.

2 Warm the orange juice in a pan but do not let it boil.

3 Stir the warm orange juice into the flour mixture with the plain yogurt and then bring the mixture together to form a dough.

4 Knead the dough on a lightly floured work counter for 5 minutes until smooth and elastic. Shape into a circle and place on a lightly greased cookie sheet. Cover with a clean dish towel and set aside to prove in a warm place until doubled in size.

5 Preheat the oven to 425°F/220°C. Bake the loaf for 35–40 minutes, until cooked through. Transfer to a wire rack and brush the top of the warm cake with the apricot jelly. Let the cake cool before serving.

COOK'S TIP
To test whether yeast bread or cake is done, tap the loaf from underneath. If it sounds hollow, the bread or cake is ready.

Stollen

Stollen is a spiced German fruit bread with a marzipan filling which is traditionally served at Christmas.

30 mins plus 3 hrs 40 mins proving

40 mins

SERVES 10

INGREDIENTS

½ cup currants

⅓ cup raisins

scant ¼ cup candied peel

⅓ cup cherries, rinsed, dried, and quartered

2 tbsp dark rum

4 tbsp butter

¾ cup milk

3 tbsp golden superfine sugar

3¼ cups white bread flour, plus extra for dusting

½ tsp salt

½ tsp ground nutmeg

½ tsp ground cinnamon

seeds from 3 cardamoms

2 tsp active dry yeast

finely grated rind of 1 lemon

1 egg, beaten

⅓ cup slivered almonds

oil, for greasing

6 oz/175 g marzipan

melted butter, for brushing

sifted confectioners' sugar, for dusting

COOK'S TIP

An enriched dough such as this takes longer to prove than ordinary bread dough, so do not be tempted to put it somewhere hot to try to speed up the process.

1 Put the currants, raisins, candied peel, and cherries in a bowl. Stir in the rum and set aside. Put the butter, milk, and sugar in a pan and heat gently until the sugar has dissolved and the butter has just melted. Cool until hand-hot. Sift the flour, salt, nutmeg, and cinnamon into a bowl. Crush the cardamom seeds with a pestle and mortar and add them to the flour mixture. Stir in the dry yeast. Make a well in the center and stir in the milk mixture, lemon rind, and beaten egg. Beat to form a soft dough.

2 Turn the dough on to a floured work counter. With floured hands, knead the dough for about 5 minutes. It will be quite sticky, so add more flour if necessary. Knead the soaked fruit and slivered almonds into the dough until just combined. Return the dough to the clean, lightly oiled bowl. Cover with plastic wrap and leave in a warm place for up to 3 hours until doubled in size. Turn the dough on to a floured work counter and knead lightly for 1-2 minutes, then roll out to a 10-inch/25-cm square.

3 Roll the marzipan into a sausage shape slightly shorter than the length of the dough and place down the center. Fold one side over to cover the marzipan. Repeat with the other side, overlapping in the center. Seal the ends. Place the roll, seam-side down, on a greased cookie sheet. Cover with oiled plastic wrap and leave in a warm place until doubled in size. Preheat the oven to 375°F/190°C. Bake the stollen for 40 minutes, or until it is golden and it sounds hollow when tapped underneath. Brush the hot stollen generously with melted butter and dredge heavily with confectioners' sugar. Let cool on a wire rack.

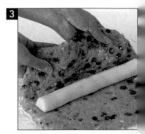

Tropical Fruit Bread

The flavors in this fruit bread will bring a touch of sunshine to your table, whatever the time of year.

15 mins plus
1 hr proving · 30 mins

SERVES 4

INGREDIENTS

2 tbsp butter, cut into small pieces, plus extra for greasing

3 cups white bread flour

½ cup bran

½ tsp salt

½ tsp ground ginger

¼ oz/7 g active dry yeast

2 tbsp brown sugar

generous 1 cup tepid water

⅓ cup candied pineapple, chopped finely

2 tbsp finely chopped dried mango

⅔ cup shredded coconut, toasted, plus extra for sprinkling

1 egg, beaten lightly

1 Grease a cookie sheet. Sift the flour into a large mixing bowl. Stir in the bran, salt, ginger, yeast, and sugar. Rub in the butter with your fingers, then add the water, and mix to form a dough.

2 On a lightly floured work counter, knead the dough for 5–8 minutes until smooth. Alternatively, use an electric mixer with a dough hook. Place the dough in a greased bowl, cover, and let prove in a warm place for 30 minutes until doubled in size.

3 Knead the pineapple, mango, and shredded coconut into the dough. Shape into a circle and place on the cookie sheet. Score the top with the back of a knife. Cover and set aside for an additional 30 minutes in a warm place.

4 Preheat the oven to 425°F/220°C. Brush the loaf with the beaten egg and sprinkle with shredded coconut. Bake in the preheated oven for about 30 minutes, or until golden brown.

5 Set the bread aside to cool on a wire rack before serving.

COOK'S TIP
To test the bread after the second proving, gently prod the dough with your finger—it should spring back if it has proved enough.

Apple & Apricot Tea Loaf

The firm texture of this cake makes it an ideal fruity snack for picnic hampers and children's lunchboxes.

15 mins plus
10 mins cooling

55–60 mins

SERVES 10

I N G R E D I E N T S

½ cup butter, softened, plus extra
for greasing

scant ¾ cup brown sugar

2 eggs, beaten

scant ⅓ cup no-soak dried apricots,
chopped

2 eating apples, peeled and grated coarsely

2 tbsp milk

generous 1½ cups self-rising flour

1 tsp ground allspice

½ tsp ground cinnamon

1 Preheat the oven to 350°F/180°C. Grease and line a 2-lb/900-g loaf pan. Place the butter and sugar in a bowl and beat until light and fluffy. Gradually beat in the eggs.

2 Reserve 1 tablespoon of the apricots, then fold the rest into the creamed mixture with the grated apples and milk. Sift in the flour, allspice, and cinnamon and fold into the mixture.

3 Spoon into the prepared pan and sprinkle over the reserved apricots. Bake in the preheated oven for 55–60 minutes, or until risen and a skewer inserted into the center comes out clean. Let cool in the pan for 10 minutes, then turn out and peel off the lining paper. Transfer to a wire rack to cool completely.

Fruit Loaf with Apple Spread

This sweet, fruity loaf is ideal served with coffee for a healthy snack.
The fruit spread can be made quickly while the cake is in the oven.

1 hr 15 mins   2 hrs

SERVES 10

INGREDIENTS

butter, for greasing

1¾ cups rolled oats

scant ½ cup molasses sugar

1 tsp ground cinnamon

scant 1 cup golden raisins

generous 1 cup raisins

2 tbsp malt extract

1¼ cups unsweetened apple juice

1½ cups self-rising whole-wheat flour

1½ tsp baking powder

FRUIT SPREAD

2 cups strawberries, washed and hulled

2 dessert apples, cored, chopped, and
mixed with 1 tbsp lemon juice to prevent
them browning

1¼ cups unsweetened apple juice

TO SERVE

strawberries

apple wedges

1 Grease and line a 2-lb/900-g loaf pan and set aside. Place the oats, sugar, cinnamon, golden raisins, raisins, and malt extract in a mixing bowl. Pour in the apple juice, stir well, and set aside to soak for 30 minutes.

2 Preheat the oven to 350°F/180°C. Sift in the flour and baking powder, adding any husks that remain in the strainer, and fold in using a metal spoon. Spoon the mixture into the prepared pan and bake in the preheated oven for 1½ hours until firm or until a skewer inserted into the center of the loaf comes out clean.

3 Remove the pan from the oven and place on a wire rack to cool for about 10 minutes, then turn the loaf out on to the rack and set aside to cool completely.

4 Meanwhile, make the fruit spread. Place the strawberries and apples in a pan and pour in the apple juice. Bring to a boil, cover, and simmer for 30 minutes. Beat the sauce well and spoon into a clean, warmed jar. Set aside to cool, then seal, and label.

5 Serve the loaf with the fruit spread and strawberries, and apple wedges.

Spiced Chocolate Yule Bread

A delicious loaf, rich with spices, chocolate, and fruit which tastes good any time of year.

15 mins plus
2 hrs 20 mins
proving

1 hr

SERVES 6

I N G R E D I E N T S

3½ cups white bread flour

pinch of salt

2 tsp each mixed spice, nutmeg, and cinnamon

4 oz/115 g cold butter, diced

¼ oz/7 g active dry yeast

½ cup superfine sugar

½ cup candied peel

grated rind of 1 orange

1 cup semisweet chocolate chips

1 egg

⅔ cup milk

oil, for greasing

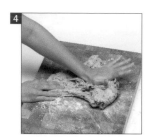

1 Sift the flour, salt, and spices together into a large bowl and rub in the butter until the mixture resembles bread crumbs.

2 Add the yeast, sugar, candied peel, orange rind, and chocolate, then add the egg. Warm the milk until tepid and add to the mixture to form a soft dough.

3 Put the dough in a floured bowl and cover. Let prove in a warm place for 2 hours. Oil two 1-lb/900-g loaf pans.

4 Tip the dough out of the bowl and knead it lightly on a floured cutting board. Shape the dough and fit it into the pans. Let rest for 20 minutes. Preheat the oven to 350°F/180°C.

5 Bake the loaves in the center of the oven for 1 hour. Remove from the oven and cool in the pans.

Chocolate Bread

For the chocoholics among us, this bread is not only great fun to make, it also has a fantastic chocolate flavor.

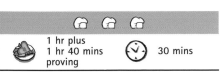

1 hr plus
1 hr 40 mins
proving

30 mins

MAKES 1 LOAF

INGREDIENTS

butter, for greasing

3½ cups white bread flour

¼ cup unsweetened cocoa

1 tsp salt

¼ oz/7 g active dry yeast

2 tbsp brown sugar

1 tbsp oil, plus extra for greasing

1¼ cups tepid water

1 Lightly grease a 2-lb/900-g loaf pan with a little butter.

2 Sift the flour and unsweetened cocoa into a large mixing bowl.

3 Stir in the salt, yeast, and brown sugar, mixing well.

4 Pour in the oil along with the tepid water and mix the ingredients together to make a dough.

5 Place the dough on a lightly floured counter and knead for 5 minutes.

6 Place the dough in a greased bowl, cover, and let prove in a warm place for about 1 hour, or until the dough has doubled in size.

7 Punch down the dough and shape it into a loaf. Place the dough in the prepared pan, cover, and let prove in a warm place for an additional 30 minutes.

8 Preheat the oven to 400°F/200°C. Bake the loaf for 25–30 minutes, or until a hollow sound is heard when the bottom of the bread is tapped. Transfer the bread to a wire rack and let cool completely. Cut into slices to serve.

COOK'S TIP
This bread can be sliced and spread with butter, or it can be lightly toasted.

Chocolate Fruit Bread

It is one of life's luxuries to sit down with a cup of coffee and a slice of fruit bread, especially if it's made with chocolate.

45 mins   1 hr

SERVES 4

INGREDIENTS

6 oz/175 g butter, softened, plus extra
   for greasing

⅔ cup brown sugar

4 eggs, beaten lightly

1¼ cups semisweet chocolate chips

½ cup raisins

½ cup chopped walnuts

finely grated rind of 1 orange

2 cups self-rising flour

1 Preheat the oven to 325°F/160°C. Grease a 2-lb/900-g loaf pan and line the bottom with parchment paper.

2 Cream together the butter and sugar in a bowl until light and fluffy.

3 Gradually add the eggs, beating well after each addition. If the mixture starts to curdle, beat in 1–2 tablespoons of the flour.

4 Stir in the chocolate chips, raisins, walnuts, and orange rind. Sift the flour and carefully fold it into the mixture.

VARIATIONS
Use white or milk chocolate chips instead of semisweet chocolate chips, or a mixture of all three, if desired. Dried cranberries instead of the raisins also work well in this recipe.

5 Spoon the mixture into the prepared loaf pan and then make a slight dip in the center of the top with the back of a spoon.

6 Bake in the preheated oven for 1 hour, or until a fine skewer inserted into the center of the loaf comes out clean.

7 Let the loaf cool in the pan for 5 minutes before carefully turning out on to a wire rack to cool completely.

8 To serve the fruit bread, cut it into thin slices.

Chocolate & Orange Teabread

This recipe makes two delicious marble loaves; one to eat now and one to freeze for another day.

20 mins   **35–45 mins**

MAKES 2 CAKES EACH SERVING 6

INGREDIENTS

5¼ oz/150 g butter, softened, plus extra for greasing

2¾ oz/75 g semisweet chocolate, broken into pieces

1¼ cups golden superfine sugar

5 large eggs, beaten

scant 1½ cups all-purpose flour

2 tsp baking powder

pinch of salt

grated rind of 2 oranges

1 Preheat the oven to 350°F/ 180°C. Grease and line 2 x 1-lb/450 g loaf pans. Put the chocolate in a heatproof bowl set over a pan of gently simmering water, making sure that the bottom of the bowl does not touch the water. Remove from the heat once the chocolate has melted.

2 Put the butter and sugar in another bowl and beat until light and fluffy. Gradually beat in the eggs. Sift the flour, baking powder, and salt into the mixture and fold in. Transfer one-third of the mixture to the melted chocolate and stir together. Stir the orange rind into the remaining mixture. Divide half the orange batter between the 2 loaf pans and spread in an even layer.

3 Drop tablespoonfuls of the chocolate batter on top, dividing it between the 2 pans, but do not smooth it out. Add the last of the orange batter to the 2 pans, then, using a knife, gently swirl the 2 mixtures together to give a marbled effect. Bake in the preheated oven for 35-40 minutes until a skewer inserted into the center of each loaf comes out clean. Let cool in the pans for 10 minutes, then turn out, remove the paper, and let cool completely on a wire rack.

COOK'S TIP
When you add the eggs, the mixture may appear to curdle. This does not matter.

Italian Chocolate Chip Bread

Serve this flavorful bread plain with butter or jelly, or Italian-style with a spoonful of mascarpone cheese.

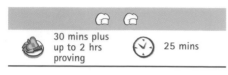

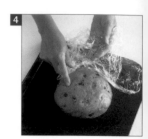

30 mins plus up to 2 hrs proving — 25 mins

MAKES 1 LOAF

INGREDIENTS

1 tsp vegetable oil, for brushing

2 cups all-purpose flour, plus extra for dusting

1 tbsp unsweetened cocoa

pinch of salt

1 tbsp butter, sweet for preference, plus ½ tsp extra, melted, for brushing

1 tbsp superfine sugar

¼ oz/7 g active dry yeast

⅔ cup lukewarm water

⅓ cup semisweet chocolate chips

1 Brush a cookie sheet with ½ teaspoon of the oil. Sift the flour, unsweetened cocoa, and salt into a bowl. Add the butter and cut it into the flour mixture, then stir in the sugar and yeast.

2 Gradually add the water, stirring well to mix. When the dough becomes too firm to stir with a spoon, gather it together with your hands. Turn it out on to a lightly floured work counter and knead thoroughly until smooth and elastic.

3 Knead the chocolate chips into the dough, distributing them throughout. Form into a round loaf, then place on the cookie sheet, cover with oiled plastic wrap, and set aside in a warm place for 1½–2 hours until doubled in bulk.

4 Preheat the oven to 425°F/220°C. Discard the plastic wrap and bake the loaf in the preheated oven for 10 minutes. Reduce the temperature to 375°F/190°C and bake for an additional 15 minutes.

5 Transfer the loaf to a wire rack and brush with melted butter. Cover with a clean dish towel until cooled.

Chocolate Fruit Loaf

A very moreish loaf that smells divine while it is baking. It is best enjoyed warm.

40 mins plus
1 hr proving   30 mins

SERVES 10

INGREDIENTS

butter, for greasing

3 cups white bread flour, plus extra
for dusting

¼ cup unsweetened cocoa

2 tbsp superfine sugar

¼ oz/7 g active dry yeast

¼ tsp salt

1 cup tepid water

2 tbsp butter, melted

5 tbsp coarsely chopped candied cherries

½ cup semisweet chocolate chips

⅓ cup golden raisins

2¾ oz/75 g no-soak dried apricots,
chopped coarsely

GLAZE

1 tbsp superfine sugar

1 tbsp water

1 Lightly grease a 2-lb/900-g loaf pan. Sift the flour and unsweetened cocoa into a large mixing bowl. Stir in the sugar, dry yeast, and salt.

2 Mix together the tepid water and butter. Make a well in the center of the dry ingredients and add the liquid. Mix well with a wooden spoon, then use your hands to bring the dough together. Turn out on to a lightly floured counter and knead for 5 minutes, until a smooth elastic dough forms. Return to a clean bowl, cover with a damp dish towel, and let prove in a warm place for about 1 hour or until doubled in size.

3 Turn the dough out on to a floured work counter and knead for 5 minutes. Roll out to a rectangle about ½-inch/1-cm thick and the same width as the length of the pan. Scatter the cherries, chocolate chips, golden raisins, and chopped apricots over the dough. Carefully roll up the dough, like a jelly roll, enclosing the filling. Transfer to the loaf pan, cover with a damp dish towel, and let prove for 20 minutes or until the top of the dough is level with the top of the pan.

4 Preheat the oven to 400°F/200°C. To make the glaze, mix together the sugar and water, then brush it over the top of the loaf. Bake in the preheated oven for 30 minutes or until well risen. Serve.

Crown Loaf

This is a rich, sweet bread combining alcohol, nuts, and fruit in a decorative wreath shape. It is ideal for serving at Thanksgiving.

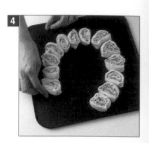

30 mins plus 1 hr 10 mins proving

30 mins

MAKES 1 LOAF

INGREDIENTS

2 tbsp butter, cut into small pieces, plus extra for greasing

generous 1½ cups white bread flour

½ tsp salt

¼ oz/7 g active dry yeast

½ cup tepid milk

1 egg, beaten lightly

FILLING

4 tbsp butter, softened

¼ cup brown sugar

2 tbsp chopped hazelnuts

1 tbsp chopped preserved ginger

⅓ cup candied peel

1 tbsp dark rum or cognac

1 cup confectioners' sugar

2 tbsp lemon juice

1 Grease a cookie sheet. Sift the flour and salt into a bowl. Stir in the yeast. Rub in the butter with your fingertips. Add the milk and egg and mix to form a dough.

2 Place the dough in a greased bowl, cover, and stand in a warm place for 40 minutes until doubled in size. Punch down the dough lightly for 1 minute. Roll out to a rectangle about 12 x 9 inches/ 30 x 23 cm.

3 To make the filling, cream together the butter and sugar until light and fluffy. Stir in the hazelnuts, ginger, candied peel, and rum or cognac. Spread the filling over the dough, leaving a 1-inch/2.5-cm border.

4 Roll up the dough, starting from one of the long edges, into a sausage shape. Cut into slices at 2-inch/5-cm intervals and place in a circle on the cookie sheet with the slices just touching. Cover and stand in a warm place to prove for 30 minutes.

5 Preheat the oven to 375°F/190°C. Bake the loaf for 20–30 minutes, or until golden. Meanwhile, mix the confectioners' sugar with enough lemon juice to form a thin frosting.

6 Let the loaf cool slightly before drizzling with frosting. Let the frosting set slightly before serving.

Cinnamon & Currant Loaf

This spiced teabread is quick and easy to make. Serve it buttered and with a drizzle of honey for an afternoon snack.

1 hr   1 hr 10 mins

SERVES 8

I N G R E D I E N T S

6 oz/175 g butter, cut into small pieces, plus extra for greasing

2¾ cups all-purpose flour

pinch of salt

1 tbsp baking powder

1 tbsp ground cinnamon

¾ cup brown sugar

¾ cup currants

finely grated rind of 1 orange

5–6 tbsp orange juice

6 tbsp milk

2 eggs, beaten lightly

1 Preheat the oven to 350°F/180°C. Grease a 2-lb/900-g loaf pan and line the bottom with parchment paper.

2 Sift the flour, salt, baking powder, and ground cinnamon into a bowl. Rub in the butter with your fingertips until the mixture resembles bread crumbs.

3 Stir in the sugar, currants, and orange rind. Beat the orange juice, milk, and eggs together and add to the dry ingredients. Mix well together.

4 Spoon the batter into the prepared pan. Make a slight dip in the center of the batter to help it rise evenly.

5 Bake in the preheated oven for about 1–1 hour 10 minutes, until a fine metal skewer inserted into the center of the loaf comes out clean.

6 Let the loaf cool before turning it out of the pan. Transfer to a wire rack and let cool completely before slicing.

COOK'S TIP
Once you have added the liquid to the dry ingredients, work as quickly as possible, because the baking powder is activated by the liquid.

Pains au Chocolat

These croissants can be a bit fiddly to make, but the flaky pastry enclosing a fabulous rich chocolate filling makes them worth the effort.

20 mins plus 3 hrs chilling and proving

20–25 mins

MAKES 12

INGREDIENTS

6 oz/175 g butter, softened, plus extra for greasing

4 cups white bread flour

½ tsp salt

¼ oz/7 g active dry yeast

2 tbsp shortening

1 egg, beaten lightly

1 cup tepid water

3½ oz/100 g semisweet chocolate, broken into 12 squares

beaten egg, for glazing

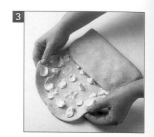

1 Lightly grease a cookie sheet. Sift the flour and salt into a mixing bowl and stir in the yeast. Rub in the fat with your fingertips. Add the egg and enough of the water to mix to a soft dough. Knead for about 10 minutes to make a smooth elastic dough.

2 Roll out to form a 15 x 8 inch/38 × 20 cm rectangle. Divide the butter into 3 portions and dot one portion over two-thirds of the rectangle, leaving a small border around the edge.

3 Fold the rectangle into 3 by first folding the plain part of the dough over and then the other side. Seal the edges of the dough by pressing with a rolling pin. Give the dough a quarter turn so the sealed edges are at the top and bottom. Re-roll and fold (without adding butter), then wrap the dough and chill for 30 minutes.

4 Repeat steps 2 and 3 until all of the butter has been used, chilling the dough each time. Re-roll and fold twice more without butter. Chill for a final 30 minutes.

5 Roll the dough to a 18 x 12 inch/45 x 30 cm rectangle, trim, and halve lengthwise. Cut each half into 6 rectangles and brush with beaten egg. Place a chocolate square at one end of each rectangle and roll up to form a sausage. Press the ends together and place, seam-side down, on the cookie sheet. Cover and let prove for 40 minutes in a warm place. Preheat the oven to 425°F/220°C. Brush each pastry roll with egg and bake in the preheated oven for 20–25 minutes, until golden. Cool on a wire rack. Serve warm or cold.

Orange & Currant Brioches

Brioche is a light rich French bread which can be made as one large loaf or small buns. They are usually served with coffee for breakfast.

30 mins plus
1 hr 40 mins
proving

15 mins

MAKES 12

INGREDIENTS

2 cups white bread flour, plus extra
   for dusting

½ tsp salt

¼ oz/7 g active dry yeast

1 tbsp golden superfine sugar

⅓ cup raisins

grated rind of 1 orange

2 tbsp tepid water

2 eggs, beaten

4 tbsp butter, melted

vegetable oil, for greasing

beaten egg, for glazing

butter, to serve

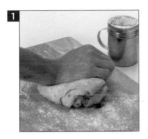

1 Butter 12 individual brioche molds. Sift the flour and salt into a warm bowl. Add the yeast, sugar, raisins, and orange rind. Make a well in the center. Mix the water, eggs, and melted butter, and add to the well. Beat vigorously to make a soft dough. Turn on to a lightly floured work counter and knead for 5 minutes until smooth and elastic. Put the dough in an oiled bowl, cover with plastic wrap, and leave in a warm place for 1 hour until doubled in size.

2 Turn out on to a lightly floured work counter, knead lightly for 1 minute, then roll into a sausage shape. Cut into 12 equal pieces. Shape three-quarters of each piece into a ball and place in the prepared molds. With a floured finger, press a hole in the center of each. Shape the remaining pieces of dough into a little plug and press into the holes.

3 Place the molds on a cookie sheet, cover lightly with oiled plastic wrap, and leave in a warm place until the dough comes almost to the top of the molds. Preheat the oven to 425°F/220°C. Brush the brioches with beaten egg and bake in the oven for 15 minutes, until golden brown. Serve warm with butter.

COOK'S TIP
If you do not have brioche molds, use a muffin pan instead.

Teacakes

These popular snacks are ideal split in half and toasted, then spread with butter. A mixture of luxury dry fruits gives them a rich taste.

20 mins plus
2 hrs 30 mins
proving

20 mins

MAKES 12

INGREDIENTS

2 tbsp butter, cut into small pieces, plus extra for greasing

3½ cups white bread flour, plus extra for dusting

¼ oz/7 g active dry yeast

¼ cup superfine sugar

1 tsp salt

1¼ cups tepid milk

½ cup mixed dry fruits

honey, for brushing

butter, to serve

1 Grease several cookie sheets with a little butter.

2 Sift the flour into a large bowl. Stir in the yeast, sugar, and salt. Rub in the butter with your fingertips until the mixture resembles fine bread crumbs. Add the milk and mix all of the ingredients together to form a soft dough.

3 Place the dough on a lightly floured work counter and knead for about 5 minutes. Alternatively, you can knead the dough with an electric mixer with a dough hook.

4 Form the dough into a ball and place in a greased bowl, cover, and let prove in a warm place for about 1–1½ hours until it has doubled in size.

5 Knead the dough again for a few minutes and knead in the fruit. Divide the dough into 12 circles and place on the

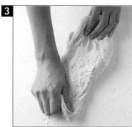

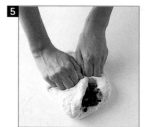

cookie sheets. Cover and let stand for 1 hour, or until springy to the touch.

6 Preheat the oven to 400°F/200°C. Bake the teacakes for 20 minutes.

7 Transfer the teacakes to a wire rack and brush with the honey while they are still warm. Let cool before serving them split in half, toasted if liked, and spread with butter.

COOK'S TIP

It is important to have the milk at the right temperature: heat it until you can put your little finger into the milk and leave it there for 10 seconds without it feeling too hot.

Cinnamon Swirls

These cinnamon-flavored buns are delicious if they are served warm
a few minutes after they come out of the oven.

20 mins plus
1 hr 20 mins
proving

20–30 mins

MAKES 12

INGREDIENTS

2 tbsp butter, cut into small pieces,
  plus extra for greasing

generous 1½ cups white bread flour

½ tsp salt

¼ oz/7 g active dry yeast

1 egg, beaten lightly

½ cup tepid milk

2 tbsp maple syrup

FILLING

4 tbsp butter, softened

2 tsp ground cinnamon

¼ cup brown sugar

⅓ cup currants

1 Grease a 9-inch/23-cm square baking pan with a little
  butter.

2 Sift the flour and salt into a mixing bowl. Stir in the
  yeast. Rub in the butter with your fingertips until the
mixture resembles bread crumbs. Add the egg and milk and
mix to form a dough.

3 Form the dough into a ball, place in a greased bowl,
  cover, and let stand in a warm place for about
40 minutes or until doubled in size.

4 Punch down the dough lightly for 1 minute, then roll
  out to a rectangle measuring 12 x 9 inches/30 x 23 cm.

5 To make the filling, cream together the softened butter,
  cinnamon, and brown sugar until light and fluffy.
Spread the filling evenly over the dough rectangle, leaving
a 1-inch/2.5-cm border all around. Sprinkle the currants
evenly over the top.

6 Roll up the dough from one of the long edges, and
  press down to seal. Cut the roll into 12 slices. Place
them in the pan, cover, and let stand for 30 minutes.

7 Preheat the oven to 375°F/190°C. Bake the buns for
  20–30 minutes, or until well risen. Brush with the
syrup and let cool slightly before serving.

Double-Chocolate Swirls

These rich, chocolate buns are very quick to make for breakfast because the dough is prepared the night before.

30 mins plus
8 hrs proving

25 mins

SERVES 24

INGREDIENTS

4½ cups white bread flour, plus extra for dusting

¼ oz/7 g active dry yeast

½ cup superfine sugar

½ tsp salt

1 tsp ground cinnamon

3 oz/85 g sweet butter

2 large eggs, beaten, plus 1 egg, beaten, for glazing

1¼ cups milk

6 tbsp chocolate hazelnut spread

7 oz/200 g milk chocolate, chopped

oil, for greasing

1 Mix the flour, yeast, sugar, salt, and cinnamon together in a large bowl.

2 Melt the butter and cool slightly, then whisk in the 2 eggs and milk. Pour into the flour and mix well.

3 Turn on to a floured work counter and knead for 10 minutes until smooth. Put into a large floured bowl, cover with plastic wrap and put in a warm place for 8 hours, or overnight.

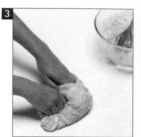

4 When you are ready to make the buns, take the dough from the bowl and punch down. Preheat the oven to 425°F/220°C and lightly oil 2 cookie sheets.

5 Divide the dough into 4 pieces and roll each piece into a rectangle about 1-inch/2.5-cm thick. Spread each rectangle with the chocolate hazelnut spread and scatter with the chopped chocolate. Roll up each piece like a jelly roll, then cut into 6 pieces. Place each swirl, cut-side down, on the cookie sheets and brush each one well with the beaten egg. Bake in the preheated oven for 20 minutes and serve warm.

Hot Cross Buns

There is nothing more tempting than the aroma of spicy hot cross buns straight from the oven.

35 mins plus 2 hrs 45 mins proving

20 mins

MAKES 12

INGREDIENTS

1 lb 2 oz/500 g white bread flour, plus extra for dusting

½ tsp salt

2 tsp ground allspice

1 tsp ground nutmeg

1 tsp ground cinnamon

¼ oz/7 g active dry yeast

¼ cup golden superfine sugar

finely grated rind of 1 lemon

1 cup currants

½ cup candied peel

2¾ oz/75 g butter, melted, plus extra for greasing

1 egg

1 cup tepid milk

vegetable oil, for greasing

CROSSES

⅓ cup all-purpose flour

2 tbsp butter, cut into pieces

GLAZE

3 tbsp milk

3 tbsp golden superfine sugar

1 Sift the flour, salt, allspice, nutmeg, and cinnamon into a bowl. Stir in the yeast, sugar, lemon rind, currants, and candied peel. Make a well in the center. Mix together the melted butter, egg, and milk and pour into the dry ingredients. Mix to form a soft dough, adding a little more milk if necessary. Turn the dough on to a floured work counter and knead for about 10 minutes until the dough is smooth and elastic. Place the dough in a lightly oiled bowl, cover with plastic wrap, and leave in a warm place for 1½–2 hours until doubled in size.

2 Turn the dough on to a floured work counter and knead lightly. Divide the dough into 12 equal-size pieces and knead each one into a ball. Place them on a greased cookie sheet and flatten slightly. Cover loosely with oiled plastic wrap and leave in a warm place for about 45 minutes until doubled in size. Preheat the oven to 425°F/220°C.

3 To make the crosses, sift the flour into a bowl and rub in the butter. Stir in 1 tablespoon of cold water to make a dough. Divide the dough to form 24 strips, about 7 inches/18 cm long. To make the glaze, put the milk and sugar in a small pan and heat gently until the sugar has dissolved. Brush some of the glaze over the buns and lay the pastry strips on the buns to form crosses. Bake for 15–20 minutes until golden. Brush with the remaining glaze and return to the oven for 1 minute. Transfer to a wire rack to cool.

Chelsea Buns

These sweet and sticky buns, with a hint of spice, are irresistible. Perfect, served at any time of day!

30 mins plus
1 hr 45 mins
proving

30 mins

MAKES 9

INGREDIENTS

2 tbsp butter, plus extra for greasing

2 cups white bread flour, plus extra for dusting

½ tsp salt

¼ oz/7 g active dry yeast

1 tsp golden superfine sugar

½ cup tepid milk

vegetable oil, for greasing

1 egg, beaten

FILLING

scant ½ cup light muscovado sugar

generous ½ cup luxury mixed dry fruits

1 tsp allspice

4 tbsp butter, softened

GLAZE

generous ½ cup confectioners' sugar

1 Grease a 7-inch/18-cm square cake pan. Sift the flour and salt into a warmed bowl, stir in the yeast and sugar, and rub in the butter. Make a well in the center. In another bowl, mix together the milk and egg and pour into the dry ingredients. Beat vigorously to make a soft dough. On a floured work counter, knead the dough for 5-10 minutes until smooth. Put the dough in an oiled bowl, cover with plastic wrap, and leave in a warm place for about 1 hour until doubled in size.

2 Turn the dough out on to a floured work counter and knead lightly for 1 minute. Roll out to a rectangle measuring 12 x 9 inches/30 x 23 cm.

To make the filling, put the sugar, dry fruits, and allspice in a bowl and mix together. Spread the dough with the softened butter and sprinkle the fruit mixture on top. Roll up from a long side and cut into 9 pieces. Place in the prepared pan, cut-side up. Cover with oiled plastic wrap and leave in a warm place for 45 minutes until well risen.

3 Preheat the oven to 375°F/190°C. Bake the buns in the oven for 30 minutes until golden. Let cool in the pan for 10 minutes, then transfer, in one piece, to a wire rack to cool. To make the glaze, sift the confectioners' sugar into a bowl and stir in enough water to make a thin glaze. Brush over the buns and let set. Pull the buns apart, to serve.

Cherry Biscuits

These are an alternative to traditional biscuits, using sweet candied cherries which not only create color but add a distinct flavor.

10 mins   8-10 mins

MAKES 8

INGREDIENTS

3 oz/85 g butter, cut into small pieces, plus extra for greasing

generous 1½ cups self-rising flour, plus extra for dusting

1 tbsp superfine sugar

pinch of salt

3 tbsp candied cherries, chopped

3 tbsp golden raisins

1 egg, beaten lightly

scant ¼ cup milk

1 Preheat the oven to 425°F/220°C. Lightly grease a cookie sheet with a little butter.

2 Sift the flour, sugar, and salt into a mixing bowl and rub in the butter with your fingertips until the mixture resembles bread crumbs.

3 Stir in the candied cherries and golden raisins. Add the beaten egg.

4 Reserve 1 tablespoon of the milk for glazing, then add the remainder to the mixture. Mix well together to form a soft dough.

5 On a lightly floured work counter, roll out the dough to a thickness of ¾ inch/2 cm and cut out 8 circles, using a 2-inch/5-cm cutter.

6 Place the biscuits on the prepared cookie sheet and brush the tops with the reserved milk.

7 Bake in the preheated oven for 8–10 minutes, or until the biscuits are golden brown.

8 Transfer the biscuits to a wire rack to cool completely, then serve them split and buttered.

COOK'S TIP
These biscuits will freeze very successfully, but they are best thawed and eaten within 1 month.

Molasses Biscuits

These biscuits are light and buttery like traditional biscuits, but the molasses gives them a deliciously rich flavor.

15 mins   8-10 mins

SERVES 8

I N G R E D I E N T S

3 oz/85 g butter, cut into small pieces, plus extra for greasing

generous 1½ cups self-rising flour

1 tbsp superfine sugar

salt

all-purpose flour, for dusting

1 dessert apple, peeled, cored, and chopped

1 egg, beaten lightly

2 tbsp molasses

5 tbsp milk

1 Preheat the oven to 425°F/220°C. Lightly grease a cookie sheet with a little butter.

2 Sift the flour, sugar, and a pinch of salt into a mixing bowl.

3 Add the butter and rub it in with your fingertips until the mixture resembles fine bread crumbs.

4 Add the chopped apple to the mixture and stir until thoroughly combined.

5 Mix the beaten egg, molasses, and milk together in a large pitcher. Add to the dry ingredients and mix to form a soft dough.

6 On a lightly floured work counter, roll out the dough to a thickness of ³/₄ inch/2 cm and cut out 8 circles, using a 2-inch/5-cm cutter.

7 Arrange the biscuits on the prepared cookie sheet and bake in the preheated oven for about 8–10 minutes.

8 Transfer the biscuits to a wire rack and let cool slightly. Serve split in half and spread with butter.

COOK'S TIP
These biscuits can be frozen, but are best thawed and eaten within 1 month.

Chocolate Biscuits

A plain biscuit mixture is transformed into a chocoholic's treat by the simple addition of chocolate chips.

🕐 10 mins   🕐 10–12 mins

MAKES 4

INGREDIENTS

2½ oz/70 g butter, plus extra for greasing

2 cups self-rising flour, sifted

1 tbsp superfine sugar

⅓ cup chocolate chips

about ⅔ cup milk

all-purpose flour, for dusting

1 Preheat the oven to 425°F/220°C. Lightly grease a cookie sheet. Place the flour in a mixing bowl. Cut the butter into small pieces and rub it into the flour with your fingertips until the biscuit mixture resembles fine bread crumbs.

2 Stir in the superfine sugar and chocolate chips.

3 Mix in enough of the milk to form a soft dough.

4 On a lightly floured work counter, roll out the dough to form a 4 x 6-inch/ 10 x 15-cm rectangle, about 1 inch/2.5 cm thick. Cut the dough into 9 squares.

5 Place the biscuits spaced well apart, on the prepared cookie sheet.

6 Brush the tops with a little milk and bake in the preheated oven for 10–12 minutes, until risen and golden.

Buttermilk Biscuits

Buttermilk makes these biscuits extra light, and gives them a tangy flavor. Serve with whipped cream and strawberry jelly.

🍰 15 mins   🕐 12–15 mins

MAKES 8

INGREDIENTS

4 tbsp cold butter, cut into pieces,
  plus extra for greasing

1¼ cups self-rising flour

1 tsp baking powder

pinch of salt

¼ cup golden superfine sugar

1¼ cups buttermilk

all-purpose flour, for dusting

2 tbsp milk

TO SERVE

whipped cream

strawberry jelly

1 Preheat the oven to 425°F/220°C. Grease a cookie sheet. Sift the flour, baking powder, and salt into a bowl. Add the butter and rub in until the mixture resembles fine bread crumbs. Add the sugar and buttermilk and quickly mix together.

2 Turn on to a floured work counter and knead lightly. Roll out to a thickness of 1 inch/2.5 cm. Using a 2½-inch/6-cm plain or fluted cutter, cut out biscuits and place on the prepared cookie sheet. Gather the trimmings, re-roll, and cut out more biscuits until you have used up all the dough.

3 Brush the tops of the biscuits with milk. Bake in the oven for 12–15 minutes, until well risen and golden. Transfer to a wire rack to cool. Split and serve with whipped cream and strawberry jelly.

COOK'S TIP

If you dip the cutter in a little flour it prevents it sticking when you cut out the biscuit circles.

Chinese Custard Tarts

These small custard tarts, baked in a rich, sweet dough, are equally good served either warm or cold.

20 mins   30 mins

SERVES 4

INGREDIENTS

PIE DOUGH

1¼ cups all-purpose flour, plus extra
    for dusting

scant ¼ cup superfine sugar

5 tbsp butter, sweet for preference

2 tbsp shortening

2 tbsp water

CUSTARD

2 small eggs

generous ¼ cup superfine sugar

¾ cup milk

½ tsp ground nutmeg, plus extra
    for sprinkling

cream, to serve

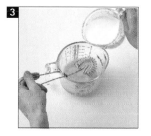

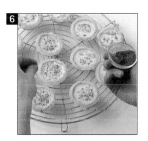

1 Preheat the oven to 300°F/150°C. To make the dough, sift the flour into a bowl. Add the sugar and rub in the butter and shortening with your fingertips until the mixture resembles bread crumbs. Add the water and mix to form a firm dough.

2 Transfer the dough to a lightly floured counter and knead for 5 minutes until smooth. Cover with plastic wrap and chill in the refrigerator while you are preparing the filling.

3 To make the custard, beat the eggs and sugar together. Gradually add the milk and ground nutmeg and beat until well combined.

4 Separate the dough into 15 even-size pieces. Flatten the dough pieces into circles and press into shallow muffin pans.

5 Spoon the custard into the tart shells and cook in the preheated oven for 25–30 minutes.

6 Transfer the custard tarts to a wire rack, let cool slightly, then sprinkle with nutmeg. Serve warm or cold with a little cream.

COOK'S TIP
For extra convenience, make the dough in advance, cover, and chill in the refrigerator until required.

Pine Nut Tartlets

Pine nuts and orange rind are popular ingredients in Mediterranean dishes—here they add a twist of flavor to luscious chocolate tartlets.

40 mins plus
1 hr 10 mins
chilling

45 mins

SERVES 8

INGREDIENTS

2 oz/55 g semisweet chocolate,
 broken into pieces

4 tbsp butter, sweet for preference

¾ cup plus 2 tbsp superfine sugar

5 tbsp brown sugar

6 tbsp milk

3½ tbsp corn syrup

finely grated rind of 2 large oranges and
 2 tbsp freshly squeezed juice

1 tsp vanilla extract

3 large eggs, beaten lightly

1 cup pine nuts

PIE DOUGH

1¾ cups all-purpose flour

pinch of salt

2¾ oz/75 g butter

1 cup confectioners' sugar

1 large egg, plus 2 large egg yolks

1 To make the pie dough, sift the flour and salt into a bowl. Make a well in the center and add the butter, confectioners' sugar, whole egg, and egg yolks. Using your fingertips, mix the ingredients in the well into a paste.

2 Gradually incorporate the surrounding flour to make a soft dough. Quickly and lightly knead the dough. Shape into a ball, wrap in plastic wrap, and chill for at least 1 hour.

3 Preheat the oven to 400°F/200°C. Roll the pie dough into 8 circles, 6 inches/15 cm across. Use to line 8 × 4-inch/10-cm loose-bottomed tartlet pans. Line each with parchment paper to fit and top with dried beans. Chill for 10 minutes.

4 Bake the tartlet shells in the preheated oven for 5 minutes. Remove the paper and beans and bake for an additional 8 minutes. Let cool on a wire rack. Reduce the oven temperature to 350°F/180°C.

5 Meanwhile, put the chocolate in a pan over medium heat. Add the butter and stir until blended.

6 Stir in the remaining ingredients. Spoon the filling into the pie dough shells on a cookie sheet. Bake for 25–30 minutes, or until the tops puff up and crack and feel set. Cover with parchment paper for the final 5 minutes if the shells are browning too much. Transfer to a wire rack and let cool for at least 15 minutes before unmolding. Serve warm or at room temperature.

Chocolate Fruit Tartlets

Chocolate pie dough trimmed with nuts makes a perfect pastry shell for fruit in these tasty individual tartlets. You can use fresh or canned fruit.

1 hr plus 30 mins chilling   20–25 mins

SERVES 4

I N G R E D I E N T S

2¼ cups all-purpose flour, plus extra for dusting

3 tbsp unsweetened cocoa

6 oz/175 g butter, cut into pieces

3 tbsp superfine sugar

2–3 tbsp water

1¾ oz/50 g semisweet chocolate, broken into pieces

½ cup chopped mixed nuts, toasted

12 oz/350 g prepared fruit

3 tbsp apricot or red currant jelly

1 Sift the flour and unsweetened cocoa into a mixing bowl. Rub the butter into the flour with your fingertips until the mixture resembles fine bread crumbs.

2 Stir in the sugar. Add enough of the water to mix to a soft dough. Cover and chill for 15 minutes.

3 Preheat the oven to 375°F/190°C. Roll out the pie dough on a lightly floured work counter and use to line 4 tartlet pans, each 4 inches/10 cm across. Prick the shells with a fork and line with a little crumpled foil. Bake in the preheated oven for 10 minutes.

4 Remove the foil and bake for an additional 5–10 minutes, until the pie dough is crisp. Place the pans on a wire rack to cool completely.

5 Put the chocolate in a heatproof bowl set over a pan of gently simmering water until melted. Spread out the chopped nuts on a plate. Remove the tartlet shells from the pans. Spread melted chocolate on the rims, then dip in the nuts. Let the chocolate set.

6 Arrange the fruit in the tartlet shells. Melt the apricot or red currant jelly with the remaining 1 tablespoon water and brush it over the fruit. Chill the tartlets until required.

VARIATION

If liked, you can fill the cases with a little sweetened cream before topping with the fruit. For a chocolate-flavored filling, blend 8 oz/225 g chocolate hazelnut spread with 5 tablespoons thick yogurt or whipped cream.

Chocolate Chip Tartlets

These little tartlets will be a big hit with the kids. Serve as a midweek supper dessert or a special treat.

1 hr plus 10 mins chilling

20 mins

MAKES 6

INGREDIENTS

scant ½ cup toasted hazelnuts

1¼ cups all-purpose flour

1 tbsp confectioners' sugar

2¾ oz/75 g soft margarine

2–3 tbsp water

FILLING

2 tbsp cornstarch

1 tbsp unsweetened cocoa

1 tbsp superfine sugar

1¼ cups semiskim milk

3 tbsp chocolate hazelnut spread

2½ tbsp semisweet chocolate chips

2½ tbsp milk chocolate chips

2½ tbsp white chocolate chips

1 Finely chop the nuts in a food processor. Add the flour, 1 tablespoon confectioners' sugar, and the margarine. Process for a few seconds until the mixture resembles bread crumbs. Add the water and process to form a soft dough. Cover and chill in the freezer for 10 minutes.

2 Preheat the oven to 400°F/200°C. Roll out the dough and use it to line 6 x 4-inch/10-cm loose-bottomed tartlet pans. Prick the bottom of the tartlet shells with a fork and line them with loosely crumpled foil. Bake in the preheated oven for 15 minutes. Remove the foil and bake for an additional 5 minutes, until the tartlet shells are crisp and golden. Remove from the oven and let cool.

3 Mix together the cornstarch, unsweetened cocoa, and sugar with enough milk to make a smooth paste. Stir in the remaining milk. Pour into a pan and cook gently over low heat, stirring until thickened. Stir in the chocolate spread.

4 Mix together the chocolate chips and reserve a quarter. Stir half of the remaining chips into the custard. Cover with damp waxed paper, let stand until almost cold, then stir in the second half of the chocolate chips. Spoon the mixture into the pastry shells and let cool. Decorate with the reserved chocolate chips, scattering them over the top.

Toffee Chocolate Puff Tarts

These crisp puff pastry tarts, with their smooth filling, are a chocolate version of the more famous Portuguese custard tarts.

30 mins plus
30 mins chilling

30 mins

MAKES 12

INGREDIENTS

15 oz/375 g ready-rolled puff pastry

5 oz/140 g semisweet chocolate

1¼ cups heavy cream

¼ cup superfine sugar

4 egg yolks

12 tsp ready-made toffee sauce

1 Line the bottoms of a 12-hole nonstick muffin pan with disks of waxed paper.

2 Cut out 12 x 2-inch/5 cm circles from the edge of the pie dough and cut the remainder into 12 strips. Roll the strips to half their thickness and line the sides of each hole with 1 strip. Put a disk of pie dough at the bottom, and press well together to seal and make a tart shell. Prick the bases and chill in the refrigerator for 30 minutes.

3 Preheat the oven to 400°F/200°C. While the pie dough is chilling, melt the chocolate in a heatproof bowl set over a pan of gently simmering water. Remove the bowl from the heat, cool slightly, then stir in the cream. Beat the sugar and egg yolks together and mix well with the melted chocolate.

4 Remove the muffin pan from the refrigerator and put a teaspoonful of toffee sauce into each tart shell. Divide the chocolate mixture among the tarts and bake for 20–25 minutes, turning the tray around halfway through the cooking, until just set. Cool the tarts in the muffin pan then remove carefully, leaving behind the waxed paper. Serve with whipped cream.

COOK'S TIP
Don't fill the tarts to the top because the chocolate will puff up in the oven then collapse back as it cools.

Chocolate Hazelnut Palmiers

These delicious chocolate and hazelnut cookies are very simple to make, yet so effective. For very young children, leave out the chopped nuts.

10 mins

10–15 mins

MAKES 26

INGREDIENTS

butter, for greasing

all-purpose flour, for dusting

13 oz/375 g ready-made puff pastry

8 tbsp chocolate hazelnut spread

½ cup chopped toasted hazelnuts

2 tbsp superfine sugar

1 Preheat the oven to 425°F/220°C. Grease a cookie sheet. On a lightly floured work counter, roll out the puff pastry to a rectangle measuring about 15 × 9 inches/38 × 23 cm.

2 Spread the chocolate hazelnut spread over the pastry using a spatula, then scatter the chopped hazelnuts over the top.

3 Roll up one long side of the pie dough to the center, then the other, so they meet in the center. Where the pieces meet, dampen the edges with a little water to join them. Using a sharp knife, cut into thin slices. Place each one on the prepared cookie sheet and flatten slightly with a spatula. Sprinkle with superfine sugar.

4 Bake in the preheated oven for about 10–15 minutes, until golden. Transfer to a wire rack to cool.

VARIATION

For an extra chocolate flavor, dip the palmiers in melted semisweet chocolate to half-cover each biscuit.

Paper-Thin Fruit Pies

These extra-crisp phyllo pastry shells, filled with slices of fruit and glazed with apricot jelly, are best served hot with lowfat custard.

🕐 20 mins   🕐 15 mins

SERVES 4

I N G R E D I E N T S

1 medium dessert apple

1 medium ripe pear

2 tbsp lemon juice

¼ cup lowfat spread

4 sheets phyllo pastry, thawed if frozen

2 tbsp reduced-sugar apricot jelly

1 tbsp unsweetened orange juice

1 tbsp finely chopped pistachios, shelled

2 tsp confectioners' sugar, for dusting

lowfat custard, to serve

1 Preheat the oven to 400°F/200°C. Core and thinly slice the apple and pear and immediately toss them in the lemon juice to prevent them turning brown. Gently melt the lowfat spread in a pan over low heat.

2 Cut the sheets of dough into 4 and cover with a clean, damp dish towel. Brush 4 nonstick muffin pans, measuring 4 inches/10 cm in diameter, with a little of the lowfat spread.

3 Working on each pie separately, brush 4 sheets of dough with lowfat spread. Press a small sheet of dough into the bottom of 1 pan. Arrange the other sheets of dough on top at slightly different angles. Repeat with the other sheets of dough to make another 3 pies.

4 Arrange the apple and pear slices alternately in the center of each pie shell and lightly crimp the edges of the dough of each pie.

5 Stir the jelly and orange juice together until smooth and brush over the fruit. Bake in the preheated oven for 12–15 minutes. Sprinkle with the pistachios, dust lightly with confectioners' sugar, and serve hot from the oven with lowfat custard.

VARIATION
Other combinations of fruit are equally delicious. Try peach and apricot, raspberry and apple, or pineapple and mango.

Phyllo Nests

Green and black grapes decorate the creamy chocolate filling in these crisp little phyllo pastry nests.

25 mins plus
20 mins cooling   15–18 mins

SERVES 4

INGREDIENTS

1 tbsp sweet butter

6 sheets phyllo pastry

1½ oz/40 g semisweet chocolate, broken into pieces

½ cup ricotta cheese

16 seedless green grapes, halved

24 seedless black grapes, halved

1 Preheat the oven to 375°F/190°C. Put the butter into a small pan and set over low heat until melted. Remove from the heat. Cut each sheet of phyllo pie dough into 4, to give 24 rectangles, each measuring about 6 × 3 inches/15 × 7.5 cm, then stack them all on top of each other. Brush 4 shallow muffin pans with melted butter. Line 1 pan with a rectangle of phyllo pie dough, brush with melted butter, place another rectangle on top at an angle to the first, and brush it with melted butter. Continue in this way, lining each pan with 6 rectangles, each brushed with melted butter. Brush the top layers with melted butter.

2 Bake in the preheated oven for 7–8 minutes, until golden and crisp. Remove from the oven and set aside to cool in the pans.

3 Put the chocolate in a heatproof bowl set over a pan of gently simmering water. Stir over a low heat until melted. Remove from the heat and cool slightly. Brush the insides of the pie dough shells with about half the melted chocolate. Beat the ricotta until smooth, then beat in the remaining melted chocolate.

4 Divide the chocolate ricotta mixture among the pie dough shells and arrange the grapes around the edges. Carefully lift the shells out of the pans and serve immediately.

Pistachio Pastries

Pistachios and rose water give these crisp little pastries a Middle Eastern flavor. Dust with confectioners' sugar just before serving.

🍮 20 mins   🕐 20 mins

MAKES 20

INGREDIENTS

4 tbsp butter, melted, plus extra for greasing

10 sheets phyllo pastry

FILLING

½ cup pistachios, ground coarsely

½ cup ground hazelnuts

2 tbsp golden granulated sugar

1 tbsp rose water

2 oz/55 g semisweet chocolate, grated

sifted confectioners' sugar, to decorate

1 Preheat the oven to 350°F/180°C. Grease 2 cookie sheets. To make the filling, put the pistachios and hazelnuts in a bowl with the sugar, rose water, and chocolate. Mix together. Cut each sheet of phyllo pastry lengthwise. Pile the rectangles on top of each other and cover with a dish towel to prevent them drying out.

2 Brush a phyllo sheet with melted butter. Spread a teaspoon of filling along one short end. Fold the long sides in, slightly over the filling and roll up from the filling end. Place on the prepared cookie sheets with the seam underneath and brush with melted butter.

3 Repeat with the remaining pastry and filling. Bake in the preheated oven for 20 minutes, or until crisp and very lightly colored. Transfer to a wire rack to cool. Dust with sifted confectioners' sugar before serving.

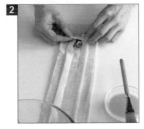

Banana & Chocolate Triangles

These crisp little parcels make a delicious snack, or could equally be enjoyed at the end of a dinner party, with coffee.

15 mins   14–16 mins

MAKES 12 SMALL TRIANGLES

INGREDIENTS

1 banana

1 oz/25 g chocolate chips

4 sheets phyllo pastry

4 tbsp butter, melted

CHOCOLATE SAUCE

⅔ cup light cream

2 oz/55 g semisweet chocolate, broken into pieces

1 Preheat the oven to 350°F/180°C. Peel the banana, put in a bowl and mash with a fork. Stir in the chocolate chips. Cover the phyllo sheets with a dish towel to prevent them drying out. Brush a phyllo sheet with melted butter and cut lengthwise into strips 2½ inches/6 cm wide.

2 Spoon a little of the banana mixture on to the bottom end of each strip, fold the corner of the pastry over to enclose it in a triangle, and continue folding along the whole length of the strip to make a triangular parcel. Place on a cookie sheet with the seam underneath. Repeat with the remaining pastry and filling. Bake in the preheated oven for 10-12 minutes, until golden.

3 To make the chocolate sauce, put the cream and chocolate in a pan and heat gently until the chocolate has melted. Stir until smooth. Serve the pastries with the chocolate sauce.

Banana Empanadas

Phyllo pastry makes these empanadas light and crisp on the outside, with a scrumptious, hot banana-chocolate filling.

10 mins   15 mins

SERVES 4

INGREDIENTS

about 8 sheets phyllo pastry,
  cut into half lengthwise

melted butter or vegetable oil, for brushing

4 ripe bananas

1–2 tsp sugar

juice of ½ lemon

6–7 oz/175–200 g semisweet chocolate,
  broken into small pieces

confectioners' sugar and ground cinnamon,
  for dusting

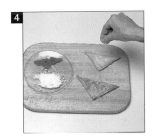

1 Preheat the oven to 375°F/190°C. Working 1 at a time, lay a sheet of phyllo pastry out in front of you, and brush it with butter or oil.

2 Peel and dice and bananas and put in a bowl. Add the sugar and lemon juice and stir well to combine. Stir in the chocolate.

3 Place 1–2 teaspoons of the banana and chocolate mixture in one corner of the phyllo pastry, then fold over into a triangle shape to enclose the filling. Continue to fold in a triangular shape, until the pastry is completely wrapped around the filling.

COOK'S TIP

You could use ready-made puff pastry instead of phyllo for a more puffed-up effect.

4 Dust the parcels with confectioners' sugar and cinnamon. Place them on a lightly greased cookie sheet and continue the process with the remaining phyllo pastry and filling.

5 Bake in the preheated oven for about 15 minutes, or until the empanadas are golden. Remove from the oven and serve immediately. The filling is very hot so do take care.

Banana Pies

These miniature pies require a little time to prepare, but are well worth the effort. A sweet banana filling is wrapped in dough and baked.

45 mins plus
30 mins chilling

25 mins

SERVES 4

I N G R E D I E N T S

PIE DOUGH

3½ cups all-purpose flour, plus extra
   for dusting

5 tbsp shortening

5 tbsp butter, sweet for preference

½ cup water

FILLING

2 large bananas

⅓ cup finely chopped no-soak dried apricots

pinch of nutmeg

dash of orange juice

1 egg yolk, beaten

confectioners' sugar, for dusting

cream or ice cream, to serve

1 To make the dough, sift the flour into a large mixing bowl. Add the shortening and butter and rub into the flour with the fingertips until the mixture resembles bread crumbs. Gradually blend in the water to make a soft dough. Wrap in plastic wrap and chill for 30 minutes.

2 Preheat the oven to 350°F/180°C. Peel and mash the bananas in a bowl with a fork and stir in the apricots, nutmeg, and orange juice, mixing well.

3 Roll the dough out on a lightly floured work counter and cut out 16 circles, each 4 inches/10 cm across.

4 Spoon a little of the banana filling on to one half of each circle and fold the dough over the filling to form semicircles. Pinch the sides together and seal by pressing the edges with the tines of a fork.

5 Arrange the pies on a nonstick cookie sheet and brush them with the beaten egg yolk. Cut a small slit in each pie and cook in the preheated oven for about 25 minutes, or until golden brown.

6 Dust the banana pies with confectioners' sugar and serve with cream or ice cream.

VARIATION
Use a fruit filling of your choice, such as apple or plum, as an alternative.

Rice Tartlets

These little tartlets have a soft semisweet chocolate ganache layer covered with creamy rice pudding for a delicious special-occasion dessert.

30 mins   50 mins

SERVES 6

INGREDIENTS

1 package frozen unsweetened pie dough, thawed

4 cups milk

pinch of salt

½ cup risotto or short-grain white rice

1 vanilla bean, split, seeds removed and reserved

1 tbsp cornstarch

2 tbsp sugar

2-3 tbsp water

unsweetened cocoa, for dusting

chocolate, broken into pieces, to decorate

GANACHE

generous ¾ cup heavy cream

1 tbsp corn syrup

6 oz/175 g semisweet or bittersweet chocolate, broken into pieces

1 tbsp butter, sweet for preference

1 Preheat the oven to 400°F/200°C. Use the pie dough to line 6 x 4-inch/ 10-cm tart pans. Fill them with dried beans and bake blind in the preheated oven for about 20 minutes, until the pie crust is set and golden at the edges. Transfer to a wire rack to cool, and remove the dried beans.

2 To make the ganache, bring the heavy cream and corn syrup to a boil. Remove from the heat and immediately stir in the chopped chocolate. Continue stirring until melted and smooth, then beat in the butter until well combined. Spoon a 1-inch/2.5-cm thick layer into each tartlet. Set aside.

3 Bring the milk and salt to a boil in a pan. Sprinkle in the rice and bring back to a boil. Add the vanilla bean and seeds. Reduce the heat and simmer until the rice is tender and the milk creamy.

4 Blend the cornstarch and sugar in a small bowl and add enough water to make a paste. Stir in a few spoonfuls of the rice mixture, then stir the cornstarch mixture into the rice. Bring to a boil and

cook for 1 minute until thickened. Cool the pan in ice water, stirring occasionally, until it has thickened.

5 Spoon into the tartlets, filling each to the brim. Let set at room temperature. Place a little chocolate in a heatproof bowl set over a pan of gently simmering water until melted. To serve, dust the tartlets with unsweetened cocoa and pipe or drizzle with melted chocolate.

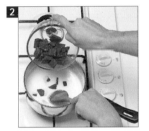

Festive Mince Pies

Serve these seasonal pastries with spiced mulled wine or eggnog. The filling is very hot when the pies come out of the oven, so let them cool.

20 mins   15 mins

MAKES 12

INGREDIENTS

1⅔ cups all-purpose flour, plus extra for dusting

3½ oz/100 g butter

¼ cup confectioners' sugar

1 egg yolk

2–3 tbsp milk

10½ oz/300 g mincemeat

1 egg, beaten, for sealing and glazing

confectioners' sugar, to decorate

1 Preheat the oven to 350°F/180°C. Sift the flour into a mixing bowl. Using your fingertips, rub in the butter until the mixture resembles bread crumbs. Mix in the confectioners' sugar and egg yolk. Stir in enough milk to form a soft dough, turn out on to a lightly floured work counter and knead lightly until smooth.

2 Shape the dough into a ball and roll out to a thickness of ½ inch/1 cm. Use fluted cutters to cut out 12 circles of 2¾-inch/7-cm diameter and 12 circles of 2-inch/5-cm diameter. Dust 12 tartlet pans with flour and line with the larger dough circles. Prick the bottoms with a fork, then half-fill each pie with mincemeat. Brush beaten egg around the pie rims, then gently press the smaller circles of dough on top to seal. Make a small hole in the top of each one, then shape any remaining dough into Christmas trees and leaves and use them to decorate the pies. Brush all over with beaten egg, then bake for 15 minutes. Remove from the oven and cool on a wire rack. Dust with confectioners' sugar and serve.

Maple Pecan Tarts

Maple syrup and pecans give a wonderful flavor to the toffee filling in these little tarts. Serve on their own, or with a little whipped cream.

20 mins plus
30 mins chilling

17–23 mins

MAKES 12

INGREDIENTS

PIE DOUGH

1¼ cups all-purpose flour, plus extra
for dusting

3 oz/85 g butter

¼ cup golden superfine sugar

2 egg yolks

FILLING

2 tbsp maple syrup

⅔ cup heavy cream

generous ½ cup golden superfine sugar

pinch of cream of tartar

6 tbsp water

1 cup pecans

14 pecan halves, to decorate

1 To make the pie dough, sift the flour into a mixing bowl and rub in the butter. Add the sugar and egg yolks, and mix to form a soft dough. Wrap and chill in the refrigerator for 30 minutes. Preheat the oven to 400°F/200°C. On a floured work counter, roll out the pie dough thinly, cut out circles, and use to line 12 tartlet pans. Prick the bottoms and press a piece of foil into each tart shell. Bake in the oven for 10–15 minutes, until light golden. Remove the foil and bake for an additional 2-3 minutes. Let cool on a wire rack.

2 To make the filling, mix half the maple syrup and half the cream in a bowl. Put the sugar, cream of tartar, and water in a pan and heat gently until the sugar dissolves. Bring to a boil and boil until light golden. Remove from the heat and stir in the maple syrup and cream mixture.

3 Return the pan to the heat and cook to the soft ball stage (240°F/116°C): that is, when a little of the mixture dropped into a bowl of cold water forms a soft ball. Stir in the remaining cream and leave until warm. Brush the remaining maple syrup over the edges of the tarts. Put the pecans in the pastry shells and spoon in the toffee. Top each one with a pecan. Let cool.

Sicilian Ricotta Tart

Pine nuts and candied peel are included in the filling of this Italian specialty.

30 mins   1 hr 10 mins

SERVES 6

INGREDIENTS

1 package frozen sweetened pie dough, thawed

FILLING

1 cup ricotta cheese

2 eggs, beaten

¼ cup golden superfine sugar

½ cup pine nuts

scant ½ cup candied mixed peel

finely grated rind of 1 lemon

½ tsp vanilla extract

confectioners' sugar, for dusting

1 Preheat the oven to 400°F/200°C. Use the pastry to line a 20-cm/8-inch tart pan. Fill with dried beans and bake blind for 20 minutes. Reduce the temperature to 350°F/180°C.

2 Press the ricotta through a strainer into a bowl. Mix in the eggs, sugar, pine nuts, candied peel, lemon rind, and vanilla extract. Pour into the pastry shell.

3 Bake for 45 minutes, until set. Cool, then dust with confectioners' sugar.

COOK'S TIP
If possible, buy whole pieces of candied peel and chop them yourself.

Cheese & Apple Tart

Chopped apples, dates, and brown sugar combined with tasty cheese make this a sweet tart with a difference.

 15 mins

 45–50 mins

SERVES 8

INGREDIENTS

butter, for greasing

1½ cups self-rising flour

1 tsp baking powder

pinch of salt

⅓ cup brown sugar

generous 1 cup pitted dates, chopped

1 lb 2 oz/500 g dessert apples,
   cored and chopped

¼ cup chopped walnuts

¼ cup sunflower oil

2 eggs

1¾ cups grated hard cheese,
   such as Cheddar

1 Preheat the oven to 350°F/180°C. Grease a 9-inch/23-cm loose-bottomed tart pan with a little butter and line with parchment paper.

2 Sift the flour, baking powder, and salt into a large bowl. Stir in the brown sugar and the dates, apples, and walnuts. Mix together until thoroughly combined.

3 Beat the oil and eggs together and add the mixture to the dry ingredients. Stir with a wooden spoon until well combined.

4 Spoon half of the batter into the prepared pan and smooth the surface with the back of a spoon.

5 Sprinkle with the grated cheese, then spoon over the remaining batter, spreading it to the edges of the pan.

6 Bake in the preheated oven for 45–50 minutes, or until golden and firm to the touch.

7 Let the tart cool slightly in the pan. Remove the tart from the pan and serve warm.

COOK'S TIP
This is a deliciously moist tart. Any leftovers should be stored in the refrigerator and heated to serve.

Chocolate Crumble Pie

This substantial tart has a crisp topping of nuts, chocolate, and almond-flavored amaretti cookies.

35 mins plus
1 hr 30 mins
resting/chilling

35 mins

SERVES 8

INGREDIENTS

1½ cups all-purpose flour

1 tsp baking powder

4 oz/115 g sweet butter

¼ cup superfine sugar

1 egg yolk

⅔ cup heavy cream

⅔ cup milk

8 oz/225 g semisweet chocolate, chopped

2 eggs

CRUMBLE TOPPING

1 cup brown sugar

1 cup toasted pecans

4 oz/115 g semisweet chocolate

3 oz/85 g amaretti cookies

1 tsp unsweetened cocoa

1 To make the pie dough, put the flour, baking powder, butter, and sugar into a food processor and pulse to mix. Add the egg and a little cold water, if necessary, to bring the dough together. (If you don't have a food processor sift the flour and baking powder into a large bowl and rub in the butter, stir in the sugar and add the egg and a little water to bring the dough together.) Turn the dough out, knead briefly and wrap in plastic wrap. Chill in the refrigerator for 30 minutes.

2 Preheat the oven to 375°F/190°C. Roll out the pie dough and use to line a 9-inch/23-cm loose-bottomed tart pan. Prick the base with a fork. Line with parchment paper, fill with dried beans, and bake blind for 15 minutes. Remove the

paper and beans and set aside. Reduce the oven temperature to 350°F/180°C.

3 In a pan bring the cream and milk to a boil, remove from the heat, and add the chocolate. Stir until melted and smooth. Beat the eggs and add to the chocolate mixture, mix thoroughly and pour into the tart shell. Bake for 15 minutes, remove from the oven, and let rest for 1 hour.

4 When you are ready to serve the tart, put the topping ingredients into the food processor and pulse to chop. (If you don't have a processor put the sugar in a large bowl, chop the nuts and chocolate with a large knife and crush the cookies, then add to the bowl with the unsweetened cocoa and mix well.) The mixture should resemble coarse bread crumbs. Scatter over the tart, then serve it sliced.

Chocolate Mousse Tart

The smooth mousse topping contrasts deliciously with the crumbly cookie base in this elegant tart.

30 mins plus 8 hrs chilling   5 mins

SERVES 8

INGREDIENTS

3 oz/85 g graham crackers, crushed

3 oz/85 g amaretti cookies, crushed

2½ oz/70 g butter, melted

TOPPING

7 oz/200 g semisweet chocolate

4 oz/115 g milk chocolate

3 large eggs, separated

¼ cup superfine sugar

3 chocolate flake bars

1   To make the base, mix the graham crackers and amaretti cookies with the butter and press well into the bottom of a 9-inch/23-cm springform cake pan. Chill in the refrigerator.

2   Melt the semisweet and milk chocolate in a heatproof bowl set over a pan of gently simmering water. Cool slightly, then add the egg yolks and mix well.

3   Whisk the egg whites until they form soft peaks, then add the superfine sugar, and whisk until stiff.

4   Fold the chocolate into the egg whites and pour over the cookie base. Chill in the refrigerator for 8 hours or overnight.

5   When you are ready to serve the tart, unmold it, transfer to a serving dish, and crumble the chocolate flake bars over the top.

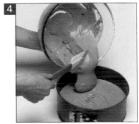

Crème Brûlée Tarts

Serve these melt-in-the-mouth tarts with fresh fruit, such as mixed summer berries, if you wish.

40 mins plus up to 12 hrs chilling | 25 mins

SERVES 6

INGREDIENTS

PIE DOUGH

1¼ cups all-purpose flour, plus extra for dusting

2 tbsp superfine sugar

4 oz/115 g cup butter, cut into small pieces

1 tbsp water

FILLING

4 egg yolks

¼ cup superfine sugar

1¾ cups heavy cream

1 tsp vanilla extract

raw sugar, for sprinkling

1 To make the pie dough, place the flour and sugar in a bowl and rub in the butter with your fingertips until the mixture resembles bread crumbs. Add the water and work the mixture together until a soft dough has formed. Wrap and chill in the refrigerator for 30 minutes.

2 On a lightly floured work counter, roll out the dough to line 6 tart pans, each 4 inches/10 cm wide. Prick the bottom of the pastry shells with a fork and chill in the refrigerator for 20 minutes.

3 Preheat the oven to 375°F/190°C. Line the shells with foil and dried beans and bake blind in the preheated oven for 15 minutes. Remove the foil and beans and cook for an additional 10 minutes, until crisp and golden. Let cool.

4 Meanwhile, make the filling. In a bowl, beat the egg yolks and sugar until

pale. Heat the cream and vanilla extract in a small pan until just below boiling point, then pour it on to the egg mixture, whisking constantly.

5 Return the mixture to a clean pan and bring to just below a boil, stirring constantly until thick. Do not let the mixture boil or it will curdle.

6 Let the mixture cool slightly, then pour it into the pastry shells. Let cool and then chill overnight in the refrigerator.

7 Sprinkle the tarts with the sugar. Place under a preheated hot broiler for a few minutes to caramelize. Let cool, then chill for 2 hours before serving.

Mini Frangipane Tartlets

These little tartlets have an unusual lime-flavored pastry, and are filled with a delicious almond frangipane mixture.

🍲 45 mins ⏰ 15 mins

SERVES 12

INGREDIENTS

scant 1 cup all-purpose flour, plus extra for dusting

2¾ oz/75 g butter, softened

1 tsp grated lime rind

1 tbsp lime juice

¼ cup superfine sugar

1 egg

¼ cup ground almonds

⅓ cup confectioners' sugar, sifted

½ tbsp water

1 Preheat the oven to 400°F/200°C. Reserve 5 teaspoons of the flour and 3 teaspoons of the butter and set aside.

2 Rub the remaining butter into the remaining flour with your fingertips until the mixture resembles fine bread crumbs. Stir in the lime rind, followed by the lime juice, and bring the mixture together to form a soft dough.

3 On a lightly floured work counter, roll out the dough thinly. Stamp out 12 circles, 3 inches/7.5 cm in diameter and line a shallow muffin pan.

4 In a bowl, cream together the reserved butter with the superfine sugar until pale and fluffy.

5 Mix in the egg, then the ground almonds, and the reserved flour.

6 Divide the mixture among the pastry shells and smooth the tops.

7 Bake in the preheated oven for 15 minutes, until set and lightly golden. Remove the tartlets from the pan, place on wire racks, and let cool completely.

8 Mix the confectioners' sugar with the water. Drizzle a little of this frosting over each tartlet and serve.

COOK'S TIP

These tartlets can be made in advance. Store them in an airtight container and decorate them just before serving.

Summer Fruit Tartlets

These small almond pastry shells filled with bright summer fruits taste as good as they look.

25 mins plus
30 mins chilling

10–15 mins

MAKES 12

INGREDIENTS

PIE DOUGH

1⅔ cups all-purpose flour

generous ½ cup confectioners' sugar

½ cup ground almonds

4 oz/115 g butter

1 egg yolk

1 tbsp milk

FILLING

1 cup cream cheese

confectioners' sugar, to taste

1½ cups fresh summer fruits, such as
    red and white currants, raspberries,
    and small strawberries

TO DECORATE

sifted confectioners' sugar

1 To make the pie dough, sift the flour and confectioners' sugar into a bowl. Stir in the ground almonds. Add the butter and rub in until the mixture resembles bread crumbs. Add the egg yolk and milk and work in with a spatula, then with fingers until the dough binds together. Wrap the dough in plastic wrap and chill for 30 minutes.

2 Preheat the oven to 400°F/200°C. On a floured work counter, roll out the pie dough and use to line 12 deep tartlet pans or individual brioche molds. Prick the bases. Press a piece of foil into each tartlet, covering the edges. Bake blind for 10–15 minutes, until light golden brown. Remove the foil and bake for an additional 2–3 minutes. Transfer to a wire rack to cool.

3 To make the filling, put the cream cheese and sugar in a bowl and mix together. Put a tablespoonful of filling in each pastry shell and arrange the fruit on top. Dust with sifted confectioners' sugar and serve at once.

VARIATION
The fruit in the tarts could be brushed with warmed red currant jelly to make an attractive glaze.

White Chocolate Tarts

These dainty little tarts make a delicious afternoon treat, and are also wonderful for serving after dinner with coffee.

25 mins plus 1 hr 35 mins chilling

15 mins

SERVES 4

I N G R E D I E N T S

generous 1 cup all-purpose flour, plus extra for dusting

2 tbsp golden superfine sugar

5½ oz/150 g chilled butter, diced

2 egg yolks

2 tbsp cold water

semisweet chocolate curls (see page 9), to decorate

unsweetened cocoa, to dust

FILLING

1 vanilla bean

1¾ cups heavy cream

12 oz/350 g white chocolate, broken into pieces

1 Place the flour and sugar in a bowl. Add the butter and rub it in until the mixture resembles fine bread crumbs. Place the egg yolks and water in a separate bowl and mix together. Stir into the dry ingredients and mix to form a dough. Knead for 1 minute, or until smooth. Wrap in plastic wrap and let chill for 20 minutes.

2 Preheat the oven to 400°F/200°C. Roll out the dough on a floured work counter and use to line 12 tartlet molds. Prick the bases, cover, and let chill for 15 minutes. Line the cases with foil and dried beans and bake for 10 minutes. Remove the beans and foil and cook for an additional 5 minutes. Let cool.

3 To make the filling, split the vanilla bean lengthwise and scrape out the black seeds with a knife. Place the seeds in a pan with the cream and heat until almost boiling. Melt the chocolate in a heatproof bowl set over a pan of gently simmering water, then pour over the hot cream. Keep stirring until smooth. Whisk the mixture with an electric whisk until thickened and the whisk leaves a trail when lifted. Let chill in the refrigerator for 30 minutes, then whisk until soft peaks form. Divide the filling between the pastry shells and let chill for 30 minutes. Decorate with chocolate curls and dust with unsweetened cocoa.

Pear Tarts

These tarts are quick to prepare because they are made with ready-made puff pastry. The finished result is rich and buttery.

35 mins plus
30 mins chilling

20 mins

SERVES 6

I N G R E D I E N T S

9 oz/250 g frozen ready-made puff pastry, thawed

all-purpose flour, for dusting

2 tbsp brown sugar

2 tbsp butter, plus extra for brushing

1 tbsp finely chopped preserved ginger

3 pears, peeled, halved, and cored

cream, to serve

1 Roll out the puff pastry on a lightly floured work counter. Cut or stamp out 6 circles, each about 4 inches/10 cm in diameter.

2 Place the circles on a large cookie sheet and chill in the refrigerator for 30 minutes.

3 Cream together the brown sugar and butter in a small bowl, then stir in the chopped preserved ginger.

4 Preheat the oven to 400°F/200°C. Prick the pastry circles with a fork and spread a little of the ginger mixture on to each one.

5 Slice the pears halves lengthwise, keeping them intact at the tip. Fan out the slices slightly.

6 Place a fanned-out pear half on top of each pie dough circle. Make small flutes around the edge of the circles with the back of a knife blade and brush each pear half with melted butter.

7 Bake in the preheated oven for 15–20 minutes, until the pastry is well risen and golden. Let cool slightly before serving the tarts warm with a little cream.

COOK'S TIP

If you prefer, serve these tarts with vanilla ice cream for a delicious dessert.

Chocolate Fudge Tart

This rich, fudgy tart is sure to become a favorite, and is quick and easy to prepare using ready-made pastry.

45 mins   1 hr 15 mins

SERVES 6–8

INGREDIENTS

12 oz/350 g ready-made unsweetened pie dough

all-purpose flour, for dusting

confectioners' sugar, for dusting

FILLING

5 oz/140 g semisweet chocolate, chopped finely

6 oz/175 g butter, diced

1¾ cups golden granulated sugar

¾ cup all-purpose flour

½ tsp vanilla extract

6 eggs, beaten

TO DECORATE

⅔ cup whipped cream

ground cinnamon

1   Preheat the oven to 400°F/200°C. Roll out the pie dough on a lightly floured counter and use to line an 8-inch/20-cm deep loose-bottomed tart pan. Prick the dough base lightly with a fork, then line with foil and fill with pie weights. Bake in the oven for 12–15 minutes, or until the dough no longer looks raw. Remove the beans and foil and bake for an additional 10 minutes, or until the dough is firm. Let cool. Reduce the oven temperature to 350°F/180°C.

2   To make the filling, place the chocolate and butter in a heatproof bowl and set over a pan of gently simmering water until melted. Stir until smooth, then remove from the heat and let cool. Place the sugar, flour, vanilla extract, and eggs in a separate bowl and whisk until well blended. Stir in the butter and chocolate mixture.

3   Pour the filling into the pastry shell and bake in the oven for 50 minutes, or until the filling is just set. Transfer to a wire rack to cool completely. Dust with confectioners' sugar before serving with a little whipped cream lightly sprinkled with cinnamon.

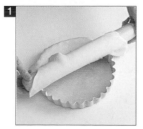

Chocolate & Chestnut Tart

This cookie crumb shell is ideal if you do not like making pastry. Try it with whipped cream, decorated with chocolate caraque.

30 mins plus 1 hr chilling

45 mins

SERVES 8

INGREDIENTS

COOKIE SHELL

3 oz/85 g butter

9 oz/250 g gingersnaps, crushed

FILLING

6 oz/175 g unsweetened chestnut purée

¼ cup golden superfine sugar

¾ cup ricotta cheese

2 eggs

3½ oz/100 g semisweet chocolate, broken into pieces

3 pieces preserved ginger, chopped very finely

¼ cup ground almonds

TO DECORATE

⅔ cup whipping cream

chocolate caraque (see page 9)

1 Preheat the oven to 350°F/180°C. Put the butter in a pan and heat gently until just melted. Stir in the crushed gingersnaps. Press the crumbs on to the bottom and up the sides of a 9-inch/23-cm loose-bottomed tart pan. Bake in the preheated oven for 10 minutes, then set aside to cool.

2 To make the filling, put the chestnut purée and sugar in a bowl and beat until smooth. Put the ricotta cheese and eggs in another bowl and beat until smooth and combined. Put the chocolate in a heatproof bowl set over a pan of gently simmering water until melted. Remove the pan from the heat and let cool slightly. Carefully stir the melted chocolate into the ricotta mixture. Add the chestnut purée mixture and mix thoroughly. Stir in the ginger and ground almonds.

3 Pour the filling into the cookie shell and bake in the preheated oven for 35 minutes, until lightly set. Let cool then chill thoroughly. Before serving, put the whipping cream in a bowl and whip until thick. Spread over the top of the tart and decorate with chocolate caraque.

Lemon & Chocolate Tart

In this tart, a crisp chocolate pastry shell is the perfect foil for the smooth creamy lemon filling. It is the perfect end to a supper party.

50 mins plus
30 mins chilling

1 hr 15 mins

SERVES 8

INGREDIENTS

¾ cup all-purpose flour

¼ cup unsweetened cocoa

2¾ oz/75 g butter

¼ cup ground almonds

¼ cup golden superfine sugar

1 egg, beaten

chocolate curls or caraque (see page 9), to decorate

FILLING

4 eggs

1 egg yolk

1 cup golden superfine sugar

⅔ cup heavy cream

grated rind and juice of 2 lemons

1 Sift the flour and unsweetened cocoa into a food processor. Add the butter, almonds, sugar, and egg and process until the mixture forms a ball. Gather the dough together and press into a flattened ball. Place in the center of an 8½-inch/22-cm loose-bottomed tart pan and press evenly over the bottom of the pan with your fingers, then work the pie dough up the sides with your thumbs. Allow any excess dough to go over the edge. Cover and let chill for 30 minutes.

2 Preheat the oven to 400°F/200°C. Trim off excess dough. Prick the dough base lightly with a fork, then line with parchment paper and fill with pie weights. Bake for 12–15 minutes, or until the dough no longer looks raw. Remove the weights and paper, return to the oven and bake for 10 minutes, or until the pastry is firm. Let cool. Reduce the oven temperature to 300°F/150°C.

3 To make the filling, whisk the whole eggs, egg yolk, and sugar together until smooth. Add the cream and whisk again, then stir in the lemon rind and juice. Pour the filling into the pastry shell and bake for 50 minutes, or until just set. When the tart is cooked, remove the tart ring and let cool. Decorate with chocolate curls or caraque before serving.

Boston Chocolate Pie

This lighter version of the popular chocolate cream pie is made with yogurt and sour cream.

25 mins

35 mins

SERVES 6

INGREDIENTS

8 oz/225 g ready-prepared pie dough

8 oz/225 g semisweet chocolate, to make caraque (see page 9)

FILLING

3 eggs

½ cup superfine sugar

½ cup flour, plus extra for dusting

1 tbsp confectioners' sugar

pinch of salt

1 tsp vanilla extract

1⅔ cups milk

⅔ cup plain yogurt

5½ oz/150 g semisweet chocolate, broken into pieces

2 tbsp kirsch

TOPPING

⅔ cup sour cream or crème fraîche (see page 9)

1 Preheat the oven to 400°F/200°C. Roll out the pie dough and use to line a 9-inch/23-cm loose-bottomed tart pan. Prick the base with a fork, line with parchment paper and fill with dried beans. Bake blind for about 20 minutes in the preheated oven. Remove the beans and paper and return the tart shell to the oven for an additional 5 minutes. Remove from the oven and place on a wire rack to cool.

2 Make the chocolate caraque (see page 9) and set aside.

3 To make the filling, beat the eggs and sugar until fluffy. Sift in the flour, confectioners' sugar, and salt. Stir in the vanilla extract.

4 Bring the milk and yogurt to a boil in a small pan and sift on to the egg mixture. Pour into a heatproof bowl set over a pan of gently simmering water. Stir until it coats the back of a spoon.

5 Gently heat the chocolate with the kirsch in a small pan until the chocolate has melted. Stir into the custard. Remove from the heat and stand the bowl in cold water. Let it cool.

6 Pour the chocolate mixture into the pastry shell. Spread the sour cream over the chocolate, and arrange the chocolate caraque on top.

Chocolate Apple Lattice Tart

This is a tempting combination of rich chocolate pie dough and a cream-rich apple filling.

25 mins plus
1–1 hr 30 mins
cooling/chilling

40–45 mins

SERVES 4–6

INGREDIENTS

PIE DOUGH

scant 1½ cups all-purpose flour, plus extra for dusting

2 tbsp unsweetened cocoa

3 tbsp superfine sugar

3½ oz/100 g sweet butter, diced, plus extra for greasing

1–2 egg yolks, beaten

FILLING

1 cup heavy cream

2 eggs, beaten

1 tsp ground cinnamon

4 oz/115 g semisweet chocolate, grated

4 dessert apples, peeled, sliced, and brushed with lemon juice

3 tbsp raw sugar

whipped cream, to serve

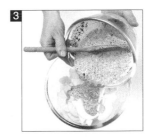

1 To make the pie dough, sift the flour and cocoa into a bowl. Add the sugar, rub in the butter and mix well. Stir in enough egg yolk to form a dough. Form into a ball, wrap in foil and chill for 45 minutes.

2 Preheat the oven to 350°F/180°C. Grease a 10-inch/25-cm loose-bottomed tart pan. Roll out the dough on a lightly floured work surface and use three-quarters of it to line the tin.

3 Beat together the cream, the eggs (reserving a little for glazing), cinnamon, and chocolate in a bowl. Stir in the apples. Spoon into the tart shell, then sprinkle over the raw sugar. Roll out the remaining dough and cut into long, thin strips, then arrange over the tart to form a lattice pattern. Brush the pastry strips with the reserved egg yolk, then bake in the preheated oven for 40–45 minutes.

4 Remove from the oven and let cool to room temperature. Serve with whipped cream.

Crispy Chocolate Pie

The rich, whiskey-flavored chocolate filling makes this delicious almond crust pie very moreish.

25 mins plus
30 mins cooling   35–40 mins

SERVES 6

INGREDIENTS

2 tsp butter, for greasing

2 egg whites

1 cup ground almonds

¼ cup ground rice

⅔ cup superfine sugar

¼ tsp almond extract

8 oz/225 g semisweet chocolate,
   broken into small pieces

4 egg yolks

4 tbsp confectioners' sugar

4 tbsp whiskey

4 tbsp heavy cream

TO DECORATE

⅔ cup whipped cream

2 oz/55 g semisweet chocolate, grated

1 Preheat the oven to 325°F/160°C. Grease an 8-inch/20-cm tart pan and line the bottom with parchment paper. Whisk the egg whites until stiff peaks form. Gently fold in the ground almonds, ground rice, superfine sugar, and almond extract. Spread the mixture over the bottom and sides of the prepared pan. Bake in the preheated oven for 15 minutes.

2 Meanwhile, put the chocolate in a heatproof bowl set over a pan of gently simmering water until melted. Remove from the heat and cool slightly, then beat in the egg yolks, confectioners' sugar, whiskey, and 4 tablespoons cream until thoroughly incorporated.

3 Remove the tart pan from the oven and pour in the chocolate mixture. Cover with foil, return to the oven, and bake at the same temperature for 20–25 minutes, until set. Remove from the oven and let cool completely.

4 Mix together the whipped cream and 1 oz/25 g of the grated chocolate, then spread over the cake. Top with the remaining grated chocolate, and serve immediately.

Chocolate & Almond Tart

This is a variation on the classic pecan pie recipe—here, almonds and chocolate are encased in a thick syrup filling.

 30 mins plus
1 hr chilling

🕐 1 hr

SERVES 8

INGREDIENTS

PIE DOUGH

1¼ cups all-purpose flour, plus extra
    for dusting

2 tbsp superfine sugar

4 oz/115 g butter, cut into small pieces

1 tbsp water

FILLING

½ cup corn syrup

4 tbsp butter

½ cup brown sugar

3 eggs, beaten lightly

½ cup whole blanched almonds,
    chopped coarsely

3½ oz/100 g white chocolate,
    chopped coarsely

cream, to serve (optional)

1 To make the pie dough, place the flour and sugar in a mixing bowl and rub in the butter with your fingers. Add the water and work the mixture together until a soft dough has formed. Wrap and let chill for 30 minutes.

2 On a lightly floured work counter, roll out the dough and line a 9½-inch/24-cm loose-bottomed tart pan. Prick the pastry shell with the tines of a fork and let chill for 30 minutes. Preheat the oven to 375°F/190°C. Line the shell with foil and dried beans and bake blind in the preheated oven for 15 minutes. Remove the foil and dried beans and cook for an additional 15 minutes.

3 To make the filling, gently melt the syrup, butter, and sugar together in a pan. Remove from the heat and let cool slightly. Stir in the beaten eggs, almonds, and chocolate.

4 Pour the chocolate and nut filling into the prepared pastry shell and cook in the oven for 30–35 minutes, or until just set. Let cool before removing the tart from the pan. Serve with cream, if wished.

VARIATION
You can use a mixture of white and semisweet chocolate for this tart if preferred.

Chocolate Orange Tart

Chocolate and orange are flavors that were made for each other. If time is limited, just serve with plain whipped cream.

SERVES 4

INGREDIENTS

PIE DOUGH

1⅔ cups all-purpose flour, plus extra for dusting

3½ oz/100 g butter, cut into small pieces, plus extra for greasing

¼ cup confectioners' sugar, sifted

finely grated rind of 1 orange

1 egg yolk, beaten

3 tbsp milk

FILLING

7 oz/200 g semisweet chocolate, broken into small pieces

2 eggs, separated

scant ½ cup milk

½ cup superfine sugar

8 amaretti cookies, crushed

1 tbsp orange-flavored liqueur, such as Cointreau

ORANGE CREAM

1 tbsp finely grated orange rind

½ cup heavy cream

finely grated orange rind, to decorate

1 To make the pie dough, sift the flour into a bowl. Rub in the butter. Mix in the confectioners' sugar, orange rind, egg yolk, and milk. Knead briefly, then let stand for 30 minutes. Preheat the oven to 350°F/180°C. Grease a 9-inch/23-cm tart pan with butter. Roll out two-thirds of the pie dough to a thickness of ¼ inch/5 mm, and use to line the bottom and sides of the pan.

2 To make the filling, melt the chocolate in a heatproof bowl set over a pan of gently simmering water. Beat in the egg yolks, then the milk. Remove from the heat. In a separate bowl, whisk the egg whites until stiff, then stir in the sugar. Fold the egg whites into the chocolate, then stir in the cookies and liqueur. Spoon into the pastry shell. Roll out the remaining pie dough, cut into strips, and use to form a lattice over the tart. Bake in the preheated oven for 1 hour. To make the orange cream, beat together the orange rind and cream. Remove the tart from the oven, decorate with orange rind, and serve with the orange cream.

Chocolate, Pear & Almond Tart

This attractive tart is filled with pears cooked in a chocolate and almond-flavored sponge. It is delicious hot or cold.

30 mins plus
10 mins freezing   35 mins

SERVES 6

INGREDIENTS

3 oz/85 g margarine, plus extra for greasing

¾ cup all-purpose flour

¼ cup ground almonds

about 3 tbsp water

FILLING

400 g/14 oz canned pear halves
   (in natural juice)

4 tbsp butter

4 tbsp superfine sugar

2 eggs, beaten

1 cup ground almonds

2 tbsp unsweetened cocoa

few drops almond extract

confectioners' sugar, for dusting

CHOCOLATE SAUCE

4 tbsp superfine sugar

3 tbsp corn syrup

generous ⅓ cup water

6 oz/175 g semisweet chocolate,
   broken into pieces

2 tbsp butter

1 Lightly grease an 8-inch/20-cm tart pan. Sift the flour into a mixing bowl and stir in the almonds. Rub in the margarine with your fingertips until the mixture resembles bread crumbs. Add enough water to mix to a soft dough. Cover, chill in the freezer for 10 minutes, then roll out and use to line the pan. Prick the bottom and chill.

2 Preheat the oven to 400°F/200°C. Meanwhile, make the filling. Drain the pears well. Beat the butter and sugar until light and fluffy. Beat in the eggs. Fold in the almonds, unsweetened cocoa, and almond extract. Spread the chocolate mixture in the pastry shell and arrange the pears on top, pressing down lightly. Bake in the center of the preheated oven for 30 minutes, or until the filling has risen. Let cool slightly and transfer to a serving dish, if wished. Dust with sugar.

3 To make the sauce, place the sugar, syrup, and water in a pan and heat gently, stirring until the sugar dissolves. Boil gently for 1 minute. Remove from the heat, add the chocolate and butter, and stir until melted. Serve with the tart.

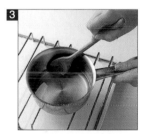

Chocolate Pear Tart

The classic partnership of chocolate and pears appears in many forms, both hot and cold. This tart will soon become a family favorite.

1 hr 15 mins   30 mins

SERVES 8

I N G R E D I E N T S

PIE DOUGH

scant 1 cup all-purpose flour, plus extra for dusting

pinch of salt

2 tbsp superfine sugar

4 oz/115 g butter, sweet for preference, cut into small pieces

1 egg yolk

1 tbsp lemon juice

TOPPING

4 oz/115 g semisweet chocolate, grated

4 pears

½ cup light cream

1 egg

1 egg yolk

½ tsp almond extract

3 tbsp superfine sugar

1 To make the pie dough, sift the flour and salt into a mixing bowl. Add the sugar and butter and mix well in an electric mixer with a dough hook or with two forks until thoroughly incorporated. Stir in the egg yolk and the lemon juice to form a dough. Form the dough into a ball, wrap in plastic wrap and chill in the refrigerator for 30 minutes.

2 Preheat the oven to 400°F/200°C. Roll out the dough on a lightly floured work counter and use it to line a 10-inch/25-cm loose-bottomed tart pan. Sprinkle the grated semisweet chocolate over the bottom of the pastry shell. Peel the pears, cut them in half lengthwise, and remove the cores. Thinly slice each pear half and fan out slightly. Using a spatula, scoop up each sliced pear half and arrange in the tart shell.

3 Beat together the cream, egg, extra yolk, and almond extract, and spoon the mixture over the pears. Sprinkle the sugar over the tart.

4 Bake in the preheated oven for 10 minutes, then reduce the temperature to 350°F/180°C and bake for an additional 20 minutes, until the pears are starting to caramelize and the filling is just set. Remove from the oven and cool to room temperature before serving.

Pear Tart

Pears are a very popular fruit in Italy. In this recipe they are flavored with almonds, cinnamon, raisins, and apricot jelly.

30 mins plus
1 hr chilling

50 mins

SERVES 6

INGREDIENTS

2¼ cups all-purpose flour

pinch of salt

½ cup superfine sugar

4 oz/115 g butter, cut into small pieces

1 egg

1 egg yolk

few drops vanilla extract

2–3 tsp water

sifted confectioners' sugar, for sprinkling

FILLING

4 tbsp apricot jelly

2 oz/55 g amaretti or ratafia
cookies, crumbled

1 lb 14 oz–2 lb 4 oz/850 g–1 kg pears,
peeled and cored

1 tsp ground cinnamon

½ cup raisins

⅓ cup brown or raw sugar

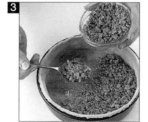

1 Sift the flour and salt on to a work counter, make a well in the center, and add the sugar, butter, egg, egg yolk, vanilla extract, and most of the water.

2 Using your fingers, gradually work the flour into the other ingredients to form a smooth dough, adding more water if necessary. Alternatively, put all the ingredients into a food processor and process until smooth. Wrap in plastic wrap and chill for 1 hour or until firm.

3 Preheat the oven to 400°F/200°C. Roll out three-quarters of the dough and use to line a shallow 10-inch/25-cm cake pan or deep tart pan. Spread the jelly over the bottom and sprinkle with the crushed cookies.

4 Slice the pears very thinly. Arrange over the cookies in the pastry shell. Sprinkle with cinnamon, then with raisins, and finally with brown sugar.

5 Roll out a thin sausage shape using one-third of the remaining pie dough, and place around the edge of the pie. Roll the remainder into thin sausages and arrange in a lattice over the pie, 4 or 5 strips in each direction, attaching them to the strip around the edge.

6 Cook in the preheated oven for 50 minutes, until golden brown and cooked through. Let cool, then serve warm or chilled, sprinkled with sifted confectioners' sugar.

Pear & Cardamom Tarte Tatin

This is a variation on Tarte Tatin, the classic French upside-down apple tart. Serve warm with cream or ice cream if desired.

20 mins   35 mins

SERVES 4

INGREDIENTS

4 tbsp butter, softened

¼ cup golden superfine sugar

seeds from 10 cardamoms

all-purpose flour, for dusting

8 oz/225 g puff pastry, thawed if frozen

3 ripe pears

1 Preheat the oven to 425°F/220°C. Spread the butter over the bottom of a 7-inch/18-cm ovenproof skillet or heavy-based cake pan. Spread the sugar evenly over the butter and scatter the cardamom seeds over the sugar. On a floured work counter, roll out the pie dough to a circle slightly larger than the skillet or pan. Prick the pie dough lightly, place it on a plate, and chill while preparing the pears.

2 Peel the pears, cut in half lengthwise, and cut out the cores. Arrange the pears, rounded-side down, on the butter and sugar. Set the skillet over medium heat until the sugar melts and starts to bubble with the butter and juice from the pears.

If any areas are browning more than others, move the skillet, but do not stir. As soon as the sugar has caramelized remove the skillet or pan carefully from the heat.

3 Place the pie dough on top, tucking the edges down the side of the skillet or pan. Transfer to the oven and bake for

25 minutes, until the pastry is well risen and golden. Leave the tart in the skillet or pan for 2–3 minutes, until the juices have stopped bubbling. Invert the skillet or pan over a plate and shake to release the tart. It may be necessary to slide a spatula underneath the pears to loosen them. Serve the tart warm with cream.

COOK'S TIP
Choose fairly large round pears for this tart, rather than the more elongated varieties.

Individual Apricot Tartes Tatin

These pretty little apricot tarts look and taste delicious drizzled with the chocolate sauce.

35 mins   20–25 mins

MAKES 12

INGREDIENTS

8 oz/225 g butter, sweet for preference, plus extra for greasing

1 cup brown sugar

6 fresh apricots, halved and pitted

1 cup all-purpose flour

pinch of salt

1 tbsp superfine sugar

1 egg yolk

1 tbsp cold water

CHOCOLATE SAUCE

4 oz/115 g semisweet chocolate

2 tbsp butter, sweet for preference

1 Preheat the oven to 400°F/200°C. To make the sauce, melt the chocolate and butter together in a heatproof bowl set over a pan of gently simmering water and whisk until smooth. Set aside.

2 Grease 2 x 6-hole muffin pans with 1 tablespoon of butter then line each with disks of waxed paper.

3 Beat 5 oz/140 g butter with the brown sugar until very soft and divide between the holes. Place an apricot half, cut-side up, in each.

4 To make the pie dough, rub in the remaining 3 oz/85 g butter to the flour and salt, then stir in the sugar. The mixture should resemble bread crumbs. Add the egg and a little cold water, if needed, to make a dough. Knead lightly and roll out. Cut out 12 x 3-inch/7.5-cm disks and fit them over the apricot halves.

5 Bake for 15–20 minutes, until crisp and golden. Remove from the oven and let stand for 5 minutes. Turn out, with the apricot on top, and drizzle with the chocolate sauce to serve.

Chocolate Nut Strudel

This is an indulgent chocolate version of a classic strudel. It is delicious served with vanilla ice cream.

20 mins   20–25 mins

SERVES 6

INGREDIENTS

1 tbsp butter, for greasing

½ cup mixed chopped nuts

4 oz/115 g each of semisweet, milk, and white chocolate, chopped

5 oz/150 g butter, sweet for preference

7 oz/200 g phyllo pastry

3 tbsp corn syrup

¼ cup confectioners' sugar

1 Preheat the oven to 375°F/190°C. Lightly grease a cookie sheet with the 1 tablespoon of butter. Reserve 1 tablespoon nuts. Mix the 3 types of chocolate together.

2 Place 1 sheet of phyllo on a clean dish towel. Melt the butter and brush the sheet of phyllo with butter, drizzle with a little syrup, and sprinkle with some nuts and chocolate. Place another sheet of phyllo on top and repeat until you have used all the nuts and chocolate.

3 Use the dish towel to help you carefully roll up the strudel and place on the cookie sheet, drizzle with a little more corn syrup, and sprinkle with the reserved nuts. Bake for 20–25 minutes. If the nuts start to brown too much, cover the strudel with foil.

4 Sprinkle with confectioners' sugar, slice and eat warm with ice cream.

Pear & Pecan Strudel

Crisp phyllo pastry is wrapped round a nutty pear filling in this easy-to-make strudel. Delicious served warm.

15 mins   30 mins

SERVE 4

INGREDIENTS

2 ripe pears

4 tbsp butter

1 cup fresh white bread crumbs

¾ cup pecans, chopped

¼ cup light muscovado sugar

finely grated rind of 1 orange

2 tbsp orange juice

3½ oz/100 g phyllo pastry

6 tbsp orange blossom honey

sifted confectioners' sugar, for dusting

1 Preheat the oven to 400°F/200°C. Peel, core, and chop the pears. Put 1 tablespoon of butter in a skillet and gently fry the bread crumbs until golden. Transfer the bread crumbs to a bowl and add the pears, nuts, sugar, and orange rind. Put the remaining butter in a small pan and heat until melted.

2 Reserve one sheet of phyllo pastry, keeping it well wrapped, and brush the remaining phyllo sheets with a little melted butter. Spoon the nut filling on to the first phyllo sheet, leaving a 1-inch/2.5-cm margin round the edge, and build up the strudel by placing buttered sheets on top of the first, spreading each one with nut filling as you build up the layers. Drizzle the honey and orange juice over the top.

3 Fold the short ends over the filling, then roll up, starting at a long side. Carefully lift on to a cookie sheet, with the

join uppermost. Brush with any remaining melted butter and crumple the reserved sheet of phyllo pastry around the strudel. Bake for about 25 minutes, until golden and crisp. Dust with sifted confectioners' sugar and serve warm with strained plain yogurt.

COOK'S TIP
When working with phyllo pastry it is important to keep it covered until you are ready to use it, otherwise it will dry out very quickly.

Pecan Pie

Pecan pie is a classic recipe. Served with a spoonful of whipped cream or ice cream, this pie is the perfect finale to a special meal.

🍳 🍳 🍳

🍯 25 mins plus 30 mins chilling ⏲ 1 hr 5 mins

SERVES 8

INGREDIENTS

PIE DOUGH

2 cups all-purpose flour

pinch of salt

4 oz/115 g butter

1 tbsp shortening

generous ¼ cup golden superfine sugar

6 tbsp cold milk

FILLING

3 eggs

2½ cups dark muscovado sugar

1 tsp vanilla extract

pinch of salt

3 oz/85 g butter, melted

3 tbsp corn syrup

3 tbsp molasses

2 cups pecans, chopped coarsely

pecan halves, to decorate

1 To make the pie dough, sift the flour and salt into a mixing bowl and rub in the butter and shortening with your fingertips until the mixture resembles bread crumbs. Work in the sugar and add the milk. Work the mixture together until a soft dough has formed. Wrap and chill in the refrigerator for 30 minutes. Preheat the oven to 400°F/200°C. Roll out the pie dough and use it to line a 9–10-inch/23–25-cm tart pan. Trim off the excess by using the rolling pin over the top of the tart pan. Line with parchment paper then fill with dried beans. Bake blind in the preheated oven for about 20 minutes. Take out of the oven and remove the paper and dried beans. Reduce the oven temperature to 350°F/180°C and place a cookie sheet in the oven.

2 Put the eggs in a bowl and beat lightly. Beat in the sugar, vanilla extract, and salt. Stir in the melted butter, syrup, molasses, and chopped nuts. Pour into the pastry shell and decorate with the pecan halves.

3 Place on the heated cookie sheet and bake in the oven for 35-40 minutes, until the filling is set. Serve warm or at room temperature with cream or vanilla ice cream.

COOK'S TIP
Cover the pie with foil if the pastry is becoming too brown before the pie is cooked.

Chocolate Pecan Pie

This version of a favorite classic is packed with deliciously contrasting flavors and textures and is simply irresistible.

40 mins plus
2 hrs chilling

1 hr 15 mins

SERVES 4

I N G R E D I E N T S

PIE DOUGH

2½ cups all-purpose flour, plus extra
  for dusting

½ cup unsweetened cocoa

1 cup confectioners' sugar

pinch of salt

7 oz/200 g butter, sweet for preference,
  cut into small pieces

1 egg yolk

FILLING

3 oz/85 g semisweet chocolate,
  broken into pieces

3 cups shelled pecans

3 oz/85 g butter, sweet for preference

generous 1 cup brown sugar

3 eggs

2 tbsp heavy cream

¼ cup all-purpose flour

1 tbsp confectioners' sugar, for dusting

1 To make the pie dough, sift the flour, unsweetened cocoa, sugar, and salt into a mixing bowl and make a well in the center. Put the butter and egg yolk in the well and gradually mix in the dry ingredients. Knead lightly into a ball. Cover with plastic wrap and chill in the refrigerator for 1 hour.

2 Unwrap the dough and roll it out on a lightly floured work counter. Use it to line a 10-inch/25-cm nonstick springform pie pan and prick the shell with the tines of a fork. Preheat the oven to 350°F/180°C.

Line the pastry shell with parchment paper and fill with dried beans. Bake blind in the preheated oven for 15 minutes. Remove from the oven, discard the beans and paper, and let cool.

3 To make the filling, put the chocolate in a heatproof bowl set over a pan of gently simmering water until melted. Remove from the heat and set aside. Roughly chop 2 cups of the pecans and set aside. Mix the butter with one-third of the brown sugar. Beat in the eggs, one at a time, then add the remaining brown sugar and mix well. Stir in the cream, flour, melted chocolate, and chopped pecans.

4 Spoon the filling into the pastry shell and smooth the surface. Cut the remaining pecans in half and arrange in concentric circles over the pie.

5 Bake in the preheated oven at the same temperature for 30 minutes, then remove the pie and cover the top with foil to prevent it burning. Bake for an additional 25 minutes. Remove the pie from the oven and let cool slightly before removing from the pan and transferring to a wire rack to cool completely. Dust with confectioners' sugar.

Chocolate & Raspberry Tart

This is a very pretty and light white chocolate tart, swirled with raspberry sauce and served with fresh raspberries.

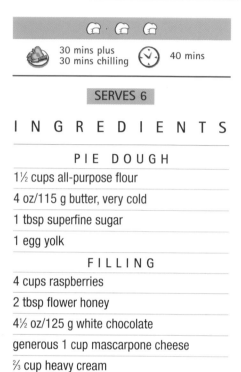

30 mins plus
30 mins chilling

40 mins

SERVES 6

INGREDIENTS

PIE DOUGH

1½ cups all-purpose flour

4 oz/115 g butter, very cold

1 tbsp superfine sugar

1 egg yolk

FILLING

4 cups raspberries

2 tbsp flower honey

4½ oz/125 g white chocolate

generous 1 cup mascarpone cheese

⅔ cup heavy cream

1 To make the pie dough, sift the flour into a bowl and grate in the butter. Rub in until the mixture resembles bread crumbs, then stir in the sugar, egg yolk, and enough cold water to form a softish ball. Roll out to fit an 8-inch/20-cm tart pan, prick the bottom with a fork, and chill in the refrigerator for 30 minutes.

2 Preheat the oven to 375°F/190°C. Line the pie dough with parchment paper, fill with dried beans, and bake blind for 15 minutes. Reduce the oven temperature to 350°F/180°C, remove the parchment paper and beans and cook for an additional 15–20 minutes. Let the tart shell cool completely and transfer from the tart pan on to a serving plate.

3 Reserve a handful of raspberries, then push the rest through a strainer into a small pan and mix with the honey. Boil until thick, then let cool completely.

4 Melt the white chocolate in a heatproof bowl set over a pan of gently simmering water, cool, then mix with the mascarpone. Whisk the cream until thick and mix into the mascarpone. Swirl in the raspberry sauce to give a marbled effect and spoon into the tart shell. Decorate with the remaining raspberries and serve.

COOK'S TIP

This tart would be equally delicious made with strawberries or blueberries.

Pine Nut Tart

This tart has a sweet filling made with creamy cheese and it is topped with pine nuts for a decorative finish and contrasting texture.

40 mins plus
1 hr chilling

1 hr 5 mins

SERVES 8

I N G R E D I E N T S

PIE DOUGH

1¼ cups all-purpose flour, plus extra for dusting

2 tbsp superfine sugar

4 oz/115 g butter, cut into small pieces

1 tbsp water

FILLING

1½ cups curd cheese

4 tbsp heavy cream

3 eggs

½ cup superfine sugar

grated rind of 1 orange

1 cup pine nuts

1 To make the pie dough, place the flour and sugar in a bowl and rub in the butter with your fingertips until the mixture resembles bread crumbs. Add the water and work the mixture together until a soft dough has formed. Wrap and chill in the refrigerator for 30 minutes.

2 On a lightly floured work counter, roll out the dough and line a 9½-inch/24-cm loose-bottomed tart pan. Prick the dough with the tines of a fork and let chill for 30 minutes.

3 Preheat the oven to 375°F/190°C. Line the pastry shell with foil and dried beans and bake in the preheated oven for 15 minutes. Remove the foil and beans and cook the pastry shell for an additional 15 minutes.

4 To make the filling, beat together the curd cheese, cream, eggs, sugar, orange rind, and half of the pine nuts. Pour the filling into the pastry shell and sprinkle over the remaining pine nuts.

5 Bake in the preheated oven for about 35 minutes or until the filling is just set. Let cool before serving.

VARIATION
Replace the pine nuts with slivered almonds, if you prefer.

Date & Apricot Tart

There is no need to add any extra sugar to this filling because the dry fruits are naturally sweet. Serve with hot custard if desired.

40 mins plus
30 mins chilling

50 mins

SERVES 8

I N G R E D I E N T S

2 cups whole-wheat flour, plus extra
for dusting

½ cup mixed nuts, ground

4 oz/115 g margarine, cut into small pieces

4 tbsp water

1 cup dried apricots, chopped

1⅓ cups chopped pitted dates

scant 1 cup unsweetened apple juice

1 tsp ground cinnamon

grated rind of 1 lemon

custard, to serve (optional)

1 Place the flour and ground nuts in a mixing bowl and rub in the margarine with your fingertips until the mixture resembles bread crumbs. Stir in the water and bring together to form a dough. Wrap the dough in plastic wrap and chill in the refrigerator for 30 minutes.

2 Meanwhile, place the apricots and dates in a pan, with the apple juice, cinnamon, and lemon rind. Bring to a boil, cover, and simmer over low heat for about 15 minutes until the fruit softens. Mash to a purée.

3 Preheat the oven to 400°F/200°C. Reserve a small ball of pie dough for making lattice strips. On a lightly floured work counter, roll out the rest of the dough to form a circle and use to line a 9-inch/23-cm loose-bottomed tart pan.

4 Spread the fruit filling evenly over the bottom of the pastry shell. Roll out the reserved pie dough and cut into strips

½ inch/1 cm wide. Cut the strips to fit the tart and twist them across the top of the fruit to form a decorative lattice pattern. Moisten the edges of the strips with a little water and seal them firmly around the rim of the tart.

5 Bake in the preheated oven for 25–30 minutes, until golden brown. Cut into slices and serve immediately with custard if wished.

Plum & Almond Tart

The flavors of plums and almonds make a particularly good combination.
This tart is delicious served warm with a spoonful of whipped cream.

20 mins plus
30 mins chilling   35–40 mins

SERVES 8

INGREDIENTS

PIE DOUGH

2 cups all-purpose flour

pinch of salt

4 oz/115 g butter

½ oz/25 g shortening

¼ cup golden superfine sugar

6 tbsp cold milk

FILLING

1 egg

1 egg yolk

½ cup golden superfine sugar

4 tbsp butter, melted

¾ cup ground almonds

1 tbsp cognac

2 lb/900 g plums, halved and pitted

3 tbsp golden superfine sugar, for sprinkling

whipped cream, to serve

1 To make the pie dough, sift the flour and salt into a mixing bowl and rub in the butter and shortening with your fingertips until the mixture resembles bread crumbs. Work in the sugar and add the milk. Work until a soft dough has formed. Wrap and chill in the refrigerator for 30 minutes. Preheat the oven to 400°F/200°C and place a cookie sheet in the oven to heat. Roll out the dough and use it to line a 9-inch/23-cm tart pan.

2 To make the filling, put the egg, the egg yolk, superfine sugar, melted butter, ground almonds, and cognac in a bowl and mix together. Spread the mixture in the tart shell.

3 Arrange the plum halves, cut-side up on top of the almond mixture. Fit them together lightly because they will shrink during cooking. Sprinkle with the superfine sugar and bake in the preheated oven for 35–40 minutes, until the filling is set and the pie crust is brown. Serve warm with whipped cream.

VARIATION
As an alternative to plums, apricots, cherries, or halved and sliced pears may be used.

Chocolate Plum Tarts

The dark rich chocolate filling in these tarts contrasts beautifully with the rich red color of the plums. Delicious served with ice cream.

30 mins plus
1 hr chilling/
freezing

35–40 mins

I N G R E D I E N T S

2¼ cups all-purpose flour

¼ cup confectioners' sugar

pinch of salt

6 oz/175 g butter, sweet for preference

F I L L I N G

4 tbsp butter

5 oz/140 g semisweet chocolate

2 egg yolks

1 whole egg

¼ cup superfine sugar, plus extra for sprinkling

3 ripe plums, halved and pitted

cream or ice cream, to serve

1 To make the pie dough, put the flour, sugar, and salt into a bowl and add the butter. Rub in until the mixture resembles bread crumbs, then add a little cold water to bring the dough together. Cover in plastic wrap and chill in the refrigerator for 30 minutes.

2 Remove the pie dough from the refrigerator and cut into 8 pieces. Roll out to fit 8 x 4-inch/10-cm individual tart pans. Freeze for 30 minutes. Preheat the oven to 350°F/180°C and bake the tart shells for 20–25 minutes until they are dried out. Remove from the oven and let cool on a wire rack.

3 Increase the oven temperature to 375°F/190°C. Melt the butter and chocolate for the filling in a heatproof bowl set over a pan of gently simmering water, stir, and let cool.

4 Whisk the egg yolks, whole egg, and sugar together, then add to the chocolate, mixing well. Divide among the tart shells. Thinly slice the plum halves, and divide the slices among the tarts, fanning out the slices for a pretty effect. Sprinkle with a little sugar and bake for 10–15 minutes, until set.

5 Remove carefully from the pans and serve with cream or ice cream.

Chocolate Almond Pithiviers

Pithiviers is a traditional French pastry stuffed with almond paste. This version adds chocolate for extra luxury.

15 mins plus
30 mins chilling

25 mins

SERVES 8

INGREDIENTS

4½ oz/125 g butter, sweet for preference, softened

½ cup superfine sugar

1 egg

scant 1 cup ground almonds

3 oz/75 g milk chocolate, grated

250 g/9 oz ready-made puff pastry

1 egg, beaten

2 tbsp superfine sugar

1 Cream the butter and sugar together until light and pale, then gradually add the egg, beating well between each addition. Fold in the ground almonds and the chocolate.

2 Roll out the pie dough and cut 2 x 10-inch/25-cm diameter disks. Place 1 pie dough disk on a cookie sheet and mound the almond mixture on top of it, leaving a 1¼-inch/3-cm edge. Brush the edges with beaten egg and put the second disk on top, seal the edges, and score the top with a swirl pattern. Let chill for 30 minutes.

3 Preheat the oven to 400°F/200°C. Bake the Pithiviers for 15 minutes, then reduce the oven temperature to 375°F/190°C for an additional 10 minutes.

4 Remove the Pithiviers from the oven and sprinkle with the sugar. Place under a preheated broiler and let the sugar caramelize—if your broiler is really hot this should take less than 1 minute. Slice and serve warm with ice cream.

Candied Peel & Nut Tart

This very rich tart is not for the faint-hearted. Keep your portions small—even for dessert enthusiasts and those with a sweet tooth.

40 mins plus
1 hr chilling

50 mins

SERVES 8

INGREDIENTS

PIE DOUGH

1¼ cups all-purpose flour, plus extra
for dusting

2 tbsp superfine sugar

4 oz/115 g butter, cut into small pieces

1 tbsp water

FILLING

3 oz/85 g butter

¼ cup superfine sugar

2¾ oz/75 g set honey

generous ¾ cup heavy cream

1 egg, beaten

scant 1 cup mixed nuts

generous 1 cup candied peel

1 To make the dough, place the flour and sugar in a bowl and rub in the butter with your fingertips until the mixture resembles bread crumbs. Add the water and work the mixture together until a soft dough has formed. Wrap and chill in the refrigerator for 30 minutes.

2 On a lightly floured work counter, roll out the dough and line a 9½-inch/24-cm loose-bottomed tart pan. Prick the dough with a fork and chill in the refrigerator for 30 minutes.

3 Preheat the oven to 375°F/190°C. Line the pastry shell with foil and dried beans and bake in the preheated oven for 15 minutes. Remove the foil and dried beans and cook for an additional 15 minutes.

4 To make the filling, melt the butter, sugar, and honey in a small pan over low heat. Stir in the cream and beaten egg, then add the nuts and candied peel. Cook over low heat, stirring constantly, for 2 minutes until the mixture is a pale golden color.

5 Pour the filling into the pastry shell and return the tart to the oven for 15–20 minutes, or until the filling is just set. Let cool, then serve in slices.

VARIATION
Substitute walnuts or pecans for the mixed nuts, if you prefer.

Fruit Crumble Tart

This tart has a double helping of flavors, with a succulent fruit filling covered in a rich crumbly topping.

20 mins plus
1 hr chilling   25 mins

SERVES 8

INGREDIENTS

PIE DOUGH

1¼ cups all-purpose flour, plus extra
   for greasing

2 tbsp superfine sugar

4 oz/115 g butter, cut into small pieces

1 tbsp water

FILLING

1½ cups raspberries

1 lb/450 g plums, halved, pitted, and
   chopped coarsely

⅓ cup raw sugar

TOPPING

scant 1 cup all-purpose flour

⅓ cup raw sugar

4 oz/115 g butter, cut into small pieces

⅔ cup chopped mixed nuts

1 tsp ground cinnamon

light cream, to serve

1 To make the dough, place the flour, sugar, and butter in a bowl and rub in the butter with your fingertips. Add the water and work the mixture together until a soft dough has formed. Wrap and let chill in the refrigerator for 30 minutes.

2 Roll out the dough on a lightly floured work counter and line the bottom of a 9½-inch/24-cm loose-bottomed tart pan. Prick the bottom of the dough with a fork and let chill for about 30 minutes.

3 Preheat the oven to 400°F/200°C. To make the filling, toss the raspberries and plums together with the sugar and spoon into the pastry shell.

4 To make the crumble topping, combine the flour, sugar, and butter in a bowl. Work the butter into the flour with your fingertips until the mixture resembles coarse bread crumbs. Stir in the nuts and ground cinnamon.

5 Sprinkle the topping over the fruit and press down gently with the back of a spoon. Bake in the preheated oven for 20–25 minutes, until the topping is golden. Serve the tart immediately with light cream.

Forest Fruit Pie

This pie is brimming with fruit. Ground hazelnuts and lime rind are added to the pie dough for extra flavor.

20 mins plus
30 mins resting

45 mins

SERVES 4

INGREDIENTS

1 cup blueberries

1 cup raspberries

1 cup blackberries

½ cup superfine sugar

1⅔ cups all-purpose flour, plus extra for dusting

¼ cup ground hazelnuts

3½ oz/100 g butter, cut into pieces, plus extra for greasing

finely grated rind of 1 lemon

1 egg yolk, beaten

4 tbsp milk

2 tbsp confectioners' sugar, to decorate

whipped cream, to serve

1 Put the fruit in a pan with 3 tablespoons of superfine sugar and simmer, stirring, for 5 minutes. Remove from the heat. Sift the flour into a bowl, then add the hazelnuts. Rub in the butter, then sift in the remaining sugar. Add the lemon rind, egg yolk, and 3 tablespoons of milk and mix. Turn out on to a lightly floured work counter and knead briefly. Leave to rest for 30 minutes.

2 Preheat the oven to 375°F/190°C. Grease an 8-inch/20-cm ovenproof pie dish with butter. Roll out the pie dough to a thickness of ¼ inch/5 mm and use it to line the bottom and sides of the dish. Spoon the fruit into the pastry shell. Brush the rim with water, then roll out the remaining pie dough and use it to cover the pie. Trim and crimp round the edges, then make 2 small slits in the top and decorate with 2 leaf shapes cut out from the dough trimmings. Brush all over with the remaining milk.

Bake for 40 minutes. Remove from the oven, sprinkle over the confectioners' sugar and serve with whipped cream.

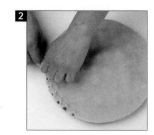

One Roll Fruit Pie

This is an easy way to make a pie—once you have rolled out the pie dough and filled it with fruit, you just turn the edges in.

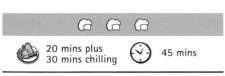

20 mins plus
30 mins chilling

45 mins

SERVES 8

INGREDIENTS

PIE DOUGH

⅓ cup butter, cut into small pieces, plus extra for greasing

1½ cups all-purpose flour

1 tbsp water

1 egg, separated

sugar lumps, crushed, for sprinkling

FILLING

1½ lb/600 g prepared fruit (rhubarb, gooseberries, plums, damsons)

⅓ cup brown sugar

1 tbsp ground ginger

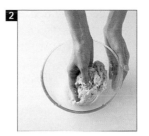

1 Grease a large cookie sheet with a little butter and set aside until required.

2 To make the pie dough, place the flour and butter in a mixing bowl and rub in the butter with your fingertips until the mixture resembles bread crumbs. Add the water and work the mixture together until a soft dough has formed. Wrap and chill in the refrigerator for 30 minutes.

3 Preheat the oven to 400°F/200°C. Roll out the chilled dough to a circle about 14 inches/35 cm in diameter.

4 Transfer the dough circle to the center of the prepared cookie sheet. Brush the dough with the egg yolk.

5 To make the filling, mix the prepared fruit with the brown sugar and ground ginger and pile it into the center of the dough.

6 Turn in the edges of the dough circle all the way around. Brush the surface of the dough with the egg white and sprinkle with the crushed sugar lumps.

7 Bake in the preheated oven for 35 minutes, or until golden brown. Serve warm.

COOK'S TIP

If the pie dough breaks when you are shaping it into a circle, don't panic—just patch and seal, because the overall effect of this tart is quite rough.

Chocolate Blueberry Tarts

The combination of chocolate pie dough, rich filling, and glistening berries makes these tarts very impressive.

40 mins plus
1 hr chilling/
freezing

20–25 mins

MAKES 10

INGREDIENTS

1½ cups all-purpose flour

¼ cup unsweetened cocoa

¼ cup superfine sugar

pinch of salt

4½ oz/125 g butter

1 large egg yolk

1½ cups blueberries

2 tbsp cassis

¼ oz/10 g confectioners' sugar, sifted

FILLING

5 oz/140 g semisweet chocolate

1 cup heavy cream

⅔ cup sour cream (or crème fraîche, see page 9)

1 To make the pie dough, put the flour, unsweetened cocoa, sugar, and salt in a food processor and pulse to mix. Add the butter, pulse again, then add the egg and a little cold water to form a dough. (If you do not have a processor put the flour, unsweetened cocoa, sugar, and salt in a

large bowl and rub in the butter until the mixture resembles bread crumbs. Add the egg and a little cold water to form a dough). Cover the pie dough in plastic wrap and chill in the refrigerator for 30 minutes.

2 Preheat the oven to 350°F/180°C. Remove the pie dough from the refrigerator and roll out. Use to line 10 x 4-inch/10-cm tart shells. Freeze for 30 minutes, then bake in the oven for 15–20 minutes. Let cool.

3 Put the blueberries, cassis, and confectioners' sugar in a pan and

warm through so the berries become shiny, but do not burst. Let cool.

4 Melt the chocolate in a heatproof bowl set over a pan of gently simmering water, then cool slightly. Whip the cream until stiff and fold in the sour cream and chocolate.

5 Remove the tart shells to a serving plate and divide the chocolate filling among them, smoothing the surface, then top with the blueberries.

COOK'S TIP
These tarts also look pretty with a little confectioners' sugar sifted over them just before serving.

Peach & Strawberry Tart

Peaches and strawberries make this the perfect choice for a summer lunch. Serve with a spoonful or two of whipped cream.

20 mins plus 1 hr 15 mins resting/chilling

15 mins

SERVES 4

INGREDIENTS

PIE DOUGH

1⅔ cups all-purpose flour, plus extra for dusting

3½ oz/100 g butter, cut into pieces, plus extra for greasing

¼ cup confectioners' sugar, sifted

finely grated rind of 1 orange

1 egg yolk, beaten

3 tbsp milk

4 tbsp strawberry jelly

FILLING

¾ cup heavy cream

4 tbsp confectioners' sugar

1 tbsp peach cognac

2 peaches, pitted and sliced

scant ½ cup strawberries, hulled and sliced

confectioners' sugar, to decorate

whipped cream, to serve

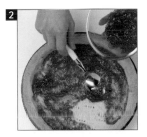

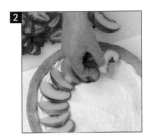

1 To make the pie dough, sift the flour into a bowl. Rub in the butter, then mix in the confectioners' sugar, orange rind, egg yolk, and milk. Knead briefly, then leave for 30 minutes. Preheat the oven to 350°F/180°C. Grease a 9-inch/ 23-cm tart pan with butter. Roll out the pie dough to a thickness of ¼ inch/5 mm and use to line the bottom and sides of the pan. Prick all over with a fork, line with parchment paper and fill with dried beans. Bake for 15 minutes. Remove from the oven and set aside.

2 To make the filling, put the cream into a bowl and beat in the confectioners' sugar. Stir in the peach cognac. Spread the bottom of the pastry shell with strawberry jelly, then spoon in the cream filling. Arrange the sliced peaches and strawberries over the top, then cover with plastic wrap and let chill for 45 minutes. Remove from the refrigerator, and dust with confectioners' sugar, then serve with whipped cream.

Apricot & Cranberry Tart

This frangipane tart, made with fresh cranberries, would be ideal for Thanksgiving. If you wish, brush the warm tart with melted apricot jelly.

20 mins plus
1 hr chilling

1 hr 30 mins

SERVES 8

INGREDIENTS

PIE DOUGH

1¼ cups all-purpose flour

2 tbsp superfine sugar

4 oz/115 g butter, cut into small pieces

1 tbsp water

FILLING

8 oz/225 g butter, sweet for preference

1 cup superfine sugar

1 egg

2 egg yolks

⅓ cup all-purpose flour, sifted

1⅔ cups ground almonds

4 tbsp heavy cream

14½ oz/410 g canned apricot halves, drained

generous 1 cup fresh cranberries

1 To make the dough, place the flour and sugar in a bowl and rub in the butter with your fingertips until the mixture resembles bread crumbs. Add the water and work the mixture together until a soft dough has formed. Wrap and chill in the refrigerator for 30 minutes.

2 Roll out the dough and line a 9½-inch/24-cm loose-bottomed tart pan. Prick the dough with a fork and chill in the refrigerator for 30 minutes.

3 Preheat the oven to 375°F/190°C. Line the pastry shell with foil and dried beans and bake in the preheated oven for 15 minutes. Remove the foil and dried beans and cook for an additional 10 minutes.

4 To make the filling, cream together the butter and sugar until light and fluffy. Beat in the egg and egg yolks, then stir in the flour, almonds, and cream.

5 Place the apricot halves and cranberries on the bottom of the pastry shell and spoon the filling over the top.

6 Return the tart to the oven and bake for about 1 hour, or until the topping is just set. Let cool slightly, then serve warm or cold.

Apple Tarte Tatin

This attractive, French upside-down apple tart is always a popular choice for a comforting dessert.

🍎 25 mins   🕐 30 mins

SERVES 8

INGREDIENTS

4 oz/115 g butter

scant ⅔ cup superfine sugar

4 dessert apples, cored and quartered

9 oz/250 g ready-made pie dough, thawed if frozen

all-purpose flour, for dusting

sour cream or cream, to serve

1 Preheat the oven to 400°F/200°C. Heat the butter and sugar in a 9-inch/23-cm ovenproof skillet over medium heat for about 5 minutes until the mixture starts to caramelize. Remove the skillet from the heat.

2 Arrange the apple quarters, skin-side down, in the skillet, taking care as the butter and sugar will be very hot. Place the skillet back on the heat and simmer for 2 minutes.

3 Roll out the pie dough on a lightly floured work counter to form a circle just a little larger than the skillet.

4 Place the pie dough over the apples, press down, and carefully tuck in the edges to seal the apples under the layer of pie dough.

5 Bake in the preheated oven for 20–25 minutes, until the pie dough is golden. Remove from the oven and let cool for about 10 minutes.

6 Place a serving plate over the skillet and, holding them firmly together, invert so that the dough forms the bottom of the turned-out tart. Serve warm with sour cream or cream.

VARIATION
Replace the apples with pears, if you prefer. Leave the skin on the pears, cut them into quarters, and then remove the core.

Traditional Apple Pie

This apple pie has a double crust and can be served either hot or cold.
The apples can be flavored with other spices or grated citrus rind.

**30 mins plus
30 mins chilling**   **50 mins**

SERVES 6

INGREDIENTS

1 lb 10 oz–2 lb 4 oz/750 g–1 kg cooking
apples, peeled, cored, and sliced

generous ½ cup brown or superfine sugar,
plus extra for sprinkling

½–1 tsp ground cinnamon, allspice,
or ground ginger

1–2 tbsp water

PIE DOUGH

3 cups all-purpose flour

pinch of salt

6 tbsp butter or margarine

⅓ cup shortening

about 6 tbsp cold water

beaten egg or milk, for glazing

1 To make the pie dough, sift the flour
and salt into a mixing bowl. Add the
butter (or margarine) and shortening and
rub in with the fingertips until the mixture
resembles fine bread crumbs. Add the
water and gather the mixture together into
a dough. Wrap the dough and let chill for
30 minutes.

2 Preheat the oven to 425°F/220°C.
Roll out almost two-thirds of the
pie dough thinly and use to line an
8–9-inch/20–23-cm deep pie plate or
shallow pie pan.

3 Mix the apples with the sugar and
spice and pack into the pastry shell;
the filling can come up above the rim. Add
the water if liked, particularly if the apples
are a dry variety.

4 Roll out the remaining pie dough to
form a lid. Dampen the edges of the
pie rim with water and position the lid,
pressing the edges firmly together. Trim
and crimp the edges.

5 Use the trimmings to cut out leaves
or other shapes to decorate the top of
the pie, dampen and attach. Glaze the top
of the pie with beaten egg or milk, make

1–2 slits in the top, and put the pie on a
cookie sheet.

6 Bake in the preheated oven for
20 minutes, then reduce the
temperature to 350°F/180°C and cook for
about 30 minutes, until the pie crust is a
light golden brown. Serve hot or cold,
sprinkled with sugar.

Spiced Apple Tart

Apples and spice are a classic, ever-popular combination. This tart makes a fabulous dessert, whatever the occasion.

20 mins plus
30 mins resting   35 mins

SERVES 4

INGREDIENTS

PIE DOUGH

1⅔ cups all-purpose flour, plus extra
  for dusting

3½ oz/100 g butter, diced, plus extra
  for greasing

generous ¼ cup confectioners' sugar, sifted

finely grated rind of 1 lemon

1 egg yolk, beaten

3 tbsp milk

FILLING

3 medium tart cooking apples

2 tbsp lemon juice

finely grated rind of 1 lemon

⅔ cup honey

1¾ cups white or whole-wheat fresh
  bread crumbs

1 tsp allspice

pinch of ground nutmeg

whipped cream, to serve

1 To make the pie dough, sift the flour into a bowl. Rub in the butter, then mix in the confectioners' sugar, lemon rind, egg yolk, and milk. Knead briefly, then leave for 30 minutes. Preheat the oven to 400°F/200°C. Grease an 8-inch/20-cm tart pan with butter. Roll out the pie dough to a thickness of ¼ inch/5 mm and use to line the bottom and sides of the pan.

2 To make the filling, core 2 apples and grate them into a bowl. Add 1 tablespoon of lemon juice and all the lemon rind, along with the honey, bread crumbs, and allspice. Mix together well. Spoon evenly into the pastry shell. Core and slice the remaining apple, and use to decorate the top of the tart. Brush the apple slices with lemon juice, then sprinkle over the nutmeg. Bake in the preheated oven for 35 minutes, or until firm. Remove from the oven and serve with cream.

Apple & Mincemeat Tart

The fresh apple brings out the flavor of the sweet rich mincemeat and makes it a beautifully moist filling for pies and tarts.

15 mins plus
1 hr chilling

50 mins

SERVES 8

I N G R E D I E N T S

PIE DOUGH

1¼ cups all-purpose flour, plus extra
for dusting

2 tbsp superfine sugar

4 oz/115 g butter, cut into small pieces

1 tbsp water

FILLING

14½ oz/410 g mincemeat

3 dessert apples

1 tbsp lemon juice

2 tbsp corn syrup

3 tbsp butter

1 To make the pie dough, place the flour and superfine sugar in a large mixing bowl and rub in the butter with your fingertips until the mixture resembles bread crumbs.

2 Add the water and work the mixture together until a soft dough has formed. Wrap and chill in the refrigerator for 30 minutes.

3 On a lightly floured work counter, roll out the dough and line a 9½-inch/24-cm loose-bottomed tart pan. Prick the base of the tart with the tines of a fork and chill in the refrigerator for 30 minutes.

4 Preheat the oven to 375°F/190°C. Line the pastry shell with foil and dried beans. Bake the shell in the preheated oven for 15 minutes. Remove the foil and beans and cook for an additional 15 minutes.

5 Core and grate the apples then combine with the mincemeat and lemon juice and spoon into the baked tart shell.

6 Melt the syrup and butter together in a small pan over low heat. Pour the syrup mixture over the mincemeat filling in the tart.

7 Return the tart to the oven and bake for about 20 minutes or until firm. Serve warm.

VARIATION

Add 2 tablespoons of sherry to spice up the mincemeat, if you wish.

Custard Tart

This is a classic egg custard tart which should be served as fresh as possible for the best flavor and texture.

15 mins plus 1 hr chilling   1 hr

SERVES 8

INGREDIENTS

PIE DOUGH

1¼ cups all-purpose flour

2 tbsp superfine sugar

4 oz/115 g butter, cut into small pieces

1 tbsp water

FILLING

3 eggs

⅔ cup light cream

⅔ cup milk

freshly grated nutmeg

whipped cream (optional), to serve

1 To make the pie dough, place the flour and sugar in a mixing bowl and rub in the butter with your fingertips.

2 Add the water and mix together until a soft dough has formed. Wrap and let chill in the refrigerator for about 30 minutes.

3 Roll out the dough to form a circle slightly larger than a 9½-inch/ 24-cm loose-bottomed tart pan.

4 Line the pan with the dough, trimming off the edges. Prick the base of the tart with the tines of a fork and chill in the refrigerator for 30 minutes.

5 Preheat the oven to 375°F/190°C. Line the pastry shell with foil and dried beans. Bake in the preheated oven for 15 minutes. Remove the foil and dried beans and bake the pastry shell for an additional 15 minutes.

6 To make the filling, whisk together the eggs, cream, milk, and nutmeg. Pour the filling into the prepared pastry shell.

7 Return the tart to the oven and cook for an additional 25–30 minutes, or until the filling is just set. Serve with whipped cream, if wished.

COOK'S TIP
Baking the pie shell blind ensures that the finished tart has a crisp base.

Orange Tart

This is a variation of the classic lemon tart—in this recipe fresh bread crumbs are used to create a thicker texture. Serve with whipped cream.

20 mins plus
1 hr chilling

1 hr 15 mins

SERVES 6–8

INGREDIENTS

PIE DOUGH

1¼ cups all-purpose flour, plus extra
    for dusting

2 tbsp superfine sugar

4 oz/115 g butter, cut into small pieces

1 tbsp water

FILLING

grated rind of 2 oranges

scant ⅔ cup orange juice

scant 1 cup fresh white bread crumbs

2 tbsp lemon juice

⅔ cup light cream

4 tbsp butter

¼ cup superfine sugar

2 eggs, separated

salt

whipped cream, to serve

1 To make the pie dough, place the flour and sugar in a bowl and rub in the butter until the mixture resembles bread crumbs. Add enough water to form a soft dough. Cover in plastic wrap and let chill in the refrigerator for 30 minutes.

2 Roll out the pie dough on a lightly floured work counter to a circle and line a 9½-inch/24-cm loose-bottomed tart pan. Prick the pie dough with a fork and let chill in the refrigerator for 30 minutes.

3 Preheat the oven to 375°F/190°C. Line the pastry shell with foil and dried beans and bake in the preheated oven for 15 minutes. Remove the foil and beans and cook for an additional 15 minutes.

4 To make the filling, combine the orange rind and juice with the bread crumbs in a bowl. Stir in the lemon juice and light cream. Melt the butter and sugar in a small pan over low heat. Remove the pan from the heat, add the 2 egg yolks, a pinch of salt, and the bread crumb mixture, and stir.

5 In a mixing bowl, whisk the egg whites with a pinch of salt until soft peaks form. Fold them into the egg yolk mixture.

6 Pour the filling mixture into the pastry shell. Reduce the oven temperature to 325°F/160°C and bake for about 45 minutes, or until just set. Let cool slightly and serve warm with cream.

Tarte au Citron

Few desserts can be more appealing to round off a meal on a hot evening than this creamy, tangy tart.

🍰 20 mins plus 1 hr chilling   🕐 35 mins

SERVES 6–8

INGREDIENTS

grated rind of 2–3 large lemons

⅔ cup lemon juice

½ cup superfine sugar

½ cup heavy cream or sour cream

3 large eggs

3 large egg yolks

confectioners' sugar, for dusting

PIE DOUGH

1¼ cups all-purpose flour, plus extra for dusting

½ tsp salt

4 oz/115 g cold sweet butter, cut into small pieces

1 egg yolk beaten with 2 tbsp ice water

1 To make the pie dough, sift the flour and salt into a bowl. Using your fingertips, rub the butter into the flour until the mixture resembles fine crumbs. Add the egg yolk and water and stir to form a dough. Gather the dough into a ball, cover in plastic wrap and let chill for at least 1 hour.

2 Preheat the oven to 400°F/200°C. Roll out on a lightly floured work counter and use to line a 9–10-inch/23–25-cm fluted tart pan with a removable bottom. Prick the bottom all over with a fork and line with a sheet of parchment paper and dried beans.

3 Bake in the preheated oven for 15 minutes, until the pie crust looks

set. Remove the paper and beans. Reduce the oven temperature to 375°F/190°C.

4 Beat the lemon rind, lemon juice, and sugar together until blended. Slowly beat in the cream or sour cream, then beat in the eggs and yolks, one by one.

5 Set the pastry shell on a cookie sheet and pour in the filling. Transfer to the preheated oven and bake for 20 minutes, until the filling is set.

6 Let cool completely on a wire rack. Dust with confectioners' sugar.

Lemon Meringue Pie

A combination of tangy lemon and soft meringue, this is a classic dessert which is ideal for both dinner parties or family gatherings.

20 mins plus
30 mins resting

1 hr

SERVES 4

INGREDIENTS

PIE DOUGH

7 oz/200 g all-purpose flour, plus extra
  for dusting

3½ oz/100 g butter, cut into small pieces,
  plus extra for greasing

¼ cup confectioners' sugar, sifted

finely grated rind of 1 lemon

1 egg yolk, beaten

3 tbsp milk

FILLING

3 tbsp cornstarch

1¼ cups cold water

juice and grated rind of 2 lemons

scant 1 cup superfine sugar

2 eggs, separated

1 To make the pie dough, sift the flour into a bowl. Rub in the butter. Mix in the remaining ingredients. Knead briefly on a lightly floured work counter. Leave to rest for 30 minutes. Preheat the oven to 350°F/180°C. Grease an 8-inch/20-cm ovenproof pie dish with butter. Roll out the pie dough to a thickness of ¼ inch/ 5 mm; use it to line the bottom and sides of the dish. Prick all over with the tines of a fork, line with parchment paper and fill with dried beans. Bake for 15 minutes. Remove from the oven. Reduce the temperature to 300°F/150°C.

2 To make the filling, mix the cornstarch with a little water. Put the remaining water in a pan. Stir in the lemon juice and rind and cornstarch paste. Bring to a boil, stirring. Cook for 2 minutes. Cool a little. Stir in 5 tablespoons of sugar and the egg yolks; pour into the pastry shell. In a separate bowl, whisk the egg whites until stiff. Gradually whisk in the remaining sugar and spread over the pie. Bake for 40 minutes. Remove from the oven and serve.

Chocolate Meringue Pie

This pretty tart, with its three contrasting layers, is surprisingly light. Use plain graham crackers if preferred.

25 mins   35 mins

SERVES 8

INGREDIENTS

9 oz/250 g chocolate graham crackers, crushed

3 oz/85 g butter, sweet for preference, melted

5 oz/140 g semisweet chocolate, chopped

⅔ cup heavy cream

½ cup mascarpone cheese

2 large eggs

2 large egg whites

pinch of salt

¼ cup superfine sugar

1 Preheat the oven to 325°F/160°C. To make the cookie base, mix the graham cracker crumbs and butter together and press well down into the bottom of a 9-inch/23-cm springform cake pan. Put the chocolate into a heatproof bowl.

2 Heat the cream to boiling point and pour it over the chocolate, stirring until the chocolate is melted and smooth. Beat the mascarpone cheese until smooth and mix in the whole eggs. Stir the mixture into the chocolate. Pour over the cookie base and bake for 15–20 minutes, until just set.

3 Meanwhile, make the meringue. Whisk the egg whites with a pinch of salt until they form soft peaks. Gradually add the sugar, whisking between additions, until the meringue is stiff and glossy.

4 After the chocolate filling has cooked for 15–20 minutes remove the tart from the oven and increase the oven temperature to 400°F/200°C. Pile the meringue on top of the chocolate filling and bake for an additional 10–15 minutes, until the meringue is lightly browned.

5 Remove from the oven and let cool. Carefully remove the springform pan and serve.

Lime & Coconut Meringue Pie

There is a Caribbean flavor to this variation on a classic lemon meringue pie. Serve it hot or cold.

30 mins plus
30 mins chilling

50 mins

SERVES 6-8

INGREDIENTS

PIE DOUGH

1½ cups all-purpose flour

pinch of salt

4 tbsp butter

4 tbsp shortening

2–3 tbsp cold water

FILLING

4 tbsp cornstarch

1¾ cups canned coconut milk

grated rind and juice of 2 limes

2 large eggs, separated

scant 1 cup superfine sugar

1 To make the pie dough, place the flour and salt in a bowl and rub in the butter and shortening with your fingertips until the mixture resembles bread crumbs. Add the water and work the mixture together until a soft dough has formed. Wrap and let chill in the refrigerator for 30 minutes. Preheat the oven to 350°F/180°C. Roll out the pie dough and use to line a 9-inch/23-cm tart pan. Line with parchment paper and dried beans. Bake blind in the preheated oven for 15 minutes. Remove from the oven and remove the beans and discard the paper. Reduce the oven temperature to 325°F/160°C. To make the filling, put the cornstarch in a pan with a little of the coconut milk and stir to make a paste.

2 Stir in the rest of the coconut milk. Bring to a boil slowly, stirring constantly. Cook, stirring, for 3 minutes until thickened. Remove from the heat and add the lime rind and juice, the egg yolks, and one-quarter cup of the sugar. Pour into the pastry shell.

3 Put the egg whites in a bowl and whisk until very stiff, then gradually whisk in the remaining sugar. Spread over the filling and swirl with a spatula. Bake in the oven for 20 minutes, or until lightly browned. Serve hot or cold.

VARIATION
Add a teaspoon of coconut liqueur to the filling with the sugar in step 2, if you like.

Coconut Tart

Coconut makes the filling in this tart beautifully moist. If you buy a ready-cooked tart shell, this recipe is quickly prepared.

5 mins plus 1 hr resting   40 mins

SERVES 8

INGREDIENTS

PIE DOUGH

1 x 9 inch/23-cm ready-cooked tart shell

FILLING

2 eggs

grated rind and lime of 2 lemons

1 cup golden superfine sugar

1¾ cups heavy cream

1 cup dry unsweetened coconut

1 Preheat the oven to 350°F/180°C. To make the filling, put the eggs, lemon rind and sugar in a bowl and beat together for 1 minute.

2 Gently stir in the cream, then the lemon juice and, finally, the coconut.

3 Spread the mixture into the pastry shell and bake in the oven for 40 minutes, until set and golden. Let cool for about 1 hour to firm up. Serve at room temperature.

COOK'S TIP
This tart is particularly good served accompanied by passion fruit pulp.

Coconut Cream Tart

Decorate this tart with some fresh tropical fruit, such as mango or pineapple, and extra shredded coconut, toasted.

20 mins plus 1 hr chilling   **40 mins**

SERVES 6–8

I N G R E D I E N T S

PIE DOUGH

1¼ cups all-purpose flour, plus extra for dusting

2 tbsp superfine sugar

4 oz/115 g butter, cut into small pieces

1 tbsp water

FILLING

scant 2 cups milk

4½ oz/125 g creamed coconut

3 egg yolks

½ cup superfine sugar

generous ⅓ cup all-purpose flour, sifted

¼ cup shredded coconut

generous ¼ cup chopped candied pineapple

2 tbsp dark rum or pineapple juice

1⅓ cups whipping cream, whipped

1 To make the pie dough, place the flour and sugar in a bowl and rub in the butter until the mixture resembles bread crumbs. Add the water and work the mixture together until a soft dough has formed. Wrap and chill for 30 minutes.

2 On a lightly floured work counter, roll out the dough to a circle and line a 9½-inch/24-cm loose-bottomed tart pan. Prick the pie dough the tines of a fork and chill in the refrigerator for 30 minutes.

3 Preheat the oven to 375°F/190°C. Line the pastry shell with foil and dried beans and bake in the preheated oven for 15 minutes. Remove the foil and beans and cook for an additional 15 minutes. Let cool.

4 To make the filling, bring the milk and creamed coconut to just below boiling point in a small pan over low heat, stirring to melt the coconut.

5 In a bowl, whisk the egg yolks with the sugar until pale and fluffy. Whisk in the flour. Pour the hot milk over the egg mixture, stirring constantly. Return the mixture to the pan and heat gently, stirring constantly, for about 8 minutes until thick. Let cool.

6 Stir the coconut, pineapple, and rum or juice into the coconut cream filling. Spread the filling in the pastry shell. Cover with the whipped cream and chill in the refrigerator until required.

Chocolate Walnut Tart

This rich chocolate nut tart is served with a caramel sauce as an unusual alternative to cream. It makes a fantastic dinner-party dessert.

30 mins plus 1½ hrs chilling

55 mins

SERVES 12

INGREDIENTS

4½ oz/125 g butter

2¼ cups all-purpose flour

½ cup confectioners' sugar

2 egg yolks

FILLING

1¾ cups heavy cream

¼ cup superfine sugar

pinch of salt

4½ oz/125 g softened butter

14 oz/400 g semisweet chocolate, chopped

1 cup chopped walnuts

CARAMEL SAUCE

¾ cup brown sugar

1 cup maple syrup

4 oz/115 g butter

2 tbsp boiling water

1 To make the pie dough, put the butter, flour and sugar in a food processor and pulse until the mixture resembles bread crumbs, add the egg and a little cold water to bring the dough together. (If you do not have a processor rub the butter into the flour and sugar until the mixture resembles bread crumbs. Add the egg and a little cold water to form a dough.) Cover the pie dough in plastic wrap and chill in the refrigerator for 30 minutes.

2 Preheat the oven to 375°F/190°C. Remove the pie dough from the refrigerator and roll out. Use to line a 9½-inch/24-cm square tart pan and line with parchment paper, fill with dried beans and bake blind for 10 minutes. Remove the paper and beans and bake for an additional 10–15 minutes, until the pie dough has dried out. Remove and let cool.

3 Put the cream, sugar, and salt in a pan and bring to a boil. Remove from the heat and add the butter and chocolate, stirring well to combine. Let cool and add the walnuts, stir well, and pour into the tart shell. Smooth the surface and let chill in the refrigerator for at least 1 hour.

4 To make the caramel sauce, heat the sugar and maple syrup until the sugar has melted, remove from the heat, and stir in the butter and hot water. Let cool.

5 Slice the tart into squares and pour a little caramel sauce over to serve.

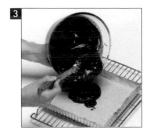

Chocolate & Coffee Tarts

These tarts have a crisp chocolate pastry and a smooth coffee filling topped with cream and a few semisweet chocolate sticks.

30 mins plus
30 mins chilling

45 mins

MAKES 10

INGREDIENTS

2¼ cups all-purpose flour

1½ oz/40 g confectioners' sugar

1 tsp ground cinnamon

1 tbsp unsweetened cocoa

6 oz/175 g butter

1 egg yolk

FILLING

¼ cup all-purpose flour

pinch of salt

3 egg yolks

½ cup superfine sugar

1 cup milk

2 tbsp instant coffee powder, mixed to a paste with a little boiling water

1 tbsp coffee liqueur (optional)

⅔ cup heavy cream

4 oz/115 g semisweet chocolate

1 Put the flour, sugar, cinnamon, and unsweetened cocoa in a food processor and pulse to combine. Add the butter and pulse until the mixture resembles bread crumbs, then add the egg and a little cold water to form a dough. (If you do not have a processor sift the flour, sugar, cinnamon, and unsweetened cocoa into a large bowl and rub in the butter until the mixture resembles bread crumbs, then add the egg and a little cold water to form a dough.) Cover the pie dough in plastic wrap and let chill in the refrigerator for 30 minutes.

2 Preheat the oven to 350°F/180°C. Remove the pie dough from the refrigerator and roll out. Use to line 10 x 4-inch/10-cm tart pans. Line each tart with parchment paper and dried beans and bake blind for 10 minutes. Remove the paper and beans and bake for an additional 5–10 minutes. Remove and let cool.

3 To make the filling, sift the flour and salt into a bowl. In a separate bowl whisk the eggs and sugar together with an electric whisk until pale and thick. Gradually add the flour and mix well. Heat the milk to boiling point, then set aside to cool slightly. Pour the milk in a steady stream into the egg mixture, whisking constantly, add the coffee and return to the pan. Bring the mixture to a boil, stirring all the time, and boil for 2 minutes. Pour into a clean bowl, let cool, and stir in the liqueur (if using).

4 Whip the cream until thick. Spoon the coffee filling in to the tart shells and transfer to individual serving plates. Top with a teaspoonful of cream and, use a vegetable peeler to make decorative sticks from the semisweet chocolate.

Treacle Tart

This is an old-fashioned dessert, which still delights people time after time. It is very quick to make if you use ready-made pie dough.

20 mins plus
30 mins chilling

40 mins

SERVES 8

INGREDIENTS

9 oz/250 g ready-made pie dough, thawed if frozen

1 cup corn syrup

scant 2 cups fresh white bread crumbs

½ cup heavy cream

finely grated rind of ½ lemon or orange

2 tbsp lemon or orange juice

custard or light cream, to serve

1 Roll out the pie dough to line an 8-inch/20-cm loose-bottomed tart pan, reserving the dough trimmings. Prick the bottom of the pie dough with a fork and let chill in the refrigerator for 30 minutes. Preheat the oven to 375°F/190°C.

2 Cut out small shapes from the reserved dough trimmings, such as hearts, leaves, or stars, to decorate the top of the tart.

3 In a bowl, combine the corn syrup, bread crumbs, heavy cream, grated lemon or orange rind, and lemon or orange juice.

4 Pour the mixture into the pastry shell and decorate the edges of the tart with the reserved dough shapes.

5 Bake in the preheated oven for 35–40 minutes, or until the filling is just set.

6 Let the tart cool slightly in the pan. Turn out and serve hot or cold, with custard or light cream.

VARIATION
Use the pie dough trimmings to create a lattice pattern on top of the tart if preferred.

Treacle & Orange Tart

An irresistibly sweet combination of corn syrup and orange. It is the perfect finale to a special occasion meal.

SERVES 6

INGREDIENTS

PIE DOUGH

1 cup all-purpose flour, plus extra for greasing

pinch of salt

2 tbsp butter

2 tbsp shortening

2 tbsp cold water

FILLING

8 tbsp corn syrup

finely grated rind of 1 orange

1 tbsp orange juice

6 tbsp fresh white bread crumbs

1 To make the pie dough, put the flour and salt in a bowl and rub in the butter and shortening until the mixture resembles bread crumbs. Add the water and work the mixture together until a soft dough has formed. Wrap and let chill for 30 minutes. Preheat the oven to 375°F/190°C. Roll out the pie dough and use to line an 8-inch/20-cm tart pan. Reserve the trimmings. To make the filling, put the syrup, orange rind, and juice in a pan and heat very gently until runny. Remove from the heat and stir in the bread crumbs.

2 Leave for 10 minutes until the crumbs have absorbed the syrup. If the mixture looks stodgy, add a little more syrup; and if it looks thin, add some more bread crumbs. It should have the consistency of thick honey.

3 Spread the mixture in the pastry shell. Roll out the pie dough trimmings and cut into narrow strips. Use to make a lattice pattern across the top of the tart. Bake in the oven for 30 minutes, or until the filling is almost set and the edge of the pastry is brown. Serve warm or cold.

COOK'S TIP

When the tart is removed from the oven, the filling should still be on the soft side if the tart is to be eaten cold, because it hardens as it cools.

Bakewell Tart

Strawberry jelly topped with a delicious almond mixture make this pie very moreish. It is best served warm.

20 mins plus
30 mins resting   40 mins

SERVES 4

INGREDIENTS

PIE DOUGH

1⅔ cups all-purpose flour, plus extra
  for dusting

3½ oz/100 g butter, cut into small pieces,
  plus extra for greasing

generous ¼ cup confectioners' sugar, sifted

finely grated rind of 1 lemon

1 egg yolk, beaten

3 tbsp milk

4 tbsp strawberry jelly

FILLING

3½ oz/100 g butter

¾ cup brown sugar

2 eggs, beaten

1 tsp almond extract

generous ½ cup ground rice

3 tbsp ground almonds

3 tbsp slivered almonds, toasted

confectioners' sugar, to decorate

1 To make the pie dough, sift the flour into a bowl. Rub in the butter. Mix in the confectioners' sugar, lemon rind, egg yolk, and milk. Knead briefly on a lightly floured work counter. Let rest for 30 minutes.

2 Preheat the oven to 375°F/190°C. Grease an 8-inch/20-cm ovenproof tart pan. Roll out the pie dough to a thickness of ¼ inch/5 mm and use it to line the bottom and sides of the pan. Prick all over the bottom with a fork, then spread with jelly.

3 To make the filling, cream together the butter and sugar until fluffy. Gradually beat in the eggs, followed by the almond extract, rice, and ground almonds. Spread the mixture evenly over the jelly-covered pastry, then scatter over the slivered almonds. Bake in the preheated oven for 40 minutes, until golden. Remove from the oven, dust with confectioners' sugar, and serve.

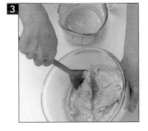

Hazelnut Cream Tarts

These elegant little tarts look particularly attractive with their sprinkling of chopped toasted hazelnuts.

40 mins plus
50 mins chilling   25 mins

MAKES 8

INGREDIENTS

1 cup self-rising flour

4 oz/115 g butter

1 tbsp confectioners' sugar, sifted

1 small egg yolk

FILLING

3 egg yolks

¼ cup superfine sugar

3 tbsp all-purpose flour

1 cup milk

3 oz/85 g chocolate

1 tbsp honey

¼ cup heavy cream

½ cup toasted hazelnuts, chopped

1 Place the flour, butter, and confectioners' sugar in a food processor and process until the mixture resembles bread crumbs. Add the egg yolk and a little cold water to form a dough. (If you do not have a processor sift the flour into a bowl and rub in the butter and sugar until the mixture resembles bread crumbs, add the egg and a little cold water to form a dough). Cover the pie dough in plastic wrap and let chill in the refrigerator for 30 minutes.

2 Preheat the oven to 375°F/190°C. Roll out the pie dough and use it to line an 8-cup muffin pan. Chill in the refrigerator for 20 minutes, then bake for 12–15 minutes. Let cool in the muffin pan.

3 To make the filling, beat the egg yolks and sugar in a bowl until pale and thick, add the flour a little at a time and mix to combine. Bring the milk to a boil and pour over the eggs, whisking all the time and beat well. Pour back into a clean pan and bring to a boil over low heat, stirring constantly. Boil for 1 minute, then pour into a cold bowl and stir. Let cool, stirring occasionally.

4 Melt the chocolate with the honey in a heatproof bowl set over a pan of gently simmering water. When melted, remove from the heat and stir in the cream. Let cool.

5 Spoon the cream filling into each tart, cover with the melted chocolate, sprinkle with the nuts and transfer to a serving dish.

Chocolate Chestnut Angel Pie

Chestnut purée adds an unusual flavor to this smooth, dense tart. A pile of white chocolate caraquc in the center adds the finishing touch.

🥧 🥧 🥧

⏱ 40 mins plus 1 hr chilling   🕐 35 mins

SERVES 8

INGREDIENTS

4½ oz/125 g butter

2¼ cups all-purpose flour, sifted, plus extra for dusting

1 cup confectioners' sugar

2 egg yolks, beaten

FILLING

7 oz/200 g semisweet chocolate

1 lb/450 g canned unsweetened chestnut purée

1 cup confectioners' sugar

1 cup heavy cream, whipped

5 oz/140 g white chocolate caraque (see page 9)

1 To make the pie dough, rub the butter into the sifted flour and sugar and add enough egg yolk to form a dough. Cover in plastic wrap and let chill in the refrigerator for 30 minutes.

2 Preheat the oven to 350°F/180°C. Remove the pie dough from the refrigerator and roll out. Use to line a 9-inch/23-cm loose-bottomed tart pan, prick the bottom with a fork, line with parchment paper, fill with dried beans and bake for 10 minutes. Remove the paper and beans and bake for an additional 10–15 minutes, until the tart shell has dried out. Remove from the oven and let cool.

3 Melt the semisweet chocolate in a heatproof bowl set over a pan of gently simmering water.

4 Put the chestnut purée and sugar in a large bowl and stir together until smooth. Fold in the chocolate, then the whipped cream.

5 Remove the tart shell from the tart pan on to a serving plate. Spoon the chestnut mixture into the shell and let chill in the refrigerator.

6 Make the caraque (see page 9) using the white chocolate. When you are ready to serve the pie, pile up the white chocolate caraque in the center of the chestnut filling.

Banoffee Pie

A melt-in-the-mouth combination of toffee and bananas, topped with grated semisweet chocolate, this pie has become a classic.

1 hr 20 mins   2 hrs 15 mins

SERVES 4

INGREDIENTS

28 fl oz/800 ml canned sweetened condensed milk

3 oz/85 g butter, melted

5½ oz/150 g graham crackers, crushed into crumbs

scant ½ cup almonds, toasted and ground

scant ½ cup hazelnuts, toasted and ground

4 ripe bananas

1 tbsp lemon juice

1 tsp vanilla extract

2 cups thick heavy cream, whipped

2¾ oz/75 g semisweet chocolate, grated

1 Place the unopened cans of milk in a large pan and cover them with water. Bring to a boil, then reduce the heat and simmer for 2 hours, topping up the water level to keep the cans covered. Lift out the hot cans and let cool.

2 Preheat the oven to 350°F/180°C. Grease a 9-inch/23-cm tart pan with butter. Put the remaining butter in a bowl and add the crushed cookies and ground nuts. Mix together well, then press the mixture evenly into the bottom and sides of the tart pan. Bake for 10–12 minutes, then remove from the oven and let cool.

3 Peel and slice the bananas and put them in a bowl. Sprinkle over the lemon juice and vanilla and mix together gently. Spread the banana mixture over the cookie crust in the pan, then open the cooled tins of condensed milk and spoon the contents over the bananas. Sprinkle over 1¾ oz/50 g of the chocolate, then top with a layer of whipped cream. Scatter over the remaining chocolate and serve.

Magic Cheesecake

This superb dessert proves that you can indulge in a wonderful creamy and luxurious cheesecake and still stick to a healthy, lowfat diet.

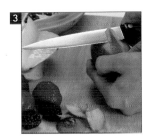

🍞 🍞 🍞

15 mins   5 mins

SERVES 6

INGREDIENTS

4 tbsp lowfat spread

6 tbsp apple juice

4 oz/115 g bran flakes

10 oz/280 g tofu or bean curd

scant 1 cup lowfat plain yogurt

1 tbsp powdered gelatin

12 oz/350 g prepared mixed fruits, such as star fruit, strawberries, kiwi fruits, papayas, and blackberries

1 Using a rolling pin, crush the branflakes in a polythene bag. Place the lowfat spread and 2 tablespoons of the apple juice in a pan and set over very low heat. When the spread has melted, stir in the bran flakes. Turn the mixture into a 9-inch/23-cm loose-bottomed tart pan and press down firmly with a wooden spoon or your fingertips to cover the bottom. Set aside.

2 Put the tofu and yogurt in a food processor and process until smooth, then scrape into a bowl. Pour the remaining apple juice into a small heatproof bowl, sprinkle the gelatin over the surface, and set aside for 5 minutes to soften. Set the bowl over a pan of gently simmering water for 5 minutes, or until the gelatin has dissolved completely. Pour the gelatin in a steady stream into the tofu mixture, beating constantly. Spread the tofu mixture evenly over the bottom in the tart pan and chill in the refrigerator until set.

3 Remove the cheesecake from the pan and place on a serving plate. Peel the kiwi fruits and papayas and slice thinly, along with the strawberries and starfruit. Arrange the slices on the cheesecake, together with the blackberries.

Hot Chocolate Cheesecake

This rich cheesecake has chocolate in the pie dough and in the filling. Your guests will want to come back for more.

25 mins plus
30 mins chilling

1 hr 30 mins

SERVES 8–10

INGREDIENTS

PIE DOUGH

4 tbsp butter, plus extra for greasing

scant 1½ cups all-purpose flour, plus extra for dusting

2 tbsp unsweetened cocoa

2 tbsp golden superfine sugar

¼ cup ground almonds

1 egg yolk

FILLING

2 eggs, separated

scant ½ cup golden superfine sugar

1½ cups cream cheese

4 tbsp ground almonds

⅔ cup heavy cream

¼ cup unsweetened unsweetened cocoa, sifted

1 tsp vanilla extract

confectioners' sugar, for dusting

1 Grease an 8-inch/20-cm loose-bottomed cake pan. To make the pie dough, sift the flour and unsweetened cocoa into a bowl and rub in the butter until the mixture resembles fine bread crumbs. Stir in the sugar and ground almonds. Add the egg yolk and sufficient water to make a soft dough.

2 Roll the pie dough out on a lightly floured work counter and use to line the prepared pan. Let chill for 30 minutes. Preheat the oven to 325°F/160°C. To make the filling, put the egg yolks and sugar in a large bowl and whisk until thick and pale. Whisk in the cream cheese, ground almonds, cream, unsweetened cocoa, and vanilla extract until well combined.

3 Put the egg whites in a large bowl and whisk until stiff but not dry. Stir a little of the egg white into the cheese mixture, then fold in the remainder. Pour into the pastry shell. Bake in the oven for 1 hour 30 minutes, until well risen and just firm to the touch. Carefully remove from the pan and dust with confectioners' sugar. Serve warm.

Chocolate Amaretto Cheesecake

Amaretto is an Italian almond-flavored liqueur which complements the semisweet chocolate perfectly.

30 mins plus
3 hrs chilling

1 hr 10 mins

SERVES 10-12

INGREDIENTS

BASE

vegetable oil, for oiling

6 oz/175 g graham crackers

2 oz/55 g amaretti cookies

3 oz/85 g butter

FILLING

8 oz/225 g semisweet chocolate,
 broken into pieces

1¾ cups cream cheese, at room temperature

generous ½ cup golden superfine sugar

4 eggs

1¼ cups heavy cream

¼ cup amaretto

TOPPING

1 tbsp amaretto

1¼ cups sour cream

crushed amaretti cookies

1 Line the bottom of a 9-inch/23-cm springform cake pan with foil and brush the sides of the pan with oil. Place the graham crackers and amaretti cookies in a polythene bag and crush with a rolling pin. Place the butter in a pan, and heat gently until just melted, then stir in the crushed cookies. Press into the bottom of the pan and chill for 1 hour.

2 Melt the chocolate in a heatproof bowl set over a pan of gently simmering water, then set aside to cool slightly. Preheat the oven to 325°F/160°C. To make the filling, put the cream cheese in a bowl and beat until fluffy, then add the sugar and beat until smooth.

Gradually add the eggs, beating until well blended. Blend in the melted chocolate, cream, and amaretto. Pour the mixture over the chilled cookie shell and bake in the oven for 50 minutes—1 hour, until set.

3 Leave the cheesecake in the oven with the door slightly ajar, until cold. Run a knife round the inside of the pan to loosen the cheesecake. Chill for 2 hours, then remove from the pan and place the cheesecake on a serving plate. To make the topping, stir the amaretto into the sour cream and spread over the cheesecake. Sprinkle the crushed cookies round the edge to decorate.

COOK'S TIP
If you do not have amaretto, use another liqueur or cognac instead.

Irish Cream Cheesecake

This is an unbaked cheesecake and although it uses no gelatin, its high chocolate content ensures that it sets perfectly.

45 mins plus
3 hrs chilling

5 mins

SERVES 12

INGREDIENTS

BASE

vegetable oil, for oiling

6 oz/175 g chocolate chip cookies

4 tbsp butter

FILLING

8 oz/225 g semisweet chocolate, broken into pieces

8 oz/225 g milk chocolate, broken into pieces

generous ¼ cup golden superfine sugar

1½ cups cream cheese

scant 2 cups heavy cream, whipped lightly

3 tbsp Baileys Irish Cream

TO SERVE

sour cream

fresh fruit

1 Line the bottom of an 8-inch/20-cm springform pan with foil and brush the sides with oil. Place the cookies in a polythene bag and crush with a rolling pin. Put the butter in a pan and heat gently until melted. Stir in the crushed cookies. Press into the bottom of the pan and chill for 1 hour.

2 Put the semisweet and milk chocolate into a heatproof bowl set over a pan of gently simmering water until melted. Let cool. Put the sugar and cream cheese in a bowl and beat together until smooth, then fold in the cream. Fold the melted chocolate into the cream cheese mixture, then stir in the Baileys Irish Cream.

3 Spoon into the prepared pan and smooth the surface. Let chill in the refrigerator for 2 hours, or until quite firm. Transfer to a serving plate and cut into small slices. Serve with sour cream and fresh fruit.

COOK'S TIP
Look out for miniature bottles of Baileys Irish Cream.

Chocolate Cheesecake

This cheesecake takes a little time to prepare, but is well worth the effort.
It is quite rich and is good served with a little fresh fruit.

🕐 1 hr 15 mins
plus 2 hrs chilling

🕐 1 hr–
1 hr 15 mins

SERVES 12

INGREDIENTS

6 oz/175 g margarine, plus extra
for greasing

generous ¾ cup all-purpose flour

scant 1 cup ground almonds

scant 1 cup molasses sugar

1 lb 8 oz/675 g firm tofu or beancurd

¾ cup vegetable oil

½ cup orange juice

¾ cup cognac

6 tbsp unsweetened cocoa, plus extra to
decorate

2 tsp almond extract

TO DECORATE

confectioners' sugar

cape gooseberries

1 Preheat the oven to 325°F/160°C. Lightly grease and line the bottom of a 9-inch/23-cm springform cake pan. Put the flour, ground almonds, and 1 tablespoon of the sugar in a bowl and mix well. Rub the margarine into the mixture to form a dough.

2 Press the dough into the bottom of the pan to cover, pushing the dough right up to the edge of the pan.

3 Coarsely chop the tofu and put in a food processor with the vegetable oil, orange juice, cognac, unsweetened cocoa, almond extract, and remaining sugar and process until smooth and creamy. Pour into the pastry shell and cook in the preheated oven for about 1–1¼ hours, or until set.

4 Let cool in the pan for 5 minutes, then remove from the pan, and chill in the refrigerator. Dust with confectioners' sugar and unsweetened cocoa. Decorate with cape gooseberries and serve.

COOK'S TIP
Cape gooseberries make an attractive decoration for many desserts. If you peel open the papery husks to expose the orange fruits they are even brighter.

Ginger Cheesecake

Chocolate has a natural affinity with spices. Vanilla seeds and bay leaves in this recipe add an enticing flavor.

20 mins plus 3 hrs chilling   10 mins

SERVES 6–8

INGREDIENTS

6 oz/175 g gingersnaps

sunflower oil, for oiling

2 oz/55 g butter, sweet for preference

14 oz/400 g good-quality bittersweet chocolate

½ cup confectioners' sugar

2 tbsp maple syrup or corn syrup

3 bay leaves

seeds from 1 vanilla pod, soaked in 4 tsp milk or dark rum

7 oz/200 g cream cheese

½ cup heavy cream, whipped

½ cup candied ginger pieces, sliced thinly, plus extra to decorate

TO SERVE

whipped cream

unsweetened cocoa

1 To make the base, crush the gingersnaps in a food processor, or place them in a polythene bag, loosely seal the end, and pound with a rolling pin to reduce them to crumbs. Oil an 8-inch/

20-cm loose-bottomed cake pan, line the bottom with waxed paper and oil again.

2 Melt the butter, stir in the crushed cookies, then press the mixture over the bottom of the pan. Refrigerate to set while you make the filling.

3 Break the chocolate into pieces and place in a large heatproof bowl set over a pan of gently simmering water. Add the confectioners' sugar, syrup, bay leaves, vanilla seeds, and their soaking liquid, and stir until the chocolate has melted and the mixture is smooth and glossy. Remove

from the heat and let cool, stirring occasionally. Remove and discard the bay leaves.

4 Beat in the cream cheese, then fold in the lightly whipped cream and the candied ginger. Pour into the pan, cover with plastic wrap and return to the refrigerator for about 3 hours. When it is firm, carefully remove the cheesecake from the pan.

5 Decorate the cheesecake with slices of ginger and serve with cream, dusted with unsweetened cocoa.

COOK'S TIP

To remove the vanilla seeds, slit the bean lengthwise and run the tip of a teaspoon or knife point down the length. You can use ¼ teaspoon vanilla extract instead of the soaked seeds for convenience, though the flavor will be less intense. You still need to add the milk or rum.

Marble Cheesecake

A dark and white chocolate cheesecake filling is marbled together to give an attractive finish to this rich and decadent dessert.

2 hrs 30 mins   5 mins

SERVES 10

INGREDIENTS

BASE

8 oz/225 g toasted oat cereal

½ cup toasted hazelnuts, chopped

4 tbsp butter

1 oz/25 g semisweet chocolate

FILLING

1½ cups cream cheese

½ cup superfine sugar

generous ¾ cup plain yogurt

1¼ cups heavy cream

¼ oz/7 g powdered gelatin

3 tbsp water

6 oz/175 g semisweet chocolate, melted

6 oz/175 g white chocolate, melted

1 Place the toasted oat cereal in a polythene bag and crush with a rolling pin. Pour the crushed cereal into a mixing bowl and stir in the hazelnuts.

2 Melt the butter and chocolate together over low heat and stir into the cereal mixture, stirring until well coated.

3 Using the bottom of a glass, press the mixture into the bottom and up the sides of an 8-inch/20-cm springform pan.

4 Beat together the cheese and sugar with a wooden spoon until smooth. Beat in the yogurt. Whip the cream until just holding its shape and fold into the mixture. Sprinkle the gelatin over the water in a heatproof bowl and let it go spongy. Place over a pan of hot water and stir until dissolved. Stir into the mixture.

5 Divide the mixture in half and beat the semisweet chocolate into one half and the white chocolate into the other half.

6 Place alternate spoonfuls of mixture on top of the cereal base. Swirl the filling together with the tip of a knife to give a marbled effect. Decorate the top using a serrated scraper. Let chill for at least 2 hours, until set, before serving.

Strawberry Cheesecake

Sweet strawberries are teamed with creamy mascarpone cheese and luxurious white chocolate to make this mouthwatering cheesecake.

3 hrs   1 hr 30 mins

SERVES 8

INGREDIENTS

BASE

2 oz/55 g butter, sweet for preference

2⅔ cups crushed graham crackers

½ cup chopped walnuts

FILLING

2 cups mascarpone cheese

2 eggs, beaten

3 tbsp superfine sugar

9 oz/250 g white chocolate, broken into pieces

2 cups strawberries, hulled and quartered

TOPPING

¾ cup mascarpone cheese

chocolate caraque (see page 9)

16 whole strawberries

1 Melt the butter over low heat and stir in the crushed crackers and the nuts. Spoon the mixture into a 9-inch/23-cm springform cake pan and press evenly over the bottom with the back of a spoon. Set aside.

2 Preheat the oven to 300°F/150°C. To make the filling, beat the cheese until smooth, then beat in the eggs and sugar. Put the chocolate in a heatproof bowl set over a pan of gently simmering water. Stir over low heat until melted and smooth. Remove from the heat and cool slightly, then stir into the cheese mixture. Finally, stir in the strawberries.

3 Spoon the mixture into the cake pan, spread out evenly, and smooth the surface. Bake in the preheated oven for 1 hour, until the filling is just firm. Turn off the oven and let the cheesecake cool inside with the door slightly ajar until completely cold.

4 Transfer the cheesecake to a serving plate and spread the mascarpone on top. Decorate with chocolate caraque and whole strawberries.

Berry Cheesecake

Use a mixture of berries, such as blueberries, blackberries, raspberries, and strawberries, for a really fruity cheesecake.

15 mins plus
2 hrs chilling

5 mins

SERVES 8

INGREDIENTS

BASE

3 oz/85 g margarine

6 oz/175 g oatmeal cookies

⅔ cup dry unsweetened coconut

TOPPING

1½ tsp powdered gelatin

generous ½ cup cold water

½ cup evaporated milk

1 egg

6 tbsp brown sugar

2 cups soft cream cheese

3 cups mixed berries

2 tbsp honey

1 Melt the margarine in a pan. Put the cookies into a food processor and process until crushed, or crush finely with a rolling pin. Stir the crumbs into the margarine with the coconut.

2 Press the mixture evenly into a base-lined 8-inch/ 20-cm springform cake pan and set aside to chill in the refrigerator.

3 To make the topping, sprinkle the gelatin over the water in a heatproof bowl and let it go spongy. Place over a pan of hot water and stir until dissolved. Set aside to cool slightly.

4 Beat the milk with the egg, sugar, and cream cheese until smooth. Stir in ½ cup of the berries. Add the gelatin in a thin stream, stirring constantly.

5 Spoon the mixture on to the cookie base and return to the refrigerator to chill for 2 hours, or until set.

6 Remove the cheesecake from the pan and transfer to a serving plate. Arrange the remaining berries on top of the cheesecake and drizzle the honey over the top. Serve.

Lime Cheesecakes

These cheesecakes are flavored with lime and mint, and set on a base of crushed graham crackers mixed with bittersweet chocolate.

30 mins plus 2 hrs 30 mins chilling

5 mins

SERVES 2

I N G R E D I E N T S

BASE

2 tbsp butter, plus extra for greasing

1 oz/25 g bittersweet chocolate

1½ cups crushed graham crackers

FILLING

finely grated rind of 1 lime

⅓ cup strained cottage cheese

⅓ cup lowfat cream cheese

1 fresh mint sprig, chopped very finely (optional)

1 tsp gelatin

1 tbsp lime juice

1 egg yolk

3 tbsp superfine sugar

TO DECORATE

whipped cream

kiwi fruit slices

fresh mint sprigs

1 Grease 2 fluted, loose-bottomed 4½-inch/11-cm tart pans thoroughly. To make the base, melt the butter and chocolate in a heatproof bowl set over a pan of gently simmering water. Stir until smooth.

2 Stir the crushed crackers evenly through the melted chocolate and then press into the bottoms of the tart pans, smoothing the surface. Chill until set.

3 Put the lime rind and cheeses into a bowl and beat until smooth and blended, then beat in the mint (if using).

4 Dissolve the gelatin in the lime juice in a heatproof bowl set over a pan of gently simmering water.

5 Beat the egg yolk and sugar together until creamy and fold into the cheese mixture, followed by the dissolved gelatin. Pour over the base and let chill until set.

6 To serve, remove the cheesecakes carefully from the tart pans. Decorate with whipped cream, slices of kiwi fruit, and mint sprigs.

Marbled Chocolate Cheesecake

Cheesecake is always a popular dessert, and this one, with marbled swirls of semisweet and white chocolate, is no exception.

45 mins plus 3 hrs chilling

1 hr 10 mins

SERVES 10–12

INGREDIENTS

BASE

vegetable oil, for oiling

8 oz/225 g semisweet chocolate graham crackers

3 oz/85 g butter

FILLING

1 lb 9 oz/700 g cream cheese

scant 1 cup golden superfine sugar

3 tbsp all-purpose flour

2 tsp vanilla extract

3 eggs, beaten

4 oz/115 g semisweet chocolate

4 oz/115 g white chocolate

1 Line the bottom of a 9-inch/23-cm springform cake pan with foil and brush the sides of the pan with oil. Place the cookies in a polythene bag and crush with a rolling pin. Place the butter in a pan and heat gently until just melted and stir in the crushed cookies. Press into the bottom of the pan and chill for 1 hour.

2 Preheat the oven to 325°F/160°C. To make the filling, put the cream cheese in a bowl and beat until fluffy, then add the sugar, flour, and vanilla extract and beat until smooth. Gradually add the eggs, beating until well blended. Place half the mixture in another bowl. Put the semisweet chocolate and white chocolate in 2 separate heatproof bowls set over 2 pans of gently simmering water until melted and let cool. Stir the semisweet chocolate into one bowl of cream cheese mixture and the white chocolate into the other.

3 Spoon the 2 mixtures alternately over the chilled cracker base, then swirl with a knife to give a marbled effect. Bake in the oven for 50 minutes–1 hour, until set. Leave the cheesecake in the oven with the door slightly ajar, until cold. Run a knife round the inside of the pan to loosen the cheesecake. Chill for 2 hours before removing from the pan to serve.

COOK'S TIP
Leaving the cheesecake in the oven to cool helps to prevent it cracking.

Manhattan Cheesecake

This is a classic baked cheesecake. The combination of juicy blueberries and baked cheese is sure to impress your guests at a dinner party.

1 hr plus 8 hrs chilling **35 mins**

SERVES 8–10

INGREDIENTS

BASE
vegetable oil, for brushing

3 oz/85 g butter

7 oz/200 g graham crackers, crushed

FILLING
1¾ cups cream cheese

2 large eggs

¾ cup superfine sugar

1½ tsp vanilla extract

2 cups sour cream

TOPPING
¼ cup superfine sugar

1 cup fresh blueberries

1 tsp arrowroot

1 Preheat the oven to 375°F/190°C. Lightly brush an 8-inch/20-cm springform cake pan with oil. To make the base, put the butter in a pan and heat gently until melted. Stir in the crushed crackers, then place in the prepared pan and spread evenly over the bottom. To make the filling, put the cream cheese,

eggs, ½ cup of the sugar, and ½ teaspoon of the vanilla extract in a food processor and process until smooth. Pour over the cookie base and smooth the top. Place the cheesecake on a rimmed cookie sheet and bake in the oven for 20 minutes, until just set. Remove from the oven, leaving it turned on, and set aside for 20 minutes.

2 Put the sour cream, remaining sugar, and vanilla extract in a bowl and mix together. Spoon over the cheesecake and return to the oven for 10 minutes. Remove from the oven and let cool. Chill overnight. To make the topping, put the sugar in a pan with 2 tablespoons water and heat gently until the sugar has dissolved. Increase the heat and add the blueberries. Cover and cook for a few minutes until they start to soften. Remove from the heat.

3 Put the arrowroot and 2 tablespoons water in a small bowl and blend together. Add to the blueberries and stir until smooth. Return to low heat and cook until the juice thickens and turns translucent. Set aside to cool. One hour before serving, remove the cheesecake from the pan and place on a serving plate. Spoon the blueberries on top and return the cheesecake to the refrigerator until ready to serve.

VARIATION
As an alternative to blueberries, other fruit such as raspberries, black currants or cranberries may be used in the topping.

Almond Cheesecakes

These creamy cheese desserts are so delicious that it's hard to believe that they are low in fat—a healthy and flavorful option.

15 mins plus 1 hr chilling	10 mins

SERVES 4

INGREDIENTS

12 amaretti cookies

1 egg white, beaten lightly

1 cup skim milk cream cheese

½ tsp almond extract

½ tsp finely grated lime rind

scant ¼ cup ground almonds

2 tbsp superfine sugar

⅓ cup golden raisins

2 tsp powdered gelatin

2 tbsp cold water

2 tbsp lime juice

TO DECORATE

2 tbsp slivered almonds, toasted

strips of lime rind

1 Preheat the oven to 350°F/180°C. Place the cookies in a polythene bag, seal, and crush with a rolling pin.

2 Place the amaretti crumbs in a bowl and stir in the egg white to bind them together.

3 Put 4 nonstick cooking rings or poached egg rings, 3½ inches/9 cm across, on a cookie sheet.

4 Divide the amaretti mixture into 4 equal portions and spoon it into the rings, pressing it down well. Bake in the preheated oven for about 10 minutes, until crisp. Remove from the oven and let cool in the rings.

5 Put the cream cheese, almond extract, lime rind, ground almonds, sugar, and golden raisins in a bowl and beat thoroughly until well mixed.

6 Sprinkle the gelatin over the water in a heatproof bowl and let it go spongy. Place over a pan of hot water and stir until dissolved then stir in the lime juice. Fold into the cheese mixture and spoon over the amaretti bases. Smooth over the tops and let chill for 1 hour or until set.

7 Loosen the cheesecakes from the rings using a small spatula and transfer to serving plates. Decorate with toasted slivered almonds and strips of lime rind and serve.

Ricotta Lemon Cheesecake

Italian bakers pride themselves on their baked ricotta cheesecakes, studded with fruit soaked in spirits.

🍰 3 hrs 45 mins   🕐 30–40 mins

SERVES 6–8

INGREDIENTS

generous ⅓ cup golden raisins

3 tbsp Marsala or grappa

butter, for greasing

2 tbsp semolina, plus extra for dusting

1½ cups ricotta cheese, drained

3 large egg yolks, beaten

½ cup superfine sugar

3 tbsp lemon juice

2 tbsp candied orange peel, chopped finely

finely grated rind of 2 large lemons

TO DECORATE

confectioners' sugar

fresh mint sprigs

red currants or berries (optional)

1 Soak the golden raisins in the Marsala or grappa in a small bowl for about 30 minutes, or until the liquid has been absorbed and the fruit is swollen.

2 Preheat the oven to 350°F/180°C. Cut out a circle of parchment paper to fit the bottom of a loose-based 8-inch/20-cm round cake pan that is about 2 inches/5 cm deep. Grease the sides and bottom of the pan and line the base. Lightly dust with semolina and tip out the excess.

3 Using a wooden spoon, press the ricotta cheese though a nylon strainer into a bowl. Beat in the egg yolks, sugar, semolina, and lemon juice and continue beating until blended.

4 Fold in the golden raisins, orange peel, and lemon rind. Pour into the prepared pan and smooth the surface.

5 Bake the cheesecake in the center of the preheated oven for 30–40 minutes, until firm to the touch and coming away slightly from the side of the pan.

6 Turn off the oven and open the door. Let the cheesecake cool in the turned-off oven for 2–3 hours. To serve, remove from the pan and transfer to a plate. Sift over a layer of confectioners' sugar from at least 12 inches/30 cm above the cheesecake to dust the top and sides lightly. Decorate with mint leaves and red currants, if wished.

Mascarpone Cheesecake

The mascarpone gives this baked cheesecake a wonderfully tangy flavor.
Ricotta cheese could be used as an alternative.

🍰 15 mins   🕐 50 mins

SERVES 8

INGREDIENTS

4 tbsp butter, sweet for preference, plus extra for greasing

3 cups gingersnap crumbs

1 tbsp chopped preserved ginger

2¼ cups mascarpone cheese

finely grated rind and juice of 2 lemons

½ cup superfine sugar

2 large eggs, separated

fruit coulis (see Cook's Tip), to serve

1 Preheat the oven to 350°F/180°C. Grease and line the bottom of a 10-inch/25-cm springform cake pan or loose-bottomed cake pan.

2 Melt the butter in a pan and stir in the cookie crumbs and chopped ginger. Use the mixture to line the pan, pressing the mixture about ¼ inch/ 5 mm up the sides.

3 Beat together the cheese, lemon rind and juice, sugar, and egg yolks until quite smooth.

4 Whisk the egg whites until they are stiff and fold into the cheese and lemon mixture.

5 Pour the mixture into the pan and bake in the preheated oven for 35–45 minutes, until just set. Don't worry if it cracks or sinks—this is quite normal.

6 Leave the cheesecake in the pan to cool. Serve with fruit coulis (see Cook's Tip).

COOK'S TIP
Fruit coulis can be made by cooking 1½ cups fruit, such as blueberries, for 5 minutes with 2 tablespoons of water. Strain the mixture, then stir in 1 tablespoon (or more, to taste) of sifted confectioners' sugar. Let cool before serving.

Pineapple Cheesecake

A delicious summer dessert, this cheesecake will have your guests coming back for another serving.

20 mins plus
4 hrs chilling

0 mins

SERVES 4

INGREDIENTS

4 tbsp butter, melted, plus extra
  for greasing

4 oz/115 g graham crackers, crushed finely

½ cup superfine sugar

juice of 1 lemon

2 tbsp grated lemon rind

1½ cups cream cheese

1½ cups curd cheese

⅔ cup heavy cream, whipped

14 oz/400 g canned pineapple slices,
  drained

pinch of ground nutmeg, to decorate
  (optional)

1 Grease an 8-inch/20-cm loose-bottomed tart pan with butter, put the crushed crackers in a large bowl and mix in the melted butter, then press the cookie mixture evenly over the bottom.

2 Put the sugar in a separate bowl and stir in the lemon juice and half of the lemon rind. Add the cheeses and beat until thoroughly combined. Fold in the cream. Spread the cream mixture evenly over the cracker layer. Cover with plastic wrap and let chill in the refrigerator for at least 4 hours.

3 Remove the cheesecake from the refrigerator, turn out on to a serving platter and arrange the pineapple slices over the top. Sprinkle over a little ground nutmeg (if using). Serve immediately.

Banana Coconut Cheesecake

The exotic combination of banana and coconut goes well with chocolate.
Fresh coconut gives a better flavor than shredded coconut.

30 mins plus
2 hrs chilling   5 mins

SERVES 10

I N G R E D I E N T S

8 oz/225 g chocolate chip cookies

4 tbsp butter

1½ cups medium-fat cream cheese

⅓ cup superfine sugar

1¾ oz/50 g grated fresh coconut

2 tbsp coconut-flavored liqueur

2 ripe bananas

4½ oz/125 g semisweet chocolate

¼ oz/7 g powdered gelatin

3 tbsp water

⅔ cup heavy cream

T O   D E C O R A T E

1 banana

lemon juice

a little semisweet chocolate, melted

1 Place the cookies in a polythene bag and crush with a rolling pin. Pour into a mixing bowl. Melt the butter and stir into the cookie crumbs until well coated. Firmly press the cookie mixture into the bottom and up the sides of an 8-inch/20-cm springform cake pan.

2 Beat together the cream cheese and superfine sugar until well combined, then beat in the grated coconut and coconut-flavored liqueur. Mash the 2 bananas and beat them in. Melt the semisweet chocolate and beat in until well combined.

3 Sprinkle the gelatin over the water in a heatproof bowl and let it go spongy. Place over a pan of gently simmering water and stir until dissolved. Stir into the chocolate mixture. Whisk the cream until just holding its shape and stir into the chocolate mixture. Spoon over the cookie base and let chill for 2 hours, until set.

4 To serve, carefully transfer to a serving plate. Slice the banana, toss in the lemon juice, and arrange around the edge of the cheesecake. Put a little chocolate, broken into pieces, in a heatproof bowl set over a pan of gently simmering water until melted. Drizzle with melted chocolate and let set.

COOK'S TIP
To crack the coconut, pierce 2 of the "eyes" and drain off the liquid. Tap hard around the center with a hammer until it cracks and lever it apart.

Hot Desserts

If you like hot desserts, you will be spoiled for choice in

this section. Light or filling, the range of exciting recipes

will bring family meals or formal gatherings to

a contented close. There are favorites such as

steamed desserts or creamy rice puddings, with

 exotic twists and tempting

flavorings to stimulate your taste buds.

Fusions of East and West cuisine come

together to create unusual warm salads

and grilled fruit kabobs, hot fudgy chocolate sauces and

wobbly soufflés. Whatever you choose, you can be sure

your guests will be back for more.

Chocolate Rum Bananas

A simple and quick dessert, ideal to prepare when unexpected guests drop in. Sprinkle with ground cinnamon, if preferred.

5 mins 5–10 mins

SERVES 4

INGREDIENTS

1 tbsp butter, melted

8 oz/225 g semisweet chocolate

4 large bananas

2 tbsp dark rum

grated nutmeg, to decorate

crème fraîche (see page 9), mascarpone cheese, or ice cream, to serve

1 Take 4 x 10-inch/25-cm squares of foil and brush them with butter.

2 Cut the chocolate into very small pieces. Make a careful slit lengthwise in the peel of each banana, and open just wide enough to insert the chocolate. Place the chocolate pieces inside the bananas, along their lengths, then close them up.

3 Wrap each stuffed banana in a square of foil, then grill them over hot coals for about 5–10 minutes, until the chocolate has melted inside the bananas. Remove from the grill, place the bananas on individual serving plates, and pour some rum into each banana. Serve at once with crème fraîche, mascarpone cheese, or ice cream, topped with a little grated nutmeg.

Coconut Bananas

This elaborate dessert is the perfect finale for a Chinese banquet.
Bananas are fried in a citrus-flavored butter and served with coconut.

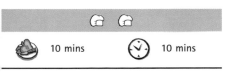

10 mins   10 mins

SERVES 4

INGREDIENTS

3 tbsp shredded coconut

2 oz/55 g butter, sweet for preference

1 tbsp grated gingerroot

grated rind of 1 orange

½ cup superfine sugar

4 tbsp fresh lime juice

6 bananas

6 tbsp orange-flavored liqueur, such as
Cointreau or Grand Marnier

3 tsp toasted sesame seeds

lime slices, to decorate

ice cream, to serve (optional)

1 Heat a small nonstick skillet until hot. Add the coconut and cook, stirring constantly, for 1 minute until lightly colored. Remove from the pan and let cool.

2 Melt the butter in a large skillet and add the ginger, orange rind, sugar, and lime juice. Mix well.

3 Peel and slice the bananas lengthwise (and cut in half if they are very large). Place the bananas cut-side down in the butter mixture and cook for 1-2 minutes, or until the sauce mixture starts to become sticky. Turn the bananas to coat in the sauce.

4 Remove the bananas and place on heated serving plates. Keep warm.

5 Return the skillet to the heat and add the orange liqueur, blending well. Ignite with a taper, let the flames die down, then pour over the bananas.

6 Sprinkle with the reserved coconut and sesame seeds and serve at once, decorated with slices of lime.

COOK'S TIP
For a very special treat
try serving this with a
flavored ice cream such as
coconut, ginger, or praline.

Grilled Chocolate Bananas

This is a very simple dessert to serve at the end of a summer grill with family and friends. Open the parcels carefully as they will be very hot.

5 mins   10 mins

SERVES 4

I N G R E D I E N T S

4 bananas

¼ cup chocolate drops

12 mini marshmallows

whipped cream, to serve

1 With a sharp knife, slit the banana skins and cut almost through the bananas. Push chocolate drops and marshmallow into the slits and wrap the bananas in foil.

2 Place the foil parcels on the grill and cook for 10 minutes, turning after 5 minutes.

3 Open up the parcels and serve the bananas with cream.

VARIATION
The bananas can also be baked in an oven at 425°F/220°C for 15–20 minutes.

Chargrilled Pineapple

Fresh pineapple slices are cooked on the grill, and brushed with a buttery fresh ginger and brown sugar baste. Serve immediately.

🍍 10 mins ⏲ 10 mins

SERVES 4

INGREDIENTS

1 pineapple

GINGER BUTTER BASTE

4½ oz/125 g butter

½ cup light muscovado sugar

1 tsp finely grated gingerroot

TOPPING

1 cup mascarpone cheese

½ tsp ground cinnamon

1 tbsp light muscovado sugar

1 Prepare the pineapple by cutting off the spiky top. Peel the pineapple with a sharp knife, remove the "eyes" and cut the flesh into thick slices.

2 To make the ginger-flavored butter, put the butter, sugar, and ginger into a small pan and heat gently until melted. Transfer to a heatproof bowl and keep warm at the side of the grill, ready for basting the fruit.

3 To prepare the topping, mix together the mascarpone cheese, cinnamon, and sugar. Cover and chill until ready to serve.

4 Grill the pineapple slices for about 2 minutes on each side, brushing them well with the ginger butter baste.

5 Serve the chargrilled pineapple with a little extra ginger butter baste poured over. Top with a spoonful of the spiced mascarpone cheese.

VARIATION
If you prefer, substitute ½ teaspoon ground ginger for the grated gingerroot. Light muscovado sugar gives the best flavor, but you can use ordinary brown sugar instead. You can make this dessert indoors by cooking the pineapple under a hot broiler.

Charbroiled Fruit

Fruit is the obvious choice for a lowfat dessert, but it can be rather unexciting. Liven it up with a flavorful glaze and serve hot.

10 mins   10 mins

SERVES 4

INGREDIENTS

4 fresh pineapple rings

4 slices mango

4 kiwi fruit, peeled and sliced

4 slices papaya

2 nectarines, peeled, pitted, and halved

2 bananas, peeled and halved

6 tbsp honey

grated rind of 1 orange

grated rind of 1 lemon

1-inch/2.5-cm piece gingerroot, grated

1 Prepare the fruit. Combine the honey, orange and lemon rind, and ginger in a small bowl. Brush the mixture over all the fruit.

2 Cook under a preheated broiler for about 10 minutes, brushing with the glaze and turning frequently.

3 Divide the fruit among individual serving plates and serve immediately.

COOK'S TIP
Use a single flower honey, if possible. Try clover, acacia, orange blossom or lavender.

Broiled Fruit with Lime Butter

This delicious variation of a hot fruit salad includes wedges of tropical fruits, dusted with dark brown sugar and a pinch of spice before broiling.

15 mins plus
30 mins resting

10 mins

SERVES 4

INGREDIENTS

1 baby pineapple

1 ripe papaya

1 ripe mango

2 kiwi fruit

4 finger bananas

4 tbsp dark rum

1 tsp allspice

2 tbsp lime juice

4 tbsp dark muscovado sugar

LIME "BUTTER"

2 oz/55 g lowfat spread

½ tsp finely grated lime rind

1 tbsp confectioners' sugar

1 Quarter the pineapple, trimming away most of the leaves, and place in a shallow dish. Peel the papaya, cut it in half, and scoop out the seeds. Cut the flesh into thick wedges and place in the same dish as the pineapple.

2 Peel the mango, cut either side of the smooth, central flat pit, and remove the pit. Slice the flesh into thick wedges. Peel the kiwi fruit and cut in half. Peel the bananas. Add all of these fruits to the dish.

3 Sprinkle over the rum, allspice and lime juice, cover, and leave at room temperature for 30 minutes, turning occasionally, to allow the flavors to develop.

4 Meanwhile, make the butter. Place the lowfat spread in a small bowl and beat in the lime rind and sugar until well mixed. Let chill until required.

5 Preheat the broiler to hot. Drain the fruit, reserving the juices, and arrange in the broiler pan. Sprinkle with the sugar and broil for 3–4 minutes until hot, bubbling, and starting to char.

6 Transfer the fruit to a serving plate and spoon over the juices. Serve with the lime butter.

VARIATION
Serve with a light sauce of 1¼ cups tropical fruit juice thickened with 2 tsp arrowroot.

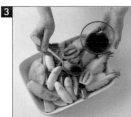

Grilled Apples

Easy to prepare and delicious to eat, these apples will be enjoyed by both adults and children.

10 mins   10 mins

SERVES 4

INGREDIENTS

4 dessert apples

3 tbsp lemon juice

3 tbsp butter

4 tsp brown sugar

8 tbsp mincemeat

plain yogurt, crème fraîche (see page 9), or mascarpone cheese, to serve

1 Wash the apples, then cut them in half from top to bottom. Remove the cores and pips, then brush the cut sides of the apples with lemon juice to prevent discoloration.

2 Put the butter in a small pan and gently melt it over low heat. Remove from the heat, then brush the cut sides of the apples with half of the butter. Reserve the rest of the melted butter.

3 Sprinkle the apples with sugar, then transfer them to the grill, cut-side down, and cook over hot coals for about 5 minutes. Brush the apples with the remaining butter, then turn them over. Add 1 tablespoon of mincemeat to the center of each apple, then cook for an additional 5 minutes, or until they are cooked to your taste.

4 Remove from the heat and transfer to serving plates. Serve at once with plain yogurt, crème fraîche, or mascarpone cheese.

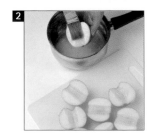

Grilled Baked Apples

When they are wrapped in foil, apples bake to perfection on the grill and make a delightful finale to any meal.

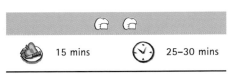

🍓 15 mins   🕐 25–30 mins

SERVES 4

INGREDIENTS

4 medium tart cooking apples

4 tbsp chopped walnuts

4 tbsp ground almonds

2 tbsp molasses sugar

¼ cup cherries, chopped

2 tbsp chopped preserved ginger

1 tbsp amaretto (optional)

2 tbsp butter

light cream or thick plain yogurt, to serve

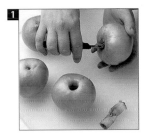

1 Core the apples and using a knife, score each around the center to prevent the skins from splitting while they are grilling.

2 To make the filling, combine the walnuts, almonds, sugar, cherries, ginger, and amaretto (if using) in a small bowl.

3 Spoon the filling mixture into each apple, pushing it down into the hollowed-out core. Mound a little of the filling mixture on top of each apple.

4 Place each apple on a large square of double-thickness foil and generously dot all over with the butter. Wrap up the foil so that the apple is completely enclosed.

5 Grill the foil packages over hot coals for 25–30 minutes, or until the apples are tender.

6 Transfer the apples to warm, individual serving plates. Serve immediately with lashings of light cream or thick plain yogurt.

COOK'S TIP

If the coals are dying down, place the foil packages directly on them, raking them up around the apples. Grill for 25–30 minutes and serve with the cream or yogurt.

Baked Apples with Berries

This winter dessert is a classic dish. Large, fluffy apples are hollowed out and filled with spices, almonds, and blackberries.

10 mins   55 mins

SERVES 4

INGREDIENTS

4 medium tart cooking apples

1 tbsp lemon juice

scant ½ cup prepared blackberries, thawed if frozen

⅓ cup slivered almonds

½ tsp allspice

½ tsp finely grated lemon rind

2 tbsp raw sugar

1¼ cups ruby port

1 cinnamon stick, broken

2 tsp cornstarch blended with 2 tbsp cold water

lowfat custard, to serve

1 Preheat the oven to 400°F/200°C. Wash and dry the apples. Using a small sharp knife, make a shallow cut through the skin around the center of each apple—this will help the apples to cook through.

2 Core the apples, brush the centers with the lemon juice to prevent them browning, and stand them in an ovenproof dish.

3 In a bowl, mix together the blackberries, almonds, allspice, lemon rind, and sugar. Using a teaspoon, spoon the mixture into the center of each apple.

4 Pour the port into the dish, add the cinnamon stick and bake the apples in the preheated oven for 35–40 minutes, or until tender and soft.

5 Drain the cooking juices into a pan and keep the apples warm.

6 Discard the cinnamon stick and add the cornstarch mixture to the cooking juices. Cook over medium heat, stirring constantly, until thickened.

7 Heat the custard until piping hot. Pour the sauce over the apples and serve with the custard.

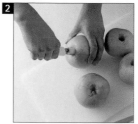

Stuffed Baked Apples

Baked apples are a family favorite, often stuffed with golden raisins and brown sugar. Try this ginger-flavored flapjack stuffing for a change.

🍎 10 mins   🕐 45 mins

SERVES 4

INGREDIENTS

1 tbsp honey

1 tbsp syrup from the preserved ginger jar (see below)

4 tbsp rolled oats

scant ½ cup no-soak dried apricots

¼ cup blanched almonds

1 piece preserved ginger, drained

4 large cooking apples

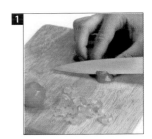

1 Preheat the oven to 350°F/180°C. Finely chop the apricots, almonds and ginger. Put the honey and syrup in a pan and heat gently until the honey has melted. Stir in the oats and cook over low heat for 2 minutes. Remove the pan from the heat and stir in the apricots, almonds, and preserved ginger.

2 Core the apples, widen the tops slightly, and score around the circumference of each to prevent the skins bursting during cooking. Place them in an ovenproof dish and fill the cavities with the stuffing. Pour in just enough water to come about one-third of the way up the apples.

3 Bake in the preheated oven for 40 minutes, or until tender. Serve immediately.

VARIATION
Omit the preserved ginger and ginger syrup. Use 2 tablespoons of honey, substitute chopped walnuts for the almonds, and add ½ teaspoon of ground cinnamon to the stuffing.

Coconut Apples

A grill variation on baked apples, but instead of being filled with dry fruits, they are layered with jelly and dry, unsweetened coconut.

🕙 10 mins   ⏱ 15–20 mins

SERVES 4

INGREDIENTS

2 tsp butter, sweet for preference

4 tbsp ginger and apple jelly

1½ cups dry unsweetened coconut

pinch of ground cinnamon

4 tart cooking apples

heavy cream or ice cream, to serve (optional)

1 Cut 4 squares of foil, each large enough to enclose 1 apple, and lightly grease with the butter. Combine the jelly and coconut in a small bowl and stir in cinnamon to taste.

2 Core the apples, but don't peel them. Cut each apple horizontally into 3 slices. Spread the mixture among the apple slices and reassemble the apples. Place 1 apple on each sheet of foil and fold up the sides to enclose securely.

3 Cook the apples on a hot grill for 15–20 minutes. Serve immediately, with cream or ice cream, if you like.

VARIATION
Substitute large, firm pears for the apples.

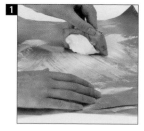

Summer Fruit Nectarines

These easily prepared nectarines taste as good as they look and will soon become a favorite for the grill.

5 mins   10–15 mins

SERVES 4

INGREDIENTS

4 large nectarines

¾ cup frozen summer fruits, such as blueberries and raspberries, thawed

3 tbsp lemon juice

3 tbsp honey

crème fraîche (see page 9), mascarpone cheese, or ice cream, to serve

1 Cut out 8 x 7-inch/18-cm squares of foil. Wash the nectarines, cut them in half, and remove the pits. Place each nectarine half on a square of foil.

2 Fill each nectarine half with summer fruits, then top each one with 1 teaspoon of lemon juice, then 1 teaspoon of honey.

3 Close the foil around each nectarine half to make a parcel, then grill them over hot coals for about 10–15 minutes, according to your taste. Remove from the grill, place the nectarines on serving plates, and serve at once with crème fraîche, mascarpone cheese, or ice cream.

Stuffed Nectarines

This delectable combination of juicy fruit, crunchy amaretti cookies, and bittersweet chocolate is an irresistible summer treat.

🧤 15 mins   🕐 40–45 mins

SERVES 6

INGREDIENTS

3 oz/85 g bittersweet chocolate, chopped finely

1 cup amaretti cookie crumbs

1 tsp finely grated lemon rind

1 large egg, separated

6 tbsp amaretto

6 nectarines, halved and pitted

1¼ cups white wine

2 oz/55 g milk chocolate, grated

whipped cream or ice cream, to serve

1 Preheat the oven to 375°F/190°C In a large bowl, mix together the chocolate, amaretti crumbs, and lemon rind. Lightly beat the egg white and add it to the mixture with half the amaretto. (Use the yolk in another recipe.) Using a small sharp knife, slightly enlarge the cavities in the nectarines. Add the removed nectarine flesh to the chocolate and crumb mixture and mix together well.

2 Place the nectarines, cut-side up, in an ovenproof dish just large enough to hold them in a single layer. Pile the chocolate and crumb mixture into the cavities, dividing it equally among them. Mix the wine and remaining amaretto together and pour it into the dish around the nectarines. Bake in the preheated oven for 40–45 minutes, until the nectarines are tender. Transfer 2 nectarine halves to each individual serving plate and spoon over a little of the cooking juices. Sprinkle over the grated milk chocolate and serve immediately with a spoonful of whipped cream or ice cream.

Baked Bananas

The orange-flavored cream can be prepared in advance, but do not make up the banana packages until just before you need to cook them.

🍊 20 mins 🕐 10 mins

SERVES 4

INGREDIENTS

4 bananas

2 passion fruit

4 tbsp orange juice

4 tbsp orange-flavored liqueur

ORANGE-FLAVORED CREAM

⅔ cup heavy cream

3 tbsp confectioners' sugar

2 tbsp orange-flavored liqueur

1 Preheat the oven to 350°F/180°C. To make the orange-flavored cream, pour the heavy cream into a mixing bowl and sprinkle with the confectioners' sugar. Whisk the mixture until it is standing in soft peaks. Carefully fold in the orange-flavored liqueur and chill in the refrigerator until required.

2 Peel the bananas and place each on a sheet of foil.

3 Cut the passion fruit in half and squeeze the juice of each half over each banana. Spoon over the orange juice and liqueur.

4 Fold the foil over the top of the bananas so that they are completely enclosed.

5 Place the packages on a cookie sheet and bake the bananas in the oven for about 10 minutes, or until they are just tender (test by inserting a toothpick).

6 Transfer the foil packages to warm, individual serving plates. Open out the foil packages at the table and then serve immediately with the chilled orange-flavored cream.

VARIATION
Try using different-flavored liqueurs, such as coconut liqueur, to make the cream. The results can be both delicious and exotic.

Fried Bananas

This wonderfully sticky dessert of bananas deep-fried in sesame batter will bring out the child in every member of the family.

🕐 10 mins   🕐 10 mins

SERVES 4

INGREDIENTS

1 cup all-purpose flour

½ tsp baking soda

salt

2 tbsp sugar

1 egg

1 tbsp sesame seeds

4 bananas

peanut or sunflower oil, for deep-frying

2 tbsp honey, to serve

1   Sift the flour into a bowl with the baking soda and a pinch of salt. Stir in the sugar, then whisk in the egg and 4–6 tablespoons of water to make a smooth, thin batter. Whisk in the sesame seeds.

2   Peel the bananas and halve lengthwise, then cut in half across the centers. Dip the bananas in the batter to coat completely.

3   Meanwhile, heat the oil in a wok or deep, heavy-based skillet to 350-375°F/180-190°C, or until a cube of bread browns in 30 seconds. Deep-fry the bananas, in batches, until golden brown. Remove with a slotted spoon and drain on paper towels. Transfer to plates and drizzle with the honey before serving.

VARIATION
Fresh pineapple rings are also delicious prepared in this way.

Banana Sizzles

Bananas are particularly sweet and delicious when grilled—and conveniently come with their own protective wrapping.

10 mins   6–8 mins

SERVES 4

INGREDIENTS

3 tbsp butter, softened

2 tbsp dark rum

1 tbsp orange juice

4 tbsp dark muscovado sugar

pinch of ground cinnamon

4 bananas

1 Beat the butter with the rum, orange juice, sugar, and cinnamon in a small bowl until thoroughly combined and smooth.

2 Place the bananas, without peeling, on a hot grill and cook, turning frequently, for 6–8 minutes, until the skins are blackened.

3 Transfer the bananas to serving plates, slit the skins, and cut partially through the flesh lengthwise. Divide the flavored butter among the bananas and serve.

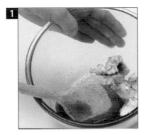
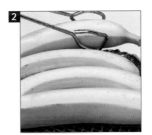

VARIATION
You can also cook the bananas wrapped in foil. Cut them in half lengthwise without peeling. Spread the flavored butter of the cut surfaces and reassemble the bananas. Wrap in foil parcels and cook on a medium grill for 5–10 minutes.

Battered Bananas

These bananas are quite irresistible, therefore it may be wise to make double quantities for weak-willed guests!

10 mins   20 mins

SERVES 4

INGREDIENTS

8 medium bananas

2 tsp lemon juice

⅔ cup self-rising flour

⅔ cup rice flour

1 tbsp cornstarch

½ tsp ground cinnamon

1 cup water

oil, for deep-frying

4 tbsp brown sugar

cream or ice cream, to serve

1 Cut the bananas into even-size chunks and place them in a large mixing bowl.

2 Sprinkle the lemon juice over the bananas to prevent discoloration.

3 Sift the self-rising flour, rice flour, cornstarch, and cinnamon into a mixing bowl. Gradually stir in the water to make a thin batter.

4 Heat the oil in a preheated wok until smoking, then reduce the heat slightly.

5 Place a piece of banana on the end of a fork and carefully dip it into the batter, draining off any excess. Repeat with the remaining banana pieces.

6 Sprinkle the brown sugar on to a large plate.

7 Carefully place the banana pieces in the oil and cook for 2–3 minutes, until golden. Remove the banana pieces from the oil with a slotted spoon and roll them in the sugar.

8 Transfer the battered bananas to serving bowls and serve immediately with cream or ice cream.

COOK'S TIP
Rice flour can be bought from wholefood stores or from Chinese supermarkets.

Peaches & Mascarpone

If you prepare these peaches in advance, all you have to do is pop them on the grill when you are ready to serve them.

🍮 10 mins   🕐 10 mins

SERVES 4

INGREDIENTS

4 peaches

¾ cup mascarpone cheese

⅓ cup pecans or walnuts, chopped

1 tsp sunflower oil

4 tbsp maple syrup

1 Cut the peaches in half and remove the pits. If you are preparing this recipe in advance, press the peach halves together again and wrap them in plastic wrap until required.

2 Combine the mascarpone cheese and pecans or walnuts in a small bowl. Chill in the refrigerator until required.

3 Brush the peaches with a little oil and place on a rack set over medium-hot coals. Grill for 5–10 minutes, turning once, until hot.

4 Transfer the peaches to a serving dish and top with the mascarpone cheese mixture.

5 Drizzle the maple syrup over the peaches and mascarpone filling and serve immediately.

VARIATION
You can use nectarines instead of peaches for this recipe. Remember to choose ripe but firm fruit which won't go soft and mushy when it is grilled. Prepare the nectarines in the same way as the peaches and grill for 5–10 minutes.

Piña Colada Pineapple

The flavors of pineapple and coconut blend as well together on the grill as they do in the well-known cocktail.

15 mins   25 mins

SERVES 4

INGREDIENTS

1 small pineapple

2 tbsp butter, sweet for preference

2 tbsp molasses sugar

½ cup shredded coconut

2 tbsp coconut-flavored liqueur or dark rum

1 Using a very sharp knife, cut the pineapple into quarters and then remove the tough core from the center, leaving the leaves attached.

2 Carefully cut the pineapple flesh away from the skin. Remove any "eyes" with a small sharp knife. Make horizontal cuts across the flesh of the pineapple quarters.

3 Place the butter in a pan and heat gently until melted, stirring constantly. Brush the melted butter over the pineapple and sprinkle with the sugar.

4 Cover the pineapple leaves with foil in order to prevent them burning and transfer the pineapple quarters to a rack set over hot coals.

5 Grill the pineapple for about 10 minutes.

6 Sprinkle the coconut over the pineapple and grill, cut-side up, for an additional 5–10 minutes, or until the pineapple is piping hot.

7 Transfer the pineapple to serving plates and remove the foil from the leaves. Spoon a little coconut-flavored liqueur or rum over the pineapple and serve immediately.

COOK'S TIP

Fresh coconut has the best flavor for this dish. If you prefer, however, you can use dry unsweetened coconut.

Flambéed Peaches

A fabulous end to a dinner party, this is a luxurious but, at the same time, refreshing dessert.

 5 mins 5 mins

SERVES 4

INGREDIENTS

3 tbsp butter, sweet for preference

3 tbsp light muscovado sugar

4 tbsp orange juice

4 peaches, peeled, halved, and pitted

2 tbsp amaretto or peach cognac

4 tbsp slivered almonds, toasted

1 Heat the butter, sugar, and orange juice in a large, heavy-based skillet until the butter has melted and the sugar has dissolved.

2 Add the peach halves and cook for 1–2 minutes on each side until turning golden.

3 Add the amaretto or peach cognac and give it time to get warm before igniting with a match or taper. When the flames have died down, transfer to a plate, sprinkle with the slivered almonds, and serve.

VARIATION
Igniting the spirit burns off the alcohol and mellows the flavor. However, if you are serving this dessert to children, you can omit the amaretto or cognac.

Poached Allspice Pears

These pears are moist and delicious from being poached in an orange juice, sugar, and allspice mixture.

🥧 5 mins   🕐 15 mins

SERVES 4

INGREDIENTS

4 large ripe pears

1¼ cups orange juice

2 tsp allspice

⅓ cup raisins

2 tbsp brown sugar

grated orange rind, to decorate

1 Using an apple corer, core the pears. Using a sharp knife, peel the pears and cut them in half.

2 Place the pear halves in a large pan.

3 Add the orange juice, allspice, raisins and sugar to the pan and heat gently, stirring, until the sugar has dissolved. Bring the mixture to the boil for 1 minute.

4 Reduce the heat to low and leave to simmer for about 10 minutes, or until the pears are cooked, but still fairly firm—test them by inserting the tip of a sharp knife.

COOK'S TIP
This dessert is refreshing at the end of a big meal. It can also be served cold.

5 Remove the pears from the pan with a slotted spoon and transfer to individual serving plates. Decorate and serve hot with the syrup.

Spiced Baked Pears

This simple, well-flavored dessert is delightful hot, but can also be prepared in advance and served cold.

5 mins   30 mins

SERVES 4

INGREDIENTS

4 large firm pears

⅔ cup apple juice

1 cinnamon stick

4 cloves

1 bay leaf

1 Preheat the oven to 350°F/180°C.

2 Peel and core the pears and cut them into quarters. Place in an ovenproof dish and add the remaining ingredients.

3 Cover the dish and bake in the preheated oven for 30 minutes.

4 Serve the pears hot or cold.

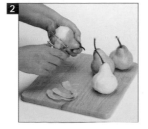

Caramelized Fruit

It is unusual to include strawberries in a chargrilled fruit salad, but they work surprising well. Choose large ripe berries and don't hull them.

15 mins plus
1 hr marinating

5 mins

SERVES 4

INGREDIENTS

⅔ cup medium sherry

generous ½ cup superfine sugar

1 Ogen melon, halved and seeded

4 peaches, halved and pitted

scant 1 cup strawberries

1 Combine the sherry and sugar in a large bowl, stirring until the sugar has dissolved.

2 Cut the melon halves into wedges and cut the flesh away from the skin. Peel the peaches (see Cook's Tip). Add the melon wedges, peach halves, and strawberries to the bowl, tossing gently to coat. Cover with plastic wrap and set aside to marinate for 1 hour.

3 Drain the fruit, reserving the marinade. Cook the melon and peaches on a hot grill for 3 minutes, then add the strawberries and cook for an additional 2 minutes. Turn the fruit and brush frequently with the reserved marinade. Serve immediately.

COOK'S TIP

To peel peaches, make a tiny nick in the skin with the point of a sharp knife. Place in a bowl and cover with boiling water. Leave for 15–30 seconds, then remove with a slotted spoon. Peel off the skin.

Pineapple Rings with Cognac

In this recipe, pineapple rings are marinated in a delicious mixture of honey and cognac, then grilled.

15 mins plus 1 hr–1 hr 15 mins marinating · **10 mins**

SERVES 4

INGREDIENTS

1 pineapple

MARINADE

2 tbsp honey

3 tbsp cognac

2 tsp lemon juice

fresh mint sprigs, to decorate

1 Peel and core the pineapple and cut into rings. For the marinade, put the honey, cognac, and lemon juice into a large, nonmetallic (glass or ceramic) bowl, which will not react with acid. Stir together until well combined. Put the pineapple rings into the bowl and turn them in the mixture until thoroughly coated. Cover with plastic wrap, transfer to the refrigerator and let marinate for 1–1½ hours.

2 When the pineapple rings are thoroughly marinated, lift them out and grill them over hot coals for about 10 minutes, turning them frequently and basting with more marinade if necessary.

3 Remove the pineapple rings from the grill, arrange them on individual serving plates and decorate with fresh mint sprigs.

Totally Tropical Pineapple

The delicious aroma of fresh pineapple and dark rum as the succulent dessert is cooking will transport your imagination to a Caribbean beach.

15 mins   6–8 mins

SERVES 4

INGREDIENTS

1 pineapple

3 tbsp dark rum

2 tbsp light muscovado sugar

1 tsp ground ginger

4 tbsp melted butter, sweet for preference

1 Using a sharp knife, cut off the crown of the pineapple, then cut the fruit into ¾-inch/2-cm thick slices. Cut away the peel from each slice and flick out the "eyes" with the point of the knife. Stamp out the cores with an apple corer or small cookie cutter.

2 Combine the rum, sugar, ginger, and butter in a pitcher, stirring until the sugar has dissolved. Brush the pineapple rings with the mixture.

3 Cook the pineapple rings on a hot grill for 3-4 minutes on each side. Serve immediately with the remaining rum mixture poured over them.

VARIATION
If you prefer, you can cut the pineapple into cubes or quarter slices and thread on metal skewers before brushing with the rum mixture and cooking.

Glazed Pineapple Slices

Pineapple slices brushed with melted butter and honey then cooked in a griddle pan—simple but delicious. Cook on a grill if preferred.

5 mins   5 mins

SERVES 4

I N G R E D I E N T S

1 pineapple

¼ cup honey

4 oz/115 g butter, melted

mint leaves, to decorate

S E R V I N G   S U G G E S T I O N S

fruit sherbet

crème fraîche (see page 9)

whipped cream

ice cream

1 Peel and core the pineapple. Cut into thick slices, about 1 inch/2.5 cm wide.

2 Preheat the griddle over medium heat. Meanwhile, heat the honey in a small pan over medium heat, until it is liquid.

3 Brush both sides of the pineapple slices with the melted butter. Place in the griddle pan and cook for 2 minutes on each side, brushing with honey before and after turning so that both sides are well coated and sticky.

4 Remove the hot pineapple slices from the griddle pan. Decorate with mint leaves and serve with a scoop of fruit sorbet, crème fraîche, whipped cream, or ice cream.

Caribbean Pineapple

Complement fresh pineapple with a fabulous dark rum and raisin chocolate sauce for a simple but special dessert.

🍍 15 mins   🕐 5–6 mins

SERVES 6

INGREDIENTS

2 tbsp raisins

4 tbsp rum

175 g/6 oz good-quality
  semisweet chocolate

1 fresh pineapple

4 tbsp sweet butter

6 tbsp corn syrup

fresh mint sprigs, to decorate

1 Place the raisins in a heatproof bowl and add the rum. Set aside to soak and plump up. Break up the chocolate into fairly small pieces.

2 Meanwhile, cut off the leafy top and the base of the pineapple. Stand the pineapple up and slice off the skin. Remove any remaining eyes with a small, sharp knife. Cut the pineapple in half lengthwise and cut out the hard, woody core, then slice the flesh.

3 Arrange the pineapple slices on a cookie sheet in a single layer and dot with half the butter. Cook under a preheated broiler for 5–6 minutes, until just beginning to brown.

4 Meanwhile, make the sauce. Add the syrup and the remaining butter to the raisins and set the bowl over a pan of gently simmering water. Stir until the syrup has melted, then add the chocolate. Continue to stir until the chocolate has melted.

5 Divide the broiled pineapple between warm serving plates, spoon over the chocolate sauce, decorate with mint sprigs, and serve immediately.

VARIATION
This would also work well with other fruit, such as halved nectarines, wedges of fresh mango, or peeled bananas halved lengthwise.

Grilled Fruit with Maple Syrup

Slices of juicy fruit are coated in a rich maple syrup sauce as they cook in little parcels on the grill.

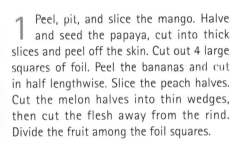 20 mins   10 mins

SERVES 4

INGREDIENTS

1 mango

1 papaya

2 bananas

2 peaches, peeled and pitted

1 Ogen melon, halved and seeded

4 oz/115 g butter, sweet for preference, cut into pieces

4 tbsp maple syrup

pinch of ground allspice

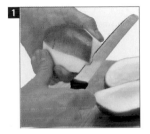

1 Peel, pit, and slice the mango. Halve and seed the papaya, cut into thick slices and peel off the skin. Cut out 4 large squares of foil. Peel the bananas and cut in half lengthwise. Slice the peach halves. Cut the melon halves into thin wedges, then cut the flesh away from the rind. Divide the fruit among the foil squares.

2 Put the butter and maple syrup in a food processor and process until thoroughly combined and smooth. Divide the flavored butter among the fruit parcels and sprinkle with a little allspice. Fold up the sides of the foil to enclose the fruit securely.

3 Cook on a medium grill, turning occasionally, for 10 minutes. Serve immediately.

COOK'S TIP
Look for "pure" or "100 percent" maple syrup. Cheaper varieties may be blended with other types of syrup.

Mexican Glazed Pumpkin

This simple dessert looks and smells wonderful and makes an unusual and tasty finale to a meal. Serve with sour cream or plain yogurt.

20 mins   10 mins

SERVES 4

INGREDIENTS

2 lb/900 g pumpkin

2¼ cups light muscovado sugar

1 tsp ground allspice

1 cup water

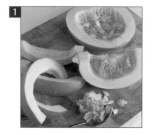  

1 Cut the pumpkin into wedges and scrape out the seeds with a spoon. Arrange the wedges in a large, flameproof casserole.

2 Combine the sugar and allspice in a bowl, then spoon it into the spaces between the wedges. Add the water, pouring it down the side of the casserole so that it doesn't wash away the sugar.

3 Cover and cook over low heat for 20 minutes, until the pumpkin is tender. Transfer the wedges to a serving dish and pour the sugary glaze over them. Serve immediately.

COOK'S TIP
Keep an eye on the water level while the pumpkin is cooking and top up with more hot water, if necessary.

Crunchy Ginger Apples

The flavor of ginger complements apples very well and this dessert can be quickly assembled. Serve warm with a little whipped or ice cream.

5 mins   10 mins

SERVES 4

I N G R E D I E N T S

4 dessert apples

2 tbsp lemon juice

2 tbsp butter, melted

2 tbsp raw sugar

4 tbsp diced preserved ginger

mint leaves, to decorate

S E R V I N G   S U G G E S T I O N S

crème fraîche (see page 9)

whipped cream

ice cream

1 Cut the apples in half through their circumference. Carefully remove the pips and core.

2 Place the lemon juice, butter, and raw sugar in 3 separate small dishes. Dip the cut side of the apples first in the lemon juice, then in the melted butter and, finally, in the sugar.

3 Preheat the griddle over medium heat. Add the apples, cut-side down, and cook for 5 minutes, or until the sugar caramelizes and the apple surfaces are dark. Turn and cook for an additional 5 minutes to blacken the skin. The cooked apples should still retain their crunch.

4 Arrange the apple halves in individual dishes (allowing 2 halves per serving), cut-side up, and spoon diced ginger over each half. Decorate with mint leaves and serve with a bowl of crème fraîche, whipped cream, or ice cream.

Pears with Chocolate Custard

Whole pears baked in a red wine and allspice syrup and served with a chocolate custard sauce—wonderful!

15 mins   30 mins

SERVES 4

INGREDIENTS

4 ripe pears

1 tbsp lime juice

2 tbsp red wine

2 oz/55 g butter

4 tbsp light brown sugar

1 tsp ground allspice

CHOCOLATE CUSTARD

2 cups milk

4 egg yolks

½ cup superfine sugar

2 tbsp grated semisweet chocolate

thin strips of lime rind, to decorate

1 Preheat the oven to 400°F/200°C. Peel and core the pears, leaving them whole, then brush with lime juice. Put the pears into a small, nonstick baking pan, then pour over the wine.

2 Heat the butter, sugar, and allspice in a small pan over low heat, stirring, until melted. Pour the mixture over the pears. Bake in the oven, basting occasionally, for 25 minutes, or until golden and cooked through.

3 Heat the milk until very hot. Beat the egg yolks while slowly adding the sugar until the mixture is pale and thick. Gradually add the milk, stirring constantly. Return the mixture to the pan and cook over medium heat, stirring constantly, until it is thickened. Add the chocolate and stir until melted.

4 Divide the custard between serving dishes. Remove the pears from the oven and put a pear in the center of each pool of custard. Decorate with strips of lime rind and serve.

Spun Sugar Pears

Whole pears are poached in a Madeira syrup in the microwave, then served with a delicate spun sugar surround.

20 mins   35 mins

SERVES 4

INGREDIENTS

⅔ cup water

⅔ cup Madeira

scant ⅔ cup superfine sugar

2 tbsp lime juice

4 ripe pears, peeled, stalks left on

fresh mint sprigs, to decorate

SPUN SUGAR

scant ⅔ cup superfine sugar

3 tbsp water

1 Combine the water, Madeira, sugar, and lime juice in a large bowl. Cover and cook on Full Power for 3 minutes. Stir well until the sugar dissolves.

2 Peel the pears and cut a thin slice from the base of each, so that they stand upright.

3 Add the pears to the bowl, spooning the wine syrup over them. Cover and cook on Full Power for about 10 minutes, turning the pears over every few minutes, until they are tender. The cooking time may vary slightly depending on the ripeness of the pears. Set aside to cool, covered, in the syrup.

4 Remove the cooled pears from the syrup and set aside on serving plates. Cook the syrup, uncovered, on Full Power for about 15 minutes, until reduced by half and thickened slightly. Set aside for 5 minutes. Spoon the syrup over the pears.

5 To make the spun sugar, combine the sugar and water in a bowl. Cook, uncovered, on Full Power for 1½ minutes. Stir until the sugar has dissolved completely. Continue to cook on Full Power for about 5–6 minutes, or until the sugar has caramelized.

6 Wait for the bubbles to subside and set aside for 2 minutes. Dip a teaspoon in the caramel and spin the caramelized sugar around each pear in a circular motion. Serve decorated with mint.

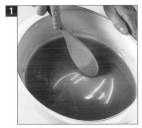
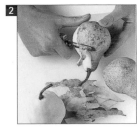
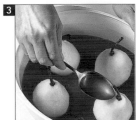

Baked Pears with Cinnamon

This simple, healthy recipe is easy to prepare and cook, but is deliciously warming. For a treat, serve hot on a pool of lowfat custard.

10 mins   25 mins

SERVES 4

INGREDIENTS

4 ripe pears

2 tbsp lemon juice

¼ cup molasses sugar

1 tsp ground cinnamon

¼ cup lowfat spread

finely shredded lemon rind, to decorate

lowfat custard, to serve

1 Preheat the oven to 400°F/200°C. Core and peel the pears, then slice them in half lengthwise, and brush them all over with the lemon juice to prevent them discoloring. Place the pears, cored-side down, in a small nonstick roasting pan.

2 Place the sugar, cinnamon, and lowfat spread in a small pan and heat gently, stirring constantly, until the sugar has dissolved. Keep the heat very low to stop too much water evaporating from the lowfat spread as it gets hot. Spoon the mixture over the pears.

VARIATION
For alternative flavors, replace the cinnamon with ground ginger and serve the pears sprinkled with chopped preserved ginger in syrup. Alternatively, use ground allspice and spoon over some warmed dark rum to serve.

3 Bake the pears in the preheated oven for 20–25 minutes, or until they are tender and golden, occasionally spooning the sugar mixture over the fruit during the cooking time.

4 To serve, heat the lowfat custard in a small pan over low heat until it is piping hot and spoon a little over the surface of each of 4 warm dessert plates. Then arrange 2 pear halves on each plate.

5 Decorate the pears with a little finely shredded lemon rind and serve immediately.

Stuffed Pears

It has long been a popular practice to sprinkle strawberries with pepper to bring out their flavor. This is equally effective with pears.

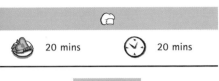

20 mins   20 mins

SERVES 4

INGREDIENTS

2 tsp butter, sweet for preference

4 firm pears

2 tbsp lemon juice

4 tbsp rosehip syrup

1 tsp green peppercorns, crushed lightly

½ cup red currants

4 tbsp superfine sugar

ice cream, to serve

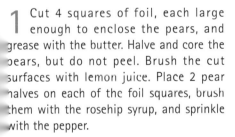

1 Cut 4 squares of foil, each large enough to enclose the pears, and grease with the butter. Halve and core the pears, but do not peel. Brush the cut surfaces with lemon juice. Place 2 pear halves on each of the foil squares, brush them with the rosehip syrup, and sprinkle with the pepper.

2 Put the red currants in a bowl and sprinkle with the sugar. Spoon the red currant mixture into the cavities of the pears. Fold up the sides of the foil to enclose the pears securely.

3 Cook on a hot grill for 20 minutes. Serve with ice cream.

VARIATION
Substitute your own favorites, such as blueberries or black currants, for the red currants.

Stuffed Pears with Mincemeat

Pears quickly go soft and lose their shape when they are cooked, so choose fruit with good firm flesh for this recipe.

🦔

🍲 20 mins   🕐 25–30 mins

SERVES 4

I N G R E D I E N T S

4 firm pears

1 tsp lemon juice

2 tbsp mincemeat

5 tbsp cake crumbs or 4 amaretti cookies, crushed

1 tbsp butter

ice cream, to serve

1 Using a sharp knife, cut the pears in half. Using a teaspoon, scoop out the core and discard.

2 Brush the cut surface of each of the pear halves with a little lemon juice to prevent discoloration.

3 Mix together the mincemeat and cake crumbs, or crushed amaretti cookies.

4 Divide the mixture among the pear halves, spooning it into a mound where the core has been removed.

5 Place 2 pear halves on a large square of double-thickness foil and generously dot all over with the butter.

6 Wrap up the foil around the pears so that they are completely enclosed.

7 Transfer the foil packages to a rack set over hot coals. Cook for 25–30 minutes, or until the pears are hot and just tender.

8 Transfer the pears to individual serving plates. Serve with 2 scoops of ice cream per serving.

COOK'S TIP
If the coals are dying down, place the foil packages directly on to the coals and grill for 25–30 minutes.

Pears with Chocolate Sauce

Pears and chocolate were made for each other, and the partnership is seen at its best in this simple dessert.

20 mins   20 mins

SERVES 4

INGREDIENTS

4 pears

2 cups water

¾ cup golden superfine sugar

4-inch/10-cm piece gingerroot, peeled and sliced

½ cinnamon stick

squeeze of lemon juice

CHOCOLATE SAUCE

4 tbsp light cream

7 oz/200 g semisweet chocolate, broken into pieces

1 Peel the pears, leaving the stalks intact. Cut the base of each pear so that it sits flat. Carefully remove as much of the core as possible with a small spoon.

2 Put the water, sugar, gingerroot, cinnamon stick, and lemon juice in a large pan. Bring to a boil and boil for 5 minutes. Add the pears and cook, turning occasionally, for about 15–20 minutes until softened. Place each pear on a serving plate.

3 To make the chocolate sauce, put the cream and chocolate in a heatproof bowl set over a pan of gently simmering water and heat until the chocolate has melted. Stir until smooth and serve with the warm pears.

COOK'S TIP
Choose pears which are ripe but still firm.

Chocolate Fudge Pears

Melt-in-the-mouth, spicy poached pears are enveloped in a wonderfully self-indulgent chocolate fudge sauce. Serve immediately.

🕐 10 mins | ⏰ 30–35 mins

SERVES 4

INGREDIENTS

4 pears

1–2 tbsp lemon juice

1¼ cups water

5 tbsp superfine sugar

2-inch/5-cm piece cinnamon stick

2 cloves

scant 1 cup heavy cream

½ cup milk

scant 1 cup brown sugar

2 tbsp butter, sweet for preference, cut into pieces

2 tbsp maple syrup

7 oz/200 g semisweet chocolate, broken into pieces

1 Peel the pears using a swivel vegetable peeler. Carefully cut out the cores from underneath, but leave the stalks intact because they look more attractive. Brush the pears with the lemon juice to prevent discoloration.

2 Pour the water into a large, heavy-based pan and add the superfine sugar. Stir over low heat until the sugar has dissolved. Add the pears, cinnamon, and cloves and bring to a boil. (Add a little more water if the pears are not almost covered.) Reduce the heat and simmer for 20 minutes.

3 Meanwhile, pour the cream and milk into another heavy-based pan and add the brown sugar, butter, and maple syrup. Stir over low heat until the sugar has dissolved and the butter has melted. Still stirring, bring to a boil and continue to boil, stirring constantly, for 5 minutes, until thick and smooth. Remove the pan from the heat and stir in the chocolate, a little at a time, waiting until each batch has melted before adding the next. Set aside.

4 Transfer the pears to individual serving plates using a slotted spoon and keep warm. Bring the poaching syrup back to a boil and cook until reduced. Remove and discard the cinnamon and cloves, then fold the syrup into the chocolate sauce. Pour the sauce over the pears and serve immediately.

Pears with Maple Cream

These spicy cinnamon pears are accompanied by a delicious melt-in-your-mouth maple and ricotta cream—you won't believe it's low in fat!

10 mins   25 mins

SERVES 4

INGREDIENTS

1 lemon

4 firm pears

1¼ cups hard cider or unsweetened apple juice

1 cinnamon stick, broken in half

fresh mint leaves to decorate

MAPLE RICOTTA CREAM

½ cup low-fat ricotta cheese

½ cup farmer's cheese

½ tsp ground cinnamon

½ tsp grated lemon rind

1 tbsp maple syrup

lemon rind, to decorate

1 Using a vegetable peeler, remove the rind from the lemon and place in a nonstick skillet. Squeeze the lemon and pour into a shallow bowl.

2 Peel the pears, then halve, and core them. Toss them in the lemon juice to prevent discoloration. Place in the skillet and pour over the remaining lemon juice.

3 Add the hard cider or apple juice and cinnamon stick halves. Gently bring to a boil, lower the heat so the liquid just simmers, and cook the pears for 10 minutes. Remove the pears using a slotted spoon. Reserve the cooking liquid. Place the pears in a warmed heatproof serving dish, cover with foil, and put in a warming drawer or low oven.

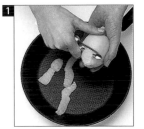

4 Return the skillet to the heat, bring to a boil, then simmer for 8–10 minutes until reduced by half. Spoon the mixture over the pears.

5 To make the maple ricotta cream, combine all the ingredients. Decorate the cream with lemon rind, and the pears with mint leaves, and serve together.

COOK'S TIP
Red Anjou and Packham's pears are suitable for this recipe. Pears ripen quickly and can bruise easily. It's best to buy them just before you plan to cook them.

Pears Poached in Blush Wine

This elegant dessert can be served hot or cold. The pears can be poached 2 days in advance and stored in their poaching juices in the refrigerator.

🍐 10 mins 🕐 25 mins

SERVES 6

INGREDIENTS

6 firm ripe pears

½ cup superfine sugar

2 cinnamon sticks

rind of 1 orange

2 cloves

1 bottle blush wine

CHOCOLATE SAUCE

6 oz/175 g semisweet chocolate

9 oz/250 g mascarpone cheese

2 tbsp orange-flavored liqueur

1 Carefully peel the pears, leaving the stalks intact.

2 Place the sugar, cinnamon sticks, orange rind, cloves, and wine in a pan that will hold the 6 pears snugly.

3 Heat gently until the sugar has dissolved, then add the pears to the liquid and bring to a simmer. Cover and poach gently for 20 minutes. If serving them cold, let the pears cool in the liquid, then chill until required. If serving hot, leave the pears in the hot liquid while preparing the chocolate sauce.

4 To make the sauce, melt the chocolate. Beat together the mascarpone cheese and the orange-flavored liqueur. Beat the mascarpone mixture into the chocolate.

5 Remove the pears from the poaching liquid and place on a serving plate. Add a generous spoonful of sauce on the side and serve the remainder separately.

COOK'S TIP
There is no need to waste the poaching liquid. Boil it rapidly in a clean pan for about 10 minutes to reduce to a syrup. Use the syrup to sweeten a fresh fruit salad or spoon it over ice cream.

Baked Peaches with Liqueur

Peaches are stuffed with a nut stuffing and baked, then served with a hot honey syrup and a contrasting cold orange cream. Sheer luxury.

20 mins | 30 mins

SERVES 4

INGREDIENTS

½ cup shelled pistachios, chopped finely

½ cup toasted hazelnuts, chopped finely

1 tbsp grated orange rind

1 tbsp brown sugar

pinch of ground allspice

4 large ripe (but firm) peaches

1 tbsp butter, sweet for preference

HONEY SYRUP

½ cup water

1 tbsp honey

2 tsp freshly squeezed orange juice

¾ cup superfine sugar

ORANGE LIQUEUR CREAM

1 tbsp finely grated orange rind

1 cup heavy cream

1 tbsp orange-flavored liqueur

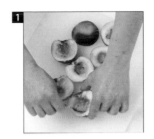
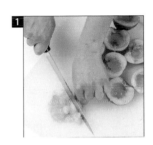

1 Preheat the oven to 350°F/180°C. Put the nuts, orange rind, brown sugar, and allspice in a mixing bowl and stir together well. Halve and stone the peaches. Remove a little more of the flesh in the center of each peach. Chop the flesh and stir into the nut mixture. Transfer the peaches to an ovenproof dish and dot with butter. Bake in the preheated oven for 30 minutes.

2 About halfway through the cooking time, put the water, honey, orange juice, and superfine sugar into a pan and bring to a boil, stirring constantly. Reduce the heat and simmer, without stirring, for about 15 minutes.

3 To make the orange liqueur cream, put the orange rind and cream in a bowl and beat together, then stir in the orange liqueur. Remove the peaches from the oven and divide among serving dishes. Pour over the honey syrup and serve with the orange liqueur cream.

Special Peach Melba

The elegant simplicity of this dessert makes it the perfect end to a special-occasion alfresco party.

15 mins plus
1 hr marinating

3–5 mins

SERVES 4

INGREDIENTS

2 large peaches, peeled, halved, and pitted

1 tbsp brown sugar

1 tbsp amaretto

1¾ cups raspberries

scant 1 cup confectioners' sugar

2½ cups vanilla ice cream

1 Put the peach halves in a large shallow dish and sprinkle with the brown sugar. Pour the amaretto over them, cover with plastic wrap and set aside for 1 hour.

2 Meanwhile, using the back of a metal spoon, press the raspberries through a fine strainer set over a bowl. Discard the contents of the strainer. Stir the confectioners' sugar into the raspberry purée. Cover the bowl with plastic wrap and chill in the refrigerator until required.

3 Drain the peach halves, reserving the marinade. Cook on a hot grill, turning and brushing frequently with the reserved marinade, for 3–5 minutes. To serve, put 2 scoops ice cream in each of 4 sundae glasses, top with a peach half, and spoon the raspberry sauce over it.

Apples in Red Wine

This simple combination of apples and raspberries cooked in red wine makes a colorful and tempting dessert.

5 mins | 20 mins

SERVES 4

INGREDIENTS

4 dessert apples

2 tbsp lemon juice

3 tbsp lowfat spread

¼ cup molasses sugar

1 small orange

1 cinnamon stick, broken

⅔ cup red wine

1⅓ cups raspberries, hulled, thawed if frozen

fresh mint sprigs, to decorate

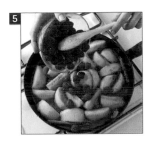

1 Peel and core the apples, then cut them into thick wedges. Place the apples in a bowl and toss thoroughly in the lemon juice to prevent the fruit turning brown.

2 In a skillet, gently melt the lowfat spread over low heat, add the sugar, and stir to form a paste.

3 Stir the apple wedges into the skillet and cook, stirring, for 2 minutes until well coated in the sugar paste.

4 Using a vegetable peeler, pare off a few strips of orange rind. Add the orange rind to the skillet with the cinnamon pieces. Squeeze the juice from the orange and pour into the skillet with the red wine. Bring to a boil, then simmer for 10 minutes, stirring constantly.

5 Add the raspberries and cook for 5 minutes, until the apples are tender.

6 Discard the orange rind and cinnamon pieces. Transfer the apple and raspberry mixture to a serving plate with the wine sauce. Decorate with a sprig of fresh mint and serve hot.

VARIATION

For other fruity combinations, cook the apples with blackberries, black currants, or red currants. You may need to add more sugar if you use currants because they are not as sweet as raspberries.

Warm Currants in Cassis

Cassis is a black currant liqueur which comes from France and is an excellent flavoring for fruit dishes.

10 mins   10 mins

SERVES 4

INGREDIENTS

3 cups black currants

2 cups red currants

4 tbsp superfine sugar

grated rind and juice of 1 orange

2 tsp arrowroot

2 tbsp cassis

whipped cream or lowfat yogurt, to serve

1 Using a fork, strip the black currants and red currants from their stalks and put in a pan.

2 Add the superfine sugar and orange rind and juice and heat gently, stirring, until the sugar has dissolved. Bring to a boil and simmer gently for 5 minutes.

3 Strain the currants and place in a bowl, then return the juice to the pan.

4 Blend the arrowroot with a little water and mix into the juice in the pan. Boil the mixture until thickened.

5 Set aside to cool slightly, then stir in the cassis and pour over the fruit.

6 Serve in individual dishes with whipped cream or yogurt.

Hot Chocolate Cherries

A gloriously self-indulgent dessert, perfect for rounding off a celebration dinner party.

🍨 15 mins 🕐 25 mins

SERVES 4

INGREDIENTS

4 tbsp water

generous ¼ cup superfine sugar

1 strip pared lemon rind

1 lb/450 g sweet black cherries, pitted

1 tbsp unsweetened cocoa

salt

4 tbsp heavy cream

4 tbsp maraschino or cherry cognac

1 Put the water, sugar, and lemon rind into a heavy-based pan and bring to a boil over low heat, stirring constantly until the sugar has dissolved. Add the cherries and cook, stirring constantly, for 1 minute. Remove the pan from the heat and, using a slotted spoon, transfer the cherries to a flameproof dish. Reserve the syrup.

2 Preheat the broiler to medium. Put the unsweetened cocoa in a bowl and mix in a pinch of salt. Whisking constantly, pour in the cream in a steady stream. Remove and discard the lemon rind from the syrup, then stir in the cream mixture. Return the pan to the heat and bring to a boil, stirring constantly. Simmer over very low heat, stirring occasionally, for 10–15 minutes, or until reduced by about half.

3 Remove from the heat, stir in the maraschino, and pour the sauce over the cherries. Place under the preheated broiler for 2 minutes, then serve.

VARIATION
Instead of pared lemon rind, flavor the syrup with a split vanilla bean and remove it in step 2 or add ½ teaspoon vanilla extract with the liqueur in step 3.

Red Fruits with Frothy Sauce

A colorful combination of soft fruits, served with a marshmallow sauce, is an ideal dessert when summer fruits are in season.

15 mins plus
1 hr chilling

20 mins

SERVES 4

INGREDIENTS

2 cups red currants, trimmed, thawed
   if frozen

2 cups cranberries

⅓ cup molasses sugar

scant 1 cup unsweetened apple juice

1 cinnamon stick, broken

2⅔ cups small strawberries, hulled
   and halved

SAUCE

1⅓ cups raspberries, thawed if frozen

2 tbsp red berry fruit cordial

3½ oz/100 g marshmallows

1 Place the red currants, cranberries, and sugar in a pan. Pour in the apple juice and add the cinnamon stick. Bring the mixture to a boil and simmer gently for 10 minutes, until the fruit is soft.

2 Stir the strawberries into the fruit mixture and mix well. Transfer the mixture to a bowl, cover with plastic wrap, and set aside to chill in the refrigerator for about 1 hour. Remove and discard the cinnamon stick.

3 Just before serving, make the sauce. Put the raspberries and fruit cordial in a small pan, bring to a boil, and simmer for 2–3 minutes, until the fruit just starts to soften. Stir the marshmallows into the raspberry mixture and heat through, stirring constantly, until the marshmallows start to melt.

4 Transfer the fruit salad to serving bowls. Spoon over the raspberry and marshmallow sauce and serve.

COOK'S TIP
This sauce is delicious poured over lowfat ice cream. For an extra-colorful sauce, replace the raspberries with an assortment of summer berries.

Caramelized Omelets

This sophisticated dessert looks wonderful and tastes delicious. You will need six small individual tart rings to shape the omelets.

25 mins | 15 mins

SERVES 6

INGREDIENTS

4 oz/115 g butter, sweet for preference,
  cut into pieces, plus extra for greasing

½ cup superfine sugar, plus extra
  for dusting

4 oz/115 g semisweet chocolate

2 eggs

6 x 3-inch/7.5-cm round plain cookies

confectioners' sugar, for dusting

FRUIT COULIS

1 lb/450 g kiwi fruit

1½–1¾ cups superfine sugar

TO DECORATE

2 oz/55 g semisweet chocolate

6 cape gooseberries

1 To make the decoration, break the chocolate into pieces and melt in a heatproof bowl. Remove from the heat. Peel back the papery coverings of the cape gooseberries and dip the fruits, 1 at a time, into the melted chocolate to half-coat. Let set on nonstick parchment paper.

2 To make the coulis, halve the kiwi fruit and scoop their contents into a blender using a teaspoon. Add about half the sugar and process to a purée, taste, and gradually add more sugar, if necessary, processing again to mix. Push the purée through a metal strainer into a bowl, if you want to remove the seeds, or simply scrape into a bowl. Cover and chill in the refrigerator.

3 Preheat the oven to 375°F/190°C. Grease 6 x 3-inch/7.5-cm round small individual tart rings and dust with superfine sugar. Arrange the tart rings on a cookie sheet.

4 To make the omelets, break the chocolate into pieces and melt in a heatproof bowl over a pan of simmering water. Remove from the heat and let cool slightly.

5 Beat the eggs with the sugar in another heatproof bowl set over a pan of gently simmering water until thickened and frothy. Remove from the heat. Stir the butter into the warm chocolate, then fold into the eggs.

6 Preheat the broiler to medium. Place a cookie inside each tart ring and top with the egg mixture, filling the ring about two-thirds full. Dredge generously with confectioners' sugar and bake for 6 minutes. Transfer to a preheated broiler and cook for a few seconds to caramelize the sugar.

7 To serve, spoon a little of the fruit coulis on to each of 6 serving plates. Run a knife around the inside of each tart ring, remove the rings and carefully transfer the omelets to the plates. Decorate with the chocolate-dipped cape gooseberries and serve immediately.

Warm Fruit Compôte

Serve this dish of lightly cooked summer fruits with light cream or vanilla ice cream for a simple and flavorful dessert.

8–10 mins   10 mins

SERVES 4

INGREDIENTS

4 plums, halved and pitted

scant 1 cup raspberries

scant 1 cup strawberries, hulled and halved

2 tbsp light muscovado sugar

2 tbsp dry white wine

2 star anise

1 cinnamon stick

4 cloves

1 Put the fruit, sugar, white wine, and spices in a large heavy-based pan and set over low heat until the sugar has dissolved.

2 Cover tightly and simmer very gently for about 5 minutes, until the fruit is tender but still retains its shape. Do not let the mixture boil.

3 Remove and discard the star anise, cinnamon, and cloves and serve the compôte warm.

Thai Bananas

Bananas go well with coconut, as this easy-to-make dessert shows.
Drizzle with maple syrup for a deliciously gooey treat, if liked.

🕙 10 mins   ⏱ 10 mins

SERVES 6

I N G R E D I E N T S

6 slightly underripe bananas

1½ cups coconut milk

2 tbsp granulated sugar

½ tsp salt

T O D E C O R A T E

1 tbsp toasted sesame seeds

maple syrup to drizzle

1 Peel the bananas and cut into 2-inch/5-cm lengths. Place the coconut milk, sugar, and salt in a pan and heat gently until the sugar has dissolved. Add the banana pieces and cook gently for 5 minutes, or until the bananas are soft but not mushy.

2 Divide the mixture among 6 small bowls. Scatter the sesame seeds over, drizzle with maple syrup (if using), and serve.

Rum Bananas

Rum and bananas is a classic combination, but orange-flavored liqueur partners bananas just as successfully.

1 min   5–10 mins

SERVES 4

INGREDIENTS

4 bananas

4 tsp dark rum or orange-flavored liqueur

SERVING SUGGESTIONS

peach slices

sherbet

ice cream

heavy cream

crème fraîche (see page 9)

1 Preheat a ridged griddle pan over high heat.

2 Place the bananas, still in their skins, on the griddle pan. Cook for 5–10 minutes, or until the skins are black, turning occasionally.

3 Remove the bananas from the griddle pan, peel, and place in individual serving bowls. Pour 1 teaspoonful of rum or orange-flavored liqueur over each banana and serve while still hot, with the peach slices. Top with sherbet, ice cream, heavy cream, or crème fraîche.

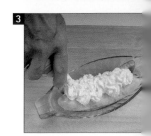

Toffee Bananas

These deep-fried banana morsels coated in sesame toffee mixture are sweet and delicious. They are best served hot.

20 mins   15–20 mins

SERVES 4

INGREDIENTS

generous ½ cup self-rising flour

1 egg, beaten

½ cup ice water, plus an extra bowl of ice water for setting

4 large ripe bananas

3 tbsp lemon juice

2 tbsp rice flour

vegetable oil, for deep-frying

generous ½ cup superfine sugar

2 tbsp sesame seeds

1 Sift the flour into a bowl. Make a well in the center, add the egg and 5 tablespoons water, and beat from the center outward until thoroughly combined.

2 Peel the bananas and cut into 2-inch/5-cm pieces. Using your hands, gently shape them into balls. Brush all over with lemon juice to prevent discoloration, then roll them in rice flour until coated. Pour enough oil into a deep-fryer to cover the bananas and heat to 375°F/190°C. Coat the balls in the batter and deep-fry for about 2 minutes until golden (you may need to do this in batches). Lift them out and drain on waxed paper.

3 To make the toffee, put the sugar in a small pan over low heat. Add 4 tablespoons of ice water and heat, stirring constantly, until the sugar dissolves. Simmer for 5 minutes, then remove from the heat and stir in the sesame seeds. Toss the banana balls in the toffee, scoop them out with a slotted spoon, and drop into the bowl of ice water to set. Lift them out and divide among individual serving bowls. Serve hot.

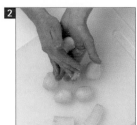

Bananas in Coconut Milk

An unusual dessert which is equally good served hot or cold, this is a classic Thai combination of fruits and vegetables.

10 mins

3–5 mins

SERVES 4

I N G R E D I E N T S

4 large bananas

1½ cups coconut milk

2 tbsp superfine sugar

pinch of salt

½ tsp orange flower water

1 tbsp shredded fresh mint

2 tbsp mung beans, cooked

fresh mint sprigs, to decorate

1 Peel the bananas and cut them into short chunks. Place in a large, heavy-based pan with the coconut milk, superfine sugar, and salt. Heat gently until boiling, then simmer for 1 minute. Remove the pan from the heat.

2 Sprinkle the orange flower water over, stir in the mint, and spoon into a serving dish.

3 Place the mung beans in a heavy based skillet and cook over high hea until turning crisp and golden, shaking th skillet occasionally. Remove, cool slightly and crush lightly with a pestle and mortar.

4 Sprinkle the toasted beans over th bananas and serve warm or cold decorated with fresh mint sprigs.

COOK'S TIP
If you prefer, the mung beans could be replaced with sliced, toasted almonds or hazelnuts.

Fruit with Chocolate Malt Dip

Use your favorite fresh fruit in season and dip the pieces in this wonderful malted chocolate mixture.

20 mins   5 mins

SERVES 4

INGREDIENTS

2 oz/55 g semisweet chocolate,
   broken into pieces

2 large bananas

1 tbsp malt extract

selection of fresh fruit, cut into chunks or
   slices, as necessary

1 Put the chocolate in a heatproof bowl set over a pan of gently simmering water. Stir over low heat until melted. Remove from the heat and let cool for 10 minutes.

2 Peel and slice the bananas. Place them in a food processor and process until smooth. With the motor still running, pour the malt extract through the feed tube. Continue to process until thick and frothy, and fully incorporated. With the motor still running, pour the melted chocolate through the feed tube in a slow, steady stream. Continue to process until thoroughly combined.

3 Scrape the dip into a small serving bowl and stand on a large serving plate. Arrange the fruit around the bowl and serve immediately.

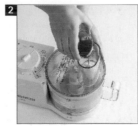

Chocolate Fondue

This is a fun dessert to serve at the end of a meal. You can prepare the fondue in advance, then just warm through before serving.

5 mins   5 mins

SERVES 4

INGREDIENTS

8 oz/225 g semisweet chocolate

generous ¾ cup heavy cream

2 tbsp cognac

TO SERVE

selection of fruit

white and pink marshmallows

sweet cookies

1 Break the chocolate into small pieces and place in a small pan with the heavy cream.

2 Heat the mixture gently, stirring constantly until the chocolate has melted and blended with the cream.

3 Remove the pan from the heat and stir in the cognac.

4 Pour into a fondue pot or a small flameproof dish and keep warm, preferably over a small burner.

5 Serve with a selection of fruit, marshmallows, and cookies for dipping. The fruit and marshmallows can be spiked on fondue forks, wooden skewers, or ordinary forks, for dipping into the chocolate fondue.

COOK'S TIP

To prepare the fruit for dipping, cut larger fruit into bite-size pieces. Fruit that discolors, such as bananas, apples, and pears, should be dipped in a little lemon juice as soon as it is cut.

Chocolate Fruit Dip

These warm, lightly grilled fruit kabobs are served with a delicious rich chocolate dipping sauce. It is best to use metal skewers.

 10 mins   5–10 mins

SERVES 4

INGREDIENTS

selection of fruit (oranges, bananas, apples, strawberries, pineapple pieces, apricots (fresh or canned), pears, kiwi fruit)

1 tbsp lemon juice

CHOCOLATE SAUCE

4 tbsp butter

1¾ oz/50 g semisweet chocolate, broken into small cubes

½ tbsp unsweetened cocoa

2 tbsp corn syrup

BASTE

4 tbsp honey

grated rind and juice of ½ orange

1 To make the chocolate sauce, place the butter, chocolate, unsweetened cocoa, and syrup in a small pan. Heat gently on the stove or at the side of a grill, stirring constantly, until all of the ingredients have melted and combined.

2 To prepare the fruit, peel and core if necessary, then cut into large, bite-size pieces or wedges as appropriate. Dip apples, pears, and bananas in lemon juice to prevent discoloration. Thread the pieces of fruit on to skewers.

3 To make the baste, mix together the honey, orange rind, and orange juice, heat gently if wished and brush over the fruit.

4 Grill the fruit skewers over warm coals for 5–10 minutes until hot. Serve with the chocolate dipping sauce.

COOK'S TIP
If the coals are too hot, raise the rack so that it is about 6 inches/15 cm above the coals, or spread out the coals a little to reduce the heat. Do not assemble the fruit kabobs more than 1–2 hours before they are required.

Toasted Tropical Fruit

Spear some chunks of exotic tropical fruits on to kabob skewers, sear them over a barbecue grill, and serve with this amazing chocolate dip.

45 mins   5 mins

SERVES 4

INGREDIENTS

DIP

4½ oz/125 g semisweet chocolate, broken into pieces

2 tbsp corn syrup

1 tbsp unsweetened cocoa

1 tbsp cornstarch

generous ¾ cup milk

KABOBS

1 mango

1 papaya

2 kiwi fruit

½ small pineapple

1 large banana

2 tbsp lemon juice

⅔ cup white rum

1 Put all the ingredients for the chocolate dip into a heavy-based pan. Heat over the grill or over low heat on the stove, stirring constantly, until thickened and smooth. Keep warm at the edge of the grill.

2 Slice the mango on each side of its large, flat pit. Cut the flesh into chunks, removing the peel. Halve, seed, and peel the papaya and cut it into chunks. Peel the kiwi fruit and slice into chunks. Peel and cut the pineapple into chunks. Peel and slice the banana and dip the pieces in the lemon juice to prevent it discoloring.

3 Thread the pieces of fruit alternately on to 4 wooden skewers. Place them in a shallow dish and pour over the rum. Set aside to soak up the flavor of the rum for at least 30 minutes, until ready to cook.

4 Cook the kabobs over the hot coals, turning frequently, for about 2 minutes, until seared. Serve, accompanied by the hot chocolate dip.

Toffee Fruit Kabobs

Serve these fruit kabobs with a sticky toffee sauce. They are perfect for fall celebrations such as Hallowe'en.

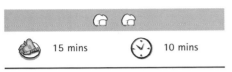

15 mins   10 mins

SERVES 4

INGREDIENTS

2 dessert apples, cored and cut into wedges

2 firm pears, cored and cut into wedges

juice of ½ lemon

2 tbsp light muscovado sugar

¼ tsp ground allspice

1 oz/25 g butter, sweet for preference, melted

SAUCE

4½ oz/125 g butter

1½ tbsp light muscovado sugar

6 tbsp heavy cream

1 Toss the apple and pears in the lemon juice to prevent any discoloration.

2 Mix the sugar and allspice together and sprinkle over the fruit.

3 Thread the fruit pieces on to skewers.

4 To make the toffee sauce, place the butter and sugar in a pan and heat, stirring gently, until the butter has melted and the sugar has dissolved.

5 Add the cream to the pan and bring to a boil. Boil for 1–2 minutes, then set aside to cool slightly.

6 Meanwhile, place the fruit kabobs over hot coals and grill for about 5 minutes, turning and basting frequently with the melted butter, until the fruit is just tender.

7 Transfer the fruit kabobs to warm serving plates and serve with the slightly cooled toffee sauce.

COOK'S TIP
Firm apples that will keep their shape are needed for this dish. Soft apples and pears will become mushy as they cook.

Fruit Skewers

These easily assembled skewers are served with delicious almond-flavored chocolate sauce. Use other combinations of fruits if preferred.

15–20 mins   10 mins

SERVES 4

INGREDIENTS

SKEWERS

6 tbsp brown sugar

pinch of ground allspice

8 whole strawberries, hulled

3 nectarines, pitted and cut into
   bite-size chunks

14 oz/400 g canned pineapple pieces,
   drained

4 plums, pitted and cut into
   bite-size chunks

3 oz/85 g butter, melted

CHOCOLATE
ALMOND SAUCE

4½ oz/125 g semisweet chocolate, broken
   into small pieces

2½ tbsp butter

6 tbsp water

1 tbsp amaretto

chopped mixed nuts, to decorate

1 Preheat the grill or broiler to medium. Combine the sugar and allspice and spread out on a large plate. Thread the whole strawberries on to skewers, alternating with the chunks of nectarine, pineapple, and plum. When the skewers are full (leave a small space at either end), brush them with melted butter and then turn them in the sugar until lightly coated. Transfer to the preheated grill or broiler pan and cook, turning occasionally, for 8–10 minutes.

2 To make the sauce, gently melt the chocolate, butter, and water together in a small pan, stirring constantly, until smooth. Stir in the amaretto. Remove the skewers from the heat, divide among individual plates, decorate with chopped mixed nuts, and serve hot with the chocolate almond sauce.

Fruit Kabobs

The sugar in which these kabobs are rolled melts to a deliciously sticky coating. If using wooden skewers, remember to presoak them.

🍓 10 mins 🕐 10 mins

SERVES 4

INGREDIENTS

1 lb/450 g assorted fruit such as peaches, apricots, plums, apples, pears

2 oz/55 g butter, melted

2 tbsp sugar

pinch of cinnamon, optional

SERVING SUGGESTIONS

crème fraîche (see page 9)

plain yogurt

ice cream

1 Select skewers that will fit comfortably on your grill. If using wooden skewers, remember to presoak them in water for 30 minutes to prevent them burning.

2 Preheat the griddle over a medium heat.

3 Pit the fruit as necessary, or remove cores, and cut into similar-size pieces. Small fruit may be left whole. Arrange alternating pieces on the skewers. Brush the fruit with melted butter.

4 Spread the sugar on a plate large enough to take the skewers. Mix in the cinnamon (if using). Roll the fruit kabobs in the sugar, pressing gently to coat.

5 Cook the kabobs on the grill, turning occasionally. Cook for about 10 minutes, or until the sugar has melted and started to bubble. The fruit should still be firm.

6 Serve hot, with crème fraîche, plain yogurt, or ice cream.

Mixed Fruit Kabobs

You can use almost any combination of firm-fleshed fruits to make these colorful, quick, and easy-to-assemble kabobs.

20 mins plus
1 hr marinating

5–7 mins

SERVES 4

INGREDIENTS

2 nectarines

2 kiwi fruit, peeled

4 red plums

1 mango, peeled, halved, and pitted

2 bananas, peeled and sliced thickly

8 strawberries, hulled

1 tbsp honey

3 tbsp orange-flavored liqueur

1 Halve and pit the nectarines. Cut the nectarine halves in half again and place in a large, shallow dish. Peel and quarter the kiwifruit. Cut the plums in half and remove the pits. Cut the mango flesh into chunks and add to the dish with the kiwifruit, plums, bananas, and strawberries.

2 Mix the honey and orange-flavored liqueur together in a measuring cup until blended. Pour the mixture over the fruit and toss to coat. Cover with plastic wrap and let marinate in the refrigerator for 1 hour.

3 Preheat the barbecue. Drain the fruit, reserving the marinade. Thread the fruit onto several presoaked wooden skewers and cook over medium hot coals, turning and brushing frequently with the reserved marinade, for 5–7 minutes, then serve.

Apple & Melon Kabobs

These fresh-tasting kabobs are ideal to serve as a light dessert to follow a barbecue. Perfect served with vanilla ice cream.

  5–10 mins 10 mins

SERVES 4

INGREDIENTS

6 tbsp butter

1–2 tbsp brown sugar

pinch of ground allspice

½ melon, such as Galia or Charentais

2 apples

1 tbsp lemon juice

plain yogurt, crème fraîche (see page 9),
   mascarpone cheese, or ice cream,
   to serve

1 In a small pan, melt the butter gently over low heat. Stir in the brown sugar and allspice, then remove from the heat and pour into a large bowl.

2 Cut the melon flesh into small chunks. Wash and core the apples, and cut into small chunks. Brush the fruit with lemon juice.

3 Thread the melon chunks on to skewers, alternating with pieces of apple. When the skewers are full (leave a small space at either end), transfer them to the bowl and turn them in the butter mixture until they are well coated.

4 Grill the kabobs over hot coals, turning them frequently, for about 10 minutes or until they are cooked to your taste. Serve with plain yogurt, crème fraîche, mascarpone cheese, or ice cream.

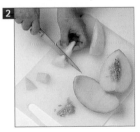

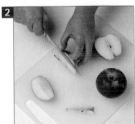

Butterscotch Melts

This delicious dessert will appeal to children of all ages. Bananas and marshmallows taste fantastic with butterscotch sauce.

5 mins

5 mins

SERVES 4

INGREDIENTS

4 bananas

4 tbsp lemon juice

8 oz/225 g marshmallows

SAUCE

4½ oz/125 g butter

⅔ cup light muscovado sugar

⅓ cup golden corn syrup

4 tbsp hot water

1 Slice the bananas into large chunks and dip them into the lemon juice to prevent them going brown.

2 Thread the marshmallows and pieces of banana alternately on to kabob sticks or bamboo skewers, placing 2 marshmallows and 1 piece banana on to each one.

3 To make the sauce, melt the butter, sugar, and syrup together in a small pan. Add the hot water, stirring until blended and smooth. Do not boil or else the mixture will become toffeelike. Keep the sauce warm at the edge of the grill, stirring from time to time.

4 Sear the kabobs over the hot coals for 30–40 seconds, turning constantly, so that the marshmallows are just starting to brown and melt.

5 Serve the kabobs with a little of the butterscotch sauce spooned over them. (Use half of the sauce to serve 4; the remainder can be used later.)

COOK'S TIP

The warm butterscotch sauce tastes wonderful with vanilla ice cream. Make double the quantity of sauce if you plan to serve ice cream at a barbecue.

Banana Coconut Fritters

These sweet banana fritters need only a dusting of confectioners' sugar and ground cinnamon to complete them.

15 mins   10 mins

SERVES 4

INGREDIENTS

9 tbsp all-purpose flour

2 tbsp rice flour

1 tbsp superfine sugar

1 egg, separated

⅔ cup coconut milk

sunflower oil, for deep-frying

4 large bananas

TO DECORATE

1 tsp confectioners' sugar

1 tsp ground cinnamon

1 Sift the all-purpose flour, rice flour, and sugar into a bowl and make a well in the center. Add the egg yolk and coconut milk and beat until a smooth, thick batter forms.

2 Whisk the egg white in a clean, dry, greasefree bowl until soft peaks form. Fold it into the batter lightly and evenly

3 Heat a 2½-inch/6-cm depth of oil in a large heavy-based skillet to 350° F/ 180°C, or until a cube of bread browns in 30 seconds. Cut the bananas in half crosswise, then dip them quickly into the batter to coat. Drop them carefully into the hot oil and fry in batches for 2–3 minutes, until golden brown, turning once.

4 Drain well on paper towels. Sprinkle with confectioners' sugar and cinnamon, and serve immediately.

COOK'S TIP
If you can buy the baby finger bananas that are popular in this dish in the East, leave them whole for coating and frying.

Apple Fritters

This is a popular choice for family meals, as children and adults alike love the flavor and crispness of the apple rings.

15 mins plus
30 mins resting

4–6 mins

SERVES 4

INGREDIENTS

salt

1 cup all-purpose flour

2 egg yolks

1 egg white

1 tbsp sunflower oil

⅔ cup milk

1 lb/450 g tart cooking apples

juice of 1 lemon

superfine sugar, for sprinkling

4 oz/115 g butter, sweet for preference

1 Sift the flour with a pinch of salt into a bowl. Make a well in the center and add the egg yolks, egg white, and oil. Gradually incorporate the flour into the liquid with a wooden spoon. Gradually beat in the milk and continue beating to make a smooth batter. Cover with plastic wrap and set aside for 30 minutes.

2 Peel and core the apples, then cut them into rings about ¼-inch/5-mm thick. Spread them out on a plate and sprinkle with the lemon juice and superfine sugar.

3 Melt the butter in a large, heavy-based skillet. Dip the apple rings, one at a time, into the batter and then drop them into the pan. Cook for 2–3 minutes on each side, until golden brown. Transfer to a platter, sprinkle with more superfine sugar, and serve immediately.

COOK'S TIP

You can prepare the batter and the apples in advance. Keep the apples covered in plastic wrap until you are ready to dip them into the batter.

Deep-Fried Apple Chunks

These apple fritters are coated in a light, spiced batter and deep-fried until crisp and golden. Serve warm with an unusual almond sauce.

🍮 15 mins 🕐 15 mins

SERVES 4

INGREDIENTS

¾ cup all-purpose flour

pinch of salt

½ tsp ground cinnamon

¾ cup warm water

4 tsp vegetable oil

2 egg whites

2 dessert apples, peeled

vegetable or sunflower oil, for deep-frying

superfine sugar and cinnamon, to decorate

SAUCE

⅔ cup plain yogurt

½ tsp almond extract

2 tsp honey

1 Sift the flour and salt together into a large mixing bowl.

2 Add the cinnamon and mix well. Stir in the warm water and vegetable oil to make a smooth batter.

3 Whisk the egg whites until stiff peaks form and fold into the batter.

4 Using a sharp knife, cut the apples into chunks and dip the pieces of apple into the batter to coat.

5 Heat the oil for deep-frying to 350°F/180°C, or until a cube of bread browns in 30 seconds. Fry the apple chunks, in batches if necessary, for about 3–4 minutes, until light golden-brown and puffy.

6 Remove the apple chunks from the oil with a slotted spoon and drain on paper towels. Mix together the superfine sugar and cinnamon and sprinkle over the apple chunks.

7 Mix the sauce ingredients in a serving bowl and serve with the apple chunks.

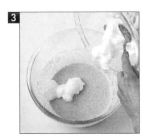

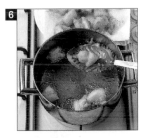

Apricot & Chocolate Fritters

Despite their appearance, both Hunza apricots from Afghanistan and Kashmir and Turkish dried apricots have a wonderful flavor.

15 mins plus 30 minutes soaking   10–15 mins

SERVES 4

INGREDIENTS

6 oz/175 g dried Turkish apricots, pitted

¾ cup all-purpose flour

3 tbsp ground almonds

3 tbsp melted butter, sweet for preference

1 egg white

vegetable oil, for deep-frying

1 tbsp unsweetened cocoa

3 tbsp superfine sugar

WHITE SAUCE

6 oz/175 g white chocolate

4 tbsp butter, sweet for preference

⅔ cup heavy cream

3 tbsp superfine sugar

2 tbsp apricot cognac

1 Place the apricots in a bowl, pour over boiling water to cover, and set aside for at least 30 minutes to plump up.

2 To make the white chocolate sauce, break the chocolate into pieces and set aside. Cut the butter into pieces and place in a heavy-based pan with the cream and sugar. Melt over low heat, stirring frequently, until smooth. Stir in the chocolate and continue to stir until melted and smooth. Remove from the heat, let cool slightly, then stir in the apricot cognac. Set aside until required.

3 Sift the flour into a bowl, add the almonds, melted butter, and egg white and mix well. Gradually add 3–4 tablespoons water, beating well until the mixture forms a smooth batter.

4 Heat the oil for deep-frying to 350°F/180°C, or until a cube of bread browns in about 45 seconds. Meanwhile, drain the apricots and pat dry with paper towels.

5 Dip the apricots a few at a time into the batter and carefully lower into the hot oil. Cook until they rise to the surface and are golden brown. Remove with a slotted spoon and drain on paper towels. Keep warm while you cook the remaining apricots.

6 Divide the apricots among warm serving plates. Mix together the unsweetened cocoa and sugar in a small bowl, then sift the mixture over the fritters. Serve immediately, with the sauce at room temperature.

Chocolate & Apple Dumplings

A melt-in-the-mouth combination of tart fruit and sweet chocolate pie dough, these dumplings are sensational.

20 mins plus
30 mins chilling

35 mins

SERVES 4

INGREDIENTS

4 large tart cooking apples

4 tbsp mincemeat

2 tbsp chopped walnuts

1 egg, beaten lightly

crème fraîche (see page 9), to serve

PIE DOUGH

6 oz/175 g semisweet chocolate

scant ½ cup all-purpose flour, plus extra
  for dusting

1 tsp ground cinnamon

4 tbsp butter

1 egg yolk, or 1–2 tbsp cold water

1 First, make the pie dough. Break the chocolate into squares and place in a heatproof bowl. Set over a pan of simmering water and heat, stirring occasionally, until melted. Remove from the heat and set aside to cool slightly. Sift the flour into a bowl and stir in the cinnamon. Rub in the butter with your fingertips until the mixture resembles bread crumbs. Make a well in the center

and pour in the cooled chocolate and the egg yolk and mix to form a dough. Knead lightly, then form into a ball, wrap, and chill in the refrigerator for 30 minutes.

2 Preheat the oven to 400°F/200°C. Divide the pie dough into 4 equal pieces and roll each out on a lightly floured work counter to a circle large enough to enclose 1 apple.

3 Core the apples and place 1 apple on each dough circle. Mix together the mincemeat and chopped walnuts and spoon into the cavities of the apples.

Brush the edges of the dough with the beaten egg, then wrap the dough around the apples, pressing the edges together to seal.

4 Transfer the dumplings to a cookie sheet and brush all over with beaten egg to glaze. Bake for about 35 minutes, until golden. Serve immediately, with crème fraîche.

VARIATION
This recipe would also work well with pears. Omit the cinnamon from the pie dough.

Chocolate Polenta Pudding

This rich dessert is delicious when served with a generous scoop of chocolate or vanilla ice cream.

🕐 25 mins   🕐 1 hr 10 mins

SERVES 8

INGREDIENTS

1 lb/450 g good quality bittersweet
  chocolate

4 oz/115 g chocolate hazelnut spread

4 oz/115 g sweet butter,
  plus extra for greasing

generous ½ cup quick-cook polenta

1¼ cups milk

6 egg yolks

½ cup superfine or confectioners' sugar,
  plus extra for dusting

8 egg whites

vanilla or chocolate ice cream, to serve

1 Preheat the oven to 350°F/180°C.

2 Break the chocolate into pieces and place in a heatproof bowl set over a pan of gently simmering water until melted. Stir the chocolate hazelnut spread into the melted chocolate

3 Melt the butter in a heavy-based pan, stir in the polenta, and cook for 2–3 minutes. Stir in the milk, reduce the heat and cook, stirring constantly, over low heat for 5–10 minutes, until thickened. Stir the chocolate mixture into the cooked polenta. Beat in the egg yolks one at a time.

4 Grease a 4½-cup soufflé dish with butter, then dust with superfine or confectioners' sugar and set aside.

5 Whisk the egg whites until stiff, adding the sugar gradually. Fold the egg whites into the chocolate polenta mixture.

6 Fill the prepared soufflé dish with the mixture and bake for 45-60 minutes, until the top starts to split open. Serve hot, dusted with the remaining sugar over the top.

Stuffed Pooris

Pooris are puffy Indian dumplings. They freeze well, so it pays to make a large quantity and reheat them in the oven.

🍰 30 mins plus
3 hrs soaking   ⏱ 1 hr

MAKES 10

INGREDIENTS

POORIS

1 cup whole-wheat flour

¾ cup all-purpose flour, plus extra for dusting

½ tsp salt

1½ tbsp ghee, plus extra for frying

⅔ cup milk

FILLING

8 tbsp chana dal

3¾ cups water

5 tbsp ghee

2 green cardamoms, peeled

4 cloves

8 tbsp sugar

2 tbsp ground almonds

½ tsp saffron strands

¼ cup golden raisins

1 To make the pooris, place the whole-wheat flour, all-purpose flour, and salt in a bowl and mix. Add the ghee and rub in with your fingers. Add the milk and mix to form a dough. Knead the dough for 5 minutes, cover, and let prove for about 3 hours. Knead the dough on a floured work counter for 15 minutes.

2 Roll out the dough until it measures 10 inches/25 cm and divide into 10 portions. Roll out each of these into 5-inch/13-cm circles and set aside.

3 To make the filling, soak the chana dal for at least 3 hours if time allows. Place the dal in a pan and add water. Bring to a boil over medium heat until all of the water has evaporated and the dal is soft enough to be mashed into a paste.

4 In a separate pan, heat the ghee and add the cardamom seeds and cloves. Reduce the heat, add the chana dal paste, and stir for 5–7 minutes.

5 Fold in the sugar and almonds and cook, stirring, for 10 minutes. Add the saffron and golden raisins and blend until thickened, stirring, for 5 minutes.

6 Spoon the filling on to one half of each pastry circle. Dampen the edges with water and fold the other half over to seal.

7 Heat the extra ghee in a skillet and cook the filled pooris over low heat until golden. Transfer to paper towels, drain, and serve.

Apple Strudel & Cider Sauce

This light, crisp and spicy strudel, delicious either hot or cold, is served with a hot sauce made with hard cider.

15 mins

20–25 mins

SERVES 2–4

INGREDIENTS

8 crisp eating apples

1 tbsp lemon juice

⅔ cup golden raisins

1 tsp ground cinnamon

½ tsp grated nutmeg

1 tbsp brown sugar

6 sheets phyllo pastry

vegetable oil spray

SAUCE

1 tbsp cornstarch

2 cups hard cider

confectioners' sugar, to serve

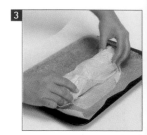

1 Preheat the oven to 375°F/190°C. Line a cookie sheet with parchment paper.

2 Peel and core the apples and chop them into ½-inch/1-cm dice. Toss the pieces in a bowl, with the lemon juice, golden raisins, cinnamon, nutmeg, and sugar.

3 Lay out a sheet of phyllo pastry, spray with vegetable oil, and lay a second sheet on top. Repeat with a third sheet. Spread over half the apple mixture and roll up lengthwise, tucking in the ends to enclose the filling. Repeat to make a second strudel. Slide on to the cookie sheet, spray with oil, and bake for 15–20 minutes.

4 Blend the cornstarch in a pan with a little hard cider until smooth. Add the remaining cider and heat gently, stirring, until the mixture boils and thickens. Serve the strudel warm or cold, dredged with confectioners' sugar and accompanied by the cider sauce.

Fruit Parcels

If you don't have a spare grill, cooking fruit in a parcel is a good idea for dessert, as it avoids any contamination from foods cooked earlier.

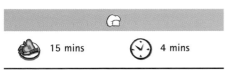

15 mins   4 mins

SERVES 4

INGREDIENTS

2 oranges

2 dessert apples

juice of 1 lemon

2 pears

4 tsp light muscovado sugar

1 Peel the oranges, carefully removing all the pith. Cut each horizontally into 6 slices. Core the apples, but do not peel. Cut each horizontally into 6 slices. Brush the slices with lemon juice. Peel and core the pears, then cut each of them horizontally into 6 slices. Brush the slices with lemon juice.

2 Cut out 4 large squares of foil. Divide the fruit slices equally among the squares and sprinkle each pile with 1 teaspoon of the sugar. Fold up the sides of the squares to enclose the fruit securely.

3 Cook the parcels on a medium grill for about 4 minutes. Serve immediately.

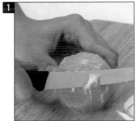

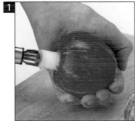

Exotic Fruit Parcels

Delicious pieces of exotic fruit are warmed through in a deliciously scented sauce to make a fabulous barbecue dessert.

10 mins
plus 30 mins
marinating

15–20 mins

SERVES 4

INGREDIENTS

1 papaya

1 mango

1 star fruit

1 tbsp grenadine

3 tbsp orange juice

light cream or lowfat plain yogurt,
  to serve

1 Cut the papaya in half, scoop out the seeds and discard them. Peel the papaya and cut the flesh into thick slices.

2 Prepare the mango by cutting it in half lengthwise around the central stone and carefully twisting the fruit off the pit.

3 Score each mango half in a criss-cross pattern. Push each mango half inside out to separate the cubes and cut them away from the skin.

4 Using a sharp knife, thickly slice the star fruit.

5 Place all of the fruit in a bowl and mix them together.

6 Mix the grenadine and orange juice together and pour over the fruit. Let marinate for at least 30 minutes.

7 Divide the fruit among 4 double-thickness squares of foil and gather up the edges to form a parcel that encloses the fruit.

8 Place the foil parcel on a rack set over warm coals and grill the fruit for 15–20 minutes.

9 Serve the fruit in the parcel, with the lowfat plain yogurt.

COOK'S TIP

Grenadine is a sweet syrup made from pomegranates. If you prefer you could use pomegranate juice instead. To extract the juice, cut the pomegranate in half and squeeze gently with a lemon squeezer—do not press too hard or the juice may become bitter.

Warm Fruit Nests

These attractive pastry shells are filled with a delicious mixture of summer berries. Serve with cream if you like.

🍓 15–20 mins ⏱ 10 mins

SERVES 4

INGREDIENTS

2–3 tbsp lemon oil

8 sheets of phyllo pastry, thawed if frozen

1 cup blueberries

1 cup raspberries

1 cup blackberries

3 tbsp superfine sugar

1 tsp allspice

fresh mint sprigs, to decorate

heavy cream, to serve

1 Preheat the oven to 350°F/180°C. Brush 4 small tartlet pans with oil. Cut the phyllo pastry into 16 squares measuring about 4½ inches/12 cm. Brush each square with oil and use to line the tartlet pans. Use 4 sheets in each pan, and stagger each sheet so that you have star-shaped effect. Transfer to a cookie sheet and bake in the preheated oven for 7–8 minutes until golden. Remove from the oven and set aside.

2 Meanwhile, warm the fruit in a pan with the superfine sugar and allspice over medium heat. Reduce the heat and simmer, stirring, for 10 minutes. Remove from the heat and drain. Using a slotted spoon, divide the warm fruit among the pastry shells. Decorate with sprigs of fresh mint and serve warm with fresh heavy cream.

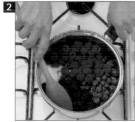

Sweet Fruit Won Tons

These sweet won tons are very adaptable and may be filled with whole, small fruits, or a spicy chopped mixture as here.

10 mins   15 mins

SERVES 4

INGREDIENTS

12 won ton wrappers

2 tsp cornstarch

6 tsp cold water

oil, for deep-frying

2 tbsp honey

selection of fresh fruit, such as kiwi fruit, limes, oranges, mango and apples, sliced, to serve

FILLING

1 cup chopped dried, pitted dates

2 tsp brown sugar

½ tsp ground cinnamon

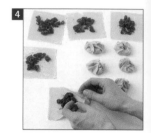

1 To make the filling, mix together the dates, sugar, and cinnamon in a bowl.

2 Spread out the won ton wrappers on a cutting board and spoon a little of the filling into the center of each wrapper.

3 Blend the cornstarch and water and brush this mixture around the edges of the wrappers.

4 Fold the wrappers over the filling, bringing the edges together, then bring the 2 corners together, sealing with the cornstarch mixture.

5 Heat the oil for deep-frying in a wok to 350°F/180°C, or until a cube of bread browns in 30 seconds. Fry the won tons, in batches, for 2–3 minutes, until golden. Remove the won tons from the oil with a slotted spoon and let drain on paper towels.

6 Place the honey in a bowl and stand it in warm water, to soften it slightly. Drizzle the honey over the sweet fruit won tons and serve with a selection of fresh fruit.

COOK'S TIP
Won ton wrappers may be found in Chinese supermarkets.

Mango Dumplings

Fresh mango and canned lychees fill these small steamed dumplings, making a really colorful and tasty treat.

🍮🍮🍮🍮

45 mins plus
1 hr resting

⏱ 20-25 mins

SERVES 4

INGREDIENTS

DOUGH

2 tsp baking powder

1 tbsp superfine sugar

⅔ cup water

⅔ cup milk

3½ cups all-purpose flour, plus extra
for dusting

FILLING AND SAUCE

1 small mango

3½ oz/100 g canned lychees, drained

1 tbsp ground almonds

4 tbsp orange juice

ground cinnamon, for dusting

1 To make the dough, place the baking powder and superfine sugar in a large mixing bowl.

2 Mix the water and milk together and then stir this mixture into the baking powder and sugar mixture until well combined. Gradually stir in the all-purpose flour to make a soft dough. Set the dough aside in a warm place for about 1 hour.

3 To make the filling, peel the mango and cut the flesh from the pit. Coarsely chop the mango flesh; reserve half and set aside for the sauce.

4 Chop the lychees and add to half of the chopped mango, together with the ground almonds. Let stand for 20 minutes.

5 Meanwhile, make the sauce. Blend the reserved mango and the orange juice in a food processor until smooth. Using the back of a spoon, press the mixture through a strainer to make a smooth sauce.

6 Divide the dough into 16 equal pieces. Roll each piece out on a lightly floured work counter into 3-inch/7.5-cm circles.

7 Spoon a little of the mango and lychee filling on to the center of each circle and fold the dough over the filling to make semicircles. Pinch the edges together to seal firmly.

8 Place the dumplings on a heatproof plate in a steamer, cover, and steam for about 20-25 minutes, or until cooked through.

9 Remove the mango dumplings from the steamer, dust with a little ground cinnamon, and serve immediately with the mango sauce.

Caramel Apple Wedges

A Thai version of a Chinese dessert, these sweet caramel-coated pieces of fruit take practice to perfect, but the trick is to get the timing right.

🍎 20 mins   🕐 10 mins

SERVES 4

INGREDIENTS

1 cup rice flour

1 medium egg

½ cup cold water

4 crisp dessert apples

2½ tbsp sesame seeds

1¼ cups superfine sugar

2 tbsp vegetable oil, plus extra vegetable oil for deep frying

1 Place the flour, egg, and water in a bowl and whisk well until a smooth, thick batter forms.

2 Core the apples and cut each into 8 wedges. Drop into the batter and stir in the sesame seeds.

3 Place the sugar and 2 tablespoons oil in a heavy-based pan and heat, stirring, until the sugar dissolves completely. Continue to stir until the syrup just starts to turn pale golden. Remove from the heat but keep warm.

4 Heat the oil for frying in a wok or deep skillet to 350°F/180°C, or until a cube of bread browns in 30 seconds. Lift the apple pieces one by one from the batter and, using chopsticks or tongs, lower into the hot oil and fry for 2–3 minutes, until golden brown and crisp.

5 Remove with a slotted spoon and dip very quickly into the sugar mixture. Dip briefly into ice water and drain on paper towels. Serve immediately.

COOK'S TIP

Take care not to over-heat the sugar syrup or it will become difficult to handle and burn. If it starts to set before you have finished dipping the apple pieces, warm it slightly over the heat until it becomes liquid again.

Mixed Fruit Brûlées

Traditionally a rich mixture made with cream, this fruit-based version is just as tempting using lowfat smetana and yogurt as a topping.

5 mins   5 mins

SERVES 4

INGREDIENTS

1 lb/450 g prepared assorted summer fruits, such as strawberries, raspberries, black currants, red currants, and cherries, thawed if frozen

⅔ cup smetana

⅔ cup lowfat plain yogurt

1 tsp vanilla extract

4 tbsp raw sugar

1 Preheat the broiler to medium. Divide the prepared strawberries, raspberries, black currants, red currants, and cherries evenly among 4 small heatproof ramekins.

2 Combine the smetana, yogurt, and vanilla extract.

3 Spoon the mixture over the fruit, to cover it completely.

4 Top each serving with 1 tablespoon of raw sugar and place the desserts under the preheated broiler until the sugar melts and starts to caramelize. Set aside for a couple of minutes before serving.

COOK'S TIP
Look out for half-fat creams, in light and heavy varieties. They are good substitutes for occasional use. Alternatively, in this recipe, double the quantity of yogurt for a lower-fat version.

Chocolate Soufflé

Served with hot chocolate custard, this is a chocoholic's dream. Do not be put off by the mystique of soufflés—this one is not difficult to make.

15 mins   50–55 mins

SERVES 4

I N G R E D I E N T S

2 tbsp butter, plus extra for greasing

3½ oz/100 g semisweet chocolate

1¼ cups milk

4 large eggs, separated

1 tbsp cornstarch

4 tbsp superfine sugar

½ tsp vanilla extract

⅔ cup semisweet chocolate chips

superfine and confectioners' sugar,
  for dusting

C H O C O L A T E   C U S T A R D

2 tbsp cornstarch

1 tbsp superfine sugar

scant 2 cups milk

1¾ oz/50 g semisweet chocolate

1 Preheat the oven to 350°F/180°C. Grease a 5-cup soufflé dish and sprinkle with superfine sugar. Break the chocolate into pieces.

2 Heat the milk with the butter in a pan until almost boiling. Mix the egg yolks, cornstarch, and superfine sugar in a bowl and pour on some of the hot milk, whisking. Return it to the pan and cook gently, stirring constantly until thickened. Add the chocolate and stir until melted. Remove from the heat and stir in the vanilla extract.

3 Whisk the egg whites until soft peaks form. Fold half of the egg whites into the chocolate mixture. Fold in the rest with the chocolate chips. Pour into the dish and bake in the preheated oven for 40–45 minutes until well risen.

4 Meanwhile, make the custard. Put the cornstarch and sugar in a small bowl and mix to a smooth paste with a little of the milk. Heat the remaining milk until almost boiling. Pour a little of the hot milk on to the cornstarch, mix well, then pour back into the pan. Cook gently, stirring until thickened. Break the chocolate into pieces and add to the custard, stirring until melted.

5 Dust the soufflé with sugar and serve immediately with the chocolate custard.

Soufflé with Coffee Sabayon

Soufflés, especially chocolate ones, are not as tricky to make as is often thought. Just make sure everyone is sitting at the table when it is ready.

🍮 25 mins · 🕐 50 mins

SERVES 4-6

INGREDIENTS

SOUFFLÉ

butter and a little superfine sugar, for coating the dish

3 tbsp cornstarch

1 cup milk

4 oz/115 g semisweet chocolate, broken into pieces

4 eggs, separated

¼ cup golden superfine sugar

confectioners' sugar, for dusting

COFFEE SABAYON

2 eggs

3 egg yolks

scant ½ cup golden superfine sugar

4 tsp instant coffee granules

2 tbsp cognac

1 Preheat the oven to 375°F/190°C. Grease a 4½-cup soufflé dish and sprinkle with superfine sugar. To make the soufflé, put the cornstarch in a bowl. Add a little of the milk and stir to make a smooth paste. Pour the remaining milk into a pan and add the chocolate. Heat gently until the chocolate has melted. Pour the chocolate milk on to the cornstarch paste, stirring. Return to the pan and bring to a boil, stirring constantly. Simmer gently for 1 minute. Remove from the heat and stir in the egg yolks, one at a time. Cover the surface closely with plastic wrap and let cool slightly.

2 Put the egg whites in a large bowl and whisk until soft peaks start to form. Gradually whisk in the superfine sugar until stiff but not dry. Stir a little of the meringue into the chocolate mixture, then carefully fold in the remainder. Pour into the prepared soufflé dish and bake in the oven for 40 minutes, until well risen and with a slight wobble when pushed.

3 Just before the soufflé is ready, make the sabayon. Put the eggs, yolks, sugar, coffee, and cognac in a heavy-based pan. Place over very low heat and whisk constantly until the mixture is thick and light. Dust a little confectioners' sugar over the soufflé and serve with the sabayon.

COOK'S TIP

A prepared soufflé will keep in the refrigerator for up to 2 hours before cooking and it will still rise.

Cappuccino Soufflé Puddings

These individual light and airy soufflés are very quick to cook and just melt in the mouth. They are perfect served with vanilla ice cream.

🍰 25 mins   🕐 15 mins

SERVES 6

I N G R E D I E N T S

butter, for greasing

6 tbsp whipping cream

2 tsp instant espresso granules

2 tbsp Kahlúa

3 large eggs, separated, plus 1 extra white

scant ¼ cup golden superfine sugar, plus extra for coating

5½ oz/150 g plain chocolate, broken into pieces

unsweetened cocoa, for dusting

vanilla ice cream, to serve

1 Preheat the oven to 375°F/190°C. Grease and coat the sides of 6 x ¼-cup ramekins with superfine sugar and place on a cookie sheet. Put the cream in a pan and warm gently. Stir in the coffee until dissolved, then add the Kahlúa.

2 Divide the mixture among the prepared ramekins. Whisk the egg whites until soft peaks form, then gradually whisk in the superfine sugar until stiff but not dry. Put the chocolate in a heatproof bowl set over a pan of gently simmering water until melted. Add the egg yolks to the melted chocolate, then stir in a little of the whisked egg white.

3 Gradually fold in the remaining egg white. Divide the mixture among the ramekins. Cook in the preheated oven for 15 minutes, until just set. Dust with unsweetened cocoa and serve at once, with vanilla ice cream.

VARIATION
Kahlúa is a coffee liqueur, but rum or cognac could be used as an alternative.

Banana Soufflés

These elegant individual soufflés would be a good choice for a dinner party dessert, especially as they are so simple to make.

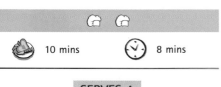

🍓 10 mins   🕐 8 mins

SERVES 4

I N G R E D I E N T S

sunflower or corn oil, for brushing

2 ripe bananas

1 tbsp lemon or lime juice

1 tbsp coconut-flavored liqueur

4 eggs, separated

¼ cup superfine sugar

1 Preheat the oven to 450°F/230°C. Lightly brush 4 x 1½-cup soufflé dishes with oil. Cut the bananas into 1-inch/2.5-cm lengths. Place the bananas, lemon juice, and liqueur in a food processor and process to a smooth purée. Add the egg yolks and 1 teaspoon of the sugar and process briefly again to mix. Scrape into a bowl.

2 Whisk the egg whites until stiff peaks form, then whisk in the remaining sugar, 1 tablespoon at a time, until stiff and glossy. Fold 1 tablespoon of the egg whites into the banana mixture to loosen it, then gently incorporate the remainder.

3 Spoon the soufflé mixture into the dishes and make a rim with the end of a teaspoon. Place on a cookie sheet and bake in preheated oven for 8 minutes, or until well risen and golden. Serve immediately.

COOK'S TIP
To whisk egg whites successfully, make sure that they are as fresh as possible and that they are at room temperature, rather than directly from the refrigerator. Some cooks like to add a pinch of salt or cream of tartar before they start to whisk.

Orange Soufflés

Light-as-air, these delicious little soufflés are the perfect choice for entertaining. As with all soufflés, they should be served immediately.

15 mins   20 mins

SERVES 6

INGREDIENTS

6 oz/175 g butter, sweet for preference, plus 1 tbsp extra for greasing

3 tbsp superfine sugar, plus 1 tbsp extra for sprinkling

6 oz/175 g semisweet chocolate, broken into small pieces

4 large eggs, separated

2 tbsp orange-flavored liqueur

¼ tsp cream of tartar

1 tbsp confectioners' sugar, for dusting

Chocolate Custard (see page 570), to serve

1 Preheat the oven to 425°F/220°C. Grease 6 ramekins and sprinkle with superfine sugar to coat the bottoms and sides. Tip out any excess. Stand the ramekins on a cookie sheet.

2 Chop the butter and place it in a heavy-based pan with the chocolate. Stir over very low heat until melted and smooth. Remove the pan from the heat and cool slightly. Beat in the egg yolks, one at a time, and stir in the orange-flavored liqueur. Set aside, stirring occasionally.

3 Gently whisk the egg whites until they are frothy, then sprinkle in the cream of tartar and whisk rapidly until soft peaks form. Add 1 tablespoon of superfine sugar and whisk rapidly again. Add the remaining superfine sugar, 1 tablespoon at a time, whisking until the whites form stiff, glossy peaks. Gently stir about one-quarter of the whites into the cooled chocolate mixture, then fold the chocolate mixture into the remaining whites using a metal spoon.

4 Divide the mixture among the ramekins and bake in the preheated oven for about 10 minutes, until risen and just set. Dust the soufflés with confectioners' sugar and serve immediately, handing the custard separately.

Chocolate Mandarin Soufflé

A perfect way to end a special-occasion meal or dinner party, this soufflé with a difference tastes and looks superb.

25 mins   35 mins

SERVES 4

INGREDIENTS

butter, sweet for preference, for greasing

3 mandarins or clementines

2½ oz/70 g semisweet chocolate

2½ cups milk

¼ cup brown sugar

⅓ cup semolina

3 eggs

6 tbsp Mandarine Napoléon liqueur

1 Grease a 7½-cup soufflé dish with butter. Place a cookie sheet in the oven and preheat to 400°F/200°C. Grate the rind of 2 of the oranges and set aside. Pare the other orange, removing all traces of pith, and cut into very fine shreds. Use the fruit for another dish (see Cook's Tip). Grate the chocolate.

2 Gently heat the milk in a heavy-based pan. Sprinkle in the sugar and semolina and bring to a boil, stirring constantly until thickened and smooth. Remove the pan from the heat and set aside to cool slightly.

3 Separate the eggs, placing the whites in a greasefree bowl. Lightly beat the yolks together, then beat them into the milk mixture with grated rind, liqueur, and most of the chocolate, reserving 2–3 teaspoons for decoration.

4 Whisk the egg whites until soft peaks form. Gently fold in about one-third of the milk mixture, then fold in the remainder. Spoon the mixture into the soufflé dish and place on the preheated cookie sheet. Bake for 30 minutes, until risen and just set. Sprinkle with the reserved chocolate and the shreds of orange rind and serve immediately.

COOK'S TIP

Separate the leftover mandarins or clementines into segments, removing all traces of pith. Half-dip in a bowl of melted semisweet chocolate and let set on nonstick parchment paper. Serve as petits fours with after-dinner coffee.

Choux Puffs with Chocolate

Sweet choux puffs are rarely served hot, which is a great shame because they are truly a special treat. Serve with your favorite ice cream.

15 mins   10–15 mins

SERVES 6–8

INGREDIENTS

2 tbsp slivered almonds

generous 1 cup all-purpose flour

2½ oz/70 g butter, sweet for preference

1 cup water

2 tsp superfine sugar

4 eggs

4 tbsp milk chocolate chips

sunflower oil, for deep-frying

2 bananas

confectioners' sugar, for dusting

ice cream, to serve

1 Spread out the almonds on a cookie sheet and toast under a preheated broiler until golden brown. Keep an eye on them because they can burn easily. Set aside to cool.

2 Sift the flour on to a sheet of waxed or parchment paper. Put the butter in a heavy-based pan, pour in the water, add the superfine sugar, and heat gently until the butter has melted. Increase the heat to medium and bring just to a boil. Immediately remove the pan from the heat and add all the flour. Mix well, then return the pan to a low heat and cook, stirring constantly, for about 1 minute, until the dough is smooth and comes away from the side of the pan. Set aside to cool slightly.

3 Beat the eggs in a pitcher, then gradually beat them into the dough. Continue to beat vigorously until the dough is thick and glossy, then beat in the toasted almonds and chocolate chips.

4 Heat the sunflower oil in a deep-fryer or large, heavy-based pan to 350°F/ 180°C, or until a cube of day-old bread browns in 45–60 seconds.

5 Meanwhile, peel and chop the bananas, then gently stir them into the dough. When the oil is hot, cook the choux puffs in batches. Scoop up tablespoonfuls of the dough and, using another spoon to help drop them into the oil. Cook for 3–5 minutes until they are puffed up, golden brown and rise to the surface of the oil. Remove drain well on paper towels and keep warm while you cook the remaining batches.

6 Transfer to serving plates, dust with confectioners' sugar, and serve immediately with scoops of ice cream.

COOK'S TIP

The secret to successful choux pastry is to stir, rather than beat the mixture when you add the flour and not to over-cook it. Remove the pan from the heat as soon as the dough comes away from the sides of the pan.

Profiteroles

A classic dessert that never goes out of style. This version, with its cognac-flavored chocolate sauce, is especially good.

25 mins   40 mins

SERVES 4

INGREDIENTS

CHOUX PASTRY

3¼ oz/90 g butter, sweet for preference, plus extra for greasing

scant 1 cup water

3½ oz/100 g all-purpose flour

3 eggs, beaten

CREAM FILLING

1¼ cups heavy cream

3 tbsp superfine sugar

1 tsp vanilla extract

CHOCOLATE AND COGNAC SAUCE

4½ oz/125 g semisweet chocolate, broken into small pieces

2½ tbsp butter

6 tbsp water

2 tbsp cognac

1 Preheat the oven to 400°F/200°C. Grease a large cookie sheet with butter. To make the pastry, put the water and butter in a pan and bring to a boil. Meanwhile, sift the flour into a bowl. Remove the pan from the heat and add in the flour all at once, beating until smooth. Let cool for 5 minutes. Beat in enough of the eggs to make a soft, dropping consistency. Transfer to a pastry bag fitted with a ½-inch/1-cm plain tip. Pipe small balls on to the cookie sheet. Bake for 25 minutes. Remove from the oven. Pierce the bottom of each ball with a skewer to let steam escape.

2 To make the filling, whip together the cream, sugar, and vanilla. Cut the pastry balls almost in half horizontally, then fill each one with the cream.

3 To make the sauce, gently melt the chocolate, butter, and water together in a small pan, stirring constantly, until smooth. Stir in the cognac. Pile the profiteroles into individual serving dishes or in a large pyramid on a raised cake stand. Pour over the sauce and serve.

Raspberry Croissants

Simple to prepare, these tasty croissants are placed on a grill to warm through until the chocolate melts.

🕑 10 mins   ⏱ 10–15 mins

SERVES 4

INGREDIENTS

4 butter croissants

4 tsp raspberry jelly

2¾ oz/75 g semisweet chocolate

oil, for greasing

½ cup raspberries

1 Slice the croissants in half. Spread the bottom half of each croissant with 1 teaspoon of the raspberry jelly.

2 Grate or finely chop the chocolate and sprinkle over the raspberry jelly.

3 Lightly grease 4 sheets of foil, brushing with a little oil.

4 Divide the raspberries equally among the croissants and replace the top half of each croissant. Place each croissant on a sheet of foil, wrapping the foil to enclose the croissant completely.

5 Place the rack 6 inches/15 cm above hot coals. Transfer the croissants to the rack and let them heat through for 10–15 minutes, or until the chocolate just starts to melt.

6 Remove the foil and transfer the croissants to individual serving plates. Serve hot.

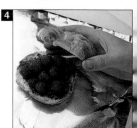

VARIATION

For a delicious chocolate and strawberry filling for the croissants, use sliced strawberries and strawberry jelly instead of the raspberries.

Chocolate French Toast

There is something very moreish about these delicious chocolate toasts, served with whipped cream and a raspberry and rum sauce.

10–15 mins

10–20 mins

SERVES 4

INGREDIENTS

1¾ oz/50 g semisweet chocolate

⅔ cup milk

1 egg

4 tbsp seedless raspberry jelly

2 tbsp dark rum (optional)

8 thick slices white bread

butter or oil, for shallow-frying

½ tsp ground cinnamon

3 tbsp superfine sugar

a little whipped cream, to serve

1 Break the chocolate into small pieces and place in a small pan with the milk. Heat gently, stirring, until the chocolate melts. Let the mixture cool slightly.

2 Beat the egg in a large mixing bowl and whisk in the chocolate milk.

3 Heat the raspberry jelly gently and stir in the rum (if using). Set aside and keep warm.

4 Remove the crusts from the bread, cut into triangles, and dip each one into the chocolate mixture. Heat the butter or oil in a skillet and cook the bread triangles for 2–3 minutes, turning once, until they are just crisp.

5 Mix together the cinnamon and superfine sugar and sprinkle it over the toast. Serve with the hot raspberry and rum sauce and a little whipped cream.

COOK'S TIP
Young children adore this dessert, made without the rum. Cut the bread into fingers to make it easier for them to handle.

Panettone & Strawberries

Panettone is a sweet Italian bread. It is delicious toasted, and when it is topped with mascarpone and strawberries it makes a sumptuous dessert.

5 mins plus
30 mins chilling   2 mins

SERVES 4

INGREDIENTS

scant 1 cup strawberries

scant ½ cup superfine sugar

6 tbsp Marsala

½ tsp ground cinnamon

4 slices panettone

4 tbsp mascarpone cheese

1 Hull and slice the strawberries and place them in a large bowl. Add the sugar, Marsala, and cinnamon to the strawberries.

2 Toss the strawberries in the sugar and cinnamon mixture until they are well coated. Let chill in the refrigerator for at least 30 minutes.

3 When ready to serve, transfer the slices of panettone to a rack set over medium hot coals. Grill the panettone for about 1 minute on each side or until golden brown.

4 Carefully remove the panettone from the grill and transfer to individual serving plates.

5 Top the panettone with the mascarpone cheese and the marinated strawberries. Serve immediately.

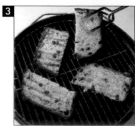

Strings of Gold

A delicate and elegant dessert with which to end a Chinese meal. Be sure that your jasmine flowers are untreated.

🍓 10 mins   🕐 10 mins

SERVES 4

INGREDIENTS

7 egg yolks

1 tbsp egg white

2½ cups granulated sugar

scant 1 cup water

handful of scented jasmine flowers

1 Press the egg yolks and egg white through a fine strainer, then whisk lightly.

2 Place the sugar and water in a large pan and heat gently until the sugar dissolves. Add the jasmine flowers, bring to a boil, and boil rapidly until a thin syrup forms. Remove the flowers with a slotted spoon.

3 Bring the syrup to simmering point. Using a pastry bag with a fine tip, or a paper frosting cone, quickly drizzle the egg mixture into the syrup in a thin steam to form loose nests or pyramid shapes.

4 As soon as the threads set, remove the nests carefully and drain well on paper towels. Arrange on a warmed serving dish. Garnish with fresh fruit.

COOK'S TIP
If you can't get hold of fresh, scented jasmine flowers, add a few drops of rose water or orange flower water to the syrup instead.

Sweet Rice

This dessert is served at banquets and celebratory meals in China, because it looks wonderful when sliced.

🍮 20 mins   🕐 1 hr 15 mins

SERVES 4

I N G R E D I E N T S

¾ cup pudding rice

2 tbsp butter, sweet for preference, plus
   extra for greasing

1 tbsp superfine sugar

8 dried dates, pitted and chopped

1 tbsp raisins

5 candied cherries, halved

5 pieces angelica, chopped

5 walnut halves

½ cup canned unsweetened chestnut purée

S Y R U P

⅔ cup water

2 tbsp orange juice

4½ tsp brown sugar

1½ tsp cornstarch

1 tbsp cold water

1 Put the rice in a pan, cover with cold water, and bring to a boil. Reduce the heat, cover, and simmer for about 15 minutes, or until the water has been absorbed. Stir in the butter and superfine sugar.

2 Grease a 2½-cup heatproof pudding bowl. Cover the bottom and sides of the bowl with a thin layer of the rice, pressing with the back of a spoon.

3 Mix the fruit and walnuts together and press them into the rice.

4 Spread a thicker layer of rice on top and then fill the center with the chestnut purée. Cover with the remaining rice, pressing the top down to seal in the purée completely.

5 Cover the bowl with pleated waxed paper and foil and secure with string. Place in a steamer, or stand the bowl in a pan and fill with hot water until it reaches halfway up the sides of the bowl. Cover and steam for 45 minutes. Let stand for 10 minutes.

6 Before serving, gently heat the water and orange juice in a small pan. Add the brown sugar and stir to dissolve. Bring the syrup to a boil.

7 Mix the cornstarch with the cold water to form a smooth paste, then stir into the boiling syrup. Cook for 1 minute until thickened and clear.

8 Turn the pudding out on to a serving plate. Pour the syrup over the top, cut into slices, and serve.

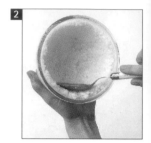

Mango with Sticky Rice

Coconut-flavored cooked rice is served in domes with cubes of fresh mango. Serve the rice cut into diamond shapes instead, if preferred.

30 mins plus
30 mins soaking   25 mins

SERVES 4

I N G R E D I E N T S

generous 1 cup glutinous rice, soaked for 30 minutes in cold water

1 cup coconut milk

2 tbsp superfine sugar

pinch of salt

2 large ripe mangoes

1 Drain the rice and rinse thoroughly. Place in a pan with the coconut milk, sugar, and salt. Bring to a boil and simmer, stirring occasionally, until the rice has absorbed all the coconut milk and is very soft.

2 Transfer the rice to a steamer set over a pan of gently simmering water. Cover and steam for 15 minutes. Let cool a little. Press the rice into the base of four ramekins and turn out onto individual plates to form rice domes. Alternatively, spread the rice out on a cookie sheet lined with foil, roll it flat with a wet rolling pin, and cut into diamond shapes.

3 Peel the mangoes and cut the flesh into cubes. To serve, pile the mango cubes around the rice domes, or arrange the rice diamonds and mango cubes on individual plates.

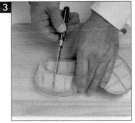

Sticky Rice Balls

Serve these sweet Chinese rice morsels as part of a dessert selection to follow a traditional Chinese banquet.

15 mins plus
3 hrs soaking

35 mins

SERVES 4

INGREDIENTS

1½ cups glutinous rice

2½ cups granulated sugar

1¼ cups water

pink and green food colorings

rose petals or jasmine flowers, to decorate

1 Place the rice in a bowl and add enough cold water to cover. Leave to soak for 3 hours, or overnight.

2 Drain the rice and rinse thoroughly in cold water.

3 Line the top part of a steamer with cheesecloth and pour the rice into it. Place over boiling water, cover, and steam the rice for 30 minutes. Remove and let cool.

4 Heat the sugar and water gently until the sugar dissolves. Bring to a boil and boil for 4–5 minutes to reduce to a thin syrup. Remove the pan from the heat and set aside.

5 Divide the rice in half and color one half pale pink, the other half pale green. Shape into small balls.

6 Using 2 forks, dip the rice balls into the syrup, drain off the excess, and pile on to a dish. Scatter with rose petals or jasmine flowers.

COOK'S TIP
If you prefer, the rice balls can be shaped in small molds like dariole molds as seen in the photo on the right.

Deep-Fried Sweetmeats

This is one of the most popular Indian sweetmeats. The flavor and beautiful aroma comes from rose water. Serve them hot or cold.

15 mins   30 mins

SERVES 8

INGREDIENTS

5 tbsp whole milk powder

1½ tbsp all-purpose flour

1 tsp baking powder

1½ tbsp butter, sweet for preference

1 medium egg

1 tsp milk to mix (if required)

10 tbsp pure or vegetable ghee

SYRUP

3¼ cups water

8 tbsp sugar

2 green cardamoms, peeled, with seeds crushed

generous pinch of saffron strands

2 tbsp rose water

1 Place the whole milk powder, flour, and baking powder in a large bowl.

2 Place the butter in a pan and heat until melted, stirring.

3 Beat the egg in a bowl. Add the melted butter and beaten egg to the dry ingredients and blend together with a fork (add the 1 teaspoon extra milk at this stage it necessary) to form a soft dough.

4 Break the dough into about 12 small pieces and shape into small, smooth balls.

5 Heat the ghee in a deep skillet. Reduce the heat and start frying the dough balls, about 3–4 at a time, tossing and turning gently with a slotted spoon until a dark golden brown color. Remove the sweetmeats from the skillet and set aside in a deep serving bowl.

6 To make the syrup, boil the water and sugar in a pan for 7–10 minutes. Add the crushed cardamom seeds and saffron, and pour the syrup over the sweetmeats.

7 Pour the rose water sparingly over the top. Let soak for about 10 minutes in order for the sweetmeats to soak up some of the syrup. Serve hot or cold.

Sweet Carrot Halva

This nutritious dessert is flavored with spices, nuts, and raisins. Serve with cream.

10 mins   55 mins

SERVES 6

INGREDIENTS

1 lb 10 oz/750 g carrots, grated

3 cups milk

1 cinnamon stick or piece cassia bark (optional)

4 tbsp vegetable ghee or oil

¼ cup granulated sugar

¼ cup unsalted pistachios, chopped

¼–½ cup blanched almonds, slivered or chopped

⅓ cup raisins

8 whole cardamoms, peeled, with seeds crushed

thick cream, to serve

COOK'S TIP

The quickest and easiest way to grate this quantity of carrots is by using a food processor fitted with the appropriate blade. This mixture may be prepared ahead of time and reheated in the microwave when required.

1 Put the grated carrots, milk, and cinnamon or cassia (if using), into a large, heavy-based pan and bring to a boil. Reduce the heat to very low and simmer, uncovered, for about 35–40 minutes, or until the mixture is thick (with no milk remaining). Stir the mixture frequently during cooking to prevent it sticking.

2 Remove and discard the cinnamon or cassia. Heat the ghee or oil in a nonstick skillet, add the carrot mixture, and stir-fry over medium heat for about 5 minutes, or until the carrots take on a glossy sheen.

3 Add the sugar, pistachios, almonds, raisins, and crushed cardamom seeds, mix thoroughly, and continue stir-frying for an additional 3–4 minutes. Serve warm or cold, with thick cream.

Carrot Dessert

This makes an impressive dinner-party dessert. It is best served warm with cream and can be made well in advance because it freezes well.

10 mins   1 hr

SERVES 6

INGREDIENTS

3 lb 5 oz/1.5 kg carrots

⅔ cup ghee

2½ cups milk

¾ cup evaporated milk

10 whole cardamoms, peeled, with seeds crushed

8–10 tbsp sugar

TO DECORATE

4 tbsp chopped pistachios

2 leaves varq (silver leaf), optional

1 Grate the carrots. Heat the ghee in a large, skillet over medium heat. Add the grated carrots and cook, stirring constantly, for about 15–20 minutes, or until the moisture from the carrots has evaporated and the carrots have darkened in color.

2 Add the milk, evaporated milk, crushed cardamoms, and sugar and cook, stirring constantly, for an additional 30–35 minutes, until the mixture is a rich brownish-red color.

3 Transfer the carrot mixture to a large shallow serving dish. Decorate with the pistachio nuts and varq (if using), and serve immediately.

COOK'S TIP
Pure ghee is best for this dessert because it will taste better. However, if you are trying to limit your fat intake, you can use vegetable ghee instead.

German Noodle Dessert

This rich and satisfying dessert is a traditional Jewish recipe that will quickly become popular with all the family.

10 mins   45 mins

SERVES 4

I N G R E D I E N T S

4 tbsp butter, plus extra for greasing

6 oz/175 g ribbon egg noodles

½ cup cream cheese

1 cup cottage cheese

scant ½ cup superfine sugar

2 eggs, beaten lightly

½ cup sour cream

1 tsp vanilla extract

pinch of ground cinnamon

1 tsp grated lemon rind

¼ cup slivered almonds

generous ⅓ cup dry white bread crumbs

confectioners' sugar, for dusting

1 Preheat the oven to 350°F/180°C. Lightly grease an oval ovenproof dish with a little butter. Bring a large pan of water to a boil. Add the noodles, bring back to a boil, and cook over medium heat for 10 minutes until tender, but still firm to the bite. Drain and set aside.

2 Beat the cream cheese with the cottage cheese and superfine sugar in a mixing bowl until the mixture is smooth. Add the beaten eggs, a little at a time, beating thoroughly after each addition.

3 Stir in the sour cream, vanilla extract, cinnamon, and lemon rind and fold in the noodles. Transfer the mixture to the prepared ovenproof dish and smooth the surface.

4 Melt the butter in a small skillet over low heat. Add the almonds and cook gently, stirring constantly, for about 1–1½ minutes until they are lightly colored. Remove the skillet from the heat and stir the bread crumbs into the almonds.

5 Sprinkle the almond and bread crumb mixture evenly over the top of the pudding and bake in the preheated oven for about 35–40 minutes, until just set. Dust the top with a little sifted confectioners' sugar and serve immediately.

VARIATION
Although not authentic, you could add 3 tablespoons raisins with the lemon rind in step 3, if desired.

Indian Vermicelli Pudding

Indian vermicelli (seviyan), which are very fine, are delicious cooked in milk and ghee. Muslims make this for a religious festival called Eid.

5 mins

20 mins

SERVES 6

INGREDIENTS

¼ cup pistachios (optional)

¼ cup slivered almonds

3 tbsp ghee

1½ cups seviyan (Indian vermicelli)

3¾ cups milk

¾ cup evaporated milk

8 tbsp sugar

6 dried dates, pitted

1 Soak the pistachios (if using) in a bowl of water for at least 3 hours. Peel the pistachios and mix them with the slivered almonds. Chop the nuts finely and set aside.

2 Melt the ghee in a large pan and lightly cook the seviyan. Reduce the heat immediately (the seviyan will turn golden brown very quickly so be careful not to burn it), and if necessary remove the pan from the heat (do not worry if some bits are a little darker than others).

3 Add the milk to the seviyan and bring to a boil over low heat, taking care that it does not boil over.

4 Add the evaporated milk, sugar, and dates to the mixture in the pan. Simmer over low heat, uncovered, stirring occasionally, for about 10 minutes. When the consistency starts to thicken, pour the pudding into a warm serving bowl.

5 Decorate the pudding with the chopped pistachios and almonds.

COOK'S TIP
You will find seviyan (Indian vermicelli) in Indian food stores. This dessert can be served warm or cold.

Sweet Potato Dessert

This unusual milky dessert is very easy to make and is equally delicious whether it is eaten hot or cold.

 15 mins   20 mins

SERVES 4

INGREDIENTS

2 lb 4 oz/1 kg sweet potatoes

3¾ cups milk

scant 1 cup sugar

chopped almonds, to decorate

1 Using a sharp knife, peel the sweet potatoes. Rinse them and then cut them into slices. Place in a large pan. Cover with 2½ cups of the milk and cook over low heat until the sweet potato is soft enough to be mashed.

2 Remove the sweet potatoes from the heat and mash thoroughly until completely smooth. Add the sugar and the remaining milk and stir gently until completely blended together.

3 Return the pan to the heat and simmer the mixture until it starts to thicken (it should reach the consistency of a creamy soup).

4 Transfer to a serving dish. Decorate with almonds and serve immediately.

COOK'S TIP

Look for the sweet potatoes with a pinkish skin and yellow flesh, which give a good colour to this dessert.

Indian Bread Pudding

This, the Indian equivalent of the English bread and butter pudding, is rather a special dessert, usually cooked for special occasions.

🍮 20 mins   🕐 25 mins

SERVES 6

INGREDIENTS

6 medium slices bread

5 tbsp ghee (preferably pure)

¾ cup sugar

1¼ cups water

3 green cardamoms, without husks

2½ cups milk

¾ cup evaporated milk or khoya
  (see Cook's Tip)

½ tsp saffron strands

heavy cream, to serve (optional)

TO DECORATE

8 pistachios, soaked, peeled, and chopped

chopped almonds

2 leaves varq (silver leaf), optional

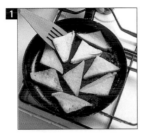

1 Cut the bread slices into quarters. Heat the ghee in a large, heavy-based skillet. Add the bread slices and cook, turning once, until crisp and golden brown. Place the fried bread in the bottom of a heatproof dish and set aside.

2 To make a syrup, place the sugar, water, and cardamom seeds in a pan and bring to a boil over medium heat, stirring constantly, until the sugar has dissolved. Boil until thickened. Pour the syrup over the fried bread.

3 Put the milk, evaporated milk or khoya (see Cook's Tip), and the saffron in a separate pan and bring to a boil over low heat. Simmer until it has halved in volume. Pour the mixture over the syrup-coated bread.

4 Decorate with the pistachios, chopped almonds, and varq (if using). Serve the bread pudding with cream, if liked.

COOK'S TIP
To make khoya, bring 3¾ cups milk to a boil in a large, heavy-based pan. Reduce the heat and boil, stirring occasionally, for 35–40 minutes, until reduced to a quarter of its volume and resembling a sticky dough.

Italian Bread Dessert

This deliciously rich dessert is cooked with cream and apples and is delicately flavored with orange.

45 mins   25 mins

SERVES 4

INGREDIENTS

1 tbsp butter

2 small dessert apples, peeled, cored, and sliced into rings

½ cup granulated sugar

2 tbsp white wine

4 thick slices bread (about 4 oz/115 g) crusts removed (day-old baguette is ideal)

1¼ cups light cream

2 eggs, beaten

pared rind of 1 orange, cut into short, thin strips

1 Lightly grease a 5-cup deep ovenproof dish with the butter.

2 Arrange the apple rings in the bottom of the dish. Sprinkle half of the sugar over the apples.

3 Pour the wine over the apples. Add the bread slices, pushing them down with your hands to flatten them slightly.

4 Mix the cream with the eggs, the remaining sugar, and the orange rind and pour the mixture over the bread. Set aside to soak for 30 minutes.

5 Preheat the oven to 350°F/180°C. Bake the pudding for 25 minutes, until golden and set. Remove from the oven, set aside to cool slightly, and serve warm.

Chocolate Bread Dessert

This chocolate sponge is served with hot fudge sauce, making it the most delicious way to use up bread that is slightly stale.

20 mins plus 2 hrs chilling

45 mins

SERVES 4

INGREDIENTS

butter, for greasing

6 thick slices white bread, crusts removed

scant 2 cups milk

¾ cup canned evaporated milk

2 tbsp unsweetened cocoa

2 eggs

2 tbsp dark muscovado sugar

1 tsp vanilla extract

confectioners' sugar, for dusting

HOT FUDGE SAUCE

2 oz/60 g semisweet chocolate, broken into pieces

1 tbsp unsweetened cocoa

2 tbsp corn syrup

¼ cup butter or margarine

2 tbsp dark muscovado sugar

⅔ cup milk

1 tbsp cornstarch

1 Grease a shallow ovenproof dish. Cut the bread into squares and layer them in the dish.

2 Put the milk, evaporated milk, and unsweetened cocoa in a pan and heat gently, stirring occasionally, until the mixture is tepid.

3 Whisk together the eggs, sugar, and vanilla extract. Add the warm milk mixture and beat well.

4 Pour into the prepared dish, making sure that all the bread is completely covered. Cover the dish with plastic wrap and chill in the refrigerator for 1–2 hours.

5 Preheat the oven to 350°F/180°C. Bake the dessert for 35–40 minutes, until set. Let stand for 5 minutes.

6 To make the sauce, put the chocolate, unsweetened cocoa, syrup, butter (or margarine), sugar, milk, and cornstarch into a pan. Heat gently, stirring until smooth.

7 Dust the dessert with confectioners' sugar and serve immediately with the hot fudge sauce.

Chocolate Marmalade Brioche

The light, buttery texture of brioche makes it the ideal basis for a rich, chocolate dessert, perfect for family meals or entertaining.

10 mins plus
1 hr soaking

1 hr 10 mins

SERVES 6

I N G R E D I E N T S

2½ oz/70 g butter, sweet for preference, plus extra for greasing

10½ oz/300 g semisweet chocolate

6 tbsp shredless Temple orange marmalade

6 individual brioches

4 large eggs

scant 2 cups milk

scant 2 cups heavy cream

3 tbsp brown sugar

1 Preheat the oven to 350°F/180°C. Grease a large ovenproof dish. Break the chocolate into pieces and place in a heatproof bowl with the marmalade. Melt over a pan of gently simmering water, stirring frequently, until melted and combined. Remove the bowl from the heat.

2 Cut the brioches in half and spread the cut sides with the chocolate and marmalade mixture, then arrange the slices evenly in the dish. Beat the eggs in a bowl, then beat in the milk and cream. Pour the mixture evenly over the brioches, pressing them down so that they are submerged. Cover the dish with plastic wrap and let soak for up to 1 hour.

3 Uncover the dish and sprinkle the sugar evenly over the surface. Bake for 50–60 minutes, until set. Remove the dish from the oven and let stand for 10 minutes, then serve.

COOK'S TIP
Temple orange marmalade is made with bitter Temple oranges. Alternatively, you could use grapefruit or a mixed citrus-fruit marmalade, but choose one that has a bitter edge.

Sunday Pudding

A popular, easy-to-make chocolate and fruit pudding that is the perfect choice for a family lunch. It can be served hot or cold.

15 mins plus
1 hr soaking

45–50 mins

SERVES 4

INGREDIENTS

2–3 tbsp butter, plus extra for greasing

6 slices brown bread

14 oz/400 g canned mangoes, drained and chopped

2 tbsp chopped blanched almonds or hazelnuts

4 tbsp golden raisins

1 tsp ground cinnamon

2 oz/55 g semisweet chocolate

2 eggs

1 tbsp superfine sugar

1½ cups light cream

1 tsp white rum (optional)

1 Grease a medium-size ovenproof dish. Cut off and discard the crusts from the bread and generously spread 1 side of each slice with butter. Cut the slices into quarters.

2 Cover the bottom of the dish with a layer of bread, buttered-side up. Spoon half the mangoes evenly over them, then sprinkle with half the nuts, half the raisins, and half the cinnamon. Cover with a second layer of bread, buttered-side up and top with the remaining mangoes, nuts, raisins, and cinnamon. Cover with the remaining bread, buttered-side up. Set aside.

3 Chop the chocolate, place in a heat-proof bowl and set over a saucepan of gently simmering water to melt. When melted, remove the saucepan from the heat and stir until smooth.

4 Beat the eggs in another heatproof bowl, then gradually whisk in the sugar and the cream. Set the bowl over a saucepan of gently simmering water and cook, whisking constantly, until thickened and a trail is left when the whisk is dragged across the surface. Remove the bowl from the heat and whisk in the melted chocolate and rum, if using. Pour the chocolate mixture evenly over the bread. Cover and let soak for up to 1 hour.

5 Preheat the oven to 375°F/190°C. Bake the pudding for 40–45 minutes, until the top is crisp and golden. Let stand for 5 minutes before serving. Alternatively, let cool and serve cold.

Brioche & Butter Pudding

Brioche gives this dessert a lovely rich flavor, but this recipe also works well with soft-baked batch bread.

20 mins   35–40 mins

SERVES 6

INGREDIENTS

8 oz/225 g brioche

1 tbsp butter

¼ cup semisweet chocolate chips

1 egg

2 egg yolks

4 tbsp superfine sugar

scant 2 cups canned evaporated milk

1 Preheat the oven to 350°F/180°C. Cut the brioche into thin slices. Lightly butter one side of each slice.

2 Place a layer of brioche, buttered-side down, in the bottom of a shallow ovenproof dish. Sprinkle a few chocolate chips over the top.

3 Continue layering the brioche and chocolate chips, finishing with a layer of brioche on top.

4 Whisk together the egg, egg yolks, and sugar until well combined. Heat the milk in a small pan until it just starts to simmer. Gradually add to the egg mixture, whisking well.

5 Pour the custard over the brioche and let stand for 5 minutes. Press the brioche down into the custard.

6 Place the dish in a roasting pan and fill with boiling water to come halfway up the side of the dish. Bake in the preheated oven for 30 minutes, or until the custard has set. Let the dessert cool for about 5 minutes before serving.

VARIATION
For a double-chocolate dessert, heat the milk with 1 tablespoon of unsweetened cocoa, stirring until well dissolved then continue from step 4.

Bread & Butter Pudding

A traditional pudding full of fruit and spices. It is the perfect way to use up day-old bread.

🍰 50 mins   🕐 45–55 mins

SERVES 6

INGREDIENTS

2½ oz/70 g butter, softened, plus extra
  for greasing

7 oz/200 g white bread, sliced

2 tbsp golden raisins

1 oz/25 g candied peel

2½ cups milk

4 egg yolks

⅓ cup superfine sugar

½ tsp allspice

1 Preheat the oven to 400°F/200°C. Grease a 5⅓-cup ovenproof dish.

2 Remove the crusts from the bread (optional), spread with butter, and cut into quarters.

3 Arrange half of the buttered bread slices in the prepared ovenproof dish. Sprinkle half of the golden raisins and candied peel over the top of the bread.

4 Place the remaining bread slices over the fruit, and then sprinkle over the reserved fruit.

5 To make the custard, bring the milk almost to a boil in a pan. Whisk together the egg yolks and the sugar in a bowl, then pour in the warm milk.

6 Strain the warm custard through a strainer. Pour the custard over the bread slices.

7 Let stand for 30 minutes, then sprinkle with the allspice.

8 Place the ovenproof dish in a roasting pan half-filled with hot water.

9 Bake in the preheated oven for 40-45 minutes, until the pudding has just set. Serve warm.

COOK'S TIP
The pudding can be prepared in advance up to step 7 and then set aside until required.

Apple Bread & Butter Pudding

Everyone has their own favorite recipe for this dish. This one has added marmalade and grated apples for a really rich and unique taste.

45 mins plus
30 mins standing

1 hr

SERVES 6

INGREDIENTS

4 tbsp butter, softened

4–5 slices white or whole-wheat bread

4 tbsp chunky orange marmalade

grated rind of 1 lemon

½–¾ cup golden raisins

¼ cup candied peel

1 tsp ground cinnamon or allspice

1 tart cooking apple, peeled, cored,
    and grated coarsely

scant ½ cup brown sugar

3 eggs

generous 2 cups milk

2 tbsp raw sugar

1 Use the softened butter to grease an ovenproof dish and to spread on the slices of bread, then spread the bread with the marmalade.

2 Place a layer of bread in the bottom of the dish and sprinkle with the lemon rind, half the golden raisins, half the candied peel, half the spice, all of the apple, and half the brown sugar. Add another layer of bread, cutting it so that it fits the dish.

3 Sprinkle over most of the remaining golden raisins and all the remaining candied peel, spice, and brown sugar, scattering it evenly over the bread. Top with a final layer of bread, again cutting to fit the dish.

4 Lightly beat together the eggs and milk and then carefully strain the mixture over the bread in the dish. If time allows, set the pudding aside to stand for 20–30 minutes. Preheat the oven to 400°F/200°C.

5 Sprinkle the top of the pudding with the raw sugar and scatter over the remaining golden raisins. Cook in the preheated oven for 50–60 minutes, until risen and golden brown. Serve immediately or let cool and serve cold.

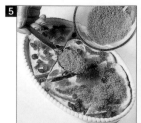

Panettone Pudding

This is a variation of bread and butter pudding, made with an Italian cross between a bread and a cake which is traditionally served at Christmas.

15 mins plus
1 hr soaking

40 mins

SERVES 6

INGREDIENTS

3 tbsp butter, softened, plus extra
for greasing

9 oz/250 g panettone, cut into slices

1 cup milk

1 cup heavy cream

1 vanilla bean, split

3 eggs

generous ⅓ cup golden superfine sugar

2 tbsp apricot jelly, warmed and strained

1 Preheat the oven to 325°F/160°C. Grease a 3¾-cup shallow baking dish. Butter the slices of panettone and arrange in the dish. Put the milk, cream, and vanilla bean in a pan and heat gently to boiling point. Put the eggs and sugar in a bowl and beat together, then pour in the milk mixture and beat together.

2 Pour the custard through a strainer over the buttered panettone. Leave for 1 hour so that the panettone soaks up the custard.

3 Bake the pudding in the oven for about 40 minutes, then brush the apricot jelly over the top. If the top crusts of the pudding are not crisp and golden, heat under the broiler for a minute.

COOK'S TIP
The vanilla bean may
be rinsed and dried
and used again.

Spiced Steamed Pudding

Steamed puddings are irresistible on a winter's day, but the texture of this pudding is so light it can be served throughout the year.

🕐 15 mins   🕐 1 hr 30 mins

SERVES 6

INGREDIENTS

4½ oz/125 g butter or margarine, plus extra for greasing

2 tbsp corn syrup, plus extra to serve

generous ½ cup superfine or brown sugar

2 eggs

1½ cups self-rising flour

¾ tsp ground cinnamon or allspice

grated rind of 1 orange

1 tbsp orange juice

½ cup golden raisins

5 tbsp preserved ginger, chopped finely

1 dessert apple, peeled, cored, and grated coarsely

1 Thoroughly grease a 3¾-cup heatproof pudding bowl. Put the corn syrup into the bowl.

2 Cream the butter or margarine and sugar together until very light and fluffy and pale in color. Beat in the eggs, one at a time, following each with a spoonful of the flour.

3 Sift the remaining flour with the cinnamon or allspice and fold into the mixture, followed by the orange rind and juice. Fold in the golden raisins, then the ginger and apple.

4 Turn the mixture into the bowl and smooth the top. Cover with a piece of pleated greased parchment paper, tucking the edges under the rim of the bowl.

5 Cover with a sheet of pleated foil. Tie securely in place with string, with a piece of string tied over the top of the bowl for a handle to make it easy to lift out of the pan.

6 Put the bowl into a pan half-filled with boiling water, cover, and steam for 1½ hours, adding more boiling water to the pan as necessary during cooking.

7 To serve the pudding, remove the foil and parchment paper, turn the pudding on to a warm serving plate, and serve immediately.

Snowdon Pudding

This old-fashioned British steamed pudding was named after the Welsh mountain, Snowdon. The story goes it was served to hungry climbers.

🍮 15 mins   🕐 2 hrs 10 mins

SERVES 6

I N G R E D I E N T S

butter, for greasing

¾ cup raisins

2 tbsp chopped angelica

2 cups fresh white bread crumbs

2 tbsp rice flour

pinch of salt

1 cup plus 2 tbsp shredded suet

2 tbsp brown sugar

grated rind of 1 large lemon

2 eggs

⅓ cup marmalade

3–4 tsp milk

L E M O N   S A U C E

1 tbsp cornstarch

1 cup plus 2 tbsp milk

grated rind and juice of 2 lemons

3 tbsp corn syrup

1 Sprinkle a well-greased 5-cup heatproof pudding bowl with 1 tablespoon of the raisins and the angelica.

2 Put the remaining raisins in a bowl with the bread crumbs, rice flour, salt, suet, sugar, and lemon rind and toss to combine. Make a well in the center.

3 Beat the eggs and marmalade for about 1 minute until starting to lighten. Beat in 3 tablespoons of the milk; pour into the well. Gently stir into the dry ingredients to form a soft dough. Add more milk if necessary. Spoon into the prepared pudding bowl.

4 Grease a sheet of waxed paper and make a pleat along the center. Cover the bowl loosely with the paper, buttered-side down; secure with string.

5 Stand the pudding bowl on a wire rack in a large pan. Fill with enough boiling water to come three-quarters of the way up the side of the bowl. Cover and steam gently over low heat for about 2 hours, until the top is risen. Top up with boiling water when needed.

6 To make the lemon sauce, mix the cornstarch with about 3 tablespoons milk to form a paste. Bring the remaining milk and the lemon rind to a simmer, then whisk into the paste until blended. Return the mixture to the pan and simmer gently for about 3 minutes, whisking, until smooth. Stir in the lemon juice and syrup. Pour into a pitcher and keep warm.

7 Remove the pudding from the pan, remove the paper, and let the pudding shrink slightly before unmolding. Serve hot, with the lemon sauce.

Steamed Coconut Cake

This steamed coconut cake, steeped in a syrup of lime and ginger, is typical of Thai desserts and sweets. It has a distinctly Chinese influence.

15 mins   30 mins

SERVES 4

INGREDIENTS

2 large eggs, separated

pinch of salt

½ cup superfine sugar

2¾ oz/75 g butter, sweet for preference, melted and cooled

5 tbsp coconut milk

scant 1½ cups self-rising flour

½ tsp baking powder

3 tbsp dry unsweetened coconut

4 tbsp syrup from the ginger jar

3 tbsp lime juice

TO DECORATE

3 pieces preserved ginger, diced

curls of freshly grated coconut

strips of lime rind

1 Cut an 11-inch/28-cm circle of parchment paper and press into a 7-inch/18-cm steamer basket to line it.

2 Whisk the egg whites with the salt until stiff. Gradually whisk in the sugar, 1 tablespoon at a time, whisking hard after each addition until the mixture forms stiff peaks.

3 Whisk in the yolks, then quickly stir in the butter and coconut milk. Sift the flour and baking powder over the mixture, then fold in lightly and evenly with a large metal spoon. Fold in the coconut.

4 Spoon the mixture into the lined steamer basket and tuck the spare paper over the top. Place the basket over boiling water, cover, and steam for 30 minutes.

5 Turn the cake on to a plate, remove the paper, and let cool slightly. Mix the ginger syrup and lime juice and spoon over the cake. Cut into squares and top with ginger, coconut curls, and lime rind.

COOK'S TIP
Coconuts grow on tropical beaches all around the world, but probably originated in Southeast Asia, and it is here that coconut is most important in cooking.

Quick Syrup Sponge

You won't believe your eyes when you see just how quickly this light-as-air sponge pudding cooks in the microwave oven!

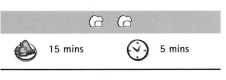

15 mins   5 mins

SERVES 4

INGREDIENTS

4½ oz/125 g butter, sweet for preference, or margarine

4 tbsp corn syrup

⅓ cup superfine sugar

2 eggs

1 cup self-rising flour

1 tsp baking powder

about 2 tbsp warm water

custard, to serve

1 Grease a 6-cup heatproof pudding bowl with a small amount of the butter or margarine. Spoon the syrup into the bowl.

2 Cream the remaining butter or margarine with the sugar until light and fluffy. Gradually add the eggs, beating well between each addition.

3 Sift the flour and baking powder together, then fold into the creamed mixture using a large metal spoon. Add enough water to give a soft, dropping consistency. Spoon into the pudding bowl and smooth the surface.

4 Cover with microwave-safe film, leaving a small space to let air escape. Microwave on Full Power for 4 minutes, then remove from the microwave and let the pudding stand for 5 minutes, while it continues to cook.

5 Turn the pudding out on to a serving plate. Serve with custard.

COOK'S TIP
If you don't have a microwave, this pudding can be steamed. Cover with a piece of pleated parchment paper and a piece of pleated foil. Place in a pan, add boiling water, and steam for 1½ hours.

Steamed Coffee Sponge

This sponge dessert is very light and is delicious served with a coffee or chocolate sauce.

10 mins   1 hr–
            1 hr 15 mins

SERVES 4

INGREDIENTS

2 tbsp margarine

2 tbsp brown sugar

2 eggs

5½ tbsp all-purpose flour

¾ tsp baking powder

6 tbsp milk

1 tsp coffee extract

SAUCE

1¼ cups milk

1 tbsp brown sugar

1 tsp unsweetened cocoa

2 tbsp cornstarch

4 tbsp water

1 Lightly grease a 2½-cup heatproof pudding bowl. Cream the margarine and sugar until the mixture is light and fluffy, then beat in the eggs.

2 Gradually stir in the flour and baking powder, then stir in the milk and coffee extract to make a smooth batter.

3 Spoon the mixture into the bowl and cover with a pleated piece of parchment paper and then a pleated piece of foil, securing around the bowl with tightly tied string.

4 Place in a steamer or large pan half full of boiling water. Cover and steam for 1–1¼ hours, or until cooked through.

5 To make the sauce, put the milk, sugar, and unsweetened cocoa in a pan and heat until the sugar dissolves. Blend the cornstarch with 4 tablespoons water to a paste and stir into the pan. Bring the sauce to a boil, stirring until thickened. Cook for 1 minute.

6 Turn the pudding out on to a warm serving plate and spoon the sauce over the top. Serve immediately.

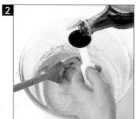

Chocolate Cranberry Sponge

The sharpness of the fruit contrasts deliciously with the sweetness of the chocolate in this wonderful, fluffy sponge pudding.

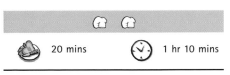

20 mins   1 hr 10 mins

SERVES 4

INGREDIENTS

4 tbsp butter, sweet for preference, plus
  1 tsp extra for greasing

4 tbsp brown sugar, plus 2 tsp
  for sprinkling

¾ cup cranberries, thawed if frozen

1 large tart cooking apple

2 eggs, beaten lightly

⅔ cup self-rising flour

3 tbsp unsweetened cocoa

SAUCE

6 oz/175 g semisweet chocolate, broken
  into pieces

1¾ cups evaporated milk

1 tsp vanilla extract

½ tsp almond extract

1 Grease a 5-cup heatproof pudding bowl, sprinkle with brown sugar to coat the sides, and tip out any excess. Put the cranberries in a bowl. Peel, core, and dice the apple and mix with the cranberries. Put the fruit in the prepared heatproof bowl.

2 Place the butter, brown sugar, and eggs in a large bowl. Sift in the flour and unsweetened cocoa and beat well until thoroughly mixed. Pour the mixture into the heatproof bowl on top of the fruit, cover the top with foil, and tie with string. Steam for about 1 hour, until risen, topping up with boiling water if necessary.

3 Meanwhile, to make the sauce, put the semisweet chocolate and milk in a double boiler or a heatproof bowl set over a pan of gently simmering water. Stir until the chocolate has melted, then remove from the heat. Whisk in the vanilla and almond extracts and continue to beat until the sauce is thick and smooth.

4 To serve, remove the sponge from the heat and discard the foil. Run a palette knife around the side of the bowl, place a serving plate on top of the sponge and, holding them together, invert. Serve immediately, with the sauce on the side.

German Chocolate Dessert

This heavenly confection from southern Germany is definitely not for those who are watching their weight.

25 mins   1 hr 30 mins–2 hrs

SERVES 6

INGREDIENTS

1 tsp vegetable oil, plus extra for oiling

6 oz/175 g semisweet chocolate

6 slices white bread

1 cup heavy cream

4 oz/115 g butter, sweet for preference

scant 1 cup superfine sugar

1½ cups ground almonds

½ tsp instant coffee

6 eggs

1 Brush a 5-cup metal mold with a little vegetable oil. Break the chocolate into pieces and place in a heatproof bowl with the vegetable oil. Set over a pan of gently simmering water, stirring occasionally, until melted. Remove from the heat and set aside.

2 Cut off and discard the crusts from the bread and cut the slices into cubes. Place in a bowl, pour in the cream, stir well, and let soak for 5 minutes.

3 Meanwhile, cream the butter with the sugar until fluffy, then add the bread and cream and beat until smooth and creamy. Then gradually beat in the melted chocolate, ground almonds, and instant coffee. Continue to beat until smooth and thoroughly incorporated. Gradually beat in the eggs, 1 at a time.

4 Pour the mixture into the prepared mold. Cut out a circle of foil about 4 inches/10 cm larger than the rim of the mold. Make a pleat in the center of the circle, place on top of the mold and tie securely in place with kitchen string.

5 Place the mold in a large pan and pour in enough boiling water to come about halfway up the sides. Cover and steam over low heat for 1½–2 hours, topping up the boiling water, as necessary.

6 Turn off the heat and remove the mold from the pan. Remove and discard the foil circle. Run a round-bladed knife around the edge of the mold to loosen, then invert the dessert on to a warm serving plate. Serve immediately.

Austrian Chocolate Dessert

This is rather like a very rich soufflé, traditionally served with chocolate sauce and fruit bottled in cognac.

25 mins | **1 hr**

SERVES 8

INGREDIENTS

PUDDING

2 oz/55 g semisweet chocolate

3½ oz/100 g butter, sweet for preference, plus extra for greasing

scant ½ cup superfine sugar, plus extra for sprinkling

1 cup milk

1 tsp vanilla extract

pinch of salt

¾ cup all-purpose flour

6 eggs, separated

confectioners' sugar, for dusting

apricots or prunes in cognac, to serve

SAUCE

6 oz/175 g semisweet chocolate

2 tbsp butter, sweet for preference

½ cup water

3 tbsp sugar

5 tbsp light cream

½ tsp vanilla extract

1 To make the pudding, break the chocolate into pieces and melt in a heatproof bowl set over a pan of gently simmering water. Remove from the heat and let cool slightly. Grease a 7½-cup soufflé dish, sprinkle with sugar, tapping the sides to coat, and tipping out any excess. Preheat the oven to 325°F/160°C.

2 Place the milk, butter, vanilla extract, and salt in a large, heavy-based pan and bring to a boil over low heat, stirring occasionally. Gradually stir in the flour and continue to stir until the mixture is just coming away from the sides of the pan. Remove from the heat and stir in the melted chocolate, then stir in the egg yolks, 1 at a time.

3 Whisk the egg whites in a clean, greasefree bowl until soft peaks form, then gradually whisk in the sugar until stiff. Spoon about one-quarter of the egg white into the chocolate mixture to lighten it, then gently fold in the remainder in 2 batches.

4 Spoon the mixture into the prepared dish, place in a large roasting pan, and pour in enough hot water to come halfway up the sides of the dish. Bake for 50 minutes.

5 Just before serving, make the sauce. Break the chocolate into pieces and dice the butter. Pour the water into a pan, add the sugar, and bring to a boil, stirring until the sugar has dissolved. Stir in the chocolate and butter, then remove the pan from the heat and stir well until smooth. Stir in the cream and vanilla extract.

6 Divide the chocolate pudding among warm serving plates and dust the top with a little confectioners' sugar. Spoon over a little of the sauce, add 1 or 2 pieces of cognac-soaked fruit and serve immediately.

Golden Pudding

A comforting pudding, perfect for a winter's day. The corn syrup gives this delicious dessert a golden glow.

   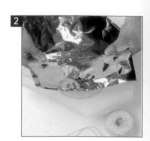

10–15 mins   1hr 30 mins

SERVES 4–6

I N G R E D I E N T S

3 tbsp butter, plus extra for greasing

2 tbsp superfine sugar

2 eggs

6 tbsp all-purpose flour

1 tsp baking powder

6 tbsp milk

1 tsp vanilla extract

4 tbsp corn syrup

thin strips of candied orange rind, to decorate

hot custard, to serve

1 Lightly grease a large heatproof pudding bowl with butter. Put the remaining butter in a large bowl with the sugar and beat until light and fluffy. Add the eggs and beat together well. Mix in the flour and baking powder, then stir in the milk and vanilla extract. Continue to stir until smooth.

2 Pour the corn syrup into the heatproof pudding bowl, then spoon the pudding mixture over the top. Cover with waxed paper, top with a piece of foil, and tie it on securely with string. Transfer to a large pan of gently simmering water that comes halfway up the side of the heatproof pudding bowl. Simmer gently for about 1½ hours until cooked right through, topping up the water level when necessary.

3 Lift out the pudding and let rest for 5 minutes, then turn it out on to a serving plate. Decorate with thin strips of candied orange rind and serve hot with custard.

New Age Spotted Dick

This is a deliciously moist lowfat pudding. The sauce is in the center of the pudding, and will spill out when the pudding is cut.

🍮 25 mins 🕐 1 hrs 15 mins

SERVES 6–8

INGREDIENTS

¾ cup raisins

½ cup water

generous ½ cup corn oil, plus extra for brushing

¼ cup cuporfino cugar

¼ cup ground almonds

2 eggs, beaten lightly

1½ cups self-rising flour

SAUCE

½ cup walnuts, chopped

½ cup ground almonds

1¼ cups semiskim milk

4 tbsp granulated sugar

1 Preheat the oven to 350°F/160°C. Brush a 4-cup heatproof pudding bowl with oil, or line with parchment paper. Put the raisins in a pan with ½ cup water. Bring to a boil, then remove from the heat. Let soak for 10 minutes, then drain.

2 Whisk together the oil, sugar, and ground almonds until thick and syrupy; this will need about 8 minutes of beating (on medium speed if using an electric whisk).

3 Add the eggs, one at a time, beating well after each addition. Combine the flour and raisins. Stir into the mixture. Put all the sauce ingredients into a pan. Bring to a boil, stir, and simmer for 10 minutes.

4 Transfer the sponge mixture to the oiled bowl and pour on the hot sauce. Place on a cookie sheet.

5 Bake in the preheated oven for about 1 hour. Lay a piece of parchment paper across the top if it starts to brown too fast.

6 Let cool for 2–3 minutes in the bowl before turning out on to a serving plate.

COOK'S TIP
Always soak raisins before baking them, as they retain their moisture nicely and you taste the flavor of them instead of biting on a dried-out raisin.

Mocha Pudding

This delectable mixture of dried and candied fruit in a coffee- and chocolate-flavored sponge is guaranteed to warm you up on a cold day.

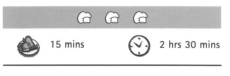

15 mins   2 hrs 30 mins

SERVES 4

INGREDIENTS

butter, sweet for preference, for greasing

4 egg yolks

2 egg whites

generous ½ cup superfine sugar

½ cup unsweetened cocoa

scant 2 cups milk

⅔ cup strong black coffee

¼ cup candied cherries, chopped

½ cup chopped walnuts

⅓ cup golden raisins

2 tsp very finely chopped candied peel

2 tbsp Marsala

heavy cream or custard, to serve

1 Preheat the oven to 350°F/150°C. Grease a medium-size ovenproof dish. Beat together the egg yolks, egg whites, sugar, and unsweetened cocoa until thoroughly combined. Beat in the milk and coffee. Stir in the candied cherries, walnuts, golden raisins, candied peel, and Marsala and mix well.

2 Spoon the mixture into the dish, smoothing the top. Cover the top of the pudding with lightly greased foil. Stand the dish in a roasting pan and pour in enough water to come about halfway up the sides of the dish. Bake for 2½ hours, until just set.

3 Discard the foil and serve the pudding immediately, with a jug of heavy cream or custard.

COOK'S TIP

You can also steam this pudding very gently for the same length of time. Place in a pan of water, keep the water barely simmering, and do not let boil. Top up the water as necessary.

Chocolate Pecan Pudding

This traditional American recipe tastes wonderful served with an equally traditional lemon-flavored hard sauce.

🍮 20 mins   🕐 2 hrs 30 mins

SERVES 4

I N G R E D I E N T S

butter, sweet for preference, for greasing

3 oz/85 g semisweet chocolate

3 oz/85 g shortening

2 cups all-purpose flour

4 tsp baking powder

pinch of salt

½ tsp ground cinnamon

½ tsp ground ginger

⅔ cup granulated sugar

½ cup pecans, chopped

1 tbsp finely chopped preserved ginger

2 eggs

⅔ cup milk

½ tsp vanilla extract

H A R D L E M O N S A U C E

3 oz/85 g butter, sweet for preference, softened

2 cups confectioners' sugar

juice of ½ lemon

finely grated rind of 1 lemon

1 Grease a 4-cup heatproof pudding bowl. Break the chocolate into pieces, and place in a heatproof bowl with the shortening. Set over a pan of simmering water. When melted, remove from the heat, stir until smooth, and set aside.

2 Sift together the flour, baking powder, salt, cinnamon, and ground ginger into a bowl. Stir in the sugar, nuts, and preserved ginger. Beat the eggs in a bowl, then beat in the milk. Stir the egg mixture into the dry ingredients, then stir in the chocolate mixture and vanilla extract. Spoon the mixture into the heatproof pudding bowl, smoothing the top.

3 Cut out a circle of waxed paper and a circle of foil 4 inches/10 cm larger than the rim of the pudding bowl. Grease the paper, then place on the foil circle, greased-side up. Make a pleat in the center of both circles then, still holding them together and with the foil circle upward, place them on top of the bowl. Tie securely in place with kitchen string.

4 Place the bowl in a large pan and pour in enough boiling water to come about halfway up the side. Cover and steam over low heat for 2½ hours, topping up the boiling water, as necessary.

5 Meanwhile, make the sauce. Cream the butter and confectioners' sugar in a bowl until well combined and fluffy. Gradually beat in the lemon juice and rind. Spoon into a bowl, cover, and let chill.

6 Remove the bowl from the pan and discard the foil and waxed-paper circles. Run a round-bladed knife around the edge of the pudding to loosen it, then invert on to a warm serving plate. Serve immediately with the hard lemon sauce.

Christmas Pudding

This timeless, classic pudding is an essential part of the Christmas table. Make it well in advance, because it needs to chill for at least two weeks.

🍮 20 mins plus
2 hrs soaking   🕐 6 hrs

SERVES 4

INGREDIENTS

generous 1 cup currants

generous 1 cup raisins

generous 1 cup golden raisins

⅔ cup sweet sherry

6 oz/175 g butter, sweet for preference,
   plus extra for greasing

generous 1 cup brown sugar

4 eggs, beaten

1½ cups self-rising flour

1⅔ cups fresh white or whole-wheat
   bread crumbs

¼ cup blanched almonds, chopped

juice of 1 orange

grated rind of ½ orange

grated rind of ½ lemon

½ tsp allspice

holly leaves, to decorate

whipped cream or hard sauce, to serve

1 Put the currants, raisins, and golden raisins in a glass bowl and pour over the sherry. Let soak for at least 2 hours.

2 Mix the butter and sugar in a bowl. Beat in the eggs, then fold in the flour. Stir in the soaked fruits and their sherry with the bread crumbs, almonds, orange juice and rind, lemon rind, and allspice. Grease a large heatproof pudding bowl with butter and press the mixture into it, leaving a gap of 1 inch/2.5 cm at the top. Cut a circle of waxed paper 1¼ inches/3 cm larger than the top of the pudding bowl, grease with butter, and place over the pudding. Top with 2 layers of foil then secure with string. Place the pudding in a large pan of boiling water that comes two-thirds of the way up the bowl. Reduce the heat and simmer for 6 hours, topping up the water when necessary.

3 Remove from the heat and let cool. Renew the waxed paper and foil and chill for 2–8 weeks. To reheat, steam for 2 hours as before. Decorate with holly leaves and serve with whipped cream or hard sauce.

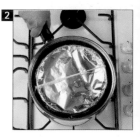

Chocolate Fudge Dessert

This dessert has a hidden surprise when cooked because it separates to give a rich chocolate sauce at the bottom of the dish.

🍲 10 mins   🕐 35–40 mins

SERVES 4

INGREDIENTS

4 tbsp margarine, plus extra for greasing

½ cup brown sugar

2 eggs, beaten

1¼ cups milk

⅓ cup chopped walnuts

¼ cup all-purpose flour

2 tbsp unsweetened cocoa

confectioners' sugar and unsweetened cocoa, for dusting

1 Preheat the oven to 350°F/180°C. Lightly grease a 4-cup ovenproof dish.

2 Cream together the margarine and sugar in a large mixing bowl until fluffy. Beat in the eggs.

3 Gradually stir in the milk and add the walnuts.

4 Sift the flour and cocoa into the mixture and fold in gently, with a metal spoon, until well mixed.

5 Spoon the mixture into the dish and cook in the preheated oven for 35–40 minutes, or until the sponge is cooked.

6 Dust with confectioners' sugar and unsweetened cocoa and serve.

VARIATION
Add 1–2 tablespoons of cognac or dark rum to the mixture for a slightly alcoholic dessert, or 1–2 tablespoons orange juice for a child-friendly version.

Chocolate Fudge Pudding

This fabulous steamed sponge pudding, served with a rich chocolate fudge sauce, is perfect for cold winter days.

10 mins

1 hr 40 mins–
2 hrs 10 mins

SERVES 6

INGREDIENTS

generous ⅓ cup soft margarine

1¼ cups self-rising flour

½ cup corn syrup

3 eggs

¼ cup unsweetened cocoa

CHOCOLATE FUDGE SAUCE

3½ oz/100 g semisweet chocolate

½ cup condensed milk

4 tbsp heavy cream

1 Lightly grease a 5-cup heatproof pudding bowl.

2 Place the ingredients for the sponge pudding in a separate mixing bowl and beat until well combined and smooth.

3 Spoon into the prepared bowl and smooth the top. Cover with a disk of waxed paper and tie a pleated sheet of foil over the bowl. Steam for 1½-2 hours, until the sponge is cooked and springy to the touch.

4 To make the sauce, break the chocolate into small pieces and place in a small pan with the condensed milk. Heat gently, stirring constantly, until the chocolate melts. Remove the pan from the heat and stir in the heavy cream.

5 To serve the dessert, turn it out on to a serving plate and pour over a little of the chocolate fudge sauce. Serve the remaining sauce separately.

Pecan Fudge Ring

Although this can be served cold as a cake, it is absolutely delicious served as a hot dessert.

🍰 35 mins   🕐 35 mins

SERVES 6

INGREDIENTS

FUDGE SAUCE

3 tbsp butter, sweet for preference

3 tbsp brown sugar

4 tbsp corn syrup

2 tbsp milk

1 tbsp unsweetened cocoa

1½ oz/40 g semisweet chocolate, broken into pieces

⅓ cup finely chopped pecans

CAKE

generous ⅓ cup soft margarine

⅔ cup brown sugar

1 cup self-rising flour

2 eggs

2 tbsp milk

1 tbsp corn syrup

1 Preheat the oven to 350°F/180°C. Lightly grease an 8-inch/20-cm ovenproof ring mold.

2 To make the fudge sauce, place the butter, sugar, syrup, milk, and unsweetened cocoa in a small pan and heat gently, stirring until well combined.

3 Add the chocolate to the mixture and stir until melted, then stir in the pecans. Pour into the mold and let cool.

4 To make the cake, place all of the ingredients in a mixing bowl and beat until smooth. Carefully spoon the cake mixture over the chocolate fudge sauce.

5 Bake in the preheated oven for 35 minutes, or until the cake is springy to the touch.

6 Let the fudge ring cool in the mold for 5 minutes, then turn out on to a serving dish and serve.

Steamed Chocolate Pudding

This is a rich pudding, perfect for chocolate lovers. Serve it with this delicious sauce, flavored with hazelnuts, cognac, and dry fruits.

25 mins

1 hr 30 mins

SERVES 4–6

INGREDIENTS

4 oz/115 g butter, sweet for preference, softened, plus extra for greasing

¾ cup light muscovado sugar

2 eggs, beaten

⅔ cup self-rising flour

¼ cup unsweetened cocoa

a little milk

½ cup semisweet chocolate chips

SAUCE

4 tbsp butter

scant ½ cup light muscovado sugar

3 tbsp cognac

scant ¾ cup blanched whole hazelnuts

⅓ cup luxury dry fruits

1 Butter a 5-cup heatproof pudding bowl and line the bottom with a small circle of waxed paper. Put the butter and sugar in a mixing bowl and beat together until light and fluffy. Gradually beat in the beaten eggs. Sift the flour and unsweetened cocoa into the mixture and fold in carefully. Add a little milk, if necessary, to make a dropping consistency. Stir in the chocolate chips.

2 Spoon the mixture into the prepared bowl. Cut a large circle of waxed paper and one of foil about 3 inches/7.5 cm larger than the top of the bowl. Grease the paper and make a fold in the center of both. Use to cover the bowl and secure with string. Place the bowl in a pan and pour in boiling water to come halfway up the bowl. Cover the pan and simmer for 1½ hours. Check the water from time to time and top up with boiling water as necessary.

3 To make the sauce, place the butter and sugar in a small pan and heat gently until the sugar has dissolved and the mixture looks slightly caramelized. Add the cognac and let bubble for 1 minute. Stir in the nuts and dry fruits. Carefully unmold the pudding on to a plate and spoon the sauce over. Serve at once.

COOK'S TIP
You can make the pudding in advance. Simply put the covered bowl back into a pan of boiling water for 20–30 minutes before serving.

Chocolate Phyllo Parcels

Not only do these little phyllo parcels look delightful, they taste superb and are sure to impress dinner-party guests.

🍮 25 mins   🕐 15 mins

SERVES 6

INGREDIENTS

2 oz/55 g semisweet chocolate

¾ cup ground hazelnuts

1 tbsp finely chopped fresh mint

½ cup sour cream

2 dessert apples

9 sheets phyllo pastry,
    about 6 inches/15 cm square

2–3 oz/55–85 g butter, sweet for
    preference, melted

confectioners' sugar, for dusting

fresh mint sprigs, to decorate

whipping cream, to serve

1 Preheat the oven to 375°F/190°C. Break up the chocolate and melt in a heatproof bowl set over a pan of gently simmering water. Remove from the heat and let cool slightly.

2 Mix together the hazelnuts, mint, and sour cream in a bowl. Peel the apples and grate them into the bowl, then stir in the melted chocolate and mix well.

3 Cut each sheet of phyllo pastry into 4 squares. Keep the squares you are not using covered with a damp dish towel. Brush 1 square with melted butter, place a second square on top, and brush with melted butter. Place a tablespoonful of the chocolate mixture in the center, then bring up the corners of the squares and twist together to enclose the filling

completely. Continue making parcels in the same way until you have used up all the pastry and filling.

4 Brush a cookie sheet with melted butter and place the parcels on it. Bake for about 10 minutes, until crisp and golden. Let cool slightly, then dust with confectioners' sugar. Serve with cream.

COOK'S TIP
These parcels are best served warm, rather than hot, and can also be served cold.

Saucy Chocolate Pudding

When you take this pudding out of the oven it doesn't look very impressive, but when you cut into it you find a lovely pool of sauce.

10 mins   50–60 mins

SERVES 4–6

INGREDIENTS

½ cup self-rising flour

¼ cup unsweetened cocoa

1 tsp ground cinnamon

3 oz/85 g butter, sweet for preference, softened

generous ½ cup golden superfine sugar

1 egg

¼ cup dark muscovado sugar

½ cup pecans, chopped

1¼ cups hot black coffee

confectioners' sugar, for dusting

whipped cream, to serve

1 Preheat the oven to 325°F/160°C. Butter a 5-cup ovenproof dish. Sift the flour, unsweetened cocoa, and cinnamon into a bowl. Add the butter, 6 tbsp of the superfine sugar, and the egg and beat together thoroughly until well blended.

2 Turn into the prepared dish and sprinkle with the muscovado sugar and the pecans. Pour the coffee into a large pitcher, stir in the remaining superfine sugar, and carefully pour over the pudding.

3 Bake in the preheated oven for 50–60 minutes, until firm to the touch in the center. Sprinkle with confectioners' sugar and serve at once, with whipped cream.

COOK'S TIP
Take care not to open the oven for the first 40 minutes of the cooking time.

Sticky Chocolate Sponges

These rich individual desserts served with a cream sauce always look and taste impressive at the end of a meal.

20 mins   1 hr

SERVES 6

INGREDIENTS

4 oz/115 g butter, softened, plus extra for greasing

1 cup brown sugar

3 eggs, beaten

pinch of salt

¼ cup unsweetened cocoa

1 cup self-rising flour

1 oz/25 g semisweet chocolate, chopped finely

2¾ oz/75 g white chocolate, chopped finely

SAUCE

⅔ cup heavy cream

½ cup brown sugar

2 tbsp butter

1 Preheat the oven to 350°F/180°C. Lightly grease 6 individual ¾-cup dessert molds.

2 In a bowl, cream together the butter and sugar until pale and fluffy. Beat in the eggs a little at a time, beating well after each addition.

3 Sift the salt, unsweetened cocoa, and flour into the creamed mixture, and fold through the mixture. Stir the chopped chocolate into the mixture until evenly combined throughout.

4 Divide the mixture among the prepared molds. Lightly grease 6 squares of foil and use them to cover the tops of the molds. Press around the edges to seal.

5 Place the molds in a roasting pan and pour in boiling water to come halfway up the sides of the molds.

6 Bake in the preheated oven for 50 minutes, or until a skewer inserted into the center of the sponges comes out clean.

7 Remove the molds from the roasting pan and set aside while you prepare the sauce.

8 To make the sauce, put the cream, sugar, and butter into a pan and bring to a boil over gentle heat. Simmer gently until the sugar has dissolved.

9 To serve, run a knife around the edge of each sponge, then turn out on to individual plates and serve, handing the sauce round separately.

Coffee & Walnut Puddings

These little coffee puddings with a butterscotch sauce are guaranteed to delight your guests.

20 mins 30–40 mins

SERVES 6

INGREDIENTS

4 tbsp butter, sweet for preference, softened, plus extra for greasing

scant 1½ cups self-rising flour

1 tsp ground cinnamon

½ cup light muscovado sugar, sifted

2 large eggs, beaten

1 tbsp instant coffee granules dissolved in 2 tbsp boiling water

½ cup walnuts, chopped finely

SAUCE

¼ cup walnuts, chopped coarsely

4 tbsp butter, sweet for preference

¼ cup light muscovado sugar

⅔ cup heavy cream

1 Preheat the oven to 375°F/190°C. Grease 6 individual heatproof metal pudding bowls. Sift the flour and cinnamon into a bowl. Put the butter and sugar in a bowl and beat together until light and fluffy. Gradually beat in the eggs. Add a little flour if the mixture shows signs of curdling. Fold in half of the flour then fold in the remaining flour, alternately with the coffee. Gently stir in the walnuts.

2 Divide the mixture between the prepared bowls. Place a piece of buttered foil over each bowl and secure with an elastic band. Stand the bowls in a roasting pan and pour in boiling water to come half way up the sides of the bowls. Cover the whole roasting pan with foil, folding it under the rim. Bake in the oven for 30–40 minutes, until well risen and firm to the touch.

3 Meanwhile, prepare the sauce. Put the walnuts, butter, sugar, and cream in a pan and heat gently, stirring, until the ingredients melt and blend together. Bring to a simmer then remove from the heat. Turn the puddings out on to a serving plate, spoon over the hot sauce, and serve.

COOK'S TIP

This mixture could be cooked as one large pudding, in which case the mixture should be put into a heatproof pudding bowl, covered, and steamed for 1½ hours.

Sticky Toffee Pudding

This delicious fruit-studded pudding has a rich toffee sauce poured over it. The cold whipped cream contrasts well with the hot pudding.

10–15 mins   35–40 mins

SERVES 4

I N G R E D I E N T S

PUDDING

½ cup golden raisins

generous ½ cup pitted dates, chopped

1 tsp baking soda

2 tbsp butter, plus extra for greasing

1 cup brown sugar

2 eggs

1⅔ cups self-rising flour, sifted

grated orange rind, to decorate

whipped cream, to serve

STICKY TOFFEE SAUCE

2 tbsp butter

¾ cup heavy cream

1¼ cups brown sugar

1 To make the pudding, put the golden raisins, dates, and baking soda in a heatproof bowl. Cover with boiling water and set aside to soak.

2 Preheat the oven to 350°F/180°C. Grease an 8-inch/20-cm cake pan with butter. Put the remaining butter in a separate bowl, add the sugar, and mix together well. Beat in the eggs then fold in the flour. Drain the soaked fruits and add to the bowl. Spoon the mixture evenly into the prepared cake pan. Transfer to the preheated oven and bake for 35–40 minutes or until a skewer inserted into the center comes out clean.

3 About 5 minutes before the end of the cooking time, make the sauce. Melt the butter in a pan over medium heat. Stir in the cream and sugar and bring to a boil, stirring constantly. Reduce the heat and simmer for 5 minutes.

4 Turn out the pudding on to a serving plate and pour over the sauce. Decorate with grated orange rind and serve with whipped cream.

Individual Chocolate Molds

These little puddings are served with a delicious chocolate sauce flavored with coffee liqueur.

10–15 mins   50 mins

SERVES 4

INGREDIENTS

PUDDINGS

¾ cup superfine sugar

3 eggs

scant ⅔ cup all-purpose flour

½ cup unsweetened cocoa

3½ oz/100 g butter, sweet for preference, melted, plus extra for greasing

3½ oz/100 g semisweet chocolate, melted

CHOCOLATE SAUCE

2 tbsp butter, sweet for preference

3½ oz/100 g semisweet chocolate

5 tbsp water

1 tbsp superfine sugar

1 tbsp coffee-flavored liqueur, such as Kahlúa

coffee beans, to decorate (optional)

1 To make the puddings, put the sugar and eggs in a heatproof bowl and place over a pan of simmering water. Whisk for about 10 minutes until frothy. Remove the bowl from the heat and fold in the flour and unsweetened cocoa. Fold in the melted butter, then the melted chocolate. Mix together well. Grease 4 small heatproof pudding bowls with butter. Spoon the mixture into the pudding bowls, then cover with waxed paper. Top with foil and secure with string. Place the puddings in a large pan filled with enough simmering water to come halfway up the pudding bowls. Steam for about 40 minutes, or until cooked through.

2 About 2–3 minutes before the end of the cooking time, make the sauce. Put the butter, chocolate, water, and sugar into a small pan and warm over low heat, stirring constantly, until melted together. Stir in the liqueur.

3 Remove the puddings from the heat, turn out on to serving dishes, and pour over the sauce. Decorate with coffee beans, if using, and serve.

Chocolate Castles

Covered in a rich chocolate sauce, these light-as-air individual desserts are a delicious treat on a cold day.

25 mins   40 mins

SERVES 4

INGREDIENTS

3 tbsp butter, plus 2 tsp extra for greasing

3 tbsp superfine sugar

1 large egg, beaten lightly

⅔ cup self-rising flour

2 oz/55 g semisweet chocolate, melted

SAUCE

2 tbsp cornstarch

2 tbsp unsweetened cocoa

⅔ cup light cream

1¼ cups milk

1–2 tbsp brown sugar

1 Grease 4 small heatproof pudding bowls or baba molds with butter. In a mixing bowl, cream together the butter and sugar until pale and fluffy. Gradually add the egg, beating well after each addition.

2 In a separate bowl, sift the flour, fold it into the butter mixture with a metal spoon, then stir in the melted chocolate. Divide the mixture among the bowls, filling them to about two-thirds full to allow for expansion during cooking. Cover each cup with a circle of foil, and tie in place with string.

3 Bring a large pan of water to a boil and set a steamer over it. Place the bowls in the steamer and cook for 40 minutes. Check the water level from time to time and top up with boiling water when necessary.

4 To make the sauce, put the cornstarch, unsweetened cocoa, cream, and milk in a heavy-based pan. Bring to a boil, then reduce the heat and simmer over low heat, whisking constantly, until thick and smooth. Cook for an additional 2–3 minutes, then stir in brown sugar to taste. Pour the sauce into a pitcher.

5 Lift the bowls out of the steamer and remove the foil circles from them. Run a knife blade around the sides of the cups and turn out the chocolate castles on to warm individual plates. Serve immediately, with the sauce on the side.

Eve's Pudding

This is a popular family dessert which has soft apples on the bottom and a light buttery sponge-cake topping.

15 mins   4–45 mins

SERVES 4

INGREDIENTS

6 tbsp butter, plus extra for greasing

1 lb/450 g tart cooking apples, peeled, cored, and sliced

½ cup granulated sugar

1 tbsp lemon juice

scant ½ cup golden raisins

scant ½ cup superfine sugar

1 egg, beaten

1⅓ cups self-rising flour

3 tbsp milk

¼ cup slivered almonds

custard or heavy cream, to serve

1 Preheat the oven to 350°F/180°C. Grease a 3¾-cup round ovenproof dish with a little butter.

2 Mix the apples with the granulated sugar, lemon juice, and golden raisins. Spoon the mixture into the dish.

3 In a bowl, cream the butter and superfine sugar together until pale. Add the beaten egg, a little at a time. Carefully fold in the self-rising flour and stir in the milk to give a soft, pourable consistency.

4 Spread the mixture over the apples and sprinkle with the slivered almonds.

5 Bake in the preheated oven for 40–45 minutes, until the sponge cake topping is golden brown.

6 Serve the pudding piping hot, accompanied by homemade custard or heavy cream.

COOK'S TIP
To increase the almond flavor of this pudding, add ¼ cup ground almonds with the flour in step 4.

Chocolate Eve's Pudding

Eve's Pudding is traditionally made with apples; this one has raspberries and white chocolate sponge, with a semisweet chocolate sauce.

🕒 15 mins   ⏰ 40–45 mins

SERVES 4

I N G R E D I E N T S

8 oz/225 g fresh or frozen raspberries

2 eating apples, peeled, cored, and thickly sliced

4 tbsp seedless raspberry jelly

2 tbsp port, optional

S P O N G E   T O P P I N G

4 tbsp soft margarine

4 tbsp superfine sugar

⅔ cup self-rising flour, sifted

1¾ oz/50 g white chocolate, grated

1 egg

2 tbsp milk

S E M I S W E E T
C H O C O L A T E   S A U C E

3 oz/85 g semisweet chocolate, broken into pieces

⅔ cup light cream

1 Preheat the oven to 350°F/180°C. Place the raspberries and apple slices in a shallow 5-cup ovenproof dish.

2 Place the raspberry jelly and port (if using) in a small pan and heat gently until the jelly melts into the port. Pour the mixture over the fruit.

3 Place all of the ingredients for the sponge topping in a large mixing bowl and beat until the mixture is smooth.

4 Spoon the sponge mixture over the fruit and level the top. Bake in the preheated oven for 40–45 minutes, or until the sponge is springy to the touch.

5 To make the sauce, place the chocolate in a heavy-based pan with the cream. Heat gently, beating until a smooth sauce is formed. Serve warm with the dessert.

VARIATION
Use semisweet chocolate in the sponge and top with apricot halves, covered with peach schnapps and apricot jelly.

Chocolate Sponge with Rum

A warming way to end supper on a wintry evening, this steamed sponge pudding is very easy to make.

15 mins   1 hr 20 mins

SERVES 4

INGREDIENTS

4 tbsp butter, sweet for preference, plus
extra for greasing

1¼ cups self-rising flour, plus extra
for dusting

2 oz/55 g semisweet chocolate

¼ tsp vanilla extract

scant ⅔ cup superfine sugar

2 eggs, beaten lightly

5 tbsp milk

SAUCE

1¼ cups milk

2 tbsp cornstarch

2 tbsp superfine sugar

2 tbsp dark rum

1 Grease and flour a 5-cup heatproof bowl. Put the butter, chocolate, and vanilla in a heatproof bowl set over a pan of gently simmering water. Heat gently until the butter and sugar have melted, then remove from the heat and cool slightly. Stir the sugar into the chocolate mixture, then beat in the eggs. Sift in the flour, stir in the milk, and mix well. Pour the mixture into the prepared heatproof bowl, cover the top with foil, and tie with string. Steam the sponge for 1 hour, topping up with more boiling water if necessary.

2 To make the sauce, pour the milk into a small pan set over medium heat. Stir in the cornstarch, then stir in the sugar until dissolved. Bring to a boil, stirring constantly, then reduce the heat and simmer until thickened and smooth. Remove from the heat and stir in the rum.

3 To serve, remove the sponge from the heat and discard the foil. Run a palette knife around the side of the bowl, place a serving plate on top of the sponge, and, holding them together, invert. Serve immediately, with the sauce on the side.

Fail-Safe Puddings

Many people don't serve hot desserts when entertaining because of time or fear of failure. These little moulds are absolutely trouble free.

🍮 15 mins   🕐 10 mins

SERVES 6

I N G R E D I E N T S

6½ oz/190 g butter, sweet for preference

6½ oz/190 g semisweet or bittersweet chocolate, broken into pieces

3 eggs

3 egg yolks

scant ½ cup superfine sugar

1 tbsp all-purpose flour

O R A N G E   S A U C E

4–5 blood oranges

2 tsp cornstarch

2 tbsp water

superfine sugar, to taste

1 For the sauce, squeeze the juice from the oranges, pouring it into a measuring cup until you have about 1¼ cups. Cover with plastic wrap and place in the refrigerator until required.

2 To make the puddings, put the butter and chocolate into a small heatproof bowl. Melt over a pan of gently simmering water, stirring occasionally. When the mixture is smooth, remove from the heat and set aside to cool slightly.

3 Whisk the eggs, egg yolks, and sugar in a separate bowl until thickened and pale. Whisk in the chocolate mixture, then sift over the flour and fold in with a metal spoon. Grease 6 ramekins or ovenproof molds and divide the mixture among them. When cool, cover and place in the refrigerator until required.

4 When you are ready to cook, preheat the oven to 450°F/230°C. Uncover the molds and bake for 6–8 minutes, until just set.

5 Meanwhile, make the orange sauce. Pour the measured orange juice into a heavy-based pan. Mix the cornstarch with the water to a smooth paste in a small bowl, then add to the orange juice. Bring just to simmering point, stirring constantly. Remove from the heat, taste, and stir in sugar, if required.

6 Invert the puddings on to 6 warm plates. Serve immediately with the orange sauce on the side.

Pears & Chocolate Meringue

This will quickly become a family favorite, so keep a can of pears and a block of chocolate handy to make it whenever you like.

10 mins   45 mins

SERVES 4–6

INGREDIENTS

4 oz/115 g butter, sweet for preference, plus extra for greasing

7 oz/200 g semisweet chocolate

14 oz/400 g canned pear halves, drained

4 eggs, separated

generous ½ cup superfine sugar

1 Preheat the oven to 325°F/160°C. Grease an ovenproof dish. Place the butter in a heatproof bowl. Break up the chocolate and add it to the bowl, then set over a pan of gently simmering water, stirring occasionally until melted. Remove from the heat and set aside to cool. Slice the pears.

2 Whisk the egg yolks with the sugar until pale and thickened, then beat in the melted chocolate. Whisk the egg white in a separate greasefree bowl until stiff. Stir a spoonful of the whites into the chocolate mixture to slacken it, then fold in the remainder with a metal spoon. Fold in the sliced pears.

3 Spoon the mixture into the dish and bake for about 40 minutes, until just set and golden brown on top. Serve immediately.

VARIATION
You could also make this meringue dessert with canned apricots or fresh peaches.

Chocolate & Nut Meringue Pie

This gloriously rich and self-indulgent dessert is best served warm, rather than hot.

25 mins plus
30 mins chilling   40 mins

SERVES 6

I N G R E D I E N T S

PIE DOUGH

salt

2 cups all-purpose flour, plus extra
for dusting

5 oz/140 g butter, sweet for preference

½ cup superfine sugar

2 egg yolks

FILLING

5 oz/140 g semisweet chocolate

2 tbsp butter, sweet for preference

generous 1 cup superfine sugar

2 tsp cornstarch

4 egg yolks

¾ cup ground hazelnuts

3 egg whites

1 To make the pie dough, sift the flour with a pinch of salt into a bowl. Cream the butter and sugar together in a separate bowl until pale and fluffy. Sift over the flour, in 2 batches, and mix in, alternating with the egg yolks. Add a little cold water, a teaspoonful at a time, if necessary to make a dough.

2 Roll out the pie dough on a lightly floured cutting board and use to line a 9-inch/23-cm tart pan. Chill for 30 minutes. Preheat the oven to 375°F/190°C.

3 Prick the tart shell with a fork, line with waxed or parchment paper, and partly fill with dried beans. Place on a cookie sheet and bake blind for 10 minutes.

4 To make the filling, break the chocolate into pieces and melt in a heatproof bowl set over a pan of gently simmering water. Remove from the heat and let cool slightly.

5 Cream the butter with 6 tablespoons of the sugar until pale and fluffy. Beat in the cornstarch and egg yolks, 1 at a time. Fold in the melted chocolate and the nuts.

6 Remove the dried beans and lining from the tart shell and spoon in the chocolate filling. Return to the oven and bake for 10 minutes.

7 Whisk the egg whites in a clean, greasefree bowl until soft peaks form. Gradually whisk in the remaining sugar and continue to whisk until stiff and glossy. Spoon the meringue over the filling in the tart shell, covering it completely. Return to the oven and bake for an additional 15 minutes, until lightly set and golden on top.

Chocolate Meringue Pie

Crumbly cracker base, rich creamy chocolate filling topped with fluffy meringue—what could be more indulgent than this fabulous dessert?

25 mins   35 mins

SERVES 6

INGREDIENTS

8 oz/225 g semisweet chocolate graham crackers

4 tbsp butter

FILLING

3 egg yolks

4 tbsp superfine sugar

4 tbsp cornstarch

2½ cups milk

3½ oz/100 g semisweet chocolate, broken into pieces

MERINGUE

2 egg whites

½ cup superfine sugar

¼ tsp vanilla extract

1 Preheat the oven to 375°F/190°C. Place the graham crackers in a polythene bag and crush with a rolling pin. Put in a bowl. Melt the butter and stir into the cracker crumbs until well mixed. Press the mixture firmly into the bottom and up the sides of a 9-inch/23-cm tart pan or dish.

2 To make the filling, beat the egg yolks, sugar, and cornstarch in a large bowl until they form a smooth paste. Heat the milk until almost boiling, then slowly pour it on to the egg mixture, whisking well.

3 Put the mixture in a pan and cook gently, whisking constantly until it thickens. Remove from the heat. Put the chocolate in a heatproof bowl set over a pan of gently simmering water until melted. Whisk the melted chocolate into the egg mixture, then pour on to the graham cracker pie shell.

4 To make the meringue, whisk the egg whites in a large mixing bowl until soft peaks form. Gradually whisk in about two-thirds of the sugar until the mixture is stiff and glossy. Fold in the remaining sugar and vanilla extract.

5 Spread the meringue over the filling, swirling the surface with the back of a spoon to give it an attractive finish. Bake in the center of the preheated oven for 30 minutes, or until the meringue is golden. Serve the pie hot or just warm.

Chocolate Apple Pie

Easy-to-make crumbly chocolate pie dough encases a delicious apple filling studded with chocolate chips—a guaranteed family favorite.

45 mins   40 mins

SERVES 6

INGREDIENTS

CHOCOLATE PIE DOUGH

4 tbsp unsweetened cocoa

1¾ cups all-purpose flour, plus extra for dusting

generous ⅓ cup softened butter, sweet for preference

4 tbsp superfine sugar

2 egg yolks

few drops vanilla extract

cold water, for mixing

FILLING

1 lb 10 oz/750 g tart cooking apples

2 tbsp butter

½ tsp ground cinnamon

¾ cup semisweet chocolate chips

little egg white, beaten

½ tsp superfine sugar

whipped cream or vanilla ice cream, to serve

1 To make the pie dough, sift the unsweetened cocoa and flour into a mixing bowl and rub in the butter until the mixture resembles fine bread crumbs. Stir in the sugar. Add the egg yolks, vanilla extract, and enough water to mix to a dough.

2 Roll out the dough on a lightly floured work counter and use to line a deep 8-inch/20-cm tart or cake pan. Chill for 30 minutes. Roll out any trimmings and cut out some pie dough leaves to decorate the top of the pie.

3 Preheat the oven to 350°F/180°C. Peel, core, and thickly slice the apples. Place half of the apple slices in a pan with the butter and cinnamon and cook over gentle heat, stirring occasionally, until the apples soften.

4 Stir in the uncooked apple slices, let cool slightly, then stir in the chocolate chips.

Prick the base of the pie shell and pile the apple mixture into it. Arrange the pie dough leaves on top. Brush the leaves with a little egg white and sprinkle with superfine sugar.

5 Bake in the preheated oven for 35 minutes, until the pastry is crisp. Serve warm or cold, with whipped cream or vanilla ice cream

Pantry Chocolate Pudding

Just the thing for unexpected guests—a rich pudding made with pantry ingredients, complete with its own delicious sauce.

🍰 10 mins   🕐 35–40 mins

SERVES 4

INGREDIENTS

2 tbsp butter, sweet for preference

⅔ cup milk

1¼ cups self-rising flour

⅔ cup unsweetened cocoa

1 cup superfine sugar

1 cup brown sugar

¼ cup crème de menthe (optional)

confectioners' sugar, for dusting

1 Preheat the oven to 350°F/180°C. Melt the butter in a small pan over low heat, then combine it with the milk in a pitcher.

2 Sift together the flour and half the unsweetened cocoa into a bowl, stir in the superfine sugar and make a well in the center. Gradually pour the milk mixture into the well, beating with a wooden spoon until the dry ingredients are thoroughly combined.

3 Divide the mixture among 4 x 1-cup ramekins or individual ovenproof dishes. Place on a cookie sheet and set aside.

COOK'S TIP

These puddings look attractive in individual dishes and they also cook more quickly than they would in a single large dish. However, if you are not in a hurry, you could use a 5-cup ovenproof dish and bake the pudding for an additional 20 minutes.

4 Sift the remaining unsweetened cocoa into a pitcher and add the brown sugar. If you are going to use the liqueur, pour in 1¼ cups boiling water; if not, pour in 1½ cups boiling water. Stir until the sugar has dissolved, then add the liqueur (if using), and stir until smooth.

5 Very carefully pour the mixture evenly over the tops of the puddings. Bake for 30–35 minutes, until risen and just firm to the touch. Dust with a little confectioners' sugar and serve immediately.

Queen of Puddings

This is a slightly different version of an old favorite made with the addition of orange rind and marmalade to give a delicious orange flavor.

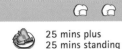

25 mins plus 25 mins standing

45 mins

SERVES 8

INGREDIENTS

2 tbsp butter, plus extra for greasing

2½ cups milk

1¼ cups superfine sugar

finely grated rind of 1 orange

4 eggs, separated

1⅔ cups fresh white bread crumbs

salt

6 tbsp orange marmalade

1 Preheat the oven to 350°F/180°C. Grease a 6-cup ovenproof dish.

2 To make the custard, heat the milk in a pan with the butter, ¼ cup of the superfine sugar, and the grated orange rind, until just warm.

3 Whisk the egg yolks in a bowl. Gradually pour the warm milk over the eggs, stirring constantly.

4 Stir the bread crumbs into the pan, then transfer the mixture to the prepared dish and let stand for about 15 minutes.

5 Bake in the preheated oven for 20–25 minutes, until the custard has just set. Remove the dish from the oven but do not turn off the oven.

6 To make the meringue, whisk the egg whites with a pinch of salt until soft peaks form. Whisk in the remaining sugar, a little at a time.

7 Spread the orange marmalade over the cooked custard. Top with the meringue, spreading it right to the edges of the dish.

8 Return the pudding to the oven and bake for an additional 20 minutes, until the meringue is crisp and golden.

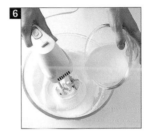 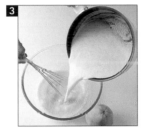 

COOK'S TIP
If you prefer a crisper meringue, bake the pudding in the oven for an extra 5 minutes.

Fruity Queen of Puddings

A delicious version of a classic British dessert, made here with fresh bananas and apricot jelly.

15 mins plus
15 mins standing   1 hr

SERVES 4

INGREDIENTS

2 cups fresh white bread crumbs

2½ cups milk

3 eggs

½ tsp vanilla extract

4 tbsp superfine sugar

2 bananas

1 tbsp lemon juice

3 tbsp apricot jelly

1 Preheat the oven to 350°F/180°C. Sprinkle the bread crumbs evenly into a round 4-cup ovenproof dish. Heat the milk until just tepid, then pour it over the bread crumbs.

2 Separate 2 of the eggs and beat the yolks with the remaining whole egg. Add to the casserole with the vanilla extract and half the sugar, stirring well to mix. Set aside for 10 minutes.

3 Bake in the preheated oven for 40 minutes until set. Remove the dish from the oven.

4 Slice the bananas and sprinkle with the lemon juice. Spoon the apricot jelly on to the pudding and spread out to cover the surface. Arrange the banana slices on top of the apricot jelly.

5 Whisk the egg whites until stiff, then add the remaining sugar. Continue whisking until the meringue is very stiff and glossy.

6 Pile the meringue on top of the pudding, return to the oven, and cook for an additional 10–15 minutes, until the meringue is just set and golden brown. Serve immediately.

COOK'S TIP

The meringue will have a soft, marshmallowlike texture, unlike a hard meringue, which is cooked slowly for 2–3 hours until dry. Always use a greasefree whisk and bowl for beating egg whites.

Chocolate Queen of Puddings

An old time favorite with an up-to-date twist, this dessert makes the perfect end to a special family meal.

🍰 25 mins   🕐 40–45 mins

SERVES 4

INGREDIENTS

1¾ oz/50 g semisweet chocolate

2 cups chocolate-flavored milk

1¾ cups fresh white or whole-wheat bread crumbs

½ cup superfine sugar

2 eggs, separated

4 tbsp cherry jelly

1 Preheat the oven to 350°F/180°C. Break the chocolate into small pieces and place in a pan with the chocolate-flavored milk. Heat gently, stirring until the chocolate melts. Bring almost to a boil, then remove the pan from the heat.

2 Place the bread crumbs in a large mixing bowl with 5 teaspoons of the sugar. Pour over the chocolate milk and mix well. Beat in the egg yolks.

3 Spoon into a 5-cup pie dish and bake in the preheated oven for 25–30 minutes, or until set and firm to the touch.

4 Whisk the egg whites in a large greasefree bowl until soft peaks form. Gradually whisk in the remaining superfine sugar and whisk until you have a glossy, thick meringue.

5 Spread the cherry jelly over the surface of the chocolate mixture and pile the meringue on top. Return the dessert to the oven for about 15 minutes, or until the meringue is crisp and golden.

VARIATION

If you prefer, add ½ cup shredded coconut to the bread crumbs and omit the jelly.

Ginger & Apricot Alaskas

There is no ice cream in this Alaska but a mixture of apples and apricots poached in orange juice enclosed in meringue.

🍞 🍞 🍞

🍲 15 mins   ⏱ 10 mins

SERVES 2

INGREDIENTS

2 slices rich, dark ginger cake, about ¾-inch/2-cm thick

1–2 tbsp ginger wine or dark rum

1 dessert apple

6 ready-to-eat dried apricots, chopped

4 tbsp orange juice or water

1 tbsp slivered almonds

2 small egg whites

⅓ cup superfine sugar

1 Preheat the oven to 400°F/200°C. Place each slice of ginger cake on an ovenproof plate and sprinkle with the ginger wine or rum.

2 Quarter, core, and slice the apple into a small pan. Add the chopped apricots and orange juice or water, and simmer over low heat for about 5 minutes, or until tender.

3 Stir the almonds into the fruit and spoon the mixture equally over the slices of soaked cake, piling it up in the center.

VARIATION
A slice of vanilla, coffee, or chocolate ice cream can be placed on the fruit before adding the meringue, but this must be done at the last minute and the dessert must be eaten immediately after it is removed from the oven.

4 Whisk the egg whites until very stiff and dry, then whisk in the sugar, a little at a time, making sure the meringue has become stiff again before adding any more sugar.

5 Either pipe or spread the meringue over the fruit and cake, making sure that both are completely covered.

6 Place in the preheated oven for 4–5 minutes, until golden brown. Serve hot.

Pecan & Chocolate Pie

Pecan pie is an all-time American favorite, and with the addition of chocolate it is even more delicious.

25 mins plus
1 hr 30 mins
chilling

35–45 mins

SERVES 6-8

INGREDIENTS

PIE DOUGH

1½ cups all-purpose flour, plus extra
for dusting

3½ oz/100 g butter

1 tbsp golden superfine sugar

1 egg yolk, beaten with 1 tbsp water

FILLING

4 tbsp butter

3 tbsp unsweetened cocoa

1 cup corn syrup

3 eggs

½ cup dark muscovado sugar

1¼ cups shelled pecans

cinnamon or coffee ice cream, to serve

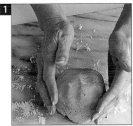

1 To make the pie dough, sift the flour into a bowl. Rub in the butter until it resembles bread crumbs, stir in the sugar, then the beaten egg yolk. Knead lightly to form a firm dough. Cover and chill for 90 minutes. Preheat the oven to 375°F/190°C.

2 On a lightly floured work counter, roll out the pie dough and use to line an 8-inch/20-cm tart pan. Put a cookie sheet in the oven to heat.

3 To make the filling, put the butter in a pan and heat gently until melted. Sift in the unsweetened cocoa and add the corn syrup. Put the eggs and sugar in a bowl and beat together. Stir in the syrup mixture and the nuts. Pour the mixture into pie shell and bake on the hot cookie sheet for 35–40 minutes, until the filling is just set. Let cool slightly and serve warm, with cinnamon or coffee ice cream.

COOK'S TIP
Cover the pie with foil
if the pastry becomes
too dark.

Peach & Almond Pie

This is a very elegant and luxurious dessert that would make a grand finale to a dinner party or celebration meal.

40 mins plus
30 mins chilling

55 mins

SERVES 6

INGREDIENTS

PIE DOUGH

4 oz/115 g semisweet chocolate

2 cups all-purpose flour, plus extra
  for dusting

4 oz/115 g sweet butter

4 tbsp ground almonds

few drops almond extract

1–2 tbsp cold water

FILLING

4 oz/115 g blanched almonds

¼ cup superfine sugar

2½ oz/70 g sweet butter

1 egg yolk

2 egg whites

few drops almond extract

5–6 ripe peaches

4 tbsp peach jelly

1 tbsp peach cognac

1 First, make the pie dough. Break the chocolate into pieces and melt in a heatproof bowl over a pan of simmering water. Remove from the heat and let cool slightly. Sift the flour into a bowl and rub in the butter with your fingers until the mixture resembles bread crumbs. Make a well in the center and add the melted chocolate, ground almonds, almond extract, and enough water to mix to a dough. Knead the dough lightly, cover, and chill for 30 minutes.

2 Roll out the dough on a lightly floured counter and use to line a 9-inch/23-cm loose-based tart pan. Chill.

3 Preheat the oven to 375°F/190°C and place a cookie sheet in it. Process the blanched almonds and sugar in a food processor, pulsing until finely ground. Do not over-process or they will become oily. Add the butter and process until smooth. Add the egg yolk, egg whites, and almond extract and process briefly until combined.

4 Peel and halve the peaches and remove the pits. Thinly slice the peach halves crosswise, keeping the halves in shape.

5 Spoon the almond mixture into the tart shell. Using a spatula, transfer the sliced peach halves to the tart, keeping them in shape as much as possible, then spread them out slightly like the spokes of a wheel.

6 Place on the heated cookie sheet and bake for about 50 minutes, until set and golden brown. Remove from the oven and let cool slightly on a wire rack.

7 Meanwhile, make the glaze. Heat the jelly and peach cognac in a small pan, stirring constantly until melted and combined. Brush the glaze over the top of the pie and serve warm.

Ginger & Lemon Sponges

These little puddings are very light and make a good choice to serve at the end of a heavy meal.

🍋 20 mins   🕐 30–40 mins

SERVES 8

INGREDIENTS

½ cup butter, softened, plus extra
    for greasing

2 lemons

3 oz/85 g drained preserved ginger,
    chopped, plus 1 tbsp syrup from the
    ginger jar

2 tbsp corn syrup

1¼ cups self-rising flour

2 tsp ground ginger

generous ½ cup golden superfine sugar

2 eggs, beaten

3–4 tbsp milk

vanilla custard, to serve

1 Preheat the oven to 325°F/160°C. Grease 8 individual metal dessert cups. Grate the rind from the lemons and reserve in a bowl. Remove all the pith from one of the lemons and slice the flesh into 8 thin circles. Squeeze the juice from half of the second lemon and reserve. Place the ginger syrup, corn syrup, and 1 teaspoon of the lemon juice in a bowl and mix together.

2 Divide the mixture between the prepared dessert cups. Place a slice of lemon in the bottom of each cup. Sift the flour and ground ginger into a bowl. Place the butter and sugar in a separate bowl and beat together until light and fluffy. Gradually beat in the eggs, then fold in the flour mixture and add enough milk to give a soft dropping consistency. Stir in the reserved grated lemon rind and the preserved ginger.

3 Divide the batter among the prepared cups. Place a piece of buttered foil over each cup and secure with an elastic band. Stand the cups in a roasting pan and pour in enough boiling water to reach halfway up the sides of the cups. Cover the roasting pan with a tent of foil, folding it under the rim. Bake in the oven for 30–40 minutes, or until well risen and firm to the touch. Turn the sponges out on to a serving dish and serve with vanilla custard.

COOK'S TIP
When grating the rind from the lemons, be careful not to include any of the white pith, otherwise the finished dish will taste bitter.

Chocolate Rosemary Cake

This cake is good cold, but when served warm with a rosemary-flavored custard it is even more special.

25 mins plus
30 mins infusing

60–70 mins

SERVES 8

INGREDIENTS

CAKE

4 oz/115 g sweet butter, plus extra
for greasing

5½ oz/150 g semisweet chocolate,
broken into pieces

3 large eggs, separated,
plus 1 extra egg white

½ cup golden superfine sugar

¾ tsp cream of tartar

3 tbsp all-purpose flour

1 tsp ground cinnamon

¼ cup ground almonds

confectioners' sugar, for dusting

rosemary sprigs, to decorate

CUSTARD

2 sprigs rosemary

1 vanilla bean, split

¾ cup light cream

⅔ cup milk

5 large egg yolks

¼ cup golden superfine sugar

1 Preheat the oven to 350°F/180°C. Grease and base-line an 8-inch/22-cm round cake pan. Put the chocolate and butter in a heatproof bowl and set over a pan of gently simmering water until melted. Stir until smooth. Stir in the egg yolks and half the sugar. Put the egg whites and cream of tartar in a large bowl and beat until soft peaks form. Gradually beat in the remaining sugar until stiff but not dry. Sift the flour and cinnamon into a bowl and stir in the ground almonds. Fold into the egg white mixture, then fold this mixture into the chocolate.

2 Spoon into the prepared cake pan and stand it in a roasting pan. Pour in hot water to come half way up the sides of the cake pan. Bake in the oven for 60–70 minutes, until firm to the touch in the center. Remove from the roasting pan, cover with a clean dish towel and leave for 10 minutes, before turning out and placing on a wire rack to cool slightly.

3 Meanwhile, make the custard. Put the rosemary, vanilla bean, light cream, and milk in a pan and heat until almost boiling. Remove from the heat and leave to infuse for 30 minutes. Put the egg yolks and sugar in a bowl and beat together until thick and pale. Reheat the cream mixture and strain it on to the yolk mixture, whisking. Set the bowl over a pan of gently simmering water and cook, stirring constantly, until the custard thickens. Dust the cake with confectioners' sugar and decorate with the sprigs of rosemary. Serve, cut into slices, with the warm custard.

VARIATION
As an alternative to rosemary, the custard could be flavored with orange rind, bay leaves, cognac, or liqueur.

Chocolate Half-Pay Pudding

This variation of a traditional English dessert is warming, filling, and comforting on a cold winter's evening.

15 mins   3 hrs

SERVES 6-8

INGREDIENTS

⅔ cup self-rising flour

¼ cup unsweetened cocoa

pinch of salt

½ tsp ground cinnamon

2 cups fresh white bread crumbs

⅔ cup shredded suet

scant 1 cup raisins

¼ cup currants

⅓ cup chopped candied peel

1¼ cups milk

2 tbsp corn syrup

butter, for greasing

custard or light cream, to serve

1 Sift together the flour, unsweetened cocoa, and salt into a large bowl, add the cinnamon, bread crumbs, suet, raisins, currants, and candied peel, and stir until thoroughly combined. Gradually stir in the milk and syrup until well mixed.

2 Grease a 5-cup heatproof pudding bowl with butter and spoon the mixture into it, smoothing the top. Cut out a circle of waxed paper and a circle of foil about 4 inches/10 cm larger than the rim of the bowl. Grease the paper with butter, then place on the foil circle, greased-side up. Make a pleat in the center of both circles then, still holding them together and with the foil circle upward, place them on top of the bowl. Tie securely in place with kitchen string.

3 Place the bowl in a large pan and add boiling water to come about halfway up the sides of the bowl. Cover and steam over low heat for 3 hours, topping up the pan with more boiling water, as necessary.

4 Turn off the heat and remove the bowl from the pan. Remove and discard the foil and waxed paper circles. Run a round bladed knife around the edge of the pudding to loosen it, then invert on to a warm serving plate. Serve immediately, with custard or cream.

COOK'S TIP
For an extra treat, put 2 tablespoons of corn syrup in the bottom of the bowl before adding the mixture. When the pudding is turned out, the syrup will run down the sides like a sauce.

Upside-Down Cake

This recipe shows how a classic favorite can be adapted for vegans by using vegetarian margarine and oil instead of butter and eggs.

15 mins   50 mins

SERVES 6

INGREDIENTS

3 tbsp vegetarian margarine, cut into small pieces, plus extra for greasing

15 oz/425 g canned pineapple pieces in natural juice, drained, juice reserved

4 tsp cornstarch

¼ cup brown sugar

½ cup water

grated rind of 1 lemon

CAKE

4 tbsp sunflower oil

⅓ cup brown sugar

⅔ cup water

1¼ cups all-purpose flour

2 tsp baking powder

1 tsp ground cinnamon

1 Preheat the oven to 350°F/180°C. Grease a deep 7-inch/18-cm cake pan with a little vegetarian margarine.

2 Mix the reserved pineapple juice with the cornstarch to a smooth paste. Put the paste in a pan with the sugar, margarine, and water and stir over low heat until the sugar has dissolved. Bring to a boil and simmer for 2–3 minutes until thickened. Let cool slightly.

3 To make the cake, heat the oil, sugar, and water in a pan until the sugar has dissolved, but do not let boil. Remove from the heat and let cool. Sift the flour, baking powder, and ground cinnamon into a bowl. Pour in the cooled sugar syrup and beat well to form a batter.

4 Place the pineapple pieces and lemon rind on the bottom of the prepared cake pan and pour over 4 tablespoons of the pineapple syrup. Spoon the sponge batter on top, smoothing the surface.

5 Bake in the preheated oven for 35–40 minutes, until firm and a skewer inserted into the center comes out clean. Invert on to a plate, let stand for 5 minutes, then remove the pan. Serve with the remaining syrup.

Apple Upside-Down Cake

Perfect for either a celebration meal or a more informal occasion, this cake tastes as good as it looks.

15 mins plus
15 mins cooling   45 mins

SERVES 4–6

INGREDIENTS

1 lb 9 oz/700 g apples

8 cloves

5 oz/140 g butter

1¼ cups superfine sugar

2 eggs

¼ cup slivered almonds, toasted lightly

¼ cup hazelnuts, toasted lightly and ground

½ cup heavy cream

½ cup milk

½ tsp ground mixed spice

scant 1½ cups self-rising flour

heavy cream, to serve

1 Preheat the oven to 350°F/180°C. Bring a large pan of water to a boil. Peel and core the apples, cut into slices, then add them to the pan with the cloves. Reduce the heat and simmer for 5 minutes, then remove from the heat. Drain well. Discard the cloves. Let the apple cool a little.

2 Grease an 8-inch/20-cm cake pan with butter, then arrange the apple slices over the bottom of the pan. Sprinkle over 2 tablespoons of the sugar. In a separate bowl, cream together the remaining butter and sugar. Gradually mix in the eggs, then the nuts, cream, milk, and mixed spice. Gradually add the flour, beating until smooth.

3 Spread the mixture evenly over the apples, then bake in the preheated oven for about 40 minutes until golden, or when a skewer inserted into the center comes out clean. Remove the pan from the oven and let cool for 5 minutes, then turn out the cake on to a serving plate. Serve hot with heavy cream.

Mini Chocolate Gingers

Individually made desserts look professional and are quick to cook.
If you do not have small ovenproof bowls, use small teacups instead.

20 mins   45 mins

SERVES 4

I N G R E D I E N T S

3 oz/85 g soft margarine, plus extra
 for greasing

¾ cup self-rising flour, sifted

½ cup superfine sugar

2 eggs

¼ cup unsweetened cocoa, sifted

1 oz/25 g semisweet chocolate

1¾ oz/50 g preserved ginger

C H O C O L A T E   C U S T A R D

2 egg yolks

1 tbsp superfine sugar

1 tbsp cornstarch

1¼ cups milk

3½ oz/100 g semisweet chocolate,
 broken into pieces

confectioners' sugar, for dusting

1 Lightly grease 4 small individual
 ovenproof bowls. Place the margarine,
flour, sugar, eggs, and unsweetened cocoa
in a mixing bowl and beat until well
combined and smooth. Chop the chocolate
and ginger and stir into the mixture.

2 Spoon the mixture into the prepared
 bowls and smooth the tops.
The mixture should three-quarters fill the
bowls. Cover the bowls with disks of
parchment paper and cover with a
pleated sheet of foil. Steam for 45 minutes,
until the sponges are cooked and springy
to the touch.

3 Meanwhile, make the custard. Beat
 together the egg yolks, sugar, and
cornstarch to form a smooth paste. Heat
the milk until boiling and pour over the
egg mixture. Return to the pan and cook
over very low heat, stirring until thick.
Remove from the heat and beat in the
chocolate. Stir until the chocolate melts.

4 Lift the mini chocolate gingers from
 the steamer, run a knife around the
edge of the bowls, and turn out on to
serving plates. Dust with sugar and drizzle
chocolate custard over the top. Serve the
remaining custard on the side.

Tuscan Puddings

These baked mini ricotta puddings are delicious served warm or chilled and will keep in the refrigerator for 3–4 days.

20 mins plus
10 mins soaking

15 mins

SERVES 4

INGREDIENTS

1 tbsp butter

⅔ cup mixed dry fruits

generous 1 cup ricotta cheese

3 egg yolks

¼ cup superfine sugar

1 tsp ground cinnamon

finely grated rind of 1 orange,
plus longer strips to decorate

crème fraîche (see page 9), to serve

1 Preheat the oven to 350°F/180°C. Lightly grease 4 mini ovenproof bowls or ramekins with the butter.

2 Put the dry fruits in a bowl and cover with warm water. Set aside to soak for 10 minutes.

3 Beat the ricotta cheese with the egg yolks in a bowl. Stir in the superfine sugar, cinnamon, and orange rind and mix to combine.

4 Drain the dry fruits in a strainer set over a bowl. Mix the drained fruits with the ricotta cheese mixture.

5 Spoon the mixture into the bowls or ramekins.

6 Bake in the preheated oven for 15 minutes. The tops should just be firm to the touch, but not brown.

7 Decorate the puddings with strips of orange rind. Serve warm or chilled with a spoon of crème fraîche, if liked.

COOK'S TIP

Crème fraîche has a slightly sour, nutty taste and is very thick. It is suitable for cooking, but has the same fat content as heavy cream. Use sour cream if you do not want to make your own.

Semolina Dessert

This dish is eaten with pooris and potato curry for breakfast in northern India, but you can serve it with fresh cream for a delicious dessert.

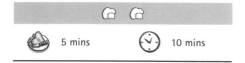

5 mins | 10 mins

SERVES 4

INGREDIENTS

6 tbsp pure ghee

3 cloves

3 cardamoms

8 tbsp coarse semolina

½ tsp saffron

½ cup golden raisins

10 tbsp granulated sugar

1¼ cups water

1¼ cups milk

cream, to serve

TO DECORATE

½ cup dry unsweetened coconut, toasted

¼ cup chopped almonds

¼ cup pistachios, soaked and chopped (optional)

1 Place the ghee in a pan and melt over medium heat.

2 Add the cloves and cardamoms to the melted butter and reduce the heat, stirring to mix.

3 Add the semolina to the mixture in the pan and stir-fry until it turns a little darker.

4 Add the saffron, golden raisins, and the sugar to the semolina mixture, stirring to mix well.

5 Pour in the water and milk and stir-fry the mixture continuously until the semolina has softened. Add a little more water if required.

6 Remove the pan from the heat and transfer the semolina to a warmed serving dish.

7 Decorate the semolina dessert with the toasted coconut, and chopped almonds and pistachios. Serve with a little cream drizzled over the top.

Baked Semolina Dessert

Succulent plums simmered in orange juice and spices complement this rich and creamy semolina dessert perfectly.

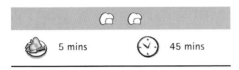

5 mins   45 mins

SERVES 4

INGREDIENTS

2 tbsp butter or margarine, plus extra for greasing

2½ cups milk

finely pared rind and juice of 1 orange

⅓ cup semolina

pinch of grated nutmeg

2 tbsp superfine sugar

1 egg, beaten

TO SERVE

1 small piece butter

grated nutmeg

SPICED PLUMS

8 oz/225 g plums, halved and pitted

⅔ cup orange juice

2 tbsp superfine sugar

½ tsp ground allspice

1 Preheat the oven to 375°F/190°C. Grease an oval 4-cup ovenproof dish with a little of the butter (or margarine). Put the milk, the remaining butter (or margarine), and the orange rind in a pan. Sprinkle in the semolina and bring to a boil over low heat, stirring constantly. Simmer gently for about 2–3 minutes. Remove the pan from the heat.

2 Add the nutmeg, orange juice, and sugar, stirring well. Add the egg and stir to mix.

3 Transfer the mixture to the prepared dish and bake in the preheated oven for about 30 minutes, until lightly browned.

4 To make the spiced plums, put the plums, orange juice, sugar, and allspice into a pan and simmer gently for about 10 minutes, until the plums are just tender. Remove the pan from the heat and set aside to cool slightly.

5 Top the dessert with the piece of butter and a sprinkling of grated nutmeg, and serve with the spiced plums.

Chocolate Almond Dessert

This is a very rich combination of light, delicate cake and glossy cognac sauce, and would be a good choice for entertaining guests.

20 mins

1 hr 5 mins

SERVES 6

INGREDIENTS

4 oz/115 g sweet butter, plus extra for greasing

⅔ cup superfine sugar

3 oz/85 g semisweet chocolate, broken into pieces

6 eggs, separated

1 cup ground almonds

6 amaretti cookies, crushed

COGNAC SAUCE

4 tbsp sweet butter

generous ½ cup superfine sugar

4 oz/115 g semisweet chocolate, broken into pieces

¼ cup milk

2 tbsp cognac

1 Grease a 5-cup heatproof pudding bowl and sprinkle with 1 tablespoon of the sugar. Turn the bowl to coat, then tip out any excess. Melt the chocolate in a heatproof bowl set over a pan of gently simmering water. Remove from the heat and let cool slightly.

2 Cream the butter and remaining sugar together until pale and fluffy, then beat in the egg yolks, 1 at a time. Beat in the melted chocolate, then fold in the ground almonds and amaretti crumbs. Put the egg whites in a clean, greasefree bowl and whisk until stiff, then fold into the chocolate mixture.

3 Spoon the mixture into the prepared pudding bowl. Cut a circle of waxed paper and a circle of foil about 4 inches/ 10 cm larger than the rim of the bowl. Butter the paper, then place on the foil circle, greased-side up. Make a pleat in the center of both circles then, still holding them together and with the foil circle upward, place them on top of the bowl. Tie securely in place with kitchen string.

4 Place the bowl in a large pan and add boiling water to come about halfway up the sides of the bowl. Cover and steam over low heat for 1 hour, topping up the pan with more boiling water, as necessary.

5 Meanwhile, make the sauce. Melt the butter with the sugar in a small pan over low heat, stirring constantly. Remove from the heat. Melt the chocolate in a heatproof bowl set over a pan of gently simmering water. Stir in the butter mixture. Gradually stir in the milk, ¼ cup water, and cognac. Remove the pan from the heat.

6 Lift the bowl out of the pan and discard the paper and foil. Invert the dessert on to a warm serving dish, pour over the sauce, and serve.

Ground Almonds in Milk

Traditionally served at breakfast in India, this almond-based dish is said to sharpen the mind. It is also delicious served as a dessert.

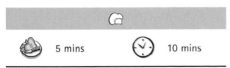

5 mins   10 mins

SERVES 4

INGREDIENTS

2 tbsp vegetable or pure ghee

4 tbsp all-purpose flour

scant 1 cup ground almonds

1¼ cups milk

4 tbsp sugar

fresh mint leaves, to decorate

1 Place the ghee in a small, heavy-based pan and melt over gentle heat, stirring constantly so that it doesn't burn.

2 Reduce the heat and add the flour, stirring vigorously to remove any lumps. Stir in the almonds.

3 Gradually stir in the milk and sugar. Bring to a boil, stirring constantly. Continue cooking, stirring constantly, for 3–5 minutes or until the mixture is smooth and has the consistency of a creamy soup.

4 Transfer to a serving dish, decorate with fresh mint leaves, and serve hot.

Raspberry Almond Spirals

This is the ultimate in self-indulgence—a truly delicious dessert that tastes every bit as good as it looks.

10 mins   20 mins

SERVES 4

INGREDIENTS

salt

½ cup fusilli

4 cups raspberries

2 tbsp superfine sugar

1 tbsp lemon juice

4 tbsp slivered almonds

3 tbsp raspberry-flavored liqueur

1 Bring a large pan of lightly salted water to a boil. Add the fusilli and cook until tender, but still firm to the bite. Drain the fusilli thoroughly, then return to the pan and set aside to cool.

2 Using a spoon, firmly press 1⅓ cups of the raspberries through a strainer set over a large mixing bowl to form a smooth paste.

3 Put the raspberry purée and sugar in a small pan and simmer over low heat, stirring occasionally, for 5 minutes. Stir in the lemon juice and set the sauce aside until required.

4 Add the remaining raspberries to the fusilli in the pan and mix together well. Transfer the raspberry and fusilli mixture to a serving dish.

5 Preheat the broiler to high. Spread the almonds out on a cookie sheet and toast under the broiler until golden brown. Remove and set aside to cool slightly.

6 Stir the raspberry liqueur into the reserved raspberry sauce and mix together well until very smooth. Pour the raspberry sauce over the fusilli, then generously sprinkle over the toasted almonds and serve.

COOK'S TIP

You could use almost any sweet, ripe berry for making this dessert. Strawberries and blackberries are especially suitable, combined with the correspondingly flavored liqueur. Alternatively, you could use a different berry mixed with the fusilli, but still pour over the raspberry sauce.

Teacup Pudding

This dessert is simple to make, because everything, except the allspice, is measured in the same cup. It tastes best served with warm custard.

10 mins   3 hrs

SERVES 4

INGREDIENTS

butter, for greasing

1 cup self-rising flour

1 tsp allspice

1 cup brown sugar

1 cup shredded suet

1 cup currants

1 cup milk

custard, to serve

1 Grease a 4-cup ovenproof bowl with butter. Sift the flour and allspice into a bowl and stir in the sugar, suet, and currants, then add the milk and mix thoroughly. Spoon the mixture into the prepared bowl.

2 Cut out a circle of waxed paper and a circle of foil about 3 inches/7.5 cm larger than the rim of the bowl. Grease the paper circle, place it on top of the foil circle, greased-side up, and pleat both circles across the center. Place them over the bowl, with the foil circle upward, and tie securely in place with kitchen string.

3 Place the bowl on a trivet in a large pan and fill with boiling water to come halfway up the sides of the bowl. Alternatively, place it in a steamer over a pan of boiling water. Steam for 3 hours, then carefully remove from the pan. Discard the covering, turn out the pudding on to a warmed serving dish, and serve with custard.

COOK'S TIP
It doesn't matter whether you use a standard measuring cup or an ordinary teacup to measure the ingredients, because the proportions remain the same.

Baked Sweet Ravioli

These unusual and scrumptious little parcels are the perfect dessert for anyone with a really sweet tooth.

1 hr 15 mins   20 mins

SERVES 4

I N G R E D I E N T S

PASTA

3¾ cups all-purpose flour, plus extra
   for dusting

6 oz/175 g butter, plus extra for greasing

¾ cup superfine sugar

4 eggs

1 oz/25 g yeast

½ cup tepid milk

FILLING

⅔ cup chestnut purée

½ cup unsweetened cocoa

generous ¼ cup superfine sugar

½ cup chopped almonds

1 cup crushed amaretti cookies

generous ½ cup orange marmalade

1 To make the sweet pasta dough, sift the flour into a mixing bowl, then add the butter, sugar, and 3 of the eggs and mix well to combine.

2 Mix together the yeast and tepid milk in a small bowl and when thoroughly combined, mix into the dough.

3 Knead the dough for 20 minutes, cover with a clean dish towel, and set aside in a warm place for 1 hour to rise.

4 In a separate bowl, mix together the chestnut purée, unsweetened cocoa, sugar, almonds, crushed amaretti cookies, and orange marmalade.

5 Preheat the oven to 350°F/180°C. Grease 1 or 2 cookie sheets with a little butter.

6 Lightly flour the work counter. Roll out the pasta dough into a thin sheet and cut into 2-inch/5-cm circles with a plain cookie cutter.

7 Put a spoonful of filling on to each circle and then fold in half, pressing the edges to seal. Arrange on the prepared cookie sheet, spacing the ravioli out.

8 Beat the remaining egg and brush all over the ravioli to glaze. Bake in the preheated oven for 20 minutes. Serve hot.

Jelly Roly Poly

A classic dessert, warming and comforting, which is delicious served with plenty of hot custard.

20 mins   1 hr 30 mins

SERVES 4

INGREDIENTS

1½ cups self rising flour,
   plus extra for dusting

pinch of salt

¾ cup shredded suet

3–4 tbsp hot water

6 tbsp raspberry jelly

2 tbsp milk

butter, for greasing

raspberries, to decorate

custard, to serve

1 Put the flour and salt in a bowl and mix together well. Add the suet and then stir in enough hot water to give a light dough. Using your hands, shape the dough into a ball. Turn out the dough on to a lightly floured work counter and knead gently until smooth. Roll out into a rectangle about 11 x 9 inches/28 x 23 cm.

2 Spread the jelly over the dough, leaving a border about ½ inch/1 cm all round. Brush the border with milk. Starting with the short side, roll up the dough evenly until you have one large roll.

3 Lightly grease a large piece of foil with butter, then place the dough roll in the center. Gently close up the foil around the dough, leaving room for expansion, and seal tightly. Transfer to a steamer on top of a pan of boiling water.

Steam for 1½ hours, keeping the water level topped up, until cooked.

4 Turn out the roly poly on to a serving platter and decorate with raspberries. Serve with hot custard.

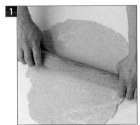

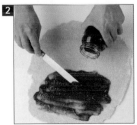

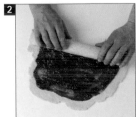

Creamy Rice Pudding

A well-made rice pudding is always popular. Even adults will come back for a second helping.

10–15 mins   2 hrs 30 mins

SERVES 4

INGREDIENTS

1 tbsp butter, sweet for preference

½ cup golden raisins

5 tbsp superfine sugar

scant ½ cup pudding rice

5 cups milk

1 tsp vanilla extract

finely grated rind of 1 large lemon

nutmeg

pistachios, chopped, to decorate

1 Preheat the oven to 325°F/160°C. Grease an 4-cup ovenproof dish with the butter.

2 Put the golden raisins, sugar, and rice into a mixing bowl, then stir in the milk and vanilla. Sprinkle over the lemon rind and grate in the nutmeg, then bake in the preheated oven for 2½ hours.

3 Remove from the oven and transfer to individual serving bowls. Decorate with chopped pistachios and serve.

Indian Rice Pudding

Indian rice pudding is cooked in a pan over low heat rather than in the oven like the Western version—which is also far less sweet.

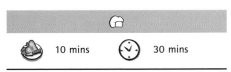

🍴 10 mins　　🕐 30 mins

SERVES 8–10

INGREDIENTS

¼ cup basmati rice

5 cups milk

8 tbsp sugar

varq (silver leaf) or chopped pistachios, to decorate

1 Rinse the rice and place in a large pan. Add 2½ cups of the milk and bring to a boil over very low heat. Cook until the milk has been completely absorbed by the rice, stirring occasionally.

2 Remove the pan from the heat. Mash the rice, making swift, round movements in the pan, for at least 5 minutes until all the lumps have been removed.

3 Gradually add the remaining 2½ cups milk and return the pan to the heat. Bring to a boil over low heat, stirring occasionally.

4 Add the sugar and continue to cook, stirring constantly, for 7–10 minutes, or until the mixture is quite thick in consistency.

5 Transfer the rice pudding to a heatproof serving bowl. Decorate with varq (silver leaf) or chopped pistachios and serve on its own or with Pooris (see page 561).

VARIATION
If desired, you can substitute white or patna long-grain rice for the basmati rice, but the result won't be as good.

Basmati & Bay Leaf Pudding

Don't be put off by the bay leaves in this recipe. They add an interesting depth of flavor to the pudding.

🕐 10 mins   ⏱ 1 hr 10 mins

SERVES 4

INGREDIENTS

2½ cups milk

1 cup light cream

4 fresh bay leaves, washed and bruised gently

4 tbsp basmati or long-grain white rice

2 tbsp golden raisins or raisins

¼ cup sugar

grated rind of 1 orange

1 tsp vanilla extract

2 tbsp pine nuts or green pistachios

sweet cookies, to serve

1 Put the milk and cream in a medium heavy-based pan and bring to a boil over medium heat, stirring occasionally to prevent sticking.

2 Add the bay leaves, then sprinkle in the rice. Reduce the heat to low and simmer gently for about 1 hour, stirring occasionally, until the rice is tender and the mixture is thickened and creamy.

3 Stir in the golden raisins, sugar, and orange rind and stir frequently until the sugar is dissolved and the fruit is plump. Remove from the heat, discard the bay leaves, and stir in the vanilla.

4 Meanwhile, toast the pine nuts in a small skillet until golden.

5 Spoon the pudding into individual bowls and sprinkle with the toasted nuts. Serve warm, or refrigerate to thicken and chill. Serve the cookies separately.

VARIATION
Bay has a lovely flavor and goes well with rice but, if preferred, you can substitute a cinnamon stick, lightly crushed cardamom seeds, freshly grated nutmeg, or seeds from a vanilla bean.

Baked Coconut Rice Pudding

A wonderful baked rice pudding cooked with flavorful coconut milk and a little lime rind. Serve hot or chilled with fresh or stewed fruit.

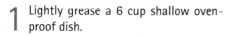

SERVES 4–6

INGREDIENTS

piece of butter, plus extra for greasing

scant ⅓ cup short or round-grain pudding rice

2½ cups coconut milk

1¼ cups milk

1 large strip lime rind

¼ cup superfine sugar

pinch of ground star anise (optional)

fresh or stewed fruit, to serve

1 Lightly grease a 6 cup shallow oven-proof dish.

2 Mix the pudding rice with the coconut milk, milk, lime rind, and superfine sugar until all the ingredients are well blended.

3 Pour the rice mixture into the greased ovenproof dish and dot the surface with a little butter. Bake in the oven for about 30 minutes.

4 Remove the dish from the oven. Remove and discard the strip of lime from the rice pudding.

5 Stir the pudding well, add the pinch of ground star anise (if using), return to the oven, and cook for an additional 1–2 hours, or until almost all the milk has been absorbed and a golden brown skin has formed on the top of the pudding.

6 Cover the top of the pudding with foil if it starts to brown too much toward the end of the cooking time.

7 Serve the baked coconut rice pudding warm, or chilled if you prefer, with fresh or stewed fruit.

COOK'S TIP
As the mixture cools it thickens. If you plan to serve the rice chilled then fold in about 3 tablespoons cream or extra coconut milk before serving, to give a thinner consistency.

Honeyed Rice Puddings

These small rice puddings are quite sweet, and have a wonderful flavor thanks to the combination of ginger, honey, and cinnamon.

10 mins   50 mins

SERVES 4

I N G R E D I E N T S

1½ cups pudding rice

2 tbsp clear honey, plus extra for drizzling

large pinch of ground cinnamon

butter, for greasing

15 no-soak apricots, chopped

3 pieces preserved ginger, drained and chopped

8 whole no-soak apricots, to decorate

1 Put the rice in a pan and just cover with cold water. Bring to a boil, reduce the heat, cover, and cook for about 15 minutes, or until the water has been absorbed. Stir the honey and cinnamon into the rice.

2 Grease 4 x ²/₃ cup ramekin dishes.

3 Blend the chopped apricots and ginger in a food processor to make a smooth paste.

4 Divide the paste into 4 equal portions and shape each into a flat round to fit into the bottom of the ramekins.

5 Divide half of the rice between the ramekins and place the apricot paste on top.

6 Cover the apricot paste with the remaining rice. Cover the ramekins with waxed paper and foil and steam for 30 minutes, or until set.

7 Remove the ramekins from the steamer and let stand for 5 minutes.

8 Turn the puddings out on to warm serving plates and drizzle with honey. Decorate with apricots and serve.

COOK'S TIP

The puddings may be left to chill in their ramekin dishes in the refrigerator, then turned out and served with ice cream or cream.

Rice Pudding Brûlée

Brown sugar sprinkled over the finished rice puddings caramelizes to an irresistible brûlée topping.

20 mins plus
2hrs chilling

35 mins

SERVES 6–8

INGREDIENTS

1 cup pudding rice

pinch of salt

1 vanilla bean, split

scant 3 cups milk

1 cup superfine sugar

2 egg yolks

½ cup heavy or whipping cream

grated rind of 1 large lemon

4 tbsp butter

2 tbsp cognac

brown sugar, for glazing

1 Put the rice in a large heavy-based pan with a pinch of salt and add enough cold water to just cover. Bring to a boil, then reduce the heat and simmer gently for about 12 minutes until the water is absorbed.

2 Scrape the seeds from the split vanilla bean into the milk. Bring to a simmer and pour over the rice. Add the sugar and cook over low heat, stirring, until the rice is tender and the milk thickened.

3 In a small bowl, beat the egg yolks with the cream and lemon rind. Stir in a large spoonful of the rice mixture and beat well to blend. Return the mixture to the pan and cook very gently until the pudding is thick and creamy; do not let boil. Stir in the butter.

4 Remove from the heat and stir in the cognac; remove the vanilla bean. Carefully spoon the mixture into 6–8 flameproof ramekins or crème brulée pots. Let cool, then chill for at least 2 hours.

5 Sprinkle a very thin layer of brown sugar on top of each ramekin, to cover completely. Wipe the edge of each ramekin, as the sugar may stick and burn.

6 Place the ramekins in a small roasting pan filled with about ½ inch ice water. Place under a preheated broiler, close to the heat, and broil until the sugar melts and caramelizes. Alternatively, use a small kitchen blowtorch to caramelize the sugar.

7 Cool the ramekins for 2–3 minutes before serving.

Indonesian Rice Pudding

Also known as sticky rice, glutinous rice is available from Chinese supermarkets and may be black or white—the former is unpolished.

45 mins   5 mins

SERVES 4

INGREDIENTS

½ cup black glutinous rice

2 cups water

scant ½ cup brown sugar

¼ cup superfine sugar

1¼ cups coconut milk, to serve

1 Rinse the rice under cold running water, drain and place in a large pan. Add the measured water and bring to a boil, stirring constantly. Cover and simmer for 30 minutes.

2 Stir in the sugars and cook for an additional 15 minutes. If necessary, add a little more water to prevent the rice sticking.

3 Ladle the rice into warm bowls and serve immediately with the coconut milk. Alternatively, let cool and serve cold.

VARIATION
Add a small piece of bruised ginger-root when cooking the rice to add extra flavor. Remove and discard before serving.

Black Rice Pudding with Fruit

This pudding is like congee, the traditional rice porridge eaten all over Southeast Asia for breakfast or as a basc for other dishes.

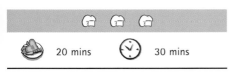

20 mins

30 mins

SERVES 6–8

INGREDIENTS

1½ cups black glutinous rice

3¾ cups boiling water

1 vanilla bean, split, black seeds removed and reserved

I cup brown sugar

¼ cup coconut powder

14 fl oz/400 ml canned thick coconut milk

2 ripe mangoes

6 passion fruit

TO DECORATE

shredded fresh coconut (optional)

fresh mint leaves

1 Put the rice in a large heavy-based pan and pour the boiling water over. Add the vanilla bean and seeds to the pan. Return to a boil, stirring once or twice. Reduce the heat to low and simmer, covered, for about 25 minutes until the rice is tender and the liquid almost absorbed; do not uncover during cooking.

2 Remove from the heat and stir in the sugar, coconut powder, and half the coconut milk. Stir until the sugar is dissolved. Cover and let stand for 10 minutes. If the rice becomes too thick, add a little more of the coconut milk or a little milk or water.

3 Cut each mango lengthwise along each side of the large pit to remove the flesh. Peel the mangoes, slice thinly, and arrange on a serving plate.

4 Cut the passion fruit crosswise in half and scoop out the pulp and juice; spoon over the mango slices. Decorate with shredded coconut, if desired, and a few mint leaves.

5 Spoon the warm pudding into wide shallow bowls and decorate with shredded coconut and mint leaves. Drizzle some of the remaining coconut milk around the edges, if desired. Serve with the mango and passion fruit salad.

Florentine Rice Pudding

This delicious pudding is flavored with orange, and baked in the oven until puffed.

15 mins   15 mins

SERVES 6

INGREDIENTS

¾ cup long-grain white rice or risotto rice

pinch of salt

4 cups milk

5 eggs

2 cups sugar or 2 cups honey, or a mixture

8 tbsp butter, melted and cooled, plus extra for greasing

2 tbsp orange flower water or 4 tbsp orange-flavored liqueur

8 oz/225 g candied orange peel

about 1 cup orange marmalade

2–3 tablespoons water

confectioners' sugar, for dusting

1 Preheat the oven to 350°F/180°C. Put the rice and salt in a large heavy-based pan. Add the milk and bring to a boil, stirring occasionally. Reduce the heat to low and simmer gently for about 25 minutes until the rice is tender and creamy. Remove from the heat.

2 Pass the cooked rice through a food mill into a large bowl. Alternatively, process in a food processor for about 30 seconds until smooth. Set aside. Stir from time to time to prevent a skin forming.

3 Meanwhile, using an electric whisk, beat the eggs with the sugar in a large bowl for about 4 minutes until very light and creamy. Gently fold into the rice with the melted butter. Stir in half the orange flower water, then stir in the candied orange peel.

4 Pour into a well-buttered 8-cup soufflé dish or charlotte mold. Place the dish in a roasting pan and pour in enough boiling water to come 1½ inches/ 4 cm up the side of the dish.

5 Bake in the preheated oven for about 25 minutes, until puffed and lightly set. Transfer the dish to a wire rack to cool slightly.

6 Heat the marmalade with the water, stirring until dissolved and smooth. Stir in the remaining orange flower water and pour into a boat or pitcher. Dust the top of the pudding with the confectioners' sugar and serve warm with the marmalade sauce.

Raspberry Risotto

The combination of coconut milk, raspberry-flavored liqueur, and fresh raspberries make this a memorable sweet risotto.

🥄 15 mins   ⏱ 50 mins

SERVES 4–6

INGREDIENTS

2 cups milk

2 cups canned unsweetened coconut milk

pinch of salt

1 vanilla bean, split

2–3 strips lemon rind

2 tbsp unsalted butter

⅔ cup arborio rice

¼ cup dry white vermouth

½ cup sugar

½ cup heavy or whipping cream

2–3 tbsp raspberry-flavored liqueur

about 2 cups fresh raspberries

2 tbsp good-quality raspberry jam
    or preserve

squeeze of lemon juice

toasted slivered almonds,
    to decorate (optional)

1 Heat the milk in a heavy-based pan with the coconut milk, salt, vanilla bean, and lemon rind until bubbles start to form around the edge of the pan. Reduce the heat to low and keep the milk mixture hot, stirring occasionally.

2 Heat the butter in another large heavy-based pan over medium heat until foaming. Add the rice and cook, stirring, for 2 minutes to coat well.

3 Add the vermouth; it will bubble and steam rapidly. Cook, stirring, until the wine is completely absorbed. Gradually add the hot milk, about ½ cup at a time, allowing each addition to be absorbed completely before adding the next.

4 When half the milk has been added, stir in the sugar until dissolved. Continue stirring and adding the milk until the rice is tender, but still firm to the bite; this should take about 25 minutes. Remove from the heat; remove the vanilla bean and lemon strips. Stir in half the cream, the liqueur, and half the fresh raspberries; cover.

5 Heat the raspberry jam with the lemon juice and 1–2 tablespoons water, stirring until smooth. Remove from heat, add the remaining raspberries and mix. Stir the remaining cream into the risotto and serve with the glazed raspberries. Decorate if desired.

Thai Rice Dessert

This Thai-style version of rice dessert is mildly spiced and creamy, with a rich custard topping. It's excellent served warm or cold.

10 mins   1–1 hr 15 mins

SERVES 4

INGREDIENTS

½ cup short-grain rice

2 tbsp palm sugar

1 cardamom, split

1¼ cups coconut milk

⅔ cup water

3 eggs

scant 1 cup coconut cream

1½ tbsp superfine sugar

sweetened coconut flakes, to decorate

fresh fruit, to serve

1 Preheat the oven to 350°F/180°C. Place the rice and palm sugar in a pan. Crush the seeds from the cardamom using a pestle and mortar and add to the pan. Stir in the coconut milk and water.

2 Bring to a boil, stirring to dissolve the sugar. Reduce the heat and simmer, uncovered, stirring occasionally, for about 20 minutes until the rice is tender and most of the liquid is absorbed.

3 Spoon the rice into 4 individual oven-proof dishes and spread evenly. Place the dishes in a wide roasting pan with water to come about halfway up the sides.

4 Beat the eggs with the coconut cream and superfine sugar and spoon over the rice. Cover with foil and bake in a preheated oven for about 45–50 minutes, until the custard sets.

5 Serve the rice desserts warm or cold, with fresh fruit and decorated with coconut flakes.

COOK'S TIP
Cardamom is quite a powerful spice, so if you find it too strong, it can be left out altogether or replaced with a little ground cinnamon.

Creamed Rice Pudding

This is real comfort food for cold winter days. Serve it with canned or stewed fruit or just enjoy it on its own.

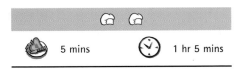

5 mins   1 hr 5 mins

SERVES 4

INGREDIENTS

¾ cup short-grain rice

4½ cups milk

½ cup superfine sugar

1 tsp vanilla extract

ground cinnamon, to decorate

1 Rinse the rice well under cold running water and drain. Pour the milk into a large, heavy-based pan, add the sugar and bring to a boil, stirring constantly.

2 Add the rice, reduce the heat, cover, and simmer gently, stirring occasionally, for 1 hour, until all the milk has been absorbed.

3 Stir in the vanilla extract and serve immediately, sprinkled with a light dusting of cinnamon.

Meringue-Topped Rice Pudding

Probably Scandinavian in origin, this mouthwatering pudding is thickened with cornstarch and egg yolks, making it extra rich and comforting.

15 mins   1 hr 20 mins

SERVES 6–8

INGREDIENTS

½ cup water

5 cups milk

½ cup long-grain white rice

2–3 strips of lemon rind

1 cinnamon stick

1 vanilla bean, split

⅔ cup sugar

3 tbsp cornstarch

4 egg yolks

MERINGUE

6 egg whites

¼ tsp cream of tartar

1 cup plus 2 tbsp superfine sugar

1 Preheat oven to 300°F/150°C. Bring the water and 1 cup of the milk to a boil in a large heavy-based pan. Add the rice, lemon rind, cinnamon stick, and vanilla bean and reduce the heat to low. Cover and simmer for about 20 minutes, until the rice is tender and all the liquid is absorbed. Remove the lemon rind, cinnamon stick, and vanilla bean and add the remaining milk; return to a boil.

2 Stir together the sugar and the cornstarch. Stir in a little of the hot rice-milk to make a paste, then stir into the pan with the rice. Cook, stirring constantly, until the mixture boils and thickens. Boil for 1 minute, then remove from the heat to cool slightly.

3 Beat the egg yolks until smooth. Stir a large spoonful of the hot rice mixture into the yolks, beating until well blended, then stir into the rice mixture. Pour into a 12-cup baking dish.

4 To make the meringue, beat the egg whites with the cream of tartar in a large bowl until stiff peaks form. Add the sugar, 2 tablespoons at a time, beating well after each addition, until stiff and glossy.

5 Gently spoon the meringue over the top of the rice pudding, spreading evenly. Make swirls with the back of the spoon.

6 Bake in the preheated oven for about 1 hour, until the top is golden and set. Turn off the oven, open the door, and let the pudding cool in the oven. Serve warm, at room temperature, or cold.

Saffron-Spiced Rice Pudding

This rich pudding is cooked in milk delicately flavored with saffron, then mixed with dry fruits, almonds, and cream, before baking.

🍮 5 mins   🕐 1 hr

SERVES 4

INGREDIENTS

2½ cups creamy whole milk

several pinches of saffron strands, crushed finely (see Cook's Tip)

¼ cup pudding rice

1 cinnamon stick or piece cassia bark

¼ cup sugar

¼ cup seedless raisins or golden raisins

¼ cup no-soak apricots, chopped

1 egg, beaten

5 tbsp light cream

1 tbsp butter, cut into small pieces, plus extra for greasing

2 tbsp slivered almonds

freshly grated nutmeg, for sprinkling

cream, to serve (optional)

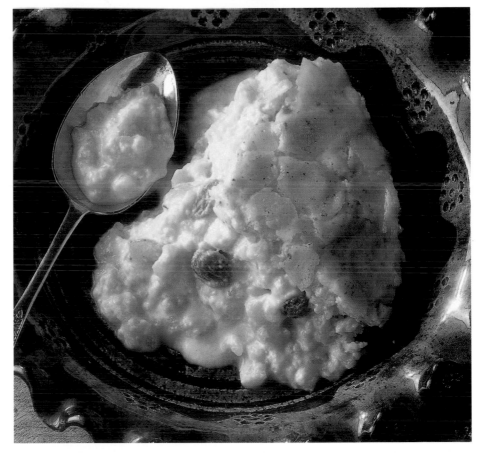

1 Preheat the oven to 350°F/180°C. Place the milk and crushed saffron in a nonstick pan and bring to a boil. Stir in the rice and cinnamon stick, or cassia bark, reduce the heat, and simmer very gently, uncovered, stirring frequently, for 25 minutes, until tender.

2 Remove the pan from the heat. Remove and discard the cinnamon stick from the rice mixture. Stir in the sugar, raisins or golden raisins and apricots, then beat in the egg, cream, and diced butter.

3 Transfer the mixture to a greased ovenproof pie or flan dish, and sprinkle with the almonds and freshly grated nutmeg to taste. Cook in the preheated oven for 25–30 minutes, until set and lightly golden. Serve hot with extra cream, if wished.

COOK'S TIP
For a slightly stronger flavor, place the saffron strands on a small piece of kitchen foil and toast them lightly under a hot broiler for a few moments, then crush them between your fingers and thumb.

Sweet Saffron Rice

This is a traditional dessert, which is easy to make and looks very impressive, especially decorated with pistachios and varq (silver leaf).

5 mins 35 mins

SERVES 4

INGREDIENTS

1 cup basmati rice

1 cup sugar

pinch of saffron strands

1¼ cups water

2 tbsp vegetable ghee

3 cloves

3 cardamoms

2 tbsp golden raisins

TO DECORATE

few pistachios (optional)

varq (silver leaf) (optional)

1 Rinse the rice twice and bring to a boil in a pan of water, stirring constantly. Remove the pan from the heat when the rice is half-cooked, drain the rice thoroughly, and set aside.

2 In a separate pan, boil the sugar and saffron in the water, stirring constantly, until the syrup thickens. Set the syrup aside until required.

3 In another pan, heat the ghee, cloves, and cardamoms, stirring occasionally. Remove the pan from the heat.

4 Return the rice to low heat and stir in the golden raisins.

5 Pour the syrup over the rice mixture and stir to mix.

6 Pour the ghee mixture over the rice and simmer over low heat for about 10–15 minutes. Check to see whether the rice is cooked. If it is not, add a little boiling water, cover, and continue to simmer until tender.

7 Serve warm, decorated with pistachios and varq (silver leaf), if desired.

COOK'S TIP
Basmati rice is the "prince of rices" and comes from the Himalayan foothills. Its name means fragrant, and it has a superb texture and flavor.

Apricot Crumble

In this delicious dessert, fresh apricots flavored with cinnamon are topped with a hazelnut crumble topping.

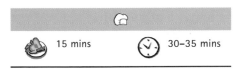

🕐 15 mins   🕐 30–35 mins

SERVES 4

I N G R E D I E N T S

4½ oz/125 g butter, plus extra for greasing

generous 1 cup brown sugar

3 cups fresh apricots, pitted and sliced

1 tsp ground cinnamon

1½ cups whole-wheat flour

½ cup hazelnuts, toasted and chopped finely

thick cream, to serve

1 Preheat the oven to 400°F/200°C. Grease a 5-cup ovenproof dish with a little butter.

2 Put 3 tablespoons of the butter and ¾ cup of the sugar in a pan, and melt together, stirring, over low heat. Add the apricots and cinnamon, cover the pan and simmer for 5 minutes.

3 Meanwhile, put the flour in a bowl and rub in the remaining butter. Stir in the remaining sugar and then the hazelnuts. Remove the fruit from the heat and arrange in the bottom of the prepared dish. Sprinkle the crumble topping evenly over the fruit until it is covered all over. Transfer to the preheated oven and bake for about 25 minutes, until golden. Remove from the oven and serve hot with thick cream.

Apple & Blackberry Crumble

A crumble is one of the easiest puddings to make and it is always popular. Delicious served with custard or cream.

15 mins   40–45 mins

SERVES 4–6

I N G R E D I E N T S

2 lb/900 g tart cooking apples

2 cups blackberries

½ cup light muscovado sugar

1 tsp ground cinnamon

custard or light cream, to serve

C R U M B L E

⅔ cup self-rising flour

⅔ cup plain whole-wheat flour

4 oz/115 g butter

scant ½ cup raw sugar

1 Preheat the oven to 400°F/200°C. Peel and core the apples and cut into chunks. Place in a bowl with the blackberries, sugar, and cinnamon and mix together and place in an ovenproof dish.

2 To make the crumble, sift the self-rising flour into a bowl and stir in the whole-wheat flour. Add the butter and rub in until the mixture resembles coarse bread crumbs. Stir in the sugar.

3 Spread the crumble over the apples and bake in the oven for 40–45 minutes, until the apples are soft and the crumble is golden brown and crisp. Serve with custard or light cream.

COOK'S TIP

When making a crumble, keep rubbing in the butter until the crumbs are quite coarse. This ensures that the crumble will be crunchy.

Fruit Crumble

Any fruits in season can be used in this wholesome dessert. It is suitable for vegans because it contains no dairy produce.

🖐 🖐

🍽 10 mins   🕐 30 mins

SERVES 6

INGREDIENTS

vegan margarine, for greasing

6 dessert pears

1 tbsp chopped preserved ginger

1 tbsp molasses

2 tbsp orange juice

soy custard, to serve

CRUMBLE

1½ cups all-purpose flour

6 tbsp vegan margarine, cut into small pieces

¼ cup slivered almonds

⅓ cup rolled oats

scant ½ cup molasses sugar

1 Preheat the oven to 375°F/190°C. Lightly grease a 4-cup ovenproof dish with vegan margarine.

2 Peel, core, quarter, and slice the pears. In a bowl, mix together the pears, ginger, molasses, and orange juice. Spoon the mixture into the prepared dish.

3 To make the crumble topping, sift the flour into a mixing bowl. Add the margarine and rub it in with your fingertips until the mixture resembles fine bread crumbs. Stir in the slivered almonds, rolled oats, and molasses sugar. Mix well until thoroughly combined.

4 Sprinkle the crumble topping evenly over the pear and ginger mixture in the dish, pressing it down gently with the back of a spoon.

5 Bake in the preheated oven for 30 minutes, until the topping is golden and the fruit tender. Serve the crumble immediately with soy custard (if using).

VARIATION
Stir 1 teaspoon of ground allspice into the crumble mixture in step 3 for added flavor, if you prefer.

Tropical Fruit Crumble

In this crumble, tropical fruits are flavored with ginger and coconut, for something a little different and very tasty.

10 mins   50 mins

SERVES 4

INGREDIENTS

2 mangoes, sliced

1 papaya, seeded and sliced

8 oz/225 g fresh pineapple, cubed

1½ tsp ground ginger

7 tbsp margarine

scant ½ cup brown sugar

1½ cups all-purpose flour

⅔ cup dry unsweetened coconut, plus extra to decorate

1 Preheat the oven to 350°F/180°C. Place the fruit in a pan with ½ teaspoon of the ground ginger, 2 tablespoons of the margarine, and 4 tablespoons of the sugar. Cook over low heat for 10 minutes until the fruit softens. Spoon the fruit into the bottom of a shallow ovenproof dish.

2 Combine the flour and remaining ginger. Rub in the remaining margarine until the mixture resembles fine bread crumbs. Stir in the remaining sugar and the coconut and spoon over the fruit to cover completely.

3 Cook the crumble in the preheated oven for about 40 minutes or until the top is crisp. Decorate with a sprinkling of dry unsweetened coconut and serve immediately.

Rhubarb & Orange Crumble

A mixture of rhubarb and apples flavored with orange rind, brown sugar, and spices and topped with a crunchy crumble topping.

15 mins

45 mins

SERVES 6

INGREDIENTS

1 lb 2 oz/500 g rhubarb

1 lb 2 oz/500 g tart cooking apples

grated rind and juice of 1 orange

½–1 tsp ground cinnamon

scant ½ cup brown sugar

CRUMBLE

2 cups all-purpose flour

½ cup butter or margarine

generous ½ cup light soft brown sugar

⅓–½ cup toasted chopped hazelnuts

2 tbsp raw sugar (optional)

1 Preheat an oven to 400°F/200°C. Cut the rhubarb into 1-inch/2.5-cm lengths and place in a large pan.

2 Peel, core, and slice the apples and add to the rhubarb, together with the grated orange rind and juice. Bring to a boil, reduce the heat and simmer for 2–3 minutes, until the fruit softens.

3 Add the cinnamon and sugar to taste and turn the mixture into an ovenproof dish, so it is not more than two-thirds full.

4 Sift the flour into a bowl and rub in the butter (or margarine) until the mixture resembles fine bread crumbs (this can be done by hand or in a food processor). Stir in the sugar, followed by the nuts.

5 Spoon the crumble mixture evenly over the fruit in the dish and smooth the top. Sprinkle with raw sugar, if liked.

6 Cook in the preheated oven for 30–40 minutes, until the topping is browned. Serve hot or cold.

VARIATION
Other flavorings, such as generous ¼ cup chopped preserved ginger, can be added either to the fruit or the crumble mixture. Any fruit, or mixtures of fruit, can be topped with crumble.

Chocolate Fruit Crumble

The addition of chocolate to a crumble topping makes it even more of a treat, and is a good way of enticing children to eat a fruit dessert.

5–10 mins   40–45 mins

SERVES 4

I N G R E D I E N T S

6 tbsp butter, plus extra for greasing

14 oz/400 g canned apricots, in natural juice

1 lb/450 g tart cooking apples, peeled and sliced thickly

¾ cup all-purpose flour

⅔ cup rolled oats

4 tbsp superfine sugar

⅔ cup semisweet or milk chocolate chips

1 Preheat the oven to 350°F/180°C. Lightly grease an ovenproof dish with a little butter.

2 Drain the apricots, reserving 4 tablespoons of the juice. Place the apples and apricots in the prepared ovenproof dish with the reserved apricot juice and toss to mix.

3 Sift the flour into a mixing bowl. Cut the butter into small pieces and rub in with your fingertips until the mixture resembles fine bread crumbs. Stir in the rolled oats, sugar, and chocolate chips.

4 Sprinkle the crumble mixture over the apples and apricots and smooth the top coarsely. Do not press the crumble into the fruit.

5 Bake in the preheated oven for 40–45 minutes, or until the topping is golden. Serve hot or cold.

VARIATION
Other fruits can be used to make this crumble—fresh pears mixed with fresh or frozen raspberries work well. If you do not use canned fruit, add 4 tablespoons of orange juice to the fresh fruit.

Golden Baked Apple Pudding

A lowfat dessert, perfect for those who enjoy sweet things but are watching their weight.

15 mins   30–35 mins

SERVES 4

INGREDIENTS

1 lb/450 g tart cooking apples

1 tsp ground cinnamon

2 tbsp golden raisins

4 oz/115 g whole-wheat bread, about 4 thick slices

generous ½ cup lowfat cottage cheese

4 tbsp light brown sugar

generous 1 cup lowfat milk

1 Preheat the oven to 425°F/220°C.

2 Peel and core the apples and chop the flesh into ½-inch/1-cm pieces. Put the apple pieces in a bowl and toss with the cinnamon and golden raisins.

3 Remove the crusts and cut the bread into ½-inch/1-cm cubes. Add to the apples with the cottage cheese and 3 tablespoons of the brown sugar, and mix together. Stir in the milk.

4 Turn the mixture into an ovenproof dish and sprinkle with the remaining sugar. Bake in the oven for 30–35 minutes, or until golden brown. Serve hot.

Chocolate Cherry Betty

This is a variation of the famous American dessert, apple brown betty, which is, in turn, a variation of the French apple charlotte.

10 mins   45 mins

SERVES 4

INGREDIENTS

2½ oz/70 g butter, plus extra for greasing

3 cups chocolate cake crumbs

2 cups cherries, pitted

½ cup brown sugar

½ tsp ground cinnamon

grated rind of ½ orange

2 tbsp orange juice

5 tbsp sherry

whipped cream or custard, to serve

1 Preheat the oven to 375°F/190°C. Grease a medium-size ovenproof dish with butter.

2 Sprinkle one-third of the cake crumbs over the bottom of the dish and dot with one-third of the butter. Arrange half the cherries evenly on top and sprinkle with half the sugar, cinnamon, orange rind, and orange juice. Make another layer with half the remaining cake crumbs, dot with half the remaining butter, and top with the remaining cherries, sugar, cinnamon, orange rind, and orange juice. Cover with the remaining crumbs and dot with butter.

3 Bake for 40 minutes, until the cherries are tender. Remove the betty from the oven, pour the sherry over the top, and return to the oven for 5 minutes. Serve hot, with cream or custard.

VARIATION
Substitute sliced peaches or nectarines for the cherries.

Chocolate Apple Dessert

This light and airy dessert is surprisingly filling—just the thing to cheer you up on a cold winter's evening.

🍎 25 mins 　 🕐 1 hr

SERVES 4

INGREDIENTS

3 tbsp butter, plus extra for greasing

2 oz/55 g semisweet chocolate

¾ cup milk

4 tbsp all-purpose flour

1 tbsp grated orange rind

1 tsp all spice

2 tbsp light muscovado sugar

2 eggs, separated

⅓ cup golden raisins

1 large tart cooking apple

whipping cream, to serve

1 Preheat the oven to 325°F/160°C. Grease a 5-cup ovenproof dish. Break the chocolate into pieces and place in a pan with the milk. Set over low heat and bring to just below simmering point, stirring constantly. Remove from the heat.

2 Melt 2 tablespoons of the butter in another pan over low heat. When the butter is foamy, stir in the flour and cook, stirring constantly, for 1 minute. Remove the pan from the heat and gradually stir in the chocolate-flavored milk. Return to the heat, add the orange rind, and all spice and cook, stirring constantly, for 2–3 minutes, until thickened and smooth.

3 Remove the pan from the heat and stir in the muscovado sugar. Add the egg yolks, 1 at a time, beating well until thoroughly blended. Stir in the golden raisins. Set aside.

4 Melt the remaining butter in a heavy-based skillet. Meanwhile, peel, core, and chop the apple. Add the apple to the pan and cook over medium heat, stirring frequently, for 4–5 minutes, until golden. Remove from the pan with a slotted spoon and drain on paper towels. Stir the apples into the chocolate mixture.

5 Whisk the egg whites in a clean, greasefree bowl until stiff. Stir about

quarter into the chocolate and apple mixture to lighten it, then fold in the remainder with a metal spoon. Spoon the mixture into the prepared dish and spread out evenly.

6 Place the dish in a roasting pan and add hot water to come about halfway up the sides of the dish. Bake for 1 hour, or until just set. Remove the dish from the oven, invert on to a warm serving plate, and serve immediately with cream.

Cherry Dessert with Sauce

This is a good way to use up slightly stale cake. You can use plain or chocolate cake crumbs—whichever are available.

🍰 15 mins   ⏱ 55 mins

SERVES 6

INGREDIENTS

sweet butter, for greasing

2⅔ cups raspberries

¾ cup superfine sugar

4 eggs, separated

2 cups cake crumbs

½ cup ground almonds

1 tbsp light cream

1 tbsp sweet butter

¼ cup candied cherries, to decorate

SAUCE

6 oz/175 g semisweet chocolate

1¾ cups evaporated milk

½ tsp almond extract

1 Preheat the oven to 350°F/180°C. Grease a 5-cup soufflé dish. Place the raspberries in the dish and sprinkle with ¼ cup of the sugar. Stir gently and set aside.

2 Whisk together the egg yolks and remaining sugar until pale and fluffy. Stir in the cake crumbs, ground almonds, cream, and butter.

3 Whisk the egg white in a clean, greasefree bowl until stiff. Stir one-quarter of the whites into the egg yolk mixture to lighten, then gently fold in the remainder. Spoon the mixture over the raspberries. Cut the candied cherries in half and use to decorate the dessert. Bake for 50 minutes, until the top is golden brown and set.

4 Meanwhile, make the sauce. Break the chocolate into pieces and place in a heatproof bowl with the evaporated milk. Set over a pan of gently simmering water, stirring frequently until melted. Remove the bowl from the heat and whisk in the almond extract. Continue to whisk until thick and smooth. Serve warm, with the dessert.

COOK'S TIP

You can use frozen raspberries or mixed berries, but thaw them completely first.

Plum Pot Pie

This is another popular dessert which can be adapted to suit almost all types of fruit if plums are not available.

10 mins | 35–40 mins

SERVES 6

INGREDIENTS

butter, for greasing

2 lb 4 oz/1 kg plums, pitted and sliced

½ cup superfine sugar

1 tbsp lemon juice

2¼ cups all-purpose flour

2 tsp baking powder

½ cup granulated sugar

1 egg, beaten

⅔ cup buttermilk

6 tbsp butter, melted and cooled

heavy cream, to serve

1 Preheat the oven to 375°F/190°C. Lightly grease an 8¾-cup ovenproof dish with butter.

2 In a large bowl, combine the plums, superfine sugar, lemon juice, and ¼ cup of the all-purpose flour.

3 Spoon the coated plums into the bottom of the prepared ovenproof dish, spreading them out evenly.

4 Sift the remaining flour, together with the baking powder, into a large bowl and add the granulated sugar. Stir well to combine.

5 Add the beaten egg, buttermilk, and cooled melted butter. Mix everything gently together to form a soft dough.

6 Place tablespoonfuls of the dough on top of the fruit mixture until it is almost completely covered.

7 Bake the pot pie in the preheated oven for 35–40 minutes, until the topping is golden brown and the plums are bubbling.

8 Serve the pot pie piping hot, with heavy cream.

COOK'S TIP
If you cannot find buttermilk, try using sour cream.

Clafoutis

Although recipes for this dessert may use a variety of fruits, cherries are the classic filling in Limousin, France, where this dish originates.

🍫 🍫 🍫

🔥 15 mins plus 1hr standing   🕐 45 mins

SERVES 4

INGREDIENTS

1 lb/450 g sweet black cherries

2 tbsp cherry cognac

1 tbsp confectioners' sugar, plus extra for dusting

butter, for greasing

BATTER

3 tbsp all-purpose flour

3 tbsp sugar

¾ cup light cream

2 eggs, beaten lightly

grated rind of ½ lemon

¼ tsp vanilla extract

1 Pit the cherries. Combine them with the cherry cognac and confectioners' sugar in a bowl, cover with plastic wrap and set aside for 1 hour.

2 Meanwhile, preheat the oven to 375°F/190°C. Grease a shallow, ovenproof dish with butter. To make the batter, sift the flour into a bowl and stir in the sugar. Gradually whisk in the

cream, eggs, lemon rind, and vanilla essence. Whisk constantly until the batter is smooth.

3 Spoon the cherries into the dish and pour the batter over them. Bake in the preheated oven for 45 minutes, until golden and set. Dust with extra confectioners' sugar and serve warm or leave to cool to room temperature.

COOK'S TIP

Traditionally the cherries are not pitted before cooking, because the pits are though to add extra flavor to the batter.

Blackberry Clafoutis

A delicious dessert to make when blackberries are in abundance.
If blackberries are unavailable, try using currants or gooseberries.

15-20 mins   30 mins

SERVES 4

INGREDIENTS

butter, for greasing

1 lb/450 g blackberries

⅓ cup superfine sugar, plus extra
   for sprinkling

1 egg

⅓ cup brown sugar

6 tbsp butter, melted

½ cup milk

scant 1 cup self-rising flour

1 Lightly grease a large 3½-cup ovenproof dish with a little butter.

2 In a large mixing bowl, gently mix together the blackberries and superfine sugar until well combined.

3 Transfer the blackberry and sugar mixture to the prepared ovenproof dish, spreading it out evenly.

4 Beat the egg and brown sugar in a separate mixing bowl. Stir in the melted butter and milk.

5 Sift the flour into the egg and butter mixture and fold together lightly to form a smooth batter.

6 Carefully spread the batter over the blackberry and sugar mixture In the ovenproof dish.

7 Bake the pudding in a preheated oven, 350°F/180°C, for about 25–30 minutes, until the topping is firm and golden.

8 Sprinkle the pudding with a little sugar and serve hot.

Blueberry Clafoutis

A good dessert to make when blueberries are in season. Serve with light cream.

15 mins   30 mins

SERVES 4

I N G R E D I E N T S

2 tbsp butter, plus extra for greasing

generous ½ cup superfine sugar

3 eggs

generous ½ cup all-purpose flour

generous 1 cup light cream

½ tsp ground cinnamon

1 lb/450 g blueberries

confectioners' sugar, to decorate

light cream, to serve

1 Preheat the oven to 350°F/180°C. Grease a 4½-cup ovenproof dish with butter.

2 Put the remaining butter in a bowl with the sugar and cream together until fluffy. Add the eggs and beat together well. Mix in the flour, then gradually stir in the cream followed by the cinnamon. Continue to stir until smooth.

3 Arrange the blueberries in the bottom of the prepared dish, then pour over the cream batter. Transfer to the preheated oven and bake for about 30 minutes, or until puffed and golden.

4 Remove from the oven, dust with confectioners' sugar and serve with light cream.

Summer Fruit Clafoutis

Serve this mouthwatering French-style fruit-in-batter dessert hot or cold with lowfat yogurt.

🍧 1 hr 45 mins   🕐 50 mins

SERVES 4

I N G R E D I E N T S

1 lb 2 oz/500 g prepared fresh assorted soft fruits, such as blackberries, raspberries, strawberries, blueberries, cherries, gooseberries, red currants, black currants

4 tbsp soft fruit liqueur such as cassis, or kirsch

4 tbsp lowfat milk powder

1 cup all-purpose flour

pinch of salt

¼ cup superfine sugar

2 eggs, beaten

1¼ cups skim milk

1 tsp vanilla extract

2 tsp superfine sugar, for dusting

T O   S E R V E

assorted soft fruits

lowfat yogurt

1 Place the assorted fruits in a mixing bowl and spoon over the fruit liqueur. Cover and let soak for 1 hour in the refrigerator.

2 In a large bowl, combine the lowfat milk powder, flour, salt, and sugar. Make a well in the center and gradually whisk in the eggs, milk, and vanilla extract, using a balloon whisk, until smooth. Transfer to a pitcher and set aside for 30 minutes.

3 Preheat the oven to 400°F/200°C. Line the bottom of a 9-inch/23-cm round ovenproof dish with parchment paper and spoon in all the fruits and their juices.

4 Whisk the batter again and pour it over the fruits, stand the dish on a cookie sheet, and bake in the preheated oven for 50 minutes, until firm, risen, and golden brown.

5 Dust with superfine sugar. Serve immediately with extra fruits and lowfat yogurt.

Cherry & Chocolate Clafoutis

Clafoutis is a classic dessert from France, typically filled with cherries.
Here it is given a new twist, with the addition of unsweetened cocoa.

15 mins   50–60 mins

SERVES 6–8

INGREDIENTS

1 lb/450 g black cherries, pitted

2 tbsp golden granulated sugar

3 eggs

¼ cup golden superfine sugar

½ cup self-rising flour

scant ¼ cup unsweetened cocoa

¾ cup heavy cream

1¼ cups milk

2 tbsp kirsch (optional)

confectioners' sugar, for sifting

cream, to serve

1 Preheat the oven to 375°F/190°C. Lightly butter a 9-inch/23-cm ovenproof tart dish. Arrange the cherries in the dish, sprinkle with the granulated sugar, and set aside.

2 Put the eggs and superfine sugar in a bowl and whisk together until light and frothy. Sift the flour and unsweetened cocoa on to a plate and add, all at once, to the egg mixture. Beat in thoroughly, then whisk in the cream followed by the milk and kirsch (if using). Pour the batter over the cherries.

3 Bake in the oven for 50–60 minutes, until slightly risen and set in the centre. Sift confectioners' sugar over and serve warm, with cream.

Chocolate Mirabelle Clafoutis

Mirabelles are a French variety of sweet, firm-fleshed, yellow plums, also used for making slivovitz liqueur.

15 mins plus
2 hrs soaking

1 hr

SERVES 6

INGREDIENTS

1 lb 8 oz/675 g ripe mirabelle plums, halved and pitted

3 tbsp slivovitz

1½ tbsp confectioners' sugar

2 oz/55 g semisweet chocolate

generous 1 cup light cream

butter, for greasing

⅓ cup all-purpose flour

generous ¼ cup superfine sugar

3 eggs

grated rind of 1 lemon

pinch of grated nutmeg

1 Place the plums in a bowl and add the slivovitz and confectioners' sugar. Mix well and set aside to soak for about 2 hours.

2 Break the chocolate into pieces and place in a small pan with the cream. Heat gently, stirring frequently, until the chocolate has melted, but do not let boil. Remove from the heat and set aside to cool.

3 Preheat the oven to 375°F/190°C. Thoroughly grease a 10-inch/25-cm ovenproof dish.

4 Sift the flour into a bowl and stir in the superfine sugar. Gradually whisk in the chocolate-flavored cream until smooth. Whisk in the eggs, lemon rind, and nutmeg.

5 Arrange the plums on the bottom of the dish, then pour over the batter. Bake for about 55 minutes, until puffed up around the edges and set in the center. Remove from the oven and let cool slightly, then serve warm.

VARIATION
If Mirabelles are unavailable, use any small ripe plums. You can also substitute amaretto for the slivovitz, if you prefer.

Chocolate & Orange Surprise

A classic combination with a twist, this rich, tangy pudding will delight and intrigue friends and family.

🍮 15 mins ⏱ 2 hrs 20 mins

SERVES 6

INGREDIENTS

1 unwaxed, seedless orange, such as Valencia

6 oz/175 g sweet butter, plus extra for greasing

2 oz/55 g semisweet chocolate

1½ cups self-rising flour

½ cup unsweetened cocoa

scant 1 cup light muscovado sugar

2 eggs

2 tbsp milk

½ cup superfine sugar

light cream, to serve

1 Bring a pan of water to a boil. Add the orange, cover, and boil for 20 minutes. Grease a 5-cup pudding bowl with butter.

2 Meanwhile, break the chocolate into pieces and place in a heatproof bowl with half the butter. Melt over a pan of gently simmering water, then remove from the heat and set aside to cool slightly.

3 Sift together the flour and unsweetened cocoa into a large bowl and stir in the sugar. Make a well in the center. Lightly beat the eggs together in a pitcher and pour into the well with the milk and melted chocolate mixture. Stir well to mix.

4 Spoon about half the mixture into the pudding bowl and make a fairly shallow indentation with the back of the spoon. Drain the orange and, holding it with tongs, pat dry with paper towels, then

prick all over with a fork. Place the orange in the bowl. Dice the remaining butter and dot it over the orange, then sprinkle with the superfine sugar. Spoon in the remaining chocolate mixture smoothing the surface.

5 Cut out a circle of waxed paper and a circle of foil about 4 inches/10 cm larger than the rim of the bowl. Grease the paper with butter, then place on the foil circle, greased-side up. Make a pleat in the center of both circles, then, still holding them together and with the foil circle

upward, place them on top of the bowl. Tie securely in place with kitchen string.

6 Place the bowl in a large pan and pour in enough boiling water to come about halfway up the side. Cover and steam over low heat for 2 hours, topping up the boiling water, as necessary.

7 Turn off the heat and remove the bowl. Remove and discard the paper and foil. Invert the pudding on to a warmed serving dish and serve immediately, with cream.

Zabaglione

This well-known dish is really a light but rich egg mousse flavored with Marsala or sweet sherry.

🥚 10 mins   🕐 5 mins

SERVES 4

INGREDIENTS

5 egg yolks

½ cup superfine sugar

⅔ cup Marsala or sweet sherry

amaretti cookies, to serve (optional)

1 Place all the egg yolks in a large mixing bowl.

2 Add the superfine sugar to the egg yolks and whisk until the mixture is thick and very pale and has doubled in volume.

3 Set the bowl containing the egg yolk and sugar mixture over a pan of gently simmering water.

4 Add the Marsala or sherry to the egg yolk and sugar mixture and continue whisking until the foam mixture becomes warm. This process may take as long as 10 minutes.

5 Pour the mixture, which should be frothy and light, into 4 wine glasses.

6 Serve the zabaglione warm with fresh fruit or amaretti cookies, if you wish.

Chocolate Zabaglione

As this recipe only uses a little chocolate, choose one with a minimum of 70 percent cocoa solids for a good flavor.

10 mins   5 mins

SERVES 4

INGREDIENTS

4 egg yolks

4 tbsp superfine sugar

1¾ oz/50 g semisweet chocolate

½ cup Marsala

unsweetened cocoa, for dusting

1 In a large glass heatproof mixing bowl, whisk together the egg yolks and superfine sugar using an electric whisk, until you have a very pale mixture.

2 Grate the chocolate finely and fold into the egg mixture.

3 Fold the Marsala gradually into the chocolate mixture.

4 Set the mixing bowl over a pan of gently simmering water and set the electric whisk on the lowest speed or change to a hand-held balloon whisk. Cook gently, whisking constantly until the mixture thickens; take care not to over-cook or the mixture will curdle.

5 Spoon the hot mixture into warm individual glass dishes or coffee cups and dust with unsweetened cocoa. Serve the zabaglione as soon as possible so that it is warm, light, and fluffy.

COOK'S TIP

Make the dessert just before serving because it will separate if you let it stand. If it starts to curdle, remove it from the heat immediately and place it in a bowl of cold water to stop the cooking. Whisk furiously until the mixture comes together.

Italian Drowned Ice Cream

Vanilla ice cream topped with hot coffee makes a wonderful instant dessert. The ice cream will keep frozen for up to 3 months.

30 mins plus 2 hrs 30 mins freezing

10 mins

SERVES 4

INGREDIENTS

2 cups freshly made espresso coffee

chocolate-coated coffee beans, to decorate

VANILLA ICE CREAM

1 vanilla bean

6 large egg yolks

⅔ cup superfine sugar or vanilla-flavored sugar

2¼ cups milk

1 cup plus 2 tbsp heavy cream

1 To make the ice cream, slit the vanilla bean lengthwise and scrape out the tiny brown seeds. Set aside.

2 Put the yolks and sugar in a heatproof bowl that will sit over a pan with plenty of room underneath. Beat the eggs and sugar together until thick and creamy.

3 Put the milk, cream, the vanilla seeds, and their pods in the pan over low heat and bring to a simmer. Pour the milk over the egg mixture, whisking. Pour 1 inch/2.5 cm of water in the bottom of a pan. Place the bowl on top, ensuring that the base does not touch the water. Increase the heat to medium-high.

4 Cook the mixture, stirring constantly, until it is thick enough to coat the back of the spoon. Remove from the heat, transfer to a bowl, and let cool. Remove and discard the vanilla pods.

5 Churn the mixture in an ice-cream maker, following the manufacturer's instructions. Alternatively, place it in a freezerproof container and freeze for 1 hour. Turn out into a bowl and whisk to break up the ice crystals, then return to the freezer. Repeat 4 times at 30-minute intervals.

6 Transfer the ice cream to a freezerproof bowl, smooth the top, and cover with plastic wrap or foil.

7 Soften in the refrigerator for 20 minutes before serving. Place scoops of ice cream in heatproof serving bowls. Pour over coffee and sprinkle with chocolate-coated coffee beans.

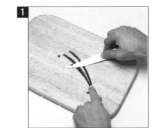

Almond Rice Custard

This traditional Turkish dessert is simply an almond milk thickened with ground rice. Serve with the traditional decoration of strawberries.

🝡 🝡 🝡

🍴 50 mins   🕐 30 mins

SERVES 6

INGREDIENTS

¾ cup whole blanched almonds

4 cups milk

¼ cup rice flour

pinch of salt

¼ cup sugar

½ tsp almond extract or 1 tbsp amaretto

toasted slivered almonds, to decorate

3 cups fresh strawberries, sliced, sprinkled with 2 tbsp sugar, and chilled, to serve (optional)

1 Put the almonds in a food processor and process until a thick paste forms. Bring 1 cup of the milk to a boil. Gradually pour into the almond paste through the feed tube, with the machine running, until the mixture is smooth. Set aside for about 10 minutes.

2 Combine the rice flour, salt, and sugar in a large bowl, then stir in about 4–5 tablespoons of the milk to form a smooth paste.

3 Bring the remaining milk to a boil in a heavy-based pan. Pour the hot milk into the rice flour paste and stir constantly, then return the mixture to the pan, and bring to a boil. Reduce the heat and simmer for about 10 minutes until smooth and thickened. Remove from the heat.

4 Strain the almond milk through a very fine strainer into the simmering rice custard, pressing through the almonds with the back of a spoon. Return to the heat and simmer for an additional 7–10 minutes or until the mixture becomes thick.

5 Remove from the heat and stir in the almond extract. Cool slightly, stirring, then pour into individual bowls. Sprinkle with the almonds and serve with the strawberries, if wished. Serve immediately, or chill until required.

French Chocolate Sauce

This rich, warm—and alcoholic—sauce is superb with both hot and cold desserts and positively magical with ice cream.

🔥 5 mins   🕐 10–15 mins

MAKES ⅔ CUP

I N G R E D I E N T S

6 tbsp heavy cream

3 oz/85 g semisweet chocolate, broken into small pieces

2 tbsp orange-flavored liqueur

1 Bring the cream gently to a boil in a small, heavy-based pan over low heat. Remove the pan from the heat, add the chocolate and stir until smooth.

2 Stir in the liqueur and serve immediately, or keep the sauce warm until required.

Glossy Chocolate Sauce

This simple sauce is a deliciously rich accompaniment to hot and cold desserts and is suitable for all the family.

5 mins   10–15 mins

MAKES ⅔ CUP

INGREDIENTS

½ cup superfine sugar

4 tbsp water

6 oz/175 g semisweet chocolate, broken into pieces

2 tbsp sweet butter, for preference cut into small pieces

2 tbsp orange juice

1 Put the sugar and water into a small, heavy-based pan set over low heat and stir until the sugar has dissolved. Stir in the chocolate, a few pieces at a time, waiting until each batch has melted before adding the next. Stir in the butter, a few pieces at a time, waiting until each batch has been incorporated before adding the next. Do not allow the sauce to boil.

2 Stir in the orange juice and remove the pan from the heat. Serve immediately or keep warm until required. Alternatively, let cool, transfer to a freezerproof container, and freeze for up to 3 months. Thaw at room temperature before reheating to serve.

Chocolate Fudge Sauce

This creamy white chocolate sauce adds a touch of sophistication and luxury to the dinner table.

  5 mins plus 15–20 mins cooling   10–15 mins

MAKES SCANT 1 CUP

I N G R E D I E N T S

¾ cup heavy cream

4 tbsp butter, sweet for preference cut into small pieces

3 tbsp superfine sugar

6 oz/175 g white chocolate, broken into pieces

2 tbsp cognac

1 Pour the cream into the top of a double boiler or a heatproof bowl set over a pan of barely simmering water. Add the butter and sugar and stir until the mixture is smooth. Remove from the heat.

2 Stir in the chocolate, a few pieces at a time, waiting until each batch has melted before adding the next. Add the cognac and stir the sauce until smooth. Cool to room temperature before serving.

Cold Desserts

Dessert is not an essential part of the menu but for many

people this is the part of the meal they particularly

look forward to, and it gives you, the cook, the chance

to indulge your creative juices. Most of these cold

desserts are easy to master and represent a treat

because so many of us are too busy, or conscious of our

weight or health, to enjoy dessert at

every meal. So when you do want to

make the effort, spend a little time

on the presentation. Use chocolate

leaves or curls, fresh or crystallized fruit or flowers,

a sprig of mint, or a light dusting of confectioners'

sugar—and present your

mouthwatering creations in style.

Cannoli

No Sicilian celebration is complete without cannoli. If you can't find the molds, use large, dried pasta tubes covered with foil, shiny-side out.

45 mins plus 1 hr chilling

15–20 mins

MAKES 20

INGREDIENTS

3 tbsp lemon juice

3 tbsp water

1 large egg

1¾ cups all-purpose flour

1 tbsp superfine sugar

1 tsp allspice

pinch of salt

2 tbsp butter, softened

sunflower oil, for deep-frying

1 small egg white, beaten lightly

confectioners' sugar

FILLING

3¼ cups ricotta cheese, drained

4 tbsp confectioners' sugar

1 tsp vanilla extract

finely grated rind of 1 large orange

4 tbsp very finely chopped candied fruit

1¾ oz/50 g semisweet chocolate, grated

pinch of ground cinnamon

2 tbsp Marsala or orange juice

1 Combine the lemon juice, water, and egg. Put the flour, sugar, spice, and salt in a food processor and quickly process. Add the butter, then, with the motor running, pour the egg mixture through the feed tube. Process until the mixture just forms a dough.

2 Turn the dough out on to a lightly floured work counter and knead lightly. Wrap and chill for at least 1 hour.

3 Meanwhile, make the filling. Beat the ricotta cheese until smooth. Sift in the confectioners' sugar, then beat in the remaining ingredients. Cover and chill until required.

4 Roll out the dough on a floured work counter until ¹⁄₁₆ inch/2 mm thick. Using a ruler, cut out 3½ × 3-inch/ 9 × 7.5-cm pieces, re-rolling and cutting the trimmings; the dough should make about 20 pieces.

5 Heat 2 inches/5 cm oil in a heavy-based skillet to 375°F/190°C. Roll a piece of dough around a greased cannoli mold, to just overlap the edge. Seal with egg white, pressing firmly. Repeat with all the molds you have. Fry 2 or 3 molds until the cannoli are golden, crisp, and bubbly.

6 Remove with a slotted spoon and drain on paper towels. Let cool, then carefully slide off the molds. Repeat with the remaining cannoli.

7 Store unfilled in an airtight container for up to 2 days. Pipe in the filling no more than 30 minutes before serving to prevent the cannoli becoming soggy. Sift confectioners' sugar over the top and serve.

Moroccan Orange Cake

This moist cake is made with semolina and ground almonds, then soaked in a fragrant orange and cardamom syrup.

20 mins plus 40 mins cooling/standing

35–40 mins

SERVES 4

INGREDIENTS

4 oz/115 g butter, softened, plus extra for greasing

1 orange

generous ½ cup golden superfine sugar

2 eggs, beaten

scant 1 cup semolina

generous 1 cup ground almonds

1½ tsp baking powder

confectioners' sugar, for dusting

strained plain yogurt, to serve

SYRUP

1¼ cups orange juice

⅔ cup superfine sugar

8 cardamoms, crushed

1 Preheat the oven to 350°F/180°C. Grease and line the bottom of an 8-inch/20-cm cake pan. Grate the rind from the orange, reserving some for the decoration, and squeeze the juice from one half. Place the butter, orange rind, and superfine sugar in a bowl and beat together until light and fluffy. Gradually beat in the eggs. In a separate bowl, mix the semolina, ground almonds, and baking powder, then fold into the creamed mixture with the orange juice. Spoon the batter into the prepared pan and bake in the preheated oven for 30–40 minutes, or until well risen and a skewer inserted into the center comes out clean. Let cool in the pan for 10 minutes.

2 To make the syrup, place the orange juice, sugar, and cardamom pods in a pan over low heat and stir until the sugar has dissolved. Bring to a boil and simmer for 4 minutes, or until syrupy.

3 Turn out the cake into a deep serving dish. Use a skewer to make holes over the surface of the warm cake. Strain the syrup into a separate bowl and spoon three-quarters of it over the cake. Let stand for 30 minutes. Dust the cake with confectioners' sugar and cut into slices. Serve with the remaining syrup drizzled around, accompanied by the plain yogurt decorated with the reserved orange rind.

COOK'S TIP
Do not be tempted to rush this cake—make sure that you give the orange syrup plenty of time to soak into the sponge.

Cherry Baskets

In this dessert, cherries and cream sit in little baskets sealed with a shiny red currant glaze.

25 mins plus 1 hr setting

20 mins

SERVES 4

I N G R E D I E N T S

B A S K E T S

3 tbsp sweet butter, plus extra for greasing

3 tbsp superfine sugar

4 tbsp corn syrup

½ tsp allspice

1 tsp almond extract

5 tbsp all-purpose flour

1 tbsp cherry cognac

F I L L I N G

10 oz/300 g cherries, pitted

1 tbsp cherry cognac

⅔ cup heavy cream, whipped

G L A Z E

⅔ cup red currant jelly

1 tbsp water

1 To make the baskets, put the butter, sugar, and corn syrup in a pan and stir over medium heat until melted. Simmer for 3 minutes, then remove from the heat. Stir in the allspice, almond extract, flour, and cherry cognac, and mix until smooth. Set aside for 10 minutes.

2 Preheat the oven to 350°F/180°C. Grease a large cookie sheet with butter. Drop enough of the mixture on the cookie sheet to make 4 circles, each measuring 4 inches/10 cm in diameter. Allow plenty of space between them because they will spread during cooking. Shape the remaining mixture into 4 "handles" and arrange on the cookie sheet. Bake for 15 minutes, or until golden. Remove from the oven, then mold them into basket shapes over 4 upturned cups or ramekins. Add the handles and press to secure. Let set for 1 hour.

3 To make the filling, mix together the cherries and cherry cognac. Just before serving, spoon whipped cream into each basket and top with cherries. To glaze, gently melt the red currant jelly with the water, brush it over the cherries and serve.

Almond & Pistachio Dessert

Rich and mouthwatering, this dessert can be prepared well in advance of the meal. It is best served cold.

 15 mins plus 1 hr setting   15 mins

SERVES 6

I N G R E D I E N T S

2¾ oz/75 g sweet butter

1¾ cups ground almonds

⅔ cup light cream

1 cup sugar

8 almonds, chopped

10 pistachios, chopped

1 Place the butter in a medium-size pan, preferably nonstick. Melt the butter, stirring well.

2 Add the ground almonds, cream, and sugar to the melted butter in the pan, stirring to combine. Reduce the heat and stir constantly for 10-12 minutes, scraping the bottom of the pan.

3 Increase the heat until the mixture turns a little darker in color.

4 Transfer the almond mixture to a shallow serving dish and smooth the top with the back of a spoon.

5 Decorate the top of the dessert with the chopped almonds and pistachios.

6 Leave the dessert to set for about 1 hour, then cut into diamond shapes and serve cold.

COOK'S TIP
This dessert can be made in advance and stored in an airtight container in the refrigerator for several days. You could use a variety of shaped cookie cutters, to cut the dessert into different shapes, if you prefer.

Pistachio Dessert

Rather an attractive-looking dessert, especially when decorated with varq (silver leaf), this is another dish that can be prepared in advance.

15 mins   10 mins

SERVES 6

INGREDIENTS

3¾ cups water

2 cups pistachios

1¾ cups dried milk

2⅓ cups sugar

seeds of 2 cardamoms, crushed

2 tbsp rose water

few saffron strands

TO DECORATE

¼ cup slivered almonds (optional)

mint leaves

1 Put about 2½ cups of water in a pan and bring to a boil. Remove the pan from the heat and soak the pistachios in this water for about 5 minutes. Drain the pistachios thoroughly, then remove their skins.

2 Process the pistachios in a food processor or grind in a mortar with a pestle.

3 Add the milk powder to the ground pistachios and mix well.

COOK'S TIP

It is best to buy whole pistachios and grind them yourself, rather than using packages of ready-ground nuts. Freshly ground nuts have the best flavor because grinding releases their natural oils.

4 To make the syrup, place the remaining water and the sugar in a pan and heat gently. When the liquid starts to thicken, add the cardamom seeds, rose water, and saffron.

5 Add the syrup to the pistachio mixture and cook, stirring constantly, for

about 5 minutes, until the mixture thickens. Set the mixture aside to cool slightly.

6 Once cool enough to handle, roll the mixture into balls in the palms of your hands. Let set before serving, decorated with the slivered almonds (if using) and fresh mint leaves.

Banana Splits

A perennial favorite, all the more special when made with homemade vanilla ice cream, and a rum and nut chocolate sauce.

🕐 1hr 45 mins– 4 hrs   🕐 5–10 mins

SERVES 4

INGREDIENTS

4 bananas

VANILLA ICE CREAM

1¼ cups milk

1 tsp vanilla extract

3 egg yolks

½ cup superfine sugar

1¼ cups heavy cream, whipped

CHOCOLATE RUM SAUCE

4½ oz/125 g semisweet chocolate, broken into small pieces

2½ tbsp butter

6 tbsp water

1 tbsp dark rum

6 tbsp chopped mixed nuts, to decorate

1 To make the ice cream, heat the milk and vanilla in a pan until almost boiling. Beat together the egg yolks and sugar, remove the milk from the heat, and stir a little into the egg mixture. Return the mixture to the pan and stir over low heat until thick. Do not let it boil. Remove from the heat. Cool for 30 minutes, fold in the cream, then cover with plastic wrap and chill for 1 hour. Transfer to an ice-cream maker and churn for 15 minutes. Alternatively, transfer to a freezerproof container and freeze for 1 hour. Take it out of the freezer, transfer to a bowl, and beat to break up the ice crystals. Put it back in the container and freeze for 30 minutes. Repeat the process twice more, freezing for 30 minutes and whisking each time. Store in the freezer.

2 To make the sauce, gently melt the chocolate, butter, and water together in a small pan, stirring constantly. Remove from the heat. Stir in the rum. Peel the bananas, slice them lengthwise and arrange on 4 serving dishes. To serve, top with ice cream, drizzle with the sauce, and decorate with chopped nuts.

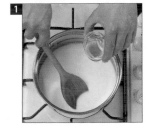

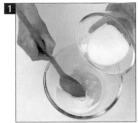

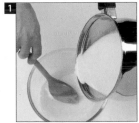

Fresh Figs & Hard Sauce

In this unusual but simple dessert, fresh figs are deliciously partnered by hard sauce.

🥘 10 mins	🕐 0 mins

SERVES 4

I N G R E D I E N T S

4 oz/115 g butter, softened slightly

scant ½ cup confectioners' sugar

1 tbsp cognac

12 fresh figs

fresh mint leaves, to decorate

1 To make the hard sauce, put the butter and sugar in a small bowl and cream together well. Stir in the cognac.

2 Using a sharp knife, cut the figs into quarters and arrange in 4 individual serving dishes. Top each serving with the hard sauce, decorate with fresh mint leaves, and serve.

Baklava

These nut and spice pastries are sticky and delicious. Serve them with coffee or tea.

🍴 25 mins   🕐 1 hr 20 mins

MAKES 12 PIECES

INGREDIENTS

2 cups walnut halves

1¾ cups shelled pistachios

¾ cup blanched almonds

4 tbsp pine nuts, chopped finely

finely grated rind of 2 large oranges

6 tbsp sesame seeds

1 tbsp sugar

½ tsp ground cinnamon

½ tsp allspice

9 oz/250 g butter, melted, plus extra for greasing

23 sheets phyllo pastry, thawed if frozen

SYRUP

3 cups superfine sugar

2 cups water

5 tbsp honey

3 cloves

2 large strips lemon rind

1 To make the filling, put the walnuts, pistachios, almonds, and pine nuts in a food processor and process gently, until finely chopped but not ground. Transfer the ground nuts to a bowl and stir in the orange rind, sesame seeds, sugar, cinnamon, and allspice.

2 Grease a 10-inch/25 cm square (or similar) ovenproof dish that is 2-inches/5-cm deep. Preheat the oven to 325°F/160°C. Cut the stacked phyllo sheets to size, using a ruler. Keep the sheets covered with a damp dish towel.

Place a sheet of phyllo on the bottom of the dish and brush with melted butter. Top with 7 more sheets, brushing with butter between each layer.

3 Sprinkle with a generous 1 cup of the filling. Top with 3 sheets of phyllo, brushing each one with butter. Continue layering until you have used up all the phyllo and filling, ending with a top layer of 3 sheets of phyllo. Brush with butter.

4 Using a sharp knife and a ruler, cut the baklava into 2-inch/5-cm squares.

Brush again with butter. Bake in the preheated oven for 1 hour.

5 Meanwhile, put all the syrup ingredients in a pan, stirring to dissolve the sugar. Bring to a boil, then simmer for 15 minutes, without stirring, until a thin syrup forms. Cool.

6 Remove the baklava from the oven and pour the syrup over the top. Let set in the dish, then remove the squares to serve.

Coconut Custard Squares

This tempting dessert is especially luxurious served with a few slivers of mango or papaya on the side.

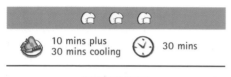

10 mins plus
30 mins cooling   30 mins

SERVES 6

INGREDIENTS

1 tsp butter, melted

6 large eggs

1³⁄₄ cups coconut milk

³⁄₄ cup light brown sugar

pinch of salt

shredded fresh coconut and lime rind

1 Preheat the oven to 350°F/180°C. Brush the butter over the inside of a 7¹⁄₂-inch/19-cm square ovenproof dish or pan, about 1¹⁄₂ inches/4 cm deep.

2 Beat the eggs in a large bowl and beat in the coconut milk, sugar, and salt. Set the bowl over a pan of gently simmering water and stir with a wooden spoon for 15 minutes, or until it starts to thicken. Pour into the prepared dish or pan.

3 Bake the custard in the preheated oven for 20–25 minutes, until just set. Remove from the oven. Let cool completely.

4 Cut the custard into squares and serve scattered with the shredded coconut and lime rind.

COOK'S TIP
Keep an eye on the custard as it bakes, because if it overcooks the texture will be spoiled. When it comes out of the oven it should be barely set and still slightly wobbly in the center, then it will firm up slightly as it cools.

Coconut Cream Molds

Smooth, creamy, and refreshing—these tempting little custards are made with an unusual combination of coconut milk, cream, and eggs.

10 mins plus
8 hrs chilling   1 hr

SERVES 8

INGREDIENTS

CARAMEL

½ cup granulated sugar

⅔ cup water

CUSTARD

1¼ cups water

3 oz/85 g creamed coconut, chopped

2 eggs

2 egg yolks

1½ tbsp superfine sugar

1¼ cups light cream

sliced banana or slivers of fresh pineapple

1 Have ready 8 small ovenproof dishes about ⅔ cup capacity. To make the caramel, place the granulated sugar and water in a pan and heat gently to dissolve the sugar, then boil rapidly, without stirring, until the mixture turns a rich golden brown.

2 Immediately remove the pan from the heat and dip the bottom into a bowl of cold water to prevent it cooking further. Quickly, but carefully, pour the caramel into the ovenproof dishes to coat the bases. Preheat the oven to 300°F/150°C.

3 To make the custard, place the water in the same pan, add the coconut and heat, stirring constantly, until the coconut dissolves. Place the eggs, egg yolks, and superfine sugar in a bowl and beat well with a fork. Add the hot coconut milk and stir well to dissolve the sugar. Stir in the cream and strain the mixture into a pitcher.

4 Arrange the dishes in a roasting pan and fill with enough cold water to come halfway up the sides of the dishes. Pour the custard mixture into the caramel-lined dishes, cover with waxed paper or foil and cook in the preheated oven for about 40 minutes, or until the tops are set.

5 Remove the dishes, set aside to cool, then chill overnight. To serve, run a knife around the edge of each dish and turn out on to a serving plate. Serve with slices of banana or slivers of fresh pineapple.

Cottage Cheese Hearts

These little molds look very attractive when they are made in the French coeur à la crème china molds, but you could use small ramekins instead.

50 mins   30 mins

SERVES 6

INGREDIENTS

15½ oz/440 g lowfat cottage cheese

⅔ cup low-fat unsweetened yogurt

1 medium egg white

2 tbsp superfine sugar

1–2 tsp vanilla extract

rose-scented geranium leaves, to decorate

SAUCE

8 oz strawberries

4 tbsp unsweetened orange juice

2–3 tsp confectioners' sugar

1 Line 4 heart-shaped molds or ramekins with clean cheesecloth. Place strainer over a mixing bowl and using the back of a metal spoon, press the cottage cheese through. Mix in the yogurt.

2 Whisk the egg white until stiff. Fold into the cheeses, with the superfine sugar and vanilla extract.

3 Spoon the cheese mixture into the molds and smooth over the tops. Place on a wire rack over a tray and chill for 1 hour, until firm and drained.

4 Meanwhile, make the sauce. Wash the strawberries under cold running water. Reserving a few strawberries for decoration, hull and chop the remainder. Place the strawberries in a blender or food processor with the orange juice and process until smooth. Alternatively, push through a strainer to purée. Mix with the confectioners' sugar to taste. Cover and chill until the sauce is required.

5 Remove the cheese hearts from the molds and transfer to serving plates. Gently remove the cheesecloth, taking care not to damage the heart shapes, decorate with strawberries and geranium leaves, and serve with the sauce.

Blueberry Coeur à la Crème

This simple combination of sweetened cream, egg white, and vanilla marries well with the tartness of blueberries and looks divine.

20 mins plus
2 hrs chilling

0 mins

SERVES 4

INGREDIENTS

scant 1 cup cream cheese

scant 1 cup crème fraîche
or mascarpone cheese

2 egg whites, whisked

2 tbsp superfine sugar

1 tsp vanilla extract

BLUEBERRY COULIS

7 oz/200 g blueberries

juice of ½ lemon

1 tbsp confectioners' sugar

whole blueberries, to decorate

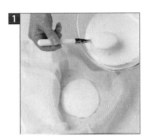
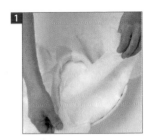

1 Put the cream cheese, crème fraîche, and egg whites into a bowl and mix well. Stir in the superfine sugar and vanilla extract. Line a large coeur à la crème mold with cheesecloth, spoon in the cheese mixture, and smooth the surface. Fold the edges of the cheesecloth over the top.

2 Place a wire rack over a tray, then place the mold on the wire rack. Transfer to the refrigerator to drain and chill for at least 2 hours.

3 To make the coulis, put the blueberries into a food processor and process into a paste, then press through a strainer into a bowl. Stir in the lemon juice and confectioners' sugar, then cover with plastic wrap and chill until required.

4 To serve, carefully turn out the cheese from the mold and discard the cloth. Decorate with whole blueberries and serve with the blueberry coulis.

White Chocolate Molds

These pretty, colorful desserts are deliciously refreshing and would make a good finale to an alfresco meal.

20 mins plus
4 hrs chilling

10–15 mins

SERVES 4

I N G R E D I E N T S

4½ oz/125 g white chocolate, broken into pieces

scant 1 cup heavy cream

3 tbsp crème fraîche or sour cream

2 eggs, separated

3 tbsp water

1½ tsp powdered gelatin

1 tsp oil, for brushing

1 cup sliced strawberries

scant 1 cup raspberries

1¼ cups black currants

5 tbsp superfine sugar

½ cup raspberry liqueur

12 black currant leaves, if available

1 Put the chocolate in a heatproof bowl set over a pan of gently simmering water. Stir over low heat until melted and smooth. Remove from the heat and set aside.

2 Meanwhile, pour the cream into a pan and bring to just below boiling point over low heat. Remove from the heat, then stir the cream and crème fraîche into the chocolate and cool slightly. Beat in the egg yolks, one at a time.

3 Pour the water into a small, heatproof bowl and sprinkle the gelatin on the surface. Let stand for 2–3 minutes to soften, then set over a pan of gently simmering water until completely dissolved. Stir the gelatin into the chocolate mixture and let stand until nearly set.

4 Brush the inside of 6 timbales, dariole molds, or small cups with oil, and line the bottoms with parchment paper. Whisk the egg whites until soft peaks form, then fold them into the chocolate mixture. Divide the mixture evenly among the prepared molds and smooth the surface. Cover with plastic wrap and chill in the refrigerator for 2 hours, until set.

5 Put the strawberries, raspberries, and black currants in a bowl and sprinkle with the superfine sugar. Pour in the liqueur and stir gently to mix. Cover with plastic wrap and chill in the refrigerator for 2 hours.

6 To serve, run a round-bladed knife around the sides of the molds and carefully turn out on to individual serving plates. Arrange the prepared fruit around the base of each dessert and serve immediately, decorated with black currant leaves, if available.

Citrus Meringue Crush

This is an excellent way to use up leftover meringue shells and is quite simple to prepare. Serve with a spoonful of tangy fruit sauce.

20 mins plus
2 hrs chilling

10 mins

SERVES 4

INGREDIENTS

8 ready-made meringue nests

1¼ cups lowfat plain yogurt

½ tsp finely grated orange rind

½ tsp finely grated lemon rind

½ tsp finely grated lime rind

2 tbsp orange-flavored liqueur or unsweetened orange juice

SAUCE

2 oz/55 g kumquats

½ cup unsweetened orange juice

2 tbsp lemon juice

2 tbsp lime juice

2 tbsp water

2–3 tsp superfine sugar

1 tsp cornstarch mixed with 1 tbsp water

TO DECORATE

sliced kumquats

grated lime rind

1 Place the meringues in a polythene bag and using a rolling pin, crush into small pieces. Place in a mixing bowl. Stir in the yogurt, grated citrus rinds, and the liqueur or juice. Spoon the mixture into 4 mini bowls and freeze for 1½–2 hours, until firm.

2 To make the sauce, thinly slice the kumquats and place them in a small pan with the fruit juices and water. Bring gently to a boil and then simmer over low heat for 3–4 minutes until the kumquats have softened.

3 Sweeten with sugar to taste, stir in the cornstarch mixture, and cook, stirring, until thickened. Pour into a small bowl, cover the surface with plastic wrap, and set aside to cool—the plastic wrap will help prevent a skin forming. Chill in the refrigerator until required.

4 To serve, dip the meringue bowls in hot water for 5 seconds or until they loosen. Turn on to serving plates. Spoon over a little sauce, decorate with slices of kumquat and lime rind, and serve.

Apricot & Orange Jello

These bright fruity little desserts are easy to make and taste so much better than store-bought jello. Serve them with lowfat ice cream.

4 hrs 15 mins   25 mins

SERVES 4

INGREDIENTS

1½ cups no-soak dried apricots

1¼ cups unsweetened orange juice

2 tbsp lemon juice

2–3 tsp honey

1 tbsp powdered gelatin

4 tbsp boiling water

CINNAMON "CREAM"

4½ oz/125 g medium-fat ricotta cheese

4½ oz/125 g lowfat natural fromage frais (unsweetened yogurt)

1 tsp ground cinnamon, plus extra for dusting

1 tbsp honey

TO DECORATE

orange segments

sprigs of mint

1 Place the apricots in a pan and pour in the orange juice. Bring to a boil, cover and simmer for 15–20 minutes until plump and soft. Let cool for 10 minutes.

2 Transfer the mixture to a blender or food processor and blend until smooth. Stir in the lemon juice and add the honey. Pour the mixture into a measuring cup and make up to 2½ cups with cold water.

3 Dissolve the gelatin in the boiling water and stir into the apricot mixture.

4 Pour the mixture into 4 individual molds, each ⅔ cup, or 1 large (2½ cup) mold. Let chill until set.

5 Meanwhile, make the cinnamon "cream". Mix all the ingredients together and place in a small serving bowl. Cover the mixture and let chill until firm.

6 To turn out the jellos, dip the molds in hot water for a few seconds and invert on to serving plates.

7 Decorate with the orange segments and mint sprigs. Serve with the cinnamon "cream", dusted with extra cinnamon.

Orange Crème à Catalana

This Spanish dessert will please all those who favor oranges. Serve it immediately, while the caramel topping is hard.

🍮 20 mins plus 8 hrs chilling
🕐 50 mins

SERVES 6

INGREDIENTS

4 cups milk

finely grated rind of 6 large oranges

9 large egg yolks

1 cup superfine sugar, plus extra for the topping

3 tbsp cornstarch

1 Put the milk and orange rind in a pan over medium-high heat. Bring to a boil, then remove from the heat, cover, and let cool for 2 hours.

2 Return the milk to the heat and simmer for 10 minutes. Put the egg yolks and sugar in a heatproof bowl set over a pan of gently simmering water. Whisk until the mixture is creamy and the sugar has dissolved.

3 Add 5 tablespoons of the flavored milk to the cornstarch, stirring until smooth. Stir into the milk. Strain the milk into the eggs, whisking until blended.

4 Rinse out the milk pan and put a layer of water in the bottom. Put the bowl on top of the pan, making sure that the bottom does not touch the water. Simmer over medium heat, whisking, for about 20 minutes, until the custard is thick enough to coat the back of a wooden spoon. Do not boil.

5 Pour into 8 × ⅔-cup ramekins and let cool. Cover each with a piece of plastic wrap and put in the refrigerator to chill for at least 6 hours.

6 When ready to serve, sprinkle the top of each ramekin with a layer of sugar. Use a kitchen blowtorch to melt and caramelize the sugar. Let stand for a few minutes until the caramel hardens, then serve at once. Do not return to the refrigerator or the topping will become soft.

COOK'S TIP
A kitchen blowtorch is the best way to melt the sugar quickly and guarantee a crisp topping. Blowtorches are sold at good kitchen-supply stores. Alternatively, you can melt the sugar under a preheated hot broiler.

Apricot Brûlée

Serve this melt-in-the-mouth dessert with crisp-baked meringues for an extra-special occasion.

15 mins plus
2 hrs soaking/
chilling

35 mins

SERVES 4

INGREDIENTS

⅔ cup dried apricots

⅔ cup orange juice

4 egg yolks

2 tbsp superfine sugar

⅔ cup plain yogurt

⅔ cup heavy cream

1 tsp vanilla extract

½ cup raw sugar

meringues, to serve (optional)

1 Place the apricots and orange juice in a bowl and set aside to soak for at least 1 hour. Pour into a small pan, bring slowly to the boil and simmer for 20 minutes. Process in a blender or food processor or chop very finely and push through a strainer.

2 Beat together the egg yolks and sugar in a heatproof bowl until the mixture is light and fluffy. Place the yogurt in a small pan, add the cream and vanilla and bring to a boil over low heat.

3 Pour the yogurt mixture over the eggs, beating all the time, then set the bowl over a pan of gently simmering water. Stir until the custard thickens. Divide the apricot mixture among 6 ramekins and carefully spoon on the custard. Cool, then chill in the refrigerator for at least 1 hour.

4 Preheat the broiler. Sprinkle the raw sugar evenly over the custard and place under preheated broiler until the sugar caramelizes. Set aside to cool. To serve the brûlée, crack the hard caramel topping with the back of a tablespoon.

Raspberry Brûlées

This dessert is quick to make and extremely enjoyable. It can be served hot or cold.

10 mins   7–8 mins

SERVES 4

INGREDIENTS

1 cup raspberries

1 tbsp lemon juice

2 tbsp raspberry jelly

½ cup crème fraîche or sour cream

¼ cup heavy cream

1 tsp vanilla extract

6 tbsp superfine sugar

whole raspberries, to decorate

1 Put the raspberries and lemon juice in a pan and stir over low heat for about 5 minutes until they start to soften. Remove from the heat, stir in the jelly, then divide among 4 ramekins.

2 Preheat the broiler to hot. In a separate bowl, mix together the crème fraîche, cream, and vanilla. Spoon it over the raspberries and smooth the surfaces. Sprinkle the sugar over the top, allowing 1½ tablespoons per ramekin. Grill under the preheated broiler, as close to the flames as possible, for 2–3 minutes until the sugar caramelizes. Remove from the broiler, decorate with whole raspberries and serve immediately. Alternatively, to serve chilled, let cool to room temperature, then cover with plastic wrap and refrigerate for 3–4 hours.

Fruit Brûlée

This is a cheat's brûlée, in that plain yogurt is used to cover a base of fruit, before being sprinkled with sugar and grilled.

10 mins plus
1 hr chilling

10–15 mins

SERVES 4

I N G R E D I E N T S

4 plums, pitted and sliced

2 cooking apples, peeled and sliced

2 tbsp water

1 tsp ground ginger

2½ cups strained plain yogurt

2 tbsp confectioners' sugar, sifted

1 tsp almond extract

⅓ cup raw sugar

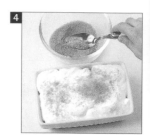

1 Put the plums and apples in a pan with the water and cook gently for 7–10 minutes, until the fruit is tender, but not mushy. Set aside to cool, then stir in the ground ginger.

2 Using a slotted spoon, spoon the mixture into the bottom of a shallow heatproof serving dish.

3 Combine the yogurt, confectioners' sugar, and almond extract and spoon on to the fruit to cover.

4 Preheat the broiler. Sprinkle the raw sugar over the top of the yogurt and cook under the preheated broiler for 3–4 minutes, or until the sugar has melted and formed a crust.

5 Set aside to chill in the refrigerator for 1 hour before serving.

Lemon & Red Currant Brûlées

Beneath the caramelized topping is a surprise fruity sauce. Made with yogurt rather than cream, these desserts are wonderful lowfat treats.

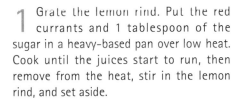

10 mins plus
30 mins chilling

10 mins

SERVES 4

INGREDIENTS

1 lemon

⅔ cup red currants

3 tbsp superfine sugar

2½ cups strained plain yogurt

¼ tsp ground cinnamon

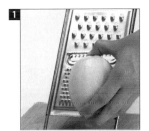

1 Grate the lemon rind. Put the red currants and 1 tablespoon of the sugar in a heavy-based pan over low heat. Cook until the juices start to run, then remove from the heat, stir in the lemon rind, and set aside.

2 Preheat the broiler. Combine the yogurt and cinnamon in a bowl. Divide the red currants among 4 ramekins or small flameproof dishes. Top with the yogurt and sprinkle with the remaining sugar.

3 Place under the preheated broiler for 4–5 minutes, or until the sugar is golden and bubbling. Chill in the refrigerator for at least 30 minutes before serving.

VARIATION
These brûlées are equally delicious made with black currants, white currants, bilberries, or blueberries.

Rice & Banana Brûlée

Take canned creamed rice, flavor it with orange rind, preserved ginger, raisins, and sliced bananas, and top with a brown sugar glaze.

50 mins   2–3 mins

SERVES 2

INGREDIENTS

14 oz/400 g canned creamed rice

grated rind of ½ orange

2 pieces of preserved ginger, chopped finely

2 tsp syrup from the ginger jar

⅓ cup raisins

1–2 bananas

1–2 tsp lemon juice

4–5 tbsp raw sugar

1 Empty the creamed rice into a bowl and stir in the grated orange rind, ginger, ginger syrup, and raisins.

2 Cut the bananas diagonally into slices, toss in the lemon juice to prevent them discoloring, drain, and divide among 2 individual flameproof dishes.

3 Spoon the rice mixture in an even layer over the bananas so that the dishes are almost full.

4 Sprinkle an even layer of sugar over the rice in each dish. Preheat the broiler to medium.

COOK'S TIP
Canned creamed rice is very versatile and is delicious heated with orange segments and grated apples added. Try it served cold with grated chocolate and mixed chopped nuts stirred through it.

5 Place the dishes under the preheated broiler and heat until the sugar melts, taking care the sugar does not burn.

6 Set aside to cool until the caramel sets, then chill in the refrigerator until ready to serve. Tap the caramel with the back of a spoon to break it.

Spanish Flan

This is a classic Spanish recipe which would be delicious served with a glass of sweet dessert wine.

30 mins plus 8 hrs chilling

2 hrs

SERVES 4

I N G R E D I E N T S

butter, for greasing

¾ cup plus 2 tbsp superfine sugar

4 tbsp water

juice of ½ lemon

2 cups milk

1 vanilla bean

2 large eggs

2 large egg yolks

TO DECORATE

red currants

fresh mint sprigs

1 Lightly grease the sides of a 5-cup soufflé dish. To make the caramel, put a scant ⅓ cup sugar with the water in a pan over medium-high heat and cook, stirring, until the sugar dissolves. Boil until the syrup becomes deep golden-brown.

2 Immediately remove from the heat and add a few drops of lemon juice. Pour into the soufflé dish and swirl around. Set aside.

3 Pour the milk into a pan. Slit the vanilla bean lengthwise and add it to the milk. Bring to a boil, remove the pan from the heat, and stir in the remaining sugar, stirring until it dissolves. Set the pan aside. Preheat the oven to 325°F/160°C.

4 Beat the eggs and egg yolks together in a bowl. Pour the milk mixture over them, whisking. Remove the vanilla bean. Strain the egg mixture into a bowl, then transfer to the soufflé dish.

5 Place the dish in a roasting pan filled with enough boiling water to come two-thirds up the side.

6 Bake in the preheated oven for 1¼–1½ hours, until a knife inserted into the center comes out clean. Cool completely. Cover with plastic wrap and refrigerate for at least 24 hours.

7 Run a spatula knife around the edge of the dish. Place an upturned serving plate with a rim over the top of the soufflé dish, then invert the plate and dish, giving a sharp shake halfway over. Lift off the soufflé dish and serve, decorated with the red currants and mint sprigs.

Coconut Cream Custard

Here is an easy, fresh-tasting dessert. Serve it with a selection of seasonal fruits.

🕐 40 mins   🕐 20–30 mins

SERVES 4

I N G R E D I E N T S

4 large eggs

generous ½ cup superfine sugar

scant 1 cup coconut cream

1 tbsp rose water

fresh fruit, to serve

1   Preheat the oven to 350°F/180°C.

2   In a bowl, beat together the eggs, sugar, coconut cream, and rose water and stir until the sugar is dissolved.

3   Divide the custard among 4 ramekins. Place in a roasting pan and pour in boiling water to come halfway up the sides of the ramekins. Bake in the preheated oven for 20–30 minutes, or until set. Remove from the pan and let cool.

4   To turn out, run a sharp knife around the edge of each custard and turn out on to a serving dish. Serve with fresh fruit.

Cream Custards

These individual cream custards are flavored with nutmeg and topped with caramelized orange strips.

15 mins plus
2 hrs chilling

25 mins

SERVES 4

INGREDIENTS

2 cups light cream

generous ½ cup superfine sugar

1 orange

2 tsp grated nutmeg

3 large eggs, beaten

1 tbsp honey

1 tsp ground cinnamon

2 tbsp water

1 Place the cream and sugar in a large nonstick pan and heat gently, stirring, until the sugar caramelizes.

2 Finely grate half of the orange rind and stir it into the pan with the nutmeg.

3 Add the eggs and cook over low heat for 10–15 minutes, stirring constantly until thickened.

4 Strain the custard through a fine strainer into 4 shallow serving dishes. Set aside to chill in the refrigerator for 2 hours.

5 Meanwhile, pare the remaining orange rind with a vegetable peeler and cut it into thin sticks.

6 Place the honey and cinnamon in a pan with the water and heat gently. Add the orange rind and cook for 2–3 minutes, stirring constantly, until the mixture has caramelized.

7 Pour the mixture into a bowl and separate out the orange strips. Let cool until set.

8 Once the custards have set, decorate them with the caramelized orange rind, and serve.

COOK'S TIP
The cream custards will keep for 1–2 days in the refrigerator. Decorate with the caramelized orange rind just before serving.

Mung Bean Custards

Mung beans give this sweet custard an unusual texture. Serve it with a generous spoonful of sour or whipped cream.

40 mins   50–60 mins

SERVES 6

INGREDIENTS

⅔ cup dried mung beans

2 eggs, beaten

¾ cup coconut milk

½ cup superfine sugar

1 tbsp ground rice

1 tsp ground cinnamon

butter, for greasing

TO DECORATE

ground cinnamon

whipped cream or sour cream

finely grated lime rind

sliced star fruit

pomegranate seeds

1 Place the beans in a pan with enough water to cover. Bring to a boil, then reduce the heat, and simmer for about 30–40 minutes, until the beans are very tender. Drain well. Preheat the oven to 350°F/180°C.

2 Mash the beans, then press through a strainer to make a smooth purée. Place the bean purée, eggs, coconut milk, sugar, ground rice, and cinnamon in a large bowl and beat well until mixed.

3 Grease and base-line 4 × ⅔-cup molds or ramekins and pour in the mixture. Place on a cookie sheet and bake in the preheated oven for 20–25 minutes, or until just set.

4 Cool the custards in the molds or ramekins, then run a spatula around the edges to loosen, and turn out on to a serving plate. Sprinkle with cinnamon. Top with sour cream or whipped cream and sprinkle with lime rind. Serve with star fruit and pomegranate seeds.

COOK'S TIP
To save time, use canned mung beans. Omit step 1, drain the beans thoroughly, and continue with step 2.

Summer Pudding

Use whatever summer fruit you have available, but avoid strawberries because they do not give a good result. Pitted cherries are delicious.

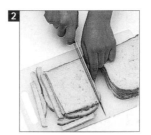

20 mins plus
8 hrs chilling

10 mins

SERVES 4–6

INGREDIENTS

2 lb 4 oz/1 kg mixed summer fruit, such as blackberries, red currants, black currants, raspberries, loganberries, and cherries

¾ cup superfine sugar

8 small slices white bread

lowfat yogurt, to serve

1 Stir the fruit and superfine sugar together in a large pan, cover and bring to a boil. Simmer for 10 minutes, stirring once.

2 Cut the crusts off the bread slices.

3 Line a 4½-cup pudding bowl with the bread, ensuring there are no gaps between the bread slices.

4 Add the fruit and as much of the cooking juices as will fit into the bread-lined bowl.

5 Cover the fruit with the remaining bread slices.

6 Put the pudding bowl on to a large plate or a shallow cookie sheet. Place a plate on top and weigh it down with cans. Let chill overnight in the refrigerator.

7 When ready to serve, turn the summer pudding out on to a serving plate or shallow bowl, cut into slices, and serve cold with lowfat yogurt.

COOK'S TIP
To give the pudding a more lasting set, dissolve 2 tablespoons of powdered gelatin in water and stir into the fruit mixture. This enables you to turn it out on to the serving plate a couple of hours before serving.

Banana & Ginger Cream

This lusciously rich and incredibly simple dessert is made almost entirely from pantry ingredients.

10 mins plus
30 mins chilling

2–3 mins

SERVES 6

INGREDIENTS

6 slices chocolate sponge cake

6 bananas

juice of ½ lemon

4 pieces preserved ginger, plus 4 tbsp syrup from the ginger jar

1¼ cups heavy cream

3 tbsp brown sugar

1 Break up the slices of cake and put them into the bottom of a large gratin dish or 6 individual heatproof dishes. Peel and slice the bananas. Place them in a bowl, add the lemon juice, and toss lightly to coat. Chop the preserved ginger and add it to the bananas.

2 Whisk the cream in a separate bowl until soft peaks form. Using a metal spoon, fold in the ginger syrup, then fold in the banana and ginger mixture.

3 Preheat the broiler. Spread the cream mixture to cover the cake base in the gratin dish or dishes. Sprinkle the sugar over the top and flash under the preheated broiler for about 2 minutes, until the sugar has melted and caramelized. Chill in the refrigerator for 30 minutes before serving.

VARIATION
For a more sophisticated flavor, substitute 4 tablespoons of Cointreau for the ginger syrup.

Rose Water Yogurt Dessert

Yogurt with Middle Eastern flavorings makes a delicious, lowfat dessert—the perfect ending to a summer meal.

25 mins plus
2–3 hrs infusing
& 4 hrs chilling   10 mins

SERVES 6–8

INGREDIENTS

1 heaping tbsp green cardamoms

⅔ cup milk

1 tbsp superfine sugar

2 lb 4 oz/1 kg plain yogurt

5 tbsp rose water

rind of ½ lime

2 medium egg whites

pinch of salt

5 tsp powdered gelatin

3 tbsp hot water

honey, to serve

fresh fruit, to decorate

1 Remove the seeds from the cardamoms and crush them with a pestle and mortar. Put the seeds and the milk in a small pan and bring to a boil over low heat. Remove from the heat, cover, and let infuse for at least 2–3 hours.

2 Pour the milk through a fine strainer, retaining the cardamom seeds. Pound the seeds with the sugar.

3 In a large bowl, whisk the yogurt, milk, cardamom sugar mix, rose water and the lime rind together.

4 In a separate bowl, whisk the egg whites with the salt until soft peaks form. Set aside.

5 Dissolve the gelatin in the hot water. Let it cool slightly, then stir into the yogurt mixture. Fold one-third of the yogurt mixture into the egg whites, then stir it into the remaining yogurt mixture.

6 Transfer the mixture to a large ring mold or soufflé dish. Cover with plastic wrap and chill thoroughly in the refrigerator until set.

7 To serve, run a round-bladed knife round the edge of the mold or dish then invert it on to a serving plate. Drizzle with honey and fill with fresh fruit.

Iced Chocolate Soufflés

Individual iced soufflés look very special, and they are far easier to serve than a hot one!

 30 mins plus 8 hrs freezing   5 mins

SERVES 6

INGREDIENTS

3½ oz/100 g semisweet chocolate, broken into pieces

1 tbsp instant coffee powder

2 tbsp water

4 eggs, separated

½ cup confectioners' sugar, sifted

1 cup heavy cream

2 tbsp Tia Maria

white chocolate caraque, to decorate (see page 9)

1 Tie a double band of foil very tightly around 6 ramekins, to stand 1 inch/2.5 cm above the rim. Put the chocolate, coffee powder and 2 tablespoons of water in a small pan and heat very gently until melted. Let cool slightly.

2 Put the egg yolks and confectioners' sugar in a bowl and whisk together, using an electric whisk, until thick and light. Whisk in the chocolate. Put the cream and Tia Maria in a bowl and whisk until thick. Set aside.

3 In another bowl, whisk the egg whites until stiff but not dry. Stir 1 tablespoon of egg whites into the chocolate mixture, then gently fold in the remaining egg whites with the cream. Pour into the prepared ramekins and freeze overnight.

4 When ready to serve, remove the foil carefully and decorate the tops of the soufflés with the chocolate caraque.

Frozen Citrus Soufflés

These delicious desserts are a refreshing way to end a meal. They can be made in advance and kept in the freezer until required.

🍧 🍧 🍧

🍨 35 mins plus
2 hrs freezing

🕐 0 mins

SERVES 4

INGREDIENTS

1 tbsp gelozone

6 tbsp very hot water

3 eggs, separated

⅓ cup superfine sugar

finely grated rind and juice of 1 lemon,
½ lime and ½ orange

⅔ cup heavy cream

½ cup plain yogurt

thin lemon, lime, and orange slices,
to decorate

1 Tie waxed paper collars around 4 individual soufflé dishes or ramekins or around 1 large (6-inch/15-cm diameter) soufflé dish.

2 Sprinkle the gelozone into the very hot (not boiling) water, stirring well to disperse. Let stand for 2–3 minutes, stirring occasionally, to give a completely clear liquid. Let cool for 10–15 minutes.

3 Meanwhile, whisk the egg yolks and sugar, using a hand-held electric or wire whisk until very pale and light in texture. Add the rind and juice from the fruits, mixing well. Stir in the cooled gelozone liquid, making sure that it is thoroughly incorporated.

4 Put the cream into a large chilled bowl and whip until it holds its shape. Stir the yogurt and then add it to the cream, mixing it in gently. Fold the cream mixture into the citrus mixture, using a large metal spoon.

5 Using a clean whisk, beat the egg whites in a clean bowl until stiff and then gently fold them into the citrus mixture, using a metal spoon.

6 Spoon the mixture into the prepared dishes, almost to the top of their collars. Allow some room for the mixture to expand on freezing. Transfer the dishes to the freezer and open-freeze for about 2 hours, until frozen.

7 Remove from the freezer 10 minutes before serving. Peel away the paper collars carefully and decorate with the slices of lemon, lime, and orange.

Chocolate Ice Cream Roll

This is a family favorite—spiral slices of moist sponge cake and chocolate ice cream never fail to please.

35 mins plus
35–40 mins
standing

20–25 mins

SERVES 8

INGREDIENTS

butter, for greasing

generous ¾ cup all-purpose flour,
  plus extra for dusting

4 eggs

generous ½ cup superfine sugar

3 tbsp unsweetened cocoa

confectioners' sugar, for dusting

2½ cups chocolate ice cream

semisweet chocolate curls,
  (see page 9), to decorate

1 cup Chocolate Fudge Sauce,
  (see page 693), to serve

1 Line a 15 × 10-inch/38 × 25-cm jelly roll pan with waxed paper. Grease the bottom and dust with flour. Put the eggs and superfine sugar in a heatproof bowl set over a pan of gently simmering water. Whisk over low heat for 5–10 minutes until the mixture is pale and fluffy. Remove from the heat and continue beating for 10 minutes until the mixture is cool and the whisk leaves a ribbon trail when lifted. Sift the flour and unsweetened cocoa over the surface and gently fold it in.

2 Preheat the oven to 375°F/190°C. Pour the mixture into the prepared pan and spread out evenly with a spatula. Bake in the preheated oven for 15 minutes, until firm to the touch and starting to shrink from the sides of the pan.

3 Spread out a clean dish towel and cover with a sheet of parchment paper. Lightly dust the parchment paper with confectioners' sugar. Turn out the cake on to the parchment paper and carefully peel off the lining paper. Trim off any crusty edges. Starting from a short side, pick up the cake and the parchment paper and roll them up together. Wrap the dish towel around the rolled cake and place on a wire rack to cool.

4 Remove the ice cream from the freezer and put it in the refrigerator for 15–20 minutes to soften slightly. Remove the dish towel and unroll the cake. Spread the ice cream evenly over the cake, then roll it up again, this time without the parchment paper. Wrap the cake in foil and place in the freezer.

5 Remove the cake from the freezer about 20 minutes before serving. Unwrap, place on a serving plate, and dust with confectioners' sugar. Make the chocolate quick curls and arrange them over the top. Place the cake in the refrigerator until required. Serve in slices with Chocolate Fudge Sauce.

Strawberry Petits Choux

These little chocolate puffs are filled with a melting mixture of strawberry mousse and fresh fruit.

35–40 mins plus
2 hrs chilling/
cooling

40–45 mins

SERVES 6

I N G R E D I E N T S

2 tsp powdered gelatin

2 tbsp water

3 cups strawberries

1 cup ricotta cheese

1 tbsp superfine sugar

2 tsp strawberry-flavoured liqueur

P E T I T S   C H O U X

¾ cup all-purpose flour

2 tbsp unsweetened cocoa

pinch of salt

6 tbsp sweet butter

1 cup water

2 eggs, plus 1 egg white

confectioners' sugar, for dusting

1 Sprinkle the gelatin over the water in a heatproof bowl. Let it soften for 2–3 minutes. Place the bowl over a pan of gently simmering water and stir until the gelatin dissolves. Remove from the heat.

2 Place scant 1 cup of the strawberries in a blender with the ricotta, sugar, and liqueur. Process until blended. Add the gelatin and process briefly. Transfer the mousse to a bowl, cover with plastic wrap, and chill for 1–1½ hours, until set.

3 Meanwhile, make the petits choux. Line a cookie sheet with parchment paper. Sift the flour, unsweetened cocoa, and salt on to a sheet of waxed paper. Put the butter and water into a heavy-based pan and heat gently until the butter has melted.

4 Preheat the oven to 425°F/220°C. Remove the pan from the heat and add the flour mixture all at once, beating vigorously with a wooden spoon. Return the pan to the heat and continue to beat vigorously until the mixture comes away from the sides of the pan. Remove from the heat and cool slightly.

5 In a separate bowl, beat the eggs with the extra egg white, then gradually add them to the chocolate mixture, beating hard until a glossy paste forms. Drop 12 rounded tablespoonfuls of the mixture on to the prepared cookie sheet and bake for 20–25 minutes, until puffed up and crisp.

6 Remove from the oven and make a slit in the side of each petit chou. Return the petits choux to the oven for 5 minutes to dry out. Transfer to a wire rack to cool.

7 Slice the remaining strawberries. Slice the petits choux in half, removing any uncooked dough from the centers, and divide the set strawberry mousse among them. Add a layer of strawberry slices and replace the tops. Dust lightly with confectioners' sugar and place in the refrigerator. Serve within 1½ hours.

Chocolate Shortcake Towers

Stacks of crisp shortcake are sandwiched with chocolate-flavored cream and fresh raspberries, and served with a fresh raspberry coulis.

30 mins | 10 mins

SERVES 6

INGREDIENTS

SHORTCAKE

7 oz/200 g butter, plus extra for greasing

½ cup brown sugar

1¾ oz/50 g semisweet chocolate, grated

scant 2½ cups all-purpose flour, plus extra for dusting

TO FINISH

scant 1½ cups fresh raspberries

2 tbsp confectioners' sugar

1¼ cups heavy cream

3 tbsp milk

3½ oz/100 g white chocolate, melted

confectioners' sugar, for dusting

1 Lightly grease a cookie sheet and preheat the oven to 400°F/200°C. Beat together the butter and sugar until light and fluffy. Beat in the chocolate. Mix in the flour to form a stiff dough.

2 Roll out the dough on a lightly floured work counter and stamp out 18 circles, 3-inches/7.5-cm across, with a plain cookie cutter. Place the circles on the cookie sheet and bake in the preheated oven for 10 minutes, until crisp and golden. Let cool on the sheet.

3 To make the coulis, set aside about ½ cup of the raspberries. Blend the remainder in a food processor with the confectioners' sugar, then push through a strainer to remove the seeds. Chill. Set aside 2 teaspoons of the cream. Whip the remainder until just holding its shape. Fold in the milk and the melted chocolate.

4 For each tower, spoon a little coulis on to a serving plate. Drop small dots of the reserved cream into the coulis around the edge of the plate and use a skewer to drag through the cream to make an attractive pattern.

5 Place a shortcake circle on the plate and spoon on a little of the chocolate cream. Add 2 or 3 raspberries and more cream, top with another shortcake, and repeat the layers. Place a third shortcake on top. Dust with confectioners' sugar.

Chocolate Wafer Layers

Crisp delicate wafers of chocolate layered with a rich pistachio cream filling taste as impressive as they look.

🍰 50 mins
plus chilling

🕐 5 mins

SERVES 6

INGREDIENTS

6 oz/175 g semisweet chocolate,
  broken into pieces

9 oz/250 g mascarpone cheese

1 tbsp superfine sugar

4 tbsp Tia Maria

1¼ cups heavy cream

¾ cup pistachios, chopped

4 oz/115 g milk chocolate, grated

1 Put the chocolate in a heatproof bowl set over a pan of gently simmering water until melted. Let cool. Cut 6 strips of nonstick parchment paper 2½ × 10½ inches/6 × 26 cm. Brush evenly with melted chocolate. Mark each strip with a knife every 3½ inches/9 cm. Leave in the refrigerator to set, then carefully peel the paper off the chocolate wafers.

2 Put the mascarpone cheese and sugar in a bowl and beat until smooth, then beat in the Tia Maria and cream until forming soft peaks. Fold in the pistachios and grated chocolate.

3 Carefully break each chocolate strip along the marked lines to make 3 wafers, giving 18 in total. Spread a little pistachio cream over 1 wafer and top with a second. Spread cream on a third wafer and stack it, cream-side down, on top of the second wafer. Repeat to make 6 stacks. Chill until ready to serve.

COOK'S TIP
Do not over-beat the mascarpone filling or it will be difficult to spread over the chocolate wafers.

Chocolate Fingers

Tasty bread fingers flavored with sherry and coated with chocolate and sugar are surprisingly tasty and very popular.

15 mins

30 mins

MAKES 24

INGREDIENTS

4 eggs, beaten lightly

2½ cups milk

5 tbsp sherry

8 slices day-old white bread,
½-inch/1-cm thick, crusts removed

4 tbsp sunflower oil

generous ½ cup superfine sugar

8 oz/225 g semisweet chocolate, grated

vanilla ice cream, to serve (optional)

1 Pour the beaten eggs, milk, and sherry into a shallow dish and beat lightly to mix. Cut each slice of bread lengthwise into 3 fingers. Soak the bread fingers in the egg mixture until soft, then drain on paper towels.

2 Heat the oil in a large, heavy-based skillet. Carefully add the bread fingers to the skillet, in batches, and cook over medium heat for 12 minutes on each side, until golden. Using tongs, transfer the fingers to paper towels to drain.

3 When all the fingers are cooked and thoroughly drained, roll them first in the sugar and then in the grated chocolate. Pile them on a warm serving plate and serve immediately, with ice cream if desired.

Blackberry Chocolate Tart

This richly flavored tart looks superb and tastes wonderful—a perfect choice for a special occasion.

30 mins plus 2 hrs chilling/cooling • 15 mins

SERVES 6

INGREDIENTS

2 cups all-purpose flour, plus extra for dusting

½ cup unsweetened cocoa

1 cup confectioners' sugar

pinch of salt

6 oz/175 g butter, sweet for preference, cut into pieces

1 egg yolk

4 cups blackberries

1 tbsp lemon juice

2 tbsp superfine sugar

2 tbsp cassis

FILLING

1¼ cups heavy cream

⅔ cup blackberry jelly

8 oz/225 g semisweet chocolate, broken into pieces

2 tbsp butter, sweet for preference, cut into pieces

1 First, make the pie dough. Sift the flour, unsweetened cocoa, confectioners' sugar, and salt into a mixing bowl and make a well in the center. Put the butter and egg yolk in the well and gradually mix in the dry ingredients, using a pie dough blender or two forks. Knead lightly and form into a ball. Cover with plastic wrap and chill in the refrigerator for 1 hour.

2 When chilled, unwrap the dough. Preheat the oven to 350°F/180°C. Roll out the dough on a lightly floured workcounter. Use it to line a 12 x 4-inch/ 30 x 10-cm rectangular tart pan and prick the pastry shell with a fork. Line the shell with parchment paper and fill with dried beans. Bake in the preheated oven for 15 minutes. Remove from the oven, remove the beans and parchment paper and set aside to cool.

3 To make the filling, put the cream and jelly into a pan and bring to a boil over low heat. Remove the pan from the heat and stir in the chocolate until melted and smooth. Stir in the butter until melted and smooth. Pour the mixture into the pastry shell and set aside to cool.

4 Put 1⅓ cups of the blackberries, the lemon juice, and superfine sugar into a food processor and process until smooth. Transfer to a bowl and stir in the cassis. Set aside.

5 Remove the tart from the pan and place on a serving plate. Arrange the remaining blackberries on top and brush with a little blackberry and liqueur sauce. Serve the tart with the sauce on the side.

Banana & Mango Tart

Bananas and mangoes are a great combination of colors and flavors, especially when topped with toasted coconut chips.

15 mins plus
1 hr chilling

5 mins

SERVES 8

INGREDIENTS

8-inch/20-cm ready-prepared pastry shell

FILLING

2 small ripe bananas

1 mango, peeled and sliced

3½ tbsp cornstarch

6 tbsp raw sugar

1¼ cups soy milk

⅔ cup coconut milk

1 tsp vanilla extract

toasted coconut chips, to decorate

1 Slice the bananas and arrange half of them in the pastry shell with half of the mango pieces.

2 Put the cornstarch and sugar in a pan and mix together. Gradually, whisk in the soy milk and coconut milk until combined. Simmer over low heat, whisking constantly, for 2–3 minutes until the mixture thickens.

3 Stir in the vanilla extract, then spoon the mixture over the fruit.

4 Top with the remaining fruit and toasted coconut chips. Chill in the refrigerator for 1 hour before serving.

COOK'S TIP

Coconut chips are available in some supermarkets and most health food stores. They are worth using as they look more attractive than as dry unsweetened coconut.

Chocolate Chiffon Pie

The nutty crust of this delectable pie contrasts with the tempting, creamy chocolate filling.

🕐 35 mins plus 4 hrs chilling/cooling

🕐 12–15 mins

SERVES 8

INGREDIENTS

1½ cup shelled Brazil nuts

2 tbsp granulated sugar

2 tsp melted butter

scant 1 cup milk

2 tsp powdered gelatin

generous ½ cup superfine sugar

2 eggs, separated

8 oz/225 g semisweet chocolate, chopped coarsely

1 tsp vanilla extract

⅔ cup heavy cream

2 tbsp chopped Brazil nuts

1 Preheat the oven to 400°F/200°C. Put the Brazil nuts into a food processor and process until finely ground. Add the granulated sugar and melted butter and process briefly to combine. Tip the mixture into a 9-inch/23-cm round springform pan and press it on to the bottom and sides with a spoon or your fingertips. Bake in the preheated oven for 8–10 minutes, until light golden brown. Set aside to cool.

2 Pour the milk into a heatproof bowl and sprinkle the gelatin over the surface. Let it soften for 2 minutes, then set over a pan of barely simmering water. Stir in half the superfine sugar, both the egg yolks, and all the chocolate. Stir constantly over low heat for 4–5 minutes, until the gelatin has dissolved and the chocolate has melted. Remove from the heat and beat until the mixture is smooth and thoroughly blended. Stir in the vanilla extract, cover with plastic wrap, and chill

in the refrigerator for 45–60 minutes, until just starting to set.

3 Whip the cream until it is stiff, then fold all but about 3 tablespoons into the chocolate mixture. Whisk the egg whites in another bowl until soft peaks form. Add 2 teaspoons of the remaining

sugar and whisk until stiff peaks form. Fold in the remaining sugar, then fold the egg whites into the chocolate mixture. Pour the filling into the pie dish and chill in the refrigerator for 3 hours, or until set. Decorate the pie with the remaining whipped cream and the chopped nuts before serving.

Chocolate Charlotte

This chocolate dessert, consisting of a rich chocolate mousse-like filling enclosed in ladyfingers, is a variation of a popular classic.

40 mins plus
5 hrs chilling

5 mins

SERVES 8

INGREDIENTS

about 22 ladyfingers

4 tbsp orange-flavored liqueur

9 oz/250 g semisweet chocolate

⅔ cup heavy cream

4 eggs

⅔ cup superfine sugar

TO DECORATE

⅔ cup whipping cream

2 tbsp superfine sugar

½ tsp vanilla extract

semisweet chocolate curls (see page 9)

chocolate decorations (see page 9), optional

1 Line the bottom of a charlotte mold or a deep 7-inch/18-cm round cake pan with a piece of parchment paper.

2 Place the ladyfingers on a cookie sheet and sprinkle with half of the orange-flavored liqueur. Use to line the sides of the mold or pan, trimming if necessary to make a tight fit.

3 Put the chocolate in a heatproof bowl set over a pan of gently simmering water until melted. Remove from the heat and stir in the heavy cream.

4 Separate the eggs and place the whites in a large greasefree bowl. Beat the egg yolks into the chocolate mixture.

5 Whisk the egg whites until stiff peaks form, then gradually add the superfine sugar, whisking until stiff and glossy. Carefully fold the egg whites into the chocolate mixture in 2 batches, taking care not to knock out all of the air. Pour into the center of the mold. Trim the ladyfingers so that they are level with the chocolate mixture. Chill for at least 5 hours.

6 To decorate, whisk the cream, sugar, and vanilla extract until soft peaks form. Turn out the charlotte on to a serving dish. Pipe cream rosettes around the bottom and decorate with chocolate curls and other decorations of your choice.

Passion Fruit Charlotte

If passion fruit are not in season, use clear apple juice for the jello and flavor the cream filling with either vanilla or orange.

30 mins plus 4 hrs chilling

15 mins

SERVES 6

I N G R E D I E N T S

1¼ cups passion fruit juice

4 tsp powdered gelatin

2–3 fresh strawberries, sliced

1⅓ cups fresh raspberries

20 ladyfingers

2 eggs, separated

¼ cup superfine sugar

⅔ cup light cream, warmed

3 passion fruit

3 oz/85 g semisweet chocolate

⅔ cup heavy cream

1 To make the jello, heat the fruit juice until almost boiling, remove from the heat, and sprinkle in 2 teaspoons of the gelatin. Stir until the gelatin has dissolved, then pour a thin layer into a rinsed 2-pint/1.2-liter charlotte mold. Let set.

2 Dip the sliced strawberries with a few raspberries in jello, then arrange on top of the layer of jello in the mold. Let set, then pour over half of the remaining jello. Let stand until completely set.

3 Dip each side of the ladyfingers into the remaining jello and place, sugar-side out, round the edge of the mold. Let chill while you prepare the filling.

4 Whisk the egg yolks and sugar until very thick and creamy. Stir in the warm cream, then strain into a heavy-based pan and cook, stirring, until the mixture thickens and coats the back of a wooden spoon. Remove and cool slightly.

5 Sprinkle the remaining gelatin over 3 tablespoons of very hot water. Stir until dissolved. Cool slightly, then stir into the custard. Halve the passion fruit, and add the juice to the custard. Melt the chocolate in a heatproof bowl set over a pan of gently simmering water. Stir into the custard with the remaining raspberries.

6 Whip the cream until soft peaks form and stir two-thirds of it into the custard. Whisk the egg whites until soft peaks form and stir into the mixture. Mix lightly, then spoon into the mold. Chill for at least 4 hours, or until set.

7 To unmold, dip the base of the mold in a pan of very hot water for a few seconds then invert on to a serving plate. To decorate, pipe the remainder of the whipped cream between the ladyfingers and around the top, then serve.

Mississippi Mud Pie

An all-time favorite with chocoholics—the "mud" refers to the moist, rich chocolate layer of the cake.

30 mins plus
3 hrs chilling

1 hr 10 mins

SERVES 8

INGREDIENTS

2 cups all-purpose flour, plus extra for dusting

¼ cup unsweetened cocoa

5 oz/140 g butter

2 tbsp superfine sugar

about 2 tbsp cold water

FILLING

6 oz/175 g butter

2⅓ cups dark brown sugar

4 eggs, beaten lightly

4 tbsp unsweetened cocoa, sifted

5½ oz/150 g semisweet chocolate

1¼ cups light cream

1 tsp chocolate extract

TO DECORATE

1¾ cups heavy cream, whipped

chocolate flakes and chocolate curls (see page 9)

1 To make the pie dough, sift the flour and unsweetened cocoa into a mixing bowl. Rub in the butter until the mixture resembles fine bread crumbs. Stir in the sugar and enough cold water to mix to a soft dough. Chill for 15 minutes.

2 Preheat the oven to 375°F/190°C. Roll out the dough on a lightly floured counter and use to line a deep 9-inch/23-cm loose-bottomed tart pan or ceramic pie dish. Line with foil or parchment paper and baking beans. Bake blind in the preheated oven for 15 minutes. Remove the beans and foil or parchment and cook for a further 10 minutes until crisp.

3 To make the filling, beat the butter and sugar in a bowl and gradually beat in the eggs with the unsweetened cocoa. Melt the chocolate and beat it into the mixture with the light cream and the chocolate extract.

4 Reduce the oven temperature to 325°F/160°C. Pour the mixture into the cooked pastry shell and bake for 45 minutes, or until the filling is set.

5 Let the mud pie cool completely, then transfer the pie to a serving plate if preferred. Cover with the whipped cream and let chill.

6 Decorate the pie with quick chocolate curls and chocolate flakes and then let it chill.

Chocolate Freezer Cake

Hidden in a ring of chocolate sponge lies the secret of this freezer cake—
a chocolate-mint ice cream. Use orange or coffee ice cream if preferred.

30 mins plus
3 hrs freezing/
cooling

30 mins

SERVES 8

INGREDIENTS

butter, for greasing

4 eggs

¾ cup superfine sugar

¾ cup self-rising flour

scant ⅓ cup unsweetened cocoa

2¼ cups chocolate-mint ice cream

chocolate sauce (see page 9), to serve

1 Preheat the oven to 350°F/180°C. Lightly grease a 9-inch/23-cm ring pan. Place the eggs and sugar in a large mixing bowl. Using an electric whisk if you have one, whisk the mixture until it is very thick and a trail is left when the whisk is dragged across the surface. If using a balloon whisk, use a heatproof bowl, set over a pan of gently simmering water while whisking.

2 Sift the flour and unsweetened cocoa together and fold into the egg mixture. Pour into the prepared pan and bake in the preheated oven for 30 minutes, or until springy to the touch. Let cool in the pan before turning out on to a wire rack to cool completely.

3 Rinse the cake pan and line with a strip of plastic wrap, overhanging slightly. Carefully cut off the top ½ inch/ 1 cm of the cake in one slice, and then set aside.

4 Return the cake to the pan. Using a spoon, scoop out the center of the cake, leaving a shell about 1 cm/½ inch thick.

5 Remove the ice cream from the freezer and let stand for a few minutes, then beat with a wooden spoon until softened a little. Fill the center of the cake with the ice cream, smoothing the top. Replace the top of the cake.

6 Cover with the overhanging plastic wrap and freeze for at least 2 hours.

7 To serve, turn the cake out on to a serving dish and drizzle over some of the chocolate sauce in an attractive pattern, if you wish. Cut the cake into slices and then serve the remaining sauce on the side.

Tiramisu Layers

This is a modern version of the well-known and very traditional chocolate- and coffee-flavored dessert from Italy.

25 mins plus
1 hr chilling

5 mins

SERVES 6

INGREDIENTS

⅔ cup heavy cream

1¾ cups mascarpone cheese

10 oz/300 g semisweet chocolate

1¾ cups hot black coffee

¼ cup superfine sugar

6 tbsp dark rum or cognac

54 ladyfingers

unsweetened cocoa, for dusting

1 Whip the cream until it just holds its shape. Beat the mascarpone to soften slightly, then fold in the whipped cream. Melt the chocolate in a heatproof bowl set over a pan of simmering water, stirring occasionally. Let the chocolate cool slightly, then stir it into the mascarpone and cream.

2 Mix the hot coffee and sugar in a pan and stir until dissolved. Let cool then add the dark rum. Dip the ladyfingers into the mixture briefly so that they absorb the coffee and rum mixture, but do not become soggy.

3 Place 3 ladyfingers on 6 serving plates.

4 Spoon a layer of the chocolate, mascarpone, and cream mixture over the ladyfingers.

5 Place 3 more ladyfingers on top of the chocolate and mascarpone mixture. Spread another layer of chocolate and mascarpone and place 3 more ladyfingers on top.

6 Let the tiramisu chill in the refrigerator for at least 1 hour. Dust with a little unsweetened cocoa just before serving.

VARIATION
Try adding ⅓ cup chopped, toasted hazelnuts to the chocolate and mascarpone mixture in step 1, if you prefer.

Traditional Tiramisu

A favorite Italian dessert flavored with coffee and amaretto. You could substitute the amaretto with cognac or marsala.

2 hrs 15 mins

5 mins

SERVES 6

INGREDIENTS

20–24 ladyfingers

2 tbsp cold black coffee

2 tbsp coffee extract

2 tbsp amaretto

4 egg yolks

6 tbsp superfine sugar

few drops vanilla extract

grated rind of ½ lemon

1½ cups mascarpone cheese

2 tsp lemon juice

1 cup heavy cream

1 tbsp milk

½ cup slivered almonds, lightly toasted

2 tbsp unsweetened cocoa

1 tbsp confectioners' sugar

1 Arrange half of the ladyfingers in the base of a glass bowl or serving dish.

2 Combine the black coffee, coffee extract and amaretto together and sprinkle just over half of the mixture over the ladyfingers.

3 Put the egg yolks into a heatproof bowl with the sugar, vanilla and lemon rind. Stand over a pan of gently simmering water and whisk until very thick and creamy and a trail is left when the whisk is dragged across the surface.

4 Put the mascarpone cheese in a bowl with the lemon juice and beat until smooth.

5 Combine the egg and mascarpone cheese mixtures and when evenly blended pour half over the ladyfingers and spread out evenly.

6 Add another layer of ladyfingers, sprinkle with the remaining coffee mixture and then cover with the rest of the egg and mascarpone cheese mixture. Chill for at least 2 hours and preferably longer, or overnight.

7 To serve, whip the cream and milk together until fairly stiff and spread or pipe over the dessert. Sprinkle with the slivered almonds and then sift an even layer of unsweetened cocoa so the top is completely covered. Finally sift a light dusting of confectioners' sugar over the unsweetened cocoa.

Chocolate & Cherry Tiramisu

There are now several variations on the original tiramisu theme. This one has the delectable flavors of chocolate, cherry, and coffee.

20 mins plus 2 hrs to chill   **0 mins**

SERVES 4

INGREDIENTS

scant 1 cup strong black coffee, cooled to room temperature

6 tbsp cherry cognac

4 trifle sponges or 16 ladyfingers

generous 1 cup mascarpone cheese

1¼ cups heavy cream, whipped lightly

3 tbsp confectioners' sugar

1½ cups sweet cherries, halved and pitted

2½ oz/65 g chocolate, grated

whole cherries, to decorate

1 Pour the cooled coffee into a pitcher and stir in the cherry cognac. Put 2 of the sponges or half of the ladyfingers in the bottom of a serving dish, then pour over half of the coffee mixture.

2 Put the mascarpone cheese in a separate bowl along with the cream and sugar and mix together well. Spread half of the mascarpone mixture over the coffee-soaked sponges or ladyfingers, then top with half of the cherries. Arrange the remaining ladyfingers on top. Pour over the remaining coffee mixture and top with the remaining cherries. Finish with a layer of mascarpone. Scatter over the grated chocolate, cover with plastic wrap, and chill in the refrigerator for at least 2 hours.

3 Remove from the refrigerator and serve decorated with whole cherries.

 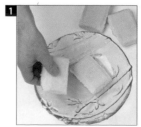 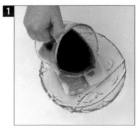

Quick Tiramisu

This quick and simple version of one of the most popular Italian desserts is ready in minutes.

15 mins   0 mins

SERVES 4

INGREDIENTS

1 cup mascarpone or full-fat soft cheese

1 egg, separated

2 tbsp plain yogurt

2 tbsp superfine sugar

2 tbsp dark rum

2 tbsp strong black coffee

8 ladyfingers

2 tbsp grated semisweet chocolate

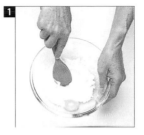

1 Put the mascarpone cheese in a large bowl, add the egg yolk and yogurt and beat until smooth.

2 Whisk the egg white until stiff but not dry, then whisk in the sugar and fold into the mascarpone mixture.

3 Spoon half of the mixture into 4 sundae glasses.

4 Mix together the rum and coffee in a shallow dish. Dip the ladyfingers into the rum mixture, break them in half, or into smaller pieces if necessary, and divide among the glasses.

5 Stir any remaining coffee mixture into the remaining cheese and spoon over the top.

6 Sprinkle with grated chocolate. Serve immediately or chill until required.

COOK'S TIP
Mascarpone is an Italian soft cream cheese made from cow's milk. It has a rich, silky smooth texture and a deliciously creamy flavor. It can be eaten as it is with fresh fruits or flavored with coffee or chocolate.

Chestnut & Chocolate Terrine

Chestnut and chocolate is a classic combination, seen at its best in this layered terrine.

30 mins plus chilling

5 mins

SERVES 6

INGREDIENTS

4 oz/115 g semisweet chocolate, broken into pieces

scant 1 cup heavy cream

1 package rectangular plain sweet cookies

scant ½ cup dark rum

8 oz/225 g canned sweetened chestnut purée

unsweetened cocoa and confectioners' sugar for dusting

COOK'S TIP

When soaking the cookies take care not to dip them into the rum for too long, otherwise they will disintegrate.

1 Line a 1-lb/450-g loaf pan with plastic wrap. Put the chocolate in a heatproof bowl set over a pan of gently simmering water until melted. Set aside to cool. Put the cream in a bowl and whip lightly until soft peaks form. Fold in the cooled chocolate.

2 Place the rum in a shallow dish. Lightly dip 4 cookies into the rum and arrange on the bottom of the pan. Then repeat with 4 more cookies. Spread half the chocolate cream over the cookies. Make another layer of 8 cookies dipped in

rum and spread the chestnut purée over, followed by another layer of cookies. Spread the remaining chocolate cream over and top with a final layer of cookies. Chill overnight.

3 Turn the terrine out on to a serving dish. Dust with unsweetened cocoa then cut strips of paper and place randomly on top of the terrine and sift confectioners' sugar over to make a pattern. Remove the paper and cut the terrine into slices with a sharp knife dipped in hot water.

Three Chocolate Terrine

Contrasting bands of white, milk and semisweet chocolate look stunning when the terrine is sliced and surrounded with orange cream.

45 mins plus 3 hrs chilling   10 mins

SERVES 10-12

INGREDIENTS

6 tbsp water

3 tsp powdered gelatin

4 oz/115 g each of milk chocolate, white chocolate, and semisweet chocolate

2 cups whipping cream

6 eggs, separated

scant ½ cup superfine sugar

ORANGE CREAM

2 tbsp superfine sugar

1 tbsp cornstarch

2 egg yolks

⅔ cup milk

⅔ cup heavy cream

1 orange

1 tbsp orange-flavored liqueur

a little orange juice (optional)

chocolate-coated coffee beans, to decorate

1 To make the milk chocolate mousse, put 2 tablespoons of the water in a small heatproof bowl, sprinkle on the gelatin and leave until spongy, then set the bowl over a pan of gently simmering water until the gelatine is dissolved. Let cool. Break the milk chocolate into pieces and place in a heatproof bowl set over a pan of gently simmering water until melted. Let cool. Put one-third of the cream in a bowl and whip until thick. Put 2 egg whites in another bowl and whisk until stiff but not dry. Put 2 egg yolks and one-third of the superfine sugar in a bowl and whisk until thick and pale, then stir in the cooled melted chocolate, the gelatin and finally the cream. Gently fold in the egg whites.

2 Pour the mixture into a 5-cup loaf pan lined with plastic wrap. Put in the freezer for 20 minutes. Make the white chocolate mousse in the same way and pour over the milk chocolate layer. Freeze as before then make the semisweet chocolate mousse and pour on top. Chill in the refrigerator for 2 hours or until set.

3 To make the orange cream, put the sugar, cornstarch and egg yolks in a bowl and stir until smooth. Grate the rind from the orange, reserving a little for decoration. Put the milk and cream in a pan with the rind and heat gently until almost boiling then pour over the yolk mixture, whisking. Strain back into the pan and return to the heat. Heat gently, stirring until thickened. Cover the surface with plastic wrap and let cool. Stir in the liqueur. The cream should be a pouring consistency. If it is too thick, stir in a little orange juice. Turn out the terrine and cut into slices. Serve with the orange cream, decorated with the chocolate-coated coffee beans and reserved orange rind.

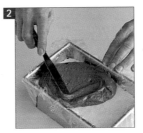

White Chocolate Terrine

This iced dessert is somewhere between a chocolate mousse and an ice cream. Serve it with a chocolate sauce or a fruit coulis and fresh fruit.

50 mins plus
8 hrs freezing

5 mins

SERVES 8

INGREDIENTS

2 tbsp granulated sugar

5 tbsp water

10 oz/300 g white chocolate

3 eggs, separated

1¼ cups heavy cream

1 Line a 1-lb/450-g loaf pan with foil or plastic wrap, pressing out as many creases as you can.

2 Place the granulated sugar and water in a heavy-based pan and heat gently, stirring until the sugar has dissolved. Bring to a boil and boil for 1–2 minutes until syrupy, then remove from the heat.

3 Break the white chocolate into small pieces and stir it into the hot syrup, continuing to stir until the chocolate has melted and combined with the syrup. Let the mixture cool slightly.

4 Beat the egg yolks into the chocolate mixture. Let cool completely.

5 Lightly whip the cream until it is just holding its shape, and fold it into the chocolate mixture.

6 Whisk the egg whites in a greasefree bowl until soft peaks form. Fold the whites into the chocolate mixture. Pour into the prepared loaf pan and freeze overnight.

7 To serve, remove the terrine from the freezer about 10–15 minutes before serving. Turn out of the pan and cut into slices. Serve with a fruit coulis, if liked (see Cook's Tip).

COOK'S TIP

To make a coulis, place 1 cup soft fruit (strawberries, mangoes, or raspberries are ideal) in a food processor. Add 1–2 tablespoons of confectioners' sugar and blend to a paste. If the fruit contains seeds, push the paste through a strainer to remove them. Chill until required.

Chocolate Salami

This Italian cold chocolate "sausage" dish gets its name from its appearance, which looks just like salami.

25 mins
plus 6–8 hrs
standing/freezing

5–7 mins

SERVES 10

INGREDIENTS

12 oz/350 g semisweet chocolate, broken into small pieces

4 tbsp amaretto or cognac

6 oz/175 g butter, sweet for preference, cut into small pieces

2 egg yolks

24 plain sweet cookies, such as Petit Beurre, crushed coarsely

½ cup toasted slivered almonds, chopped

¼ cup ground almonds

1 tsp vegetable oil or olive oil, for greasing

1 Put the chocolate in a heatproof bowl set over a pan of gently simmering water. Add the amaretto and 2 tablespoons of the butter. Stir over low heat until melted and smooth. Remove from the heat and cool slightly.

2 Stir in the egg yolks, then add the remaining butter, a little at a time, making sure each addition is fully incorporated before adding more. Stir in about three-quarters of the crushed cookies and all the toasted almonds. Cover with plastic wrap, then set aside for 45–60 minutes, until starting to set. Meanwhile, put the remaining crushed cookies into a food processor and process until finely crushed. Transfer them to a bowl and stir in the ground almonds. Set aside.

3 Lightly oil a sheet of parchment paper and turn out the chocolate mixture on to it. Using a spatula, shape the mixture into a salami about 14 inches/ 35 cm long. Wrap the salami in the parchment paper and place in the freezer for 4–6 hours, until set.

4 About 1¼ hours before serving, spread out the ground almond mixture on a sheet of parchment paper.

Remove the salami from the freezer and unwrap. Roll it over the ground almond mixture until thoroughly and evenly coated. Cover with plastic wrap, then set aside for 1 hour at room temperature. Cut into slices and serve.

Chocolate & Almond Terrine

Full of flavor and contrasting textures, this classic Italian dessert is very quick and easy to prepare.

30–40 mins
plus 4–5 hrs
chilling/cooling

5 mins

SERVES 8

INGREDIENTS

vegetable oil, for brushing

8 oz/225 g semisweet chocolate, broken into pieces

4 tbsp dark rum

7 oz/200 g sweet butter

⅔ cup superfine sugar

2 eggs, separated

1½ cups ground almonds

pinch of salt

2 cups crushed amaretti or ratafia cookies

2 tbsp confectioners' sugar

TO DECORATE

2¾ oz/75 g semisweet chocolate

8 cherries

8 chocolate leaves (see page 9)

1 Line a 2-lb/900-g loaf pan with parchment paper, letting it overlap the sides. Brush with oil. Put the chocolate in a heatproof bowl set over a pan of gently simmering water. Stir over low heat until melted. Remove the pan from the heat, stir in the rum and set aside to cool.

2 Cream together the butter and superfine sugar until pale and fluffy, then beat in the egg yolks, one at a time. Add the almonds and then beat in the cooled chocolate.

3 Whisk the egg whites with a pinch of salt until stiff peaks form. Gently fold the whites into the chocolate mixture, then fold in the cookie crumbs. Spoon the mixture into the prepared pan, spread it out evenly, and smooth the top. Cover with plastic wrap and chill in the refrigerator for 4–5 hours, until firm.

4 To serve, uncover the pan and run a round-bladed knife around the sides.

Dip the bottom in hot water. Place a serving plate on top of the pan, then, holding them firmly together, invert. Remove the parchment paper. Dust with the confectioners' sugar.

5 To decorate, melt the semisweet chocolate as before, and put spoonfuls along the top of the cake. Top with cherries and chocolate leaves.

Chocolate Brownie Roulade

The addition of nuts and raisins has given this dessert extra texture, making it similar to that of chocolate brownies.

20 mins   30 mins

SERVES 4

INGREDIENTS

5½ oz/150 g semisweet chocolate, broken into pieces

3 tbsp water

¾ cup superfine sugar

5 eggs, separated

2 tbsp raisins, chopped

¼ cup pecans, chopped

pinch of salt

1¼ cups heavy cream, whipped lightly

confectioners' sugar, for dusting

1   Grease a 12 x 8-inch/30 x 20-cm jelly roll pan, line with parchment paper and grease the parchment.

2   Melt the chocolate with the water in a small pan over low heat until the chocolate has just melted. Let cool.

3   In a bowl, whisk the sugar and egg yolks for 2-3 minutes with a hand-held electric whisk until thick and pale.

4   Fold in the cooled chocolate, raisins, and pecans.

5   In a separate bowl, whisk the egg whites with the salt. Fold one quarter of the egg whites into the chocolate mixture, then fold in the rest of the whites, working lightly and quickly.

6   Transfer the mixture to the prepared pan and bake in a preheated oven, 350°F/180°C, for 25 minutes until risen and just firm to the touch. Let cool before covering with a sheet of nonstick parchment paper and a damp clean dish cloth. Leave until completely cold.

7   Turn the roulade out on to another piece of parchment paper dusted with confectioners' sugar and remove the lining paper.

8   Spread the cream over the roulade. Starting from a short end, roll the sponge away from you using the paper to guide you. Trim the ends of the roulade to make a neat finish and transfer to a serving plate. Leave to chill in the refrigerator until ready to serve. Dust with a little confectioners' sugar before serving, if wished.

Strawberry & Almond Roulade

A light, flourless almond sponge is wrapped around a filling of strawberries and mascarpone cheese in this variation on a classic, popular dessert.

40 mins   15 mins

SERVES 4

INGREDIENTS

butter, for greasing

6 eggs

1 cup golden superfine sugar

2 tsp baking powder

2 cups ground almonds

confectioners' sugar, for dusting

FILLING

⅔ cup mascarpone cheese

⅔ cup heavy cream

3 cups fresh strawberries

1 Preheat the oven to 350°F/180°C. Grease and line the bottom and sides of a 15 × 10-inch/38 × 25-cm jelly roll pan. Separate the eggs, placing the whites in a large bowl and the yolks in a separate bowl. Add the sugar to the yolks and whisk together until pale and thick. Place the baking powder and ground almonds in a bowl and mix together. Stir gently into the yolk mixture, taking care not to over-mix. Carefully fold in the egg whites.

2 Spread in the pan and bake in the preheated oven for 15 minutes, or until firm. Cover with a clean dish towel and let cool in the pan. To make the filling, place the mascarpone cheese and cream in a bowl and stir together to give a spreading consistency. Place half the strawberries in a separate bowl and mash. Coarsely chop the remainder and reserve. Stir the mashed strawberries into the cream.

3 Place a sheet of waxed paper on the work counter and dust thickly with confectioners' sugar. Turn the roulade out on to the paper and peel off the lining paper. Spread the cream over the roulade and scatter the chopped strawberries over. Roll up and serve, cut into slices, within 1–2 hours of assembling.

VARIATION
Raspberries will also complement the flavor of almonds, and make a good alternative to strawberries.

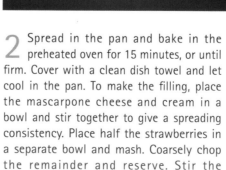

Chocolate Christmas Pudding

This is a wonderful alternative for anyone who dislikes a traditional Christmas pudding, but it can be enjoyed at any time.

🍰 15 mins plus
8 hrs chilling

🕐 5 mins

SERVES 10

INGREDIENTS

⅔ cup mixed candied fruits, chopped

⅓ cup raisins

grated rind of ½ orange

3 tbsp orange juice

3 tbsp light cream

12 oz/350 g semisweet chocolate, cut into pieces

½ cup cream cheese

4 oz/115 g amaretti cookies, broken into rough pieces

TO SERVE

½ cup whipping cream

2 tbsp amaretto

1 tsp grated semisweet chocolate

1 Grease a 4½-cup pudding bowl. Put the candied fruit, raisins, orange rind, and juice in a bowl and mix together. Put the light cream and chocolate into a pan and heat very gently until melted. Stir until smooth then stir in the fruit mixture. Let cool.

2 Put the cream cheese and a little of the chocolate mixture in a bowl and beat together until smooth, then stir in the remaining chocolate mixture. Stir in the amaretti cookies. Pour into the prepared bowl, cover, and chill overnight.

3 To serve, turn the pudding out on to a chilled serving plate. Pour the whipping cream into a bowl and add the amaretto. Whip lightly until slightly thickened. Pour some over the pudding and sprinkle grated chocolate on top before serving.

COOK'S TIP
Because this pudding is very rich it should be cut into thin slices. To make it easier to slice, dip a sharp knife into hot water.

Chocolate & Orange Slices

Contrasting flavors, textures, and colors are combined to create this delectable masterpiece.

30–40 mins plus
3–4 hrs chilling

10 mins

SERVES 8

I N G R E D I E N T S

2 tsp butter, for greasing

1 lb/450 g semisweet chocolate,
  broken into pieces

3 small, loose-skinned oranges, such as
  tangerines, mandarins, or satsumas

4 egg yolks

scant 1 cup sour cream

2 tbsp raisins

1¼ cups whipped cream, to serve

1 Lightly grease a 1-lb/450-g terrine or loaf pan and line it with plastic wrap. Put 14 oz/400 g of the chocolate in a heatproof bowl set over a pan of gently simmering water. Stir over a low heat until melted. Remove from the heat and let cool slightly.

2 Meanwhile, peel the oranges, removing all traces of pith. Cut the rind into very thin snips. Beat the egg yolks into the chocolate, one at a time, then add most of the orange rind (reserve the rest for decoration), and all the sour cream and raisins, and beat until thoroughly combined. Spoon the mixture into the prepared pan, cover with plastic wrap, and chill in the refrigerator for 3–4 hours, until set.

3 While the chocolate mixture is chilling, put the remaining chocolate in a heatproof bowl set over a pan of gently simmering water until melted. Remove the pan from the heat and cool slightly. Meanwhile, segment the oranges. Dip each segment into the

melted chocolate and spread out on a sheet of parchment paper for about 30 minutes, until set.

4 To serve, remove the pan from the refrigerator and turn out the

chocolate mold. Remove the plastic wrap and cut the mold into slices. Place a slice on individual serving plates and decorate with the chocolate-coated orange segments and the remaining orange rind. Serve immediately with whipped cream.

Chocolate Rice Dessert

What could be more delicious than creamy, tender rice cooked in a rich chocolate sauce? This dessert is almost like a dense chocolate mousse.

🍳 🍳 🍳

🍮 30 mins plus
2 hrs chilling

🕐 1 hr 10 mins

SERVES 8

INGREDIENTS

½ cup long-grain white rice

pinch of salt

2½ cups milk

generous ½ cup superfine sugar

7 oz/200 g bittersweet or semisweet chocolate, chopped

3 oz/85 g butter, cut into pieces

1 tsp vanilla extract

2 tbsp cognac

scant ¾ cup heavy cream

whipped cream, for piping (optional)

chocolate curls or leaves, to decorate (see page 9), optional

1 Bring a pan of water to a boil. Sprinkle in the rice and add the salt, then reduce the heat and simmer gently for 15–20 minutes, or until the rice is just tender. Drain, rinse, then drain again.

2 Heat the milk and the sugar in a large heavy-based pan over medium heat until the sugar dissolves, stirring frequently. Add the chocolate and butter and stir until they are melted and smooth.

3 Stir in the cooked rice and reduce the heat to low. Cover and simmer, stirring occasionally, for 30 minutes, or until the milk is absorbed and the mixture thickened. Stir in the vanilla extract and cognac. Remove the mixture from the heat and let cool to room temperature.

4 Using an electric whisk, beat the cream until soft peaks form. Stir one heaping tablespoonful of the cream into the chocolate rice mixture to lighten it, then fold in the remaining cream.

5 Spoon the dessert into glass serving dishes, cover them, and chill for about 2 hours. If wished, decorate with whipped cream and top with curls of chocolate or chocolate leaves.

VARIATION
To mold the dessert, soften ½ oz/15 g of gelatin in ¼ cup of cold water and heat gently until dissolved. Stir into the chocolate rice just before folding in the cream. Pour into a rinsed mold, let set, then unmold.

Rice Pudding with Lemon

Rice is transformed into a creamy, family-style dessert. At the height of summer, serve well chilled with a mixture of summer berries.

30 mins plus
1 hr chilling

25 mins

SERVES 4

INGREDIENTS

1 tsp cornstarch

3¾ cups milk, plus an extra 2 tbsp

generous ½ cup pudding rice

about 2 tbsp sugar or 1 tbsp honey

finely grated rind of 1 large lemon

freshly squeezed lemon juice

½ cup shelled pistachios

1 Place the cornstarch in a small bowl and stir in 2 tablespoons of the milk, stirring until there are no lumps. Rinse a pan with cold water.

2 Place the remaining milk and the cornstarch mixture in the rinsed pan over medium–high heat and heat, stirring occasionally, until small bubbles form all around the edge. Do not boil.

3 Stir in the rice, reduce the heat, and continue stirring for 20 minutes or until all but about 2 tablespoons of the excess liquid has evaporated and the rice is tender.

4 Remove from the heat and pour into a heatproof bowl. Stir in sugar to taste. Stir in the lemon rind, then stir in lemon juice to taste. Set the bowl aside to cool completely.

5 Tightly cover the top of the cool rice with a sheet of plastic wrap and chill in the refrigerator for at least 1 hour—the colder the rice is, the better it tastes with fresh fruit.

6 Meanwhile, finely chop the pistachios. To serve, spoon the rice pudding into individual bowls and sprinkle with the chopped nuts.

COOK'S TIP
It is important to rinse the pan in step 1 to prevent the milk from scorching on the sides or bottom.

Orange-Scented Rice

This delicious creamy dessert is flavored with fresh oranges, orange-flavored liqueur, and two kinds of ginger.

2 hrs   45 mins

SERVES 6

INGREDIENTS

1¼ cups pudding rice

1 cup freshly squeezed orange juice

pinch of salt

1¼ cups milk

1 vanilla bean, split

2-inch/5-cm piece gingerroot, gently bruised

1 cup sugar

¼ cup heavy cream

4 tbsp orange-flavored liqueur

2 tbsp butter

4–6 seedless oranges

2 pieces preserved ginger, sliced thinly, plus 2 tbsp syrup from the ginger jar

ground ginger, for dusting (optional)

1 Put the rice in a pan with the orange juice and salt. Bring to a boil, skimming off any foam. Reduce the heat and simmer for about 10 minutes, stirring occasionally, until the juice is absorbed.

2 Gradually stir in the milk, add the vanilla bean and gingerroot, and simmer for 30 minutes, stirring frequently, until the milk is absorbed and the rice is very tender. Remove from the heat. Remove the vanilla bean and gingerroot.

3 Stir in half the sugar, half the cream, the orange-flavored liqueur, and butter until the sugar is dissolved and the butter is melted. Set aside to cool, then stir in the remaining cream, and pour into a bowl. Cover and set aside at room temperature.

4 Pare the rind from the oranges and set aside. Working over a bowl to catch the juices, remove the pith from all the oranges. Cut out the segments and drop into the bowl. Stir in the preserved ginger and syrup. Chill in the refrigerator.

5 Cut the pared orange rind into thin strips and blanch for 1 minute. Drain and rinse. Bring 1 cup water to a boil with the remaining sugar. Add the rind strips and simmer gently until the syrup is reduced by half. Set aside to cool.

6 Serve the rice with the chilled oranges and top with the caramelized orange rind strips. Lightly dust with ground ginger, if liked.

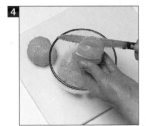

Portuguese Rice Pudding

This buttery, egg-rich rice pudding is quite irresistible, and makes a deliciously different dessert for a dinner party.

10 mins   35 mins

SERVES 6–8

I N G R E D I E N T S

1 cup valencia, risotto, or pudding rice

pinch of salt

1 lemon

2 cups milk

⅔ cup light cream

1 cinnamon stick

6 tbsp butter

¾ cup sugar, or to taste

8 egg yolks

ground cinnamon, for dusting

T O   D E C O R A T E

fresh mint leaves

a few strawberries, hulled and sliced

1 Bring a pan of water to a boil. Sprinkle in the rice and salt, and return to a boil, then reduce the heat and simmer for about 15 minutes or until just tender. Drain the rice, rinse it, then drain again.

2 Using a small sharp knife or vegetable peeler, try to peel the rind off the lemon in one piece, working round the fruit. Alternatively, peel it off in strips.

3 Place the milk and cream in a pan, and bring to a simmer over medium heat. Add the rice, cinnamon stick, butter, and the lemon rind "curl" or strips. Reduce the heat to low, and simmer the mixture very gently for about 20 minutes, or until it becomes thick and creamy in consistency. Remove from the heat; remove and discard the cinnamon stick and the lemon rind. Stir in the sugar until it is dissolved.

4 In a large bowl, beat the egg yolks until well blended. Gradually beat in the rice mixture until smooth. Stir frequently, to prevent the eggs curdling, until slightly cooled, then pour into a bowl or 6–8 individual glasses. Dust with ground cinnamon, decorate with the mint and fruit, and serve at room temperature.

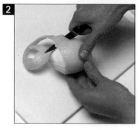

Flummery

This charming, traditional English dessert looks pretty and tastes delicious. It would be a good choice for a summer dinner party.

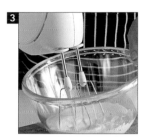

  10 mins
plus 2–3 hrs
cooling/chilling   1 hr

SERVES 4

INGREDIENTS

½ cup pudding rice

1¼ cups milk

1¼ cups heavy cream, plus extra
   for decoration

generous ¼ cup superfine sugar

1 tbsp grated lemon rind

1 tsp ground cinnamon, plus extra
   for dusting

whipped cream, to serve

1 Wash the rice well and place in the top of a double boiler with the milk, cream, sugar, lemon rind, and cinnamon. Set over a pan of gently simmering water, cover and cook, stirring occasionally, for 55 minutes, until most of the liquid has been absorbed and the rice is tender.

2 Remove the pan from the heat and transfer the rice mixture to a serving bowl or individual cups. Set aside to cool, then cover with plastic wrap and chill in the refrigerator for 2–3 hours, until set.

3 To serve, top the flummery with a swirl of whipped heavy cream, lightly dusted with ground cinnamon.

Kesari Kheer

This exotic dessert combines the flavor of cardamom, saffron, and pistachios. Decorate with silver leaf (varq).

40 mins   1 hr

SERVES 4–6

INGREDIENTS

2 tbsp clarified butter or pure ghee

⅓ cup basmati rice, rinsed and well drained

6¼ cups milk

½ cup sugar, or to taste

the seeds of 10–12 green cardamoms

½ cup golden raisins or raisins

generous pinch saffron strands,
    about ½ tsp, soaked in 2–3 tbsp milk

½ cup green pistachios, toasted lightly

⅔ cup heavy cream, whipped (optional)

ground cinnamon, for dusting

silver leaf (varq), to decorate (optional)

1 Melt the butter in a large, heavy-based pan over medium heat. Pour in the rice and cook, stirring almost constantly, for about 6 minutes, until the rice grains are translucent and a deep golden brown.

2 Pour in the milk and bring to a boil over high heat. Reduce the heat and simmer for about 30 minutes, stirring occasionally, until the milk has reduced by about half.

3 Add the sugar, cardamom seeds, and golden raisins and cook for about 20 minutes until reduced and thick. Stir in the saffron-milk mixture and simmer over low heat until as thick as possible, stirring almost constantly. Remove from the heat and stir in half the pistachios.

4 Place the pan in a larger pan of ice water and stir until cool. If using, stir in the cream, then spoon into a serving bowl and chill.

5 To serve, dust the top of the pudding with cinnamon. Sprinkle with the remaining pistachios. If using, decorate with pieces of silver leaf.

COOK'S TIP
Silver leaf (varq), which is edible, is available in some Asian or Indian food stores or specialty stores.

Passion Fruit Rice

This creamy rice pudding, adapted for the microwave, is spiced with cardamom, cinnamon, and bay leaf, and served with passion fruit.

1 hr 15 mins   30 mins

SERVES 4

INGREDIENTS

scant 1 cup jasmine fragrant rice

2½ cups milk

½ cup superfine sugar

6 cardamoms, split open

1 bay leaf

1 cinnamon stick

⅔ cup heavy cream, whipped

4 passion fruit

berries, to decorate

1 Place the jasmine fragrant rice in a large bowl with the milk, superfine sugar, cardamoms, bay leaf, and cinnamon stick. Cover and place in the microwave, cook on Medium power for 25–30 minutes, stirring occasionally. The rice should be just tender and have absorbed most of the milk. Add a little extra milk, if necessary.

2 Leave the rice to cool, still covered. Remove the bay leaf, cardamom husks, and cinnamon stick.

3 Gently fold the cream into the cooled rice mixture.

4 Halve the passion fruits and scoop out the centers into a bowl.

5 Layer the rice with the passion fruit in 4 tall glasses, finishing with a layer of passion fruit. Leave to chill in the refrigerator for 30 minutes.

6 Decorate the passion fruit rice with berries and serve immediately.

COOK'S TIP
If you are unable to obtain passion fruit, you can use a purée of another fruit of your choice, such as kiwi fruit, raspberry, or strawberry.

Tropical Fruit Rice Mold

A rice pudding with a twist. Light flakes of rice with a tang of pineapple and lime. You can serve it with any selection of your favorite fruits.

4 hrs 30 mins   25 mins

SERVES 8

INGREDIENTS

1 cup plus 2 tbsp short-grain or pudding rice, rinsed

3¾ cups skim milk

1 tbsp superfine sugar

4 tbsp white rum with coconut or unsweetened pineapple juice

¾ cup lowfat plain yogurt

14 oz/400 g canned pineapple pieces in natural juice, drained and chopped

1 tsp grated lime rind

1 tbsp lime juice

½ oz/15 g powdered gelatin dissolved in 3 tbsp very hot water

lime wedges, to decorate

mixed tropical fruits such as passion fruit, baby pineapple, papaya, mango, lime, star fruit, to serve

1 Place the rice and milk in a pan. Bring to the boil, then simmer gently, uncovered, for 20 minutes until the rice is soft and the milk is absorbed.

2 Stir the mixture occasionally and keep the heat low to prevent sticking. Transfer to a mixing bowl and leave to cool.

3 Stir the sugar, white rum with coconut or pineapple juice, yogurt, pineapple pieces, lime rind and juice into the rice, then fold in the gelatin mixture.

4 Rinse a 1½-quart nonstick ring mold with water and spoon in the rice mixture. Press down well and chill for 2 hours until firm.

5 To serve, loosen the rice from the mold with a small palette knife and invert on to a serving plate.

6 Decorate with lime wedges and fill the center of the rice ring with assorted tropical fruits.

COOK'S TIP

Try serving this dessert with a light sauce made from 1¼ cups tropical fruit or pineapple juice, heated gently then thickened with 2 teaspoons arrowroot.

Riz à l'Impératrice

A sublime combination of rice, cherry-flavored liqueur, dry fruits, and cream that is certain to win compliments.

30 mins plus 2–8 hrs chilling

40 mins

SERVES 6–8

INGREDIENTS

½ cup kirsch or other liqueur of your choice

4 oz/115 g candied or dry fruits, such as sour cherries, cranberries, blueberries, raisins, or candied peel

½ cup long-grain white rice

pinch of salt

3 cups milk

¼ cup superfine sugar

1 vanilla bean

½ oz/15 g powdered gelatin

¼ cup cold water

2 egg yolks, beaten lightly

1 cup heavy cream, whipped until soft peaks form

4 tbsp apricot jelly or preserve

candied cherries, to decorate

fruit coulis (optional), to serve

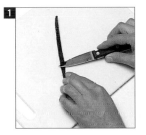

1 Split open the vanilla bean, scrape out the seeds, and reserve. Combine 2–3 tablespoons of the kirsch with the candied or dry fruits and set aside.

2 Bring a pan of water to a boil. Sprinkle in the rice and salt; simmer gently for 15 minutes or until the rice is just tender. Drain, rinse, and drain again.

3 Bring the milk and sugar to a boil in a large nonstick pan. Add the vanilla seeds and bean and stir in the rice. Reduce the heat to low and simmer, covered, until the rice is very tender and the milk reduced by about a third. Remove from the heat and discard the vanilla bean.

4 Soften the gelatin in the water in a heatproof bowl, then heat gently over a pan of hot water until it is completely dissolved.

5 Add about 2 tablespoons of the hot rice to the egg yolks and whisk to blend, then beat into the rice with the dissolved gelatin, until the mixture thickens slightly. Pour into a large mixing bowl. Place the bowl in a roasting pan half-filled with ice water and stir until starting to set.

6 Fold in the soaked fruits and cream. Stir until it starts to set again, then immediately pour into a rinsed 5–6¼-cup mold. Smooth the surface, cover, and chill for at least 2 hours or overnight.

7 Unmold the rice on to a serving plate. Heat the jelly with the remaining kirsch and 2 tablespoons of water to make a smooth glaze. Brush over the top of the unmolded rice. Decorate the dessert with the cherries and let stand for 15 minutes before serving with fruit coulis if liked.

Chocolate Dairy Wraps

Light chocolate sponge is wrapped around a dairy cream filling. These individual cakes can be served for dessert, if desired.

40 mins   6–8 mins

SERVES 6

INGREDIENTS

2 eggs

4 tbsp superfine sugar

⅓ cup all-purpose flour

1½ tbsp unsweetened cocoa

4 tbsp apricot jelly

⅔ cup heavy cream, whipped

confectioners' sugar, for dusting

1 Preheat the oven to 425°F/220°C. Line 2 cookie sheets with pieces of parchment paper. Whisk the eggs and sugar together until the mixture is very light and fluffy and the whisk leaves a trail when lifted.

2 Sift together the flour and unsweetened cocoa. Using a metal spoon or a spatula, gently fold it into the eggs and sugar in a figure-of-eight movement.

3 Drop rounded tablespoonfuls of the mixture on to the lined cookie sheets and spread them into oval shapes, allowing room for the cookies to spread during cooking.

4 Bake in the preheated oven for about 6–8 minutes, or until springy to the touch. Let cool on the cookie sheets.

5 When cold, slide the parchment paper with the cakes on to a damp dish towel and let stand until cold. Carefully remove the cakes from the dampened parchment paper. Spread the flat side of the cakes with apricot jelly, then spoon or pipe the whipped cream down the center of each one.

6 Fold the cakes in half and place them on a serving plate. Dust with a little confectioners' sugar and serve.

VARIATIONS

Fold 4 teaspoons crème de menthe or 2 oz/55 g melted chocolate into the cream for fabulous alternatives to plain cream.

Fruit & Fiber Layers

A good, hearty dessert, guaranteed to fill you up. Use your own favorite dry fruits in the compôte.

1 hrs plus
1 hr chilling

15 mins

SERVES 4

INGREDIENTS

½ cup no-soak dried apricots

½ cup no-soak dried prunes

½ cup no-soak dried peaches

2 cups dried apple

½ cup dried cherries

2 cups unsweetened apple juice

6 cardamoms

6 cloves

1 cinnamon stick, broken

1¼ cups lowfat plain yogurt

1 cup crunchy oat cereal

apricot slices, to decorate

1 Place the apricots, prunes, peaches, apples, and cherries in a pan and pour in the apple juice. Add the cardamoms, cloves, and cinnamon stick, bring to a boil, and simmer for 10–15 minutes until the fruits are plump and tender.

2 Remove and discard the spices from the fruits. Remove the pan from the heat and set aside to cool completely, then transfer the mixture to a bowl and chill in the refrigerator for 1 hour.

3 Spoon the compôte into 4 dessert glasses, layering it alternately with yogurt and oat cereal, finishing with the oat cereal on top.

4 Decorate each dessert with slices of apricot and serve immediately.

COOK'S TIP
Check the ingredients labels of dry fruits because several types have added sugar or are rolled in sugar and this will affect the sweetness of the dish that you use them in.

Raspberry Shortcake

For this lovely summery dessert, two crisp rounds of shortbread are sandwiched together with fresh raspberries and lightly whipped cream.

40 mins   15 mins

SERVES 8

INGREDIENTS

5 oz/140 g butter, cut into pieces, plus extra for greasing

1½ cups self-rising flour

scant ½ cup superfine sugar

1 egg yolk

1 tbsp rose water

all-purpose flour, for dusting

2½ cups whipping cream, whipped lightly

1⅓ cups raspberries, plus a few extra to decorate

TO DECORATE

confectioners' sugar

1 Preheat the oven to 375°F/190°C. Lightly grease 2 cookie sheets with a little butter.

2 To make the shortcake, sift the self-rising flour into a bowl. Add the butter and rub it into the flour with your fingertips until the mixture resembles fine bread crumbs.

3 Stir the sugar, egg yolk, and rose water into the mixture and bring together with your fingers to form a soft dough. Divide the dough in half.

4 Roll out each piece of dough to an 8-inch/20-cm round on a lightly floured work counter. Carefully lift each of them with the rolling pin on to the prepared cookie sheets. Gently crimp the edges of the dough with your finger.

5 Bake in the preheated oven for 15 minutes until lightly golden. Transfer the shortcakes to a wire rack and set aside to cool completely.

6 Mix the whipped cream with the raspberries and spoon the mixture on top of 1 of the shortcakes, spreading it out evenly. Top with the other shortcake round, dust with a little confectioners' sugar, and decorate with the extra raspberries.

COOK'S TIP

The shortcake can be made a few days in advance and stored in an airtight container until required.

Cherry & Chocolate Meringue

A luscious, sticky chocolate meringue base smothered in cream and sticky cherries.

30 mins plus
45 mins cooling   1 hr 30 mins

SERVES 4

INGREDIENTS

4 large egg whites

1 cup superfine sugar

1 tsp cornstarch, sifted

1 tsp white wine vinegar

1 tbsp unsweetened cocoa

5 oz/150 g semisweet chocolate, chopped

TOPPING

1¾ cups heavy cream

¼ cup confectioners' sugar, sifted

4 tbsp maple syrup

4 tbsp sweet butter

1 lb/450 g black cherries

semisweet chocolate caraque (see page 9),
    to decorate

1 Preheat the oven to 275°F/140°C. Line a cookie sheet with parchment paper.

2 Whisk the egg whites until stiff. Gradually add the sugar, whisk until stiff and shiny. Fold in the cornstarch, vinegar, cocoa, and chocolate. Spread the meringue on to the cookie sheet to form a 9½-inch/24-cm disk. Make a hollow in the center. Bake for 1½ hours.

3 Turn off the oven and leave the meringue in the oven for 45 minutes.

4 Whisk the cream and confectioners' sugar until stiff, then chill in the refrigerator. Pit most of the cherries, reserving a few whole. Melt the maple syrup with the butter in a skillet and stir in the pitted cherries to coat, then set aside.

5 Make the chocolate caraque (see page 9) and set aside until you are ready to assemble the meringue. Peel off the paper from the meringue when cold.

6 To serve, put the meringue on a dish. Spoon the cream into the center, pile on the cherries, using the whole ones around the edge. Top with the caraque.

Pavlova

This fruit meringue was created for Anna Pavlova, and it looks very impressive. Use fruits of your choice to make a colorful display.

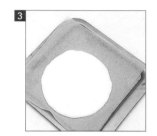
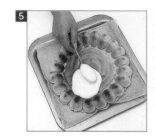

1 hr 30 mins   1 hr 30 mins

SERVES 8

INGREDIENTS

6 egg whites

½ tsp cream of tartar

1 cup superfine sugar

1 tsp vanilla extract

1¼ cups whipping cream

2½ cups strawberries, hulled and halved

3 tbsp orange-flavored liqueur

fruit of your choice, to decorate

1 Preheat the oven to 275°F/140°C for a chewy meringue, or 225°F/110°C for a drier meringue. Line a cookie sheet with parchment paper and mark out a circle to fit your serving plate. The recipe makes enough meringue for a 12-inch/30-cm circle.

2 Whisk the egg whites and cream of tartar together until stiff. Gradually beat in the superfine sugar and vanilla extract. Whisk well until glossy and stiff.

3 Either spoon or pipe the meringue mixture into the marked circle, in an even layer, slightly raised at the edges.

COOK'S TIP

If you like a dry meringue, you can also leave it in the oven on the lowest setting overnight. However, do not use this technique with a gas oven—but in an electric oven or solid fuel cooker it would be fine.

4 Baking the meringue depends on your preference. If you like a soft chewy meringue, bake in the preheated oven for about 1½ hours, until dry but slightly soft in the center, or for 3 hours, until dry.

5 Before serving, whip the cream to a piping consistency, and either spoon or pipe on to the meringue base, leaving a border of meringue all around the edge.

6 Stir the strawberries and liqueur together and spoon on to the cream. Decorate with fruit of your choice.

Brown Sugar Pavlovas

This simple combination of fudgy meringue topped with mascarpone and raspberries is the perfect finale to any meal.

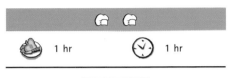

🍰 1 hr   🕐 1 hr

SERVES 4

INGREDIENTS

2 large egg whites

1 tsp cornstarch

1 tsp raspberry vinegar

½ cup light brown sugar, crushed free of lumps

2 tbsp rcd currant jelly

2 tbsp unsweetened orange juice

¾ cup lowfat mascarpone cheese

1 cup raspberries, thawed if frozen

rose-scented geranium leaves, to decorate (optional)

1 Preheat the oven to 300°F/150°C. Line a large cookie sheet with parchment paper. Whisk the egg whites until very stiff and dry. Gently fold in the cornstarch and vinegar.

2 Gradually whisk in the sugar, a spoonful at a time, until the mixture is thick and glossy.

3 Divide the mixture into 4 and spoon on to the prepared cookie sheet, spaced well apart. Smooth each heap into a circle, about 4 inches/10 cm in diameter, and bake in the preheated oven for 40–45 minutes until crisp and a light golden-brown color. Let cool on the cookie sheet.

4 Place the red currant jelly and orange juice in a small pan and heat, stirring, until melted. Let cool for 10 minutes.

5 Using a spatula, carefully remove each pavlova from the parchment paper and transfer to a serving plate. Top with the mascarpone and the raspberries. Glaze the fruit with the red currant jelly mixture, and decorate with the rose-scented geranium leaves (if using).

COOK'S TIP
Make a large pavlova by forming the meringue into a circle, measuring 7 inches/18 cm across, on a lined cookie sheet, and baking it for 1 hour.

Strawberry Meringues

The combination of aromatic strawberries and rose water with crisp caramelized sugar meringues makes this a truly irresistible dessert.

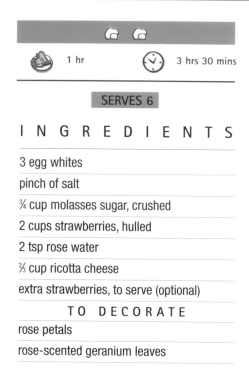

1 hr   3 hrs 30 mins

SERVES 6

INGREDIENTS

3 egg whites

pinch of salt

¾ cup molasses sugar, crushed

2 cups strawberries, hulled

2 tsp rose water

⅔ cup ricotta cheese

extra strawberries, to serve (optional)

TO DECORATE

rose petals

rose-scented geranium leaves

1 Preheat the oven to 250°F/120°C. In a large grease-free bowl, whisk the egg whites with the salt until very stiff and dry. Gradually whisk in the sugar, a spoonful at a time, until the mixture is stiff again.

2 Line a cookie sheet with parchment paper and drop 12 tablespoonfuls of the meringue mixture on to it. Bake in the preheated oven for 3–3½ hours, until completely dried out and crisp. Set aside to cool.

3 Reserve ½ cup of the strawberries. Place the remaining strawberries in a blender or food processor and blend for a few seconds until smooth.

4 Alternatively, mash the strawberries with a fork and press through a strainer to form a purée. Stir in the rose water. Chill until required.

5 Slice the reserved strawberries lengthwise. Sandwich the meringues together with ricotta and strawberries.

6 To serve, spoon the strawberry rose purée on to 6 serving plates and top with a meringue.

7 Decorate with rose petals and rose-scented geranium leaves, and serve with extra strawberries (if using).

Raspberry Meringue

This meringue makes an easy yet elegant dessert, perfect for a celebration dinner.

15 mins plus
2 hrs 15 mins
cooling/chilling

30 mins

SERVES 4

INGREDIENTS

6 egg whites

generous 1 cup superfine sugar

generous 1 cup ground almonds

butter, for greasing

3¾ cups heavy cream

5 tbsp confectioners' sugar

2¼ cups raspberries

TO DECORATE

whole raspberries

fresh mint leaves

1 Preheat the oven to 300°F/150°C. Put the egg whites into a bowl and whisk until stiff peaks form. Gradually whisk in the superfine sugar, then fold in the almonds.

2 Grease 2 x 8-inch/20-cm layer cake pans with butter and line with waxed paper. Divide the egg mixture among the 2 pans and smooth the surfaces. Transfer to the preheated oven and bake for 30 minutes. Remove from the oven and let cool on a wire rack.

3 Put the cream into a bowl, add the confectioners' sugar, and mix well. Put one of the meringues on a cake stand or serving plate and spread over a generous layer of cream. Cover with a generous layer of raspberries and then top with the remaining meringue. Spread the remaining cream evenly over the top of the cake, and chill in the refrigerator for at least 2 hours.

4 Remove from the refrigerator, decorate with the remaining raspberries and fresh mint leaves, and serve.

Satsuma & Pecan Pavlova

Make this spectacular dessert for the perfect way to round off a special occasion. You can make the meringue base well in advance.

2 hrs 15 mins   3 hrs

SERVES 8

INGREDIENTS

4 egg whites

1 cup light muscovado sugar

1¼ pint cups heavy or whipping cream

½ cup pecans

4 satsumas, peeled

1 passion fruit or pomegranate

1 Preheat the oven to 275°F/140°C. Line 2 cookie sheets with parchment paper or waxed paper. Draw a 9-inch/23-cm circle on one of them.

2 Whisk the egg whites in a large grease-free bowl until stiff. Add the sugar gradually, continuing to beat until the mixture is very glossy.

3 Pipe or spoon a layer of meringue mixture on to the circle marked on the parchment paper; then pipe large rosettes or place spoonfuls on top of the meringue's outer edge. Pipe any remaining meringue mixture in tiny rosettes on the second cookie sheet.

4 Bake in the preheated oven for 2–3 hours, making sure that the oven is well-ventilated by using a folded dish towel to keep the door slightly open. Remove from the oven and let cool completely. When cold, peel off the parchment paper carefully.

5 Whip the heavy or whipping cream in a large chilled bowl until thick. Spoon about one-third into a piping bag, fitted with a star tip. Reserve a few pecans and 1 satsuma for decoration. Chop the remaining nuts and fruit, and fold into the remaining cream.

6 Pile on top of the meringue base and decorate with the tiny meringue rosettes, piped cream, segments of satsuma, and pecans. Scoop the seeds from the passion fruit or pomegranate with a teaspoon and sprinkle them on top.

Black Forest Trifle

Try all the delightful flavors of a Black Forest gâteau in this new guise—the results are stunning.

15 mins plus 1 hr chilling

10 mins

SERVES 6

INGREDIENTS

6 thin slices chocolate buttercream roll

1 lb 12 oz/800 g canned black cherries

2 tbsp kirsch

1 tbsp cornstarch

2 tbsp superfine sugar

generous 1¾ cups milk

3 egg yolks

1 egg

2¾ oz/75 g semisweet chocolate

1¼ cups heavy cream, whipped lightly

TO DECORATE

chocolate caraque (see page 9)

maraschino cherries (optional)

1 Place the slices of chocolate roll in the bottom of a glass serving bowl.

2 Drain the black cherries, reserving 6 tablespoons of the juice. Place the cherries and the reserved juice on top of the cake. Sprinkle with the kirsch.

3 In a heatproof bowl, mix the cornstarch and superfine sugar. Stir in enough milk to mix to a smooth paste. Beat in the egg yolks and the whole egg.

4 Heat the remaining milk in a small pan until almost boiling, then gradually pour it on to the egg mixture, whisking well until it is combined.

5 Set the bowl over a pan of hot water and cook over low heat until the custard thickens, stirring. Add the chocolate and stir until melted.

6 Pour the chocolate custard over the cherries and cool. When cold, spread the cream over the custard, swirling with the back of a spoon. Chill before decorating.

7 Decorate with chocolate caraque and whole maraschino cherries (if using) before serving.

Chocolate Trifle

This is a wonderful dessert for a party and makes a change from a conventional trifle.

45 mins plus
2 hrs chilling

10 mins

SERVES 8

INGREDIENTS

10 oz/280 g store-bought chocolate loaf cake

3–4 tbsp seedless raspberry jelly

4 tbsp amaretto

9 oz/250 g package frozen mixed red fruits, thawed

CHOCOLATE CUSTARD

6 egg yolks

¼ cup golden superfine sugar

1 tbsp cornstarch

generous 2 cups milk

2 oz/55 g semisweet chocolate, broken into pieces

TOPPING

1 cup heavy cream

1 tbsp golden superfine sugar

½ tsp vanilla extract

ready-made chocolate truffles, to decorate

COOK'S TIP

Frozen packages of fruit are available in most supermarkets. Sometimes they are described as "summer fruits" or "fruits of the forest." Try to find a variety that includes cherries.

1 Cut the cake into slices and make "sandwiches" with the raspberry jelly. Cut the "sandwiches" into cubes and place in a large glass serving bowl. Sprinkle with amaretto. Spread the fruit over the cake.

2 To make the custard, put the egg yolks and sugar in a bowl and whisk until thick and pale. Stir in the cornstarch. Put the milk in a pan and heat until almost boiling. Pour on to the yolk mixture, stirring. Return the mixture to the pan and

bring just to a boil, stirring constantly, until it thickens. Remove from the heat and let cool slightly. Put the chocolate in a heatproof bowl set over a pan of gently simmering water until melted, then add to the custard. Pour over the cake and fruit. Cool, cover, and chill for 2 hours to set.

3 Put the cream in a bowl and whip until soft peaks form. Beat in the sugar and vanilla. Spoon over the trifle. Decorate with truffles and chill until ready to serve.

Chocolate & Orange Trifle

The slight tartness of satsumas beautifully counterbalances the richness of this trifle, but you could use clementines if preferred.

25 mins plus 1 hr 30 mins chilling	15 mins

SERVES 6

INGREDIENTS

6 slices sponge cake

2 large chocolate coconut macaroons, crumbled

4 tbsp sweet sherry

8 satsumas

7 oz/200 g semisweet chocolate, broken into pieces

2 egg yolks

2 tbsp superfine sugar

2 tbsp cornstarch

scant 1 cup milk

generous 1 cup mascarpone cheese

1 cup heavy cream

TO DECORATE

marbled chocolate shapes (see page 821)

10–12 satsuma segments

1 Break up the sponge cake slices and place in a large glass serving dish. Sprinkle the crumbled macaroons on top, then sprinkle with the sherry. Squeeze the juice from 2 of the satsumas and sprinkle it over the crumbled macaroons. Peel and segment the remaining satsumas and arrange them in the dish.

2 Put the chocolate in a heatproof bowl set over a pan of gently simmering water. Stir over low heat until melted and smooth. Remove from the heat and let cool completely.

3 In a separate bowl, mix together the egg yolks, sugar, and cornstarch to make a smooth paste. Bring the milk to just below boiling point in a small pan. Remove from the heat and pour it into the egg yolk mixture, stirring constantly. Return the custard to a clean pan and cook over low heat, stirring constantly, until thickened and smooth. Return to the bowl, then stir in the mascarpone cheese until thoroughly combined. Stir in the cooled melted chocolate. Spread the chocolate custard evenly over the satsuma segments and transfer to the refrigerator to chill for 1 hour until set.

4 Whip the cream until thick, then spread it over the top of the trifle, swirling it with the back of a spoon. Decorate with marbled chocolate shapes and satsuma segments.

Almond Trifles

Amaretti cookies made with ground almonds have a high fat content. Use cookies made from apricot kernels for a lower fat content.

15 mins plus
1 hr standing/
cooling

0 mins

SERVES 4

INGREDIENTS

8 amaretti cookies

4 tbsp brandy or amaretto

1⅓ cups raspberries

1¼ cups lowfat custard

1¼ cups lowfat plain thick yogurt

1 tsp almond extract

2 tbsp slivered almonds, toasted

1 tsp unsweetened cocoa

1 Place the cookies in a mixing bowl and using the end of a rolling pin, carefully crush them into small pieces.

2 Divide the crushed cookies among 4 serving glasses. Sprinkle over the brandy or amaretto and set aside for about 30 minutes to soften.

3 Top with a layer of raspberries and spoon over enough custard just to cover the fruit.

4 Combine the yogurt with the almond extract and spoon the mixture over the custard, smoothing the surface. Chill in the refrigerator for about 30 minutes.

5 Sprinkle with the toasted almonds and dust with unsweetened cocoa. Decorate the trifles with extra fruit, if liked, and serve immediately.

VARIATION
Try this trifle with assorted summer fruits. If they are a frozen mix, use them frozen so that as they thaw the juices soak into the cookie base—it will taste delicious.

Sherry Trifle

This is a classic, timeless, and elegant dessert which is always a dinner-party favorite.

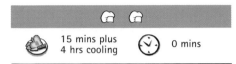

15 mins plus
4 hrs cooling

0 mins

SERVES 4

INGREDIENTS

FRUIT LAYER

6 slices sponge cake

2 tbsp strawberry jelly

6 large strawberries, hulled and sliced

2 bananas, peeled and sliced

14 oz/400 g canned sliced peaches, drained

6 tbsp sherry

CUSTARD LAYER

generous 1¼ cups heavy cream

1 tsp vanilla extract

3 egg yolks

4 tbsp superfine sugar

TOPPING

1 cup heavy cream

2 tbsp superfine sugar

chopped mixed nuts, to decorate

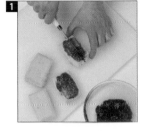

1 To make the fruit layer, spread the sponge cake with jelly and cut into bite-size pieces. Arrange them in the bottom of a large glass serving bowl or 4 serving glasses and scatter over the strawberries, bananas, and peaches. Pour over the sherry and set aside.

2 To make the custard, put the cream and vanilla into a pan and bring almost to a boil over low heat. Meanwhile, put the egg yolks and sugar into a bowl and whisk together well. Remove the cream from the heat and gradually stir into the egg mixture. Return the mixture to the pan and warm over low heat, stirring, until thickened. Remove the custard from the heat and let cool for at least 20 minutes, then pour it evenly over the fruit layer. Cover with plastic wrap and chill for 2½ hours.

3 Remove the trifle from the refrigerator. Whip together the cream and sugar, then spread it evenly over the custard layer. Scatter over the chopped mixed nuts, then cover again with plastic wrap and chill for an additional 1½ hours. Serve chilled.

Festive Trifle

It is quite unusual to use vodka in desserts, but it works well, especially with raspberries and cherries. Substitute sherry, if you prefer.

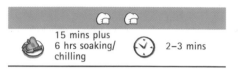

15 mins plus
6 hrs soaking/
chilling

2–3 mins

SERVES 4

INGREDIENTS

FRUIT LAYER

3½ oz/100 g trifle sponges

⅔ cup raspberry jelly

3–4 tbsp vodka or sherry

5½ oz/150 g frozen raspberries, thawed

14 oz/400 g mixed fruit, frozen or canned

CUSTARD LAYER

6 egg yolks

¼ cup superfine sugar

generous 2 cups milk

1 tsp vanilla extract

TOPPING

1¼ cups mascarpone cheese

1–2 tbsp superfine sugar

toasted mixed nuts, chopped, to decorate

1 Spread the trifle sponges with jelly, cut them into bite-size cubes, and arrange in the bottom of a large glass serving bowl. Pour over the vodka or sherry and let stand for 30 minutes.

2 Combine the raspberries and other fruits and place on the sponges. Cover with plastic wrap and chill for 30 minutes.

3 To make the custard, put the egg yolks and sugar into a bowl and whisk together. Pour the milk into a pan and warm gently over low heat. Remove from the heat, stir into the egg mixture, then return it all to the pan and stir constantly

over low heat until thickened. Do not boil. Remove from the heat, pour into a bowl, and stir in the vanilla. Cool for 1 hour. Spread the custard over the trifle, cover with plastic wrap, and chill for 2 hours.

4 For the topping, turn the mascarpone into a bowl and beat in sugar to taste. Spread over the trifle, then scatter over the nuts. Cover with plastic wrap and chill for 2 hours before serving.

Sticky Sesame Bananas

These tasty morsels are a real treat. Pieces of banana are dipped in caramel and then sprinkled with sesame seeds.

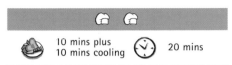

10 mins plus
10 mins cooling

20 mins

SERVES 4

INGREDIENTS

4 ripe medium bananas

3 tbsp lemon juice

generous 1 cup superfine sugar

4 tbsp cold water

2 tbsp sesame seeds

⅔ cup lowfat plain yogurt

1 tbsp confectioners' sugar

1 tsp vanilla extract

TO DECORATE

shredded lemon rind

shredded lime rind

1 Peel the bananas and cut into 2-inch/ 5-cm pieces. Place the banana pieces in a bowl, spoon over the lemon juice, and stir well to coat—this will help prevent the bananas discoloring.

2 Place the sugar and water in a small pan and heat gently, stirring constantly, until the sugar dissolves. Bring to a boil and cook for 5–6 minutes, until the mixture turns golden brown.

3 Meanwhile, drain the bananas and blot with paper towels to dry. Line a cookie sheet or cutting board with parchment paper and arrange the bananas, spaced well apart, on top.

4 When the caramel is ready, drizzle it over the bananas, working quickly because the caramel sets almost instantly. Sprinkle the sesame seeds over the caramelized bananas and set aside to cool for 10 minutes.

5 Combine the yogurt, confectioners' sugar, and vanilla extract.

6 Peel the bananas away from the parchment paper and arrange on serving plates.

7 Serve the yogurt as a dip, decorated with the shredded lemon and lime rind.

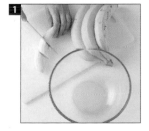

Caramelized Oranges

The secret of these oranges is to let them marinate in the syrup for at least 3 hours, and preferably up to 2 days, so the flavors amalgamate.

15 mins plus at least 3 hrs chilling

20 mins

SERVES 6

I N G R E D I E N T S

6 large oranges

1 cup granulated sugar

1 cup water

6 cloves (optional)

2–4 tbsp orange-flavored liqueur

1 Using a citrus zester or potato peeler, pare the rind from 2 of the oranges in narrow strips without any white pith attached. If using a potato peeler, cut the peel into very thin julienne strips.

2 Put the strips into a small pan and barely cover with water. Bring to a boil and simmer for 5 minutes. Drain the strips and reserve the water.

3 Cut away all the white pith and peel from the remaining oranges using a very sharp knife. Then cut horizontally into 4 slices. Reassemble the oranges and hold in place with wooden toothpicks. Stand in a heatproof dish.

4 Put the sugar and water into a heavy-based pan with the cloves (if using). Bring to a boil and simmer gently until the sugar has dissolved, then boil hard without stirring until the syrup thickens and starts to color. Continue to cook until a light golden brown, then quickly remove from the heat and carefully pour in the reserved orange rind liquid.

5 Place over gentle heat until the caramel has fully dissolved again, then remove from the heat and add the liqueur. Pour over the oranges.

6 Sprinkle the orange strips over the oranges, cover with plastic wrap, and leave until cold. Chill for at least 3 hours and preferably for 24–48 hours before serving. If time allows, spoon the syrup over the oranges several times while they are marinating. Discard the toothpicks before serving.

Aztec Oranges

Simplicity itself, this refreshing orange dessert is hard to beat and is the perfect follow-up to a hearty, spiced entrée.

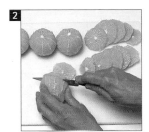

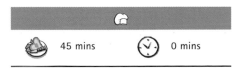

45 mins

0 mins

SERVES 4–6

INGREDIENTS

6 oranges

1 lime

2 tbsp tequila

2 tbsp orange-flavored liqueur

brown sugar, to taste

fine lime rind strips, to decorate
(see Cook's Tip)

1 Using a sharp knife, cut a slice off the top and bottom of the oranges, then remove the peel and pith, cutting downward and taking care to retain the shape of the oranges.

2 Holding the oranges on their side, cut them horizontally into slices.

3 Place the oranges in a bowl. Cut the lime in half and squeeze over the oranges. Sprinkle with the tequila and liqueur, then sprinkle with sugar to taste.

4 Cover with plastic wrap and chill in the refrigerator until ready to serve, then transfer to a serving dish, and decorate with lime strips.

COOK'S TIP
To make the decoration, finely pare the rind from a lime using a vegetable peeler, then cut into thin strips. Blanch in boiling water for 2 minutes. Drain and rinse under cold running water. Drain again and pat dry with paper towels.

Minted Pears

Choose firm but ripe pears that will hold their shape when poached and leave the stalk intact after peeling for an attractive appearance.

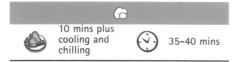

10 mins plus cooling and chilling

35–40 mins

SERVES 4

INGREDIENTS

4 large pears, peeled

4 tbsp superfine sugar

4 tbsp honey

2 tbsp green crème de menthe

fresh mint sprigs, to decorate

1 Stand the pears upright in a heavy-based pan and add enough water to cover. Bring to a boil, reduce the heat, cover and simmer for 25–30 minutes, until tender. Pour away half the water and add the sugar to the pan. Simmer for an additional 10 minutes.

2 Transfer the pears to a bowl using a slotted spoon. Measure ⅔ cup of the cooking water. Stir in the honey and crème de menthe. Pour the syrup over the pears.

3 Set the pears aside to cool, then cover with plastic wrap and chill in the refrigerator for 1–2 hours. Transfer the pears to individual serving bowls, spoon over the mint syrup, and serve, decorated with fresh mint sprigs.

Mangoes in Syrup

A simple, fresh-tasting fruit dessert to round off a rich meal perfectly.
Serve the mango lightly chilled.

15 mins   5 mins

SERVES 4

INGREDIENTS

2 large ripe mangoes

1 lime

1 lemongrass stem, chopped

3 tbsp superfine sugar

1 Peel the mangoes, then cut away the flesh from either side of the large pits. Slice the flesh into long, thin slices and arrange them in a large, chilled serving dish.

2 Remove a few shreds of the rind from the lime and reserve for decoration, then cut the lime in half and squeeze out the juice.

3 Place the lime juice in a small pan with the lemongrass and sugar. Heat gently, without boiling, until the sugar is completely dissolved. Remove from the heat and set aside to cool completely.

4 Strain the cooled syrup into a pitcher and pour evenly over the mango slices. Sprinkle with the lime rind strips, cover, and chill before serving.

COOK'S TIP
To serve this dessert on a hot day, particularly if it is to stand for a while, place the dish on a bed of crushed ice to keep the fruit and syrup chilled.

Poached Peaches

Soaking the peaches overnight is an old Turkish tip to prevent the fruit becoming too soft and falling apart while they are being poached.

15 mins plus
24 hrs chilling

10 mins

SERVES 4–6

INGREDIENTS

8–12 ripe peaches

1 large lime

2 cups fruity dry white wine

1 tbsp black peppercorns, crushed lightly

3-inch/7.5-cm cinnamon stick, halved

finely pared rind of 1 unwaxed lemon

½ cup superfine sugar

fresh mint sprigs, to decorate

AMARETTO-MASCARPONE CREAM

2 tbsp amaretto

generous 1 cup mascarpone cheese

1 Fill a large bowl with ice water. Bring a large pan of water to a boil. Add the peaches and cook for 1 minute. Using a slotted spoon, immediately transfer the peaches to the ice water to stop the cooking process.

2 Squeeze the juice from the lime into a bowl of water. Peel the peaches, then quarter each, and remove the pit. Drop the fruit into the lime water as it is prepared. Cover and let chill in the refrigerator for 24 hours.

3 Meanwhile, make the amaretto-mascarpone cream. Stir the amaretto into the mascarpone cheese until thoroughly incorporated, cover, and chill.

4 Place the wine, peppercorns, cinnamon, lemon rind, and sugar in a pan over medium-high heat and stir until the sugar dissolves.

5 Boil the syrup for 2 minutes then reduce to a simmer. Remove the peaches from the refrigerator, add them to the syrup. Poach for 2 minutes or until tender—they should not be falling apart.

6 Using a slotted spoon, transfer the peaches to a bowl. Bring the syrup to a boil and continue boiling until thickened and reduced to about ½ cup. Pour the syrup into a heatproof bowl and set aside to cool. When cool, pour over the peaches. Cover and chill until required. To serve, decorate with mint sprigs.

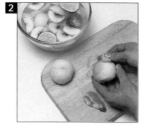

Figs with Orange Blossom

Luscious, sweet fresh figs are piled high on market stalls throughout the Mediterranean during the summer.

🍰 10 mins   🕐 5 mins

SERVES 4

INGREDIENTS

8 large fresh figs

4 large fresh fig leaves, rinsed and dried

ORANGE-BLOSSOM CREAM

½ cup crème fraîche (see page 9), or sour cream

4 tbsp orange flower water

1 tsp orange-blossom honey

finely grated rind of ½ orange

2 tbsp slivered almonds, to decorate (optional)

1 If you are making the crème fraîche at home, start at least a day ahead (see page 9).

2 To toast the almonds for the decoration, place in a dry skillet over medium heat and stir until lightly browned. Take care that the almonds do not burn. Immediately tip them out of the pan and set aside.

3 To make the orange-blossom cream, put the crème fraîche or sour cream in a small bowl and stir in 4 tablespoons of orange flower water, with the honey and the orange rind. Taste and add a little extra orange flower water if necessary, and sweeten with a little more honey, if liked.

4 To serve, cut the stems off the figs, but do not peel them. Stand the figs upright with the pointed end upward. Cut each into quarters without cutting all the way through, so you can open them out into attractive "flowers."

5 If you are using fig leaves, place one in the center of each serving plate. Arrange 2 figs on top of each leaf, and spoon a small amount of the orange-flavored cream alongside them. Sprinkle the cream with the toasted slivered almonds, if desired, just before serving.

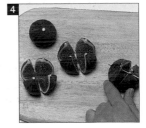

Balsamic Strawberries

Generations of Italian cooks have known that the unlikely combination of freshly ground black pepper and ripe, juicy strawberries is fantastic.

| 30 mins plus 4 hrs chilling | 0 mins |

SERVES 4–6

INGREDIENTS

1 lb/450 g fresh strawberries

2–3 tbsp balsamic vinegar

pepper

fresh mint leaves, torn, plus extra to decorate (optional)

½–¾ cup mascarpone cheese

1 Wipe the strawberries with a damp cloth, rather than rinsing them, so they do not become soggy. Using a paring knife, cut off the green stalks at the top and use the tip of the knife to remove the core or hull.

2 Cut each strawberry in half length-wise or into quarters if large. Transfer to a bowl.

3 Add the balsamic vinegar, allowing ½ tablespoon per person. Add several twists of ground black pepper, then gently stir together. Cover with plastic wrap and chill for up to 4 hours.

4 Just before serving, stir in torn mint leaves to taste. Spoon the mascarpone cheese into bowls and the berries on top. Decorate with a few mint leaves, if wished. Sprinkle with extra pepper to taste.

COOK'S TIP

This is most enjoyable when it is made with the best-quality balsamic vinegar, one that has aged slowly and has turned thick and syrupy. Unfortunately, the genuine mixture is always expensive. Less expensive versions are artificially sweetened and colored with caramel.

Autumn Fruit Bread Pudding

This is like a summer pudding, but it uses fruits which appear later in the year, such as apples, pears, and blackberries, as a succulent filling.

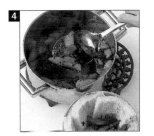

12 hrs   10 mins

SERVES 8

INGREDIENTS

4 cups mixed blackberries, chopped apples, chopped pears

¾ cup brown sugar

1 tsp ground cinnamon

8 oz/225 g white bread, sliced thinly, crusts removed

scant ½ cup water

1 Place the prepared fruit in a large pan with the brown sugar, cinnamon, and scant ½ cup water, stir, and bring to a boil.

2 Reduce the heat and simmer for 5–10 minutes so that the fruits soften but still hold their shape.

3 Meanwhile, line the base and sides of a 3³/₄-cup pudding bowl with the bread slices, ensuring that there are no gaps between the pieces of bread.

4 Spoon the fruit into the center of the bread-lined bowl and cover the fruit with the remaining bread.

5 Place a saucer on top of the bread and weight it down. Let the pudding chill in the refrigerator overnight.

6 Turn the pudding out on to a serving plate and serve immediately.

VARIATION
You can use thin slices of plain sponge cake instead of the sliced bread. The sponge will turn a pinkish color from the fruit juices and the brown edges of the cake will form an attractive pattern of irregular brown lines.

Winter Desserts

An interesting alternative to the familiar and ever-popular summer dessert that uses dry fruits and a tasty malt loaf.

40 mins plus
8 hrs chilling

15 mins

SERVES 4

INGREDIENTS

11½ oz/325 g fruit malt loaf

scant ¾ cup no-soak dried apricots,
   chopped coarsely

6 cups coarsely chopped dried apple

generous 1¾ cups orange juice

1 tsp grated orange rind,
   plus extra to decorate

2 tbsp orange-flavored liqueur

lowfat crème fraîche (see page 9)
   or lowfat natural yogurt, to serve

1 Cut the malt loaf into ½-inch/5-mm thick slices.

2 Place the apricots, apple, and orange juice in a pan. Bring to a boil, then simmer for 10 minutes. Remove the fruit, using a slotted spoon, and reserve the liquid. Place the fruit in a dish and set aside to cool. Stir in the orange rind and orange-flavored liqueur.

3 Line 4 x ¾-cup bowls or ramekins with parchment paper.

4 Cut 4 circles from the malt loaf slices to fit the tops of the molds and cut the remaining slices to line them.

5 Soak the malt loaf slices in the reserved fruit syrup, then arrange around the base and sides of the molds. Trim away any crusts which overhang the edges. Fill the centers with the chopped

fruit, pressing down well, and place the malt loaf circles on top.

6 Cover with parchment paper and weigh each bowl down with an 8-oz/225-g weight or a food can. Chill in the refrigerator overnight.

7 Remove the weight and parchment paper. Carefully turn the puddings out on to 4 serving plates. Remove the parchment paper.

8 Decorate with orange rind and serve with lowfat crème fraîche or yogurt.

Orchard Fruits Bristol

An elegant fruit salad of poached pears and apples, oranges, and strawberries in a wine and caramel syrup topped with crumbled caramel.

🍰🍰🍰🍰

🍧 50 mins   🕐 20 mins

SERVES 4

INGREDIENTS

4 oranges

generous ¾ cup granulated sugar

4 tbsp water

⅔ cup white wine

4 firm pears

4 dessert apples

1 cup strawberries

1   Pare the rind thinly from 1 orange and cut into narrow strips. Cook in the minimum of boiling water for 3–4 minutes until tender. Drain and reserve the cooking liquid. Squeeze the juice from this and 1 other orange.

2   Lay a sheet of parchment paper on a cookie sheet or cutting board.

3   Heat the sugar gently in a pan until it melts, then continue without stirring until it turns a pale golden brown. Pour half the caramel quickly on to the parchment paper and set aside to set.

4   Add the water and squeezed orange juice immediately to the caramel left in the pan with ⅔ cup of the reserved cooking liquid. Heat until it melts, then add the wine, and remove the pan from the heat.

5   Peel, core, and slice the pears and apples thickly (you can leave the apple skins on, if you prefer) and add to the caramel syrup. Bring gently to a boil and simmer for 3–4 minutes until just starting to soften—they should still be firm in the center. Transfer the pears and apples to a bowl.

6   Cut away the peel and pith from the remaining oranges and either ease out the segments or cut into slices, discarding any pits. Add to the other fruits. Hull the strawberries and halve, quarter, or slice thickly, depending on the size, and add to the other fruits.

7   Add the orange rind strips to the syrup and return to a boil for 1 minute, then pour over the fruits. Set aside until cold, then break up the caramel and sprinkle it over the fruit. Cover and chill until ready to serve.

Oranges & Strawberries

Ideal as a summery dessert, this dish can also be served as a fresh fruit dish with brunch. The oranges enhance the delicate flavor of the berries.

45 mins   0 mins

SERVES 4

INGREDIENTS

3 sweet oranges

2 cups strawberries

grated rind and juice of 1 lime

1–2 tbsp superfine sugar

1 fresh mint sprig, to decorate

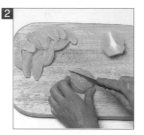

1 Using a sharp knife, cut a slice off the top and bottom of the oranges, then remove the peel and all the pith, cutting downward and taking care to retain the shape of the oranges.

2 Using a small sharp knife, cut down between the membranes of the oranges to remove the segments. Discard the membranes.

3 Hull the strawberries, pulling the leaves off with a pinching action. Cut into slices, along the length of the strawberries.

VARIATION
An optional hint of orange-flavored liqueur is delicious on this—reduce or omit the sugar. You can replace the oranges with mangoes, and the strawberries with blackberries, for a dramatically colored dessert.

4 Put the oranges and strawberries in a bowl, then sprinkle with the lime rind, lime juice, and sugar. Chill in the refrigerator until ready to serve.

5 To serve, transfer to a serving bowl and decorate the dish with the fresh mint sprig.

Oranges in Spiced Caramel

This flavorful and refreshing dessert is suitable to serve at the end of dinner in summer or winter.

15 mins   10 mins

SERVES 4

I N G R E D I E N T S

4 large juicy oranges

4–6 tbsp shelled pistachios, chopped, to decorate

S P I C E D   C A R A M E L

1¼ cups superfine sugar

5 black peppercorns, crushed lightly

4 cloves

1 green cardamom, crushed lightly

1¼ cups water

1 To make the spiced caramel, put the sugar, peppercorns, cloves, cardamom, and ⅔ cup of the water in a pan and stir over medium heat to dissolve the sugar. When it has dissolved, increase the heat, and boil, without stirring, until the syrup thickens and turns a deep caramel color. Use a wet pastry brush to brush the syrup down from the sides of the pan if necessary.

2 Carefully pour in an additional ⅔ cup water, standing back because it will splatter. Remove from the heat and, using a long-handled wooden spoon, stir until all the caramel has dissolved. Let cool.

3 Pare off the orange rind and pith, cutting carefully so that the oranges retain their shape. Leave the oranges whole, or, working over a bowl, cut into segments, cutting the flesh away from the membranes.

4 Pour over the caramel syrup with the spices and stir together. Cover and chill, until ready to serve. Serve the dessert in individual bowls with chopped pistachios sprinkled over the tops at the last minute.

VARIATION
Turn this Spanish dessert into a Sicilian-style one by using the blood oranges that grow in great profusion on the island.

Nectarine Crunch

This incredibly easy and nutritious dessert is very popular with children, who enjoy making it themselves.

10 mins   10 mins

SERVES 4

INGREDIENTS

4 nectarines

6 oz/175 g raisin and nut crunchy oat cereal

1¼ cups lowfat plain yogurt

2 tbsp peach jelly

2 tbsp peach nectar

1 Cut the nectarines in half and remove the stones. Chop the flesh into bite-size pieces. Reserve 12–16 pieces for decoration and divide the remainder among 4 sundae glasses or individual bowls.

2 Divide the crunchy oat cereal between the glasses or bowls and top with the yogurt.

3 Combine the jelly and peach nectar in a pitcher, stirring well to mix. Drizzle the sauce over the yogurt and decorate with the reserved nectarine pieces. Serve immediately.

Peaches in White Wine

A very simple but incredibly pleasing dessert, which is especially good for a dinner party on a hot summer day.

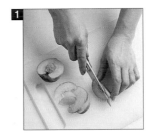

15 mins plus
10 mins chilling

0 mins

SERVES 4

INGREDIENTS

4 large ripe peaches

2 tbsp confectioners' sugar, sifted

pared rind and juice of 1 orange

¾ cup medium or sweet white wine, chilled

1 Using a sharp knife, halve the peaches, remove the pits, and discard them. Peel the peaches if you prefer. Slice the peaches into thin wedges.

2 Place the peach wedges in a glass serving bowl and sprinkle the sugar over.

3 Using a sharp knife, pare the rind from the orange. Cut the rind into matchsticks, place them in a bowl of cold water, and set aside.

4 Squeeze the juice from the orange and pour over the peaches, together with the wine.

5 Let the peaches marinate and chill in the refrigerator for at least 1 hour.

6 Remove the orange peel from the cold water and pat dry with paper towels.

7 Decorate the peaches with the strips of orange rind and serve immediately.

COOK'S TIP
There is absolutely no need to use expensive wine in this recipe, so it can be quite economical to make.

Fruit in Lemongrass Syrup

This simple tropical fruit salad with its oriental flavors makes a refreshing and exotic dessert.

15 mins plus
8 hrs chilling

15 mins

SERVES 4

INGREDIENTS

LEMONGRASS SYRUP

1½ cups superfine sugar

⅔ cup water

2 lemongrass stalks, bruised

2 kaffir lime leaves

juice of 1 lime

TROPICAL FRUIT SALAD

1 honeydew melon

1 small pineapple

1 papaya

14 oz/400 g lychees, pitted

3 passion fruit

TO DECORATE

1 tbsp lime rind

small handful of fresh mint leaves

1 To make the syrup, place the sugar, water, lemongrass, and lime leaves and lime juice in a pan. Heat gently until the sugar has dissolved. Bring to a boil and boil, uncovered, for 5 minutes. Chill in refrigerator overnight.

2 Cut the melon in half, then remove the seeds and scoop out the flesh with a melon baller. Place in a bowl. Peel the pineapple, then cut into fourths lengthwise and remove the core. Cut into cubes and add to the melon. Peel the papaya, then remove the seeds and cut the flesh into cubes and add to the other fruit.

3 Add the lychees. Cut the passion fruit in half and scoop the pulp and seeds into the bowl of fruit. Stir to combine, then transfer to a serving bowl. Remove the lemongrass stalks and lime leaves from the syrup and pour over the fruit. Decorate with the lime rind and fresh mint leaves and serve.

Pineapple with Lime

Pineapples are sweet and fragrant, and feature regularly as a dessert in Thailand, usually served very simply, as in this recipe.

🥧 15 mins plus
30 mins chilling   ⏱ 2 mins

SERVES 4

INGREDIENTS

1 pineapple

2 cardamoms

1 strip lime rind, pared thinly

4 tbsp water

1 tbsp brown sugar

3 tbsp lime juice

fresh mint sprigs and whipped cream,
to decorate

1 Using a sharp knife, cut the top and bottom from the pineapple, then cut away the peel and remove all the "eyes" from the flesh. Cut into quarters and remove the core. Slice the pineapple flesh lengthwise.

2 Crush the cardamoms in a mortar with a pestle and place in a small pan with the lime rind and water. Heat gently until the mixture is boiling, then simmer for 30 seconds.

3 Remove the pan from the heat and stir in the sugar until it has dissolved, then cover, and set aside to steep for 5 minutes.

4 Add the lime juice, stir well to mix, then strain the syrup over the pineapple. Chill for 30 minutes.

5 Arrange the pineapple on a serving dish, spoon the syrup over it, and serve decorated with fresh mint sprigs and whipped cream.

COOK'S TIP
To remove the "eyes" from pineapple, cut off the peel, then use a small sharp knife to cut a V-shaped channel down the pineapple. Cut diagonally through the lines of brown "eyes" in the flesh, to make spiraling cuts around the fruit.

Pineapple Compôte

For a more elaborate dish, accompany the pineapple with a scoop of good-quality pineapple sherbet.

15 mins   0 mins

SERVES 4–6

INGREDIENTS

1 ripe pineapple

sugar

juice of 1 lemon

2–3 tbsp tequila or few drops vanilla extract

several fresh mint sprigs, leaves removed and cut into thin strips

fresh mint sprig, to decorate

1 Using a sharp knife, cut off the top and bottom of the pineapple. Place upright on a cutting board, then slice off the skin, cutting downward. Cut in half, remove the core, then cut the flesh into slices. Cut the fruit into chunks.

2 Put the pineapple in a bowl and sprinkle with the sugar, lemon juice, and tequila or vanilla extract.

3 Toss the pineapple to coat well, then chill until ready to serve.

4 To serve, arrange on a serving plate and sprinkle with the mint strips. Decorate the dish with a mint sprig.

COOK'S TIP
Make sure you slice off the "eyes" when removing the skin from the pineapple.

Compôte of Dry Fruits

Dry fruits, soaked in tea and orange juice, make a fragrant compôte.
This is a good dessert, and can also be served with cereal for breakfast.

 25 mins
plus 24 hrs
marinading

 0 mins

SERVES 4

INGREDIENTS

1 tbsp jasmine tea

1¼ cups boiling water

¼ cup dried apricots

¼ cup dried apple rings

¼ cup prunes

1¼ cups fresh orange juice

1 Put the tea in a pitcher and pour in the boiling water. Let steep for 20 minutes, then strain.

2 Put the dry fruits in a serving bowl and pour the jasmine tea and orange juice over them. Cover and let marinate in the refrigerator for 24 hours.

3 Serve the compôte well chilled.

Fresh Fruit Compôte

Elderflower cordial is used in the syrup for this refreshing fruit compôte, giving it a delightfully summery flavor.

20 mins   15 mins

SERVES 4

INGREDIENTS

1 lemon

¼ cup superfine sugar

4 tbsp elderflower cordial

1¼ cups water

4 dessert apples

1 cup blackberries

2 fresh figs

TOPPING

⅔ cup strained plain yogurt

2 tbsp honey

1 Thinly pare the rind from the lemon using a vegetable peeler. Squeeze the juice. Put the lemon rind and juice into a pan, together with the sugar, elderflower cordial, and water. Set over low heat and simmer, uncovered, for 10 minutes.

2 Peel, core, and slice the apples. Add the apples to the pan. Simmer gently for about 4–5 minutes, until just tender. Remove the pan from the heat and set aside to cool.

3 When cold, transfer the apples and syrup to a serving bowl and add the blackberries. Slice and add the figs. Stir gently to mix. Cover and chill in the refrigerator until ready to serve.

4 Spoon the yogurt into a small serving bowl and drizzle the honey over the top. Cover and chill before serving.

COOK'S TIP

Strained plain yogurt may be made from cow's or ewe's milk. The former is often strained to make it more concentrated and has a high fat content, which perfectly counterbalances the sharpness and acidity of fruit.

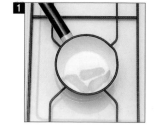

Fruit Compôte with Port

Port complements the flavor of berries very well. This delicious compôte is topped with sweetened whipped cream and grated chocolate.

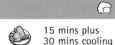

15 mins plus
30 mins cooling   15 mins

SERVES 4

INGREDIENTS

1 tbsp butter

¾ cup blueberries

¾ cup blackberries

scant ½ cup strawberries

6 tbsp port

3 tbsp blueberry jelly

1 tbsp cornstarch

1 tsp allspice

TOPPING

2 cups heavy cream

3–4 tbsp superfine sugar

grated chocolate, to decorate

1 Preheat the oven to 375°F/190°C. Grease a baking dish with butter and add all the fruit.

2 In a bowl, mix together the port, jelly, cornstarch and allspice. Pour over the fruit and mix together well. Bake in the preheated oven for 15 minutes, stirring from time to time. Remove from the oven and let cool to room temperature, then divide among 4 decorative serving glasses.

3 For the topping, put the cream in a mixing bowl and beat in enough sugar to taste. Spoon the mixture over the fruit, top with grated chocolate and serve.

Blueberry Compôte

Serve this easy dish with whipped cream or ice cream and cookies. It is perfect for entertaining, as it has to be made in advance and chilled.

10 mins plus 3 hrs chilling

5 mins

SERVES 6

INGREDIENTS

2½ cups blueberries

generous 1⅓ cups superfine sugar

1 tbsp water

2 tbsp gin

dessert cookies, to serve

1 Place the blueberries, superfine sugar, and water in a heavy-based pan over low heat, shaking the pan occasionally, until the sugar has dissolved completely. Remove the pan from the heat and gradually stir in the gin, then let the fruit mixture cool completely.

2 Transfer the compôte to dishes, cover, and let chill in the refrigerator for 2–3 hours before serving with dessert cookies.

VARIATION

You can substitute fresh red currants for the blueberries and brandy for the gin, if you prefer.

Fig & Watermelon Salad

Fruit salads are always popular and easy to prepare. Ring the changes with this summery combination that looks almost too pretty to eat.

15 mins
plus chilling

5 mins

SERVES 4

I N G R E D I E N T S

I watermelon, weighing about
3 lb 5 oz/1.5 kg

¾ cup seedless black grapes

4 figs

1 lime

1 orange

1 tbsp maple syrup

2 tbsp honey

4 fresh mint sprigs, to decorate (optional)

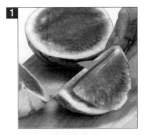

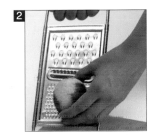

1 Cut the watermelon into quarters and scoop out and discard the seeds. Cut the flesh away from the rind, then chop the flesh into 1-inch/2.5-cm cubes. Place the watermelon cubes in a bowl with the grapes. Cut each fig lengthwise into 8 wedges and add to the bowl.

2 Grate the rind from the lime and orange and squeeze the juice from the orange. Mix the lime rind with the orange rind and juice, maple syrup, and honey in a small pan. Bring to a boil over low heat. Pour the mixture over the fruit and stir. Let cool. Stir again, cover, and let chill in the refrigerator for at least 1 hour, stirring occasionally.

3 To serve, divide the fruit salad equally among 4 glass dishes and decorate with a fresh mint sprig, if you like.

VARIATION
Add 2 pieces of finely chopped preserved ginger to the fruit in step 1 and substitute 1 tablespoon of the syrup from the jar for the maple syrup.

Mango & Passion Fruit Salad

The rich mascarpone cream which accompanies the exotic fruit salad gives this Chinese dessert an Italian twist.

1 hrs 15 mins   0 mins

SERVES 4

INGREDIENTS

1 large mango

2 oranges

4 passion fruit

2 tbsp orange-flavored liqueur

mint or geranium leaves, to decorate

MASCARPONE CREAM

½ cup mascarpone cheese

1 tbsp clear honey

4 tbsp strained plain yogurt

few drops vanilla extract

1 Using a sharp knife, cut the mango in half lengthwise as close to the pit as possible. Remove the pit, using a sharp knife.

2 Peel off the mango skin, cut the flesh into slices, and place into a large bowl.

3 Peel the oranges, removing all the pith, and cut into segments. Add to the bowl with any juices.

4 Halve the passion fruit, scoop out the flesh, and add to the bowl with the orange-flavored liqueur. Mix together all the ingredients in the bowl.

5 Cover the bowl with plastic wrap and chill in the refrigerator for 1 hour. Turn into glass serving dishes.

6 To make the mascarpone cream, blend the mascarpone cheese and honey together. Stir in the strained plain yogurt and vanilla extract until thoroughly blended.

7 Serve the fruit salad with the mascarpone cream, decorated with mint or geranium leaves.

COOK'S TIP

Passion fruit are ready to eat when their skins are well dimpled. They are most readily available in the summer. Substitute guava or pineapple for the passion fruit, if you prefer.

Melon & Kiwi Salad

A refreshing fruit salad, ideal to serve after a rich meal. Charentais or Cantaloupe melons are also good.

🍴 1 hr 15 mins   🕐 0 mins

SERVES 4

I N G R E D I E N T S

½ Galia melon

2 kiwi fruit

1 cup seedless green grapes

1 papaya, halved

3 tbsp orange-flavored liqueur

1 tbsp chopped lemon verbena, lemon balm, or mint

sprigs of lemon verbena, or cape gooseberries, to decorate

1 Remove the seeds from the melon, cut into 4 slices, and cut away the skin. Cut the flesh into cubes and put into a bowl.

2 Peel the kiwi fruit and cut across into slices. Add to the melon with the green grapes.

3 Remove the seeds from the papaya and cut off the skin. Slice the flesh thickly and cut into diagonal pieces. Add to the fruit bowl and mix well.

4 Mix together the liqueur and lemon verbena, pour over the fruit, and set aside for 1 hour, stirring occasionally.

5 Spoon the fruit salad into glasses, pour over the juices, and decorate with lemon verbena sprigs or cape gooseberries.

COOK'S TIP

Lemon balm or sweet balm is a fragrant lemon-scented plant with slightly hairy serrated leaves and a pronounced lemon flavor. Lemon verbena can also be used—this has an even stronger lemon flavor and smooth, elongated leaves.

Orange & Grapefruit Salad

Sliced citrus fruits with a delicious lime and honey dressing make an unusual and refreshing dessert.

🕐 15 mins plus 2 hrs chilling   🕐 3 mins

SERVES 4

I N G R E D I E N T S

2 grapefruit, ruby or plain

4 oranges

pared rind and juice of 1 lime

4 tbsp honey

2 tbsp warm water

1 fresh mint sprig, chopped coarsely

½ cup chopped walnuts

1 Using a sharp knife, slice the top and bottom from the grapefruits, then slice away the rest of the skin and pith.

2 Cut between each segment of the grapefruit and remove the fleshy part only, discarding the membranes.

3 Using a sharp knife, slice the top and bottom from the oranges, then slice away the rest of the skin and pith.

4 Cut between each segment of the oranges to remove the fleshy part, discarding the membranes. Add the orange segments to the grapefruit.

5 Place the lime rind, 2 tablespoons lime juice, the honey, and the warm water in a small bowl. Whisk with a fork to mix the dressing.

6 Pour the dressing over the segmented fruit, add the chopped mint, and mix well. Set aside to chill in the refrigerator for 2 hours for the flavors to mingle.

7 Preheat the broiler to medium. Place the chopped walnuts on a cookie sheet. Toast lightly under the preheated broiler for 2–3 minutes, or until browned.

8 Sprinkle the toasted walnuts over the fruit and serve.

Aromatic Fruit Salad

The fruits in this salad are arranged attractively on serving plates with a spicy syrup spooned over.

25 mins   5 mins

SERVES 6

INGREDIENTS

3 tbsp granulated sugar

⅔ cup water

1 cinnamon stick or large piece cassia bark

4 cardamoms, crushed

1 clove

juice of 1 orange

juice of 1 lime

½ honeydew melon

1 large wedge watermelon

2 ripe guavas

3 ripe nectarines

about 18 strawberries

toasted shredded coconut, for sprinkling

sprigs of mint or rose petals, to decorate

strained plain yogurt, to serve

1 First prepare the syrup. Put the sugar, water, cinnamon, cardamoms and clove into a pan and bring to a boil, stirring to dissolve the sugar. Simmer for 2 minutes, then remove from heat.

2 Add the orange and lime juices to the syrup and let cool and infuse while you prepare the fruits.

3 Peel and remove the seeds from the melons and cut the flesh into neat slices.

4 Cut the guavas in half, scoop out the seeds, then peel and slice the flesh neatly.

5 Cut the nectarines into slices and hull and slice the strawberries.

6 Arrange the slices of fruit attractively on 6 serving plates.

7 Strain the cooled prepared syrup and spoon over the sliced fruits.

8 Sprinkle the fruit salad with a little toasted coconut. Decorate each serving with sprigs of mint or rose petals, and serve with yogurt.

Summer Fruit Salad

A mixture of soft summer fruits in an orange-flavored syrup with a dash of port. Serve with a spoonful of lowfat plain yogurt.

5 mins   10 mins

SERVES 6

INGREDIENTS

6 tbsp superfine sugar

5 tbsp water

grated rind and juice of 1 small orange

2¼ cups red currants, stripped from their stalks

2 tsp arrowroot

2 tbsp port

1 cup blackberries

1 cup blueberries

1 cup strawberries

1⅓ cups raspberries

lowfat yogurt, to serve

1 Put the sugar, water, and grated orange rind into a heavy-based pan and heat gently, stirring until the sugar has completely dissolved.

2 Add the red currants and orange juice, bring to a boil, and simmer gently for 2–3 minutes.

3 Strain the fruit, reserving the syrup, and put into a bowl.

4 Blend the arrowroot with a little water. Return the syrup to the pan, add the arrowroot, and bring to a boil, stirring constantly, until thickened.

5 Add the port and mix together well. Then pour the syrup over the red currants in the bowl.

6 Add the blackberries, blueberries, strawberries, and raspberries. Mix the fruit together and set aside to cool until required. Serve in individual glass dishes with lowfat yogurt.

COOK'S TIP

Although this salad is really best made with fresh fruits in season, you can achieve an acceptable result with frozen equivalents, with perhaps the exception of strawberries. You can buy frozen fruits of the forest, which would be ideal, in most supermarkets.

Tropical Salad

Papayas are ready to eat when they yield to gentle pressure. Serve in the shells of baby pineapples for a stunning effect.

10 mins   0 mins

SERVES 8

INGREDIENTS

1 papaya

2 tbsp fresh orange juice

3 tbsp dark rum

2 bananas

2 guavas

1 small pineapple or 2 baby pineapples

2 passion fruit

pineapple leaves, to decorate

1 Cut the papaya in half and remove the seeds. Peel and slice the flesh into a bowl.

2 Pour over the orange juice together with the rum.

3 Slice the bananas, peel and slice the guavas, and add both to the bowl.

4 Cut the top and base from the pineapple, then cut off the skin.

5 Slice the pineapple flesh, discard the core, cut into pieces and add to the bowl.

6 Halve the passion fruit, scoop out the flesh with a teaspoon, add to the bowl and stir well to mix.

7 Spoon the salad into glass bowls and decorate with pineapple leaves.

COOK'S TIP
Guavas have a heavenly smell when ripe—their scent will fill a whole room. They should give to gentle pressure when ripe, and their skins should be yellow. The canned varieties are very good and have a pink tinge to the flesh.

Exotic Fruit Salad

This colorful, exotic salad is infused with the delicate flavors of jasmine tea and ginger. Ideally, it should be chilled about an hour before serving.

15–20 mins plus 1 hr chilling

0 mins

SERVES 6

I N G R E D I E N T S

1 tsp jasmine tea leaves

1 tsp grated gingerroot

1 strip lime rind

½ cup boiling water

2 tbsp superfine sugar

1 papaya

1 mango

½ small pineapple

1 star fruit

2 passion fruit

1 Place the tea leaves, ginger, and lime rind in a heatproof pitcher and pour over the boiling water. Let stand to infuse for 5 minutes, then strain the liquid.

2 Add the sugar to the liquid and stir well to dissolve. Let the syrup stand until it is completely cool.

3 Halve, seed, and peel the papaya. Halve the mango, remove the pit, and peel. Peel and remove the core from the pineapple. Cut the fruits into regular, bite-size pieces.

4 Slice the star fruit crosswise. Place all the prepared fruits in a wide serving bowl and pour over the cooled syrup. Cover the bowl with plastic wrap and chill for about 1 hour.

5 Cut the passion fruit in half, scoop out the flesh, and mix with the lime juice. Spoon over the salad, and serve.

COOK'S TIP
Star fruit have little flavor when unripe and green, but when ripe and yellow they are sweet and fragrant. The tips of the ridges often turn brown, so run a vegetable peeler along each ridge before slicing.

Chinese Fruit Salad

The syrup for this colorful dish is filled with Chinese flavors for a refreshing and mouthwatering dessert.

45 mins plus
1 hr chilling

10 mins

SERVES 4

INGREDIENTS

scant ½ cup Chinese rice wine or dry sherry

grated rind and juice of 1 lemon

3¾ cups water

generous cup superfine sugar

2 cloves

1-inch/2.5-cm piece cinnamon
   stick, bruised

1 vanilla bean

pinch of ground allspice

1 star anise pod

1-inch/2.5-cm piece of gingerroot, sliced

scant ½ cup unsalted cashews

2 kiwi fruits

1 star fruit

scant ½ cup strawberries

14 oz/400 g canned lychees in
   syrup, drained

1 piece preserved ginger, drained and sliced

chopped fresh mint, to decorate

1 Put the Chinese rice wine or sherry, lemon rind and juice, and water into a heavy-based pan.

2 Add the superfine sugar, cloves, cinnamon stick, vanilla bean, allspice, star anise, and gingerroot to the pan.

3 Heat the mixture in the pan gently, stirring constantly, until the sugar has dissolved and then bring to a boil. Reduce the heat and simmer for 5 minutes. Set aside to cool completely.

4 Strain the syrup, discarding the flavorings. Stir in the cashews, cover with plastic wrap and chill in the refrigerator.

5 Meanwhile, prepare the fruits: halve and slice the kiwi fruit, slice the star fruit, and hull and slice the strawberries.

6 Spoon the prepared fruit into a dish with the lychees and preserved ginger. Stir through gently to mix.

7 Pour the syrup over the fruit, decorate with chopped mint, and serve.

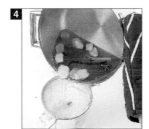

Green Fruit Salad

This delightfully refreshing fruit salad is the perfect finale for a Chinese meal. It has a lovely light syrup made with fresh mint and honey.

🍰 30 mins 🕐 15 mins

SERVES 4

INGREDIENTS

SYRUP

1 orange

⅔ cup white wine

⅔ cup water

4 tbsp honey

fresh mint sprigs

FRUIT

1 small Charentais or honeydew melon

2 green apples

2 kiwi fruit

1 cup seedless white grapes

fresh mint sprigs, to decorate

1 To make the syrup, pare the rind from the orange using a vegetable peeler.

2 Put the orange rind in a pan with the white wine, water, and honey. Bring to a boil, then simmer gently for 10 minutes.

3 Remove the syrup from the heat. Add the mint sprigs and set aside to cool.

4 To prepare the fruit, first slice the melon in half and scoop out the seeds. Use a melon baller or a teaspoon to make melon balls.

5 Core and chop the apples. Peel and slice the kiwi fruit.

6 Strain the cooled syrup into a serving bowl, removing and reserving the orange rind, and discarding the mint sprigs.

7 Add the apple, grapes, kiwi fruit, and melon to the serving bowl. Stir through gently to mix.

8 Serve the fruit salad, decorated with sprigs of fresh mint and some of the reserved orange rind.

COOK'S TIP

Single-flower honey has a better, more individual flavor than blended honey. Acacia honey is typically Chinese, but you could also try clove, lemon blossom, lime flower, or orange blossom.

Fruit Salad & Ginger Syrup

This is a very special fruit salad made from the most exotic and colorful fruits that are soaked in a syrup made with gingerroot and ginger wine.

30 mins plus 2–4 hrs chilling

5 mins

SERVES 4

INGREDIENTS

1-inch/2.5-cm piece gingerroot, peeled and chopped

¼ cup superfine sugar

⅔ cup water

grated rind and juice of 1 lime

⅓ cup ginger wine

1 fresh pineapple, peeled, cored, and cut into bite-size pieces

2 ripe mangoes, peeled, pitted, and diced

4 kiwi fruit, peeled and sliced

1 papaya, peeled, seeded and diced

2 passion fruit, halved and flesh removed

12 oz/350 g lychees, peeled and pitted

¼ fresh coconut, grated

cape gooseberries, to decorate (optional)

coconut ice cream, to serve (optional)

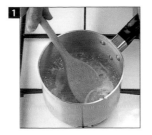

1 Place the gingerroot, sugar, water, and lime juice in a pan and bring slowly to a boil. Simmer for 1 minute, remove from the heat, and let cool slightly.

2 Strain the syrup, add the ginger wine, and mix well. Cool completely.

3 Place the prepared fruit in a serving bowl. Add the cold syrup and mix well. Cover and chill in the refrigerator for 2–4 hours.

4 Just before serving, add half of the grated coconut to the salad and mix well. Sprinkle the remainder on top.

5 If using cape gooseberries to decorate the salad, peel back each calyx to form a flower. Wipe the berries clean, then arrange them around the side of the fruit salad before serving with coconut ice cream.

COOK'S TIP
Despite their name, cape gooseberries are golden in color and more similar in appearance to ground cherries. They make a delightful decoration to many fruit-based desserts.

Creamy Fruit Parfait

On the tiny Greek island of Kythera, this luscious combination of summer fruits and yogurt is served at tavernas as well as in homes.

15 mins plus 1 hr cooling

0 mins

SERVES 4–6

INGREDIENTS

1⅓ cups cherries

2 large peaches

2 large apricots

3 cups plain thick yogurt

½ cup walnut halves

2 tbsp flower-scented honey

fresh red currants or berries, to decorate (optional)

1 To prepare the fruit, use a cherry or olive pitter to remove the cherry pits. Cut each cherry in half. Cut the peaches and apricots in half lengthwise and remove the pits, then finely chop the flesh of all the fruit.

2 Place the finely chopped cherries, peaches, and apricots in a bowl and gently stir together.

3 Spoon one-third of the yogurt into an attractive glass serving bowl. Top with half the fruit mixture.

4 Repeat with another layer of yogurt and fruit and, finally, top with the remaining yogurt.

5 Place the walnuts in a small food processor and pulse until chopped, but not finely ground. Take care not to over-process. Sprinkle the walnuts over the top layer of the yogurt.

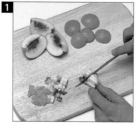

6 Drizzle the honey over the nuts and yogurt. Cover the bowl with plastic wrap and chill in the refrigerator for at least 1 hour. Decorate the bowl with a small bunch of red currants (if using), just before serving.

Chocolate Hazelnut Parfait

Richly flavored molded ice creams make a scrumptious and attractive summertime dessert for all the family.

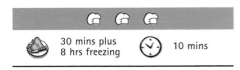

30 mins plus
8 hrs freezing

10 mins

SERVES 6

INGREDIENTS

1½ cups blanched hazelnuts

6 oz/175 g semisweet chocolate, broken into small pieces

2½ cups heavy cream

3 eggs, separated

2½ cups confectioners' sugar

1 tbsp unsweetened cocoa, for dusting

6 small fresh mint sprigs, to decorate

wafer cookies, to serve

1 Preheat the broiler to medium. Spread out the hazelnuts on a cookie sheet and toast under the broiler for about 5 minutes, shaking the sheet from time to time, until golden all over. Set aside to cool.

2 Put the chocolate in a heatproof bowl set over a pan of gently simmering water. Stir over low heat until melted, then remove from the heat and cool. Put the toasted hazelnuts in a food processor and process until finely ground.

3 Whisk the cream until it is stiff, then fold in the ground hazelnuts and set aside. Add 3 tablespoons of the sugar to the egg yolks and beat for 10 minutes until pale and thick.

4 Whisk the egg whites in a separate bowl until soft peaks form. Whisk in the remaining sugar, a little at a time, until the whites are stiff and glossy. Stir the

cooled chocolate into the egg yolk mixture, then fold in the cream and finally, fold in the egg whites. Divide the mixture among 6 freezerproof timbales or molds, cover with plastic wrap, and freeze for at least 8 hours, or overnight, until firm.

5 Transfer the parfaits to the refrigerator about 10 minutes before serving to soften slightly. Turn out on to individual serving plates, dust the tops lightly, with unsweetened cocoa, decorate with mint sprigs, and serve with wafers.

Oeufs à la Neige au Chocolat

In this dessert, poached meringues float on a richly flavored chocolate custard like little snowballs.

15 mins plus
2 hrs chilling

15–20 mins

SERVES 6

INGREDIENTS

2½ cups milk

1 tsp vanilla extract

scant 1 cup superfine sugar

2 egg whites

CUSTARD

¼ cup superfine sugar

3 tbsp unsweetened cocoa

4 egg yolks

1 Put the milk, vanilla extract, and 5 tablespoons of the superfine sugar into a heavy-based pan and stir over low heat until the sugar has dissolved. Simmer gently.

2 Whisk the egg whites until stiff peaks form. Whisk in 2 teaspoons of the remaining sugar and continue to whisk until glossy. Gently fold in the rest of the superfine sugar.

3 Drop large spoonfuls of the meringue mixture on to the simmering milk mixture and cook, stirring once, for 4–5 minutes, until the meringues are firm. Remove with a slotted spoon and set aside on paper towels to drain. Poach the remaining meringues in the same way, then reserve the milk mixture.

4 To make the custard, mix the sugar, unsweetened cocoa, and egg yolks in a heatproof bowl. Place over gently simmering water. Gradually whisk in the reserved milk mixture and cook for 5–10 minutes, whisking constantly, until thickened. Remove from the heat and cool slightly. Divide the chocolate custard among individual serving glasses and top with the meringues. Cover with plastic wrap and chill in the refrigerator for at least 2 hours before serving.

Chocolate Marquise

This classic French dish is part way between a mousse and a parfait. It is usually chilled in a large mold, but here it is made in individual molds.

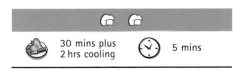

🍮 30 mins plus 2 hrs cooling 🕐 5 mins

SERVES 6

INGREDIENTS

7 oz/200 g semisweet chocolate, broken into pieces

3 oz/85 g butter

3 egg yolks

⅓ cup superfine sugar

1 tsp chocolate extract or 1 tbsp chocolate-flavored liqueur

1¼ cups heavy cream

TO SERVE

chocolate-dipped fruits

sour cream

unsweetened cocoa, for dusting

1 Put the chocolate and butter in a heatproof bowl set over a pan of gently simmering water and stir until melted and well combined. Remove from the heat and let cool.

2 Place the egg yolks in a mixing bowl with the sugar and whisk until pale and fluffy. Using an electric whisk running on low speed, slowly whisk in the cool chocolate mixture. Stir in the chocolate extract or chocolate-flavored liqueur.

3 Whip the cream until just holding its shape. Fold into the chocolate mixture. Spoon into 6 small custard pots, or individual metal molds. Chill the desserts for at least 2 hours.

4 To serve, turn out the desserts on to individual serving dishes. If you have difficulty turning them out, dip each pot or mold into a bowl of warm water for a few seconds to help the marquise to slip out. Serve with chocolate-dipped fruits and sour cream and dust with unsweetened cocoa.

COOK'S TIP
The slight tartness of the sour cream contrasts well with this very rich dessert. Dip the fruit in melted white chocolate to give a good color contrast.

Coffee Panna Cotta

Panna cotta, which means "cooked cream," is an Italian dessert. Here it is flavored with coffee and served with a chocolate sauce.

25 mins plus
8 hrs chilling

5 mins

SERVES 6

INGREDIENTS

2½ cups heavy cream

1 vanilla bean

¼ cup golden superfine sugar

2 tsp instant espresso coffee powder dissolved in 4 tbsp water

2 tsp powdered gelatin

chocolate-coated coffee beans, to serve

CHOCOLATE CREAM SAUCE

2 oz/55 g semisweet chocolate

⅔ cup light cream

1 Put the cream in a pan. Split the vanilla bean and scrape the black seeds into the cream. Add the vanilla bean and the sugar and heat gently until almost boiling. Strain the cream into a bowl. Put the coffee into a small heatproof bowl, sprinkle on the gelatin, and leave for 5 minutes until spongy. Set the bowl over a pan of gently simmering water until the gelatin is dissolved.

2 Stir a little of the cream into the gelatin mixture, then stir the gelatin into the rest of the cream. Divide the mixture between 6 lightly oiled ⅔-cup molds, filling them only two-thirds full, and let cool. Chill in the refrigerator overnight.

3 Make the chocolate cream sauce. Put the chocolate in a heatproof bowl set over a pan of gently simmering water until melted. Put a quarter of the cream into a bowl and stir in the melted chocolate. Gradually stir in the remaining cream, reserving about 1 tablespoon. To serve the panna cotta, dip the molds briefly into hot water and turn out on to 6 plates. Pour the chocolate cream around. Dot drops of the reserved cream on to the sauce and feather it with a skewer. Decorate with chocolate coffee beans and serve.

COOK'S TIP

Individual metal pudding bowl shaped molds are ideal for this, and the panna cotta turns out more easily than from china molds.

Chocolate Ice Cream Bombe

An ice cream bombe is a spectacular dessert to serve at a dinner party and the combination of white and semisweet chocolate is a winner.

50 mins plus
6 hrs freezing   20 mins

SERVES 4

INGREDIENTS

SEMISWEET CHOCOLATE ICE CREAM

2 eggs

2 egg yolks

generous ½ cup golden superfine sugar

1¼ cups light cream

8 oz/225 g semisweet chocolate, chopped

1¼ cups heavy cream

WHITE CHOCOLATE ICE CREAM

5 oz/140 g white chocolate, broken into pieces

⅔ cup milk

2 oz/55 g golden superfine sugar

1¼ cups heavy cream

chocolate leaves, to decorate

1 Put a 6¼-cup bombe mold into the freezer and turn the freezer to its lowest setting. Place the eggs, egg yolks, and sugar in a heatproof bowl and beat together until well blended. Put the light cream and chocolate in a pan and heat gently until the chocolate has melted, then continue to heat, stirring constantly, until almost boiling. Pour on to the egg mixture, stirring vigorously, then place the bowl over a pan of simmering water, making sure that the bottom of the bowl does not touch the water. Cook, stirring constantly, until the mixture lightly coats the back of the spoon. Strain into another bowl and let cool. Place the heavy cream in a bowl and whisk until slightly thickened, then fold into the cooled chocolate mixture.

2 Either freeze in an ice-cream maker, following the manufacturer's directions, or pour the mixture into a freezerproof container, cover, and freeze for 2 hours until just frozen. Spoon into a bowl and beat with a fork to break down the ice crystals. Return to the freezer until almost solid. Line the bombe mold with the chocolate ice cream and return to the freezer. Transfer from the freezer to the refrigerator 30 minutes before serving.

3 To make the white chocolate ice cream, put the chocolate and half the milk in a pan and heat gently until the chocolate has just melted. Remove from the heat and stir. Put the sugar and remaining milk in another pan and heat gently until the sugar has melted. Set aside to cool, then stir into the cooled chocolate mixture. Place the cream in a bowl and whisk until slightly thickened, then fold into the chocolate mixture. Spoon into the center of the bombe, cover, and freeze for about 4 hours, until firm. To serve, dip the mold briefly into warm water, then turn out on to a serving plate. Decorate with chocolate leaves.

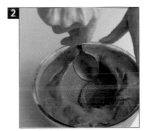

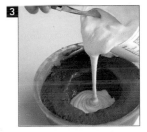

Chocolate & Orange Pots

These little pots of rich chocolate cream will satisfy the most serious chocolate lovers. Decorate with orange rind, if liked.

15 mins plus
1 hr chilling

5 mins

SERVES 8

INGREDIENTS

7 oz/200 g semisweet chocolate, broken into pieces

grated rind of 1 orange

1¼ cups heavy cream

¾ cup golden superfine sugar

3 tbsp orange-flavored liqueur

3 large egg whites

strips of orange rind, to decorate

crisp dessert cookies, to serve

1 Melt the chocolate in a heatproof bowl set over a pan of gently simmering water until melted. Stir in the orange rind. Put the cream in a bowl with ½ cup of the sugar and the liqueur and whisk until thick.

2 Put the egg whites in a clean bowl and whisk until soft peaks form, then gradually whisk in the remaining sugar until stiff but not dry. Fold the melted chocolate into the cream, then beat in a spoonful of the whisked whites. Fold in the remaining whites until thoroughly mixed in.

3 Spoon the mixture into 8 small ramekins or demi-tasse coffee cups. Chill for 1 hour, then decorate with strips of orange rind, before serving with crisp dessert cookies.

COOK'S NOTE
Chill the chocolate pots for no more than 2 hours otherwise the mixture becomes too firmly set.

Chocolate Coeur à la Crème

This classic French dessert is traditionally made in special pierced heart-shaped porcelain molds.

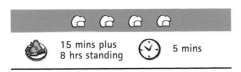

15 mins plus
8 hrs standing

5 mins

SERVES 8

INGREDIENTS

1 cup ricotta cheese

½ cup confectioners' sugar, sifted

1½ cup heavy cream

1 tsp vanilla extract

2 oz/55 g semisweet chocolate, grated

2 egg whites

few strawberries, halved, to decorate

RASPBERRY COULIS

scant 1 cup raspberries

confectioners' sugar, to taste

1 Line 8 individual heart shaped molds with cheesecloth. Press the cheese through a strainer into a bowl. Add the confectioners' sugar, heavy cream and vanilla extract and beat together thoroughly. Stir in the grated chocolate. Place the egg whites in a large bowl and whisk until stiff but not dry. Gently fold into the cheese mixture.

2 Spoon the mixture into the prepared molds. Stand the molds on a tray or dish and let stand in the refrigerator overnight to drain. The cheesecloth will absorb most of the liquid. To make the raspberry coulis, put the raspberries in a blender or food processor and process to a purée. Press the purée through a strainer into a bowl and add confectioners' sugar, to taste.

3 To serve, turn each coeur à la crème on to a plate and pour the raspberry coulis round. Decorate with halved strawberries.

COOK'S TIP
If you do not have the special heart-shaped mold, use yogurt pots which have been pierced at the bottom. Alternatively, make one large mold by lining a sieve with cheesecloth.

Chocolate Rum Pots

Wickedly rich little chocolate pots, flavored with a hint of dark rum, are pure indulgence on any occasion!

20 mins plus
2 hrs chilling

5 mins

SERVES 6

I N G R E D I E N T S

8 oz/225 g semisweet chocolate

4 eggs, separated

⅓ cup superfine sugar

4 tbsp dark rum

4 tbsp heavy cream

T O   D E C O R A T E

whipped cream

Marbled Chocolate Shapes (see page 821)

1 Put the chocolate in a heatproof bowl set over a pan of gently simmering water until melted. Let cool slightly.

2 Whisk the egg yolks with the superfine sugar in a bowl until very pale and fluffy.

3 Drizzle the melted chocolate into the mixture and fold in together with the rum and the heavy cream.

4 Whisk the egg whites in a greasefree bowl until soft peaks form. Fold the egg whites into the chocolate mixture in 2 batches. Divide the mixture among 6 individual dishes, and let chill for at least 2 hours.

5 To serve, decorate with a little whipped cream and with Marbled Chocolate Shapes (see page 821).

COOK'S TIP

Make sure you use a perfectly clean, greasefree bowl for whisking the egg whites. They will not aerate if any grease is present as the smallest amount breaks down the bubbles in the whites, preventing them trapping and holding air.

Chocolate Hazelnut Pots

Chocoholics will adore these creamy desserts consisting of a rich baked chocolate custard with the delicious flavor of hazelnuts.

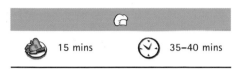

🍰 15 mins   ⏱ 35–40 mins

SERVES 4

I N G R E D I E N T S

2 eggs

2 egg yolks

1 tbsp superfine sugar

1 tsp cornstarch

2½ cups milk

3 oz/85 g semisweet chocolate

4 tbsp chocolate hazelnut spread

grated chocolate or quick chocolate curls

1 Preheat the oven to 325°F/160°C. Beat together the eggs, egg yolks, superfine sugar, and cornstarch until well combined. Heat the milk until it is almost boiling.

2 Gradually pour the milk on to the eggs, whisking as you do so. Melt the chocolate hazelnut spread in a heatproof bowl set over a pan of gently simmering water, then whisk the melted chocolate mixture into the eggs.

3 Pour into 4 small ovenproof dishes and cover the dishes with foil. Place them in a roasting pan. Fill the pan with boiling water until halfway up the sides of the dishes.

4 Bake in the preheated oven for 35–40 minutes, until the custard is just set. Remove from the pan and cool, then let chill until required. Serve decorated with grated chocolate or chocolate curls.

COOK'S TIP
This dish is traditionally made in little pots called pots de crème, which are individual ovenproof dishes with a lid. Custard pots are fine. The dessert can also be made in one large dish: cook for about 1 hour, or until set.

Chocolate Cheese Pots

These super-light desserts are just the thing if you have a craving for chocolate. Serve them on their own or with a selection of fruits.

10 mins plus
30 mins chilling   0 mins

SERVES 4

INGREDIENTS

1¼ cup ricotta cheese

⅔ cup lowfat plain yogurt

2 tbsp confectioners' sugar

4 tsp lowfat drinking chocolate powder

4 tsp unsweetened cocoa

1 tsp vanilla extract

2 tbsp dark rum (optional)

2 egg whites

4 chocolate cake decorations

TO SERVE

pieces of kiwi fruit, orange, and banana

strawberries and raspberries

1 Combine the ricotta cheese and lowfat yogurt in a bowl. Sift in the confectioners' sugar, drinking chocolate powder, and unsweetened cocoa and mix well. Add the vanilla extract and rum (if using).

2 In a clean bowl, whisk the egg whites until stiff. Using a metal spoon, gently fold the egg whites into the chocolate mixture.

3 Spoon the yogurt and chocolate mixture into 4 small china dessert pots and set aside in the refrigerator to chill for about 30 minutes.

4 Decorate each chocolate cheese pot with a chocolate cake decoration and serve with an assortment of fresh fruit, such as pieces of kiwi fruit, orange, banana, strawberries, and raspberries.

COOK'S TIP
This chocolate mixture can also be used as a cheesecake filling. Make the base out of crushed amaretti cookies and egg white, and set the filling with 2 teaspoons of powdered gelatin dissolved in 2 tablespoons of boiling water.

Lebanese Almond Rice

This delicate rice cream is flavored with almonds and rose water.
If pomegranates are in season, decorate with the gorgeous pink seeds.

30 mins plus
2 hrs chilling

10 mins

SERVES 6

INGREDIENTS

6 tbsp rice flour

pinch of salt

3 cups milk

¼ cup superfine sugar

¾ cup ground almonds

1 tbsp rose water

TO DECORATE

2 tbsp chopped pistachios or toasted
sliced almonds

pomegranate seeds (optional)

washed rose petals (optional)

1 Put the rice flour in a bowl, stir in the salt, and make a well in the center.

2 Pour about ¼ cup of the milk into the well and whisk thoroughly to form a smooth paste.

3 Bring the remaining milk to a boil in a heavy-based pan. Whisk in the rice flour paste and the sugar and cook, stirring constantly, until the mixture thickens and bubbles. Reduce the heat and simmer gently for 5 minutes.

4 Whisk in the ground almonds until the mixture is smooth and thickened, then remove from the heat to cool slightly. Stir in the rose water and cool completely, stirring occasionally.

5 Divide the mixture among 6 glasses or pour into a serving bowl. Chill for at least 2 hours before serving.

6 To serve, sprinkle with the pistachios or almonds, pomegranate seeds, and rose petals, if wished.

COOK'S TIP
For a smoother texture, this can be made without the ground almonds. Stir 2 tablespoons of cornstarch into the ground rice and use a little more of the milk to make the paste. Proceed as directed, omitting the ground almonds.

Zuccotto

This famous Italian ice cream bombe is so named because its shape resembles a pumpkin, or zucca. Serve with fresh cherries, if wished.

30 mins plus
2 hrs chilling   0 mins

SERVES 4

INGREDIENTS

2½ cups heavy cream

¼ cup confectioners' sugar

½ cup hazelnuts, toasted

1¼ cups cherries, halved and pitted

4 oz/115 g semisweet chocolate, chopped finely

2 x 8-inch/20-cm round chocolate sponge cakes

4 tbsp cognac

4 tbsp amaretto

TO DECORATE

2 tbsp confectioners' sugar

2 tbsp unsweetened cocoa

fresh cherries (optional)

1 In a large bowl, whisk the cream until it is stiff, then fold in the sugar, followed by the hazelnuts, cherries, and chocolate. Cover with plastic wrap and chill in the refrigerator until required.

2 Meanwhile, cut the sponge cakes in half horizontally and then cut the pieces to fit a 5-cup bowl, so that the bottom and sides are completely lined. Reserve the remaining sponge cake. Mix together the cognac and amaretto in a small bowl and sprinkle the mixture over the sponge cake lining.

3 Remove the cream filling from the refrigerator and spoon it into the lined bowl. Cover the top with the remaining sponge cake, cut to fit. Cover with plastic wrap and chill the bombe in the refrigerator for 2 hours, or until it is ready to serve.

4 For the decoration, sift the confectioners' sugar into a bowl and the unsweetened cocoa into another bowl. To serve, remove the bombe from the refrigerator and run a round-bladed knife around the sides to loosen it. Place a serving plate on top of the bowl and, holding them firmly together, invert. Dust opposite quarters with confectioners' sugar and unsweetened cocoa to make alternating sections of color. Decorate with fresh cherries (if using).

Chocolate & Vanilla Creams

These rich, creamy desserts are completely irresistible. Decorate with chocolate shapes and serve them with crisp dessert cookies, if liked.

🕒 40 mins plus 1 hr chilling

🕐 5–10 mins

SERVES 4

INGREDIENTS

scant 2 cups heavy cream

⅓ cup superfine sugar

1 vanilla bean

generous ¾ cup sour cream

2 tsp powdered gelatin

3 tbsp water

1¾ oz/50 g semisweet chocolate

MARBLED CHOCOLATE SHAPES

little melted white chocolate

little melted semisweet chocolate

1 Place the cream and sugar in a pan, and add the vanilla bean. Heat gently, stirring until the sugar has dissolved, then bring to a boil. Reduce the heat and simmer for 2–3 minutes.

2 Remove the pan from the heat and take out the vanilla bean. Stir in the sour cream.

3 Sprinkle the gelatin over the water in a small heatproof bowl and let it go spongy, then set over a pan of hot water and stir until dissolved. Stir into the cream mixture. Pour half of this mixture into another mixing bowl.

4 Put the semisweet chocolate in a heatproof bowl over a pan with gently simmering water until melted. Stir the melted chocolate into one half of the cream mixture. Pour the chocolate mixture into 4 individual glass serving dishes and let chill for 15–20 minutes, until just set. While it is chilling, keep the vanilla mixture at room temperature.

5 Spoon the vanilla mixture on top of the chocolate mixture and let chill until the vanilla is set.

6 Meanwhile, make the shapes for the decoration. Spoon the melted white chocolate into a paper pastry bag and snip off the tip. Spread some melted semisweet chocolate on a piece of parchment paper. While still wet, pipe a fine line of white chocolate in a scribble over the top. Use the tip of a toothpick to marble the white chocolate into the dark. When firm but not too hard, cut into shapes with a small shaped cutter or a sharp knife. Chill the shapes until firm, then use to decorate.

Chocolate & Pernod Creams

This unusual combination of flavors makes a sophisticated and tempting dessert to serve at a dinner party.

10 mins plus
2 hrs chilling

20 mins

SERVES 4

INGREDIENTS

2 oz/55 g semisweet chocolate, broken into pieces

scant 1 cup milk

1¼ cups heavy cream

2 tbsp superfine sugar

1 tbsp arrowroot dissolved in 2 tbsp milk

3 tbsp Pernod

langues de chat cookies, or chocolate-tipped rolled wafer cookies, to serve

1 Put the chocolate in a heatproof bowl set over a pan of barely simmering water. Stir over low heat until melted. Remove the pan from the heat and cool slightly.

2 Pour the milk and cream into a pan over low heat and bring to just below boiling point, stirring occasionally. Remove the pan from the heat and then set aside.

3 Beat the sugar and the arrowroot mixture into the melted chocolate. Gradually stir in the hot milk and cream mixture, then stir in the Pernod. Set the bowl over a pan of gently simmering water and cook, over low heat, for 10 minutes, stirring constantly, until thick and smooth. Remove from the heat and let cool.

4 Pour the chocolate and Pernod mixture into 4 individual serving glasses. Cover with plastic wrap and chill in the refrigerator for 2 hours before serving with langues de chat cookies or chocolate-tipped rolled wafer cookies, whichever you prefer.

Chocolate Mint Swirls

The classic combination of semisweet chocolate and mint flavors makes an attractive dessert for special occasions.

45 mins   5 mins

SERVES 6

INGREDIENTS

1¼ cups heavy cream

⅔ cup mascarpone cheese

2 tbsp confectioners' sugar

1 tbsp crème de menthe

6 oz/175 g semisweet chocolate,
    plus extra for decorating

1 Place the cream in a large mixing bowl and whisk until soft peaks form.

2 Fold in the mascarpone cheese and confectioners' sugar, then place about one-third of the mixture in a smaller bowl. Stir the crème de menthe into the smaller bowl. Put the semisweet chocolate in a heatproof bowl set over a pan of barely simmering water until melted. Stir the melted chocolate into the remaining mascarpone mixture.

3 Place alternate tablespoonfuls of the 2 mixtures into serving glasses, then swirl the mixture together to give a decorative effect. Chill until required.

4 To make the piped chocolate decorations, melt a small amount of chocolate and place in a paper pastry bag.

5 Place a sheet of parchment paper on a cutting board and pipe squiggles, stars, or flower shapes with the melted chocolate. Alternatively, to make curved decorations, pipe decorations on to a long strip of parchment paper, then carefully place the strip over a rolling pin, securing with sticky tape. Let the chocolate set, then carefully remove from the parchment paper.

6 Decorate each dessert with the piped chocolate decorations and serve. The desserts can be decorated and then chilled, if preferred.

COOK'S TIP
Pipe the patterns freehand or draw patterns on to parchment paper first, turn the parchment paper over and then pipe the chocolate, following the drawn outline.

Quick Chocolate Desserts

This rich creamy dessert takes hardly any time to prepare, but you will need to allow time for chilling before serving.

8 mins plus 2 hrs chilling

8 mins

SERVES 4

INGREDIENTS

½ cup water

4 tbsp superfine sugar

6 oz/175 g semisweet chocolate, broken into pieces

3 egg yolks

1¼ cups heavy cream

sweet cookies, to serve

1 Pour the water into a pan and add the sugar. Stir over low heat until the sugar has dissolved. Bring to a boil and continue to boil, without stirring, for 3 minutes. Remove the pan from the heat and let cool slightly.

2 Put the chocolate in a food processor and add the hot syrup. Process until the chocolate has melted, then add the egg yolks and process briefly until smooth. Finally, add the cream and process until fully incorporated.

3 Pour the mixture into 4 glasses or individual bowls, cover with plastic wrap and chill in the refrigerator for 2 hours, until set. Serve with sweet cookies.

Mocha Creams

These creamy chocolate and coffee-flavored desserts make a perfect end to an elegant meal. Serve with amaretto cookies, if liked.

30 mins   5 mins

SERVES 4

INGREDIENTS

8 oz/225 g semisweet chocolate

1 tbsp instant coffee powder

1¼ cups boiling water

1 envelope powdered gelatin

3 tbsp cold water

1 tsp vanilla extract

1 tbsp Kahlúa or other coffee-flavored liqueur (optional)

1¼ cups heavy cream

4 chocolate-covered coffee beans, to decorate

8 amaretti cookies, to serve

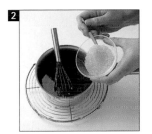

1 Break the chocolate into small pieces and place in a pan with the coffee. Stir in the boiling water and heat gently, stirring until the chocolate melts.

2 Sprinkle the gelatin over the cold water and let it go spongy, then whisk it into the hot chocolate mixture to dissolve it.

3 Stir in the vanilla extract and coffee-flavored liqueur (if using). Let stand in a cool place until just starting to thicken; whisk from time to time.

4 Whisk the cream until soft peaks form, then reserve a little for decorating the desserts and fold the remainder into the chocolate mixture. Spoon into serving dishes and let set.

5 Decorate with the reserved cream and coffee beans and serve with the amaretti cookies.

VARIATION
To add a delicious almond flavor to the dessert, replace the coffee-flavored liqueur with amaretto.

Triple Stripe Cream

Layers of chocolate, vanilla, and coffee, topped with a swirl of whipped cream, make a simple but elegant dessert for any occasion.

15 mins plus
2 hrs chilling

20 mins

SERVES 6

INGREDIENTS

1½ cups superfine sugar

6 tbsp cornstarch

3¼ cups milk

3 egg yolks

3 oz/85 g butter, sweet for preference, cut into pieces

1 heaping tbsp instant coffee powder

2 tsp vanilla extract

2 tbsp unsweetened cocoa, sifted

⅔ cup whipped cream, to decorate

1 Put ½ cup of the superfine sugar and 2 tablespoons of the cornstarch in a small, heavy-based pan. Gradually whisk in one-third of the milk. Set the pan over low heat and whisk in one of the egg yolks. Bring to a boil, whisking constantly, and boil for 1 minute. Remove the pan from the heat and stir in 1 tablespoon of the butter, and all the coffee powder. Set aside to cool slightly, then divide among 6 wine goblets and smooth the surfaces.

2 Place ½ cup of the remaining sugar and 2 tablespoons of the remaining cornstarch in a small, heavy-based pan. Gradually, whisk in 1¼ cups of the remaining milk. Set the pan over low heat and whisk in one of the remaining egg yolks. Bring to a boil, whisking constantly, and boil for 1 minute. Remove the pan from the heat and stir in 2 tablespoons of the remaining butter, and all the vanilla. Set aside to cool slightly, then divide among the goblets and smooth the surfaces.

3 Put the remaining sugar and cornstarch into a small, heavy-based pan. Gradually, whisk in the remaining milk. Set the pan over low heat and whisk in the last egg yolk. Bring to a boil, whisking constantly, and boil for 1 minute. Remove from the heat and stir in the remaining butter, and all the cocoa. Set the mixture aside to cool slightly, then divide among the goblets. Cover with plastic wrap and chill in the refrigerator for 2 hours, until set.

4 Whip the cream until thick, then pipe a swirl on top of each of the desserts. Serve immediately.

Chocolate Clouds

This unbelievably easy but delicious dessert can be made in a matter of a few minutes. Add the cream just before serving.

50 mins plus 1 hr 30 mins chilling	5 mins

SERVES 6

INGREDIENTS

4 oz/115 g semisweet chocolate, broken into pieces

4 eggs, separated

2¼ cups heavy cream

toasted slivered almonds, to decorate

1 Put the chocolate in a heatproof bowl set over a pan of gently simmering water. Stir over low heat until melted. Remove from the heat and let cool slightly, then beat in the egg yolks.

2 In a separate bowl, whisk the egg whites until they are stiff, then fold them into the chocolate mixture. Set aside for 30 minutes until starting to set.

3 Whip half the cream until thick, then fold ⅔ cup of it into the chocolate mixture. Spoon half the chocolate mixture into 6 sundae glasses. Divide another ⅔ cup of whipped cream among the glasses in a layer over the chocolate mixture, then top with the remaining chocolate mixture. Cover with plastic wrap and chill in the refrigerator for 30 minutes.

4 Just before serving, whip the remaining cream until it is thick. Pipe a swirl of cream on the top of each dessert and sprinkle with the almonds.

Chocolate Banana Sundae

A banana split in a glass! Choose the best vanilla ice cream you can find, or better still, make your own. Serve with fan wafer cookies.

15 mins   5 mins

SERVES 4

INGREDIENTS

GLOSSY CHOCOLATE SAUCE

2 oz/55 g semisweet chocolate

4 tbsp corn syrup

1 tbsp butter

1 tbsp cognac or dark rum (optional)

SUNDAE

4 bananas, peeled

⅔ cup heavy cream

8–12 scoops good-quality vanilla ice cream

¾ cup slivered or chopped almonds, toasted

grated or flaked chocolate, for sprinkling

4 fan wafer cookies, to serve

1 To make the chocolate sauce, break the chocolate into small pieces and place in a heatproof bowl with the syrup and butter. Set over a pan of gently simmering water until melted, stirring until well combined. Remove the bowl from the heat and stir in the cognac or rum (if using).

2 Whip the cream until just holding its shape, and slice the bananas. Place a scoop of ice cream in the bottom of 4 tall sundae dishes. Top with slices of banana, some chocolate sauce, a spoonful of cream, and a generous sprinkling of nuts.

3 Repeat the layers, finishing with a good dollop of cream, sprinkled with nuts, and a little grated or flaked chocolate. Serve with fan wafer cookies.

VARIATION

For a traditional banana split, halve the bananas lengthwise and place on a plate with 2 scoops of ice cream between. Top with cream and sprinkle with nuts. Serve with the glossy chocolate sauce poured over the top.

Champagne Mousse

Any dry sparkling wine made by the traditional method used for champagne can be used for this elegant dessert.

🍲 1 hr plus 2 hrs chilling   🕐 8 mins

SERVES 4

INGREDIENTS

SPONGE

2 tbsp butter, melted, plus extra for greasing

4 eggs

⅓ cup superfine sugar

⅔ cup self-rising flour

2 tbsp unsweetened cocoa

MOUSSE

1 envelope powdered gelatin

3 tbsp water

1¼ cups champagne of dry sparkling wine

1¼ cups heavy cream

2 egg whites

⅓ cup superfine sugar

2 oz/55 g semisweet chocolate-flavored cake covering, melted, to decorate

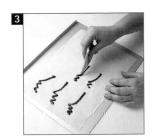

1 Preheat the oven to 400°F/200°C. Line a 15 x 10-inch/38 x 25-cm jelly roll pan with greased parchment paper. Place the eggs and sugar in a bowl and beat, using an electric whisk if you have one, until the mixture is very thick and a trail is left when the whisk is dragged across the surface. If using a balloon whisk, use a heatproof bowl set over a pan of gently simmering water while whisking. Sift the flour and unsweetened cocoa together and fold into the egg mixture. Fold in the butter. Pour into the pan and bake in the preheated oven for 8 minutes, or until springy to the touch. Cool for 5 minutes, then turn out on to a

wire rack until cold. Meanwhile, line 4 x 4-inch/10-cm baking rings with parchment paper. Line the sides with 1-inch/2.5-cm strips of cake and the bottom with circles.

2 For the mousse, sprinkle the gelatin over the water and let it go spongy. Set the bowl over a pan of gently simmering water; stir until dissolved. Stir in the champagne.

3 Whip the cream until just holding its shape. Fold in the champagne mixture. Stand in a cool place until on the point of setting, stirring. Whisk the egg whites until soft peaks form, add the sugar, and whisk until glossy. Fold into the setting mixture. Spoon into the sponge cases, letting the mixture go above the sponge. Chill for 2 hours. Pipe the cake covering in squiggles on a piece of parchment paper, let them set, then use them to decorate the mousses.

Layered Chocolate Mousse

Three layers of rich mousse give this elegant dessert extra chocolate appeal. It is a little fiddly to prepare, but well worth the extra effort.

20 mins plus 3 hrs chilling

10 mins

SERVES 4

INGREDIENTS

3 eggs

1 tsp cornstarch

4 tbsp superfine sugar

1¼ cups milk

1 envelope powdered gelatin

3 tbsp water

1¼ cups heavy cream

2¾ oz/75 g semisweet chocolate, broken into pieces

2¾ oz/75 g white chocolate, broken into pieces

2¾ oz/75 g milk chocolate, broken into pieces

chocolate caraque, to decorate (see page 9)

1 Line a 1-lb/450-g loaf pan with parchment paper. Separate the eggs, putting each egg white in a separate bowl. Place the egg yolks and sugar in a large mixing bowl and whisk until well combined. Place the milk in a pan and heat gently, stirring until almost boiling. Pour the milk on to the egg yolks, whisking.

2 Set the bowl over a pan of gently simmering water and cook, stirring until the mixture thickens enough to thinly coat the back of a wooden spoon.

3 Sprinkle the gelatin over the water in a small heatproof bowl and let it go spongy. Set over a pan of hot water and stir until dissolved. Stir into the hot mixture. Let the mixture cool.

4 Whip the cream until just holding its shape. Fold into the egg custard, then divide the mixture into 3. Put the 3 types of chocolate in separate heatproof bowls set over pans of gently simmering water until melted. Fold the semisweet chocolate into one egg custard portion. Whisk one egg white until soft peaks form and fold into the semisweet chocolate custard until combined. Pour into the prepared pan and smooth the top. Chill in the coldest part of the refrigerator until just set. The remaining mixtures should stay at room temperature.

5 Fold the white chocolate into another portion of the egg custard. Whisk another egg white and fold in. Pour on top of the semisweet chocolate layer and chill quickly. Repeat with the remaining milk chocolate and egg white. Chill for at least 2 hours, until set. To serve, carefully turn out on to a serving dish and decorate with chocolate caraque.

White Chocolate Mousse

White chocolate makes a sweet and creamy mousse and fragrant rose water adds an interesting flavor. Decorate with pretty washed rose petals.

30 mins plus
8 hrs chilling

8 mins

SERVES 6

INGREDIENTS

9 oz/250 g white chocolate, broken into pieces

½ cup whole milk

1½ cup heavy cream

1 tsp rose water

4 oz/115 g semisweet chocolate, broken into pieces

washed rose petals, to decorate

1 Put the white chocolate and milk in a pan and heat very gently until the chocolate has melted. Transfer to a large bowl and let cool.

2 Put the cream and rose water in a bowl and whisk until soft peaks form. In a large bowl, whisk the egg whites until stiff but not dry. Fold the whipped cream into the chocolate, then fold in the egg whites. Spoon the mixture into 6 small dishes or glasses, cover with plastic wrap, and place in the refrigerator for 8 hours, or overnight, to set.

3 Put the semisweet chocolate in a heatproof bowl set over a pan of gently simmering water until melted. Let cool, then spread evenly over the mousses. Leave until hardened, then decorate with rose petals and serve.

Mocha Swirl Mousse

A combination of feather-light yet rich chocolate and coffee mousses, whipped and attractively presented in serving glasses or dishes.

15 mins plus
1 hr chilling

0 mins

SERVES 4

INGREDIENTS

1 tbsp coffee and chicory extract

2 tsp unsweetened cocoa, plus extra
    for dusting

1 tsp lowfat drinking chocolate powder

⅔ cup lowfat sour cream, plus
    4 tsp to serve

2 tsp powdered gelatin

2 tbsp boiling water

2 large egg whites

2 tbsp superfine sugar

4 chocolate-coated coffee beans, to serve

1 Place the coffee and chicory extract in one bowl, and 2 teaspoons of unsweetened cocoa and the drinking chocolate in another bowl. Divide the sour cream among the 2 bowls and mix both well.

2 Dissolve the gelatin in the boiling water and set aside. In a greasefree bowl, whisk the egg whites and sugar until stiff and divide this evenly among the 2 mixtures.

3 Divide the dissolved gelatin among the 2 mixtures and, using a large metal spoon, gently fold until well mixed.

4 Spoon small amounts of the 2 mousses alternately into 4 serving glasses and swirl together gently. Let chill for 1 hour, or until set.

5 To serve, top each mousse with a teaspoon of sour cream, a chocolate coffee bean, and a light dusting of cocoa. Serve immediately.

COOK'S TIP

Vegetarians should not be denied this delicious chocolate dessert. Instead of gelatin, use the vegetarian equivalent, gelozone, available from health-food stores. Be sure to read the instructions on the package first, because it is prepared differently from gelatin.

Chocolate Mousse

This is a light and fluffy mousse with a subtle hint of orange. It is wickedly delicious served with a fresh fruit sauce.

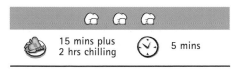

15 mins plus
2 hrs chilling

5 mins

SERVES 8

INGREDIENTS

3½ oz/100 g semisweet chocolate, broken into pieces

1¼ cups plain yogurt

⅔ cup Quark

4 tbsp superfine sugar

1 tbsp orange juice

1 tbsp cognac

1½ tsp powdered gelatin, or gelozone (vegetarian gelatin)

9 tbsp cold water

2 large egg whites

TO DECORATE

coarsely grated bittersweet and white chocolate

orange rind

1 Put the chocolate in a heatproof bowl set over a pan of gently simmering water until melted. Put the melted chocolate, yogurt, Quark, sugar, orange juice, and cognac in a food processor or blender and process for 30 seconds. Transfer the mixture to a large bowl.

2 Sprinkle the gelatin or gelozone over the water and stir until dissolved.

3 In a pan, bring the gelatin or gelozone and water to a boil for 2 minutes. Cool slightly, then thoroughly stir into the chocolate mixture.

4 Whisk the egg whites until stiff peaks form and fold into the chocolate mixture using a metal spoon.

5 Line a 1-lb 2 oz/500-g loaf pan with plastic wrap. Spoon the mousse into the pan. Chill in the refrigerator for 2 hours, until set. Turn the mousse out on to a serving plate, decorate with grated chocolate and orange rind, and serve.

COOK'S TIP
For a quick fruit sauce, process canned mandarin segments in natural juice in a food processor and press through a strainer. Stir in 1 tablespoon of honey and serve with the mousse.

Rich Chocolate Mousses

A serious dessert for dedicated chocolate lovers, they make a spectacular finale to any special-occasion meal.

10 mins plus 4 hrs chilling

5 mins

SERVES 4

INGREDIENTS

10½ oz/300 g semisweet chocolate (at least 70% cocoa solids)

5 tbsp superfine sugar

1½ tbsp unsalted butter

1 tbsp cognac

4 eggs, separated

unsweetened cocoa, to decorate

1 Break the chocolate into small pieces and put it in a heatproof bowl over a pan of gently simmering water. Add the superfine sugar, and butter and melt together, stirring, until smooth. Remove from the heat, stir in the cognac, and let cool a little. Add the egg yolks and beat until smooth.

2 In a separate bowl, whisk the egg whites until stiff peaks form, then fold them into the chocolate mixture. Place a stainless steel cooking ring on each of 4 small serving plates, then spoon the mixture into each ring and smooth the surfaces. Transfer to the refrigerator and chill for at least 4 hours, until set.

3 Remove the mousses from the refrigerator and discard the cooking rings. Dust with unsweetened cocoa and serve immediately.

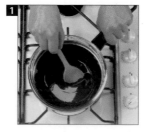

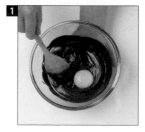

Sweet Mascarpone Mousse

A sweet cream cheese dessert that complements the tartness of fresh summer fruits rather well. Serve with amaretti cookies, if liked.

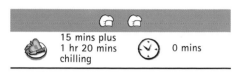

SERVES 4

I N G R E D I E N T S

2 cups mascarpone cheese

½ cup superfine sugar

4 egg yolks

1¾ cups frozen summer fruits, such as raspberries and red currants

red currants, to decorate

amaretti cookies, to serve

1 Place the mascarpone cheese in a large mixing bowl. Using a wooden spoon, beat the mascarpone cheese until smooth.

2 Stir the sugar and egg yolks into the mascarpone cheese, mixing well. Let the mixture chill in the refrigerator for 1 hour.

3 Spoon a layer of the mascarpone mixture into the bottom of 4 individual serving dishes. Spoon a layer of the summer fruits on top. Repeat the layers in the same order, reserving some of the mascarpone mixture for the top.

4 Let the mousses chill in the refrigerator for about 20 minutes. The fruits should still be slightly frozen.

5 Decorate the mascarpone mousses with red currants and serve with amaretti cookies.

VARIATION
Try adding 3 tablespoons of your favorite liqueur to the mascarpone cheese mixture in step 1, if you prefer.

Black & White Pudding

This rich dessert is a cross between a steamed pudding and a soufflé. It makes an extravagant treat whatever the occasion.

30 mins   45 mins

SERVES 4

INGREDIENTS

oil, for brushing

4 oz/115 g butter, sweet for preference

generous ½ cup golden superfine sugar

½ tsp ground cardamoms

4 eggs, separated

4 oz/115 g semisweet chocolate, broken into pieces

1 tbsp rum

⅔ cup heavy cream

¼ cup sour cream

1 Lightly brush a 3½-cup ovenproof bowl with oil. Place the butter, sugar, and cardamoms in a bowl and beat until light and thick. Gradually beat in the egg yolks. Put the chocolate in a heatproof bowl set over a pan of gently simmering water until melted. Let cool. Stir the cooled chocolate and the rum into the egg mixture. Place the egg whites in a separate greasefree bowl and whisk until stiff but not dry. Stir 1 tablespoon of the whisked egg whites into the chocolate mixture, then carefully fold in the remainder.

2 Turn the mixture into the prepared bowl. Cover with oiled parchment paper and foil and tie securely with string. Place the bowl in a large, heavy-based pan and pour in enough boiling water to come one-third of the way up the side of the bowl. Cover and let simmer for 45 minutes.

3 Leave the pudding in the bowl until cold, then turn out on to a serving dish. Cover the pudding with the sour cream or serve on the side.

Raspberry Creams

A refreshing dessert that, as well as being delicious and simple to prepare, has the advantage of being low in fat.

10 mins plus 1 hr chilling   0 mins

SERVES 4

INGREDIENTS

2⅔ cups raspberries

¾ cup lowfat cottage cheese

3 tbsp sugar

⅔ cup lowfat plain yogurt

confectioners' sugar, sifted, to decorate

1 Reserving a few whole raspberries to decorate, use the back of a spoon to push the raspberries and cottage cheese through a strainer into a bowl.

2 Stir the sugar and yogurt into the raspberry mixture and stir to blend, then spoon into individual serving dishes. Chill in the refrigerator for about 1 hour.

3 Serve chilled, decorated with the reserved raspberries and dusted with sifted confectioners' sugar.

Lime Mousse with Mango

Lime-flavored cream molds, served with a fresh mango and lime sauce, make a stunning dessert for any occasion.

10 mins   0 mins

SERVES 4

INGREDIENTS

1 cup cream cheese

grated rind of 1 lime

1 tbsp superfine sugar

½ cup heavy cream

MANGO SAUCE

1 mango

juice of 1 lime

4 tsp superfine sugar

TO DECORATE

4 cape gooseberries

strips of lime rind

1 Put the cream cheese, lime rind, and sugar in a bowl and mix together.

2 Whisk the heavy cream in a separate bowl and fold into the cream cheese.

3 Line 4 decorative molds or ramekins with cheesecloth or plastic wrap and divide the mixture evenly among them. Fold the cheesecloth over the top and press down firmly.

4 To make the sauce, slice through the mango on each side of the large flat pit, then cut the flesh from the pit. Remove the skin, cut off 12 thin slices and set aside.

5 Chop the remaining mango, and put into a food processor with the lime juice and sugar. Blend until smooth, or push the mango through a strainer, then mix with the lime juice and sugar.

6 Turn out the molds on to serving plates. Arrange 3 slices of mango on each plate, pour some sauce around, decorate with cape gooseberries and lime rind, and serve.

COOK'S TIP

Cape gooseberries have a tart and mildly scented flavor and make an excellent decoration for many desserts. Peel back the papery husks to expose the bright orange fruits.

Mango Mousse

This is a light, softly set and tangy mousse, which is perfect for clearing the palate after a Chinese meal of mixed flavors.

40 mins   0 mins

SERVES 4

INGREDIENTS

14 oz/400 g canned mangoes in syrup

2 pieces preserved ginger, chopped, plus extra to decorate

1 cup heavy cream

4 tsp powdered gelatin

2 tbsp hot water

2 egg whites

1½ tbsp light brown sugar

lime rind, to decorate

1 Drain the mangoes, reserving the syrup. Blend the mango pieces and ginger in a food processor or blender for 30 seconds, or until smooth.

2 Measure the purée and make up to 1¼ cups with the reserved mango syrup.

3 In a separate bowl, whip the cream until soft peaks form. Fold the mango mixture into the cream until well combined.

4 Dissolve the gelatin in the hot water and let cool slightly.

5 Pour the gelatin into the mango mixture in a steady stream, stirring. Let cool in the refrigerator for 30 minutes, until almost set.

6 Beat the egg whites in a clean bowl until soft peaks form, then beat in the sugar. Gently fold the egg whites into the mango mixture with a metal spoon.

7 Spoon the mousse into individual serving dishes, decorate with preserved ginger and lime rind and serve.

COOK'S TIP
The gelatin must be stirred into the mango mixture in a gentle, steady stream to prevent it from setting in lumps when it comes into contact with the cold mixture.

Orange Syllabub

A zesty, creamy whip made from yogurt and milk with a hint of orange, served with light and luscious sweet sponge cakes.

30 mins plus
2 hrs chilling

10 mins

SERVES 4

INGREDIENTS

4 oranges

2½ cups lowfat plain yogurt

6 tbsp lowfat milk powder

4 tbsp superfine sugar

1 tbsp grated orange rind

4 tbsp orange juice

2 egg whites

orange rind, to decorate

SPONGE HEARTS

2 medium eggs

6 tbsp superfine sugar

6 tbsp all-purpose flour

6 tbsp whole-wheat flour

1 tbsp hot water

1 tsp confectioners' sugar, for dusting

1 Slice off the tops and bottoms of the oranges and the skin. Then cut out the segments, removing the rind and membranes between each one. Divide the orange segments among 4 dessert glasses, then chill.

2 In a mixing bowl, combine the yogurt, milk powder, sugar, orange rind, and juice. Cover and chill for 1 hour. Whisk the egg whites until stiff, then fold into the yogurt mixture. Pile on to the orange slices and chill for 1 hour. Decorate with fresh orange rind.

3 To make the sponge hearts, preheat the oven to 425°F/220°C. Line a 6 x 10-inch/15 x 25-cm baking pan with parchment paper. Whisk the eggs and superfine sugar until thick and pale. Sift the flours, then fold in using a large metal spoon, adding the hot water at the same time.

4 Pour into the pan and bake in the preheated oven for 9–10 minutes, until golden and firm to the touch.

5 Turn on to a sheet of parchment paper. Using a 2-inch/5-cm heart-shaped cutter, stamp out hearts. Transfer to a wire rack to cool. Lightly dust with confectioners' sugar before serving with the syllabub.

Syllabub

Wine, cognac, and cream make this old-fashioned dessert wonderfully self-indulgent and it is guaranteed to impress at dinner parties.

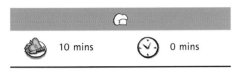

10 mins   0 mins

SERVES 6

INGREDIENTS

¼ cup Madeira

2 tbsp cognac

grated rind of 1 lemon

½ cup lemon juice

generous ½ cup superfine sugar

2½ cups heavy cream

10 amaretti or ratafia cookies, crumbled

ground cinnamon and lemon slices,
   to decorate

1 Whisk the Madeira, cognac, lemon rind, lemon juice, and sugar in a bowl until combined.

2 Add the cream and whisk until the mixture is thick.

3 Divide the cookies among 6 long-stemmed glasses or sundae dishes. Fill each glass or dish with the syllabub mixture and chill until ready to serve. Dust the surface of each dessert with a little ground cinnamon and decorate with the lemon slices.

COOK'S TIP
Madeira is a fortified wine from the island of the same name. It may be dry, medium, or sweet. Sweet madeira is best for this recipe.

Lemon & Lime Syllabub

This dessert is rich but absolutely delicious. It is not, however, for the calorie-conscious because it contains a high proportion of cream.

15 mins plus
4 hrs infusing/
chilling

0 mins

SERVES 4

I N G R E D I E N T S

¼ cup superfine sugar

grated rind and juice of 1 small lemon

grated rind and juice of 1 small lime

¼ cup Marsala or medium sherry

1¼ cups heavy cream

strips of lime and lemon rind, to decorate

 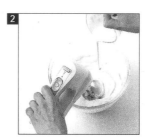 

1 Put the sugar, lemon rind and juice, lime rind and juice, and Marsala in a bowl, mix well, and set aside to infuse for 2 hours.

2 Add the cream to the fruit juice mixture and whisk until it just holds its shape.

3 Spoon the mixture into 4 tall serving glasses and chill in the refrigerator for 2 hours.

4 Decorate with strips of lime and lemon rind and serve.

Pink Syllabub

The pretty pink color of this dessert is achieved by adding black currant-flavored liqueur to the wine and cream before whipping.

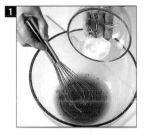

45 mins   0 mins

SERVES 2

INGREDIENTS

5 tbsp white wine

2–3 tsp black currant-flavored liqueur

finely grated rind of ½ lemon or orange

1 tbsp superfine sugar

scant 1 cup heavy cream

ladyfingers (optional)

fresh fruit, such as strawberries, raspberries, or red currants, or pecan or walnut halves

fresh mint sprigs

1 Mix together the white wine, black currant-flavored liqueur, grated lemon or orange rind, and superfine sugar in a bowl and set aside for at least 30 minutes.

2 Add the cream to the wine mixture and whip until the mixture has thickened enough to stand in soft peaks.

3 If you are using the ladyfingers, break them up coarsely and divide them among 2 glasses.

4 Put the mixture into a pastry bag fitted with a large star or plain tip and pipe it over the ladyfingers. Alternatively, simply pour the syllabub over the ladyfingers. Chill until ready to serve.

5 Before serving, decorate each syllabub with slices or small pieces of fresh soft fruit or nuts, and sprigs of mint.

COOK'S TIP
These syllabubs will keep in the refrigerator for 48 hours, so it is worth making more than you need, and keeping the extra for another day.

Baked Chocolate Alaska

A cool dessert that leaves the cook completely unflustered—assemble it in advance and keep it in the freezer until required.

50 mins   12 mins

SERVES 4

INGREDIENTS

butter, for greasing

2 eggs

4 tbsp superfine sugar

¼ cup all-purpose flour

2 tbsp unsweetened cocoa

3 egg whites

⅔ cup superfine sugar

4 cups good-quality chocolate ice cream

1 Preheat the oven to 425°F/220°C. Grease a 7-inch/18-cm round cake pan and line the bottom with parchment paper.

2 Whisk the eggs and the 4 tablespoons of sugar in a mixing bowl until very thick and pale. Sift the flour and unsweetened cocoa together and carefully fold in.

3 Pour into the prepared pan and bake in the preheated oven for 7 minutes, or until springy to the touch. Transfer to a wire rack to cool completely.

COOK'S TIP

This dessert is delicious served with a black currant coulis. Cook a few black currants in a little orange juice until soft, blend to a paste, and push through a strainer, then sweeten to taste with a little confectioners' sugar.

4 Whisk the egg whites in a greasefree bowl until soft peaks form. Gradually add the sugar, whisking until you have a thick, glossy meringue.

5 Place the sponge on a cookie sheet and pile the ice cream on to the center in a heaped dome.

6 Pipe or spread the meringue over the ice cream, making sure the ice cream is completely enclosed. (At this point the dessert can be frozen, if wished.)

7 Return it to the oven, for 5 minutes until the meringue is just golden. Serve immediately.

Apricot & Orange Fool

A simple, summery dessert that takes only minutes to make. Apricots and orange juice make a refreshing combination.

5 mins   0 mins

SERVES 4

INGREDIENTS

generous 1 cup no-soak dried apricots

1 tbsp honey

generous 1 cup fresh orange juice

generous 1 cup lowfat plain yogurt

2 tsp toasted slivered almonds, to decorate

1 Put all the ingredients, except the almonds, in a bowl and mix thoroughly until smooth.

2 Serve in individual glass dishes, decorated with the toasted almonds.

Tropical Fruit Fool

Fruit fools are always popular, and this light, tangy version will be no exception. You can use your favorite fruits in this recipe.

35 mins   0 mins

SERVES 4

INGREDIENTS

1 medium ripe mango

2 kiwi fruit

1 medium banana

2 tbsp lime juice

½ tsp finely grated lime rind, plus extra to decorate

2 egg whites

scant 2 cups canned lowfat custard

½ tsp vanilla extract

2 passion fruit

1 Peel the mango, then slice either side of the smooth, flat central pit. Coarsely chop the flesh and process the fruit in a food processor or blender until smooth. Alternatively, mash with a fork.

2 Peel the kiwi fruit, chop the flesh into small pieces, and place in a bowl. Peel and chop the banana, and add to the bowl. Toss all of the fruit in the lime juice and rind and mix well.

3 In a greasefree bowl, whisk the egg whites until stiff and then gently fold in the custard and vanilla extract until thoroughly mixed.

4 In 4 tall glasses, alternately layer the chopped fruit, mango purée, and custard mixture, finishing with the custard on top. Set aside to chill in the refrigerator for 20 minutes.

5 Halve the passion fruit, scoop out the seeds, and spoon over the fruit fools. Decorate each serving with the extra lime rind and serve.

VARIATION
Other tropical fruits to try include papaya purée, with chopped pineapple and dates or pomegranate seeds to decorate.

Raspberry Fool

This dish is very easy to make and can be prepared in advance and stored in the refrigerator until required.

15 mins plus
1 hr chilling   0 mins

SERVES 4

I N G R E D I E N T S

1⅔ cups fresh raspberries, plus extra
   to decorate

¼ cup confectioners' sugar

1¼ cups sour cream, plus extra to decorate

½ tsp vanilla extract

2 egg whites

lemon balm leaves, to decorate

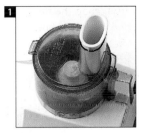

1 Put the raspberries and confectioners' sugar in a food processor or blender and process until smooth. Alternatively, press through a strainer with the back of a spoon.

2 Reserve 1 tablespoon per portion of sour cream for decorating.

3 Put the vanilla extract and remaining sour cream in a bowl and stir in the raspberry mixture.

4 Whisk the egg whites in a separate mixing bowl until stiff peaks form. Gently fold the egg whites into the raspberry mixture using a metal spoon, until fully incorporated.

5 Spoon the raspberry fool into individual serving dishes and chill for at least 1 hour. Decorate with the reserved sour cream, raspberries, and lemon balm leaves and serve.

COOK'S TIP
Although this dessert is best made with fresh raspberries in season, an acceptable result can be achieved with frozen raspberries, which are available from most stores.

Almond Sherbet

It is best to use whole almonds rather than ready-ground almonds for this dish because they give it a better texture.

45 mins plus
3–8 hrs 30 mins
soaking/chilling

0 mins

SERVES 2

INGREDIENTS

2 cups shelled almonds

2 tbsp sugar

1¼ cups milk

1¼ cups water

1 Put the almonds in a bowl, cover with water, and set aside to soak for at least 3 hours, or preferably overnight.

2 Using a sharp knife, chop the almonds into small pieces. Grind to a fine paste in a food processor or in a mortar with a pestle.

3 Add the sugar to the almond paste and grind once again to form a very fine paste.

4 Add the milk and water and mix thoroughly, in a bowl or use a blender.

5 Transfer the almond sherbet to a large serving dish.

6 Chill the almond sherbet in the refrigerator for about 30 minutes. Stir it well just before serving.

Mocha Sherbet

This mocha sherbet makes a light and refreshing yet luxurious end to any meal. Serve with some crisp cookies and freshly brewed coffee.

15 mins plus
9 hrs freezing/
chilling

10 mins

SERVES 6

INGREDIENTS

½ cup unsweetened cocoa

generous ¾ cup golden superfine sugar

2 tsp instant coffee powder

2 cups water

crisp cookies, to serve

1 Sift the unsweetened cocoa into a small, heavy-based pan and add the superfine sugar, coffee powder, and a little of the water. Using a wooden spoon, mix together to form a thin paste, then gradually stir in the remaining water. Bring the mixture to a boil over low heat and let simmer gently for 8 minutes, stirring frequently.

2 Remove the pan from the heat and let cool. Transfer the mixture to a bowl, cover with plastic wrap, and place in the refrigerator until well chilled. Freeze in an ice-cream maker, following the manufacturer's instructions. Alternatively, pour the mixture into a large freezerproof container, then cover and freeze for 2 hours. Remove the sherbet from the freezer and beat to break down the ice crystals. Freeze for an additional 6 hours, beating the sherbet every 2 hours.

3 Transfer the sherbet to the refrigerator 30 minutes before serving. Scoop into 6 small bowls and serve with cookies.

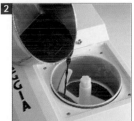

Chocolate Sherbet

This is a truly special sherbet, and it is worth buying the best possible quality bittersweet and semisweet chocolate for it.

10–12 mins plus
3 hrs 30 mins
cooling/freezing

7–10 mins

SERVES 6

INGREDIENTS

5 oz/140 g bittersweet chocolate,
chopped coarsely

5 oz/140 g semisweet chocolate,
chopped coarsely

scant 2 cups water

1 cup superfine sugar

langues de chat cookies, to serve

1 Put both types of chocolate into a food processor and process briefly until chopped very finely.

2 Pour the water into a heavy-based pan and add the sugar. Stir over medium heat to dissolve, then bring to a boil. Boil for 2 minutes, without stirring, then remove the pan from the heat.

3 With the motor of the food processor running, pour the hot syrup on to the chocolate. Process for about 2 minutes, until all the chocolate has melted and the mixture is smooth. Scrape down the sides of the food processor, if necessary. Strain the chocolate mixture into a freezerproof container and let cool.

4 When the mixture is cool, place it in the freezer for about 1 hour, until slushy but starting to become firm around the edges. Tip the mixture into the food processor and process until smooth. Return to the container and freeze for at least 2 hours until firm.

5 Remove the sherbet from the freezer about 10 minutes before serving and let stand at room temperature to let it soften slightly. Serve in scoops with langues de chat cookies.

Chocolate Orange Sherbet

Semisweet chocolate encloses liqueur-flavored sherbet to provide this very elegant and sophisticated dinner party dessert.

1 hr plus
12 hrs freezing

12–15 mins

SERVES 4

INGREDIENTS

2 tsp vegetable oil, for brushing

8 oz/225 g semisweet chocolate, broken into small pieces

4 cups crushed ice

2¼ cups freshly squeezed orange juice

⅔ cup water

¼ cup superfine sugar

finely grated rind of 1 orange

juice and finely grated rind of 1 lemon

1 tsp powdered gelatin

3 tbsp orange-flavored liqueur

fresh mint leaves, to decorate

1 Brush a 3¼-cup mold with oil, drain well, then chill in the refrigerator. Put the chocolate in a heatproof bowl set over a pan of gently simmering water. Stir over low heat until melted, then remove from the heat.

2 Remove the mold from the refrigerator and pour in the melted chocolate. Tip and turn the mold to coat the interior. Place the mold on a bed of crushed ice and continue tipping and turning until the chocolate has set. Return the mold to the refrigerator.

3 Reserve 3 tablespoons of the orange juice in a small, heatproof bowl. Pour the remainder into a pan and add the water, sugar, orange rind, and lemon juice

and rind. Stir over low heat until the sugar has dissolved, then increase the heat and bring the mixture to a boil. Remove the pan from the heat.

4 Meanwhile, sprinkle the gelatin on the surface of the orange juice in the bowl. Set aside for 2 minutes to soften, then set over a pan of gently simmering water until dissolved. Stir the dissolved gelatin and the liqueur into the orange juice mixture. Pour into a freezerproof container and place in the freezer for 30 minutes, until slushy.

5 Remove the sherbet from the freezer, transfer to a bowl, and beat

thoroughly to break up the ice crystals. Return it to the freezerproof container and put it back in the freezer for 1 hour. Repeat this process 3 more times.

6 Remove the sherbet from the freezer, transfer to a bowl, and beat well once more. Remove the mold from the refrigerator and spoon the sherbet into it. Smooth the surface with a spatula. Put the mold in the freezer overnight.

7 Remove the mold from the freezer shortly before serving. Place a chilled serving plate on top and, holding them firmly together, invert. Decorate with fresh mint leaves and serve immediately.

Orange Sherbet

Serve this fresh-tasting sherbet in scooped-out orange shells for a dramatic effect to impress your guests.

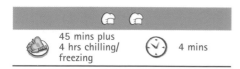

45 mins plus 4 hrs chilling/ freezing

4 mins

SERVES 4

INGREDIENTS

generous 2 cups water

1 cup superfine sugar

8 large oranges

2 tbsp orange-flavored liqueur

1 Heat the water and superfine sugar in a pan over low heat, stirring, until the sugar has dissolved, then boil without stirring for 2 minutes. Pour into a heatproof glass bowl. Cool to room temperature. While it cools, grate the rind from 2 oranges and extract the juice. Extract the juice from 2 more oranges. Mix the juice and rind in a bowl, cover with plastic wrap, and set aside. Discard the squeezed oranges. When the sugar syrup has cooled, stir in the orange juice, the grated rind, and the orange-flavored liqueur. Cover with plastic wrap and chill for 1 hour.

2 Transfer the orange mixture to an ice-cream maker and process for 15 minutes. Alternatively, transfer it into a freezerproof container and freeze for 1 hour. Transfer to a large bowl, beat to break up the crystals, then put it back in the freezerproof container and freeze for 30 minutes. Repeat twice more, freezing for 30 minutes and whisking each time. Cut the tops off the remaining 4 oranges. Scoop out the flesh, divide the frozen sherbet among the orange cups, and serve.

Orange & Campari Sherbet

Campari is a distinctive Italian drink made with the rind of bitter oranges. Combined with freshly squeezed orange juice it makes a cooling sherbet.

1 hr plus 2 hrs chilling/freezing

3–5 mins

SERVES 4–6

INGREDIENTS

3–4 large oranges

generous 1 cup superfine sugar

2½ cups water

3 tbsp Campari

2 extra large egg whites

TO DECORATE

fresh mint leaves

candied citrus rind (optional)

1 Working over a bowl to catch any juice, pare the rind from 3 of the oranges, without removing the bitter white pith. If some of the pith does come off with the rind, use the knife to scrape it off.

2 Put the sugar and water into a pan and stir over low heat until dissolved. Increase the heat and boil for 2 minutes, without stirring. Using a wet pastry brush, brush any crystals down the side of the pan, if necessary.

3 Remove the pan from the heat and pour into a heatproof nonmetallic bowl. Add the orange rind and let steep while the mixture cools to room temperature.

4 Roll the pared oranges back and forth on the work counter, pressing down firmly. Cut them in half and squeeze ½ cup juice. If you need more juice, squeeze the remaining orange.

5 When the syrup is cool, stir in the orange juice and Campari. Strain into a container, cover, and chill for at least 30 minutes.

6 Put the mixture in an ice-cream maker and churn for 15 minutes. Alternatively, follow the instructions for Orange Sherbet (opposite). Whisk the egg whites in a clean, greasefree bowl until stiff peaks form.

7 Add the egg whites to the ice-cream maker and continue churning for 5 minutes, or according to the manufacturer's instructions. Transfer to a shallow, freezerproof container, cover, and freeze for up to 2 months.

8 About 15 minutes before serving, place the ice cream in the refrigerator to soften. Scoop into bowls and serve decorated with mint leaves and candied citrus rind, if wished.

Lychees with Orange Sherbet

This dish is truly delicious! The fresh flavor of the sorbet complements the gingery lychees. Perfect for a dinner party dessert.

45 mins plus
2–3 hrs freezing

5 Mins

SERVES 4

INGREDIENTS

SHERBET

1¼ cups superfine sugar

2 cups cold water

12 oz/350 g canned mandarins, in natural juice

2 tbsp lemon juice

STUFFED LYCHEES

15 oz/425 g canned lychees, drained

2 pieces preserved ginger, drained and chopped finely

lime rind, cut into diamond shapes, to decorate

1 To make the sherbet, place the sugar and water in a pan and stir over low heat until the sugar has dissolved. Bring the mixture to a boil and boil vigorously for 2–3 minutes.

2 Blend the mandarins in a food processor or blender until smooth. Press the purée through a strainer then stir into the syrup, together with the lemon juice. Set aside to cool. Once cooled, pour the mixture into a freezerproof container and freeze until set, stirring occasionally.

3 Meanwhile, drain the lychees on absorbent paper towels. Spoon the chopped ginger into the center of the lychees.

4 Arrange the lychees on serving plates and serve with scoops of orange sherbet. Decorate with lime rind.

COOK'S TIP
It is best to leave the sherbet in the refrigerator for 10 minutes, so that it softens slightly, letting you scoop it to serve.

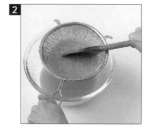

Lychee & Ginger Sherbet

A refreshing palate-cleanser after a rich meal, this sherbet couldn't be easier to make, and can be served with a fruit salad.

30 mins plus
3 hrs 30 mins
freezing

0 mins

SERVES 4

INGREDIENTS

1 lb 12 oz/800 g canned lychees in syrup

finely grated rind of 1 lime

2 tbsp lime juice

3 tbsp syrup from the ginger jar

2 egg whites

TO DECORATE

star fruit slices

slivers of preserved ginger

1 Drain the lychees, reserving the syrup. Place the fruits in a blender or food processor with the lime rind, juice, and ginger syrup and process until completely smooth. Transfer to a mixing bowl.

2 Mix the purée thoroughly with the reserved syrup, then pour into a freezerproof container, and freeze for about 1–1½ hours, until slushy in texture. Alternatively, use an ice-cream maker.

3 Remove from the freezer and whisk to break up the ice crystals. Whisk the egg whites in a clean, dry bowl until stiff, then quickly and lightly fold them into the lychee mixture.

4 Return to the freezer and freeze until firm. Remove from the freezer 15 minutes before serving to soften slightly. Serve the sherbet in scoops, with slices of star fruit and ginger to decorate.

COOK'S TIP
It is not recommended that raw egg whites are served to young children, pregnant women, the elderly, or anyone weakened by chronic illness. The egg whites may be left out of this recipe, but you will need to whisk the sherbet a second time.

Mango & Lime Sherbet

A refreshing sherbet is the perfect way to round off a spicy Thai meal, and mangoes make a deliciously smooth-textured, velvety sherbet.

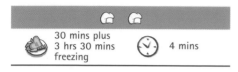

30 mins plus 3 hrs 30 mins freezing

4 mins

SERVES 4

INGREDIENTS

6 tbsp superfine sugar

scant ½ cup water

finely grated rind of 3 limes

2 tbsp coconut cream

2 large, ripe mangoes

generous ½ cup lime juice

curls of fresh coconut, toasted, to decorate

1 Place the sugar, water, and lime rind in a small pan and heat gently, stirring constantly, until the sugar dissolves. Boil rapidly for 2 minutes to reduce slightly, then remove from the heat and strain into a bowl or pitcher. Stir in the coconut cream and set aside to cool.

2 Halve the mangoes, remove the pits, and peel thinly. Chop the flesh coarsely and place in a food processor with the lime juice. Process to a smooth purée and transfer to a small bowl.

3 Pour the cooled syrup into the mango purée, mixing evenly. Tip into a freezerproof container and freeze for 1 hour, or until slushy in texture. Alternatively, use an ice-cream maker.

4 Remove the container from the freezer and beat with an electric whisk to break up the ice crystals. Freeze for an additional hour, then remove from the freezer, and beat the contents again until smooth.

5 Cover the container, return to the freezer, and freeze until firm. To serve, remove from the freezer and let stand at room temperature for about 15 minutes to soften slightly before scooping. Sprinkle with toasted coconut to serve.

COOK'S TIP
If you prefer, canned mangoes in syrup can be used to make the sherbet. Omit the sugar and water, and steep the lime rind in the syrup from the can instead.

Peach Sherbet

This is a quick, but still effective, way of making a luscious frozen dessert full of intense fruit flavor. Decorate with fresh mint leaves.

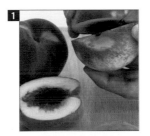

10 mins plus
1 hr freezing   0 mins

SERVES 4

INGREDIENTS

3 large ripe peaches

1 tbsp lemon juice

1 tbsp honey

1 tsp Southern Comfort or peach cognac

fresh mint leaves, to decorate

1 Cut the peaches in half, remove the pits, and place in a bowl of handhot water to loosen the skin. Peel the skin and drain the peach halves on paper towels.

2 Cut the peach halves into 1-inch/ 2.5-cm chunks and toss with the lemon juice. Spread the chunks out on a cookie sheet, cover with plastic wrap, and freeze until solid.

3 Remove the peaches from the freezer and place in a food processor. Process until granular, scraping down the sides from time to time.

4 Add the honey and Southern Comfort or peach cognac and process again until thoroughly combined and fairly firm in consistency. Decorate with fresh mint leaves and serve immediately or place in a freezerproof container and store in the freezer for up to 24 hours.

Peach & Banana Sherbet

An easy dish, perfect to make when peaches are in season. This sherbet is an ideal refreshing dessert to follow a barbecue.

20 mins plus
4 hrs freezing

0 mins

SERVES 4

INGREDIENTS

4 large peaches

2 bananas

1 tbsp peach cognac

fresh mint leaves, to decorate

1 Peel and pit the peaches, then cut the flesh into small chunks. Arrange them in a single layer on a cookie sheet. Peel and slice the bananas and arrange in a single layer on another cookie sheet. Transfer the cookie sheets to the freezer and freeze for 4 hours.

2 Remove the frozen peaches and bananas from the freezer and transfer to a food processor. Pour in the peach cognac and process until the mixture is smooth.

3 Scoop the sherbet into serving bowls, decorate with fresh mint leaves, and serve immediately.

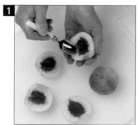

Apple & Honey Water Ice

Apples lend a refreshing tang to this quick, easy-to-make water ice.
Serve straight from the freezer on a hot summer afternoon.

10 mins plus
5–6 hrs freezing

20 mins

SERVES 4

I N G R E D I E N T S

4 crisp dessert apples

2 tbsp lemon juice

scant 1 cup water

5 tbsp sugar

2 tbsp honey

apple slices, to decorate

1 Peel and core the apples and cut them into chunks. Put in a pan with the lemon juice and 1 tablespoon of water and heat gently for about 20 minutes, stirring frequently, until soft.

2 Meanwhile, put the sugar and the remaining water in a pan and heat gently, stirring, until dissolved. Bring to a boil, then boil for 2 minutes. Remove from the heat.

3 Push the apple through a strainer into a bowl. Stir in the sugar syrup and honey. Let stand until cold.

4 When cold, pour the mixture into a freezerproof container. Freeze, uncovered, for 2 hours until the water ice mixture starts to set. Turn the mixture into a bowl and whisk until smooth. Return to the container and freeze for an additional 3–4 hours until firm.

5 Serve decorated with apple slices.

Granita

A delightful end to a meal or a refreshing way to cleanse the palate between courses, granita needs to be served very quickly.

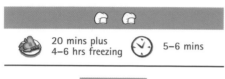

20 mins plus
4–6 hrs freezing

5–6 mins

SERVES 4

INGREDIENTS

LEMON GRANITA

3 lemons

¾ cup lemon juice

3½ oz/100 g superfine sugar

2¼ cups cold water

COFFEE GRANITA

2 tbsp instant coffee powder

2 tbsp sugar

2 tbsp hot water

2½ cups cold water

2 tbsp dark rum or cognac

1 To make the lemon granita, finely grate the lemon rind. Place the lemon rind, juice, and superfine sugar in a pan. Bring the mixture to a boil and let simmer for 5–6 minutes, or until thick and syrupy. Let cool.

2 Once cooled, stir in the cold water and pour into a shallow freezerproof container with a lid. Freeze the granita for 4–5 hours, stirring occasionally to break up the ice. Serve as a palate cleanser between dinner courses.

3 To make the coffee granita, place the coffee and sugar in a bowl and pour over the hot water, stirring constantly until dissolved.

4 Stir in the cold water and dark rum or cognac.

5 Pour the mixture into a shallow freezerproof container with a lid. Freeze the granita for at least 6 hours, stirring every 1–2 hours in order to create a grainy texture. Serve after dinner.

COOK'S TIP

If you would prefer a nonalcoholic version of the coffee granita, simply omit the dark rum or cognac and add extra instant coffee powder instead.

Espresso Granita

Enjoy this crunchy granita as a cooling light dessert at the end of an alfresco supper. Keeps in the freezer for up to three months.

10 mins plus
6 hrs freezing

5 mins

SERVES 4–6

I N G R E D I E N T S

1 cup superfine sugar

2½ cups water

½ tsp vanilla extract

2½ cups very strong espresso coffee, chilled

fresh mint, to decorate

1 Put the sugar in a pan with the water and stir over low heat to dissolve the sugar. Increase the heat and boil for 4 minutes, without stirring. Use a wet pastry brush to brush down any spatters on the side of the pan.

2 Remove the pan from the heat and pour the syrup into a heatproof nonmetallic bowl. Sit the bowl in the kitchen sink filled with ice water to speed up the cooling process. Stir in the vanilla extract and coffee and let stand until completely cool.

3 Transfer to a shallow freezerproof container, cover, and freeze for at least 6 hours, stirring occasionally.

4 Before serving, chill individual serving bowls in the refrigerator.

5 To serve, invert the container on to a cutting board. Rinse a cloth in very hot water, wring it out, then rub on the bottom of the container for 15 seconds. Give the container a sharp shake and the mixture should fall out.

6 Break up the granita with a knife and transfer to a food processor. Process until it becomes grainy and crunchy. Serve in the chilled bowls, decorated with mint.

COOK'S TIP
A very dark, full-flavored espresso is the only choice for this Italian specialty. Otherwise the flavor will be marred by the freezing.

Lemon Granita

Soft and granular, this iced dessert has a sharp, zingy flavor, which is refreshing and ideal for rounding off any rich meal.

15 mins plus 6 hrs freezing

5 mins

SERVES 4–6

INGREDIENTS

4 large unwaxed lemons

½ cup superfine sugar

3 cups water

fresh mint sprigs, to decorate (optional)

1 Pare 6 strips of rind from 1 of the lemons, then finely grate the remaining rind from the remaining lemons, being very careful not to remove any bitter white pith.

2 Roll the lemons back and forth on the work counter, pressing down firmly. Cut each in half and squeeze ½ cup juice. Add the grated rind to the juice. Set aside.

3 Put the pared strips of lemon rind, sugar, and water in a pan and stir over low heat to dissolve the sugar. Increase the heat and boil for 4 minutes, without stirring. Use a wet pastry brush to brush down any spatters on the side of the pan. Remove from the heat, pour into a nonmetallic bowl, and set aside to cool.

VARIATION
Lemon-scented herbs add a unique and unexpected flavor. Add 4 small lemon balm sprigs or 2 lemon thyme sprigs to the syrup in step 3. Remove and discard with the pared rind in step 4. Alternatively, stir ½ tablespoon of finely chopped lemon thyme into the mixture in step 4.

4 Remove the strips of rind from the syrup. Stir in the grated rind and juice. Transfer to a shallow freezerproof container, cover, and freeze for at least 6 hours, stirring occasionally.

5 Chill serving bowls 30 minutes before serving. To serve, invert the container on to a cutting board. Rinse a cloth in very hot water, wring it out, then rub on the bottom of the container for 15 seconds. Give the container a shake and the mixture should fall out.

6 Break up the granita with a knife and transfer to a food processor. Process until it becomes granular. Serve in the chilled bowls (or in scooped-out lemons). Decorate with mint sprigs, if wished.

Rose Ice

A delicately perfumed sweet granita ice, which is coarser than many ice creams. This looks very pretty on a glass dish sprinkled with rose petals.

15 mins plus
6 hrs freezing

10 mins

SERVES 4

INGREDIENTS

1⅔ cups water

2 tbsp coconut cream

4 tbsp sweetened condensed milk

2 tsp rose water

few drops pink food coloring (optional)

pink rose petals, to decorate

1 Place the water in a small pan and add the coconut cream. Heat the mixture gently without boiling, stirring.

2 Remove from the heat and let cool. Stir in the condensed milk, rose water, and food coloring (if using).

3 Pour into a freezerproof container and freeze for 1–1½ hours, until slushy.

4 Remove from the freezer and break up the ice crystals with a fork. Return to the freezer and freeze until firm.

5 Spoon the ice roughly into a pile on a serving dish and sprinkle with rose petals to decorate.

COOK'S TIP
To prevent the ice thawing too quickly at the table, nestle the bottom of the serving dish in another dish filled with crushed ice.

Forest Fruits Granita

This is a wonderfully refreshing dessert on a hot summer day. It's more cooling and less calorie-packed than ice cream, but full of flavor.

1 hr plus
2–3 hrs freezing

5 mins

SERVES 4–6

INGREDIENTS

1 cup strawberries, hulled

¾ cup raspberries

¾ cup blackberries

1–2 tbsp lemon juice (optional)

¾ cup superfine sugar

⅔ cup water

TO DECORATE

whipped cream

fresh mint sprigs

1 Put the strawberries, raspberries, and blackberries into a food processor or blender and process to a purée. Push the purée through a fine-meshed strainer into a freezerproof container to remove the seeds. Add lemon juice to taste.

2 Place the sugar and water in a small pan over low heat and stir until the sugar has dissolved. Pour the syrup over the fruit purée and stir well. Set aside to cool, stirring occasionally, then cover and freeze until set.

3 Transfer the granita to the refrigerator 30 minutes before serving. Spoon the granita into glasses and serve decorated with whipped cream and mint sprigs.

VARIATION
For a really lazy granita, replace the fruit purée with 4½ cups fruit juice, such as orange or cranberry.

Berry Yogurt Ice

This refreshing ice makes a wonderful summer dessert after a filling meal, because it is light and cooling without the richness, or fat, of ice cream.

15 mins plus
2–3 hrs freezing   5 mins

SERVES 4

INGREDIENTS

½ cup raspberries

½ cup blackberries

½ cup strawberries

1 large egg

¼ cup strained plain yogurt

½ cup red wine

2¼ tsp powdered gelatin

fresh berries, to decorate

1 Put the raspberries, blackberries, and strawberries in a food processor and process to a purée. Rub the purée through a strainer into a bowl to remove the seeds. Separate the egg and stir in the yolk and yogurt.

2 Pour the wine into a heatproof bowl and sprinkle the gelatin on the surface. Set aside for 5 minutes to soften, then set the bowl over a pan of gently simmering water until the gelatin has completely dissolved. Pour the gelatin in a steady stream into the berry purée, whisking constantly. Transfer the mixture to a freezerproof container and freeze until slushy.

3 Whisk the egg white until very stiff. Remove the berry mixture from the freezer and fold in the egg white. Return to the freezer and freeze until firm. To serve, scoop the berry yogurt ice into tall glasses and decorate with fresh berries of your choice.

VARIATION
Substitute ¼ cup red currants for half the raspberries and ¼ cup black currants for half the blackberries.

Icy Fruit Blizzard

Keep a store of prepared fruit in the freezer, then whirl it up into this refreshing dessert, which is as light and healthy as it is satisfying.

15 mins plus
2 hrs freezing

0 mins

SERVES 4

INGREDIENTS

1 pineapple, peeled and cut into small pieces

1 large piece watermelon, peeled, seeded, and cut into small pieces

2 cups strawberries or other berries, hulled and whole or sliced

1 mango, peach, or nectarine, peeled and sliced

1 banana, peeled and sliced

orange juice

superfine sugar

1 Arrange the fruit on top of 2 non stick cookie sheets and freeze for at least two hours, or until firm and icy.

2 Place 1 type of fruit in a food processor and process until it is broken up into small pieces.

3 Add a little orange juice and sugar, to taste, and continue to process until it forms a granular mixture. Repeat with the remaining fruit. Arrange in chilled bowls and serve immediately.

Rose Petal Ice Cream

This delicate ice cream is subtly flavored with coconut and rose water, and is guaranteed to impress guests at a dinner party.

1 hr plus
3–4 hrs freezing   5 mins

SERVES 4

INGREDIENTS

1¼ cups milk

2 tbsp coconut cream

3 egg yolks

½ cup superfine sugar

1¼ cups heavy cream, whipped

1 tbsp rose water

TO DECORATE

grated fresh coconut

rose petals

1 Pour the milk into a pan, stir in the coconut cream and heat gently until almost boiling. In a separate bowl, beat together the egg yolks and sugar, remove the milk from the heat, and stir a little into the egg mixture. Return the mixture to the pan and stir over low heat until thickened and smooth. Do not let it boil. Remove from the heat and let cool for 30 minutes. Add the mixture to the cream and fold in. Stir in the rose water. Cover with plastic wrap and chill for 1 hour.

2 Remove from the refrigerator. Transfer to an ice-cream maker and process for 15 minutes. Alternatively, transfer to a freezerproof container and freeze for 1 hour. Take it out of the freezer, transfer to a bowl, and beat to break up the ice crystals. Put it back in the container and freeze for 30 minutes. Repeat twice more, freezing for 30 minutes and whisking each time. Store in the freezer until required.

3 Remove from the freezer and scoop into serving dishes. Scatter over the grated coconut and rose petals and serve.

Rich Vanilla Gelato

Italy is synonymous with ice cream. This homemade version of real vanilla ice cream is absolutely delicious and so easy to make.

45 mins plus
8 hrs freezing

15 mins

SERVES 4–6

INGREDIENTS

2½ cups heavy cream

1 vanilla bean

pared rind of 1 lemon

4 eggs, beaten

2 egg yolks

scant 1 cup superfine sugar

1 Place the cream in a heavy-based pan and heat gently, whisking. Add the vanilla bean, lemon rind, eggs, and egg yolks and heat until the mixture reaches just below boiling point.

2 Reduce the heat and cook for 8–10 minutes, whisking the mixture constantly, until thickened.

3 Stir the sugar into the cream mixture, then set aside and let cool.

4 Strain the cream mixture through a fine strainer.

5 Slit open the vanilla bean and scoop out the tiny black seeds, then stir them into the cream.

6 Pour the mixture into a shallow freezerproof container with a lid and freeze overnight until set. Serve when required.

COOK'S TIP

Ice cream is one of the traditional dishes of Italy. Everyone eats it and there are numerous gelato stalls selling a wide variety of flavors, usually in a cone. It is also serve in scoops, and even sliced!

Chocolate Chip Ice Cream

This marvelous frozen dessert offers the best of both worlds, delicious chocolate chip cookies and a rich dairy-flavored ice.

45 mins plus 6 hrs freezing/chilling — 5 mins

SERVES 6

INGREDIENTS

1¼ cups milk

1 vanilla bean

2 eggs

2 egg yolks

¼ cup superfine sugar

1¼ cups plain yogurt

4½ oz/125 g chocolate chip cookies, broken into small pieces

1 Pour the milk into a small pan, add the vanilla bean, and bring to a boil over low heat. Remove from the heat, cover the pan, and set aside to cool.

2 Beat the eggs and egg yolks in a heatproof bowl set over a pan of gently simmering water. Add the sugar and continue beating until the mixture is pale and creamy.

3 Reheat the milk to simmering point and strain it over the egg mixture. Stir constantly until the custard is thick enough to coat the back of a spoon. Remove the custard from the heat and stand the pan or bowl in cold water to prevent any further cooking. Wash and dry the vanilla bean for future use.

4 Stir the yogurt into the cooled custard and beat until it is well blended. When the mixture is thoroughly cold, stir in the broken cookies.

5 Transfer the mixture to a chilled metal cake pan or freezerproof container, cover, and freeze for 4 hours.

Remove from the freezer every hour, transfer to a chilled bowl and beat vigorously to prevent ice crystals forming, then return to the freezer. Alternatively, freeze the mixture in an ice-cream maker, following the manufacturer's instructions.

6 To serve the ice cream, transfer it to the main part of the refrigerator for 1 hour. Serve in scoops.

Chocolate Fudge Ice Cream

This is an ice cream which is equally popular with adults and children. For best results, transfer to the refrigerator 15 minutes before serving.

15 mins plus
5–6 hrs freezing   0 mins

SERVES 6

INGREDIENTS

4 medium ripe bananas

juice of ½ lemon

1 cup golden superfine sugar

generous 2 cups whipping cream

3½ oz/100 g semisweet chocolate chips

3½ oz/100 g fudge, cut into small pieces

1 Peel the bananas and chop them coarsely then place in a blender or food processor with the lemon juice and superfine sugar. Process until well chopped, then pour in the cream and process again until well blended.

2 Either freeze in an ice-cream maker, following the manufacturer's directions, adding the chocolate chips and fudge just before the ice cream is ready, or pour the mixture into a freezerproof container, cover, and freeze for 2 hours until just frozen. Spoon into a bowl and beat with a fork to break down the ice crystals. Return to the freezer for an additional 2 hours, or until almost frozen.

3 Whisk again and stir in the chocolate chips and fudge. Return to the freezer until firm. Transfer from the freezer to the refrigerator for 15 minutes before serving.

COOK'S TIP
Choose bananas which are ripe but not brown.

Chocolate Kulfi

Kulfi is a delicately spiced Indian ice cream made not with cream but milk. It is traditionally made in special tube-shaped terracotta containers.

1 hr plus
12 hrs freezing

20 mins

SERVES 6

INGREDIENTS

9 cups creamy whole milk

12 whole cardamoms

scant ½ cup golden superfine sugar

3½ oz/100 g semisweet chocolate

scant ¼ cup chopped blanched almonds

¼ cup chopped unsalted pistachios

1 Place the milk and cardamoms in a large heavy-based pan. Bring to a boil, then simmer vigorously until reduced to one third of its original amount.

2 Strain the milk into a bowl, discarding the cardamoms, then stir in the sugar and chocolate until melted. Add the almonds and half the pistachios, then set aside to cool. Pour the mixture into a freezerproof container, cover, and freeze until almost firm, stirring every 30 minutes.

3 When the ice cream is almost solid, pack it into 6 yogurt pots or dariole molds, cover with plastic wrap, and freeze overnight or until completely solid. To serve, dip the molds quickly into hot water then turn out on to dessert plates. Scatter the remaining pistachios over, to decorate.

COOK'S TIP
Use a wide heavy-based pan for reducing the milk to allow plenty of room for the milk to bubble up, and to speed the evaporation.

Marbled Chocolate Ice Cream

Swirls of orange-flavored chocolate running through the white chocolate not only look attractive but taste delicious, too.

15 mins plus
9 hrs freezing

15 mins

SERVES 6

INGREDIENTS

6 oz/175 g white chocolate

1 tsp cornstarch

1 tsp vanilla extract

3 egg yolks

1¼ cups milk

2 cups heavy cream

4 oz/115 g orange-flavored
    semisweet chocolate

orange peel segments, to serve

1 Chop the white chocolate into small pieces. Place the cornstarch, vanilla extract, and egg yolks in a bowl and stir together until well blended. Pour the milk into a pan and bring to a boil. Pour over the yolk mixture, stirring.

2 Strain the mixture back into the pan and heat gently, stirring, until thickened. Remove from the heat, add the white chocolate pieces, and stir until melted. Stir in the cream. Reserve $^2/_3$ cup of the mixture and pour the remainder into a freezerproof container. Freeze until starting to set. Melt the orange-flavored chocolate and stir into the reserved mixture.

3 Remove the partially frozen ice cream from the freezer and beat with a fork. Place spoonfuls of the orange chocolate mixture over the ice cream and swirl with a knife to give a marbled effect. Freeze overnight until firm. Transfer the ice cream to the refrigerator 30 minutes before serving. To serve, scoop the ice cream into individual glasses and serve with the orange peel and segments.

VARIATION
Use mint-flavored chocolate instead of orange chocolate.

Chocolate Marshmallow Ice

Richly flavored and with a wonderful texture, this homemade ice cream really couldn't be simpler. Store for up to a month in the freezer.

10 mins plus
2 hrs 30 mins
cooling/freezing

5–10 mins

SERVES 4

INGREDIENTS

3 oz/85 g semisweet chocolate, broken into pieces

6 oz/175 g white marshmallows

⅔ cup milk

1¼ cups heavy cream

fresh fruit to serve

1 Put the chocolate and marshmallows in a pan and pour in the milk. Warm over very low heat until the chocolate and marshmallows have melted. Remove from the heat and let cool completely.

2 Whisk the cream until thick, then fold it into the cold chocolate mixture with a metal spoon. Pour into a 1-lb/450-g loaf pan and freeze for at least 2 hours, until firm (it will keep for 1 month in the freezer). Serve with fresh fruit.

White Chocolate Ice Cream

This white chocolate ice cream is served in a cookie cup. If desired, top with a chocolate sauce for a true chocolate addict's treat.

1 hr plus
4–5 hrs freezing

15 mins

SERVES 6

INGREDIENTS

ICE CREAM

1 egg

1 egg yolk

3 tbsp superfine sugar

5½ oz/150 g white chocolate, broken into pieces

1¼ cups milk

⅔ cup heavy cream

COOKIE CUPS

1 egg white

4 tbsp superfine sugar

2 tbsp all-purpose flour, sifted

2 tbsp unsweetened cocoa, sifted

2 tbsp butter, melted

1 Place parchment paper on 2 cookie sheets. To make the ice cream, beat together the egg, egg yolks, and sugar. Put the chocolate in a heatproof bowl with 3 tablespoons of milk and set over a pan of gently simmering water. Heat the milk until almost boiling and pour on to the eggs, whisking. Set over a pan of gently simmering water and cook, stirring until the mixture thickens enough to coat the back of a wooden spoon. Whisk in the chocolate. Cover with dampened parchment paper and let cool.

2 Whip the cream until just holding its shape and fold into the custard. Transfer to a freezerproof container and freeze the mixture for 1–2 hours, until frozen 1 inch/2.5 cm from the sides. Scrape into a bowl and beat again until smooth. Freeze until firm.

3 To make the cups, preheat the oven to 400°F/200°C. Beat the egg white and sugar together. Beat in the flour and unsweetened cocoa, then the butter. Place 1 tablespoon of mixture on one cookie sheet and spread out into a 5-inch/13-cm circle. Bake in the preheated oven for 4–5 minutes. Remove and mold into shape over an upturned cup. Let the cookie cup set, then cool on a wire rack. Repeat to make 6 cookie cups. Serve the ice cream in the cups. Decorate as preferred.

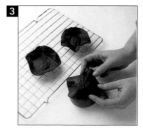

Rich Chocolate Ice Cream

This chocolate ice cream is delicious on its own or with chocolate sauce. For a special dessert, serve it in these attractive trellis cups.

45 mins plus 4–5 hrs freezing

12 mins

SERVES 6

INGREDIENTS

ICE CREAM

1 egg

3 egg yolks

scant ½ cup superfine sugar

1¼ cups whole milk

9 oz/250 g semisweet chocolate

1¼ cups heavy cream

TRELLIS CUPS

3½ oz/100 g semisweet chocolate

1 Beat together the egg, egg yolks, and superfine sugar in a heatproof bowl until well combined. Heat the milk until it is almost boiling.

2 Gradually pour the hot milk on to the eggs, whisking as you do so. Set the bowl over a pan of gently simmering water and cook, stirring until the mixture thickens enough to thinly coat the back of a wooden spoon.

3 Break the semisweet chocolate into small pieces and add to the hot custard. Stir until the chocolate has melted. Cover with a sheet of dampened parchment paper and let cool.

4 Whip the cream until just holding its shape, then fold into the cooled chocolate custard. Transfer to a freezerproof container and freeze for 1–2 hours, until the mixture is frozen 1 inch/2.5 cm from the sides.

5 Scrape the ice cream into a chilled bowl and beat again until smooth. Freeze until firm.

6 To make the trellis cups, invert a muffin pan and cover 6 alternate mounds with plastic wrap. Melt the chocolate, place it in a paper pastry bag, and snip off the end.

7 Pipe a circle around the bottom of the mound, then pipe chocolate back and forth over it to form a trellis; carefully pipe a double thickness. Pipe around the bottom again. Chill until set, then lift from the pan and remove the plastic wrap. Serve the ice cream in the trellis cups.

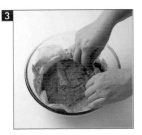

Chocolate & Honey Ice

Ice cream is always a popular summer dessert—try this rather different recipe for a change. It looks even better decorated with strawberries.

50 min plus
5 hrs freezing/
chilling

15 mins

SERVES 6

INGREDIENTS

2 cups milk

7 oz/200 g semisweet chocolate, broken into pieces

4 eggs, separated

scant ½ cup superfine sugar

2 tbsp honey

pinch of salt

12 strawberries, washed and hulled

1 Pour the milk into a pan, add 5½ oz/150 g of the chocolate and stir over medium heat for 3–5 minutes until melted. Remove the pan from the heat and set aside.

2 In a separate bowl, beat the egg yolks with all but 1 tablespoon of the sugar until pale and thickened. Gradually beat in the milk mixture, a little at a time. Return the mixture to a clean pan and cook over low heat, whisking constantly, until smooth and thickened. Remove from the heat and set aside to cool completely. Cover with plastic wrap and chill in the refrigerator for 30 minutes.

3 Whisk the egg whites with a pinch of salt until soft peaks form. Gradually whisk in the remaining sugar and continue whisking until stiff and glossy. Remove the chocolate mixture from the refrigerator and stir in the honey, then gently fold in the egg whites.

4 Divide the mixture among 6 individual freezerproof molds and place in the freezer for at least 4 hours, until frozen. Meanwhile, put the remaining chocolate in a heatproof bowl set over a pan of gently simmering water. Stir over low heat until melted and smooth, then dip the strawberries in the melted chocolate so that they are half-coated. Place on a sheet of parchment paper to set. Transfer the ice cream to the refrigerator 10 minutes before serving. Turn out on to serving plates and decorate with the strawberries.

Coconut Ice Cream

Coconut and white chocolate combine to make a smooth creamy ice cream with an exotic flavor. Serve with tropical fruit of your choice.

🍨 25 mins plus 4–5 hrs freezing   ⏱ 15 mins

SERVES 6

INGREDIENTS

2 eggs

2 egg yolks

generous ½ cup golden superfine sugar

1¼ cups light cream

4 oz/115 g white chocolate, chopped

4 oz/115 g creamed coconut, chopped

1¼ cups heavy cream

3 tbsp coconut-flavored liqueur

tropical fruit such as mango, pineapple, passion fruit, to serve

1 Place the eggs, egg yolks, and sugar in a heatproof bowl and beat together until well blended. Put the light cream, chocolate, and coconut in a pan and heat gently until the chocolate has melted, then continue to heat, stirring constantly, until almost boiling. Pour on to the egg mixture, stirring vigorously, then place the bowl over a pan of gently simmering water, making sure that the bottom of the bowl does not touch the water.

2 Cook, stirring constantly, until the mixture lightly coats the back of the spoon. Strain into another bowl and let cool. Place the heavy cream and liqueur in a bowl and whisk until slightly thickened, then fold into the cooled chocolate mixture.

3 Either freeze in an ice-cream maker, following the manufacturer's directions, or pour the mixture into a freezerproof container, cover, and freeze for 2 hours, until just frozen. Spoon into a bowl and beat with a fork to break down the ice crystals. Return to the freezer until firm. Transfer from the freezer to the refrigerator 30 minutes before serving. Serve with tropical fruit.

VARIATION
As an alternative to serving this ice cream with fruit, it is also delicious served with a semisweet chocolate sauce.

Mint-Chocolate Gelato

Rich, creamy gelati, or ice creams, are one of the great Italian culinary contributions to the world. This version is made with fresh mint.

2 hrs 45 mins plus 5 hrs freezing

20 mins

SERVES 4

INGREDIENTS

6 large eggs

¾ cup superfine sugar

1¼ cups milk

⅔ cup heavy cream

large handful fresh mint leaves, rinsed and dried

2 drops green food coloring (optional)

2 oz/55 g semisweet chocolate, chopped finely

1 Put the eggs and sugar in a heatproof bowl that will sit over a pan with plenty of room underneath. Using an electric whisk, beat the eggs and sugar together until thick and creamy.

2 Put the milk and cream in the pan and bring to a simmer, where small bubbles appear all around the edge, stirring. Pour on to the eggs, whisking constantly. Rinse the pan and put 1 inch/2.5 cm water in the bottom. Place the bowl on top, making sure the bottom does not touch the water. Turn the heat to medium–high.

3 Transfer the mixture to a pan and cook the mixture, stirring constantly, until it is thick enough to coat the back of the spoon and leave a mark when you pull your finger across it.

4 Tear the mint leaves and stir them into the custard. Remove the custard from the heat. Let cool, then cover and set aside to infuse for at least 2 hours, chilling for the last 30 minutes.

5 Strain the mixture through a small nylon strainer to remove the pieces of mint. Stir in the food coloring (if using). Transfer to a freezerproof container and freeze the mixture for 1–2 hours, until frozen 1 inch/2.5 cm from the sides.

6 Scrape into a bowl and beat again until smooth. Stir in the chocolate pieces, smooth the top, and cover with plastic wrap or foil. Freeze until set, for up to 3 months. Soften in the refrigerator for 20 minutes before serving.

Coffee Ice Cream

This wonderful Italian-style dessert tastes as if it is full of heavy cream.
In fact, it is made with ricotta and lowfat plain yogurt.

🍨 1 hr plus
6 hrs freezing   🕐 0 mins

SERVES 6

INGREDIENTS

1 oz/25 g semisweet chocolate

1 cup ricotta cheese

5 tbsp lowfat plain yogurt

scant ½ cup superfine sugar

¾ cup strong black coffee, chilled

½ tsp ground cinnamon

dash of vanilla extract

chocolate curls, to decorate (see page 9)

1 Grate the chocolate. Put the ricotta cheese, yogurt, and sugar in a food processor and process to a smooth purée. Scrape into a bowl and beat in the remaining ingredients.

2 Spoon the mixture into a freezerproof container and freeze for 1½ hours, or until slushy. Remove from the freezer, turn into a bowl and beat vigorously. Return to the container and freeze again for 1½ hours.

3 Repeat this beating and freezing process twice more, then return to the freezer for 15 minutes before serving in scoops. Alternatively, store in the freezer until 15 minutes before serving, then transfer to the refrigerator to soften slightly. Decorate with chocolate curls, and serve.

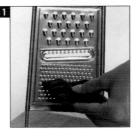  

VARIATION
Omit the cinnamon and vanilla extract and substitute 1½ oz/40 g grated mint chocolate for the semisweet chocolate.

Coconut & Ginger Ice Cream

Coconut and ginger are very compatible flavors. Serve with a few lychees, and a little ginger syrup drizzled over.

20 mins plus
6–8 hrs freezing

10 mins

SERVES 4

INGREDIENTS

1¾ cups coconut milk

1 cup whipping cream

4 egg yolks

5 tbsp superfine sugar

4 tbsp syrup from the ginger jar

6 pieces preserved ginger, drained and chopped finely

2 tbsp lime juice

fresh mint sprigs, to decorate

TO SERVE

lychees

syrup from the ginger jar

1 Place the coconut milk and cream in a medium pan. Heat gently until just starting to simmer. Remove from the heat.

2 In a large bowl, beat together the egg yolks, sugar, and ginger syrup until pale and creamy. Slowly pour in the hot milk mixture, while stirring. Return to the pan and heat gently, stirring constantly, until the mixture thickens and coats the back of a spoon. Remove from the heat and let cool. Stir in the ginger and lime juice.

3 Transfer the mixture to a freezerproof container. Cover and freeze for 2–3 hours, or until just frozen. Spoon into a bowl and mash with a fork or whisk to break down any ice crystals. Return the mixture to the container and freeze for an additional 2 hours. Mash once more, then freeze for 2–3 hours, or until firm. Remove from the freezer to the refrigerator 20–30 minutes before serving. Decorate with mint sprigs and serve with lychees and a little ginger syrup drizzled over.

Brown Bread Ice Cream

Although it sounds unusual, this yogurt-based recipe is delicious. It contains no cream and is ideal for a lowfat diet.

15 mins plus
2 hrs freezing

5 mins

SERVES 4

INGREDIENTS

3 cups fresh whole-wheat bread crumbs

¼ cup finely chopped walnuts

¼ cup superfine sugar

½ tsp ground nutmeg

1 tsp finely grated orange rind

2 cups lowfat plain yogurt

2 large egg whites

TO DECORATE

walnut halves

orange slices

fresh mint sprigs

1 Preheat the broiler to medium. Mix together the bread crumbs, walnuts, and sugar and spread over a sheet of foil in the broiler pan.

2 Broil, stirring frequently, for 5 minutes until crisp and evenly browned. (Take care that the sugar does not burn.) Remove from the heat and let cool.

3 When cool, transfer to a mixing bowl and mix in the nutmeg, orange rind, and yogurt. In another bowl, whisk the egg whites until stiff. Gently fold into the bread crumb mixture, using a metal spoon.

4 Spoon the mixture into 4 mini bowls, smoothing the surface, and freeze for 1½–2 hours, until firm.

5 To serve, hold the bottoms of the molds in hot water for a few seconds, then turn on to serving plates.

6 Serve immediately, decorated with the walnuts, oranges, and fresh mint.

COOK'S TIP
If you don't have mini bowls, use ramekins or teacups or, if you prefer, use one large bowl. Alternatively, spoon the mixture into a large, freezerproof container to freeze and serve the ice cream in scoops.

Lavender Ice Cream

Lavender is a herb that works very well in cooking. You can store this deliciously fragrant ice cream in the freezer for up to three months.

2 hrs 45 mins
plus 6–8 hrs
freezing

15 mins

SERVES 6–8

INGREDIENTS

flowers from 10–12 large fresh lavender sprigs, plus extra to decorate

6 large egg yolks

¾ cup superfine sugar, or lavender sugar (see Cook's Tip)

2 cups milk

1 cup heavy cream

1 tsp vanilla extract

1 Strip the small flowers from the stems, without any brown or green bits. Place them in a small strainer and rinse, then pat dry with paper towels. Set aside.

2 Put the egg yolks and sugar in a heatproof bowl that will sit over a pan with plenty of room underneath. Using an electric whisk, beat the eggs and sugar together, until they are thick.

3 Put the milk, cream, and vanilla in the pan over low heat and bring to a simmer, stirring. Pour the hot milk over the egg mixture, whisking constantly. Rinse the pan and place 1 inch/2.5 cm water in the bottom. Place the bowl on top, making sure that the bottom does not touch the water. Turn the heat to medium-high.

4 Cook the mixture, stirring, until it is thick enough to coat the back of a spoon.

5 Remove the custard from the heat and stir in the flowers. Cool, then cover, and set aside to infuse for 2 hours, chilling for the last 30 minutes. Strain the mixture through a nylon strainer to remove the flowers.

6 Churn in an ice-cream maker, following the manufacturer's instructions. Alternatively, freeze and whisk as in step 3 of Coconut & Ginger Ice Cream (see page 880).

7 Transfer to a freezerproof bowl, smooth the top, and cover with plastic wrap or foil. Freeze for up to 3 months. Soften in the refrigerator for 20 minutes before serving. Decorate with fresh lavender flowers.

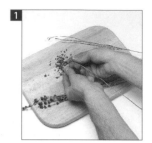

COOK'S TIP

To make lavender sugar, put 2½ cups sugar and 4½ oz/ 125 g lavender flowers in a food processor. Process until blended, then leave in a sealed container for 10 days. Sift out the flower pieces. Store the sugar in a sealed jar.

Easy Mango Ice Cream

Mangoes make excellent ice cream. Add sugar to taste, because some of the sweetness will be lost during the freezing process.

10 mins plus
6–8 hrs freezing

0 mins

SERVES 4

I N G R E D I E N T S

⅔ cup whipping cream

2½ cups ready-made traditional custard

flesh of 2 ripe mangoes, puréed

confectioners' sugar, to taste

passion fruit seeds, to serve

1 Whip the cream lightly. In a large bowl, mix together the custard, cream, and mango purée.

2 Taste for sweetness and, if necessary, add confectioners' sugar to taste, remembering that when frozen, the mixture will taste less sweet.

3 Transfer the mixture to a freezerproof container. Cover and freeze for 2–3 hours, or until just frozen. Spoon into a bowl and mash with a fork or whisk to break down any ice crystals. Return the mixture to the container and freeze for an additional 2 hours. Mash once more, then freeze for 2–3 hours, or until firm.

4 Transfer from the freezer to the refrigerator 20–30 minutes before serving. Serve with the passion fruit seeds.

Cognac & Orange Ice Cream

The cognac adds a subtle depth of flavor to this orange ice cream. You may use other fruits of your choice, if you prefer.

45 mins plus
3–4 hrs chilling/
freezing

5 mins

SERVES 4

INGREDIENTS

4 egg yolks

½ cup superfine sugar

scant 1 cup milk

generous 1 cup heavy cream

3 tbsp orange juice

3 tbsp cognac

1 tbsp finely grated orange rind

TO DECORATE

star fruit, sliced finely

pieces of candied orange peel

1 Beat the egg yolks and sugar together in a heatproof bowl until fluffy. Put the milk, cream, orange juice, cognac, and grated orange rind into a large pan and bring to a boil. Remove from the heat and whisk into the beaten egg yolks. Return the mixture to the pan and cook, stirring constantly, over very low heat until thickened. Do not let it reach a simmer. Remove from the heat, transfer to a bowl, and cool. Cover with plastic wrap and chill for 1 hour.

2 Transfer the mixture to an ice-cream maker and process for 15 minutes. Alternatively, put the mixture in a freezerproof container and freeze for 1 hour. Transfer to a bowl and beat to break up the ice crystals, then put it back in the freezerproof container and freeze for 30 minutes. Repeat twice more, freezing for 30 minutes and whisking each time. Freeze until ready to serve.

3 To serve, soften in the refrigerator for 20 minutes beforehand. Scoop into serving dishes, and decorate with star fruit slices and candied orange peel. Serve immediately.

Candied Fruit Ice Cream

This ice cream looks very effective made in a large pudding bowl, then turned out on to a serving plate to be sliced in front of your guests.

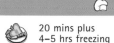

20 mins plus
4–5 hrs freezing   0 mins

SERVES 4

INGREDIENTS

½ cup golden raisins

½ cup raisins

6 tbsp amaretto

4 eggs, separated

½ cup superfine sugar

2½ cups heavy cream

⅔ cup candied cherries

¼ cup candied peel

generous ½ cup blanched almonds, chopped

lemon rind, to decorate

1 Put the golden raisins and raisins in a bowl and pour over 4 tablespoons of amaretto. Cover with plastic wrap and let soak.

2 Beat the egg yolks and sugar together in a heatproof bowl until fluffy. In a separate bowl, whisk together the cream and remaining amaretto, then whisk the mixture into the beaten egg yolks. In a separate bowl, whisk the egg whites until stiff peaks form, then fold into the cream mixture along with the soaked fruit, cherries, candied peel, and chopped almonds.

3 Transfer the mixture to a large pudding bowl, cover, and freeze for 4–5 hours, until set. To serve, dip the pudding bowl in hot water to loosen the ice cream, then turn it out on to a serving plate. Decorate with lemon rind and serve immediately.

Ice Cream Sauces

Serve plain vanilla or chocolate ice cream with one or more of these delicious sauces on the side.

15–20 mins   5–10 mins

SERVES 6

INGREDIENTS

vanilla or chocolate ice cream, to serve

BERRY SAUCE

scant 1 cup berries, such as blackberries or raspberries

2 tbsp water

2–3 tbsp superfine sugar

2 tbsp fruit liqueur, such as cassis or raspberry-flavored liqueur

MOCHA SAUCE

⅔ cup heavy cream

4 tbsp butter, sweet for preference

2 oz/55 g light muscovado sugar

scant 1 cup semisweet chocolate, broken into pieces

2 tbsp dark rum (optional)

PORT SAUCE

1½ cups ruby port

2 tsp cornstarch

1 For the berry sauce, put all the ingredients into a small, heavy-based pan and heat gently, until the sugar has dissolved and the fruit juices run. Purée with a hand-held blender or in a food processor, then push through a strainer into a serving bowl to remove the seeds. Add more sugar if necessary and serve warm or cold.

2 For the mocha sauce, pour the cream in a heatproof bowl and add the butter and sugar. Set over a pan of gently simmering water and cook, stirring constantly, until smooth. Remove from the heat and set aside to cool slightly. Stir in the chocolate and continue stirring until it has melted. Stir in the rum (if using), then leave the sauce to cool to room temperature before serving.

3 For the port sauce, combine ¼ cup of the port with the cornstarch to make a smooth paste. Pour the remainder of the port into a pan and bring to a boil. Stir in the cornstarch paste and cook, stirring constantly, for about 1 minute, until thickened. Remove from the heat and set aside to cool. Pour into a bowl, cover, and chill in the refrigerator.

4 Serve scoops of ice cream with a little of the 3 sauces on the side. Serve the remaining sauce in pitchers.

Italian Rice Ice Cream

In this ice cream, pudding rice is flavored with honey and lemon curd.
Decorate with candied peel for an elegant dinner-party dessert.

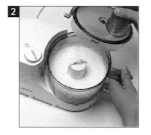

30 mins plus
9 hrs chilling/
freezing

🕐 10 mins

SERVES 4–6

I N G R E D I E N T S

½ cup pudding rice

2¼ cups milk

⅓ cup sugar

⅓ cup good-quality honey

1 tsp vanilla extract

½ tsp lemon extract

¾ cup good-quality lemon curd

2¼ cups heavy or whipping cream

grated rind and juice of 1 large lemon

TO DECORATE

candied peel

1 Put the rice and milk in a large, heavy-based pan and bring to a gentle simmer, stirring occasionally; do not let boil. Reduce the heat to low, cover, and simmer very gently for about 10 minutes, stirring occasionally, until the rice is just tender and the liquid absorbed.

2 Remove from the heat and stir in the sugar, honey, and vanilla and lemon extracts, stirring until the sugar has dissolved. Pour into a food processor and pulse 3 or 4 times. The mixture should be thick and creamy but not completely smooth.

3 Put the lemon curd in a bowl and gradually beat in about 1 cup of the cream. Stir in the rice mixture with the lemon rind and juice until blended. Lightly whip the remaining cream until it just starts to hold its shape, then fold into the lemon-rice mixture. Chill.

4 Stir the rice mixture and pour into an ice-cream maker. Churn according to the manufacturers' instructions for 15–20 minutes. Transfer to a freezerproof container and freeze for 6–8 hours, or overnight. Transfer to the refrigerator about 1 hour before serving.

COOK'S TIP

If you do not have an ice-cream maker, transfer the chilled rice mixture to a freezerproof container. Freeze for 1 hour until slightly slushy, then whisk to break up any crystals; refreeze. Repeat twice more.

Ricotta Ice Cream

The ricotta cheese adds a creamy flavor, while the nuts add a crunchy texture. This ice cream needs to be chilled in the freezer overnight.

20 mins plus
8 hrs freezing

0 mins

SERVES 6

INGREDIENTS

⅓ cup pistachios

⅓ cup walnuts or pecans

⅓ cup toasted chopped hazelnuts

grated rind of 1 orange

grated rind of 1 lemon

2 tbsp candied or preserved ginger

2 tbsp candied cherries

¼ cup no-soak dried apricots

¼ cup raisins

1 lb/450 g ricotta cheese

2 tbsp maraschino, amaretto, or cognac

1 tsp vanilla extract

4 egg yolks

½ cup superfine sugar

TO DECORATE

whipped cream

few candied cherries, pistachios,
   or mint leaves

1 Coarsely chop the pistachios and walnuts and mix with the toasted hazelnuts, orange rind, and lemon rind.

2 Finely chop the candied or preserved ginger, cherries, apricots, and raisins, and add them to the bowl.

3 Stir the ricotta cheese evenly through the fruit mixture, then beat in the liqueur and vanilla extract.

4 Put the egg yolks and sugar in a bowl and whisk hard until very thick and creamy. Use an electric whisk if you have

one, otherwise whisk over a pan of gently simmering water to speed up the process. Let cool if necessary.

5 Carefully fold the ricotta mixture evenly through the beaten eggs and sugar until smooth.

6 Line a 7 x 5-inch/18 x 12-cm loaf pan with a double layer of plastic wrap or parchment paper. Pour in the ricotta

mixture, smooth the top, cover with more plastic wrap or parchment paper, and freeze until firm—at least overnight.

7 To serve, remove the ice cream from the pan and peel off the paper.

8 Transfer the ice cream to a serving dish and decorate with whipped cream, candied cherries, pistachios, and mint leaves. Serve in slices.

Cardamom Cream Horns

A crisp chocolate cookie cone encloses a fabulous cardamom-and-ginger-flavored cream, making this an unusual dessert.

🍴 🍴 🍴

30 mins   🕐 4–5 mins

SERVES 6

I N G R E D I E N T S

2 tbsp butter, sweet for preference, melted, plus extra for greasing

1 egg white

4 tbsp superfine sugar

2 tbsp all-purpose flour

2 tbsp unsweetened cocoa

1¾ oz/50 g semisweet chocolate

C A R D A M O M   C R E A M

⅔ cup heavy cream

1 tbsp confectioners' sugar

¼ tsp ground cardamom

pinch of ground ginger

1 oz/25 g preserved ginger, chopped finely

1   Preheat the oven to 400°F/200°C. Place a sheet of parchment paper on 2 cookie sheets. Lightly grease 6 cream horn molds. To make the horns, beat the egg white and sugar in a mixing bowl until well combined. Sift the flour and unsweetened cocoa together, then beat into the egg followed by the melted butter.

2   Place 1 tablespoon of the mixture on to 1 cookie sheet and spread out to form a 5-inch/13-cm circle. Bake in the preheated oven for 4–5 minutes.

3   Working quickly, remove the cookies with a spatula and wrap around the cream horn mold to form a cone. Let the cone set, then remove from the mold. Repeat with the remaining mixture to make 6 cones.

4   Melt the chocolate and dip the open edges of the horn in the chocolate. Place on a piece of parchment paper and let the chocolate set.

5   To make the cardamom cream, place the cream in a bowl and sift the confectioners' sugar and ground spices over the surface. Whisk the cream until soft peaks form. Fold in the chopped ginger and use to fill the chocolate cones.

Zuccherini

Italians, especially Sicilians and Sardinians, are famous for having a sweet tooth—and for their superb desserts, such as this one.

30 mins plus
8 hrs 30 mins
chilling   10 mins

SERVES 6

INGREDIENTS

6 oz/175 g semisweet chocolate,
   broken into pieces

10 amaretti cookies, crushed

MOUSSE

2 oz/55 g semisweet chocolate,
   broken into pieces

1 tbsp cold strong black coffee

2 eggs, separated

2 tsp orange-flavored liqueur

TO DECORATE

⅔ cup heavy cream

6 chocolate-coated coffee beans

2 tbsp unsweetened cocoa

1 To make the chocolate cups, put the 6 oz/175 g semisweet chocolate in a heatproof bowl set over a pan of gently simmering water. Stir until melted and smooth, but not too runny, then remove from the heat. Coat the inside of 12 double paper cake cases with chocolate, using a small brush. Stand them on a plate and chill for at least 8 hours, or overnight in the refrigerator.

2 To make the mousse, put the chocolate and coffee in a heatproof bowl set over a pan of gently simmering water. Stir over low heat until the chocolate has melted and the mixture is smooth, then remove from the heat. Let cool slightly, then stir in the egg yolks and orange-flavored liqueur.

3 Whisk the egg whites in a separate bowl until stiff peaks form. Fold the

whites into the chocolate mixture with a metal spoon, then set aside to cool.

4 Remove the chocolate cups from the refrigerator and carefully peel off the paper cases. Divide the crushed amaretti cookies equally among the chocolate cups

and top with the chocolate mousse. Return to the refrigerator for at least 30 minutes. Just before serving, whip the cream and pipe a star on the top of each chocolate cup. Decorate half of the zuccherini with the chocolate-coated coffee beans and dust the other half with unsweetened cocoa.

Raspberry Chocolate Boxes

Mocha mousse, fresh raspberries, and light sponge cake, all presented in neat little chocolate boxes—almost too good to eat.

50 mins plus 3 hrs chilling/ cooling

45–55 mins

SERVES 12

INGREDIENTS

7 oz/200 g semisweet chocolate, broken into pieces

1½ tsp cold, strong, black coffee

1 egg yolk

1½ tsp Kahlúa or other coffee-flavored liqueur

2 egg whites

¾ cup raspberries

SPONGE CAKE

2 tsp butter, for greasing

1 egg, plus 1 egg white

¼ cup superfine sugar

scant ½ cup all-purpose flour

1 To make the mocha mousse, melt 2 oz/55 g of the chocolate in a heatproof bowl set over a pan of gently simmering water. Add the coffee and stir over low heat until smooth, then remove from the heat and cool slightly. Stir in the egg yolk and the coffee-flavored liqueur.

2 Whisk the egg whites in a separate bowl until stiff peaks form. Fold into the chocolate mixture, cover with plastic wrap, and chill for 2 hours, until set.

3 For the sponge cake, lightly grease an 8-inch/20-cm square cake pan and line the bottom with parchment paper. Put the egg and extra white with the sugar in a heatproof bowl set over a pan of gently simmering water. Whisk over low heat for 5–10 minutes, until pale and thick. Remove from the heat and continue whisking for

10 minutes until cold and a trail is left when the whisk is dragged across the surface.

4 Preheat the oven to 350°F/180°C. Sift the flour over the egg mixture and gently fold it in. Pour the mixture into the prepared pan and spread evenly. Bake in the preheated oven for 20–25 minutes, until firm to the touch and slightly shrunk from the sides of the pan. Turn out on to a wire rack to cool, then invert the cake, keeping the parchment paper in place.

5 To make the chocolate boxes, grease a 12 x 9-inch/30 x 23 cm jelly roll pan and line with waxed paper. Place the remaining chocolate in a heatproof bowl set over a pan of gently simmering water. Stir over low heat until melted, but not too runny. Pour it into the pan and spread

evenly with a spatula. Set aside in a cool place for about 30 minutes, until set.

6 Turn out the set chocolate on to parchment paper on a counter. Cut it into 36 rectangles, measuring 3 x 1 inches/ 7.5 x 2.5 cm. Cut 12 of these rectangles in half to make 24 rectangles measuring 1½ x 1 inches/4 x 2.5 cm.

7 Trim the crusty edges off the sponge cake, then cut it into 12 slices, measuring 3 x 1¼ inches/7.5 x 3 cm. Spread a little of the mocha mousse along the sides of each sponge rectangle and press 2 long and 2 short chocolate rectangles in place on each side to make boxes. Divide the remaining mousse among the boxes and top with raspberries. Chill until ready to use.

Mini Chocolate Tartlets

Small tartlet shells are filled with a rich chocolate cream to serve as dessert or petits fours. Use individual tartlet pans to make the shells.

20 mins plus
15 mins chilling   15 mins

SERVES 18

INGREDIENTS

1½ cups all-purpose flour, plus extra
    for dusting

⅓ cup butter

1 tbsp superfine sugar

about 1 tbsp water

FILLING

3½ oz/100 g full-fat soft cheese

2 tbsp superfine sugar

1 small egg, beaten lightly

1¾ oz/50 g semisweet chocolate

TO DECORATE

generous ⅓ cup heavy cream

semisweet chocolate curls (see page 9)

unsweetened cocoa, for dusting

1 Sift the flour into a mixing bowl. Cut the butter into small pieces and rub in with your fingertips until the mixture resembles fine breadcrumbs. Stir in the sugar. Add enough water to mix to a soft dough, then cover with plastic wrap and chill for 15 minutes.

2 Preheat the oven to 375°F/190°C. Roll out the dough on a lightly floured counter and use to line 18 mini tartlet pans or mini muffin pans. Prick the tartlet shells with a toothpick.

3 Beat together the full-fat soft cheese and the sugar. Beat in the egg. Melt the chocolate and beat it into the mixture. Spoon into the tartlet shells and bake in the preheated oven for 15 minutes, until the dough is crisp and the filling set. Place the pans on a wire rack to cool completely.

4 Chill the tartlets. Whip the cream until it is just holding its shape. Place in a pastry bag fitted with a star tip. Pipe rosettes of cream on top of the tartlets. Decorate with chocolate curls and dust with cocoa.

COOK'S TIP
The tartlets can be made up to 3 days ahead. Decorate on the day of serving, preferably no more than 4 hours in advance.

Pineapple Chocolate Rings

These pretty little fruit desserts make a perfect end to a summertime supper, but can also be served with mid-morning coffee.

25–30 mins · 30–40 mins

SERVES 10

INGREDIENTS

6 oz/175 g butter, sweet for preference

¼ cup superfine sugar

1¼ cups all-purpose flour, plus extra for dusting

3 tbsp ground almonds

½ tsp almond extract

7 oz/200 g semisweet chocolate, broken into small pieces

10 canned pineapple rings, drained and juice reserved

10 maraschino cherries

1 tsp cornstarch

1 Line a cookie sheet with parchment paper. Cream 4 oz/115 g of the butter with all the sugar until pale and fluffy. Sift in the flour, add the ground almonds and almond extract, and knead the mixture thoroughly until it forms a soft dough.

2 Preheat the oven to 375°F/190°C. Turn out the dough on to a lightly floured cutting board and roll out to ¼-inch/5-mm thick. Stamp out 20 circles with a 3-inch/7.5-cm round cookie cutter and place them on the prepared cookie sheet. Prick the surface of each almond circle with a fork, then bake in the preheated oven for 20 minutes, until lightly browned. Using a spatula, transfer the circles to a wire rack to cool.

3 Place the remaining butter and the chocolate in a heatproof bowl set over a pan of gently simmering water. Stir over low heat until melted and smooth. Remove the pan from the heat. Sandwich the almond circles together in pairs, while still moist, with the chocolate mixture spread between them. Place a pineapple ring on top of each pair of circles before the chocolate sets and place a cherry in the center of each ring.

4 Put 4 tablespoons of the reserved can juice into a small pan and stir in the cornstarch. Bring to a boil over a medium heat, stirring constantly, and cook for 5–7 minutes until thickened. Remove the pan from the heat and let it cool to room temperature. Brush the glaze over the pineapple rings and let stand for 10 minutes to set before serving.

Honey & Nut Nests

Pistachios and honey are combined with crisp cooked angel hair pasta in this unusual, delicious, and charming dessert.

10 mins   1 hr

SERVES 4

INGREDIENTS

salt

8 oz/225 g dried angel hair pasta

4 oz/115 g butter

1½ cups chopped pistachios

½ cup sugar

⅓ cup honey

⅔ cup water

2 tsp lemon juice

strained plain yogurt, to serve

1 Preheat the oven to 350°F/180°C. Bring a large pan of lightly salted water to a boil. Add the angel hair pasta, bring back to a boil, and cook for 8–10 minutes, or until tender, but still firm to the bite. Drain the pasta and return to the pan. Add the butter and toss to coat the pasta thoroughly. Let cool.

2 Arrange 4 small tart or cooking rings on a cookie sheet. Divide the angel hair pasta into 8 equal quantities and spoon 4 of them into the rings. Press down lightly. Top the pasta with half of the nuts, then add the remaining pasta.

3 Bake in the preheated oven for 45 minutes, or until golden brown.

4 Meanwhile, put the sugar, honey, and water in a pan and bring to a boil over low heat, stirring constantly until the sugar has dissolved completely. Simmer for 10 minutes, add the lemon juice and simmer for an additional 5 minutes.

5 Using a spatula, carefully transfer the angel hair nests to a serving dish. Pour over the honey syrup, sprinkle over the remaining nuts, and set aside to cool completely before serving. Serve at room temperature and hand the strained plain yogurt separately.

COOK'S TIP
Angel hair pasta is also known as capelli d'angelo. Long and very fine, it is usually sold in small bunches that already resemble nests.

Banana Cream Profiteroles

Chocolate profiteroles are a popular choice. In this recipe they are filled with a delicious banana-flavored cream—the perfect combination!

45 mins   30 mins

SERVES 4

INGREDIENTS

DOUGH

5 tbsp butter, plus extra for greasing

⅔ cup water, plus extra for sprinkling

¾ cup strong all-purpose flour, sifted

2 eggs

CHOCOLATE SAUCE

3½ oz/100 g semisweet chocolate, broken into pieces

2 tbsp water

4 tbsp confectioners' sugar

2 tbsp butter, sweet for preference

FILLING

1¼ cups heavy cream

1 banana, peeled

2 tbsp confectioners' sugar

2 tbsp crème de banane

1 Preheat the oven to 425°F/220°C. Lightly grease a cookie sheet and sprinkle with a little water. To make the dough, place the water in a pan. Cut the butter into small pieces and add to the pan. Heat gently until the butter melts, then bring to a rolling boil. Remove the pan from the heat and add the flour in one go, beating well until the mixture leaves the sides of the pan and forms a ball. Let cool slightly, then gradually beat in the eggs to form a smooth, glossy mixture. Spoon the paste into a large pastry bag fitted with a ½-inch/1-cm plain tip.

2 Pipe about 18 small balls of the paste on to the cookie sheet, allowing enough room for them to expand during cooking. Bake in the preheated oven for 15–20 minutes, until crisp and golden. Remove from the oven and make a small slit in each one for steam to escape. Cool on a wire rack.

3 To make the sauce, place all the ingredients in a heatproof bowl, set over a pan of gently simmering water and heat until combined to make a smooth sauce, stirring constantly.

4 To make the filling, whip the cream until soft peaks form. Mash the banana with the sugar and liqueur. Fold into the cream. Place in a pastry bag fitted with a ½-inch/1-cm plain tip and pipe into the profiteroles. Serve with the sauce poured over.

Petits Fours, Candy & Drinks

Here are some delightful ways to round off a meal, or

the day. There are mini bites such as Almond & Chocolate

Tuiles and Churros to appreciate with afternoon tea;

petits fours, such as Mini Minted Meringues and Praline &

Coffee Truffles to offer after dinner;

and fudge and toffee recipes which

make a welcome gift or enjoyable treat.

There are also extravagant cocktails,

including Krechma, Mona Lisa, and Chocolate Cake

Cocktail; decadent smoothies and shakes using spices,

mint, and mocha; and hot chocolate

drinks with cream and cognac.

Dry Fruits Petits Fours

Irresistibly sweet and unbelievably tempting, these fruity little chocolates can be served with coffee at the end of a dinner party.

20–25 mins plus
30 mins setting

5 mins

MAKES 30

INGREDIENTS

¾ cup no-soak dried apricots

¾ cup no-soak dried figs

¾ cup no-soak dried dates

¾ cup coarsely chopped walnuts

3 tbsp finely chopped candied orange peel

3 tbsp apricot cognac,
  plus extra for moistening

confectioners' sugar, for dusting

4 oz/115 g milk chocolate,
  broken into pieces

4 tbsp chopped toasted hazelnuts

1 Chop the dry fruits by hand or in a food processor. Place the chopped fruits in a bowl and add the walnuts, candied peel, and apricot cognac. Mix well.

2 Gather the mixture together and turn out on to a work counter lightly dusted with confectioners' sugar. Divide the mixture into 3 pieces and form each piece into a roll about 8 inches/20 cm long, then cut each roll into slices about ³/₄ inch/2 cm thick. Moisten your hands with a little apricot cognac and roll each slice into a ball between your palms.

3 Place the chocolate in a heatproof bowl set over a pan of gently simmering water. Stir over low heat until melted. Remove from the heat and cool slightly. Spear each fruit ball with a fork or skewer and dip it in the melted chocolate to coat it. Place on a sheet of parchment paper and sprinkle over the hazelnuts. Let stand for 30 minutes, or until set.

Chocolate Almond Petits Fours

These rich little petits fours are the perfect partner to serve with coffee after dinner. For the best results, use good-quality chocolate.

🍮 25 mins   🕐 5 mins

MAKES 15

INGREDIENTS

½ cup ground almonds

½ cup granulated sugar

5 tsp unsweetened cocoa

1 egg white

8 blanched almonds, halved

2 oz/55 g semisweet chocolate, broken into pieces

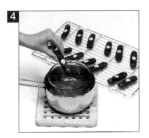

1 Preheat the oven to 375°F/190°C. Line a cookie sheet with parchment paper. Put the ground almonds, sugar, and unsweetened cocoa in a bowl and mix well together. Add the egg white and mix to form a firm mixture.

2 Fill a pastry bag, fitted with a small plain tip, with the mixture and pipe 2-inch/5-cm lengths, spaced well apart, on to the prepared cookie sheet. Place an almond half on top of each.

3 Bake in the oven for about 5 minutes, until firm. Transfer to a wire rack and let cool.

4 When the petits fours are cold, melt the chocolate in a heatproof bowl set over a pan of gently simmering water. Dip each end of the petits fours into the melted chocolate, then leave on the wire rack to set.

COOK'S TIP

You could use the remaining egg yolk from this recipe to make Chocolate Cherry Cups on page 967.

Chocolate Fruit & Nut Balls

These chocolate balls, packed with dry fruits and nuts, become favorites with everyone who tries them. Serve in paper candy cases if preferred.

20 mins plus
2 hrs chilling

5 mins

MAKES 20

INGREDIENTS

¾ cup golden raisins

¾ cup raisins

¾ cup blanched almonds

grated rind of 1 orange

8 oz/225 g semisweet chocolate, broken into pieces

1 Line a cookie sheet with parchment paper. Put the golden raisins, raisins, almonds, and orange rind in a food processor and chop very finely.

2 Take a heaping teaspoonful of the mixture at a time and roll into a ball. Place on the prepared cookie sheet. Continue until you have used up the remaining mixture. Let chill in the refrigerator for about 2 hours, until firm.

3 Melt the chocolate in a heatproof bowl set over a pan of gently simmering water. Using a dipping ring or 2 forks, carefully dip each ball into the melted chocolate. Lift it out quickly, letting any excess chocolate drain against the side of the bowl, and place on the prepared cookie sheet. Let set.

4 When the chocolate balls have set, place in paper candy cases.

Chocolate & Honey Fudge

Honey not only flavors the fudge but also gives it a smooth, soft texture.
Pieces of fudge make an ideal gift packed in a pretty box.

🥘 35–40 mins ⏱ 15–20 mins

MAKES ABOUT 64 PIECES

I N G R E D I E N T S

4 oz/115 g butter, plus extra for greasing

4 oz/115 g bittersweet chocolate, broken
  into pieces

2⅓ cups granulated sugar

¾ cup canned evaporated milk

⅓ cup honey

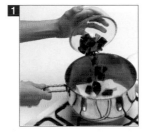

1 Grease a 7-inch/18-cm shallow
square pan or an 8 x 6-inch/20 x
15-cm shallow pan. Put all the ingredients
into a large, heavy-based pan and heat
gently, stirring all the time, until the
chocolate and butter have melted and the
sugar has dissolved.

2 Bring to a boil and boil for about
10–15 minutes, stirring occasionally,
until a little of the mixture, when dropped
into a small bowl of cold water, forms a
soft ball when rolled between the fingers.

3 Remove the pan from the heat and let
cool for 5 minutes, then beat the
mixture vigorously with a wooden spoon,
until thick, creamy, and grainy.

4 Immediately pour the mixture into
the prepared pan, let cool, then mark
into small squares. When the fudge is
cold and set, cut up the squares with a
sharp knife.

COOK'S TIP
It is better to use sweet
butter in the mixture, rather
than salted, as it has less
tendency to burn.

Chocolate & Peppermint Fudge

The addition of peppermint gives this chocolate fudge a deliciously fresh flavor. This fudge is perfect for eating at any time of the day.

40 mins   15–20 mins

MAKES ABOUT 64 PIECES

INGREDIENTS

4 oz/115 g butter, plus extra for greasing

¾ cup canned evaporated milk

2 tbsp milk

3½ cups granulated sugar

5½ oz/150 g bittersweet chocolate, broken into pieces

1 tsp peppermint flavoring

1 Grease a 7-inch/18-cm shallow square pan or an 8 x 6-inch/20 x 15-cm shallow pan. Pour the evaporated milk and milk into a large, heavy-based pan and add the sugar, butter, and chocolate. Heat gently, stirring all the time, until the sugar has dissolved and the butter and chocolate have melted.

2 Bring to a boil and boil for about 10–15 minutes, stirring occasionally, until a little of the mixture, when dropped into a small bowl of cold water, forms a soft ball when rolled between the fingers.

COOK'S TIP

For a superior flavor, use peppermint oil rather than peppermint flavoring, but only add about 3 drops at first. If preferred, add more to taste.

3 Remove the pan from the heat and let cool for 5 minutes, then add the peppermint oil. Beat the mixture vigorously with a wooden spoon until thick, creamy, and grainy.

4 Immediately pour the mixture into the prepared pan, let cool, then mark into squares. When the fudge is cold and set, cut up the squares using a sharp knife.

Ginger Chocolate Fudge

The combination of the hot ginger flavor and the sweet chocolate flavor in this fudge is a great success. Let cool completely before serving.

40 mins   15–20 mins

MAKES 49 PIECES

INGREDIENTS

4 oz/115 g butter, plus extra for greasing

6 pieces preserved ginger

1¼ cups milk

5½ oz/150 g bittersweet chocolate, broken into pieces

2⅓ cups granulated sugar

1 Grease a 7-inch/18-cm shallow square pan or an 8 x 6-inch/20 x 15-cm shallow pan. Dry the syrup off the pieces of preserved ginger on paper towels, then chop finely.

2 Pour the milk into a large, heavy-based pan and add the chocolate, butter, and sugar. Heat gently, stirring all the time, until the chocolate and butter have melted and the sugar has dissolved.

3 Bring to a boil and boil for about 10–15 minutes, stirring occasionally, until a little of the mixture, when dropped into a small bowl of cold water, forms a soft ball when rolled between the fingers.

4 Remove the pan from the heat and stir in the chopped ginger. Let cool for 5 minutes, then beat the mixture vigorously with a wooden spoon, until thick, creamy, and grainy.

5 Immediately pour the mixture into the prepared pan, let cool, then mark into small squares. Leave the fudge until cold and set, then cut up the squares with a sharp knife.

COOK'S TIP
Dipping the knife in hot water makes the fudge much easier to cut.

Light & Dark Fudge

Creamy white fudge and dark fudge, flavored with unsweetened cocoa for an intense chocolate flavor, are swirled together for a stunning effect.

🕐 35 mins   🕐 15–20 mins

MAKES ABOUT 64 PIECES

INGREDIENTS

4 oz/115 g butter, plus extra for greasing

1¼ cups milk

2¾ cups granulated sugar

½ tsp vanilla extract

2 tbsp unsweetened cocoa

1 Grease a 7-inch/18-cm shallow square pan or an 8 x 6-inch/20 x 15-cm shallow pan. Pour the milk into a large, heavy-based pan. Add the sugar and butter and heat gently, stirring all the time, until the sugar has dissolved and the butter has melted.

2 Bring to a boil and boil for about 10–15 minutes, stirring occasionally, until a little of the mixture, when dropped into a small bowl of cold water, forms a soft ball when rolled between the fingers.

3 Remove the pan from the heat and carefully pour half the mixture into a clean pan. Stir in the vanilla extract. Sift the unsweetened cocoa into the remaining mixture, then beat the mixture vigorously with a wooden spoon, until thick, creamy, and grainy.

4 Immediately swirl the mixture over the bottom of the prepared pan, leaving gaps. Beat the vanilla mixture vigorously until thick, creamy, and grainy, then pour into the gaps in the pan.

5 Let the fudge cool, then mark into squares. When cold and set, cut up the squares with a sharp knife.

COOK'S TIP
It is important to use a heavy-based pan to help prevent the fudge sticking to the bottom of the pan.

Pecan Mocha Fudge

This recipe makes plenty of delicious fudge for eating yourself, for sharing, and for giving away as presents to your family and friends!

15 mins plus
2 hrs setting

15–20 mins

MAKES ABOUT 108 PIECES

I N G R E D I E N T S

9 oz/250 g butter, plus extra for greasing

1¼ cups milk

2 lb 4 oz/1 kg golden granulated sugar

2 tbsp instant coffee granules

2 tbsp unsweetened cocoa

2 tbsp corn syrup

14 oz/400 g canned condensed milk

½ cup shelled pecans, chopped

1 Grease a 12 x 9-inch/30 x 23-cm jelly roll pan. Place the milk, sugar, and butter in a large pan. Stir over gentle heat until the sugar has dissolved. Stir in the coffee granules, unsweetened cocoa, syrup, and condensed milk.

2 Bring to a boil and boil steadily, whisking constantly, for 10 minutes, or until a temperature of 241°F/116°C is reached on a sugar thermometer, or a small amount of the mixture forms a soft ball when dropped into cold water.

3 Let cool for 5 minutes, then beat vigorously with a wooden spoon until the mixture starts to thicken. Stir in the nuts. Continue beating until the mixture takes on a fudge-like consistency. Quickly pour into the prepared pan and let stand in a cool place to set. Cut the fudge into squares to serve.

COOK'S TIP
To test the temperature of the fudge accurately, it is best to use a sugar thermometer. These are available from specialist kitchenware stores.

Fruit & Nut Fudge

Chocolate, nuts, and dry fruits—the perfect combination—are all found in this simple-to-make fudge. Cut into even-size squares to serve.

10 mins plus
1 hr chilling

5 mins

MAKES 36 PIECES

INGREDIENTS

9 oz/250 g semisweet chocolate, broken into pieces

2 tbsp butter, plus extra for greasing

4 tbsp evaporated milk

3 cups confectioners' sugar, sifted

½ cup coarsely chopped hazelnuts

⅓ cup golden raisins

1 Lightly grease an 8-inch/20-cm square cake pan.

2 Put the chocolate in a heatproof bowl with the butter and evaporated milk and set over a pan of gently simmering water. Stir until the chocolate and butter melt and the mixture is well blended.

3 Remove the bowl from the heat and gradually beat in the confectioners' sugar. Stir the hazelnuts and golden raisins into the mixture. Press the fudge into the prepared pan and smooth the top. Chill until firm.

4 Tip the fudge out on to a cutting board and cut into squares. Chill in the refrigerator until required.

VARIATION
Vary the nuts used in this recipe; try making the fudge with almonds, Brazil nuts, walnuts, or pecans.

Chocolate Marshmallow Fudge

This fudge is not made by the traditional method of boiling because the addition of marshmallows gives the mixture its fudgelike texture.

15 mins plus
1–2 hrs setting

5 mins

MAKES 49 PIECES

INGREDIENTS

4 oz/115 g bittersweet chocolate,
  broken into pieces

2½ oz/70 g butter, plus extra for greasing

7 oz/200 g white mini marshmallows

2 tsp water

¾ cup blanched almonds, chopped coarsely

1 Grease a 7-inch/18-cm shallow square pan or an 8 x 6-inch/20 x 15-cm shallow pan. Melt the chocolate in a heatproof bowl over a pan of simmering water. Put the marshmallows, butter, and water in a large, heavy-based pan and heat gently, stirring frequently, until melted.

2 Remove the pan from the heat and pour the chocolate into the mixture. Add the almonds and stir until well mixed.

3 Pour the mixture into the prepared pan and let stand in a cool place for 1–2 hours, until set. When the fudge is cold and set, cut into squares with a sharp knife. To serve, place each piece of fudge in a small paper candy case.

COOK'S TIP

You could use large marshmallows for this recipe, cut into small pieces. The best way of doing this is to use wet scissors.

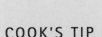

Mocha Fudge

Chocolate and coffee are a classic combination and in this fudge recipe the chocolate is made deeper in flavor by the addition of the coffee.

45 mins · 15–20 mins

MAKES 49 PIECES

INGREDIENTS

4 oz/115 g butter, plus extra for greasing

1¼ cups milk

4 oz/115 g bittersweet chocolate, broken into pieces

1¾ cups granulated sugar

2 tbsp instant coffee granules

1 Grease a 7-inch/18-cm shallow square pan or an 8 x 6-inch/20 x 15-cm shallow pan. Pour the milk into a large, heavy-based pan and add all the remaining ingredients. Heat gently, stirring all the time, until the chocolate and butter have melted and the sugar and coffee have dissolved.

2 Bring to a boil and boil for about 10–15 minutes, stirring occasionally, until a little of the mixture, when dropped into a cup of cold water, forms a soft ball when rolled between the fingers.

3 Remove the pan from the heat and let cool for 5 minutes, then beat the mixture vigorously with a wooden spoon until thick, creamy, and grainy.

4 Immediately pour the mixture into the prepared pan, let cool, then mark into squares. When the fudge is cold and set, cut up the squares with a sharp knife.

Easy Chocolate Fudge

This is the easiest fudge to make—for a really rich flavor, use a good semisweet chocolate with a high cocoa content, at least 70 percent.

🥚 10 mins plus 1 hr setting 🕐 5 mins

MAKES 64 PIECES

I N G R E D I E N T S

2¾ oz/75 g sweet butter, plus extra for greasing

1 lb 2 oz/500 g semisweet chocolate

1¾ cups condensed milk

½ tsp vanilla extract

1 Lightly grease an 8-inch/20-cm square cake pan.

2 Break the chocolate into pieces and place in a large pan with the butter and condensed milk.

3 Heat gently, stirring until the chocolate and butter melts and the mixture is smooth. Do not allow to boil.

4 Remove from the heat. Beat in the vanilla extract, then beat the mixture for a few minutes until thickened. Pour it into the prepared pan and smooth the top.

5 Chill the mixture in the refrigerator until firm.

6 Tip the fudge out on to a cutting board and cut into squares to serve.

Microwave Chocolate Fudge

This cheat's fudge takes only minutes to make. If there is any left after serving, then store in an airtight container for several days.

10 mins plus
2 hrs setting

3 mins

MAKES 49 PIECES

INGREDIENTS

sunflower oil, for oiling

4 oz/115 g semisweet chocolate,
  broken into pieces

2 tbsp sweet butter

1 lb/450 g confectioners' sugar, sifted

2 tbsp milk

½ cup chopped walnuts

1 Lightly oil a 7-inch/18-cm shallow square baking pan.

2 Place the chocolate in a large bowl. Cut the butter into pieces and add to the bowl. Add the confectioners' sugar and milk.

3 Heat in the microwave, on Full Power, for 3 minutes or until the chocolate and butter have melted. Beat until smooth.

4 Stir in the nuts and pour the mixture into the prepared pan. Smooth the top and let stand until set. Cut into squares.

COOK'S TIP

To make this fudge without a microwave, melt all the ingredients in a pan and bring to a boil, stirring constantly. Cook for 1 minute, then proceed as in the recipe.

Chocolate Creams

This soft, creamy candy is quick and simple to make, and ideal if the children want to be involved. Perfect served with a cup of coffee or tea.

20 mins plus
12 hrs setting

0 mins

MAKES ABOUT 30

INGREDIENTS

7 oz/200 g semisweet chocolate,
   broken into pieces

2 tbsp light cream

2 cups confectioners' sugar

drinking chocolate powder, for dusting

1 Line a cookie sheet with parchment paper. Melt 2 oz/55 g of the chocolate in a large heatproof bowl set over a pan of gently simmering water. Stir in the cream and remove the bowl from the heat.

2 Sift the confectioners' sugar into the melted chocolate then, using a fork, mix well together. Knead to form a firm, smooth, pliable mixture.

3 Lightly dust a work counter with drinking chocolate powder, turn out the mixture, and roll out to ¼-inch/5-mm thickness, then cut into circles, using a 1-inch/2.5-cm plain round cutter.

4 Transfer to the prepared cookie sheet and let stand for about 12 hours, or overnight, until set and dry.

5 When the chocolate creams have set, line a cookie sheet with parchment paper. Melt the remaining chocolate in a heatproof bowl set over a pan of gently simmering water. Using 2 forks, carefully dip each chocolate cream into the melted chocolate. Lift it out quickly, letting any excess chocolate drain against the side of the bowl, and place on the prepared cookie sheet. Let set.

Coffee Creams

Coffee-flavored fondant is extra special when coated with semisweet chocolate. Serve with a cappuccino or hot chocolate for a real treat.

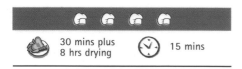

🎂 30 mins plus
8 hrs drying

⏰ 15 mins

MAKES 20

INGREDIENTS

2 cups granulated sugar

⅔ cup water

pinch of cream of tartar

3 tbsp light cream

½ tsp coffee extract

3 oz/85 g bittersweet chocolate, for coating

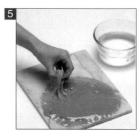

1 Put the sugar and water in a heavy-based pan and heat gently until the sugar has dissolved. Bring to a boil and add the cream of tartar.

2 Boil until the syrup registers 240°F/116°C on a sugar thermometer, or until a few drops of syrup form a soft ball when dropped into a cup of cold water. Stir the syrup into the cream.

3 Sprinkle a little water on a cutting board. Pour the syrup on to the cutting board and let cool for a few minutes until a skin forms around the edges.

4 Collect the syrup together with a spatula. Turn the mixture, working it backward and forward in a figure-of-eight movement, until it becomes opaque and grainy, then knead in the coffee extract.

5 Pull off walnut-size pieces of fondant. Roll each piece into a ball, then press to flatten slightly. Let dry for 8 hours, or overnight, on a cookie sheet lined with nonstick parchment paper.

6 Break the chocolate into pieces and place in a heatproof bowl set over a pan of gently simmering water until melted. Dip one end of each coffee cream into the melted chocolate to half-coat. Let stand on the parchment paper to dry.

Nutty Chocolate Clusters

Nuts and crisp cookies encased in chocolate make these candies rich, chocolatey, and quite irresistible at any time of the day!

🍬 30 mins plus 1 hr chilling   ⏱ 5 mins

MAKES 30

INGREDIENTS

6 oz/175 g white chocolate, broken into pieces

3½ oz/100 g graham crackers

⅔ cup chopped macadamia nuts or Brazil nuts

1 oz/25 g preserved ginger, chopped (optional)

6 oz/175 g semisweet chocolate, broken into pieces

1 Line a cookie sheet with a sheet of parchment paper. Put the white chocolate in a large heatproof bowl set over a pan of gently simmering water; stir until melted.

2 Break the graham crackers into small pieces. Stir the crackers into the melted chocolate with the chopped nuts and preserved ginger (if using).

3 Place heaping teaspoons of the mixture on the prepared cookie sheet.

4 Chill the mixture until set, then remove from the parchment paper.

5 Melt the semisweet chocolate (see step 1) and let it cool slightly. Dip the clusters into the melted chocolate, letting the excess drip back into the bowl. Return the clusters to the cookie sheet and chill in the refrigerator until set.

COOK'S TIP
Macadamia and Brazil nuts are both rich and high in fat, which makes them particularly popular for confectionery, but other nuts can be used if preferred.

Chocolate-Coated Brazil Nuts

In a box of chocolates these are often a favorite, yet they are surprisingly easy to make at home and are perfect for serving after dinner.

🥧 20 mins   🕐 5 mins

MAKES ABOUT 28

I N G R E D I E N T S

7 oz/200 g semisweet or milk chocolate, broken into pieces

1¾ cups shelled Brazil nuts

1 Line a cookie sheet with parchment paper. Break the chocolate into pieces and place in a heatproof bowl set over a pan of gently simmering water. Remove from the heat.

2 Using a fork, carefully dip and turn each Brazil nut into the melted chocolate. Lift it out quickly, letting any excess chocolate drain against the side of the bowl, and place on the cookie sheet. Let set.

3 When the chocolate has set, put the Brazil nuts into paper candy cases.

VARIATIONS
Other nuts that can be coated in the same way include walnuts, macadamia nuts, and blanched almonds.

Chocolate Almonds

This candy looks very elegant served in gold and silver foil cases.
Alternatively, use paper candy cases or place in an attractive dish.

🍰 30 mins   🕐 5 mins

MAKES 32

I N G R E D I E N T S

1½ cups confectioners' sugar, plus extra
  for dusting

½ cup unsweetened cocoa

1 tbsp milk

4 tbsp butter

½ cup whole blanched almonds

4 oz/115 g semisweet chocolate

1 Sift the confectioners' sugar and unsweetened cocoa into a bowl.

2 Place the milk and butter in a small pan and heat together until the butter has melted. Add to the confectioners' sugar mixture and beat to a stiff paste.

3 Turn the paste on to a work counter and dust your hands with confectioners' sugar. Roll the mixture into a thick rope. Cut into 32 pieces and shape each piece into an oval. Top each oval with an almond.

4 Break the chocolate into pieces and place in a heatproof bowl with 1 tablespoon of water. Set over a pan of gently simmering water until melted. Dip one side of each oval in chocolate and leave on a wire rack to set.

Chocolate Pralines

These heavenly chocolates, packed with crunchy almond praline, are wonderful served with a chocolate dessert such as a mousse or soufflé.

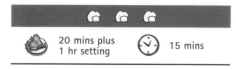

20 mins plus
1 hr setting

15 mins

MAKES 49

INGREDIENTS

sunflower oil, for brushing

1 cup granulated sugar

3 tbsp water

1 cup blanched almonds

7 oz/200 g bittersweet chocolate

1 Brush a cookie tray with oil. Put the sugar and water in a pan and heat gently, stirring, until the sugar has dissolved, then allow to bubble gently, without stirring, for 6–10 minutes, until lightly golden brown.

2 Remove the pan from the heat and stir in the almonds. Immediately pour the mixture on to the prepared cookie tray and spread out evenly. Let stand in a cool place for about 1 hour, until cold and hardened.

3 When the praline has hardened, crush it into tiny pieces in a food processor or in a polythene bag with a hammer.

4 Break the chocolate into pieces and place in a heatproof bowl set over a pan of gently simmering water. Add the crushed praline and mix together to form a stiff paste. Turn into a 7-inch/18-cm shallow square pan and let set.

5 When the chocolate praline has set, cut into squares to serve.

VARIATIONS
Instead of almonds, other nuts could be used such as blanched hazelnuts or pistachios.

Chocolate Marzipans

These delightful little morsels make the perfect gift, if you can resist eating them all yourself! Store in an airtight container.

50 mins   5 mins

MAKES 30

I N G R E D I E N T S

1 lb/450 g marzipan

⅓ cup very finely chopped candied cherries

1 oz/25 g preserved ginger, chopped very finely

confectioners' sugar, for dusting

⅓ cup no-soak dried apricots, chopped very finely

12 oz/350 g semisweet chocolate, broken into pieces

1 oz/25 g white chocolate, broken into pieces

1 Line a cookie sheet with parchment paper. Divide the marzipan into 3 balls and knead each ball to soften it.

2 Work the candied cherries into one portion of the marzipan by kneading on a work counter lightly dusted with confectioners' sugar.

3 Do the same with the preserved ginger and another portion of marzipan, and then the apricots and the third portion of marzipan.

4 Form each flavored portion of marzipan into small balls, keeping the different flavors separate.

5 Put the semisweet chocolate in a heatproof bowl and set over a pan of gently simmering water. Stir until melted. Dip one of each flavored ball of marzipan into the chocolate by spiking each one with a toothpick, letting the excess chocolate drip back into the bowl.

6 Place the balls in clusters of the 3 flavors on the cookie sheet. Repeat with the remaining balls. Chill until set.

7 Melt the white chocolate (see step 5) and drizzle a little over the tops of each cluster of marzipan balls. Let chill until hardened, then remove from the parchment paper.

VARIATIONS
Coat the marzipan balls in white or milk chocolate and drizzle with semisweet chocolate if you prefer.

Chocolate Raisin Clusters

These delicious chocolate raisin clusters are very simple to prepare and perfect for children to make on a rainy day.

 10 mins    5 mins

MAKES 36

I N G R E D I E N T S

8 oz/225 g semisweet chocolate, broken into pieces

1½ cups raisins

1 Line a cookie sheet with parchment paper. Melt the chocolate in a heatproof bowl set over a pan of gently simmering water.

2 Stir the raisins into the melted chocolate until well coated. Let cool slightly, then drop heaping teaspoonfuls of the mixture on to the prepared cookie sheet. Leave until cold and set.

3 When the chocolate raisin clusters have set, place in paper candy cases.

VARIATION
Golden raisins could be used instead of seedless raisins.

Almond Balls

The crunchy, nutty texture comes as a pleasant surprise in these balls of rich chocolate. They are ideal for serving after dinner with coffee.

🥄 15 mins   🕐 0 mins

MAKES 20

INGREDIENTS

5½ oz/150 g semisweet chocolate

½ cup finely chopped almonds

1 cup confectioners' sugar

3 tbsp light cream

1 Finely grate the chocolate. Put 4 oz/115 g of the chocolate into a bowl and spread the remaining chocolate on to a plate.

2 Add the almonds to the chocolate in the bowl, then sift in the confectioners' sugar. Stir together and add enough cream to form a firm mixture.

3 Take a heaping teaspoonful of the mixture at a time and roll into a ball. Continue until you have used up all the mixture. Drop each ball on to the plate of grated chocolate.

4 Roll the balls in the grated chocolate on the plate, to coat them. Place the balls in paper candy cases.

VARIATIONS
Other nuts, such as hazelnuts or macadamia nuts, could replace the almonds.

Chocolate Cherries

This cherry and marzipan candy is easy to make. Serve as petits fours at the end of a meal or as an indulgent nibble at any time of day.

🕐 1 hr 30 mins   🕐 2 mins

MAKES 24

INGREDIENTS

12 candied cherries

2 tbsp dark rum or cognac

9 oz/250 g marzipan

5½ oz/150 g semisweet chocolate, broken into pieces

milk, semisweet, or white chocolate, to decorate (optional)

1 Line a cookie sheet with a sheet of parchment paper.

2 Cut the cherries in half and place in a small bowl. Add the rum or cognac and stir to coat. Let the cherries soak for at least 1 hour, stirring occasionally.

3 Divide the marzipan into 24 pieces and roll each piece into a ball. Press half a cherry into the top of each marzipan ball.

4 Put the chocolate in a heatproof bowl and set over a pan of gently simmering water. Stir until all the chocolate has melted.

VARIATION
Flatten the marzipan and use it to mold around the cherries to cover them, then dip in the chocolate as above.

5 Dip each candy into the melted chocolate using a toothpick, letting the excess to drip back into the bowl. Place the coated cherries on the parchment paper and chill until set.

6 If liked, melt a little extra chocolate and drizzle it over the top of the coated cherries. Let set.

Mini Florentines

Serve these delicious cookies at the end of a meal with coffee, or arrange in a shallow presentation box for an attractive gift.

🍓 30 mins　　🕐 15–20 mins

MAKES 40

INGREDIENTS

2¾ oz/75 g butter, plus extra for greasing

all-purpose flour, for dusting

⅓ cup superfine sugar

2 tbsp golden raisins or raisins

2 tbsp chopped candied cherries

2 tbsp chopped preserved ginger

1 oz/25 g sunflower seeds

¾ cup slivered almonds

2 tbsp heavy cream

6 oz/175 g semisweet or milk chocolate, broken into pieces

1 Preheat the oven to 350°F/180°C. Grease and flour 2 cookie sheets or line with parchment paper.

2 Place the butter in a small pan and heat gently until melted. Add the sugar, stir until dissolved, then bring the mixture to a boil. Remove from the heat and stir in the golden raisins or raisins, cherries, ginger, sunflower seeds, and almonds. Mix well, then beat in the cream.

3 Place small teaspoons of the fruit and nut mixture on to the prepared cookie sheet, allowing plenty of room for the mixture to spread during baking. Bake in the preheated oven for 10–12 minutes, or until light golden in color.

4 Remove from the oven and, while still hot, use a circular cookie cutter to pull in the edges to form perfect circles. Let cool and go crisp before removing from the cookie sheet.

5 Put the chocolate in a heatproof bowl set over a pan of gently simmering water and stir until melted. Spread most of the chocolate on to a sheet of parchment paper. When the chocolate is on the point of setting, place the cookies flat-side down on the chocolate and let it harden completely.

6 Cut around the florentines and remove from the parchment paper. Spread a little more chocolate on the coated side of the florentines and use a fork to mark waves in the chocolate. Let set. Arrange the florentines on a plate (or in a presentation box for a gift) with alternate sides facing upward. Keep cool.

Italian Chocolate Truffles

These tasty morsels are flavored with almonds and chocolate, and are simplicity itself to make. Serve with coffee for the perfect end to a meal.

50 mins   5 mins

MAKES 24

INGREDIENTS

175 g/6 oz semisweet chocolate, broken into pieces

2 tbsp amaretto or orange-flavored liqueur

3 tbsp sweet butter

4 tbsp confectioners' sugar

½ cup ground almonds

1¾ oz/50 g grated chocolate

1 Melt the semisweet chocolate with the amaretto or orange-flavored liqueur in a heatproof bowl set over a pan of gently simmering water, stirring until well combined.

2 Add the butter and stir until it has melted. Stir in the confectioners' sugar and the ground almonds.

3 Let the mixture stand in a cool place until firm enough to roll into 24 balls.

4 Place the grated chocolate on a plate and roll the truffles in the chocolate to coat them.

5 Place the truffles in paper candy cases and chill.

VARIATION

The amaretto gives these truffles an authentic Italian flavor. The original Amaretto di Saronno comes from Saronno in Italy.

White Chocolate Truffles

These delicious creamy white truffles will testify to the fact that there is nothing quite as nice as homemade chocolates.

15 mins plus 2 hrs 30 mins chilling

5 mins

MAKES 20

INGREDIENTS

2 tbsp sweet butter

5 tbsp heavy cream

8 oz/225 g good-quality Swiss white chocolate

1 tbsp orange-flavored liqueur (optional)

3½ oz/100 g white chocolate, broken into pieces, for coating

1 Line a jelly roll pan with parchment paper.

2 Place the butter and cream in a small pan and bring slowly to a boil, stirring constantly. Boil for 1 minute, then remove from the heat.

3 Add the chocolate to the cream. Stir until melted, then beat in the liqueur (if using).

4 Pour into the prepared pan and chill for about 2 hours, until firm.

5 Break off pieces of the mixture and roll them into balls. Chill for an additional 30 minutes before finishing the truffles.

6 To finish, put the white chocolate in a heatproof bowl set over a pan of gently simmering water until melted. Dip the balls in the chocolate, letting the excess drip back into the bowl. Place on nonstick parchment paper, swirl the chocolate with the tines of a fork, and let it harden.

COOK'S TIP
The truffle mixture needs to be firm but not too hard to roll. If the mixture is too hard, let it stand at room temperature for a few minutes to soften slightly. During rolling the mixture will become sticky, but will reharden in the refrigerator before coating.

Chocolate Orange Truffles

These rich orange-flavored truffles make a delicious change from the more usual liqueur-flavored truffles. Serve in paper candy cases.

2 hrs 30 mins   0 mins

MAKES 36

INGREDIENTS

4 oz/115 g bittersweet chocolate,
   broken into pieces

4 tbsp butter

2 egg yolks

finely grated rind of 1 small orange

1 tbsp orange juice

½ cup cake crumbs

⅓ cup ground almonds

2 cups confectioners' sugar

chocolate vermicelli, for coating

1 Put the chocolate and butter in heatproof bowl set over a pan of gently simmering water until melted. Remove from the heat, add the egg yolks, and mix well together.

2 Add the orange rind and juice, cake crumbs, and almonds. Sift in the confectioners' sugar, then beat together until well mixed. Let cool for about 2 hours, until the mixture is firm.

VARIATION
The truffles can be coated in drinking chocolate powder as an alternative to the chocolate vermicelli.

3 Take a teaspoonful of the mixture at a time and roll into a ball between your hands. Continue until you have used up the remaining mixture.

4 Spread the chocolate vermicelli on to a plate, then roll the truffles in the chocolate vermicelli to coat them. Place the truffles in paper candy cases.

Chocolate Chestnut Truffles

Christmas is the time for eating chestnuts so make a batch of these for a festive treat. Use a package of cooked whole chestnuts for this recipe.

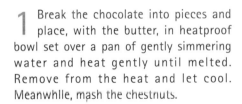

1 hr 30 mins   0 mins

MAKES 24

INGREDIENTS

3 oz/85 g bittersweet chocolate, broken into pieces

3 tbsp butter

7 oz/200 g cooked whole chestnuts

¼ cup superfine sugar

½ tsp vanilla extract

⅓ cup ground almonds, for coating

1 Break the chocolate into pieces and place, with the butter, in heatproof bowl set over a pan of gently simmering water and heat gently until melted. Remove from the heat and let cool. Meanwhile, mash the chestnuts.

2 Whisk together the butter and the sugar until pale and fluffy. Add the mashed chestnuts and vanilla extract and mix well together. Stir in the cooled chocolate until combined. Chill the mixture in the refrigerator for about 1 hour, until firm.

3 Take a heaping teaspoonful of the mixture at a time and roll into a ball between your hands. Continue until you have used up the remaining mixture.

4 Spread out the ground almonds on a plate, then roll the truffles in the ground almonds to coat them. Place the truffles in paper candy cases.

COOK'S TIP
If you find it difficult to mash the chestnuts, soften them in a microwave for 1 minute. If wished, ⅓ cup chopped almonds can be added to the mixture.

Chocolate Liqueurs

These tasty chocolate cups are filled with a delicious liqueur-flavored filling. Use your favorite liqueur to flavor the cream.

30 mins plus
20 mins chilling   5 mins

MAKES 20

INGREDIENTS

3½ oz/100 g semisweet chocolate, broken
    into pieces

20 candied cherries

20 hazelnuts or macadamia nuts

⅔ cup heavy cream

2 tbsp confectioners' sugar

4 tbsp liqueur, such as cognac

TO FINISH

1¾ oz/50 g semisweet chocolate, melted

little white chocolate, melted, or
    white chocolate curls (see page 9),
    or extra nuts and cherries

1 Line a cookie sheet with a sheet of parchment paper. Put the semisweet chocolate in a heatproof bowl and set over a pan of gently simmering water. Stir until melted. Spoon the chocolate into 20 paper candy cases, spreading up the sides with a spoon or brush. Place upside down on the cookie sheet and let set.

2 Carefully peel away the paper cases. Place a cherry or nut in each cup.

3 To make the filling, place the heavy cream in a mixing bowl and sift the confectioners' sugar on top. Whisk the cream until it is just holding its shape, then whisk in the liqueur.

4 Place the cream in a pastry bag fitted with a ½-inch/1-cm plain tip and pipe a little into each chocolate case. Let chill for 20 minutes.

5 To finish, melt a little semisweet chocolate (see step 1) over the cream to cover it, then pipe melted white chocolate on top, swirling it into the semisweet chocolate with a toothpick. Let the candies harden. Alternatively, cover the cream with melted semisweet chocolate and decorate with white chocolate curls before setting, or place a small piece of nut or cherry on top of the cream, then cover with semisweet chocolate.

COOK'S TIP
Paper candy cases can vary in size.
Use the smallest you can find
for this recipe.

Rocky Road Bites

Young children will love these chewy bites. You can vary the ingredients and use different nuts and dry fruits according to taste.

40 mins   5 mins

MAKES 20

INGREDIENTS

FILLING

4½ oz/125 g milk chocolate, broken into pieces

2½ oz/70 g mini multicolored marshmallows

¼ cup chopped walnuts

1 oz/25 g no-soak dried apricots, chopped

1 Line a cookie sheet with parchment paper and set aside.

2 Put the milk chocolate in a large heatproof mixing bowl. Set the bowl over a pan of gently simmering water and stir until the chocolate has melted.

3 Stir in the marshmallows, walnuts, and apricots, and toss in the melted chocolate until well covered.

4 Put heaping teaspoonfuls of the mixture on to the prepared cookie sheet.

5 Let the candies chill in the refrigerator until set.

VARIATION
Light, fluffy marshmallows are available in white or pastel colors. If you cannot find mini marshmallows, use large ones and snip them into smaller pieces with wet kitchen scissors before mixing them into the melted chocolate in step 3.

6 Once set, carefully remove the candies from the parchment paper.

7 The chewy bites can be placed in paper candy cases to serve, if desired.

Chocolate Popcorn

Children love popcorn, even more so when coated in chocolate.
Make sure that it is cool enough to eat before serving.

15 mins   15 mins

MAKES ABOUT 9 OZ/250 G

I N G R E D I E N T S

3 tbsp sunflower oil

⅓ cup popcorn

2 tbsp butter

⅓ cup brown sugar

2 tbsp corn syrup

1 tbsp milk

⅓ cup semisweet chocolate chips

1 Preheat the oven to 300°F/150°C. Heat the oil in a large, heavy-based pan. Add the popcorn, cover the pan, and cook, shaking the pan vigorously and frequently, for about 2 minutes, until the popping stops. Turn into a large bowl.

2 Put the butter, sugar, corn syrup, and milk in a pan and heat gently until the butter has melted. Bring to a boil, without stirring, and boil for 2 minutes. Remove from the heat, add the chocolate chips, and stir until melted.

3 Pour the chocolate mixture over the popcorn and toss together until evenly coated. Spread the mixture on to a large cookie sheet.

4 Bake the popcorn in the oven for about 15 minutes, until crisp. Let cool before serving.

Italian Amaretti Slices

Serve these delicious traditional almond-flavored chocolate slices with coffee, at the end of an Italian meal.

20 mins plus
1 hr standing/
4 hrs chilling

5 mins

MAKES 28–30 SLICES

INGREDIENTS

4 oz/115 g bittersweet chocolate, broken into pieces

3 oz/85 g butter

1 tbsp amaretto or cognac

2 tbsp toasted blanched almonds

8 oz/225 g amaretti cookies

1 Break the chocolate into pieces and place, with the butter and amaretto, in pan and heat gently. Stir occasionally, until it has all melted and mixed together. Remove from the heat.

2 Put the almonds in a food processor and chop finely. Add to the chocolate mixture.

3 Put the amaretti cookies in the food processor and chop finely. Reserve 2 tablespoons of the crumbs. Add the remaining crumbs to the chocolate mixture and mix well together. Let stand in a cool place for about 1 hour, until firm.

4 When the mixture is firm, turn out on to a sheet of waxed paper and shape into a sausage shape measuring about 9 inch/23 cm long. Wrap in the waxed paper and chill in the refrigerator for at least 4 hours or overnight, until solid.

5 Unwrap the sausage and dust with the reserved crumbs until coated, then cut into slices.

COOK'S TIP

If you are unable to buy ready-toasted almonds, toast blanched almonds under the broiler for 2–3 minutes, shaking frequently. Other nuts can be used, such as hazelnuts or walnuts if preferred.

Chocolate & Pistachio Truffles

These wickedly rich truffles add a touch of decadence at the end of a light meal. Use other types of nuts, such as almonds, if preferred.

30 mins plus 8 hrs chilling

5 mins

MAKES 26–30

INGREDIENTS

3½ oz/100 g white chocolate, broken into pieces

1 tbsp butter

¼ cup heavy cream

¼ cup shelled unsalted pistachios, chopped finely

confectioners' sugar, for dusting

1 Put the chocolate, butter, and cream in a heatproof bowl set over a pan of gently simmering water and heat, without stirring, until the chocolate has melted. Stir gently and add the nuts.

2 Remove the bowl from the heat. Let cool, then cover and chill overnight in the refrigerator. Line a cookie sheet with parchment paper.

3 Take teaspoonfuls of mixture and roll them into balls. Place them on the cookie sheet and chill until firm. Just before serving, roll the truffles in confectioners' sugar.

COOK'S TIP
The truffles look best if they are quite rough, rather than being rolled into smooth balls.

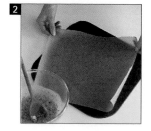

Rum Truffles

Truffles are always popular. They make a fabulous gift or, served with coffee, they are a perfect end to a special-occasion meal.

15 mins plus
30 mins chilling

5 mins

MAKES 20

INGREDIENTS

5½ oz/150 g semisweet chocolate, broken into pieces

small piece of butter

2 tbsp dark rum

½ cup dry unsweetened coconut

1⅔ cups cake crumbs

6 tbsp confectioners' sugar

2 tbsp unsweetened cocoa

1 Put the chocolate in a heatproof bowl with the butter. Set the bowl over a pan of gently simmering water, stirring until melted and combined.

2 Remove from the heat and beat in the rum. Stir in the dry unsweetened coconut, cake crumbs, and two-thirds of the confectioners' sugar. Beat until combined. Add a little extra rum if the mixture is stiff.

3 Roll the mixture into small balls and place them on a sheet of parchment paper. Chill until firm.

4 Sift the remaining confectioners' sugar on to a large plate. Sift the unsweetened cocoa on to another plate. Roll half of the truffles in the confectioners' sugar until coated and roll the remaining truffles in the unsweetened cocoa.

5 Chill the truffles in the refrigerator until ready to serve.

VARIATIONS
Make the truffles with white chocolate and replace the rum with coconut-flavored liqueur or milk if you prefer. Roll them in unsweetened cocoa or dip in melted milk chocolate.

Irish Cream Truffles

Truffles are quickly and easily made and are the ideal gift for chocoholics. They look particularly attractive arranged in alternate colors.

35 mins plus
8 hrs chilling

5–10 mins

MAKES ABOUT 24

I N G R E D I E N T S

⅔ cup heavy cream

8 oz/225 g semisweet chocolate,
  broken into pieces

2 tbsp butter

3 tbsp Bailey's Irish cream

FOR COATING

4 oz/115 g white chocolate,
  broken into pieces

4 oz/115 g semisweet chocolate,
  broken into pieces

1 Put the cream in a pan and heat without boiling. Remove from the heat and stir in the chocolate and butter. Leave for 2 minutes, then stir until melted and smooth. Stir in the liqueur. Pour the mixture into a bowl and let stand until cool. Cover and let chill in the refrigerator overnight, until firm.

2 Line a cookie sheet with parchment paper. Take teaspoonfuls of mixture and roll them into balls. Place them on the cookie sheet and chill again until firm. Put the white chocolate in a heatproof bowl set over a pan of gently simmering water until melted. Let cool a little.

3 Coat half the truffles by spearing on thin skewers and dipping in the white chocolate. Leave on nonstick parchment to set. Melt the semisweet chocolate in the same way and coat the remaining truffles. Store in the refrigerator in an airtight container, separated by layers of waxed paper, for up to 1 week.

COOK'S TIP
It is essential that the best-quality chocolate is used in this recipe.

Peanut Butter Truffles

Peanut butter combined with apricots and walnuts gives these truffles a wonderful flavor. Store in the refrigerator for several days.

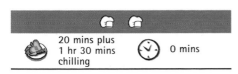

20 mins plus
1 hr 30 mins
chilling

0 mins

MAKES 24

I N G R E D I E N T S

¾ cup confectioners' sugar

½ cup no-soak dried apricots,
chopped coarsely

½ cup walnut pieces, chopped finely

8 oz/225 g smooth peanut butter

4 oz/115 g semisweet chocolate

grated chocolate, to decorate

1 Line a cookie sheet with nonstick parchment paper.

2 Sift the confectioners' sugar into a bowl. Add the apricots, walnuts, and peanut butter. Stir together to make a chunky mixture.

3 Shape teaspoonfuls of the mixture into walnut-size balls and arrange on the prepared cookie sheet. Chill in the refrigerator for 1 hour.

4 Break the chocolate into pieces and place in a heatproof bowl set over a pan of gently simmering water until melted. Using a fork, dip the truffles into the melted chocolate and set them on the parchment paper. Sprinkle with grated chocolate, then chill until firm.

Chocolate & Pistachio Biscotti

These crunchy biscuits from northern Italy are traditionally dunked into dessert wine, but they are just as good dipped into coffee or tea!

25 mins   40–45 mins

MAKES 48

INGREDIENTS

2 cups all-purpose flour, plus extra
   for dusting

1 tsp baking soda

pinch of salt

⅓ cup golden superfine sugar

½ cup ground almonds

2 eggs

3 oz/85 g semisweet chocolate, melted

½ cup shelled pistachios, chopped coarsely

1 egg white, beaten lightly

1 Preheat the oven to 375°F/190°C. Line 2 cookie sheets with nonstick parchment paper.

2 Sift the flour, baking soda, and salt into a bowl. Stir in the superfine sugar and ground almonds. Make a well in the center and break in the eggs. Stir from the center to form a rough dough.

3 Stir the melted chocolate into the dough. Turn out on to a floured cutting board and knead until well blended, then work in the chopped pistachios.

4 Divide the dough into 3 equal pieces and roll each one into a sausage shape 1 inch/2.5 cm in diameter. Place them on 1 of the prepared cookie sheets, allowing room for the biscotti to spread during cooking. Brush with beaten egg white. Bake in the preheated oven for 20 minutes.

5 Remove from the oven and leave for 5 minutes to cool and firm up. Reduce the oven temperature to 275°F/140°C. Using a serrated knife, cut the biscotti at an angle into ½-inch/1-cm thick slices. Arrange the slices on the cookie sheets and return to the oven for 20–25 minutes, turning once. Transfer to wire racks to cool.

Collettes

A creamy, orange-flavored chocolate filling in little white chocolate cups makes a wonderful treat for any occasion.

15 mins plus
1 hr setting/
chilling

5 mins

MAKES 20

INGREDIENTS

3½ oz/100 g white chocolate,
broken into pieces

FILLING

5½ oz/150 g orange-flavored semisweet
chocolate, broken into pieces

⅔ cup heavy cream

2 tbsp confectioners' sugar

1 Line a cookie sheet with parchment paper. Put the white chocolate in a heatproof bowl and set over a pan of gently simmering water. Stir until melted. Spoon the melted chocolate into 20 paper candy cases, spreading up the sides with a small spoon or brush. Place upside down on the prepared cookie sheet and let set.

2 When set, carefully peel away the paper cases.

3 To make the filling, melt the orange-flavored chocolate and place in a mixing bowl with the heavy cream and the confectioners' sugar. Beat until smooth. Chill until the mixture becomes firm enough to pipe, stirring occasionally.

4 Place the filling in a pastry bag fitted with a star tip and pipe a little into each candy case. Chill until required.

COOK'S TIP
If the chocolate cups do not hold their shape well, use 2 cases to make a double-thickness mold. Foil cases are firmer, so use these if you can find them.

Pastel Chocolate Cups

Packed in a box, these delicately colored chocolate cups make an attractive gift. Store in the refrigerator for up to a week.

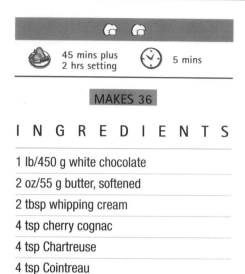

45 mins plus
2 hrs setting

5 mins

MAKES 36

INGREDIENTS

1 lb/450 g white chocolate

2 oz/55 g butter, softened

2 tbsp whipping cream

4 tsp cherry cognac

4 tsp Chartreuse

4 tsp Cointreau

pink, green, and orange food coloring

1 Place the chocolate in a heatproof bowl set over a pan of gently simmering water until melted.

2 Arrange 36 foil petit-four cases on a tray and spoon a little chocolate into each case. Using a fine brush, coat the inside of each case with chocolate. Let set.

3 Add the softened butter and cream to the remaining chocolate and stir until smooth. Divide the mixture among 3 bowls.

4 Add the cherry cognac to one bowl, Chartreuse to another, and Cointreau to the third. Color the mixtures pink, pale green, and pale orange respectively.

5 When the chocolate mixtures are set to a soft peaking consistency place each in a separate pastry bag fitted with a small star tip. Pipe swirls of each color into 12 chocolate cases. Let set.

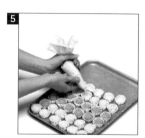

COOK'S TIP
Buy miniature liqueur bottles for this recipe.

Chocolate Mascarpone Cups

Mascarpone—the velvety smooth Italian cheese—makes a rich, creamy filling for these tasty chocolates. Dust with cocoa just before serving.

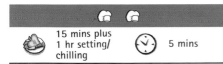

15 mins plus 1 hr setting/ chilling

5 mins

MAKES 20

INGREDIENTS

3½ oz/100 g semisweet chocolate, broken into pieces

FILLING

3½ oz/100 g milk or semisweet chocolate, broken into pieces

scant 1 cup mascarpone cheese

¼ tsp vanilla extract

unsweetened cocoa, for dusting

1 Line a cookie sheet with a sheet of parchment paper. Put the semisweet chocolate in a heatproof bowl and set over a pan of gently simmering water. Stir until melted. Spoon the chocolate into 20 paper candy cases, and spread up the sides with a spoon or brush. Place upside down on the cookie sheet and let set.

2 When set, carefully peel away the paper cases.

3 To make the filling, melt the milk or semisweet chocolate (see step 1). Put the mascarpone in a bowl and beat in the vanilla extract and melted chocolate until well combined. Let the mixture chill, beating occasionally until firm enough to pipe.

4 Put the mascarpone filling in a pastry bag fitted with a star tip and pipe the mixture into the cups. Decorate with a dusting of unsweetened cocoa.

VARIATION
Mascarpone is a rich Italian soft cheese made from fresh cream, so it has a high fat content. Its delicate flavor blends well with chocolate.

Double Chocolate Truffles

Marzipan, honey, and semisweet and milk chocolate are combined into little morsels of sheer delight. They are perfect for serving with coffee.

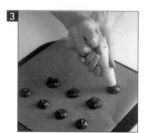

25 mins plus 2 hrs cooling

10 mins

MAKES 60

INGREDIENTS

6 oz/175 g sweet butter

⅔ cup grated marzipan

4 tbsp honey

½ tsp vanilla extract

7 oz/200 g semisweet chocolate, broken into pieces

12 oz/350 g milk chocolate, broken into pieces

1 Line 2 cookie sheets with parchment paper. Beat together the butter and marzipan until thoroughly combined and fluffy. Stir in the honey, a little at a time, then stir in the vanilla.

2 Place the semisweet chocolate and 7 oz/200 g of the milk chocolate in a heatproof bowl set over a pan of gently simmering water. Stir over low heat until melted and smooth. Remove from the heat and let cool slightly.

3 Stir the melted chocolate into the marzipan mixture, then spoon the chocolate and marzipan mixture into a pastry bag fitted with a large round tip and pipe small balls on to the prepared cookie sheets. Let cool and set.

4 Put the remaining milk chocolate in a heatproof bowl set over a pan of gently simmering water. Stir over low heat until melted, then remove from the heat.

Dip the truffles, 1 at a time, in the melted chocolate to coat them, then texture some of them by gently tapping them with a fork. Place on the cookie sheets to cool and set.

Mocha Truffles

Bittersweet chocolate and coffee are the perfect combination. Serve these delicious truffles with coffee at the end of a meal.

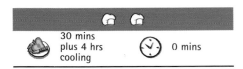

30 mins
plus 4 hrs
cooling

0 mins

MAKES 35

INGREDIENTS

2 tbsp instant coffee granules

2 tbsp boiling water

12 oz/350 g bittersweet chocolate

6 oz/175 g butter

3 tbsp heavy cream

2 tbsp unsweetened cocoa, for coating

1 In a heatproof bowl, dissolve the coffee in the boiling water. Break the chocolate into pieces and add to the bowl. Set the bowl over a pan of gently simmering water until melted.

2 Remove the bowl from the heat and gradually beat in the butter, then stir in the cream. Let the mixture cool for at least 4 hours or overnight, until the mixture is firm.

3 Take a heaping teaspoonful of the mixture at a time and roll into a ball between your hands. Continue until you have used up the remaining mixture.

4 Spread the unsweetened cocoa on to a plate, then roll the truffles in the unsweetened cocoa to coat them. Place the truffles in paper candy cases.

VARIATION
For a different effect, roll the truffles in ground almonds.

Praline & Coffee Truffles

Made with chocolate, praline, coffee, cognac, and cream, these rich truffles are pure indulgence and will surely impress your guests!

1 hr 35 mins plus 2 hrs chilling

10 mins

MAKES 40

I N G R E D I E N T S

sunflower oil, for brushing

⅓ cup granulated sugar

2 tbsp water

⅓ cup blanched almonds

12 oz/350 g bittersweet chocolate

½ cup strong black coffee

1 tbsp cognac

4 oz/115 g butter

3 tbsp heavy cream

1 tbsp unsweetened cocoa

1 tbsp confectioners' sugar

1 Brush a cookie sheet with oil. Put the sugar and water in a pan and heat gently, stirring, until the sugar has dissolved, then allow to bubble gently, without stirring, for 6–10 minutes, until lightly golden brown.

2 Remove the pan from the heat and stir in the almonds. Immediately pour the mixture on to the cookie sheet and spread out evenly. Leave in a cool place for about 1 hour, until cold and hardened.

3 When the praline has hardened, crush it to a fine powder in a food processor or in a polythene bag with a hammer.

4 Break the chocolate into small even-size pieces and place, with the coffee and cognac, in a heatproof bowl set over a pan of gently simmering water until melted. Remove the pan from the heat and let the mixture cool slightly.

5 Gradually add the butter to the chocolate mixture, then let cool, until a trail is left on the surface when lifted with a spoon.

6 Add the crushed praline and cream to the cooled chocolate mixture and stir together. Let chill in the refrigerator for about 2 hours, or until the chocolate mixture is firm.

7 Take a teaspoonful of the mixture at a time and roll into a ball between your hands. Continue until you have used up all the mixture.

8 Spread the unsweetened cocoa and confectioners' sugar on 2 separate plates, then roll half the truffles in the unsweetened cocoa and half in the confectioners' sugar to coat them. Place the truffles in paper candy cases.

Candied Citrus Peel

Strips of chocolate-coated candied citrus peel make a refreshing change from candy or chocolates with after-dinner coffee.

🍓 15 mins plus 6 hrs standing   🕐 40 mins

MAKES 60–80 PIECES

I N G R E D I E N T S

1 large unwaxed, thick-skinned orange

1 large unwaxed, thick-skinned lemon

1 large unwaxed, thick-skinned lime

3 cups superfine sugar

1¼ cups water

4½ oz/125 g best-quality semisweet chocolate, chopped (optional)

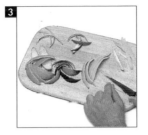

1 Cut the orange into quarters lengthwise and squeeze the juice into a cup to drink, or use in another recipe. Cut each quarter in half lengthwise to make 8 pieces in all.

2 Cut the fruit and pith away from the rind. If any of the pith remains on the rind, lay the knife almost flat on the white side of the rind and gently "saw" backward and forward to slice it off because it will make the rind taste bitter.

3 Repeat with the lemon and lime, only cutting the lime into quarters. Cut each piece into 3 or 4 thin strips to make 60–80 strips in total. Place the strips in a pan of water and boil for 30 seconds. Drain.

4 Dissolve the sugar in the water in a pan over medium heat, stirring. Increase the heat and bring to a boil, without stirring. When the syrup becomes clear, turn the heat to its lowest setting.

5 Add the citrus strips, using a wooden spoon to push them in without stirring. Simmer in the syrup for 30 minutes, without stirring. Turn off the heat and set aside for at least 6 hours until completely cool.

6 Line a cookie sheet with foil. Skim off the thin crust on top of the syrup without stirring. Remove the citrus strips, one by one, from the syrup, shaking off any excess. Place the strips on the foil to cool.

7 Put the chocolate in a heatproof bowl set over a pan of gently simmering water until melted. Working with 1 piece of candied peel at a time, dip the peel halfway into the chocolate. Drizzle a little melted chocolate over some of the strips. Return to the foil and let set. Store in an airtight container.

Rum & Chocolate Cups

Use firm foil candy cases, rather than paper ones, to make the chocolate cups, because they offer extra support. Use cognac if preferred.

40 mins plus 1 hr 45 mins chilling

10–15 mins

MAKES 12

INGREDIENTS

2 oz/55 g semisweet chocolate, broken into pieces

12 toasted hazelnuts

FILLING

4 oz/115 g semisweet chocolate, broken into pieces

1 tbsp dark rum

4 tbsp mascarpone cheese

1 To make the chocolate cups, place the chocolate in a heatproof bowl set over a pan of gently simmering water. Stir over low heat until the chocolate is just melted but not too runny, then remove from the heat. Spoon about ½ teaspoon of melted chocolate into a foil candy case and brush it over the bottom and up the sides. Coat 11 more foil cases in the same way and let set for 30 minutes. Chill in the refrigerator for 15 minutes. If necessary, reheat the chocolate in the heatproof bowl to melt it again, then coat the foil cases with a second, slightly thinner coating. Let the cases chill in the refrigerator for an additional 30 minutes.

2 Meanwhile, make the filling. Place the chocolate in a heatproof bowl set over a pan of gently simmering water. Stir over a low heat until melted, then remove from the heat. Let cool slightly, then stir in the rum and beat in the mascarpone cheese until fully incorporated and smooth. Let cool completely, stirring occasionally.

3 Spoon the filling into a pastry bag fitted with a ½-inch/1-cm star tip. If preferred, carefully peel away the confectionery cases from the chocolate cups. Pipe the filling into the cups and top each one with a toasted hazelnut.

Chocolate-Dipped Prunes

A much underrated dry fruit, prunes make delicious and very attractive after-dinner treats, especially if dipped in white chocolate.

30 mins plus
30 mins cooling   55–65 mins

MAKES 24

INGREDIENTS

scant 1 cup water

⅔ cup granulated sugar

2 cinnamon sticks,
    each 3 inches/7.5 cm long

1 vanilla bean

1 lb/450 g whole prunes

2¾ oz/75 g leftover sponge cake

¾ cup ground toasted walnuts

5 tbsp slivovitz or cognac

½ tsp vanilla extract

3½ oz/100 g white chocolate,
    broken into pieces

1 Pour the water into a pan, add the sugar, and stir over low heat until the sugar has dissolved. Add the cinnamon sticks and vanilla bean, increase the heat and bring to a boil. Then reduce the heat and simmer for 5 minutes.

2 Add the prunes, bring back to a boil, and simmer for 5 minutes. Lift out 24 large, well-shaped prunes with a slotted spoon and set aside to cool. Simmer the remaining prunes for 30–40 minutes, until very tender. Meanwhile, slit the 24 reserved prunes and remove the pits, leaving a neat cavity for the filling.

3 Drain the soft-cooked prunes and discard the syrup. Remove the pits and place the prunes in a food processor with the sponge cake, ground walnuts, slivovitz or cognac, and vanilla. Process to a smooth paste. Divide the filling among the reserved prunes, carefully pressing it into the cavities and gently reshaping the prunes around it.

4 Put the chocolate in a heatproof bowl set over a pan of gently simmering water. Stir over low heat until melted, then remove from the heat. Dip each prune into the melted chocolate to half-coat, then spoon the remaining chocolate into a pastry bag fitted with a fine tip. Pipe thin lines over the tops of the prunes, then place them on a sheet of parchment paper until set.

Brazil Nut Brittle

Chunks of fudge, white chocolate, and Brazil nuts are embedded in semisweet chocolate. Serve with coffee at the end of a meal.

10 mins   20 mins

MAKES 20 PIECES

INGREDIENTS

oil, for brushing

12 oz/350 g semisweet chocolate, broken into pieces

scant ¾ cup shelled Brazil nuts, chopped

6 oz/175 g white chocolate, chopped coarsely

6 oz/175 g fudge, chopped coarsely

1 Brush the bottom of an 8-inch/20-cm square cake pan with oil and line with parchment paper. Put half the semisweet chocolate in a heatproof bowl and set over a pan of gently simmering water. Stir until melted, then spread in the prepared pan.

2 Sprinkle with the chopped Brazil nuts, white chocolate, and fudge. Melt the remaining semisweet chocolate pieces as in step 1 and pour over the top.

3 Let the brittle set, then break up into jagged pieces using the tip of a strong knife.

COOK'S TIP
Put the brittle on a serving plate or in an airtight container and keep, covered, in a cool place. Alternatively, you can store it in the refrigerator for up to 3 days.

Chocolate & Rum Tartlets

These tiny tarts filled with a delicious concoction of chocolate and rum then topped with a white frosting are very popular in France.

30 mins plus
45 mins cooling   15–20 mins

MAKES 18-20

INGREDIENTS

PIE DOUGH

4 tbsp butter

¼ cup superfine sugar

1 egg yolk

1 cup all-purpose flour, plus extra
   for dusting

FILLING

3 oz/85 g semisweet chocolate

1 tbsp sweet butter

2 tbsp light cream

2 tsp dark rum

FROSTING

1 cup confectioners' sugar

vanilla extract

chocolate curls (see page 9),
   to decorate

1 Preheat the oven to 375°F/190°C.

2 Make the pie dough. Beat together the butter and sugar in a bowl until light and fluffy. Gradually beat in the egg yolk. Sift the flour into the bowl and work into the mixture.

3 Turn the dough on to a floured cutting board and roll out quite thinly. Use to line 18–20 tiny tartlet pans with a capacity of about 1 tablespoon. Prick the bases. Bake in the oven for 10–15 minutes, until crisp and very lightly browned. Let cool in the pan for 2 minutes, then transfer to a wire rack.

4 Make the filling. Place the chocolate, butter, and cream in a pan and heat very gently, stirring, until melted and combined. Remove from the heat and stir in the rum. Let cool completely, beating occasionally until thick. Divide among the tartlet cases.

5 Make the frosting. Sift the confectioners' sugar into a bowl. Stir in a few drops of vanilla extract and enough cold water to make a thick glacé frosting. Spoon the frosting over the chocolate mixture and decorate with a chocolate curls. Let set.

Chocolate Coconut Squares

Chocolate and coconut are a perenially favorite combination. These squares are perfect served with coffee or tea at any time of the day.

15 mins

5 mins

MAKES 49 PIECES

INGREDIENTS

3½ oz/100 g bittersweet chocolate

¾ cup milk

2⅓ cups granulated sugar

2 cups dry unsweetened coconut

2 tsp unsweetened cocoa

1 Rinse out a 7-inch/18-cm shallow square pan with cold water. Break the chocolate into pieces and place in a heatproof bowl set over a pan of gently simmering water until melted. Remove from the heat.

2 Pour the milk into a pan and add the sugar. Heat gently, stirring, until the sugar dissolves, then bring to a boil and boil gently for about 5 minutes, until a little of the mixture, when dropped into a bowl of cold water, forms a soft ball when rolled between the fingers.

3 Remove the pan from the heat and stir in the melted chocolate. Beat vigorously until the mixture is thick and creamy, then immediately pour into the prepared pan.

4 Leave the mixture until half set, then mark into squares. Cut when cold and firm. Mix the coconut and unsweetened cocoa on a plate. Roll the fudge cubes in the mixture to coat them, pressing gently to make sure the coconut sticks to all sides.

Strawberry Shortbread Hearts

It is very easy to become addicted to this combination of buttery chocolate shortbread, fresh strawberries, and cream!

🍰 20 mins　　🕐 8–10 mins

MAKES 20

INGREDIENTS

⅔ cup all-purpose flour, plus extra for dusting

1 tbsp unsweetened cocoa

4 tbsp butter

¼ cup golden superfine sugar

1 cup heavy cream

2 tbsp superfine sugar

10 strawberries, halved

2 tsp confectioners' sugar, for dusting

1 Preheat the oven to 350°F/180°C.

2 Sift the flour and unsweetened cocoa into a food processor and add the butter and superfine sugar. Process until the mixture forms a ball.

3 Transfer the dough to a cutting board and roll out to a thickness of ¼ inch/5 mm. Using a 2½-inch/6-cm heart-shaped cutter, cut out 20 cookies and place on a cookie sheet.

4 Bake the cookies in the preheated oven for 8–10 minutes until firm. Transfer to a wire rack to cool.

5 In a bowl, whip together the cream and sugar until soft peaks form. Transfer to a pastry bag fitted with a large star tip and pipe 3 rosettes of cream on to each cookie. Place half a strawberry in the middle of each one.

6 Dust with confectioners' sugar just before serving.

Chocolate Peppermint Creams

Peppermint creams are a great favorite, and the addition of a chocolate coating makes them even more popular. Serve at the end of a meal.

20 mins plus
24 hrs setting

0 mins

MAKES 40

INGREDIENTS

1 egg white

2 cups confectioners' sugar, plus extra
for dusting

few drops peppermint oil

7 oz/200 g semisweet chocolate, broken
into pieces

1 Line a cookie sheet with parchment paper. Whisk the egg white until stiff. Gradually sift in the confectioners' sugar and mix together to form a firm, pliable mixture. Add the peppermint oil to taste and mix well together.

2 Lightly dust a cutting board with confectioners' sugar, turn out the mixture, and knead for 2–3 minutes. Roll out to a $^{1}/_{4}$-inch/5-mm thickness then cut into circles, using a 1-inch/2.5-cm round cutter.

3 Transfer to the prepared cookie sheet and leave for about 24 hours, or overnight, until set and dry.

4 Melt the chocolate in a heatproof bowl set over a pan of gently simmering water. When the peppermints have set carefully dip each peppermint into the melted chocolate using 2 forks.

Lift it out quickly, letting any excess chocolate drain against the side of the bowl, and place on the prepared cookie sheet. Let set.

COOK'S TIP

Peppermint oil has a very strong flavor, so must be added sparingly. To do this, dip the end of a skewer into the bottle and shake off the drops one by one. Peppermint oil is far superior to peppermint flavoring, but if you do use peppermint flavoring, you will need to add about ½ teaspoon to this recipe.

Mint Chocolate Crisps

Crushed mints give these thin chocolates a crisp texture. These little candies are a real treat at any time of the day.

15 mins plus
30 mins chilling

10 mins

MAKES 20

I N G R E D I E N T S

1 package extra-strong mints

4 oz/115 g milk chocolate

2 oz/55 g semisweet chocolate

1 Line a cookie sheet with nonstick parchment paper.

2 Place the mints in a polythene bag and, using a rolling pin, crush to a coarse powder.

3 Break the milk chocolate in pieces and place in a heatproof bowl set over a pan of gently simmering water until melted. Stir the crushed mints into the melted chocolate. Using a round-bladed knife, spread the mixture on the prepared cookie sheet to a rectangle measuring 9 x 7 inches/23 x 18 cm. Chill the mixture for 10 minutes, or until almost set.

4 Melt the semisweet chocolate in the same way as the milk chocolate, then spread in a very thin layer over the chocolate-mint mixture. Let chill in the refrigerator until set.

5 Trim the edges, then warm a knife in hot water and cut into 20 squares.

Mini Mint Meringues

Serve these tiny mint-flavored meringues with after-dinner coffee.
If there are any left, keep in the refrigerator for several days.

🕐 40 mins   🕐 1 hr

MAKES 45

INGREDIENTS

1 egg white

¼ cup superfine sugar

¼ tsp peppermint extract

4 oz/115 g semisweet chocolate

1 Preheat the oven to 275°F/140°C. Line 2 cookie sheets with nonstick parchment paper.

2 Place the egg white in a bowl and whisk until stiff. Gradually whisk in the sugar, then whisk in the peppermint extract.

3 Spoon the mixture into a pastry bag fitted with a ¹/₄-inch/5-mm plain tip. Pipe 45 small circles, about 1-inch/2.5-cm in diameter on to the prepared cookie sheets. Cook in the oven for 1 hour, until firm and easy to lift.

4 Break the chocolate into pieces and place in a heatproof bowl set over a pan of gently simmering water until melted.

5 Dip the meringues into the melted chocolate. Remove with a fork, shaking gently, and transfer to a wire rack to set.

Ginger & Chocolate Meringues

Chocolate, ginger, and meringue: a winning, melt-in-the-mouth combination. They are best assembled just before serving.

30 mins   1 hr

MAKES 20

INGREDIENTS

2 egg whites

½ cup superfine sugar

2 oz/55 g semisweet chocolate, grated

FILLING

⅔ cup heavy cream

2 tsp syrup from the ginger jar

2 pieces preserved ginger, chopped finely

1 Preheat the oven to 250°F/120°C. Line 2 cookie sheets with nonstick parchment paper.

2 Place the egg whites in a bowl and whisk until stiff. Gradually whisk in the sugar. Fold in the grated chocolate.

3 Spoon the mixture into a pastry bag fitted with a large star tip and pipe 40 meringue rosettes on to the prepared cookie sheets. Bake in the oven for 1 hour, or until crisp and dry. Cool completely before removing from the cookie sheet.

4 Make the filling. Whip the cream until thick, stir in the ginger syrup, then add the chopped preserved ginger. Use the filling to sandwich the meringues together in pairs.

Mocha Coconut Clusters

These little clusters are the perfect candy for coconut lovers, with the addition of chocolate and coffee to give them their mocha flavor.

15 mins   5 mins

MAKES 30

INGREDIENTS

4 oz/115 g milk chocolate, broken into pieces

2 tbsp butter

1 tsp instant coffee powder

1 cup dry unsweetened coconut

1 Line 2–3 cookie sheets with parchment paper. Melt the chocolate and butter in a heatproof bowl set over a pan of gently simmering water. Remove from the heat.

2 Stir the coffee granules into the chocolate until dissolved, then stir in the coconut.

3 Place heaping teaspoonfuls of the mixture on to the prepared cookie sheets and let set. Serve the clusters in paper candy cases.

COOK'S TIP

If you wish, toast the coconut before you add it to the mixture, to bring out its full flavor. To do this, put it in a large dry skillet and heat gently, stirring constantly, until golden brown.

Chocolate Eggs

Who can resist a chocolate egg? Certainly not when they are packed with praline. Wrapped in foil, these eggs make great gifts at Easter.

30 mins plus 12 hrs setting

6–10 mins

MAKES 4

INGREDIENTS

sunflower oil, for brushing

⅓ cup granulated sugar

2 tbsp water

⅓ cup blanched almonds

4 large eggs

8 oz/225 g semisweet or milk chocolate, broken into pieces

2 tbsp heavy cream

1 Brush a cookie sheet with oil. Put the sugar and water in a pan and heat gently, stirring, until the sugar has dissolved, then let bubble gently, without stirring, for 6–10 minutes, until lightly golden brown.

2 Remove the pan from the heat and stir in the almonds. Immediately pour the mixture on to the cookie sheet and spread out evenly. Leave in a cool place for about 1 hour, until cold and hardened.

3 When the praline has hardened, finely crush it to a powder in a food processor or place it in a polythene bag and crush with a hammer.

4 Using a pin, pierce a hole in the pointed end of each egg. Using small scissors, carefully enlarge the hole to about ½ inch/1 cm in diameter.

5 Using a skewer or toothpick, burst the egg yolk, then shake the raw egg into a bowl. (Use the eggs in another recipe.) Carefully pour running water into the shells, then shake out until clean.

Turn the shells upside down and let dry for 30 minutes on paper towels.

6 When the egg shells are dry, melt the chocolate in a heatproof bowl set over a pan of gently simmering water. Remove from the heat and stir in the praline and cream.

7 Fill a pastry bag, fitted with a small plain tip, with the mixture and pipe into the egg shells. Let stand for up to 12 hours until set.

8 When set, carefully crack the eggs and peel off the shells, then wrap each egg in colored foil.

Cocochoc Pyramids

This is a traditional favorite. In this recipe, coconut ice is deliciously dipped in melted chocolate to make a two-tone treat.

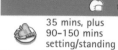

35 mins, plus
90–150 mins
setting/standing

15–25 mins

MAKES 12

I N G R E D I E N T S

⅔ cup water

2¼ cups granulated sugar

pinch of cream of tartar

generous 1 cup dry unsweetened coconut

1 tbsp heavy cream

few drops of yellow food coloring

3 oz/85 g semisweet chocolate,
broken into pieces

1 Pour the water into a heavy-based pan, add the sugar, and stir over low heat until the sugar has dissolved. Stir in a pinch of cream of tartar and bring to a boil. Boil steadily, without stirring, until the temperature reaches 238°F/119°C on a sugar thermometer. If you do not have a sugar thermometer, test the syrup frequently by dropping a small quantity into a bowl of cold water. If the mixture can then be rolled between your finger and thumb to make a soft ball, it is ready.

2 Remove the pan from the heat and beat in the coconut and cream. Continue to beat for 5–10 minutes until the mixture becomes cloudy. Beat in a few drops of yellow food coloring, then let cool. When cool enough to handle, take small pieces of the mixture and form them into pyramids. Place on a sheet of parchment paper and let harden.

3 Put the chocolate in a heatproof bowl set over a pan of gently simmering water. Stir over low heat until melted, then remove from the heat. Dip the bottom of the pyramids into the melted chocolate and let set.

Mini Chocolate Cones

These unusual cone-shaped mint-cream chocolates make a change from the more usual cup shape, and are perfect for an after-dinner chocolate.

40 mins   5 mins

MAKES 10

I N G R E D I E N T S

2¾ oz/75 g semisweet chocolate,
   broken into pieces

generous ⅓ cup heavy cream

1 tbsp confectioners' sugar

1 tbsp crème de menthe

chocolate-coated coffee beans,
   to decorate (optional)

1 Cut 10 circles, 3 inches/7.5 cm across, out of parchment paper. Shape each circle into a cone shape and secure with sticky tape.

2 Put the chocolate in a heatproof bowl and set over a pan of gently simmering water. Stir until melted. Using a small brush, coat the inside of each cone with the melted chocolate. Chill to set.

3 Brush a second layer of chocolate on the inside of the cones and chill until set. Carefully peel away the paper.

4 Place the heavy cream, confectioners' sugar, and crème de menthe in a mixing bowl and whip until just holding its shape. Place in a pastry bag fitted with a star tip and pipe the mixture into the chocolate cones.

5 Decorate the cones with chocolate-coated coffee beans (if using) and chill in the refrigerator until required.

COOK'S TIP
The chocolate cones can be made in advance and kept in the refrigerator for up to 1 week. Do not fill them more than 2 hours before you are going to serve them.

Chocolate Puff Fingers

Using ready-made puff pastry and chocolate hazelnut spread, making these crisp fingers could not be easier.

🍴 15 mins   🕐 8–10 mins

MAKES 30

I N G R E D I E N T S

1 package ready-rolled puff pastry, thawed if frozen

2 tbsp chocolate and hazelnut spread

confectioners' sugar, to decorate

1 Preheat the oven to 425°F/220°C.

2 Cut the puff pastry in half. Spread the chocolate hazelnut spread over one half and place the other half on top.

3 Cut into 30 strips. Twist each strip, arrange on a cookie sheet, and bake in the oven for 8–10 minutes, until browned and crisp. Transfer to a wire rack to cool.

4 When the fingers are cold, dust with sifted confectioners' sugar.

Chocolate Toffee

This is traditional toffee, with the addition of chocolate. It looks very attractive in paper or foil candy cases.

🍰 10 mins 🕐 20–25 mins

MAKES 36

INGREDIENTS

4 oz/115 g butter, plus extra for greasing

2 cups golden granulated sugar

⅔ cup water

2 tbsp corn syrup

4 oz/115 g semisweet chocolate, broken into pieces

1 Grease a shallow 7-inch/18-cm square pan.

2 Put the sugar, butter, water, and corn syrup in a large, heavy-based pan. Stir over low heat until the sugar has dissolved.

3 Bring slowly to a boil and cook, for 10–15 minutes, without stirring, until the temperature reaches 250°F/120°C. If you do not have a sugar thermometer, test the toffee by dropping a small amount into cold water. It is ready when it reaches the soft crack stage: that is when it separates into threads that are hard and brittle.

4 Remove the pan from the heat and stir in the chocolate. Stir gently until melted, then pour immediately into the prepared pan.

5 When the toffee is starting to set, mark into squares with a sharp knife. Let set, then cut into squares when cold.

Walnut & Chocolate Fingers

Phyllo pastry makes a lovely crisp shell round the nutty chocolate filling. Try to find the best-quality semisweet chocolate available.

20 mins   20 mins

MAKES 20

INGREDIENTS

4 tbsp sweet butter, melted, plus extra for greasing

5 large sheets phyllo pastry

1 tbsp confectioners' sugar, for dusting

FILLING

1¼ cups walnut pieces, ground coarsely

2 tbsp golden granulated sugar

½ teaspoon ground cinnamon

2 oz/55 g semisweet chocolate, grated

1 Preheat the oven to 325°F/160°C. Grease 2 cookie sheets.

2 Make the filling. In a bowl, mix together the walnuts, granulated sugar, cinnamon, and grated chocolate.

3 Cut each sheet of phyllo pastry into 4 rectangles measuring 9 x 7 inches/ 23 x 18 cm. Pile on top of each other and cover with a dish towel to prevent drying out.

4 Brush a phyllo rectangle with melted butter. Spread a teaspoon of filling along one short end. Fold the long sides in, slightly over the filling. Roll up from the end with the filling.

5 Place on the prepared cookie sheet with the seam underneath and brush with melted butter. Repeat with the remaining pastry and filling. Bake in the oven for 20 minutes, or until very lightly colored.

6 Transfer to a wire rack to cool. Dust the walnut and chocolate fingers with confectioners' sugar before serving.

VARIATIONS
Substitute ground almonds, or chopped pistachios or pine nuts, for the walnuts.

Almond & Chocolate Tuiles

These little cookies are very crisp and extremely moreish! Try them with vanilla ice cream. Make sure that they are completely cold before serving.

🕒 30 mins   ⏱ 18–24 mins

MAKES 36

INGREDIENTS

4 tbsp sweet butter, melted and cooled, plus extra for greasing

2 egg whites

½ cup golden superfine sugar

⅓ cup all-purpose flour

2 tbsp unsweetened cocoa

⅓ cup slivered almonds

1 Preheat the oven to 350°F/180°C. Grease 3 cookie sheets and a length of wooden dowelling (or similar) 1 inch/2.5 cm in diameter.

2 Put the egg whites and superfine sugar in a bowl and whisk together with a fork until the mixture is frothy. Sift the flour and unsweetened cocoa over the egg whites. Add the slivered almonds and mix with a fork. Add the melted butter and mix together thoroughly.

3 Drop half teaspoons of the mixture on to the prepared cookie sheets, allowing room for the cookies to spread during cooking. Using a round-bladed knife, spread each one out slightly.

4 Bake in the oven, 1 sheet at a time, for 6–8 minutes, until the edges feel firm.

5 Lift the cookies off carefully with a round-bladed knife and place on the wooden dowel while still warm. Leave for 2 minutes until set into a curved shape. Transfer to a wire rack to cool completely. Store in an airtight container.

Praline & Sesame Candy

The addition of sesame seeds gives this praline candy an exotic flavor.
Serve with your favorite liqueur or spirit for a special treat.

30 mins plus
1 hr hardening

15 mins

MAKES 20–24

I N G R E D I E N T S

sunflower oil, for brushing

½ cup golden superfine sugar

¼ cup whole unblanched almonds

1 tbsp sesame seeds, toasted

2 oz/55 g semisweet chocolate

1 Brush a large cookie sheet with oil.
Put the sugar and almonds in a heavy-based pan and heat very gently until the sugar has dissolved.

2 Cook gently until the almonds start to pop and turn brown and the caramel is a rich brown color, shaking the pan so the almonds are well coated.

3 Pour in the sesame seeds and shake the pan to mix. Pour on to the prepared cookie sheet and let harden.

4 Break the chocolate into pieces and place in a heatproof bowl set over a pan of gently simmering water until melted. Break the praline into large pieces and half-dip in the warm melted chocolate. Shake off the excess and place on nonstick parchment paper to set.

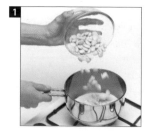

COOK'S TIP

If the praline is not going to be used immediately it should be completely coated in chocolate, otherwise it will become sticky.

Sesame Bites

These delicious, little deep-fried treats are crisp on the outside and melt-in-the mouth on the inside. Excellent served warm.

🍽 15 mins   🕐 10-15 mins

MAKES 10

I N G R E D I E N T S

½ cup sugar

2 tbsp coconut milk

2 eggs, beaten lightly

2 tbsp coconut butter, melted

2¼ cups all-purpose flour

4 tsp dry unsweetened coconut

¼ tsp baking powder

salt

4 tbsp sesame seeds

sunflower oil, for deep-frying

1 Combine the sugar, coconut milk, eggs, and coconut butter in a bowl. Combine the flour, dry unsweetened coconut, baking powder and a pinch of salt in another bowl, then stir the flour mixture into the egg mixture. Knead lightly until smooth.

2 Form the mixture into small balls with your hands or using 2 teaspoons. Spread out the sesame seeds on a plate and roll the balls in them to coat.

3 Half fill a wok or deep, heavy-based skillet or pan with oil and heat to 180-190°C/350-375°F or until a cube of bread browns in 30 seconds. Add the sesame bites, in batches, and deep-fry until golden brown. Remove with a slotted spoon and drain on paper towels. Serve warm.

Bunuelo Stars

Tortillas, cut into star shapes, deep-fried, and sprinkled with cinnamon and sugar, are simply delicious served with chocolate or vanilla ice cream.

5–10 mins   15 mins

SERVES 4

INGREDIENTS

4 flour tortillas

3 tbsp ground cinnamon

6–8 tbsp sugar

vegetable oil, for frying

chocolate ice cream, to serve

fine strips orange rind, to decorate

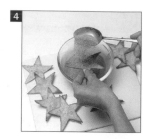

1 Using a sharp knife or kitchen scissors cut each tortilla into star shapes.

2 Mix the cinnamon and sugar together and set them aside.

3 Heat the oil in a shallow, wide skillet until it is hot enough to brown a cube of bread in 30 seconds. Working one at a time, fry the star-shaped tortillas until one side is golden, then turn and cook until golden on the other side. Remove from the hot oil with a slotted spoon and drain on paper towels.

4 Sprinkle generously with the cinnamon and sugar mixture. Serve with chocolate ice cream, sprinkled with orange rind strips.

COOK'S TIP

These star-shaped bunuelos make an attractive decoration for an ice cream sundae with Mexican flavors, caramel, cinnamon, coffee, and chocolate.

Pistachio & Chocolate Halva

The word "halva" is derived from the Arabic word *hulw* meaning sweet. For best results, try to find unsalted pistachios for this recipe.

20 mins plus
30 mins soaking

15 mins

MAKES 25 SQUARES

INGREDIENTS

1¼ cups shelled pistachios

1 cup boiling water

2 tbsp milk

½ cup golden superfine sugar

2 tbsp butter

2 oz/55 g semisweet chocolate, broken into small pieces

1 Put the pistachios in a bowl. Pour over the boiling water and let soak for 30 minutes. Grease and base-line a 7-inch/18-cm square pan.

2 Drain the pistachios thoroughly and place in a blender or food processor. Add the milk and process until finely chopped. Stir in the sugar.

3 Heat a large, nonstick skillet and add the butter. Melt over low heat and add the nut mixture. Cook for 15 minutes, stirring constantly, until the mixture is very thick.

4 Stir in the chocolate and let melt. Mix together, then spoon the mixture into the prepared pan and spread evenly. Let cool and set completely, then cut into 25 squares. Store in the refrigerator for up to 2 weeks.

Noisettes

These classic petits fours consist of a hazelnut paste encased in chocolate, then topped with a chocolate-coated hazelnut.

30 mins plus
8 hrs 30 mins
resting/setting

10 mins

MAKES 25

INGREDIENTS

8 oz/225 g semisweet chocolate, broken into pieces

1 cup blanched hazelnuts

½ cup superfine sugar

1 tbsp water

confectioners' sugar, for dusting

1 Line 2 cookie sheets with parchment paper. Melt 3 oz/85 g of the chocolate in a heatproof bowl set over a pan of gently simmering water. Remove from the heat.

2 Using 2 forks, carefully dip 25 hazelnuts, one at a time, into the melted chocolate. Lift out quickly, letting any excess chocolate drain against the side of the bowl, and place on a prepared cookie sheet. Let set.

3 Put the remaining hazelnuts in a food processor and chop until finely ground. Add to the bowl with the remaining melted chocolate, then add the superfine sugar and water and mix to form a firm paste. Let rest in the refrigerator for 30 minutes.

4 Lightly dust a cutting board with confectioners' sugar, turn out the mixture, and knead for 2–3 minutes. Using your fingers, flatten the paste to a ½-inch/1-cm thickness, then cut into circles, using a 1-inch/2.5-cm plain round cutter. Place on a prepared cookie sheet and leave overnight, until set.

5 Melt the remaining 5 oz/140 g of the chocolate in a heatproof bowl set over a pan of gently simmering water. Remove from the heat. Using 2 forks, carefully dip the hazelnut circles, one at a time, into the melted chocolate then place on the cookie sheet.

6 Place a chocolate-coated hazelnut on top of each hazelnut circle and let set. Serve in paper candy cases.

COOK'S TIP

If you are unable to buy ready-blanched hazelnuts, you can remove the skins yourself. Spread them on a sheet of foil and lightly toast under a broiler, turning them frequently, then rub in a clean dish towel to remove the skins.

Walnut Cups

If walnuts are your favorite nut, you will adore the filling of these petits fours. If not, simply choose one of the variations suggested below.

40 mins plus cooling and setting

15 mins

MAKES 14

INGREDIENTS

10 oz/300 g semisweet chocolate, broken into pieces

⅓ cup walnut pieces

3 tbsp granulated sugar

2 tsp water

1 Line a cookie sheet with parchment paper and place 14 double-thickness paper candy cases on it.

2 Melt 4 oz/115 g of the chocolate in a heatproof bowl set over a pan of gently simmering water. Spoon the melted chocolate into the prepared candy cases, spreading up the sides with a small brush. Place on the cookie sheet and let set.

3 Put ¼ cup of the walnuts in a food processor and mix until finely ground. Put the sugar and water in a small, heavy-based pan and heat gently, stirring constantly, until the sugar has dissolved. Bring to a boil and boil for 2 minutes. Remove from the heat and stir in the ground walnuts.

4 Melt an additional 4 oz/115 g of the chocolate, then stir into the walnut mixture. Let cool.

5 Spoon the walnut filling equally into the chocolate cups and smooth the surface. Leave in a cool place to set.

6 Melt the remaining 2 oz/55 g of the chocolate, then pour over the cups to completely cover the surface. Let cool, then top each cup with a small sprinkling of the remaining walnuts. Let set.

7 When the chocolate cups have set, carefully peel away the paper candy cases and place in clean cases.

VARIATIONS
If preferred use almonds, hazelnuts, or macadamia nuts instead of the walnuts.

Chocolate Orange Cups

Orange-flavored chocolate plus grated orange rind gives the filling in these chocolate cups an intense flavor. Serve at the end of a meal.

40 mins
plus 2 hrs
setting

15 mins

MAKES 24

INGREDIENTS

9 oz/250 g orange-flavored semisweet chocolate

1 egg yolk

1 tbsp sweet butter

finely grated rind of 1 small orange, plus extra for decorating

½ cup whipping cream, whipped

1 Break half the chocolate into pieces and place in a heatproof bowl set over a pan of gently simmering water until melted. Let cool.

2 Arrange 24 paper candy cases on a tray and spoon a little chocolate into each case. Using a fine brush, coat the inside of each case with chocolate. Let set. Make a small tear in each paper case, then carefully peel off.

3 Meanwhile, in a bowl set over a pan of gently simmering water, warm the remaining chocolate until almost melted. Add the egg yolk and stir until thickened. Remove from the heat and stir in the butter and orange rind. Set aside to cool to room temperature.

4 Fold the cream into the chocolate mixture and spoon into a pastry bag fitted with a star tip. Pipe the filling into each chocolate case. Let set. Decorate with a little orange rind and serve.

Chocolate Cherry Cups

These look very professional yet are incredibly easy to prepare. They look particularly attractive if placed in paper candy cases.

30 mins plus 2 hrs marinating/ setting | 10 mins

MAKES 16

INGREDIENTS

½ cup candied cherries, chopped

1 tbsp cognac

8 oz/225 g semisweet chocolate, broken into pieces

1 egg yolk

2 tsp confectioners' sugar

1 Line a cookie sheet with parchment paper and place 16 double-thickness paper candy cases on it. Put the cherries and cognac in a bowl and let marinate for about 1 hour.

2 Meanwhile, melt 4½ oz/125 g of the chocolate in a heatproof bowl set over a pan of gently simmering water. Spoon the melted chocolate into the prepared candy cases, spreading up the sides with a small brush. Place on the cookie sheet and let set.

3 When set, carefully peel away the paper cases and place the cups in clean cases. Drain the cherries, reserving the cognac, then put the cherries in the chocolate cases.

4 Melt the remaining chocolate, then remove from the heat and let cool slightly. Add the egg yolk and reserved cognac and mix well together. Sift in the confectioners' sugar, then stir together.

5 Fill a pastry bag, fitted with a star tip, with the chocolate mixture and pipe into the chocolate cups.

COOK'S TIP
Should the chocolate cases crack as you are removing them from the paper cases, you can patch them up by brushing on a little extra melted chocolate.

Chocolate Ice Cream Bites

These miniature chocolate-coated ice creams are irresistible at the end of a meal. Use your favorite ice cream flavor.

30 mins plus freezing

5 mins

SERVES 6

INGREDIENTS

2½ cups good-quality ice cream

7 oz/200 g semisweet chocolate

2 tbsp sweet butter

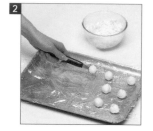
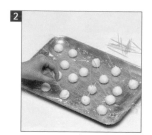

1 Line a cookie sheet with plastic wrap.

2 Using a melon baller, scoop out balls of ice cream and place them on the prepared cookie sheet. Alternatively, cut the ice cream into bite-size cubes. Stick a toothpick in each piece and return to the freezer until very hard.

3 Place the chocolate and the butter in a heatproof bowl set over a pan of gently simmering water until melted. Quickly dip the frozen ice cream balls into the warm chocolate and return to the freezer. Keep them there until ready to serve.

Chocolate & Prune Candy

Children enjoy making this candy if an adult helps with melting the syrup and butter. Coat the candy with unsweetened cocoa if preferred.

🕒 20 mins plus 1 hr chilling   ⏱ 5 mins

MAKES 20

INGREDIENTS

4 oz/115 g butter

3 tbsp corn syrup

4 oz/115 g semisweet chocolate

¾ cup no-soak dried prunes, chopped

6 oz/175 g granola

drinking chocolate powder, for coating

1 Put the butter and corn syrup in a heavy-based pan and heat gently until melted. Remove the pan from the heat.

2 Break the chocolate into pieces and add to the pan. Let melt, then beat together until smooth. Stir in the prunes and granola and mix thoroughly. Let cool, then chill in the refrigerator for 1 hour.

3 Take teaspoonfuls of the mixture and roll into balls. Roll the chocolate balls in the drinking chocolate powder, then place in paper candy cases and return to the refrigerator until firm.

Apricot & Almond Clusters

These delicious little morsels are extremely quick and easy to make. They will quickly become a firm favorite with children.

10 mins
plus setting

4–5 mins

MAKES 24–28

INGREDIENTS

4 oz/115 g semisweet chocolate, broken into pieces

2 tbsp honey

¾ cup no-soak dried apricots, chopped

½ cup blanched almonds, chopped

1 Put the chocolate and honey in a heatproof bowl set over a pan of gently simmering water and stir until melted.

2 Stir in the apricots and almonds.

3 Drop teaspoonfuls of the mixture into paper candy cases. Let set.

COOK'S TIP
These would be an easy candy for children to make, if they had some help with melting the chocolate.

Chocolate Caramel Turtles

This traditional South American candy consists of clumps of pecans with a chocolate caramel coating. Use other types of nuts if preferred.

45 mins plus
2 hrs setting   15–20 mins

MAKES 15

I N G R E D I E N T S

sunflower oil, for brushing

1 cup heavy cream

¾ cup corn syrup

2 tbsp butter

1¼ cups granulated sugar

3 tbsp brown sugar

¾ cup pecans

6 oz/175 g semisweet chocolate,
    broken into pieces

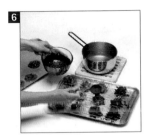

1 Oil a cookie sheet. Put the cream, corn syrup, butter, granulated and brown sugar in a heavy-based pan and heat gently, stirring constantly, until the butter has melted and the sugars have dissolved.

2 Bring to a boil and boil for about 15–20 minutes, stirring frequently, until a little of the mixture, when dropped into a cup of cold water, forms a soft ball when rolled between the fingers.

3 Remove the pan from the heat and let cool for 2–3 minutes, then gently stir in the nuts until coated in the caramel.

4 Using an oiled tablespoon, drop spoonfuls of the mixture, well apart, on to the prepared cookie sheet. Leave until cold and set.

5 When set, transfer to a wire rack and set the rack over the cookie sheet. Melt the chocolate in a heatproof bowl set over a pan of gently simmering water, then set aside to cool slightly.

6 Using a tablespoon, spoon the melted chocolate over the turtles to coat them completely. Return the chocolate on the cookie sheet to the heatproof bowl, reheat if necessary, and use to cover all the turtles. Leave for about 2 hours, until set.

Chocolate Squares

These are extremely simple to make yet, when packed into paper or foil candy cases, they look very elegant.

🕙 10 mins   🕐 4–5 mins

MAKES 64

I N G R E D I E N T S

4 oz/115 g butter, plus extra for greasing

¼ cup superfine sugar

⅔ cup unsweetened cocoa

⅔ cup drinking chocolate powder

1 Grease a 7-inch/18-cm shallow square pan or an 8 x 6-inch/20 x 15-cm shallow pan. Melt the butter in a pan. Remove from the heat and stir in the sugar.

2 Sift the unsweetened cocoa and drinking chocolate powder into the butter mixture, then beat well together until smooth.

3 Turn the mixture into the prepared pan and leave until cold and set. When the chocolate has set, cut into squares using a sharp knife.

Chocolate Coated Toffee

Real, old-fashioned toffee is delicious on its own, but coated in chocolate it becomes truly irresistible. Store in an airtight container for a few days.

🍯 15 mins ⏰ 10–15 mins

MAKES ABOUT 60

INGREDIENTS

sunflower oil, for brushing

8 oz/225 g butter

¾ cup granulated sugar

pinch of cream of tartar

1 cup semisweet chocolate chips

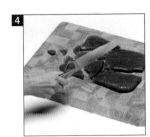

1 Invert a 9-inch/23-cm square cake pan and mold a piece of foil over the bottom and sides, then use the foil to line the pan. Brush the foil generously with oil. Put the butter, sugar, and cream of tartar in a large, heavy-based pan and heat gently, stirring constantly, until the butter has melted and the sugar has dissolved.

2 Bring the mixture to a boil, then cover the pan and leave for 2 minutes. Uncover the pan and boil for about 10–15 minutes, until a little of the mixture, when dropped into a cup of cold water, separates into threads that are hard and brittle.

3 Carefully pour the mixture into the prepared pan and leave for 1 minute. Sprinkle the chocolate chips evenly over the top and leave for 2–3 minutes, until starting to melt then, using the lines of a fork, swirl the chocolate over the top. Leave until hard and set.

4 When hard, using the foil to lift the toffee, remove from the pan and place on a board. Using the back of a heavy knife or a small hammer, break the toffee into pieces.

Torrone Molle

This is an Italian specialty, which is a wickedly rich mixture of semisweet chocolate, nuts, cognac, and plain cookies.

20 mins plus
8 hrs chilling

20 mins

MAKES 24 PIECES

INGREDIENTS

sunflower oil, for oiling

6 oz/175 g butter, softened

6 oz/175 g semisweet chocolate, melted

½ cup walnuts, ground coarsely

½ cup blanched almonds, ground coarsely

½ cup hazelnuts, ground coarsely

½ cup golden superfine sugar

3 tbsp water

1 tbsp cognac

6 oz/175 g plain cookies, such as Petit Beurre, broken into small pieces

1 Oil an 11 x 8-inch/28 x 20-cm jelly roll tin. Put the butter in a bowl and set aside. Put the chocolate in a heatproof bowl set over a pan of gently simmering water until melted, then beat with the butter until smooth. Stir in the ground walnuts, almonds, and hazelnuts. Put the sugar and water in a pan and heat until the sugar has dissolved.

2 Boil steadily until the mixture reaches the 'soft ball' stage (240°F/116°C on a sugar thermometer). To test, drop a spoonful of the mixture into cold water. A soft ball should form. Let cool for a few minutes, then beat vigorously and pour into the chocolate mixture, stirring until smooth.

3 Stir in the cognac, then the cookie pieces into the mixture. Turn into the prepared tin and press to flatten. Cover and chill overnight. Remove from the refrigerator just before serving and cut into diamond shapes.

COOK'S TIP

If you are grinding the nuts yourself in a food processor, take care not to over-process them or they will become oily.

Churros

These delicious Spanish morsels are an excellent choice with a cup of coffee as a mid-morning treat. They are best served hot.

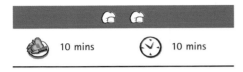

🐟 10 mins   🕐 10 mins

MAKES 4

INGREDIENTS

1 cup water

grated rind of 1 lemon

3 oz/85 g butter

⅛ tsp salt

1 cup all-purpose flour

¼ tsp ground cinnamon,
plus extra for dusting

½–1 tsp vanilla extract

3 eggs

olive oil, for frying

about 5 tbsp sugar

1 Place the water with the lemon rind in a heavy-based pan. Bring to a boil, add the butter and salt and cook for a few moments until the butter melts.

2 Add the flour all at once, with the cinnamon and vanilla, then remove the pan from the heat and stir rapidly until it forms the consistency of mashed potatoes.

3 Beat in the eggs, one at a time, using a wooden spoon; if you have difficulty incorporating the eggs to a smooth mixture, use a potato masher, then when it is mixed, return to a wooden spoon and mix until smooth.

4 Heat 1 inch/2.5 cm of oil in a deep skillet until it is hot enough to brown a cube of bread in 30 seconds.

5 Place the batter in a pastry bag with a wide star tip, then squeeze out 5-inch/12.5-cm lengths directly into the hot oil, making sure that the churros are about 3–4 inches/7.5–10 cm apart, as they will puff up as they cook. You may need to fry them in 2 or 3 batches.

6 Cook the churros in the hot oil for about 2 minutes on each side, until they are golden brown. Remove with a slotted spoon and drain on paper towels.

7 Dust generously with sugar and sprinkle with cinnamon to taste. Serve either hot or at room temperature.

Mini Cinnamon Muffins

To enjoy them at their best, serve these chocolate and spice muffins warm from the oven. They are particularly good served for breakfast.

10 mins plus
5 mins cooling

15–20 mins

MAKES 20

I N G R E D I E N T S

1¼ cups self-rising flour

1 tsp baking powder

2 tbsp unsweetened cocoa

½ tsp ground cinnamon

¼ cup brown sugar

1 small egg, lightly beaten

⅔ cup milk

4 tbsp butter, melted

1 Preheat the oven to 400°F/200°C. Line 20 mini muffin cups with mini muffin paper cases.

2 Sift the flour, baking powder, unsweetened cocoa, and cinnamon into a bowl. Stir in the sugar. Mix together the egg, milk, and melted butter.

3 Pour the egg mixture on to the dry ingredients and mix briefly. The mixture should be lumpy. Divide the mixture among the paper cases.

4 Bake in the oven for 15–20 minutes, until risen and the top springs back when lightly touched with a finger. Transfer the muffins to a wire rack to cool for 5 minutes, then serve warm.

Ginger Thins

Thin disks of chocolate studded with chopped preserved ginger are the perfect accompaniment to after-dinner coffee.

15 mins
plus setting

5 mins

MAKES 18–20

INGREDIENTS

7 oz/200 g semisweet chocolate

finely grated rind of 1 orange

3 pieces preserved ginger, chopped

1 Line a cookie sheet with nonstick parchment paper.

2 Break the chocolate into pieces and set over a pan of gently simmering water until melted. Stir the grated rind into the melted chocolate.

3 Place scant teaspoonfuls of chocolate on the prepared cookie sheet and spread them out with the back of the spoon to form thin disks.

4 Scatter the chopped ginger over the chocolate disks and let set.

Sopaipillas

These little, deep-fried puffs are popular sweet snacks in Mexico. You can serve them with honey, syrup, or sprinkled with sugar and cinnamon.

🥄 15 mins   🕐 15 mins

SERVES 6

I N G R E D I E N T S

2 cups all-purpose flour,
    plus extra for dusting

1 tbsp baking powder

salt

2 tbsp margarine, cut into pieces

¾ cup water

sunflower oil, for deep-frying

T O   S E R V E

scant ½ cup superfine sugar

1 tbsp ground cinnamon

1 Sift the flour, baking powder, and a pinch of salt into a bowl. Add the margarine and rub it in with your fingertips until the mixture resembles bread crumbs. Gradually stir in the water to form a soft dough.

2 Turn out the dough on to a floured counter and knead gently until smooth. Roll out to a large, thin rectangle, then cut into 3-inch/7.5-cm squares.

3 Heat the oil in a large, deep skillet to 350–375°F/180–190°C or until a cube of bread browns in 30 seconds. Add the dough squares, a few at a time, and cook until puffed up and golden. Turn and cook the other side. Remove with a slotted spoon and drain on paper towels. Combine the sugar and cinnamon. Serve the sopaipillas warm, sprinkled with the sugar mixture and cinnamon.

COOK'S TIP
Make sure the oil heats up again after you have cooked one batch before adding the next.

Chocolate Boxes

Guests will think you have spent hours creating these little boxes, but a few tricks (such as ready-made cake) make them quick to put together.

20 mins plus
1 hr setting/
chilling

5 mins

SERVES 4

INGREDIENTS

8 oz/225 g semisweet chocolate

about 8 oz/225 g store-bought or ready-made plain or chocolate sponge cake

2 tbsp apricot jelly

⅔ cup heavy cream

1 tbsp maple syrup

scant ½ cup prepared fresh fruit, such as small strawberries, raspberries, kiwi fruit, cherries or red currants

1 Melt the semisweet chocolate and spread it evenly over a large sheet of parchment paper. Let harden in a cool place.

2 When just set, cut the chocolate into 2-inch/5-cm squares and remove from the parchment. Make sure that your hands are cool and handle the chocolate as little as possible.

3 Cut the cake into 2 cubes, 2 inches/ 5 cm across, then cut each cube in half. Warm the apricot jelly and brush it over the sides of the cake. Carefully press a chocolate square on to each side of the cake to make 4 chocolate boxes with cake at the bottom. Chill in the refrigerator for 20 minutes.

4 Whip the heavy cream with the maple syrup until just holding its shape. Spoon or pipe a little of the mixture into each chocolate box.

5 Decorate the top of each box with the prepared fruit. If liked, the fruit can be partially dipped into melted chocolate and allowed to harden before being placed on top of the boxes.

COOK'S TIP
For the best results, keep the boxes well chilled and fill and decorate them just before you are ready to serve them.

Christmas Tree Decorations

Ribbon loops are sandwiched between chocolate shapes so that they can be hung on the Christmas tree.

40 mins plus 1 hr setting

5 mins

MAKES 20

INGREDIENTS

6 oz/175 g semisweet chocolate, broken into pieces

6 oz/175 g milk chocolate, broken into pieces

silver balls (optional)

colored ribbon

1 On nonstick parchment paper, draw around Christmas cookie cutters, such as stars and Christmas trees. Invert the paper and place on a cookie sheet.

2 Melt the semisweet and milk chocolate in 2 separate heatproof bowls set over pans of gently simmering water.

3 Half fill 2 waxed paper pastry bags with melted semisweet chocolate. Snip a small point off one bag and pipe a fine outline of chocolate, following the drawn shapes. Snip a larger point off the end of the second pastry bag and pipe chocolate into the shapes to give an over-filled and rounded appearance. Repeat with the milk chocolate. If liked, decorate with silver balls. Let set hard.

4 Carefully peel off the paper. Cut the ribbon into short lengths to make loops. Sandwich matching chocolate shapes together with the remaining melted chocolate, placing the ribbon loops in between. Let set hard before hanging on the Christmas tree.

Chocolate Cookie Baskets

Chocolate-coated cookie baskets make perfect containers for a strawberry and cream filling delicately flavored with raspberry liqueur.

40 mins plus 30 mins setting   25–33 mins

MAKES 20

INGREDIENTS

4 tbsp sweet butter

¼ cup raw sugar

2 tbsp corn syrup

½ cup all-purpose flour, sifted

6 oz/175 g semisweet chocolate, broken into pieces

FILLING

1 cup heavy cream

2 tbsp framboise

4 oz/115 g baby strawberries

1 Preheat the oven to 350°F/180°C.

2 Put the butter, raw sugar, and corn syrup in a pan and heat gently until the butter has melted and the sugar has dissolved. Let cool slightly, then beat in the flour.

3 Place 20 half teaspoonfuls of the mixture on 4 cookie sheets, allowing room for the cookies to spread during cooking, and press out with wet fingertips into 2½-inch/6-cm circles. Bake in the oven, 1 sheet at a time, for 5–7 minutes, until golden.

4 Let cool slightly, then remove with a round-bladed knife and invert over the bottom of an inverted tartlet pan or small glass. Mold the cookies to give a wavy edge. Leave for a few minutes to set, then remove carefully. If the cookies become too brittle to handle, return to the oven for 30 seconds to soften.

5 Put the chocolate in a heatproof bowl set over a pan of gently simmering water until melted. Put a spoonful of melted chocolate inside one of the baskets and rotate to coat the inside, using the back of a teaspoon to help. Repeat with the remaining chocolate and baskets. Let set.

6 Make the filling. Whip the cream and framboise together in a bowl until thick. Slice the strawberries and set aside 20 slices for decoration. Fold the rest into the cream and spoon into the baskets. Decorate with the sliced strawberries.

Real Hot Chocolate

You will never go back to store-bought drinking chocolate powder once you have tasted this! Decorate with whipped cream for a real treat.

🍰 5 mins   🕐 5 mins

SERVES 1–2

INGREDIENTS

1½ oz/40 g semisweet chocolate, broken into pieces

1¼ cups milk

2 tbsp whipped cream and drinking chocolate powder, to decorate

1 Put the chocolate into a large pitcher. Put the milk in a pan and bring to a boil. Pour about a quarter of the milk on to the chocolate and leave until the chocolate has softened.

2 Whisk until smooth. Return the remaining milk to the heat and bring back to a boil. Pour on to the chocolate, whisking.

3 Pour into warmed mugs and top with whipped cream dusted with drinking chocolate powder.

COOK'S TIP

Chocolate powder for dusting on cappuccinos is available in supermarkets alongside the coffee.

Hot Chocolate Drinks

Rich and soothing, a hot chocolate drink in the evening can be just what you need to help ease away the stresses of the day.

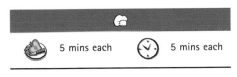

🧊 5 mins each   🕐 5 mins each

SERVES 2

I N G R E D I E N T S

SPICY HOT CHOCOLATE

2½ cups milk

1 tsp allspice

3½ oz/100 g semisweet chocolate, broken into pieces

4 cinnamon sticks

generous ⅓ cup heavy cream, whipped lightly

HOT CHOCOLATE & ORANGE TODDY

2½ oz/75 g orange-flavored semisweet chocolate

2½ cups milk

3 tbsp dark rum

2 tbsp heavy cream

grated nutmeg

1 To make Spicy Hot Chocolate, pour the milk into a pan. Add the allspice.

2 Add the semisweet chocolate to the milk. Heat the mixture over a low heat until the milk is just boiling, stirring all the time to prevent the milk burning on the bottom of the pan.

3 Place 2 cinnamon sticks in 2 cups and pour in the hot chocolate. Top with the whipped heavy cream and serve.

4 To make Hot Chocolate & Orange Toddy, put the orange-flavored chocolate in a pan with the milk. Heat the mixture over low heat until just boiling, stirring constantly.

5 Remove the pan from the heat and stir in the dark rum. Pour into cups.

6 Pour the cream over the back of a spoon or swirl on to the top so that it sits on top of the hot chocolate. Sprinkle with grated nutmeg and serve at once.

COOK'S TIP
Using a cinnamon stick as a stirrer will give any hot chocolate drink a sweet, pungent flavor of cinnamon without overpowering the flavor of the chocolate.

White Heat

It is unusual to make a hot drink with white chocolate, but this winter warmer demonstrates that it works extremely well.

5 mins   4–5 mins

SERVES 4

INGREDIENTS

4 tbsp heavy cream

7½ cups milk

6 oz/175 g white chocolate

2 tsp instant coffee

2 tsp cognac

1 tsp grated nutmeg

1 Whisk the heavy cream with an electric whisk until thickened. Set aside.

2 Pour the milk into a small pan and bring to just below boiling point, then remove from the heat. Meanwhile, finely chop the chocolate.

3 Whisk the chocolate, instant coffee, and cognac into the milk and continue to whisk until the chocolate has melted and the mixture is smooth.

4 Pour the mixture into 4 warmed glasses or mugs. Top each with a spoonful of whipped cream, sprinkle with the nutmeg, and serve immediately.

VARIATIONS
Substitute another spirit for the cognac, if you prefer. Try whiskey, crème de menthe, or Grand Marnier.

Spiced Hot Chocolate

Semisweet chocolate and spices complement each other perfectly.
Use a little ground cinnamon instead of allspice if preferred.

10 mins   5 mins

SERVES 4

INGREDIENTS

3¾ cups milk

7 oz/200 g semisweet chocolate, broken into pieces (preferably one that contains at least 70 percent cocoa solids)

2 tsp sugar

1 tsp allspice

TO DECORATE

unsweetened cocoa

grated white chocolate

1 Put the milk, chocolate, sugar, and allspice in a pan over medium heat. Whisk, stirring constantly, until the chocolate has melted and the mixture is simmering but not boiling.

2 Remove from the heat and pour into heatproof glasses. Sprinkle over some cocoa powder and grated white chocolate and serve immediately.

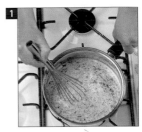

Chocolate Eggnog

The perfect pick-me-up on a cold winter's night, this delicious drink will get the taste buds tingling. Use brandy or whiskey if preferred.

10 mins   5 mins

SERVES 4

INGREDIENTS

8 egg yolks

1 cup sugar

4 cups milk

8 oz/225 g semisweet chocolate, grated

⅔ cup dark rum

1 Beat the egg yolks with the sugar until thickened.

2 Pour the milk into a large pan, add the grated chocolate, and bring to a boil. Remove from the heat and gradually beat in the egg yolk mixture. Stir in the rum and pour into heatproof glasses.

Hot Cognac Chocolate

Cognac and chocolate have a natural affinity, as this richly flavored drink amply demonstrates. For pure indulgence top with whipped cream.

10 mins   7–10 mins

SERVES 4

INGREDIENTS

4 cups milk

4 oz/115 g semisweet chocolate, broken into pieces

2 tbsp sugar

5 tbsp cognac

6 tbsp whipped cream, to decorate

4 tsp unsweetened cocoa, for sprinkling

1 Pour the milk into a pan and bring to a boil, then remove from the heat. Place the chocolate in a small pan and add 2 tablespoons of the hot milk. Stir over low heat until the chocolate has melted. Stir the chocolate mixture into the remaining milk and add the sugar.

2 Stir in the cognac and pour into 4 heatproof glasses. Top each with a swirl of whipped cream and sprinkle with a little sifted unsweetened cocoa.

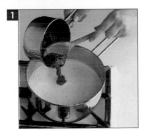

Café Mocha

This is sheer indulgence for coffee and chocolate lovers alike: the perfect nightcap. Use chocolate ice cream if preferred.

5 mins   5 mins

SERVES 2

INGREDIENTS

2 oz/55 g semisweet chocolate

2 tbsp water

2 tbsp golden superfine sugar

1 cup milk

½ cup strong freshly made black coffee

2 scoops coffee ice cream

2 tbsp whipped cream, to decorate

1 Put the chocolate, water, and sugar in a pan and heat gently until melted. Stir until smooth. Reserve a little of the chocolate sauce for decoration.

2 Stir the milk into the chocolate sauce. Divide the coffee among 2 warmed glasses and pour the chocolate mixture on the top.

3 Add the ice cream and drizzle the reserved chocolate sauce over.

Nutty Hot Chocolate

A cup of hot chocolate at bedtime will never be the same again after you have tasted this fabulous concoction.

15 mins   8 mins

SERVES 4

I N G R E D I E N T S

5 tbsp superfine sugar

2 tbsp blanched almonds, chopped coarsely

½ cup unsweetened cocoa

4½ cups milk

3 tbsp amaretto

1 Grind 1 tablespoon of the sugar and the almonds with a pestle and mortar, or pulse briefly in a food processor.

2 Place the remaining sugar and the unsweetened cocoa in a small bowl and add 3 tablespoons of the milk. Mix to smooth paste.

3 Bring the remaining milk to a boil and whisk in the cocoa paste until thoroughly combined. Pour 1 cup of the mixture into another pan and whisk in the almond mixture. Whisk over low heat for 2 minutes, then return to the main pan. Remove the pan from the heat.

4 Stir in the amaretto and pour the mixture into warmed glasses. Serve immediately.

COOK'S TIP
Be careful not to over-grind or over-process the almonds or they will become oily.

Hot Chocolate Float

It isn't only children who love the sensational combination of hot chocolate, whipped cream, and coconut ice cream.

🍳 5 mins   🕐 5 mins

SERVES 4

INGREDIENTS

2 cups milk

8 oz/225 g semisweet chocolate

2 tbsp superfine sugar

8 scoops coconut ice cream

8 scoops semisweet chocolate ice cream

whipped cream, to decorate

1 Pour the milk into a pan. Break the chocolate into pieces and add to the pan with the sugar. Stir over low heat until the chocolate has melted, the sugar has dissolved, and the mixture is smooth. Remove the pan from the heat.

2 Put 1 scoop of coconut ice cream into each of 4 heatproof glasses, top with a scoop of chocolate ice cream, then repeat the layers.

3 Pour the chocolate-flavored milk into the glasses, top with whipped cream, and serve immediately.

VARIATION

For a richer-tasting drink, substitute bittersweet chocolate for the semisweet chocolate.

Marshmallow Float

Children love this drink—let them choose which color marshmallows they want to add. Try to find the best-quality chocolate for a good flavor.

5 mins   5 mins

SERVES 4

INGREDIENTS

8 oz/225 g semisweet chocolate, broken into pieces

3¾ cups milk

3 tbsp superfine sugar

8 marshmallows

1 Finely chop the chocolate with a knife or in a food processor. Do not over-process or the chocolate will melt.

2 Pour the milk into a pan and bring to just below boiling point. Remove the pan from the heat and whisk in the sugar and the chocolate.

3 Pour into warmed mugs or heatproof glasses, top with a marshmallow or two and serve immediately.

COOK'S TIP

For an attractive finish, save 1 tablespoon of chopped chocolate to sprinkle over the marshmallows on top of the chocolate.

Alhambra Royale

This stylish version of hot chocolate is one to serve with a real flourish for a special occasion. Flame the glasses, one at a time.

5 mins   10 mins

SERVES 4

INGREDIENTS

2 cups milk

8 oz/225 g semisweet chocolate, broken into pieces

2 tbsp superfine sugar

4 wide strips orange rind

¾ cup cognac

whipped cream, to decorate

1 Pour the milk into a pan. Add the chocolate and the sugar. Stir over low heat until the chocolate has melted, the sugar dissolved, and the mixture is smooth. Remove the pan from the heat.

2 Fill 1 heatproof glass almost full with the hot chocolate. Twist a strip of orange rind over it, then drop the rind into the glass.

3 Heat one-quarter of the cognac in a ladle over a pan of simmering water. When hot, carefully ignite it and ladle the flaming cognac into the glass. Stir well and top with a spoonful of whipped cream. Repeat to make 3 more glasses. Serve immediately.

VARIATION

For an Alhambra Mocha, stir 4 teaspoons of instant coffee powder into the hot chocolate milk until completely dissolved before pouring into the glasses.

Cinnamon Mocha

This drink is equally delicious hot or cold. It looks particularly attractive served in tall heatproof glasses.

15 mins   5 mins

SERVES 6

INGREDIENTS

9 oz/250 g milk chocolate,
  broken into pieces

¾ cup light cream

4½ cups freshly brewed coffee

1 tsp ground cinnamon

whipped cream, to decorate

1 Put the chocolate in a large heatproof bowl set over a pan of gently simmering water. Add the light cream and stir until the chocolate has melted and the mixture is smooth.

2 Pour in the coffee, add the cinnamon, and whisk until foamy. If serving hot, pour into heatproof glasses or mugs, top with cream, and serve immediately. If serving cold, remove the bowl from the heat and let cool, then chill in the refrigerator until required.

VARIATIONS
You could also serve this with a scoop of chocolate ice cream or marshmallows.

Hot Ginger Chocolate

The combination of chocolate and preserved ginger is a classic one, but it is not often found in drinks, although it works extremely well.

🍴 5 mins   🕐 10 mins

SERVES 4

INGREDIENTS

8 oz/225 g semisweet chocolate, broken into pieces

3¾ cups milk

4 tbsp syrup from a preserved ginger jar

4 tbsp heavy cream

1 Put the chocolate in a heatproof bowl set over a pan of gently simmering water until it melts. Remove from the heat.

2 Heat the milk in a pan until just below boiling point, then remove the pan from the heat. Stir in the melted chocolate and ginger syrup.

3 Pour into 4 mugs or heatproof glasses, float the cream on top. Serve immediately.

COOK'S TIP
To float cream on top of a drink, hold a spoon, round-side upward, against the rim of the mug or glass. Gently pour the cream over the back of the spoon so that it floats on the surface of the drink.

Viennese Chocolate

The perfect antidote to the winter blues, this rich drink is warming and wonderfully self-indulgent. Sprinkle with grated chocolate if wished.

🕐 5 mins   🕐 15 mins

SERVES 6

INGREDIENTS

5 tbsp heavy cream

2 tbsp confectioners' sugar

few drops vanilla extract

7 oz/200 g semisweet chocolate,
  broken into pieces

4 cups milk

1 tbsp superfine sugar

1 Whisk the heavy cream until soft peaks form, then whisk in the confectioners' sugar and vanilla. Set aside.

2 Put the chocolate in a heatproof bowl with 1 cup of the milk. Set over a pan of gently simmering water until the chocolate melts, stirring occasionally.

3 Pour the remaining milk into a pan and add the superfine sugar and heat gently. Add the chocolate and milk mixture as soon as the chocolate has melted and whisk constantly over the heat for 5 minutes, until frothy.

4 Pour into warmed cups, top with the whipped cream mixture, and serve immediately.

VARIATION
If you like, you can add 1–2 tablespoons of dark rum for an extra luxurious treat.

Mexican Chocolate Corn

If you can obtain Mexican chocolate, it is worth doing so, but otherwise use any good-quality, semisweet chocolate.

5 mins

10–15 mins

SERVES 6

INGREDIENTS

scant 3 cups water

½ cup tortilla flour

2-inch/5-cm piece cinnamon stick

scant 3 cups milk

4 oz/115 g semisweet chocolate, grated

sugar, to taste

1 Pour the water into a large pan, stir in the tortilla flour and add the cinnamon. Stir over low heat for about 10–15 minutes, until thickened and smooth. Gradually stir in the milk, then beat in 3 oz/85 g of the grated chocolate, a little at a time, until melted and fully incorporated. Remove and discard the cinnamon.

2 Remove the pan from the heat and ladle the mixture into heatproof glasses. Sweeten to taste with sugar and sprinkle the remaining grated chocolate on top.

Mexicana

Chocolate, coffee, and rum make this a drink to really lift the spirits. Sprinkle the tops with cocoa or grated semisweet chocolate if preferred.

5 mins   0 mins

SERVES 2

INGREDIENTS

1 oz/25 g semisweet chocolate

1¼ cups hot black coffee

sugar

1 tbsp dark rum

TO DECORATE

2 tbsp whipped cream

ground coffee, for sprinkling

1 Put the chocolate, coffee, and sugar in a blender and process until well blended.

2 Add the rum and pour into 2 heatproof glasses.

3 Top with whipped cream and sprinkle with a little ground coffee.

Cold Chocolate Drinks

These delicious chocolate summer drinks are perfect for making a chocoholic's summer day! Use vanilla ice cream if preferred.

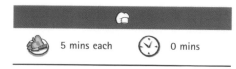

5 mins each   0 mins

SERVES 2

INGREDIENTS

CHOCOLATE MILKSHAKE

2 cups ice-cold milk

3 tbsp drinking chocolate powder

3 scoops chocolate ice cream

unsweetened cocoa, for dusting (optional)

CHOCOLATE ICE CREAM SODA

5 tbsp Glossy Chocolate Sauce (see page 692)

soda water

2 scoops of chocolate ice cream

heavy cream, whipped

semisweet or milk chocolate, grated

1 To make the Chocolate Milkshake, pour half of the milk into a blender.

2 Add the drinking chocolate powder to the blender and 1 scoop of the chocolate ice cream. Blend until frothy and well mixed. Stir in the remaining milk.

COOK'S TIP

Served in a tall glass, a milk shake or an ice cream soda makes a scrumptious snack in a drink. Serve with straws, if wished.

3 Place the remaining 2 scoops of chocolate ice cream in 2 serving glasses and carefully pour the chocolate milk over the ice cream.

4 Sprinkle a little cocoa (if using) over the top of each drink and serve.

5 To make the Chocolate Ice Cream Soda, divide the Glossy Chocolate Sauce among 2 glasses. (You could also use a ready-made chocolate dessert sauce.)

6 Add a little soda water to each glass and stir to combine. Place a scoop of ice cream in each glass and top up with more soda water.

7 Place a dollop of whipped heavy cream on the top, if liked, and sprinkle with a little grated semisweet or milk chocolate.

Quick Chocolate Milkshake

This is a great way to encourage children to drink milk, although adults will also enjoy this refreshing drink, especially on a hot summer's day.

🍓 5 mins   🕐 0 mins

SERVES 2

I N G R E D I E N T S

6 rounded tbsp vanilla ice cream

4 tbsp drinking chocolate powder

1¼ cups milk

1 chocolate flake bar, crushed coarsely

ground cinnamon, for dusting

1 Place the vanilla ice cream, drinking chocolate, and milk in a blender or food processor.

2 Process the mixture for 30 seconds, then pour into 2 tall serving glasses.

3 Sprinkle with the flake, add a light dusting of cinnamon, and serve with straws, if you like.

VARIATION

For a more chocolatey milkshake, use chocolate ice cream instead of vanilla, and decorate the top with a light dusting of unsweetened cocoa.

Iced Coffee & Chocolate Crush

Coffee, chocolate, and peppermint make a wonderful combination. Serve in tall heatproof glasses and decorate with fresh mint sprigs.

5 mins   0 mins

SERVES 2

INGREDIENTS

1¾ cups milk

generous ¾ cup coffee syrup

scant ½ cup peppermint syrup

1 tbsp chopped fresh mint leaves

4 ice cubes

TO DECORATE

grated chocolate

fresh mint sprigs

1 Pour the milk, coffee syrup, and peppermint syrup into a food processor and process gently until combined.

2 Add the mint and ice cubes and process until a slushy consistency has been reached.

3 Pour the mixture into glasses. Scatter over the grated chocolate, decorate with sprigs of fresh mint, and serve.

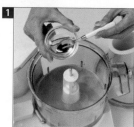

Mocha Float

This is deliciously refreshing on a hot summer's day and can double as dessert after an informal al fresco meal.

5 mins plus chilling

6 mins

SERVES 4

INGREDIENTS

1¼ cups water

generous 1 cup sugar

½ cup unsweetened cocoa, plus extra for dusting

2 tsp instant coffee powder

5 cups ice-cold milk

4 scoops vanilla ice cream

4 cinnamon sticks

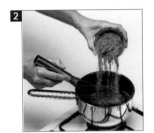

1 Pour the water into a pan and add the sugar. Stir over low heat until the sugar has completely dissolved, bring to a boil, then boil without stirring for 3 minutes.

2 Whisk in the unsweetened cocoa and instant coffee and remove the pan from the heat. Let cool, then chill in the refrigerator.

3 Measure about 6 tablespoons of the chocolate syrup into each of 4 glasses. Top with ice-cold milk. Add a scoop of ice cream. Break the cinnamon sticks in half and lay two halves crossed over, on top of each glass. Dust lightly with unsweetened cocoa and serve immediately.

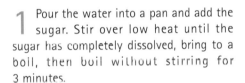

Mocha Cream

Coffee and chocolate make perfect partners. You can prepare this drink stronger or sweeter according to your own particular taste.

15 mins   0 mins

SERVES 2

INGREDIENTS

generous ¾ cup milk

scant ¼ cup light cream

1 tbsp brown sugar

2 tbsp unsweetened cocoa

1 tbsp coffee syrup or instant
   coffee powder

6 ice cubes

TO DECORATE

whipped cream

grated chocolate

1 Put the milk, cream, and sugar into a food processor and process gently until combined.

2 Add the unsweetened cocoa and coffee syrup or powder and process well, then add the ice cubes and process until smooth.

3 Pour the mixture into glasses. Top with whipped cream, sprinkle over the grated chocolate, and serve.

Cool Minty Chocolate

This is a great nonalcoholic choice for an outdoor brunch party and also a good alternative for those who don't like coffee.

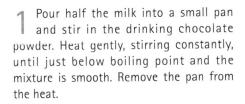

10 mins   5 mins

SERVES 4

INGREDIENTS

2½ cups ice-cold milk

6 tbsp drinking chocolate powder

1 cup light cream

1 tsp peppermint extract

6 scoops chocolate-mint ice cream

fresh mint sprigs, to decorate

1 Pour half the milk into a small pan and stir in the drinking chocolate powder. Heat gently, stirring constantly, until just below boiling point and the mixture is smooth. Remove the pan from the heat.

2 Pour the chocolate-flavored milk into a large, chilled bowl and whisk in the remaining milk. Whisk in the cream and peppermint extract and continue to whisk until cold.

3 Pour the mixture into 6 glasses, top each with a scoop of ice cream, decorate with a mint sprig, and serve immediately.

VARIATIONS
Substitute plain yogurt for the cream. Omit the peppermint extract and mint sprigs and add 4 tablespoons of lime cordial with the yogurt. Serve with scoops of chocolate or vanilla ice cream.

Chocolate & Almond Float

Drinking chocolate powder, which is already sweetened and dissolves easily, is a very quick and easy way to make both hot and cold drinks.

10 mins   0 mins

SERVES 4

INGREDIENTS

8 tsp drinking chocolate powder

3 tbsp boiling water

1 tsp almond extract, or to taste

3 cups ice-cold milk

4 scoops of chocolate-chip ice cream

1 Put the drinking chocolate powder into a bowl, add the boiling water, and stir to a smooth paste.

2 Whisk in the almond extract and milk and continue to whisk until cold and thoroughly mixed. Taste and add more almond extract if liked.

3 Pour into 4 glass, top with a scoop of chocolate-chip ice cream, and serve.

VARIATION
Substitute 4 teaspoons of maple syrup for the almond extract and top with popcorn instead of ice cream.

Egg Cream

It is difficult to know why this "mocktail" is called egg cream, since it contains no eggs. However, it does resemble eggnog in texture.

5 mins   0 mins

SERVES 2

INGREDIENTS

¼ cup chocolate syrup

scant 1 cup ice-cold milk

soda water

1 Divide the chocolate syrup equally among 2 glasses. Stir in the milk until thoroughly combined.

2 Top up with soda water and stir until foamy. Serve immediately.

COOK'S TIP
Many syrups, fruit-flavored as well as chocolate-flavored, are ideal for making milkshakes and cocktails. They are available from large supermarkets.

Wonderful Town

A nonalcoholic cocktail, which is popular with both adults and children. This drink is fabulous to serve at a barbecue party.

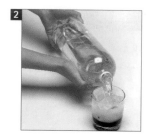

🍴 5 mins   🕐 0 mins

SERVES 4

INGREDIENTS

¼ cup chocolate syrup

½ cup peppermint syrup

ice cubes

sparkling mineral water

TO DECORATE

fresh mint sprigs

grated chocolate

1 Divide the chocolate syrup and peppermint syrup equally among 4 medium tumblers or whiskey glasses and mix well.

2 Fill the glasses with ice cubes, then top up with mineral water. Decorate with mint sprigs and grated chocolate and serve immediately.

VARIATION
For an alcoholic version of this cocktail, substitute clear crème de menthe for the peppermint syrup.

Barbary Coast

You will need a cocktail shaker to make this potent mixture. To ensure that it is properly mixed, make only one cocktail at a time.

1 min   0 mins

SERVES 1

INGREDIENTS

cracked ice

1 tbsp white crème de cacao

2 tbsp white rum

1 tbsp Scotch whisky

1 tbsp gin

1 tbsp light cream

1 Half-fill a cocktail shaker with cracked ice, then pour in the crème de cacao, rum, whisky, gin, and cream.

2 Replace the top and shake vigorously for 10–20 seconds. Strain into a chilled cocktail glass and serve immediately.

COOK'S TIP

If you are planning to serve cocktails frequently, it is worth buying a bar measure. A double measure usually has a 1½-tablespoon capacity at one end—a single—and slightly more than a 2-tablespoon capacity at the other end.

Chocolate

It is drinking chocolate powder rather than a chocolate-flavored liqueur that gives this cocktail its flavor. It's still quite potent though.

1 min 0 mins

SERVES 1

INGREDIENTS

cracked ice

1½ tbsp maraschino

1½ tbsp yellow Chartreuse

1 tsp drinking chocolate powder

1 egg

1 Half-fill a cocktail shaker with cracked ice. Pour in the maraschino and Chartreuse and add the drinking chocolate powder and egg.

2 Replace the top and shake vigorously for 10–20 seconds. Strain into a chilled cocktail glass and serve immediately.

COOK'S TIP
If you like, frost the rim of the glass before serving. Brush the rim with a little egg white, then dip into a saucer of superfine sugar to coat. Let dry.

Bushwhacker

This cocktail is based on Bailey's Irish Cream, an extremely popular chocolate-flavored liqueur made with Irish whiskey and heavy cream.

🕐 1 min   ⏱ 0 mins

SERVES 1

INGREDIENTS

cracked ice

ice cubes

1½ tbsp Bailey's Irish Cream

½ tbsp Tia Maria

1½ tbsp white rum

1½ tbsp amaretto

¾ cup light cream

slice of lemon

1 Half-fill a cocktail shaker with cracked ice and half-fill a tumbler with ice cubes. Pour in the Bailey's, Tia Maria, rum, and amaretto, then add the cream.

2 Replace the top and shake vigorously for 10–20 seconds, then strain into the tumbler, decorate with a slice of lemon and serve immediately.

VARIATION

For a Bushranger, half-fill a cocktail shaker with cracked ice, add a dash of Angostura bitters, pour in ¼ cup white rum and 1½ tablespoons of Dubonnet and shake for 10–20 seconds. Strain into a chilled glass and decorate with a slice of lemon.

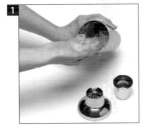

Tropical Cocktail

Crème de cacao, a chocolate-flavored liqueur from France, varies in color from pale cream to deep brown and in degrees of sweetness.

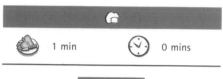

🍮 1 min   🕐 0 mins

SERVES 1

INGREDIENTS

cracked ice

dash of Angostura bitters

¼ cup white crème de cacao

1½ tbsp maraschino

1 tbsp dry vermouth

1–2 maraschino cherries, to decorate

1 Half-fill a cocktail shaker with cracked ice and add a dash of Angostura bitters. Pour in the crème de cacao, maraschino, and vermouth.

2 Replace the top and shake vigorously for 10–20 seconds. Strain into a chilled cocktail glass. Spear 1–2 maraschino cherries with a toothpick, add to the glass, and serve immediately.

VARIATION

You can add a dash of orange bitters as well as the Angostura bitters to the cracked ice if you like.

Macaroon

This cocktail, a mixture of chocolate and almond flavors, was no doubt named after the ever-popular cookie. Chill the cocktail glass before using.

1 min   0 mins

SERVES 1

INGREDIENTS

cracked ice

1½ tbsp crème de cacao

1½ tbsp amaretto

generous ½ cup vodka

thin slice of orange, to decorate

1 Half-fill a cocktail shaker with cracked ice. Pour in the crème de cacao, amaretto, and vodka.

2 Replace the top and shake vigorously for 10–20 seconds. Strain into a chilled cocktail glass, decorate with a thin slice of orange, and serve immediately.

VARIATION
Moon Landing is a similar cocktail. Substitute Bailey's Irish Cream for the crème de cacao, use only 1½ tablespoons of vodka, and add 1½ tablespoons of Tia Maria. Shake and serve as above.

Krechma

The innocent appearance and smooth taste of this cocktail can deceive you into believing that it is far less potent than it actually is.

🕐 1 min   🕐 0 mins

SERVES 1

INGREDIENTS

cracked ice

1–2 dashes grenadine

¼ cup crème de cacao

¼ cup vodka

1½ tbsp freshly squeezed lemon juice

1 Half-fill a cocktail shaker with cracked ice and add 1–2 dashes of grenadine. Pour in the crème de cacao, vodka, and lemon juice.

2 Replace the top and shake vigorously for 10–20 seconds. Strain into a chilled cocktail glass and serve immediately.

COOK'S TIP
Grenadine is a nonalcoholic syrup flavored with pomegranate juice. It is used both for coloring and flavoring alcoholic and nonalcoholic drinks.

Irish Charlie

As fans of James Bond will be aware, some cocktails are indeed stirred, not shaken. The trick is to stir just long enough to chill, as well as mix.

1 min   0 mins

SERVES 1

INGREDIENTS

ice cubes

1½ tbsp Bailey's Irish Cream

1½ tbsp white crème de menthe

fresh mint sprigs, to decorate

1 Place a few ice cubes in a large glass or pitcher. Pour in the Bailey's and crème de menthe.

2 Using a long, metal spoon, stir vigorously for 20 seconds. Strain into a chilled cocktail glass, decorate with the mint sprig, and serve immediately.

COOK'S TIP

Cocktails are almost always strained into the glass, either through a small separate strainer or the integral strainer of a cocktail shaker, to avoid including the ice. This is because as the ice melts, it dilutes the cocktail and spoils the flavor.

Mocha Mint

This tastes just like a liquid version of a rich chocolate, coffee, and mint mousse and has the same creamy texture. Perfect for a special occasion.

1 min

0 mins

SERVES 1

INGREDIENTS

cracked ice

1½ tbsp white crème de cacao

1½ tbsp Kahlúa

1½ tbsp white crème de menthe

slice of orange rind, to decorate

1 Half-fill a cocktail shaker with cracked ice. Pour in the crème de cacao, Kahlúa, and crème de menthe.

2 Replace the top and shake vigorously for 10–20 seconds. Strain into a chilled cocktail glass, decorate with a slice of orange rind, and serve immediately.

COOK'S TIP

Kahlúa is a coffee-flavored liqueur from Mexico. It is slightly sweeter than Tia Maria, the other leading brand.

Mona Lisa

Guaranteed to give you an enigmatic smile as you sip, this cocktail is traditionally served in a glass frosted with lemon juice and sugar.

🕐 1 min   🕐 0 mins

SERVES 1

INGREDIENTS

1 lemon wedge

confectioners' sugar or superfine sugar, for frosting

ice cubes

4½ tbsp dark crème de cacao

1½ tbsp Noilly Prat or other dry vermouth

1 Rub the rim of the glass with the lemon wedge, then dip in a saucer of confectioners' or superfine sugar to frost.

2 Place a few ice cubes in a pitcher or large glass. Pour in the crème de cacao and vermouth.

3 Using a long metal spoon, stir vigorously for 20 seconds, then strain into a cocktail glass and serve immediately.

VARIATION
For a Duchamp's Mona Lisa, substitute Lillet for the Noilly Prat. Lillet is quite like vermouth in that it is a herb-flavored apéritif made from wine fortified with cognac, in this case Armagnac.

Princess Mary

This is a creamy cocktail for the truly sweet-toothed. Adjust the quantity of sugar according to your particular taste.

3 mins

0 mins

SERVES 1

INGREDIENTS

1½ tbsp light cream

1–2 tsp superfine sugar

cracked ice

1½ tbsp white crème de cacao

1½ tbsp gin

grated semisweet chocolate, to decorate

1 Place the cream in a small bowl and stir in superfine sugar to taste. Half fill a cocktail shaker with cracked ice. Add the cream and pour in the crème de cacao and gin.

2 Replace the top and shake vigorously for 10–20 seconds. Strain into a chilled cocktail glass, sprinkle with grated chocolate, and serve immediately.

VARIATION

For a Queen Mary, shake together the cracked ice, crème de cacao, and gin, then float the cream on top and sprinkle with chocolate.

Panama Cocktail

Like many cocktails based on chocolate-flavored liqueurs, this one is enriched by the addition of cream. Serve in a tall glass if liked.

1 min   0 mins

SERVES 1

INGREDIENTS

cracked ice

1½ tbsp white crème de cacao

¼ cup cognac

4½ tbsp light cream

freshly grated nutmeg, to decorate

1 Half-fill a cocktail shaker with cracked ice. Pour in the crème de cacao, cognac, and cream.

2 Replace the top and shake vigorously for 10–20 seconds. Strain into a chilled cocktail glass, sprinkle with freshly grated nutmeg, and serve immediately.

COOK'S TIP
This is very similar to the well-known Brandy Alexander, which is made with dark crème de cacao and cognac.

New York Knickerbocker

This is such a richly flavored and substantial cocktail, it's almost a milkshake—but one that's strictly for adults. A great drink for a party.

🕐 1 min   🕐 0 mins

SERVES 1

INGREDIENTS

cracked ice

dash of grenadine

¼ cup white crème de cacao

1½ tbsp crème de banane

1½ tbsp Cointreau

¼ cup light cream

banana slice, to decorate (optional)

1   Half-fill a cocktail shaker with cracked ice and add a dash of grenadine. Pour in the crème de cacao, crème de banane, Cointreau, and cream.

2   Replace the top and shake vigorously for 10–20 seconds. Strain into a chilled cocktail glass, decorate with the banana slice, and serve immediately.

VARIATION
For a much simpler version, shake 1½ tablespoons of crème de cacao and 1½ tablespoons of crème de banane with ice, strain and serve.

Chocolate Cake Cocktail

You will need a steady hand to achieve the attractive layered effect of this cocktail. Chill all the ingredients well before you start.

2–3 mins   0 mins

SERVES 1

INGREDIENTS

1½ tbsp dark crème de cacao, chilled

1½ tbsp cognac, chilled

1½ tbsp heavy cream, chilled

1 Pour the crème de cacao into a chilled liqueur glass or other small glass. When it is still, carefully spoon the cognac on top. Finally, spoon on the cream. Serve immediately.

VARIATION

If you have a steady hand you can make 2 additional layers. Spoon in 1½ tablespoons of Bailey's Irish Cream before adding the crème de cacao and 1½ tablespoons of Kahlúa before adding the cream.

Savoy Hotel

This is said to be named in honor of the eponymous London hotel, where the cocktail bar has been very imaginative and creative over the decades.

2–3 mins   0 mins

SERVES 1

I N G R E D I E N T S

1½ tbsp dark crème de cacao, chilled

1½ tbsp Benedictine, chilled

1½ tbsp cognac, chilled

1 Pour the crème de cacao into a chilled liqueur glass or other small glass. When it is still, carefully spoon the Benedictine on top. Finally, spoon on the cognac. Serve immediately.

COOK'S TIP

Many cocktails that form layers in the glass have been inspired by the original Pousse-Café, which features 6 differently colored ingredients poured in layers. A small, straight-sided glass, known as a pousse-café glass, is the best one to use for this sort of cocktail.

Velvet Hammer

This smooth cocktail seems innocuous, so it is extremely tempting to have several—that's where the hammer comes in.

1 min   0 mins

SERVES 1

INGREDIENTS

cracked ice

5 tbsp vodka

1½ tbsp dark crème de cacao

1½ tbsp light cream

1 Half-fill a cocktail shaker with cracked ice. Pour in the vodka, crème de cacao, and cream.

2 Replace the top and shake vigorously for 10–20 seconds. Strain into a chilled cocktail glass and serve immediately.

COOK'S TIP
Opinion is divided about decorating cocktails, although some classics are always served in the same way. If you want to add a decoration, choose something that complements the flavor of the drink.

index